STUDIES ON VOLTAIRE AND THE EIGHTEENTH CENTURY

243

General editor

PROFESSOR H. T. MASON
Department of French
University of Bristol
Bristol BS8 1TE

RENATO G. MAZZOLINI
and SHIRLEY A. ROE

Science against the unbelievers: the correspondence of Bonnet and Needham, 1760-1780

THE VOLTAIRE FOUNDATION
AT THE TAYLOR INSTITUTION, OXFORD

1986

© *1986 University of Oxford*

ISSN 0435-2866

British Library cataloguing in publication data

Bonnet, Charles
Science against the unbelievers: the correspondence of
Bonnet and Needham, 1760-1780. — (Studies on Voltaire
and the eighteenth century; 243)
1. Bonnet, Charles   2. Needham, John Turberville
3. Science — Philosophy — Biography
I. Title   II. Needham, John Turberville
III. Mazzolini, Renato G.   IV. Roe, Shirley A.
V. Voltaire Foundation   VI. Series
501   Q175
ISBN 0-7294-0339-4

Printed in England at The Alden Press, Oxford

Contents

Illustrations

Abbreviations

AARB	Archives de l'Académie royale de Belgique, Bruxelles
AASP	Archives de l'Académie des sciences, Paris
A.D.B.	*Allgemeine deutsche Biographie*. [...] Herausgegeben durch die Historische Commission bei der k. Akademie der Wissenschaften, Leipzig 1876-1912.
AGR	Archives générales du Royaume, Bruxelles.
BAM	Biblioteca Ambrosiana, Milano
BB	Burgerbibliothek, Bern
BCL	Biblioteca Comunale, Livorno
BCRE	Biblioteca Comunale, Reggio Emilia
BD	Bibliothèque de Dunkerque, Dunkerque
BDA	Birmingham Diocesan Archives, Birmingham
Best.D	*Correspondence and related documents*. Definitive edition by Theodore Besterman. Vols 85-135 of *The Complete works of Voltaire*. Genève, Banbury, Oxford 1968-1977.
BIF	Bibliothèque de l'Institut de France, Paris
BL	British Library, London
BLUL	Brotherton Library, University of Leeds, Leeds
B.N.	*Biographie nationale*. Publiée par l'Académie royale des sciences, des lettres et des beaux-arts de Belgique. Bruxelles 1866-1944.
BNM	Biblioteca Nazionale, Milano
BNT	Biblioteca Nazionale, Torino
B.O.	Charles Bonnet, *Œuvres d'histoire naturelle et de philosophie*. 8 vols. in 10 parts (4°), Neuchatel: De l'Imprimerie de Samuel Fauche, 1779-1783; 18 vols. (8°), Neuchatel: Chez Samuel Fauche, Libraire du Roi, 1779-83. References will be given first to the 4° edition, then to the 8° edition, in the following format: B.O., 3:411/6:317.
BPUG	Bibliothèque Publique et Universitaire, Genève
B.U.	*Biographie universelle ancienne et moderne*. [Michaud]. Nouvelle édition. [1842-1865].
BUB	Biblioteca Universitaria, Bologna
C.L.	*Correspondance littéraire, philosophique et critique par Grimm, Diderot, Raynal, Meister, etc.* Ed. Maurice Tourneux. Paris 1877-1883.
C.R.S.	Catholic Record Society Publications (Record Series). London 1905-
D.B.F.	*Dictionnaire de biographie française*. Paris 1933-
D.B.I.	*Dizionario biografico degli italiani*. Roma 1960-
D.N.B.	*Dictionary of national biography*. Ed. Leslie Stephen and Sidney Lee. London 1885-1900.
D.S.B.	*Dictionary of scientific biography*. Ed. Charles Coulston Gillispie. New York 1970-1980.
Epistolario	Lazzaro Spallanzani, *Epistolario*. A cura di Benedetto Biagi. Firenze 1958-1964.

HL	Huntington Library, San Marino, California
KB	Koninklijke Bibliotheek, Den Haag
Leigh	*Correspondance complète de Jean Jacques Rousseau*. Edition critique établie et annotée par R. A. Leigh. Genève, Banbury, Oxford 1965-
LSL	Linnean Society of London, London
N.N.B.W.	*Nieuw Nederlandsch Biografisch Woordenboek*. Onder redactie van P. C. Molhuysen en P. J. Blok [and K. H. Kossmann]. Leiden 1911-1937.
PAL	Provincial Archives O.F.M., London
R.O.	Jean-Jacques Rousseau, *Œuvres complètes*. Edition publiée sous la direction de Bernard Gagnebin et Marcel Raymond. Paris 1959-
RS	Royal Society, London
SAL	Society of Antiquaries Library, London
SPKS	Staatsbibliothek Preussischer Kulturbesitz, Berlin
UCLC	Ushaw College, Lisbon Collection, Durham
UL	Universiteitsbibliotheek, Leiden
VF	Voltaire Foundation, Oxford
V.O.	*Œuvres complètes de Voltaire*. [Ed. Louis Moland]. Nouvelle édition. Paris 1883-1885.
W.C.	*The Yale Edition of Horace Walpole's Correspondence*, ed. W. S. Lewis. London, Oxford 1935-
WCRO	Warwick County Record Office, Warwick
WDA	Westminster Diocesan Archives, London
WIHM	Wellcome Institute for the History of Medicine, London
Wurzbach	Constantin von Wurzbach, *Biographisches Lexicon des Kaiserthums Oesterreich*. Wien 1856-1891.
YUL	Yale University Library, New Haven, Connecticut

Preface and acknowledgements

ALTHOUGH this edition is the product of a collaborative effort, we divided primary responsibility for various aspects of it. Shirley Roe wrote sections 1, 2, 3, 4, 5, and 7 of the Introduction, and compiled the Bonnet and Needham biographies and the Appendices. Renato Mazzolini wrote sections 6, 8, 9, and 10 of the Introduction, as well as the explanatory notes to the letters. We have, of course, mutually benefited from each other's comments and suggestions regarding both the Introduction and the notes. Concerning the transcription of the correspondence, the final checking of the Bonnet letters was done by Renato Mazzolini, and of the Needham letters by Shirley Roe.

In the course of preparing this volume, we have incurred many debts of gratitude both to individuals and to institutions. We are especially grateful to Philippe Monnier, the curator of the manuscript collection at the Bibliothèque Publique et Universitaire in Geneva, for providing us with access to the letters and for responding to numerous requests during our work on them. We would also like to thank Carlo Castellani and Francesca Bianca Crucitti Ullrich for their help in the early stages of preparing the transcription of the Bonnet-Needham correspondence. Our research could not have been completed without the resources and staffs of a number of institutions to which we are greatly indebted, among them the Taylor Institution Library, the Bodleian Library, the library of the Wellcome Institute for the History of Medicine, Widener Library, and the British Library. Archival materials were obtained from a number of libraries, and in this connection we would like to thank the Archives de l'Académie Royale de Belgique in Brussels, the Bibliothèque Publique et Universitaire in Geneva, the library of the Royal Society, the Society of Antiquaries Library in London, and the additional libraries included in the list of abbreviations.

Renato Mazzolini would like to express his appreciation to the Wellcome Trust for their generous support of this and previous projects and to St Cross College, Oxford, where he had the pleasure of being a Visiting Fellow while preparing this edition. He is also grateful for research funds received from the Consiglio Nazionale delle Ricerche and for the advice and assistance of Jean-Daniel Candaux, Jane Whitehead, and Albert E. Best. Shirley Roe would like to thank the Harvard Graduate Society, the Clark Fund (Harvard University), and the American Philosophical Society for research grants in support of this project. She is especially grateful to the Wellcome Institute for the History of Medicine for providing her with research facilities during the preparation of this volume.

R. G. Mazzolini
S. A. Roe

Charles Bonnet

1720	Born in Geneva on 13 March; first child of Pierre Bonnet and Anne-Marie Lullin, both patricians. The Bonnet family originated from France, which they left in 1572. Charles's younger sister Suzanne (1728-1807) married their cousin Jean-Jacques Bonnet (1717-1802) on 5 May 1771; they had no children.
1735	Studied at the Auditoire de belles-lettres of the Genevan Académie.
1736-1739	Studied at the Auditoire de philosophie of the Genevan Académie; took courses in philosophy from Jean-Louis Calandrini (1703-1758), in mathematics from Gabriel Cramer (1704-1752), and in logic from Ami de La Rive (1692-1763). On a private basis, studied physics with Calandrini, and algebra and geometry with Cramer.
1737	Inspired by reading the first volume of Réaumur's *Mémoires pour servir à l'histoire des insectes* (1734-1742), began studying natural history.
1738	Sent his first letter, dated 4 July 1738, to Réaumur, who became his scientific mentor. Their correspondence lasted until Réaumur's death in 1757.
1739-1743	Studied law at the Auditoire de droit. A reluctant student, pursuing law only because of his father's wishes, Bonnet nevertheless followed with interest the courses of Jean-Jacques Burlamaqui (1694-1748).
1740	Discovered parthenogenesis in aphids in a series of observations made from 20 May to 24 June.
1740	Named correspondent of Réaumur at the Paris Académie des sciences on 31 August.
1743	Elected Fellow of the Royal Society of London on 17 November.
1744-1747	Health deteriorated; developed severe eye problems that remained with him the rest of his life.
1745	Published the *Traité d'insectologie*.
1747	Began investigations in botany.
1748-1753	Dictated the *Méditations sur l'univers*, which was never published in its original form, but which gave rise to Bonnet (1755), (1762), and (1764).
1752	Elected to the Great Council in Geneva.
1753-1754	Corresponded with Montesquieu.
1754	Published *Recherches sur l'usage des feuilles dans les plantes*.
1754	Began a correspondence with Albrecht von Haller on 8 March that was to continue until the latter's death in 1777, encompassing over 900 letters.
1755	Published anonymously the *Essai de psychologie*.
1756	Married Jeanne-Marie de La Rive (1728-1796) on 30 May. The

	Bonnets had no children.
1760	Visited by Needham in June or July.
1760	Published the *Essai analytique sur les facultés de l'ame*.
1762	Published *Considérations sur les corps organisés*.
1763	On his only trip away from home, visited Haller at Roche in August.
1764	Visited by Needham in May.
1764	Published *Contemplation de la nature*.
1765	Received his first letter from Lazzaro Spallanzani, dated 18 July. Their correspondence, including nearly 200 letters, continued until 1791.
1765	Visited by Needham in September.
1765-1768	Politically active during the crisis in the Republic of Geneva.
1767	Moved permanently to his father-in-law's home at Genthod, where Bonnet and his wife had previously spent their summers.
1769	Resigned on 1 January from the Great Council.
1769	Published *La Palingénésie philosophique*.
1774-1779	Published several mémoires in the abbé Rozier's *Observations sur la physique*, on preexistent germs, on fecundation in plants, on bees, on the taenia, and on regeneration in salamanders and snails.
1779	Visited by Spallanzani at Genthod in July.
1779-1783	Published his collected works as *Œuvres d'histoire naturelle et de philosophie* in two editions (4° and 8°). Bonnet spent eight years correcting and revising his earlier published and unpublished writings for this edition.
1782	Agreed to become again a member of the Genevan Great Council.
1783	Elected Associé étranger of the Paris Académie des sciences on 22 May.
1793	Died on 20 May.

Bonnet's autobiographical mémoires have been published by Savioz (1948b). For biographies of Bonnet, see Saussure [1793], [J. Trembley] (1794), [Lévesque de Pouilly] (1794), Anspach [1793], R. Wolf (1858-1862, 3:257-90), and P. E. Pilet, *D.S.B.*, 2 (1970) 286-87. Works dealing with Bonnet's life, thought, and reputation include Caraman (1859), G. Bonnet (1930), Savioz (1948a), Rocci (1975), Marx (1976), and Anderson (1982). For Bonnet's biological theories, see Whitman (1895a and 1895b), Soleto (1966), Castellani (1969, 1969-1970, and 1972), Bowler (1973), Marx (1973b and 1974), Anderson (1976), and Belloni (1977). For Bonnet's psychology and educational theories, see Speck (1897), Fritzsche (1905), Strózewski (1905), Isenberg (1906), Schubert (1909), E. Claparède (1909), and Starobinsky (1975). Works on Bonnet's political ideas and activities include Gaullieur (1855), Humbert (1858), Savioz (1950), and Postigliola (1978). Only two of Bonnet's political speeches were published in his autobiography (Savioz 1948b:222-23, 226-29); manuscript copies of all of his speeches are in the BPUG (MS Bonnet 16). Excerpts from Bonnet's vast correspondence are included in several of the above works. For editions of his correspondence with Spallanzani, see Castellani (1971); with Fontana, see Mazzolini (1972); with Morgagni, see Usuelli (1972); and with Haller, see Sonntag (1983). For a discussion of Bonnet's correspondence with Réaumur (without copies of the letters), see Torlais (1932); and for excerpts from various letters dealing with Rousseau, see Ritter (1916-1917b). Several volumes of original letters addressed to Bonnet and draft copies of Bonnet's own letters are preserved in the BPUG, along with other Bonnet manuscripts. For a partial list of these, see Savioz (1948a:375-76 and 1948b:401-403); a typescript catalogue of all of Bonnet's manuscript remains is in the BPUG. For additional secondary literature on Bonnet, see Marx (1976:715-55).

John Turberville Needham

1713	Born in London on 10 September; eldest son of John Needham, a barrister, and Martha Lucas. Of his younger brothers, Robert became a Franciscan, adopting the name Joseph; and Francis became a bookseller, marrying Winifred Sherwood. There is no information on Needham's sister Susannah (see Appendix A).
1722	Began study under the secular clergy at the English College at Douai in Flanders.
1732	Received tonsure at Arras on 8 March.
1735-1740	Taught logic, rhetoric, and philosophy at the English College at Douai.
1738	Ordained a priest at Cambrai on 31 May.
1740-1743	Assistant master at a school for Catholic youth at Twyford near Winchester. Sent letters on scientific observations to the Royal Society.
1744-1745	Taught philosophy at the English College in Lisbon from 22 February 1744 to 21 June 1745. Made observations on marine organisms.
1745	Published *An account of some new microscopical discoveries.*
1745-1746	Attended meetings of the Royal Society in London, as a guest, from October 1745 to April 1746, where he presented some of his microscopical observations.
1746	Moved in May to Paris where he lived (with visits to London) until 1751. Became acquainted with Buffon and Réaumur.
1747	Elected Fellow of the Royal Society of London on 22 January (first English Catholic priest to be so honoured). Did not sign the Obligation until 25 May 1749, during a visit to London.
1748	Began microscopical observations with Buffon in Paris on 16 March. These continued through the summer, after Buffon's departure for the country in May.
1748	Deposited a sealed 'Memoire sur la Generation', dated 9 June, with Jean-Paul Grandjean de Fouchy, Secretary of the Paris Académie des sciences (see Appendix B).
1748	Wrote 'A summary of some late observations upon the generation, composition, and decomposition of animal and vegetable substances; communicated in a letter to Martin Folkes Esq. [...]', dated 23 November. Read by Folkes before the Royal Society on 15 and 22 December. Published in the December issue of the *Philosophical transactions* and as a separate monograph in 1749.
1750	Published *Nouvelles observations microscopiques, avec des découvertes intéressantes sur la composition & la décomposition des corps organisés.*
1751-1766	Travelled as a tutor with several young English noblemen making the Grand Tour. These included Arthur-James Plunkett, seventh Earl of Fingall (1731-1793); Philip Howard of Corby (1730-1810);

	Anthony Preston, eleventh Viscount Gormanston (1736-1786); Charles Towneley (1739-1805); and lastly Charles Dillon (1745-1813), later Viscount, with whom Needham spent five years (1762-1766). Needham's correspondence indicates that he spent much of his time during these years in Turin, Rome, Paris, Caen, and Geneva, visiting as well Naples, Parma, Venice, Brussels, London, and parts of Scotland.
1760	Visited Bonnet in Geneva in June or July.
1761	Published *De inscriptione quadam Aegyptiaca Taurini inventa et characteribus Aegyptiis olim et Sinis communibus*.
1761	Elected Honorary Fellow of the Society of Antiquaries of London on 10 December.
1764	Visited Bonnet in Geneva in May.
1765-1766	Lived in Geneva from August 1765 to May 1766. Visited Bonnet in September 1765 and on other occasions.
1765	While in Geneva, published three anonymous pamphlets on miracles directed against Voltaire.
1766-1769	Beginning in June 1766 lived in Paris (from 1767 at the English College, St Gregory's Seminary).
1768	Named correspondent of Buffon at the Paris Académie des sciences on 26 March.
1769	Published *Nouvelles recherches sur les découvertes microscopiques, et la génération des corps organisés* (a translation of Spallanzani's *Saggio di osservazioni microscopiche* [1765] with Needham's notes) together with his own *Nouvelles recherches physiques et métaphysiques sur la nature et la religion*.
1769	Moved to Brussels in March to become Director of the newly founded Société littéraire. Became canon at the collegiate church at Dendermonde.
1773	Appointed to a canonry in the collegiate and royal church of Soignes in Hainaut.
1773-1780	Director from April 1773 to May 1780 of the Brussels Académie impériale et royale des sciences et belles-lettres, which succeeded the Société littéraire. Published five papers in the Academy's *Mémoires*.
1776	Published *Idée sommaire, ou vüe générale du systeme physique, & metaphysique de Monsieur Needham sur la génération des corps organisés*, which had previously appeared as an editor's note in [Monestier] (1774 and 1775). A second edition was issued in 1781.
1781	Died in Brussels on 30 December. Buried at the abbey of Caudenberg.

Where dates presented above differ from published biographical notices they are based on manuscript sources and correspondence. The principal biography of Needham is Mann (1783). See also Pierre-Joseph Van Beneden, *B.N.*, 15 (1899) 520-28; Gillow(1885-1903, 5:157-60); Thompson Cooper, *D.N.B.*, 14 (1909) 157-59; Rachel Horowitz Westbrook, *D.S.B.*, 10 (1974) 9-11; and Anstruther (1968-1977, 4:195-96). For further information, see Knox (1878:60, 65); Croft (1902:232); Bradney (1904-1932, 1:58); Kirk (1909:171); Sharratt (1973:12-17); and C.R.S., 28:101, 115, 121, 127, 130n, 138, 145, 153, 156, 159, 161, 162, 164, 165, 166, 171, 174, 194, 196, 199, 202, 203, 209, 211, 214, 215, 218, 219, 224, 245, 292; 63:115, 118. Needham's will and other documents relating to his death are in WDA, series A, vol.42, nos.177-185. For Needham's biological and philosophical views, see Roger (1963:494-520), Solinas (1967:85-91), and Roe (1983). For the Needham-Spallanzani controversy, see in addition Rostand (1951, ch.2-4), Castellani (1969-1970 and 1973), Tega (1971), Farley (1977:22-27), Gottdenker (1980), and Roe (1982). For Needham's research on cryptobiosis, see Keilin (1959:149-61) and Mazzolini (1972:70-72). For his controversy with Voltaire, see Roger (1963:732-48), Perkins (1965), Marx (1973a and 1975), and Roe (1985). For Needham and the 'bust of Isis' episode, see Paravia (1842:35-39), Gauthier (1906:82-83), Dawson (1932 and 1935-1938), Appleton (1951:149-51), Iverson (1961:106-107), Guy (1963:390), Curto (1962-1963), and Pierce (1965:212-15). Several relevant unpublished documents are in the BL (Add. 21416) and the SAL (*Minutes*, viii:352-54, 371-72, 399-400, 422, 437-39; ix:9-14, 79, 202-203, 336-38; x:87-89; and Correspondence 1761-1770 and Thomas Jenkins F.S.A. Nine Letters to Norris 1758-1772). For Needham and the Brussels Academy of Sciences, see Gachard (1838 and 1840), Mailly (1883), Lavalleye (1973:17-18, 32, 36), and Marx (1977:58-59). Several documents relating to Needham's activities as Director of the Brussels Academy and manuscript copies of some of his reports and mémoires are in the AARB (Needham). Two letters from Needham to Antonio Vallisneri have been published in Paravia (1842:152-60); two letters to Albrecht von Haller have been edited by Mazzolini (1976). For his correspondence with Lazzaro Spallanzani, see Castellani (1973) and *Epistolario*, 1:132-33, 136-37, 152, 2:92. A list of Needham's extant manuscripts and correspondence may be found in Appendix C.

Introduction

1. The correspondence

CHARLES Bonnet and John Turberville Needham corresponded for twenty years, from 1760 to 1780, the year before Needham died. Fifty-three letters remain from this correspondence, twenty-six written by Bonnet and twenty-seven by Needham, and are published here for the first time in their entirety. Another four letters written by Needham to Bonnet are known to be missing.[1] All of Bonnet's letters to Needham have survived both in a draft form taken down by Bonnet's secretary from dictation and in a copy that was made under Bonnet's direction, probably for eventual publication.[2] The actual letters that Needham received have never been located, but comparison of other Bonnet letters with the secretary's drafts show the latter to be quite faithful to the letters as sent. All of the extant Needham letters to Bonnet, together with the drafts and copies of Bonnet's letters to Needham, are now preserved in the Bibliothèque Publique et Universitaire in Geneva.

Although both Bonnet and Needham made contributions principally to the natural sciences, especially to biology and natural history, their correspondence is not limited to scientific subjects. Rather, their letters reflect many of the major concerns of their day on philosophical, religious, and political issues. Moreover, unlike most scientists during this period, Bonnet and Needham freely discussed in their letters the relationship between their scientific work and their philosophical, religious, and social commitments.[3] Both were opposed to the contemporary philosophe movement, which they viewed as undermining the moral foundations of society. And each was, in his own way, committed to promoting science and philosophy within a clear religious framework and in direct opposition to the unbelievers. As participants in what has subsequently been termed the Age of Enlightenment, Bonnet and Needham exhibited a more cautious approach to philosophical and social innovation than did many of their French contemporaries. Even in their discussions of scientific issues, such as the generation of living organisms, their concerns about the implicit alliance of certain biological doctrines with atheism, materialism, and political change is apparent. Their letters to one another allow one not only to glimpse the motivations that underlay their own scientific work but also to understand more thoroughly the intimate, though often hidden, tie between scientific, philosophical, religious, and social concerns that existed during the second half of the eighteenth century. The Bonnet-Needham letters are thus unique among scientific correspondence from this period.

The Bonnet-Needham correspondence was initiated following a visit Needham paid to Bonnet in the summer of 1760. Thereafter, the two wrote to one another

1. See letter 9, n.1; letter 25, n.1; letter 42, n.2; and letter 44, n.1.
2. On these two extant versions of Bonnet's letters, see the Note on the text. See also letter 26, n.1, on a possible missing communication from Bonnet to Needham.
3. One can compare the correspondence, for example, of Buffon, Spallanzani, Morgagni, Fontana, Barthez, the Bernoullis, and Haller (except for some of his letters to Bonnet), which are devoted almost exclusively to scientific subjects.

on a fairly frequent basis, although there are five gaps of one year or more in their correspondence. The first main group of letters, written during the years 1760 to 1762, consists of sixteen letters. These were followed by a two-year lapse which ended when Needham visited Bonnet again in Geneva in May 1764, resulting in an exchange of two letters in the summer of 1764. Needham returned to Geneva in August 1765, and four letters passed between the two during that summer. After another one-year gap, due to Needham's presence in Geneva from August 1765 to May 1766, their correspondence resumed again in summer 1766; and twenty-three letters, the second main group, are from the years 1766 to 1770. After a three-year gap, two letters were exchanged in 1773; and, after a further six-year lapse, a final six letters passed between the two in 1779 and 1780.

During this entire twenty-year period, Bonnet lived either in Geneva or at his father-in-law's home in Genthod, which was near Geneva on the shores of Lac Léman. Needham, by contrast, wrote to Bonnet from Turin, Rome, and Geneva during the early period of their correspondence when he was a travelling tutor; then from Paris, while residing there from 1766 to 1769; and finally from Brussels, after moving there in 1769 to assume the directorship of the newly founded Société littéraire, which soon became the Brussels Academy of Sciences. Needham's frequent changes of address were not entirely the product of choice, but rather of economic necessity. Prevented from receiving an academic or ecclesiastical position in England because he was a Catholic priest, Needham remained on the Continent for almost all of his life. During his years of travel with a succession of young English gentlemen on the Grand Tour, Needham attempted several times to secure more stable employment. He tried to arrange a professorship at the University of Louvain in 1759, but was unsuccessful; and he hoped (without result) that a pension could be obtained from Paris after the publication of one of his books in 1761.[4] Thus when in 1768 Needham received the offer to become Director of the Société littéraire in Brussels, he was more than willing to accept it; and he worked hard at its organisation and at transforming it into the resulting Academy of Sciences.[5] Needham's nomadic existence was not without some detrimental effect on him, both personally and intellectually. As he wrote to a friend in 1777, 'we are both of us wanderers, I by a forced expatriation the result of iniquitous laws, without a foot of property on this globe'.[6] Moreover, the gap in his major scientific publications between 1750 and 1769 no doubt resulted from his constant travel. By contrast, Bonnet, although not always in the best of health, was free throughout his life to devote his time to scientific and philosophical research, due to his own personal wealth. Both Needham's employment as a tutor and eventual appointment in Brussels from the Austrian court, as well as Bonnet's financial independence represent very different but quite typical ways in which eighteenth-century scientific research was supported.

In relation to their correspondence with other individuals, the letters between Bonnet and Needham were extremely important to both of them. Although

4. See sections 9 and 6 of this Introduction, respectively.
5. See section 9 of this Introduction.
6. Letter to Nathaniel Pigott, 29 May 1777 (VF).

Bonnet received letters from at least three hundred correspondents during his lifetime, of the letters preserved at the Bibliothèque Publique et Universitaire, those from only eleven individuals exceed in number those that he received from Needham. Bonnet's great scientific correspondence with Albrecht von Haller, with Lazzaro Spallanzani, and with René Antoine Ferchault de Réaumur included many more letters than his correspondence with Needham. Yet in terms of the range of subjects discussed, the Needham-Bonnet letters are of a similar level of importance for our understanding of Bonnet's thought and work. Since Bonnet was continually trying to convince Needham to alter his biological and metaphysical views, these letters, taken in conjunction with contemporaneous letters to Haller, Spallanzani, and others, offer us a unique picture of Bonnet's underlying concerns and attitudes.

With regard to Needham, the Bonnet correspondence is of even greater significance for our understanding of both his biography and his intellectual development. Although much of Needham's correspondence with others and all of the letters he received apparently no longer exist, of those Needham letters that are still in existence,[7] only those to Honoré-Auguste Sabatier de Cabre, a French diplomat, total more in number than those he wrote to Bonnet. Furthermore, the letters to Bonnet include more discussion than those to Sabatier of Needham's scientific opinions and of the concerns that guided his philosophical and biological researches. Because Needham and Bonnet disagreed over scientific, philosophical, and religious issues, their letters to each other reveal more about their motivations and attitudes than do most correspondences.

Although Bonnet's and Needham's letters to one another were generally quite cordial, their differences of opinion reached a somewhat acrimonious level in 1770 and resulted in the three-year break in their correspondence previously mentioned. The ostensible point of contention was an anonymous piece Needham had written comparing Voltaire and Rousseau, which Bonnet severely criticised on stylistic grounds (see letter 44).[8] One can discern an underlying motive on Bonnet's part, which stemmed from his continuing anger at Needham over the edition Needham had published in 1769 of a work by Spallanzani.[9] Needham responded with somewhat righteous indignation to Bonnet's critique (see letter 45), and Bonnet did not reply. An exchange of letters in 1773 (letters 46 and 47) still bristled with some of this earlier ill feeling, and letters ceased once again. Finally, the correspondence concluded, after six letters written in 1779 and 1780, on a further note of disharmony, when Bonnet took offence at Needham's charge that Spallanzani had switched his allegiance from Needham's theory of generation to Bonnet's for reasons of career advancement (see letters 52 and 53).

The remainder of this Introduction is organised around the major themes that appear in the correspondence, in a more or less chronological order. We have attempted not only to highlight the issues as treated in the letters but also to provide background and contextual information that should aid in the reader's better understanding of each topic and of its significance during the period.

7. See Appendix C.
8. See section 5 of this Introduction.
9. See section 2.iv of this Introduction.

Common to nearly all of these topics is one theme that underlay the often diverging efforts of Bonnet and Needham. Both sought – in generation theory, cosmogony, metaphysics, religion, and politics – to counter the 'contagion' of unbelievers and to restore science, philosophy, and revealed religion to their rightful position as the foundations of morality and society.

2. The generation of living organisms

THE subject of generation, that is, the process whereby living things procreate, received more attention in the Bonnet-Needham letters than any other single issue.[1] For both Bonnet and Needham, this topic was the principal focal point of their biological research. Both proposed theories of generation that were widely discussed by their contemporaries; and, most significantly for their correspondence, Bonnet and Needham were on completely opposite sides in their views on the subject. Bonnet was an adamant preformationist, believing that all living creatures had been fashioned by God at the Creation; whereas Needham supported epigenesis, the idea that living organisms are formed gradually at each instance of reproduction. The religious and philosophical context of each of their positions mirrored the wider significance of the subject in their day and formed much of the basis for the discussion of generation in their correspondence.

The period from 1760 to 1780 falls in the middle of the productive careers of both Bonnet and Needham. Bonnet had carried out significant experimental studies in the 1740s and 1750s (see section 2.iii below), but it was not until 1762 that he published his first major work on theory of generation, the *Considérations sur les corps organisés*. Needham had also put forth his views on generation in the late 1740s and early 1750s (see section 2.ii below), but the first real experimental challenge to his theory did not arise until 1765, with the work of Lazzaro Spallanzani. The letters that passed between Needham and Bonnet during this twenty-year period discuss many of the important events that occurred with regard to the promulgation and defence of each of their positions. It is principally in Needham's letters to Bonnet (and in a few of his letters to Spallanzani; see Castellani 1973) that we have any evidence of the significant changes that Needham's views underwent during the late 1760s. Furthermore, Needham is more candid in his letters to Bonnet than in any others about the motivations underlying his ideas on generation. With regard to Bonnet, even though his fundamental commitment to preformation did not alter, he further refined and reinforced his theory during the period of his correspondence with Needham. Bonnet's welcoming of new evidence from Spallanzani to use in his continuing critique of epigenesis, plus a hardening of his own position in opposition to Needham, are both documented in these letters. Bonnet and Needham were also writing during these same years to Spallanzani and to Albrecht von Haller, another proponent of preformation.[2] By looking at all of this correspondence together, one can not only understand more fully the topics discussed in the Bonnet-Needham letters but also gain an appreciation for the variety of issues involved in the generation debate.

This section will be divided into four subsections. Section 2.i presents the

---

1. The principal discussions of generation, which will be highlighted later in this section, occur in letters 6, 7, 14, 15, 19, 20, 22, 24-30, 32-36, 41, and 47-53.

2. See *Epistolario*, Castellani (1971 and 1973), Mazzolini (1976), and Sonntag (1983).

general background to theories of generation in the eighteenth century and outlines the major topics that were being debated when Bonnet and Needham entered the field. Section 2.ii treats the development of Needham's ideas on generation, including the first statements of his views, up to the initiation of his correspondence with Bonnet. Section 2.iii discusses the origins of Bonnet's views and presents his reactions to Needham's theory prior to 1762. Finally, in section 2.iv, the subject of generation as treated in the correspondence is discussed, as well as the events of the Needham-Spallanzani debate.

i. Theories of generation in the eighteenth century

During the eighteenth century, the subject of generation occupied a place of importance and controversy not unlike that of evolution in the nineteenth century.[3] The two dominant, and diametrically opposed, doctrines – preformation and epigenesis – represented far more than two contrasting views of embryological development. The preformationist position was embedded in a view of the world as static, predetermined, and hierarchical, with all things in the natural (and social) world having been created and prearranged by God. Epigenesis, on the other hand, connoted the idea of a self-creative and dynamic universe, where even living things could be produced by material causes alone. The clash of such disparate world views, which reached its height in the period from the 1740s to the 1770s, thus involved religious, philosophical, and social issues as well as more specific biological controversies.

The theory of preformation, often also called the theory of preexistence, arose in the late seventeenth century during the Scientific Revolution, when the mechanical philosophy was becoming the dominant view of science. The success of mechanical explanations in physics and astronomy had led to their natural extension to the biological sphere, yet with some reservations. One difficulty in applying a strictly mechanical view to reproduction was to explain how in fact simple forces could produce a complex living creature. The most avid proponent of mechanical epigenesis in this period was René Descartes who, in *De la formation de l'animal*, published posthumously in 1664, proposed an account of embryological development based entirely on the motions of particles. Yet Descartes's theory, and others like it, was unable to explain *why* development proceeds as it does, that is, why the proper organism, with its parts perfectly arranged, is formed.

A second difficulty with mechanical epigenesis was the danger that, if it were true, then there might no longer be a place for God in the creation of life. The theory of preformation, on the other hand, first formulated in the 1670s by Nicolas Malebranche, Jan Swammerdam, Claude Perrault, and others, avoided this difficulty. One of the key aspects of many preformationist theories was that all organisms that were ever to appear on Earth had been created at the same time and either encased one within the other (encapsulation, or *emboîtement*) or scattered as germs throughout nature (panspermism). At its appointed time

3. For eighteenth-century theories of generation, see Roger (1963), Farley (1977, ch.1), and Roe (1981).

each preexistent germ would develop into an adult organism through a simple mechanical process of unfolding. The new embryo thus emerged from its tiny and invisible state by becoming more solid, opaque, and larger in size. Such an explanation of embryological development preserved both a mechanical explanatory framework and God's necessary role in each instance of reproduction. Thus preexistence avoided the atheistic and materialistic implications of development by epigenesis, while also accounting for the source of the offspring's organisation. Embryos (and seeds) developed into the proper animal or plant because all of their parts were created at one time and arranged in the proper fashion by God; yet the process of their development was based entirely on mechanical laws.

During the first half of the eighteenth century, preformation was widely accepted. Following the discovery by Anthoni van Leeuwenhoek and Nicolaas Hartsoeker of the existence of animalcules (spermatozoa) in male seminal fluid, some naturalists thought that organisms were preformed through male seminal animalcules (animalculism). Most continued to believe, however, in preexistence via the female egg (ovism). Yet in the 1740s, the notion of preexistence was challenged by three new epigenetic theories, proposed by Pierre Louis de Maupertuis, John Turberville Needham, and Georges Louis Leclerc, comte de Buffon.[4] All three accounts used recent biological evidence, especially concerning regeneration and microorganisms, to criticise preexistence. And all three theories relied on active forces to explain generation through epigenesis. In comparison with seventeenth-century mechanical epigenesis, based entirely on matter and motion, epigenesis via active forces represented a new challenge to preformation. Yet by attributing inherent activity to matter, as distinct from simply viewing matter as passive particles in motion, such an epigenetic approach ran the risk of spilling over into materialism. Consequently, Maupertuis, Buffon, and Needham were all criticised for proposing theories of generation with materialist implications. One of the principal themes we shall encounter when following the development of Needham's views on generation through the years is his continual struggle to distinguish his theory from materialism and to demonstrate that it was in fact an alternative to both preformation and materialism.

One biological discovery that lent support to the idea that material powers govern the generation of new organisms was Abraham Trembley's observation in 1740 of the unusual regenerative powers possessed by the freshwater polyp (hydra).[5] Not only did the polyp regenerate a new part when cut in two, but the cut-off part became a new organism as well. Trembley found that one could cut a polyp into several different pieces, each of which would regenerate into a complete animal. Réaumur, to whom Trembley communicated his findings in a series of letters, expressed the sense of surprise and wonder engendered by the polyp's unusual capabilities when he wrote, 'lorsque je vis pour la premiére fois deux polypes se former peu à peu de celui que j'avois coupé en deux, j'eus peine à en croire mes yeux; & c'est un fait que je ne m'accoûtume point à voir, après l'avoir vû & revû cent & cent fois' (Réaumur 1734-1742, 6:liv-lv; see also M.

4. See Maupertuis (1744 and 1745), Needham (1748), and Buffon (1749-1789, vol.ii).
5. For secondary literature on the polyp, see letter 1, n.10.

Trembley 1943). Although some, like Bonnet, attempted to reconcile such regenerative phenomena with preformation, others, such as Haller, converted (temporarily) to epigenesis because of the polyp, and still others, notably La Mettrie and Diderot, used the polyp as a central motif in their materialist theories of epigenesis.

By the time Needham and Bonnet began their correspondence in 1760, both were firmly committed to well-developed but opposing views of generation. Bonnet represented the confluence of mechanistic and religious ideas that had underlain the theory of preformation from its inception. Needham, by contrast, was part of the new approach of epigenesis by active forces, although, as we shall see, still within a definite religious and non-materialist framework. Their disagreements over the nature of generation thus reflected many of their contemporaries' concerns with these same issues.

ii. The development of Needham's views on generation

After completing his education at the English Catholic school at Douai in Flanders, Needham remained there for five years to teach rhetoric, logic, and philosophy. In 1740, he returned to England to take up a post at a Catholic school in Twyford, near Winchester, which he held until 1743. It was here that his first scientific work seems to have been carried out, for in 1743 Needham sent five letters to the Royal Society in London concerning observations he had made at Twyford.[6] Two of the letters dealt with malm, a chalky soil found in the area around Twyford, and with the process of petrifaction. Needham also reported on small white worms he had found inhabiting the stomachs of trout and on experiments he had performed on starfish regeneration, a subject that would later figure in his theory of generation. In the last of these letters from Twyford, the only one to be published in the *Philosophical transactions* (see Needham 1743), Needham briefly announced two discoveries that were subsequently to be recognised as extremely significant. The first was based on observations he had carried out with a microscope on pollen grains of the common lily. Needham found that, when immersed in water, these pollen grains immediately released a train of tiny globules. Needham's second discovery related to grains of blighted wheat, which, when viewed with a microscope, could be seen to contain a substance composed of white fibres. When adding water to separate the fibres for easier viewing, Needham saw, to his surprise, that they immediately came to life, moving in a twisting motion for several hours. He did not attempt to discuss in this early paper any explanation for these two phenomena, simply reporting his observations.

In February 1744 Needham arrived in Lisbon to take up a teaching position at the English College. There he continued his scientific work, making extensive observations on calamary (squid), on barnacles, on sole embryos that attach themselves to shrimp, and on lizards. He remained in Lisbon for only fifteen

6. Of these five letters from Needham now in the Royal Society, two were sent to the physician James Parsons, F.R.S., who was a friend of Needham's, and three to Martin Folkes, President of the Royal Society (see RS, L&P. I.167, 193, 204, 244, and Fo.2.8).

months, apparently because of ill health, returning to England in June 1745. After showing some of his specimens to Martin Folkes, President of the Royal Society, and to several other members, Needham was encouraged to write up the observations he had made in Portugal for publication. With the addition of reports on his earlier work on pollen and on blighted wheat, these observations formed the basis for his first book, *An account of some new microscopical discoveries*, which was published in 1745 by Needham's brother, Francis Needham, and dedicated to Folkes and the Fellows of the Royal Society. Needham personally presented a copy of his book to the Society when, in October 1745, he began regularly attending their meetings (as a guest); and he demonstrated his microscopical observations on the calamary to the Society the following month.

In the Introduction to his *New microscopical discoveries*, Needham explained the reasons why he became interested in studying certain marine organisms. One is struck, he commented in the opening sentence, not only with the enormous fecundity of nature but also with its 'Subordination of Worlds', where each level of size in the natural world, from the visible to the subvisible, contains a whole range of harmoniously arranged organisms. '[A] Drop of Water,' Needham remarked, 'the Diameter of which exceeds not a Line, may be a Sea, not only as daily Experience shews, in the Capacity which it has of containing, and affording Sustenance to Millions of Animals, but also in the Similitude which these very Animals may bear to several known Species in that part of the Creation, which is the Object of our naked Eyes' (Needham 1745:2). In other words, one finds numerous analogies between organisms of the microscopical realm and those that one encounters in the visible realm. This line of reasoning led Needham to the idea that one might perhaps be able to better understand some of the structures and capabilities of microscopical animals by studying larger organisms that seemed to be analogous to them. In particular, Needham wanted to be able to find a marine organism that was similar enough to the freshwater polyp for it to be used to help explain the polyp's unusual regenerative capabilities and its ability to reproduce by budding. Having already made observations on starfish regeneration while at Twyford, Needham hoped to find other organisms at the seashore in Lisbon that would help to elucidate these puzzling phenomena. He was unsuccessful in finding such an organism, although he did think that the barnacle might reproduce by budding; yet in studying the calamary, a type of squid, Needham made an even more surprising discovery. He found that during the breeding season the male calamary's milt contained small cartilaginous vessels. As they developed in the milt these tubular vessels seemed to draw into them the surrounding seminal fluid, so that eventually the milt bag, which previously contained diffused semen, contained only these milt vessels, which had absorbed all of the fluid. Needham then observed that if one placed mature milt vessels under the microscope, one could see them ejecting their contents, especially after water was added. Needham was in fact the first person to observe the spermatophores of squid, which do indeed contain a coiled mass of spermatozoa that are ejected during fertilisation. Needham's descriptions and illustrations of these milt vessels and of the sac in which they are stored (now called Needham's sac) are remarkably accurate when compared with modern micro-photographs. Needham concluded from his observations that perhaps all seminal animalcules might not in fact be true animals as Leeuwen-hoek had thought, but rather might be tiny vessels analogous to the milt vessels of the calamary. Thus, rather than playing a role in the generative process by being miniature animals, seminal animalcules might 'be nothing more than immensely less Machines analogous to these Milt-Vessels, which may be only in Large, what those are in Miniature' (Needham 1745:56).

Needham pressed this analogy further in describing his observations on the *farina foecundans*, or pollen grains, of flowering plants. Building on his earlier brief report that these pollen grains release tiny globules when immersed in water (Needham 1743), Needham now described this phenomenon in detail and expanded his discussion to include observations he had made on several different species of plants. He concluded that all pollen acts in the same way, by emitting a substance that is the true generative material. Needham suggested as well that it is this generative substance contained in the pollen grains that holds the germ of the future plant, and not the seed, as most naturalists believed (Needham 1745:78-79). Finally, Needham returned to the question of seminal animalcules, and argued that with the analogy both of pollen grains and of the milt vessels in calamary, one could not help but conclude that seminal animalcules were likewise the mere containers of the generative material. Explicitly rejecting Leeuwenhoek's and Nicolas Andry's theories of generation, which maintained that the seminal animalcules were preformed organisms destined to develop into new offspring, Needham called into question the whole basis of animalculist preformation. What does one gain, Needham asked, by attributing to these animalcules the privileged status of the future organism, since one must still explain how these animalcules are formed? And, Needham further queried, 'Why there should not be as much Reason, if we make the Wisdom of the Almighty, as far as we can possibly trace, our Standard in this Particular, in asserting that the Foetus is generated from a Lifeless Point of Matter, as in affirming that it proceeds from an Animalcule?' (Needham 1745:83). This belief, that organisms are produced through divine laws out of lifeless matter, was to guide Needham through all of his subsequent research and theorising on the subject of generation.

One further set of observations described by Needham in this book should be mentioned here, those carried out on eels in blighted wheat. Previously an-nounced, like the observations on pollen, in 1743, Needham's discovery of revivification in these organisms was of major significance. Describing again how the lifeless white fibres in grains of blighted wheat had come to life under his microscope, Needham reported that one could allow them to dry up again and be revived by the addition of water as often and as repeatedly as one liked. He even found that grains he had had in his possession for two years and had brought with him to Portugal exhibited the same phenomenon. Later still Henry Baker was to report that he was able to produce live eels after twenty-seven years from grains Needham had sent to the Royal Society in 1743.[7] The significance of Needham's discovery was not lost on him even as early as his

---

7. See H. Baker (1753:250-60), Needham (1775a:227), and Spallanzani (1776, 2:230; 1777, 2:356-57).

CHARLES BONNET.
né à Genève le 13 Mars 1720.

FUTURI SPES VIRTUTEM ALIT.

Fig. 1. Charles Bonnet (1720-1793). This engraving by Johan-Frederick Clemens, completed in 1778, was based on an oil portrait painted by Jens Juel in 1777 (now hanging in the museum of the Bibliothèque Publique et Universitaire, Geneva). (From the frontispiece to Bonnet, *Œuvres d'histoire naturelle et de philosophie*, 1779-1783, 4° ed., vol.i. Courtesy of the Syndics of Cambridge University Library.)

Fig. 2. Bonnet dictating letters to his secretary. (From Bonnet, *Œuvres d'histoire naturelle et de philosophie*, 1779-1783, 4° ed., vol.v, pt.1. Courtesy of the Taylor Institution Library, Oxford.)

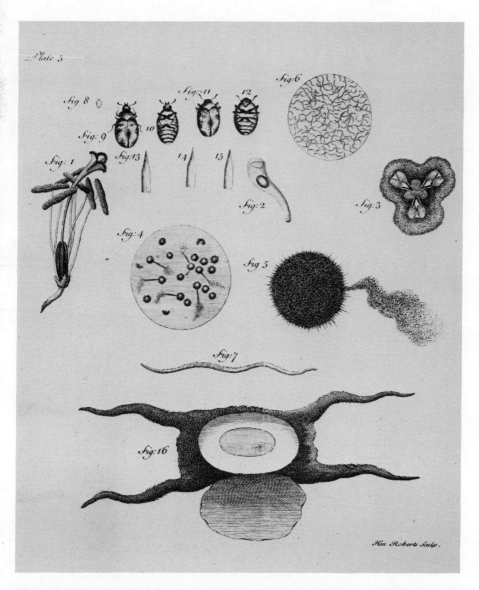

Fig. 5. Needham's early microscopical investigations. *Figs. 1, 2, 3, 4, 5*: The common white lily and its pollen grains, showing the expulsion of the generative globules. *Figs. 6, 7*: Eels in blighted wheat, as seen with low and high magnification. *Figs. 8, 9, 10, 11, 12, 13, 14, 15*: A beetle found feeding on Narcissus pollen, and its scales. *Fig. 16*: The egg of the thornback, partly opened. (From Needham, *An account of some new microscopical discoveries*, 1745, plate 5. Courtesy of the Wellcome Institute Library, London.)

discussion of it in his *New microscopical discoveries*. Yet in 1745, he was unable to explain how these eels could live for so long in a desiccated state or where they arose from and how they reproduced. The subject was, however, to be a dominant one in Needham's subsequent work, and was to play a prominent role especially in Needham's later controversy with Voltaire (see section 5 of this Introduction).

During 1745, Needham also carried out observations on eels found in flour paste jointly with James Sherwood. Needham and Sherwood found that these eels were viviparous (Sherwood 1746). In addition, Needham observed animal-cules in dog semen with John Hill, who also gave Needham a seed infusion to take home with him for his own observations (see Needham 1748:632; 1750:182n). All of these observations were to figure in the development of Needham's ideas on generation. Needham did not propose his own theory, however, until after he moved to Paris in mid-1746 and encountered Buffon. During his first year and a half in Paris, Needham seems not to have pursued his work on generation. He sent four letters to the Royal Society, two of which were published, one on electrical experiments and the other on a mirror invented by Buffon that would burn objects at a distance of sixty-six feet.[8] These letters contain evidence that Needham was in frequent contact with Buffon, whose acquaintance he had made on Folkes's recommendation. Needham also paid Réaumur several visits (see letter 20, n.7) – an interesting combination of friends, considering the dislike Buffon and Réaumur held for one another. On 22 January 1747, Needham was elected a Fellow of the Royal Society, on the basis of his *New microscopical discoveries*, the several communications he had sent to the Society, and 'his Learning and Candor, as well as [...] his dilligence in the promotion of Philo-sophical and Natural Knowledge' (RS, *Certificates*, 1731-1750, f.335).

It was not until the spring of 1748 that Needham began working again on the question of generation, through the prompting of Buffon. As Needham later reported, it was Buffon 'who first engaged me in this Enquiry, by his ingenious System, which he was pleas'd to read to me, and at the same time expressed his Desire I should pursue it, before I had myself any Thoughts of it, or any one Experiment had been try'd' (Needham 1748:633). Buffon had indeed already conceived of his own theory of generation and had written an account of it by early 1746 (see Buffon 1749-1789, 2:168; and Roger 1963:543). This account later formed the first five chapters of volume two of Buffon's *Histoire naturelle*, published in 1749; and it was these chapters that Buffon evidently read to Needham in the spring of 1748, before their joint research began (see Needham 1748:640 and Buffon 1749-1789, 2:170). The collaboration that ensued between Buffon and Needham was of immense benefit to both of them. From their observations on seminal fluid and on infusions, Buffon was able to add an experimental substratum to his otherwise speculative theory. And for Needham, these observations were to lead to the formulation of his own universal theory of generation.

As mentioned earlier in this section, Buffon's epigenetic account of generation

---

8. See Needham (1746a, 1746b, and 1747b); see also Needham's letter to James Parsons in the WIHM (Autograph Letters), and RS, *Journal book*, xx:139-40, 179-80, 258-59, 376-83.

presented a clear challenge to the predominant preformationist theories of his day. Buffon explained the generative process on the basis of two concepts, *molecules organiques* (organic particles) and the *moule intérieur* (internal mould). Buffon believed that in nature two kinds of matter exist, organic and brute, and that in digestion organisms separate out the organic particles from brute matter. These organic particles are then sent to all parts of the body for growth and repair; and excess particles are stored in special reservoirs, where they become the seminal fluid. During reproduction, these excess organic particles, acting as 'representatives' from the parts of the body from which they were sent, are organised into a new organism through the influence of the internal mould and the agency of a 'penetrating force'. No preformed or preexisting structures are thus involved, in Buffon's view, in the generative process; and each new creature is formed anew out of the parents' organic particles.

This was the view of generation that Buffon presented to Needham in early 1748. It was in many respects similar to Maupertuis's theory of generation that had been published only a few years earlier (see Maupertuis 1744 and 1745). Buffon and Maupertuis had in fact often spoken together, according to Needham, about the subject of generation and about their common dissatisfaction with the theory of preexistence (see Needham 1748:633). Buffon proposed to Needham, when explaining his theory to him, that since the seminal fluid is the reservoir for organic particles, then the spermatic animalcules that had been discovered there could not be true animals but must rather be either the organic particles themselves or assemblages of them. This idea coincided well with Needham's own earlier suggestion, in his *New microscopical discoveries* (1745), that spermatic animalcules were 'mere machines' and not the agents of generation. Buffon reasoned that if one viewed the seminal fluid with a microscope then one might perhaps be able to see the organic particles or at least their smallest combinations, since there ought to be a great concentration of them in seminal fluid. Needham seems to have suggested the idea of looking at seed infusions as well with a microscope, because seeds, analogous to seminal fluid, should contain a large number of organic particles. Needham had previously made observations on a seed infusion given to him by John Hill, and he had seen the microscopic moving bodies one finds after the seeds have been infused for a few days. 'Thus did our Enquiry commence upon Seed-Infusions,' Needham reported, 'from a Desire Mr. *de Buffon* had to find out the organical Parts, and I, if possible, to discover which among these moving Bodies were strictly to be look'd upon as Animals, and which to be accounted mere Machines' (Needham 1748:634).

Although Needham was present at some of Buffon's observations (made with Daubenton) on male and, more controversially, on female seminal fluid, the emphasis of the research he did with Buffon was on infusions (see Needham 1748:635-40, 643; Needham 1750:202-203n; and Buffon 1749-1789, 2:171, 184, 203, 221). Needham reported that he first made four infusions of almond germs, followed by fifteen other seed infusions, which he and Buffon initially observed together, after which Needham took the infusions home for further viewing. 'The Result of our first Observations was,' Needham recounted, 'that tho' the Phials had been close stopp'd, and all Communication with the exterior Air prevented, yet, in about fifteen Days Time, the Infusions swarm'd with Clouds of moving Atoms, so small, and so prodigiously active; that tho' we made use of a Magnifier of not much above half a Line focal Distance, yet I am persuaded nothing but their vast Multitude render'd them visible' (Needham 1748:636).

Needham's most famous infusion, made with mutton broth, was designed to show that microscopical beings result from the decomposition of the infused material and not from eggs deposited from the air. This latter explanation was the one favoured by preformationists, who wanted to extend to the microscopic realm the universality of reproduction via eggs. Needham sought to demonstrate that, on the contrary, microorganisms did not generate from eggs but rather through vegetative forces. 'For my Purpose therefore,' he reported, 'I took a Quantity of Mutton-Gravy hot from the Fire, and shut it up in a Phial, clos'd up with a Cork so well masticated, that my Precautions amounted to as much as if I had sealed my Phial hermetically. I thus effectually excluded the exterior Air, that it might not be said my moving Bodies drew their Origin from Insects, or Eggs floating in the Atmosphere' (Needham 1748:637). After sealing his flask, Needham heated it in hot ashes to destroy any possible existing eggs. He then left his infusion for several days. When he opened it, Needham described, 'My Phial swarm'd with Life, and microscopical Animals of most Dimensions, from some of the largest I had ever seen, to some of the least. The very first Drop I used, upon opening it, yielded me Multitudes perfectly form'd, animated, and spontaneous in all their Motions' (Needham 1748:638). He repeated these observations on 'three or four Scores' of infusions of animal and vegetable substances, obtaining the same results whether he sealed and heated the infusions or not.

During the course of these observations, Needham began to question the idea that microscopic beings are in general 'mere machines', as Buffon believed, and to abandon the concept of organic particles. He came to believe instead that all microscopic beings are actually organisms, that they arise from the decomposition of animal or vegetable substances, and that their formation results from a 'vegetative Force' present 'in every microscopical Point of Matter, and every visible Filament of which the whole animal or vegetable Texture consists' (Needham 1748:653). He began to view the production of microorganisms in infusions as a process of vegetation, resulting from the actions of a vegetative force that had been released, as it were, by the decomposition of animal or plant material. The basis for this view was a series of new infusions Needham began on his own a few days before Buffon left Paris for the country in May and that he pursued for several weeks. These infusions were made with pulverised wheat, which formed a gelatinous mass in the bottom of his flasks. When viewed with a microscope, this gelatinous mass seemed to be composed of filaments that proceeded to break up into moving bodies (fig. 6, *2*). After a few days these moving bodies disappeared, to be followed by a new production of filaments and subsequent moving bodies. Needham was enthralled with his new observations: 'I own I cannot but wonder to this Day at what I saw; and tho' I have now seen them so often, I still look upon them with new Surprize' (Needham 1748:647).

Further infusions yielded similar results and seemed to indicate that plant-like filaments produced animal-like moving bodies, which in turn vegetated anew into filaments. Needham refined his technique of observation, floating wheat grains on water by attaching them to thin slices of cork. When the seeds, from which the germ had been removed, began to vegetate, Needham detached a portion of the vegetating filaments and placed this in a watch crystal with a small amount of water (fig. 6, *3*). In this manner, Needham could put each separate infusion under his microscope without having to disturb it. 'Thus I had for the Subject of my Observations,' he wrote, 'what I may call a micro-scopical Island, whose Plants and Animals soon became so familiar to me, that I knew every animal Species, and every individual Plant almost without any Danger of Mistake' (Needham 1748:652). These infusions produced filaments that appeared to open at one end and release animated globules (fig. 6, *A, B*).[9]

Needham viewed the successive appearance of filaments and globules in his infusions as providing evidence for the universal existence of a vegetative force. Having actually observed microscopic beings emerging from the filaments, which were themselves the product of pulverised wheat, Needham thought that he had seen at first-hand the vegetative force in action. He believed he had discovered a new level of life in which generation occurred in a wholly unexpected manner. Rather than being the product of previously deposited eggs, micro-organisms demonstrated that vegetation, instead of conventional modes of generation, governed the microscopic world. As he claimed: 'I believe I can furnish, from my last Summer's Observations, a Cloud of Instances, of a new Class of Beings, whose Origin has hitherto been unknown, wherein Animals grow upon, are produc'd by, and, in the strict Sense of the Word, brought forth from Plants; then by a strange Vicissitude again become Plants of another Kind, these again Animals of another, and thus on for a Series, further than the utmost Power of Glasses can carry the most inquisitive Observer' (Needham 1748:629-30). This new class of beings formed the basis for a theory of vegetation Needham was to extend to the entire living world.

Within a month of making these observations on wheat infusions, Needham wrote a short 'Memoire sur la Generation', dated 9 June 1748, which he deposited as a sealed letter with Jean-Paul Grandjean de Fouchy, the Secretary of the Paris Académie des sciences (see Appendix B). Needham seems to have been motivated to take this precaution by a concern over protecting his priority in both his theory and his observations. He stated in the mémoire that he had communicated his results to Buffon, Réaumur, Daubenton, and others; yet, he continued, 'mais comme on a commencé a parler de cette systeme nouvelle, et que mes experiences sont plus connu que j'ai voulu d'abord pour m'assurer mes propres decouvertes, J'ai pris la precaution de sceller, et signer cette petite memoire'. Needham may also have been inspired – and perhaps worried – by the fact that Buffon had deposited in May his own sealed mémoire describing their joint experiments (Roger 1963:543 n.85).

Needham's observations continued through the summer of 1748, and it was not until November of that year that he wrote his well-known paper, 'A summary

9. Needham's descriptions and illustrations (fig. 6, *A, B*) of the production of globules from filaments indicate that he was most probably observing certain forms of water mould, which are species of fungus. These reproduce by forming filamentous structures that release flagellated zoospores into the water.

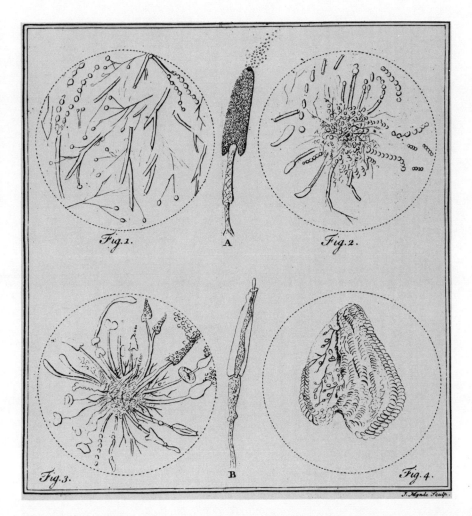

Fig. 6. Needham's illustrations of microscopical observations made on infusions and seminal fluid. His description reads: '*Fig. 1*. Represents the Origin of the spermatic Animals. *Fig. 2*. The Wheat-Infusion. *Fig. 3*. What I have called an Island in the Wheat-Infusion. *Fig. 4*. A Groupe of the Chrysalids of the Paste-Eels. *Fig. 5*. [*A, B*] Is a Draught of one of the first microscopical Plants or Zoophytes which I discover'd; wherein *A* shows the Figure of the Plant throwing out its Animals, and *B* the same again after the Animals were discharged, again putting out a new Shoot from the Stem below, through the hollow transparent Head, to form a new Head, and produce another Generation.' (From Needham, *Observations upon the generation, composition, and decomposition of animal and vegetable substances*, 1749. Courtesy of the Francis A. Countway Library of Medicine.)

of some late observations upon the generation, composition, and decomposition of animal and vegetable substances', which he sent to the Royal Society and from which the above report of his experiments has been drawn. This was read by Martin Folkes at two meetings of the Society in December and was published both in the *Philosophical transactions* for 1748 and as a separate monograph in 1749. It was translated into French by a Parisian physician, Louis-Anne Lavirotte, and was actually in press in Paris when Needham decided to add some further reflections on his system. Needham's additions became a 255-page disquisition including not only a restatement of his ideas on generation but also an explanation of his metaphysical and epistemological views (see section 3 of this Introduction). The resulting book, *Nouvelles observations microscopiques, avec des découvertes intéressantes sur la composition & la décomposition des corps organisés*, was published in 1750.[10]

Needham believed that the phenomena he had observed in the microscopic realm provided evidence for a theory of generation by vegetation that was applicable throughout the living world. He viewed all operations in nature as resulting from the combined effects of active, expansive forces and forces of resistance. When living matter decomposes, he maintained, its 'resistant' aspects separate from its 'active' ones, so that the active forces become released from the resistive ones. This process of vegetation he often described as one of 'exaltation'. He believed that, on the basis of his theory of vegetation, he could explain not only the appearance of microorganisms in infusions but also the formation of animalcules in seminal fluid and the appearance of eels in blighted wheat and in flour paste. When stored grain becomes too humid, he proposed, its contents begin to vegetate and to form the whitish filaments that Needham had seen take life under his microscope (Needham 1748:647-48 and 1750:223-25n, 226-27n). He similarly thought, although somewhat more tentatively, that eels in flour paste could be a product of a 'ductile vegetating Matter, the Produce of Wheat-Flour and Water', even though these eels later became viviparous (Needham 1748:659).[11] Needham further believed that the process of vegetation governed the formation of the embryo in higher organisms, although he did not discuss development at higher levels in any great detail. But he was firmly convinced that epigenesis was the universal method of generation and that at no level of life were any preexistent germs necessary for reproduction to occur. Although some of the particulars of his theory underwent substantial modification in future years (see section 2.iv below), Needham's firm commitment to epigenesis through vegetation was never to waver.

One further aspect of Needham's views on generation remains to be mentioned. Needham was sometimes accused of promoting a theory of equivocal generation, or, as it is more commonly termed today, spontaneous generation. What this meant in Needham's day was the origins of living organisms by accidental or chance means, hence 'equivocal'. Before the late seventeenth

10. This work contained as well a republication of Needham's *Nouvelles observations microscopiques* (1747), which was itself a translation of his *New microscopical discoveries* (1745).

11. Needham later abandoned these explanations of the origins of eels in blighted wheat and in flour paste when Roffredi clarified the life-cycles of these two organisms in 1775 (see Needham 1775a; letter 6, n.4; and letter 49, n.3).

century, the belief that maggots could arise from rotting meat, flies from mud, lice on animals and humans, even rats in piles of rags was widespread. With the rise of preexistence theories and the denial of material causation in generation, the idea of spontaneous generation fell into disrepute by the beginning of the eighteenth century (see Farley 1977). When Francesco Redi demonstrated in 1688 that the maggots on rotting meat were produced from flies depositing eggs, and when Jan Swammerdam and Marcello Malpighi further showed that plant galls were not the product of plants but rather came from insect eggs, two of the most common instances of alleged spontaneous generation were experimentally demonstrated to be false. Consequently, the belief that all organisms arise from eggs became the predominant view.

By the mid-eighteenth century, when Needham and Buffon maintained that microscopic organisms could arise from decomposing matter through vegetative forces (Needham) or organic molecules (Buffon), the spontaneous generation debate emerged once more, albeit on a different plane and with somewhat different issues involved. Although Buffon freely labelled his view as spontaneous generation (see especially Buffon 1749-1789, *Supplément*, 4:335-66), Needham consistently and strenuously denied that his theory in any way supported equivocal generation. His theory did allow for the production of organisms from decomposition; yet, he maintained, this always occurred in a lawful, regular way, not in an equivocal one. As he remarked, 'no Axiom, how much soever it may have been exploded, is more true than that of the Antients, *Corruptio unius est Generatio alterius*; though they drew it from false Principles, and so established it as to render Generation equivocal' (Needham 1748:638). Needham maintained that, in his theory, higher organisms are produced through a lawful succession of developmental events so that, even though they are formed epigenetically, offspring of the proper species always result. At the microscopic level, the same kind of lawful succession occurs, he claimed; for whenever he infused a particular substance, the same sequence of microorganisms was produced. Furthermore, different infused substances produced identifiably different sequences of microorganisms. Thus the vegetative force, Needham concluded, could operate only in definite, regular ways prescribed by God and never in an equivocal fashion.

Needham was striking out on new ground with this argument, for his contemporaries saw no middle option between lawful preformed generation and unlawful, accidental spontaneous generation. To allow matter to form organisms in a regular manner yet not by chance was a new threat to the preformation-mechanism synthesis. By proposing the views that he did on material causation, Needham became caught up in the debate over materialism that ensued in the 1750s, 1760s, and 1770s (see section 4 of this Introduction). Yet he always believed that epigenesis through vegetation was the way in which God had ordained that the natural world should operate. As he explained in a letter to Haller in 1760, in both his own theory of epigenesis and in the theory of preformation, 'the divinity equally presides over the powers of generation, and governs by infallible laws, absolutely exclusive of equivocal generation; the difference at most is but in the manner, and in the time' (Mazzolini 1976:72). On this basis, Needham mounted a lifelong campaign to demonstrate that one could sustain an epigenetic view of generation that reaffirmed, rather than challenged, the existence of God. His hope was that his theory of generation would provide an alternative both to preformation and to materialism.

iii. Bonnet's theory of preformation

Bonnet's career as a naturalist began in the field of insectology. Having read the first volume of Réaumur's *Mémoires pour servir à l'histoire des insectes* in 1737, at the youthful age of seventeen, Bonnet began in the following year a correspondence with Réaumur that was to last until the latter's death in 1757. Réaumur quickly became Bonnet's mentor and guide as the latter's interests in natural history grew. One problem that Réaumur had posed in the *Mémoires* was the generation of aphids, in which females appeared to reproduce without coupling with male aphids. Yet Réaumur had been unsuccessful in devising an experiment to test this (Réaumur 1734-1742, 3:329-30). Bonnet decided to investigate the question, and by 1740 he had succeeded in demonstrating parthenogenesis in aphids by isolating newly generated female aphids until they matured and could be observed to reproduce. Through further experiments, Bonnet was eventually able to observe parthenogenesis in nine successive generations of females. Réaumur announced Bonnet's discovery before the Paris Académie des sciences, resulting in Bonnet's being named a correspondent of Réaumur at the Académie on 31 August 1740. He was also elected a Fellow of the Royal Society of London on 17 November 1743. Two years later, Bonnet published an extensive account of his observations in his first book, *Traité d'insectologie* (1745). By the age of twenty-five, Bonnet had become a renowned naturalist (see Savioz 1948b:14 and Marx 1976:316-22).

The discovery of parthenogenesis in aphids served also to confirm Bonnet's belief in the preexistence of germs. If the female aphid could produce offspring without any contact with the male and, even more strikingly, if these offspring themselves could again reproduce in isolation (and so on for several generations), then the idea that the female egg contained successive generations enclosed one within the other received experimental confirmation. Furthermore, Bonnet extended the idea of preformed germs to account for the problem of regeneration, which he had studied in earthworms and to which the second half of the *Traité d'insectologie* was devoted. Following the discovery made by Abraham Trembley in 1740 that the freshwater polyp could regenerate into several new polyps when cut into pieces, Bonnet demonstrated the same phenomenon in earthworms. Bonnet attributed this regenerative ability to preformed germs present in the organism, and he viewed mulitiplication by division as a confirmation of 'la belle théorie des germes contenus les uns dans les autres' (Bonnet 1745:xxiii-xxiv; B.O., 1:xxviii/1:xlii).

An additional topic treated in the *Traité d'insectologie*, albeit only briefly in the Preface, was Bonnet's concept of a chain of being in nature. One thing that had impressed Bonnet about the polyp was the plant-like nature of its ability to multiply by budding and by division. As he explained, 'Les admirables propriétés qui leur sont communes avec les Plantes, je veux dire, la multiplication *de bouture* & celle *par rejettons*, indiquent suffisamment qu'ils sont le lien qui unit le regne végétal à l'animal. Cette réflexion m'a fait naître la pensée, peut-être téméraire, de dresser une Echelle des Etres naturels, qu'on trouvera à la fin de cette Préface [reproduced here as fig. 8]' (1745:xxviii; B.O., 1:xxx/1:xlv). The idea that the polyp formed the link between the animal and plant kingdoms was a common one in Bonnet's day, although Bonnet never went as far as to say, like some, that the polyp was a true zoophyte (animal-plant), arguing instead that it was an animal that simply possessed properties common to plants. Yet the notion that there exists a continuous, ascending scale of beings in nature played a powerful role in Bonnet's thought throughout his life.

Increasing difficulties with his eyesight forced Bonnet to abandon his early experimental investigations on insects. Yet his commitment to natural history did not cease but developed rather into a more encompassing philosophy of nature that he expounded in subsequent publications. In 1748, Bonnet began dictating a work titled *Méditations sur l'univers*, which, although never published in its original form, served as the basis for several of Bonnet's later works. In particular, eight chapters of the *Méditations* were devoted to the problem of generation and to elaborating Bonnet's own preformationist views. Later published in 1762 as the first eight chapters of the *Considérations sur les corps organisés*, these early writings show us Bonnet's first systematic attempt to promote the theory of preexistence as well as his initial reaction to the views of Buffon and Needham, which were published while Bonnet was in the midst of writing the *Méditations*.

The reasons for Bonnet's delay in publishing his theory of generation are explained by him in the Preface to the *Considérations sur les corps organisés*. Three factors contributed to his setting aside the *Méditations*: first, the initiation of a series of experiments on the leaves of plants, in which Bonnet studied transpiration and the movement of leaves, among other subjects, and which resulted in his *Recherches sur l'usage des feuilles dans les plantes* (1754). Second, Bonnet became increasingly interested in psychology, especially in the relationship between the nervous system, sensations, and ideas (see section 3 of this Introduction). These speculations produced the anonymously published *Essai de psychologie* (1755), which was based on a separate part of the *Méditations*, and Bonnet's *Essai analytique sur les facultés de l'ame* (1760). But the principal reason Bonnet gave for his delay in publishing his views on generation was that he did not feel that they were sufficiently confirmed by experimental demonstration, and he decided to wait until more investigations were carried out. He did not have to wait long, for 'Enfin cette découverte importante que j'attendois & que j'avois osé prédire, me fut annoncée en 1757, par M. le Baron de HALLER, qui la tenoit de la Nature elle-même' (1762, 1:vii; B.O., 3:ix/5:71-72).

Bonnet was referring to Haller's observations on the development of incubated chick embryos and to his demonstration that the tiny, invisible embryo exists in the egg before conception. Really more an argument than a discovery, Haller's demonstration was based on the continuity of certain intestinal membranes of the embryonic chick with the yolk-sac membranes. Having found membranes surrounding the unfecundated egg that Haller took to be the same membranes as those that later surrounded the yolk, Haller concluded that the tiny embryo must also exist in the unfecundated egg, connected to the membranes in

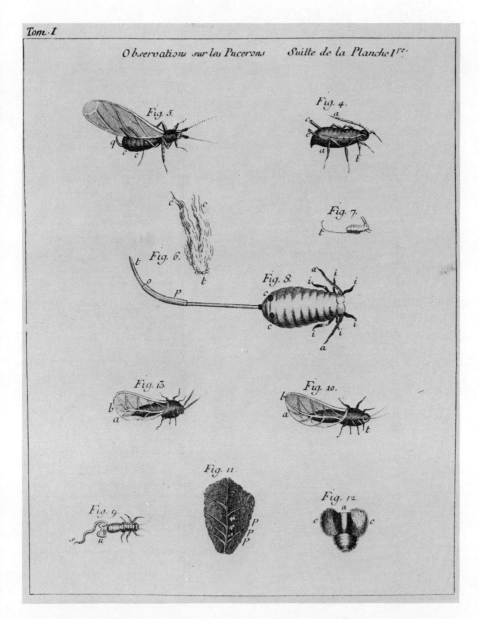

Fig. 7. Illustrations of aphids (*Figs. 4-8*) and so-called 'Faux-Pucerons', insects that resemble aphids (*Figs. 9-13*) from Bonnet's *Traité d'insectologie* (1745). All of the figures were originally published in the third volume of Réaumur's *Mémoires pour servir à l'histoire des insectes* (1734-1742). (From Bonnet, *Œuvres d'histoire naturelle et de philosophie*, 1779-1783, vol.i, plate 1, [pt. 2]. Courtesy of the Taylor Institution Library, Oxford.)

IDÉE D'UNE ÉCHELLE
DES ETRES NATURELS.

L'HOMME.

Orang-Outang.

Singe.

QUADRUPEDES

Ecureuil volant.

Chauvefouris.

Autruche.

OISEAUX.

Oifeaux aquatiques.

Oifeaux amphibies.

Poiffons volans.

POISSONS.

Poiffons rampans.

Anguilles.

Serpens d'eau.

SERPENS.

Limaces.

Limaçons.

COQUILLAGES.

Vers à tuyau.

Teignes.

INSECTES.

Gallinfectes.

Tænia, ou Solitaire.

Polypes

Orties de Mer.

Senfitive.

PLANTES.

PLANTES.

Lychens.

Moififfures.

Champignons, Agarics.

Truffes.

Coraux & Coralloïdes.

Lithophytes.

Amianthe.

Talcs, Gyps, Sélénites.

Ardoifes.

PIERRES.

Pierres figurées.

Cryftallifations.

SELS.

Vitriols.

METAUX.

DEMI-METAUX.

SOUFRES.

Bitumes.

TERRES.

Terre pure.

EAU.

AIR.

FEU.

Matieres plus fubtiles.

Fig. 8. Bonnet's table of the chain of being, from the preface to his *Traité d'insectologie* (1745). The original plate is a continuous column, here divided into two halves for reproduction. (From Bonnet, *Œuvres d'histoire naturelle et de philosophie*, 1779-1783, vol.i.)

the same fashion that would later become visible. Haller communicated this argument to Bonnet in a letter dated 1 September 1757 (Sonntag 1983:109) and published his observations on chick embryos, which formed the basis for his own conversion from the theory of epigenesis to preformation, in *Sur la formation du cœur dans le poulet* (1758).[12] Bonnet's reaction to this book was predictable: 'Vos *Poulets* m'enchantent: je n'avois pas éspéré que le secret de la Génération se découvriroit si-tôt,' he wrote to Haller on 30 October 1758. Referring to his own earlier thoughts on the subject, Bonnet continued, 'C'êst bien par vous, Monsieur, que la Nature à été prise sur le Fait. J'avois osé la déviner il y a une dizaine d'années, et j'ai été bien agréablement surpris, quand j'ai vû vos Expériences s'accorder si bien avec mes conjectures, et vôtre Hypothése avec la mienne' (Sonntag 1983:147-48).

Bonnet then sent his earlier manuscript on generation to Haller for his opinion, and, when Haller urged him to publish it, Bonnet concurred. The letters that passed between Bonnet and Haller on this matter are included by Bonnet in his Preface to the resulting *Considérations sur les corps organisés*. One's impression upon reading Bonnet's account is that he included these letters not only to demonstrate Haller's approval of his book but also to claim some priority for his own views on generation, so happily confirmed by Haller's observations. This is also very probably the reason why Bonnet included the eight chapters from the *Méditations* virtually unchanged from their original form as written over a decade earlier (see Savioz 1748b:210).

The *Considérations sur les corps organisés*, however, grew into a much larger work when Bonnet finished making his additions. The twelve new chapters dwarfed the earlier eight ones in size, increasing the length of the book four-fold. They also offer us a compendium of eighteenth-century natural history on the subject of generation. Although unable to pursue his own experimental investigations, Bonnet made much use of others' observations to support his own views. And since these views were decidedly preformationist, Bonnet's book marshalls evidence on all fronts to combat theories of epigenetic development. In his *Mémoires autobiographiques*, Bonnet explained his motives for writing this work: 'Je m'étais proposé trois choses dans la composition de cet ouvrage: la première, de rassembler en abrégé tout ce que l'histoire naturelle offrait de plus intéressant et de plus certain sur l'origine, la reproduction et le développement des êtres organisés; la deuxième, de combattre les divers systèmes fondés sur l'*épigénèse*, et en particulier ceux de MM. de Buffon et Needham; la troisième, d'opposer à ces étranges opinions une hypothèse plus conforme aux faits et aux principes d'une saine philosophie' (Savioz 1748b:210).

The first eight chapters of the *Corps organisés* (as Bonnet often referred to this work) open with a clear statement of Bonnet's preformationist position: 'La Philosophie ayant compris l'impossibilité où elle étoit d'expliquer méchanique-ment la formation des Etres organisés, a imaginé heureusement qu'ils existoient déja en petit, sous la forme de *Germes*, ou de *Corpuscules organiques*' (Bonnet 1762, 1:1; B.O., 3:1/5:83). Immediately following the initial eight chapters Bonnet

12. For the changes that Haller's views on embryological development underwent and for further discussion of his observations on incubated chicken eggs, see Roe (1975 and 1981), Mazzolini (1977), and Duchesneau (1979).

added a chapter on Haller's observations on chicken eggs and his proof that the chick preexists in the egg before fecundation. On this basis, Bonnet concluded even more decisively in favour of preformation: 'Je suis donc ramené plus fortement que jamais', he declared, 'au grand principe dont je suis parti en commençant cet ouvrage; c'est qu'il n'est point dans la Nature de véritable génération; mais, nous nommons improprement *génération*, le commencement d'un développement qui nous rend visible ce que nous ne pouvions auparavant appercevoir' (Bonnet 1762, 1:169; B.O., 3:135/5:304). Bonnet argued, like Haller, that all of the essential parts of the embryo exist in miniature in the egg before conception and that fecundation simply initiates a process of unfolding and development by stimulating the tiny embryo's heart to begin beating. The embryo may appear to form gradually; but in reality, Bonnet and Haller maintained, the observer witnesses only the gradually emerging visibility of structures that preexisted in a subvisible state.

Bonnet devoted the last two of the eight chapters taken from his *Méditations* to an exposition and critique of the system of generation presented in the second volume of Buffon's *Histoire naturelle*. Thus we have Bonnet's initial reaction upon first reading Buffon's views, since these two final chapters were written by Bonnet sometime between 1749 and 1751.[13] This would have been Bonnet's first exposure to Needham's work as well, since in the *Histoire naturelle* Buffon discussed their collaboration on observations of spermatic animalcules and infusions, and also presented Needham's observations on the calamary. Needham, however, is not mentioned in Bonnet's two chapters; and one can surmise that Bonnet had not yet read Needham's own paper on generation.

Bonnet's discussions of Buffon and Needham in the *Corps organisés* can be divided into three categories, representing his reactions to their views at three distinct times. The first discussion, just mentioned, was based on Bonnet's initial reading of Buffon. Second, Bonnet added numerous extended discussions of both Buffon and Needham in the twelve new chapters written for the publication of the *Corps organisés* in 1762. Finally, Bonnet turned again to their views even more critically in notes he added to the edition of the *Corps organisés* published in his *Œuvres* in 1779. It is instructive to separate these three discussions and to consider them in sequential order, as they reveal much about Bonnet's gathering of new evidence and arguments through the years to combat Needham and Buffon. We shall examine the first two critiques here, turning to the final one in the next section.

Bonnet opened his discussion of Buffon's system of generation by claiming that he had written the first six chapters of the *Méditations*, which outlined his own preformationist theory, before seeing the second volume of Buffon's *Histoire naturelle*. The effect of first reading this work on Bonnet was immediate: 'La conformité des matieres contenues dans ce Volume avec celles que je viens de traiter, la réputation de l'Auteur, la singularité du systême, la nouveauté des découvertes, l'air de preuves qu'elles affectent, & sur-tout la défiance où je dois

---

13. These dates are based upon the year of publication of Buffon's theory (1749) and the fact that, in a footnote to chapter eight (on Buffon), Bonnet stated that the chapter had been written before he had received a letter from Réaumur written in December 1751 (see Bonnet 1762:117-18n and B.O., 3:85-86 n.3/5:224 n.1).

être à l'égard de mes idées, m'avoient d'abord fait penser à renoncer à tout ce que j'avois écrit sur la génération' (Bonnet 1762, 1:77; B.O., 3:56/5:174). But Bonnet quickly recovered his confidence and, after presenting an account of Buffon's observations on seminal fluids and on infusions, and after summarising his theories of organic molecules and the *moule intérieur*, Bonnet turned to his own critique of the new system. It is important to remember (and if one forgets, one is reminded by footnotes Bonnet later added to these chapters) that, at the time Bonnet composed this critique, he had no reason to doubt the accuracy of Buffon's observations. Thus his comments assume the form of conjectures rather than solid rebuttal (as would his later critiques).

Two of his objections to Buffon's system reveal Bonnet's basic discomfort with a theory of generation founded on active matter and attractive forces. Given the fact that an organism is a complex whole composed of innumerable interdependent parts, Bonnet could not see how it could be formed by material forces alone. As he remarked to his readers (Bonnet 1762, 1:99; B.O., 3:71-72/5:200):

Je leur demanderai ensuite, s'ils conçoivent qu'un Tout aussi composé, aussi lié, aussi harmonique, puisse être formé par le simple concours de molécules mues ou dirigées suivant certaines loix à nous inconnues. Je les prierai de me dire s'ils ne sentent point la nécessité où nous sommes d'admettre, que cette admirable machine a été d'abord dessinée en petit par la même main qui a tracé le plan de l'Univers. Pour moi j'avoue ingénument, que je n'ai jamais conçu que la chose puisse être autrement. Lorsque j'ai voulu essayer de former un Corps organisé sans le secours d'un germe primitif, j'ai toujours été si mécontent des efforts de mon imagination, que j'ai très-bien compris que l'entreprise étoit absolument au-dessus de sa portée.

Such a reaction to Buffon's theory was independently expressed by Bonnet's ally Haller in his own review of the Buffonian system.[14]

Bonnet's second difficulty with Buffon's theory was the question of the nature of the 'moving globules' seen in seminal fluid and in infusions of vegetable seeds. Buffon had argued that these microscopic bodies were simply the most basic assemblages of organic particles, which were present in abundance in seminal fluid and in seeds. Bonnet was forced to admit, on the basis of Buffon's alleged observations, that these moving bodies might perhaps not be true animals. Yet he quickly asserted his own opinion that they were in fact animals, bolstering his claim by pointing to the magnificence of God's creation if indeed such minute creatures were animals and if all larger creatures, animal and plant, were composed of these tiny animals. By the time Bonnet finished writing this critique he was able to add some experimental basis to his speculative rejection of Buffon's opinions on animalcules. Both he and Trembley had received letters from Réaumur in December 1751, in which Réaumur described observations that he and the abbé Lignac had carried out on infusions with the intention of repeating Buffon's and Needham's observations. Réaumur reported that the moving bodies in infusions were indeed true animals that reproduced in normal fashions (see M. Trembley 1943:360-64). Quoting from Réaumur's letters in a footnote, Bonnet called on Buffon to reconsider his observations, concluding, 'Il

14. See Haller (1751) and letter 7, n.5.

a tant de sagacité, qu'il seroit bien étrange que le vrai lui échappât. Mais súrement il ne lui échappera point, s'il veut bien oublier, au moins pour un temps, ses *molécules organiques*, ses moules, & tout l'attirail d'un systême, que son génie fécond s'est plû à inventer, & que sa raison devenue sévere abandonnera peut-être quelque jour' (Bonnet 1762, 1:118n; B.O., 3:85-86 n.3/5:224-25 n.1).

In Bonnet's second set of discussions of the Buffonian system, in the new sections of the *Corps organisés*, he continued to criticise Buffon's ideas and now singled out Needham as well for extended evaluation. Bonnet was so convinced of the explanatory scope of Haller's observations on chick embryos that he gave as one of the titles to chapter 11, 'Que les observations sur la formation du Poulet achevent de détruire le systême des molécules organiques'. Because Haller had demonstrated, Bonnet argued in this chapter, that the chick embryo preexists in the egg before fecundation, how could organic molecules in the semen of the cock have any influence on the generation of the new offspring? Citing again Réaumur's report of his and Lignac's observations on the moving bodies in infusions, Bonnet rejected as well Buffon's explanation of the origins of microscopic beings. One could never believe that animalcules were produced by the material of the infusion itself, Bonnet claimed, for 'Une telle Physique choqueroit également le raisonnement & l'expérience' (Bonnet 1762, 1:174-75; B.O., 3:139-40/5:311). Microscopic animalcules reproduce from eggs present in the infusion or dropped from the air, Bonnet maintained – a contention, as we shall see, that was most happily to be confirmed by Spallanzani.

In volume two of the *Corps organisés*, Bonnet devoted an entire chapter to an examination and critique of Needham's microscopical observations and theory of generation. Here Bonnet likened the initial discovery of the microscopical level of life to the discovery of America, about which the early explorers could give only limited descriptions. Calling Needham 'un de ces Colombs modernes qui auront la gloire d'avoir les premiers côtoyé cette Région des infinimens petits', Bonnet explained that he was going to give a précis of Needham's microscopical observations because of 'La nouveauté de ces découvertes, la singularité des objets qu'elles présentent, la réputation bien méritée de leur Auteur, & le but que je me suis proposé dans cet Ouvrage' (Bonnet 1762, 2:206-207; B.O., 3:393/6:289). Bonnet proceeded to summarise Needham's theory as presented in his paper on generation of 1748, highlighting his observations on sealed, heated mutton juice, on seed and wheat infusions, on eels in blighted wheat, and on spermatic animalcules. Bonnet also presented Needham's explanation of filamentous zoophytes producing moving animalcules.

Needless to say, Bonnet raised a number of questions with regard to Needham's observations; for, as he remarked, 'Plus on réfléchit sur ces diverses expériences, & plus on sent combien il est difficile de s'assurer ici du vrai, & de dissiper tous les doutes qu'elles font naître' (Bonnet 1762, 2:212; B.O., 3:393/6:296). With regard to Needham's observations on sealed, heated infusions, Bonnet queried, were Needham's flasks really completely sealed? And was it certain that no type of egg or animal could withstand the heat Needham subjected the flasks to? Could one be positive that, when Needham extracted a drop of infusion liquid for examination, animalcules were not introduced then from the air? Bonnet even suggested that perhaps some animalcules could grow from new eggs to a visible size in the space of the few minutes it took to extract the drop of liquid and place it under the microscope. With regard to the filaments in infusions that produced animalcules, Bonnet asked, could these animalcules not simply be hidden from view among the filaments and only appear to be produced by them?

One must recall that, because his poor eyesight prevented him from making microscopical observations himself, Bonnet could only offer queries and suggestions, so that other investigators might repeat Needham's observations and disprove his theory. Many of Bonnet's objections are very similar to those presented in the abbé Lignac's *Lettres à un Amériquain* (1751), the eleventh letter of which was devoted to a critique of Needham's observations. Although Bonnet did not refer to Lignac in the chapter on Needham in the *Corps organisés*, he did remark in a letter to Needham dated 20 December 1760 that he had recently had Lignac's *Lettres* read to him and that 'plusieurs de ses remarques m'ont paru fondées' (letter 6). Thus Bonnet had certainly read Lignac before writing his own chapter on Needham and may have derived some of his criticisms from him.[15] Referring again (for the third time) to Réaumur's letters on his and Lignac's repetition of Needham's observations, Bonnet suggested in this chapter that Needham's description of the conversion of zoophytes into animalcules was only an appearance, which Needham would undoubtedly have recognised had he examined their generation more closely.

Yet Bonnet's main objection to Needham's theory was not so much to his observations as to the conclusions he had drawn from them. The existence of a vegetative force, the possibility of equivocal generation, the alleged reality of true zoophytes – these were the issues that really concerned Bonnet. 'Quand pour expliquer l'apparition de certains Animalcules dans une liqueur,' Bonnet declared, 'on recourt à des forces *productrices*, à des vertus *végétatives*, ne met-on pas des mots à la place des choses? Quelle idée a-t-on de ces forces? Comment conçoit-on qu'elles organisent la matiere, qu'elles transforment des molécules inanimées en Êtres vivans, le Végétal en Animal?' (Bonnet 1762, 2:214; B.O., 3:399/6:299). How could one believe that the numerous interdependent and interconnected organs in an animal's body could be formed successively? (Bonnet 1762, 2:215; B.O., 3:399-400/6:300):

Plus on approfondit la nature de l'Animal, plus on s'aide des lumieres de l'Anatomie, & plus on se persuade qu'un Tout si harmonique n'a pu être formé pieces après pieces. Et si l'on se retranchoit à dire que la force *génératrice* produit son effet d'un seul coup, je demanderois quel grand avantage l'on trouve à mettre une telle Force à la place du CRÉATEUR qui sûrement agit ainsi, & dont notre estimable Auteur est très éloigné de combattre l'existence? Nous avons ri d'EPICURE, qui formoit un Monde avec des atomes: faire un Animal avec du jus de Mouton, seroit-ce moins choquer la bonne Philosophie?

Bonnet's attitude toward the operation of natural forces in the process of generation was that they could never act in a formative fashion, but only in a limited, mechanical manner. This was a common position among preformationists, and Bonnet's views were reinforced by those of his friend and colleague Haller.

15. Bonnet did not finish writing the *Corps organisés* until February 1762 (see Savioz 1748b:210).

In a similar manner, Bonnet completely rejected the possibility of equivocal generation. Arguing again, as he had in his critique of Buffon's views, that animalcules could never be formed spontaneously from the material of the infusion, Bonnet proclaimed that, of all the varieties of fecundation and generation that existed in nature, none occurred equivocally; for all organisms originate from a parent of the same species. One had to assume, until rigorous experiments demonstrated otherwise, that there was no equivocal generation in the microscopic world either. 'La Nature entiere,' he concluded, 'dépose contre les générations *équivoques*' (Bonnet 1762, 2:215; B.O., 3:400/6:300).

Finally, Bonnet questioned the existence, proclaimed by Needham, of zoophytes, that is, of true animal-plants. Bonnet was quite concerned about the transformation that Needham had allegedly observed between plant-like filaments and animalcules. Although he was a strong promoter of the idea of a continuous chain of being in nature, Bonnet refused to allow the existence of truly intermediate organisms between the animal and plant kingdoms. One of the principal reasons for this refusal was that Bonnet could not accept the idea of an active, interconvertable chain of being in nature, but rather remained adamantly tied to a fixed, though nuanced, hierarchical arrangement. Thus, to counter Needham's claims on behalf of the existence of zoophytes, Bonnet queried whether one could ever define any single character that separated plants from animals and concluded by arguing that a true animal-plant would be a contradiction in terms.

Although Bonnet did not have any really decisive observational proof against the views of Needham when he wrote the new chapters for his *Corps organisés*, he undoubtedly felt that he had raised enough questions concerning both Needham's observations and his conclusions to seriously undermine his theory of generation. In a number of letters to Haller and to Spallanzani, written over the next several years, Bonnet alluded to his discussion of Needham's views in the *Corps organisés* as a solid refutation, often complaining that Needham had not bothered to read his remarks. How much Needham read of Bonnet's book is difficult to tell, but it was not until the publication of Spallanzani's critique in 1765 that Needham indicated his reaction to any of his critics. The major documentation that we have for this reaction is in Needham's letters to Bonnet, to which we shall now turn.

iv. The subject of generation in the correspondence

At the end of his chapter on Needham in the *Corps organisés*, Bonnet remarked that 'Après avoir composé ce Chapitre, j'ai cru devoir écrire à M. NEEDHAM, pour le prier de m'apprendre s'il étoit toujours dans les mêmes idées sur l'origine des Animalcules; car j'aimois à penser qu'il les avoit abandonnées' (Bonnet 1762, 2:255; B.O., 3:140/6:316). Bonnet then quoted from his own letter to Needham, dated 31 December 1761, where he had asked, 'N'avés vous rien découvert de nouveau sur les *Animalcules Microscopiques* depuis les observations que vous avés publiées dans les *Transactions Philosophiques*? Etés vous toujours dans les mêmes Idées sur l'origine de ces Animalcules?' (letter 14).[16] Bonnet further queried whether Needham still believed in his explanations of the interconversion of filaments and animalcules and of the origins of eels in blighted wheat. In a previous letter, Bonnet had in fact remarked, when discussing Lignac's critique, 'Je doute que vous soyes resté dans vos premieres idées sur l'origine des Corps organizés: vous etes trop capable de reflechir et vous aimes trop le Vrai' (20 December 1760, letter 6). Yet Bonnet's hopes were to be thwarted, for Needham replied, 'En attendant, aux questions, que vous me faites, J'ai l'honneur de vous repondre, que Je n'ai pas trouvé encore aucune raison de changer mes sentimens sur l'origine des animalcules en question; j'ai souvent depuis repeté les memes experiences toujours avec le meme succès, et encore depuis peu un professeur de Reggio me vient d'ecrire, qu'il a fait precisement les memes observations à lesquelles il a ajouté plusieures autres pour confirmer mes sentimens la dessus' (13 February 1762, letter 15).[17] This 'professor from Reggio', Needham continued, was planning to publish his own results in the form of letters addressed to Needham. After quoting this passage from Needham's letter, Bonnet remarked in the *Corps organisés*, 'En attendant la publication de ces nouvelles observations, j'oserois bien prédire qu'elles ne *démontreront* pas que les Animalcules dont il s'agit, aient une origine aussi étrange que l'a pensé & que le pense encore mon célebre Confrere. Je m'en tiens donc, sans balancer, aux réflexions que je viens de soumettre au jugement du Lecteur éclairé & impartial' (Bonnet 1762, 2:226; B.O., 3:411/6:317). With these rather prophetic words, Bonnet concluded his chapter on Needham.

The 'professor from Reggio' was in fact Lazzaro Spallanzani, but, since Needham did not give his name in his letter, Bonnet was unaware for several years who this person was. Spallanzani did eventually publish the results of his observations, but not until 1765, as his famous *Saggio di osservazioni microscopiche concernenti il sistema della generazione de' Signori di Needham, e Buffon.*[18] Yet, contrary to Needham's expectations but fully confirming Bonnet's prediction, Spallanzani's results turned out to be opposed to Needham's, and his conclusions were very critical of Needham's theory. There is no doubt, however, that Spallanzani began his infusion observations in 1761 with a view to confirming Needham's ideas on generation. Although Spallanzani's initial letter to Needham now seems to be lost, Needham's reply, date 29 August 1761, could only have been written in response to comments favourable to Needham's theory (Castellani 1973:79):

Vous m'avés fait un très grand plaisir en m'informant de vos observations microscopiques, qui viennent si bien à l'appuye de celles, que j'ai fait autrefois à Paris. Heureusement vous avez le tems, et la patience necessaire, enfin toutes les qualités requises pour faire un bon observateur, et je me felicite d'avoir contribué à la naissance des verités importantes qui sortiront de votre plume. Quant à cé, que vous me demandés, de pouvoir adresser vos lettres contenantes vos observations à moi, c'est me faire beaucoup d'honneur, et meme plus que je merite. [...] je suis d'autant bien aise de vos experiences sur des infusions prealablement assujetties à l'action violente du feu, qui sont si bien d'accord avec les miennes.

16. This passage was published (slightly altered) in Bonnet 1762, 2:225 and B.O., 3:410/6:316.
17. This passage was published (slightly altered) in Bonnet 1762, 2:225-26 and B.O., 3:411/6:317.
18. The *Saggio* formed the first part of Spallanzani's *Dissertazioni due* (1765).

Needham's account of Spallanzani's early views is confirmed by Spallanzani's own experimental notebooks, which do indeed reveal his initial support for Needham's explanation of the phenomena of infusions (see letter 40, n.13). In later years, Spallanzani always denied that he had ever reported favourable observations to Needham; and he included a full review of his relationship with Needham in a long note in his *Opuscoli di fisica animale, e vegetabile*, where he remarked that 'La trop grande précipitation de Mr. DE NEEDHAM pour présager le résultat définitif de mes observations en fit un faux Prophéte' (Spallanzani 1776, 1:290 n.a; 1777, 2:74 n.a).[19] Whatever the full story may be concerning Spallanzani's initial beliefs, his critique of Needham's work in 1765 was to touch off a chain of events that were crucial to the development of Needham's own views on generation.

Needham received from Spallanzani a copy of his *Saggio* sometime in July 1765.[20] By early August, Needham had arrived in Geneva, where he was to spend the next ten months; and he immediately sent his copy of Spallanzani's book to Bonnet, who was temporarily at Perroy (not far from Geneva). Needham's initial reading of Spallanzani's critique seems to have had a major impact on his thinking; for he wrote to Bonnet in his accompanying letter: 'Ses observations m'ont données des lumieres nouvelles, et je commence à croire, que j'ai trop étendu mes idées, en donnant des puissances à la matiere, qui ne sont pas necessaires pour expliquer les Phenomenes du monde microscopique' (letter 19). In this same letter, however, Needham reiterated his belief in epigenesis and outlined several alterations in his theory that will be discussed below. He concluded by asking Bonnet to read Spallanzani's book (and to return it), as well as to comment on his own new views. As one might expect, Bonnet was extremely pleased both with Needham's recantation of his earlier theory and with Spallanzani's confirmation of Bonnet's opinion on the nature of animalcules, as can be seen in his reply to Needham of 5 August 1765. Although Bonnet did not understand Italian and therefore could not read Spallanzani's book, he was able to gather from it what the essence of Spallanzani's views was. 'J'y ai vû avec le plus grand plaisir,' he wrote to Needham, 'qu'il confirme sans le sçavoir, mes petites Opinions sur l'origine des Animalcules' (letter 20). Still not connecting this new work with Needham's earlier nameless mention of Spallanzani, Bonnet concluded, 'L'Homme de Reggio se sera donc trompé, comme je l'avois présumé'.

Bonnet's jubilation over Spallanzani's book and Needham's new views is apparent in letters he wrote during August and early September to Haller, Schaeffer, Formey, and Allamand. To Haller, Bonnet remarked, 'Mr Néédham, qui est actuellement à Genève, m'écrit que ces nouvelles Observations l'engageront à se rapprocher de son Ami [Spallanzani] & de moi. Cela fait honneur à sa candeur' (15 August 1765; Sonntag 1983:433-34). By the end of August Bonnet had learned from Spallanzani himself that he was indeed the professor

19. See also *Epistolario*, 1:63, 227-28.
20. A letter from Needham to Spallanzani of 2 July 1765 indicates that he had not yet received a copy of the *Saggio* (see Castellani 1973:83-84). By 3 August 1765, he had received it, because he sent his copy to Bonnet (see letter 19).

from Reggio.[21] This delighted Bonnet even more, as he wrote in a letter to Formey: 'Il m'arrive une chose qui me fait grand plaisir. Vous scavés que j'avois refuté mon Ami Néédham dans le second Volume de mes *Corps Organisés*, Chap: VI. J'avois prédit à la pag.226 que le Professeur de Reggio ne confirmeroit pas par ses nouvelles Observations les idées étranges de nôtre Ami commun. Ce Professeur vient de m'écrire pour m'annoncer l'envoi de son Ouvrage, & pour m'aprendre que tout ce qu'il a vû tend à confimer mes Remarques.' Announcing as well Needham's recantation of his vegetative force, Bonnet continued, 'Voilà de la franchise philosophique & qui fait honneur à nôtre Physicien' (7 September 1765; BPUG, MS Bonnet 71:231v).[22] To Haller, Bonnet wrote again on 17 September 1765, 'Mr Spallanzani m'a écrit la Lettre la plus flateuse sur ce Livre [the *Corps organisés*]. Il se félicite beaucoup de nôtre accord singulier à refuter le *Néedhamisme*. [...] Je lui ai répondu; & je me suis fait un plaisir de lui aprendre que nôtre estimable Ami Mr Néédham commence à se rapprocher de lui & de moi. J'eu[s] samedi dernier un long entretien avec lui sur ce sujet dont je fus très satisfait. Il est à cent lieuës de Mr Buffon; je devrois dire à mille' (Sonntag 1983:439). To this Haller responded, 'Je serai charmé de la conversion de M. Needham' (28 September 1765; Sonntag 1983:441).

One thing that especially pleased Bonnet was the independent nature of Spallanzani's discoveries. Although Bonnet regretted somewhat that Spallanzani had not known of the *Corps organisés* when he was making his observations and writing the *Saggio*, Spallanzani's confirmation not only of Bonnet's views on animalcules but also of his critique of Needham's theory and his prediction about the outcome of the investigations of the 'professor from Reggio' more than made up for this minor displeasure. As Bonnet wrote in his first letter to Spallanzani, in response to two letters from Spallanzani and the receipt of the *Saggio*, 'L'accord singulier de vos observations avec mes remarques m'a donné d'autant plus de satisfaction, qu'elles ont été pour notre estimable ami la décision de la Nature elle même. Il m'écrit en honnête philosophe qu'il va se rapprocher de vous et de moi; et remanier de neuf ce sujet intéressant.' After quoting from Needham's letters on the changes in his views, Bonnet remarked succinctly, 'C'est ainsi, Monsieur, que vous avez réussi à enlever le bandeau qui couvrait les yeux de notre savant Confrère. Ce que je n'avais qu'ébauché, vous l'avez fini, et ce que je n'avais qu'entrevu, vous l'avez vu' (Castellani 1971:2-3). From these initial letters there blossomed a friendship between Bonnet and Spallanzani, and a correspondence, comprising nearly two hundred letters, that lasted until 1791. During these years, Bonnet continually encouraged and advised Spallanzani on his scientific investigations, especially those designed to further combat Needham's epigenetic views.

In the *Saggio*, Spallanzani's critique of the theories of Buffon and Needham revolved around three principal claims. Against Buffon, Spallanzani offered observational evidence that microscopic beings were true animals that possessed spontaneous motion and were not simply chance combinations of organic

21. Spallanzani wrote to Bonnet on 18 July 1765 and sent him a copy of his *Saggio* (see *Epistolario*, 1:54-55).

22. Similar comments may be found in Bonnet's letters to Schaeffer (31 August 1765; BPUG, MS Bonnet 71:228v) and to Allamand (10 September 1765; BPUG, MS Bonnet 71:232v-233r).

molecules. Proving that microscopic organisms were true animals was an important step in Spallanzani's overall plan, which was to demonstrate that microorganisms generate from eggs like all other organisms and not from material
decomposition. Against Needham, Spallanzani argued, first, that there was
no evidence to support Needham's alleged observation of microscopic plants
producing microscopic animals, and vice versa. Second, Spallanzani maintained
on the basis of new experiments that Needham's observations of animalcules in
sealed, heated infusions had been faulty.

Spallanzani devoted two chapters of the *Saggio* to examining Needham's
claims on the conversion of plant-like filaments into moving animalcules. Having
attempted to repeat Needham's observations, Spallanzani reported that, although he observed the formation of filaments in infusions and the presence of
small animated animalcules among them, he never saw these animalcules
actually being released from the filaments, as Needham had described. 'J'aurois
désiré pouvoir de même dire, avec lui,' Spallanzani declared, 'que ces petits
corps qui s'animent, ont appartenu auparavant à la plante qui végéte, & en
sont des portions détachées, comme il le prétend, afin d'adopter, de concert,
cette proposition, *qu'un végétal se convertit en un animal.* [...] Mais quelques efforts
que j'aie faits pour interroger la nature, je l'ai toujours trouvée muette sur ce
point' (Spallanzani 1765, pt.1:50; 1769, pt.1:76-77).[23] Spallanzani suggested
that these animalcules had actually arisen from eggs previously deposited in the
infusion and that their proximity to the filaments simply gave the appearance
of their production from these filaments. Spallanzani also investigated the
sediment formed at the bottom of the infusions from previously live animalcules,
from which Needham claimed that new filaments and animalcules subsequently
arose. Yet although Spallanzani agreed with Needham that one witnessed
successive populations of animalcules in infusions, he was unwilling to adopt
Needham's conclusions. 'Ne peut-il pas se faire', he asked, 'que, dans une si
grande multitude de choses, notre Auteur, naturellement incliné pour son
systême, n'ait pas toûjours vû ce qu'il a cru appercevoir [...]?' (Spallanzani
1765, pt.1:63-64; 1769, pt.1:99). When one has built a system on the basis of
favourable experiments, Spallanzani explained, one has the tendency to interpret
new observations, even ambiguous ones, in the light of the system. Thus, he
conlcuded, 'Or, seroit-il possible de soupçonner que M. *de Needham* fût tombé
dans une erreur de cette espece? On sçait que l'ame de celui qui invente est
naturellement vive & hardie, & que rarement elle marche avec une circonspec-
tion mesurée' (Spallanzani 1765, pt.1:65; 1769, pt.1:102).

The most well-known of Spallanzani's chapters in the *Saggio*, and the one to
which Needham later took the most exception, was the final chapter, which
reported Spallanzani's experiments on sealed, heated infusions. Spallanzani had
repeated Needham's observations on his famous mutton-broth infusion, with
elaborate precautions. 'Comme c'est principalement sur cette expérience qu'est
appuyé tout l'édifice de son systême,' Spallanzani explained, 'j'ai cru devoir
entrer dans tous ces détails, & en faire un examen scrupuleux' (Spallanzani
1765, pt.1:80; 1769, pt.1:127). Arguing that the air we breathe contains a myriad

23. All quotations will be from the French translation (Spallanzani 1769).

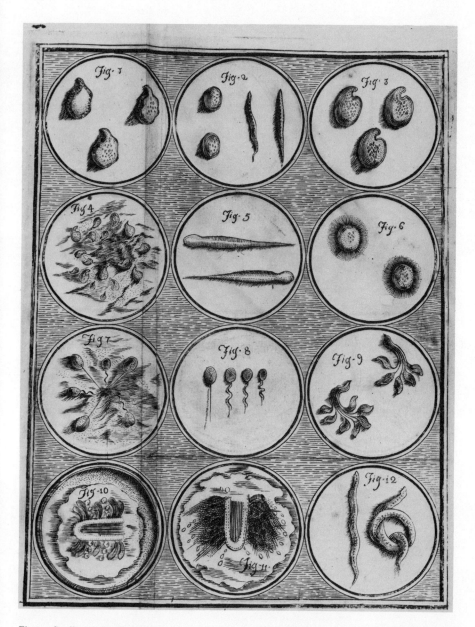

Fig. 9. Spallanzani's illustrations of various microscopic animalcules observed in infusions. To counter Needham's claim that animalcules could be produced from plant filaments, Spallanzani made infusions of legume roots (*Figs. 10, 11*), contending that the fibres that developed and the animalcules observed in the surrounding water were independent from one another. (From Spallanzani, *Saggio di osservazioni microscopiche*, in *Dissertazioni due*, 1765. Courtesy of the Royal Society, London.)

of invisible eggs that can develop into organisms given the right conditions, Spallanzani warned that one must take care to completely seal the flasks. Needham, he charged, had used cork, which from his own experiments Spallanzani had found to be porous to the outside air. Furthermore, Spallanzani maintained, one had to carefully heat each component of the infusion to destroy all existing eggs. Thus, he exposed empty flasks to heat, boiled the infusion contents (either seeds or broth), and after hermetically sealing the flasks heated them again, to eliminate any eggs in the air trapped in the infusion. As he described, 'Je scellai hermétiquement les orifices de dix-neuf vases remplis d'un aussi grand nombre d'infusions faites avec différentes graines; je les plongeai en partie dans l'eau d'un vase plus grand, & je les y fis bouillir l'espace d'une heure: par ce moyen, il me parut qu'il n'y avoit rien à desirer du côté de l'exactitude de l'expérience [...]. Je visitai mes infusions au jour marqué; elles ne me donnerent pas le moindre signe d'aucun mouvement spontanée ou d'animalité, pendant tout le tems que je les examinai avec le microscope' (Spallanzani 1765, pt.1:83-84; 1769, pt.1:132). Spallanzani claimed that he found the same results in all experiments he carried out using the same precautions. But he also found that if, after the final boiling, one allowed even a small amount of air to enter the flasks, animalcules then developed. 'Voilà,' he concluded, 'ce qui m'a empêché d'adopter en entier l'opinion de M. *de Needham*' (Spallanzani 1765, pt.1:84; 1769, pt.1:133).

On 24 September 1765, Needham wrote Spallanzani a long letter outlining the changes in his views the *Saggio* had prompted. As he had stated in his earlier letter to Bonnet, Needham informed Spallanzani that he was giving up his idea of a formative force: 'j'abandonnerai meme pour ces classes inferieures, et pour tout corps organisé quelconque jusqu'au plus simples, la force generatrice de la matiere la plus active, que j'ai cru autrefois necessaire d'adopter pour comprendre tous les phenomenes' (Castellani 1973:87). However, he continued in a postscript, 'il faut pourtant m'entendre parfaitement dans tout ce, que je viens de vous écrire. Pour avoir abandonné la puissance generatrice de la matiere dans certaines occasions, et pour avoir admis comme indispensablement necessaire la preexistance d'un être pareil specifique je n'abandonne pas pour cela le systeme de l'epigenese: je ne crois nullement ni embrions, ni œufs, ni germes, ni parties proli[fi]ques tellement formées et preexistantes depuis le commencement du monde, emboîtées les unes dans les autres, et se developpant ensuite' (Castellani 1973:87-88).

Although he had abandoned his idea of a vegetative force, Needham nevertheless was able to offer a new basis for his belief in epigenesis. This he outlined both in his letter to Bonnet of 3 August 1765 (letter 19) and in his 24 September letter to Spallanzani. Needham now argued that all organisms generate from a parent organism or, as he also described, 'un être pareil specifique' or 'individus generateurs specifiques'. At higher levels of life, this could proceed either oviparously or viviparously, with or without the concourse of two sexes. Yet at the microscopic level, Needham now claimed, all microscopic beings originate from previous ones by division. Needham based this idea on a series of observations that had been made in the summer of 1765 by Horace Benedict de Saussure, Bonnet's nephew. Needham was in Geneva at the time and was in close contact with Saussure, visiting his laboratory on at least two occasions (see letter 23, n.3). Saussure never published the results of his observations, but several years later he described them in a letter to Bonnet, which Bonnet published (see letter 41, n.26). Saussure, who was a preformationist, complained in this letter that Needham had misunderstood and misused his observations. Saussure claimed that he had seen the divided portions of an animalcule grow to the same size as the original organism, whereas Needham had erroneously described Saussure's observations as having demonstrated continual division into smaller and smaller beings. Thus Needham's account of microscopic division fitted his own views on material decomposition and exaltation in infusions, rather than preformation, as Saussure believed. Needham was never to change his description of division, and such a manner of reproduction was used in all of his future explanations of generation in the microscopic realm.

When Needham described his ideas on division to Bonnet in August 1765, Bonnet replied that it had actually been he who had first suggested the idea of division among animalcules in his *Corps organisés* (see letter 20, n.1). That Needham seemed not to have been aware of Bonnet's idea added further evidence to Bonnet's suspicions that Needham had not read his book. He brought this subject up in his letter to Needham of 5 August 1765 (letter 20), to which Needham replied that he had indeed only rapidly glanced through the *Corps organisés* (28 August 1765, letter 21). Bonnet responded that he had given Needham a copy when he was in Geneva in the spring of 1764. '[J]e m'en étonne un peu, parce que le tems qui s'est écoulé est long, et que la Matière vous interessoit beaucoup. J'ai bien des petites affaires; mais surement je ne resterois pas deux mois sans dévorer une de vos Productions' (10 September 1765, letter 22). Bonnet complained to Spallanzani as well about Needham's remiss behaviour, to which Spallanzani replied, referring also to Bonnet's *Contemplation de la nature*, 'S'il avoit médité ces Ouvrages, je suis très sur qu'en Philosophe [naïf] il auroit abandonné l'Epigenèse. Vos raisons unies à la célèbre decouverte d'Haller son si claires, si fortes, et si convaincantes, que le plus opiniatre amateur de cette Hipothèse est obligé de ceder' (17 April 1766; *Epistolario*, 1:86). With this opinion Bonnet certainly concurred, and he remarked in a later letter to Spallanzani that Needham's belief in epigenesis was 'probablement la raison secrète qui l'a empêché jusqu'ici de méditer mes idées sur la génération et sur les reproductions' (26 December 1766; Castellani 1973:49).

When Needham first sent his own copy of Spallanzani's *Saggio* to Bonnet in August 1765, he mentioned that he was going to publish a French translation of Spallanzani's treatise along with 'une dissertation à ma façon en presentant mes observations, et les siennes dans un point de vüe totalement differente de mes vües anciennes' (letter 19). Bonnet reported this to Spallanzani, and Needham mentioned it himself to Spallanzani in a letter of 24 September 1765 (see Castellani 1973:87). Both Bonnet and Spallanzani encouraged Needham in their letters to him during 1766 and 1767 to finish this publication quickly, although they seem to have had some doubts about what the final product would turn out to be. Bonnet wrote to Spallanzani on 29 April 1767, 'je l'ai fort excité à avancer ses notes sur votre traduction; il s'éloignera plus ou moins de nos principes: nous en jugerons. Je ne sais s'il m'aura lu enfin, et s'il m'aura bien entendu: sa manière de philosopher sur la Nature n'est pas précisément la mienne: nous avons pourtant bien de principes communs' (Castellani 1971:52). To this Spallanzani responded, with regard to the notes Needham was writing to develop and clarify his new views: 'Plût à Dieu qu'il le fasse d'une manière satisfaisante, mais j'en doute beaucoup. Vous verrez qu'aux notions et aux principes claires et très-reçus que nous adoptons dans nos ouvrages, il en substituera d'autres obscurs, et que presque Personne de bon sens n'admettra pas' (6 June 1767; *Epistolario*, 1:144).

Spallanzani's letter to Bonnet of 6 June contained as well a summary of a letter that Needham had written to Spallanzani in March or April 1767. Spallanzani published Needham's letter in the *Giornale d'Italia spettante alla scienza naturale* for 27 June 1767 in order to alert the learned world, Spallanzani noted in his accompanying letter to the journal, of the 'notabile cangiamento che è per dare al suo sistema' (*Giornale*, 3:409).[24] Needham's letter had outlined three principal changes he had made in his theory that would be more fully explained in his notes to the translation of Spallanzani's *Saggio*. One of these changes he had already discussed in a previous letter to Spallanzani, namely, that on the basis of Saussure's observations, he now believed that microscopic beings propagated by division in a continual process, producing populations of smaller and smaller organisms in an infusion. The other changes involved a new conception Needham had developed of the nature of 'vitality' at lower levels of life. He now argued that microscopic beings should be divided into two classes: true animals that originate from a parent of the same species and a new class of organisms, which Needham called 'vital beings', that reproduce by continual division. These vital beings were to be distinguished from true microscopic animals by not possessing a sensitive principle as all animals do, but rather by operating solely on the basis of, as Needham expressed it, 'les debris de la vitalité preexistante dans les substances organisées' (*Giornale*, 3:410; Castellani 1973:92). Needham gave as corroborating evidence for this 'principle of vitality' Haller's discovery of irritability and Adanson's observations on the spontaneous movements of the tremella, an alga.[25] Needham had actually expressed the idea of a class of organisms intermediate between plants and true animals in a letter to Bonnet of 10 January 1761 (letter 8), but the full development of this notion did not occur until he was reformulating his ideas during 1767 and 1768.

On the basis of his new principle of vitality, Needham explained as the third change in his theory that instead of appearing to argue, as he had in his previous publications, that these vital beings 'provenoi[en]t par une vraie metamorphose des substances corrompues en Etres complets & organisés', he now was claiming that they arise from 'une organisation preexistante dans les substances mêmes' (*Giornale*, 3:411; Castellani 1973:93). In other words, these microscopic beings did not arise *de novo* from corrupted substances; but rather, because they

24. Although the date given for Needham's letter in the *Giornale* (the original no longer exists) is 22 May 1767, this is clearly erroneous, since Spallanzani's reply to Needham was written on 3 May 1767 (*Epistolario*, 1:136-37). One can surmise that Needham's letter was probably written in March or April 1767.

25. For Haller's concept of irritability, see Haller (1753) and letter 7, n.7. For the tremella, see Adanson (1770) and Mazzolini (1972:80-86).

originated and propagated by division, they retained the vitality of the living substance that had decomposed in the infusion. These new ideas on vitality were apparently a topic of discussion between Needham and Bonnet while Needham was living in Geneva in 1765-1766; for, as Needham commented to Spallanzani, his notion of vitality was one 'sur la quelle j'eu d'assez longues conversations avec M. *Bonnet* à Geneve, qui me parut la gouter très-fort' (*Giornale*, 3:410). It should also be noted here that one of the motivations for Needham's creation of the class of vital beings was to counter the charge that his theory supported equivocal generation and materialism (see section 4 of this Introduction).

In August 1766, after moving to Paris, Needham reported to Bonnet that he had given Spallanzani's *Saggio* to the publishers to be translated (letter 23). In January of the following year, he commented, 'Spalanzani avance, mais lentement' (letter 26). It was not until December 1767 that Needham seems to have been working full time on his notes to Spallanzani's treatise. In a letter to Sabatier de Cabre dated 27 December 1767, he commented that he had for some time been isolated from the news of the world because of his work on this project: 'You may further imagin, that I do not thus sequester myself from mankind without some occupation, I am employed in publishing a translation from the Italian of Spalanzani's (professor of Modena) microscopical observations, which are but a repetition in a great measure, tho' by way of confirmation, of those I made formerly with Mr de Buffon' (BLUL). To Bonnet, Needham had reported the same month in a somewhat more critical vein, 'Je travaille actuellement sur Spalanzani, et je trouve beaucoup plus à faire, que j'avais prevu' (14 December 1767, letter 28). Complaining that Spallanzani's writing was imprecise, his descriptions too exhaustive, and his observations sometimes erroneous, Needham maintained that his and Buffon's ideas had been misunderstood. '[B]ref,' Needham charged, 'ses raisonnemens sont trop vagues, et par consequent nullement concluants.' Needham explained that in his notes he would attempt to clarify his own system of epigenesis, to prove its truth by reasoning and observations, and yet discuss also any weaknesses it might have. 'C'est tout ce que je puis faire pour la cause de la verité', he concluded.

In his next letter to Bonnet, written six months later, Needham was able to report that the printer had just finished setting the translation of Spallanzani's treatise and would now be beginning on the notes. Commenting that there were points in Spallanzani's argument with which he disagreed but that on the whole 'nous marchons ensemble main en main', Needham stated that his major objection was to Spallanzani's final chapter, which presented the observations on sealed, heated infusions that Spallanzani had made in an attempt to disprove Needham's theory. Concerning these, Needham complained, 'il conclut contre moi sur le poids d'une seule espece d'experience, que je trouve très equivoque, et point du tout concluante de la maniere, qu'il la conduit, dont j'ai raison de croire, qu'il était lui-meme sans dessein la dupe par trop de precautions' (8 June 1768, letter 29). Consequently, Needham continued, 'C'est pour cela que je reviens à mes principes, et que dans mes notes j'ai fait un resumé de mon système. [...] J'amene mes anciennes preuves, j'ajoute des nouvelles'. Needham proposed that Spallanzani repeat these experiments on Needham's terms, declaring that if they turned out against him, 'je renoncerai à mes principes nouveaux en revenant de bonne foi aux anciens'. Yet Needham was never to return to the fold of the preformationists. In his notes to Spallanzani's *Saggio* he completely reinstated his theory of the vegetative force, which he had formerly renounced, and attacked Spallanzani's views far more sharply than he had led Spallanzani and Bonnet to believe he would when he had first suggested publishing the translation.

Even before receiving this letter, Bonnet was worried about what Needham's edition of Spallanzani's treatise would turn out to contain. Commenting to Haller about a passage in a letter from Needham in which he said he would be defending epigenesis in his notes, Bonnet remarked, 'Que dites-vous, mon Illustre Ami, de ce brave *Epigenesiste*? Je fais le plus grand cas de sa droiture & de sa candeur; mais je n'ai jamais trouvé sa Logique assés rigoureuse sur cette Matière. Ses Idées ne sont point nettes et ses expressions trop souvent embarassées accroissent partout l'obscurité. Je ne puis nommer cela de la *profondeur*' (6 January 1768; Sonntag 1983:712). With this Haller concurred in response: 'Votre ami Needham n'a pas la netteté philosophique, qui donne un sens determiné a chaque expression. Il est confus et obscur; il pouroit faire plus de mal que de bien avec ces dispositions, meme involontairem'' (10 January 1768; Sonntag 1983:714). To Spallanzani, Bonnet wrote concerning a criticism Needham had made (in letter 29) of Spallanzani's explanation of regeneration in snails, 'Je n'ai pas grande opinion des arguments par lesquels il entreprendra de vous combattre [that regeneration must entail plastic forces]: ce brave homme a bien peu de netteté dans l'esprit, et sa logique n'est guère exacte. Mais ses intentions sont les meilleures du monde' (22 June 1768; Castellani 1971:77). Spallanzani, as one would expect, agreed, commenting on Needham's forthcoming notes in his *Saggio*, 'Il me tarde de lire son Ouvrage. Je ne doute pas de n'avoir bien attrapé quelques fois ses idées. Mais il seroit à souhaiter en elles plus de netteté. Quand il entre dans la methaphisique il est un homme des plus obscurs du mond[e]. Je verrai donc le plan plus equitable, qu'il me proposera. Comme dans ma Dissertation je l'ai combattu avec beaucoup de politesse, et sans jamais l'offenser, j'espere qu'il en usera de même avec moi' (15 July 1768; *Epistolario*, 1:160).

On 3 December 1768, Needham announced to Bonnet that he was sending the next day a package containing several copies of his edition of Spallanzani's treatise, titled *Nouvelles recherches sur les découvertes microscopiques, et la génération des corps organisés*. Bonnet was to keep one copy for himself, send one to Haller, and ship the remainder to Italy, where one copy would be sent to Spallanzani. 'Vous verrez', Needham remarked to Bonnet, 'que je soutienne l'epigenese contre vos sentimens avec toutes mes forces, et vous en verrez bientot les raisons' (letter 32). Bonnet replied on 26 December that the books had arrived and that he had sent the remaining copies to Haller and to Italy as Needham had instructed. Although he had not yet read Needham's book, Bonnet queried how Needham could have combated him with all his force, since Bonnet could not even find his name in the index. Again accusing Needham of not having read his books, Bonnet remarked, 'Je laisse au Public éclairé et impartial à juger entre vous et moi. Quand je vous aurai lu et médité, je vous dirai mon sentiment avec toute la franchise que vous aimés et que j'aime' (letter 33). Needham replied that he had not meant that he had combated Bonnet personally but rather the preformationist system, and that he customarily did not have other books around him when he wrote his own (letter 34).

On 30 December, Bonnet wrote to Haller that he had sent him a copy of Needham's book, commenting, 'Je n'en ai encore parcouru que quelques endroits: et certes j'en ai bien vû assés pour juger de cette mauvaise Physique, et de la Métaphysique plus mauvaise encore qui lui sert de fondement. [...] Néédham a les meilleures intentions du mond: mais, il est trop dépourvu de Logique *naturelle & artificielle*' (Sonntag 1983:792). Bonnet complained as well about Needham's tone, which he thought was too confident and affirmative, and about his tendency to flatter himself by citing positive comments others had made about his views. Haller wrote in reply that he had received the book and that he was 'presque faché d'etre obligé de le lire' (3 January 1769; Sonntag 1983:793). By early January, Bonnet had read more of Needham's edition, and he was even more upset, complaining to Haller that Needham's logic was faulty and that he had completely misunderstood or misrepresented what Bonnet had written on Haller's chick embryo observations. 'Au reste,' he added, 'son Stile est partout d'une obscurité & d'une barbarie qui n'ajoutera pas peu à la maussaderie de tout le reste. Il a de tems en tems des Idées ingénieuses, qu'il devoit se borner à indiquer, & qu'il gate en s'y appesantissant' (10 January 1769; Sonntag 1983:797). To this Haller replied with his characteristic succinctness, 'je ne sais pas s'il s'entend lui meme' (15 January 1769; Sonntag 1983:797). Bonnet evidently agreed, remarking, 'Non assurément; le bon Abbé Epigenesiste ne s'entend pas lui même; il devroit donc nous dispenser de l'entendre. Plus j'avance dans sa lecture, & plus je le trouve *anti-philosophique*' (24 January 1769; Sonntag 1983:800).

Bonnet was even more critical of Needham's work in his letters to Spallanzani. Writing to him in late January to tell him of the copies of Needham's edition that had been shipped to Italy, Bonnet let loose with what can only be described as a tirade against Needham. 'Ce pauvre homme', he wrote, 'parle sans cesse de la *chaîne de ses raisonnements*, et il ne se doute pas le moins du monde qu'elle n'est qu'une chaîne de paralogismes. Toujours, ou presque toujours, il tire des conclusions certaines de premesses incertaines' (18 [29] January 1769; Castellani 1971:96). For example, Bonnet wrote, Needham had argued that when vegetable matter decomposes and filaments are produced, one sees moving globules as well. From this he claimed that these globules were produced by the filaments and inferred the existence of a vegetative force. But, although Needham said that this force was not the same one that makes plants vegetate normally, Bonnet asked, 'Qu'est-elle donc? comptez qu'il n'en sait rien. Il fabrique des mots, et pense après cela avoir découvert des vérités. [...] Que résulterait-il d'anti-logique de cette physique? Il en résulterait que Dieu aurait prodigeusement multiplé les êtres sentants, et qu'il en aurait parsemé toutes les parties des Plantes et des animaux. Admirable point de vue de l'Univers!' (p.96). Criticising as well Needham's ideas on vital beings, his failure to read Bonnet's *Corps organisés*, his erroneous statements on chick development, his suggestion that animalcules propagate by division without citing Bonnet's priority on the idea, and his misunderstanding of Leibniz, Bonnet concluded: 'Cet hardi épigenésiste a un air de profondeur qu'il ne doit qu'à son extrême obscurité, et à l'emploi fréquent d'un jargon métaphysique, qui ne peut tromper que ceux qui ne savent point approfondir. [...] Que vous dirais-je encore, mon estimable Confrère? Je n'ai jamais lu en physique ni en métaphysique de livre plus essentiellement mauvais, ni plus mal fait que celui-ci' (p.98). Chiding Spallanzani for having referred to Needham as 'un *grand homme*' in his *Saggio*, Bonnet was nevertheless delighted with the translated edition of Spallanzani's treatise: 'Voilà ce que je nomme de la bonne logique: voilà comme la Nature veut-être interrogée. Les notes de votre adversaire ne font, à mon avis, que vous faire briller davantage. Vous proposez-vous de lui répliquer? Vous aurez beau jeu' (p.99). Bonnet continued to complain about Needham's book and to praise Spallanzani's in letters to Spallanzani and Haller throughout 1769.

By March 1769, Needham was beginning to wonder why he had received no response on his book from Bonnet, Spallanzani, or Haller. Concerned, he wrote to Bonnet, 'est ce que j'aurai eu le malheur de degouter une partie de mes Lecteurs, et de facher sans le vouloir, l'autre?' (letter 35). In reply Bonnet remarked simply, 'Soufrés que je n'entre point dans le détail sur votre Ouvrage. Vous sçavés que nous ne pensons point de même sur la Generation. [...] Je ne sçaurois me faire aucune Idée d'une *Force végetatrice* qui *organise*. [...] Je laisse à notre Ami M.ᵣ Spallanzani à vous répondre sur les Animalcules: plusieurs de vos Repliques me paroissent éxiger de nouvelles Expériences. Il sçaura les faire' (8 April 1769, letter 36). Aside from criticising Needham for misrepresenting Bonnet's account of Haller's chick embryo observations, briefly questioning Needham's explanation of a fungus that grew on nymphs (see letter 36, n.7), and castigating Needham's French, Bonnet said nothing more to Needham about his opinion of the edition.

Spallanzani did not receive a copy of Needham's edition until December 1769. For some reason, the copy destined for him via Needham's friend in Turin, Sabatier de Cabre, never reached Spallanzani; and he had to obtain one on his own. Writing to Bonnet before he had seen the book and in response to Bonnet's tirade against it, Spallanzani commented, 'Comme il me confute, qui scait s'il a voulu m'en envoyer une copie? En attendant je tacherai de me la pourvoir ailleurs. Le vif Portrait que vous en faites dans vôtre bel extrait me fait prendre pitié de l'original. Voilà on tombe un Homme depourvu de bonne logique, et enteté dans ses idées' (29 April 1769; *Epistolario*, 1:180). When Spallanzani finally did receive the book, his reaction was not an unexpected one: 'Quelle confusion, quelle obscurité regne-t-il dans ses Notes à mes Observations microscopiques! Quelle monstruosité dans ses pensées! Que de ridicules efforts pour expliquer les Reproductions de mes Animaux! Je vois bien que dans mon Ouvrage il foudra que je parle de nouveau de son Roman' (23 December 1769; *Epistolario*, 1:215). Announcing to Bonnet that he would be instituting a series of new experiments designed to refute Needham once and for all, Spallanzani remarked, 'Si au lieu de consulter sa tête echauffée M.r Needham avoit consulté ces fideles Secretaires de la Nature [Redi, Vallisnieri, Réaumur, and, of course, Bonnet] qu'il semble n'avoir jamais lu, je suis presque assuré qu'il auroit changé sa façon de raisonner, et qu'il seroit revenu de ses rêves' (8 March 1770; *Epistolario*, 1:228).

The notes in Needham's French edition of Spallanzani's *Saggio* present a curious and somewhat unorganised account of Needham's biological and metaphysical beliefs, with particular attention paid to responding to Spallanzani as well as to other critics, especially those who saw Needham as a materialist. To this edition of the *Saggio*, Needham also added a treatise of his own, titled *Nouvelles recherches physiques et métaphysiques sur la nature et la religion*, in which he presented his views on cosmogony, on the Deluge, and on other aspects of revealed religion (see sections 4 and 7 of this Introduction). The notes that Needham added to Spallanzani's *Saggio*, which precede his treatise on cosmogony, were so extensive that, even set in smaller type, they occupy more pages than Spallanzani's work. The notes are keyed to Spallanzani's chapters, and most are quite long, often digressing into somewhat unrelated topics. Needham also added at the end of the notes several 'Remarques' – on new discoveries relating to zoophytes that corroborated Needham's views, such as those on the vegetating fly and plant worm (both fungi) and on the tremella; on Spallanzani's more recent discoveries on regeneration; and, in an unusual concluding section, on the formation of Eve from Adam through a process of vegetation akin to multiplication by division in the polyp. Needham's notes and remarks constitute in many ways his most interesting work; for, as he moves from topic to topic, one can glimpse the underlying concerns and motivations that guided his thinking and research.

Needham's aims in his notes were, in addition to responding to Spallanzani, to restate his theory of vital beings and the vegetative force, and to show that his system entirely conformed to a world created by God and was in no way a materialist view. '[J]e ne donne aucune autre puissance à la matiere', he wrote, 'que celle qui produit la pure vitalité dénuée de toute sensation, & qui dérive, comme son existence primitive, de la seule Divinité; [...] tout corps ou partie organisée, est une procession ou prolongation d'un corps organisé, soit végétal ou animal, qui doit nécessairement préexister, & dont la souche primitive sort immédiatement des mains de Dieu' (Spallanzani 1769, pt.1:142). Needham proposed that all organisms, by being the product of a previous organism either through reproduction or through division, could be traced back to the original creation of the world by God. Yet his system, he claimed, explained how each instance of generation occurred, unlike the theory of preexistent germs, which simply maintained that all organisms had always existed: 'il est bien plus naturel & plus philosophique dans la recherche des causes immédiates, de monter aux causes générales qui lient les corps organisés avec le systême total, & de les faire dériver de celles qui ont été établies par la Divinité, que de poser pour premier principe ce qui n'est qu'une pure défaite, peu digne d'un Physicien' (Spallanzani 1769, pt.1:140).

Needham's remarks in response to Spallanzani's critique can be grouped into three principal categories: the question of whether microscopic organisms are animals, Needham's observations on filaments and globules, and the dispute over heated and sealed infusions. Spallanzani had argued in the *Saggio* that all moving microscopic organisms are true animals that exhibit spontaneous behaviour. His conclusions were based on extensive observations of the habits and movements of various infusion organisms. Needham's response, based as much on his theory of vital beings as it was on observation, was to claim that some microscopic organisms were indeed true animals, born from parents of the same species. But the vast majority of them were not animals, but rather vital beings that, being devoid of a sensitive principle, only *appeared* to behave in a spontaneous manner. Furthermore, these vital beings multiplied by dividing into smaller and smaller kinds and did not, Needham maintained, generate from eggs present in the infusion, as Spallanzani had sought to prove.

On the question of whether filaments produce moving globules in infusions of wheat and other grains, Needham again invoked his theory of vital beings to respond to Spallanzani's critique. Spallanzani had argued that he had found no evidence that microscopic plants could convert into animals and vice versa, as Needham had claimed. Needham responded by criticising Spallanzani's observations as not having been made in exactly the same manner as his own, but also by claiming that the issue was not one involving animals and plants: 'on peut dire, non pas, comme M. *Spalanzani* s'exprime, que les animaux deviennent plantes, pour paroître de nouveau sous la forme d'animaux, mais que les êtres vitaux végétent de nouveau pour en produire, par leur partage, d'autres d'une classe inférieure en volume, quoique supérieure par leur dégré d'exaltation' (Spallanzani 1769, pt.1:200). The successive appearance of filaments and globules in infusions was due simply to the vegetation and division of vital beings, not the conversion of plants into animals.

With regard to Spallanzani's experiments on sealed, heated infusions, Needham was quite critical. He had commented in a letter to Bonnet (letter 29, cited above) that he found Spallanzani's experiments on this issue very ambiguous and completely inconclusive. In his notes on the *Saggio* he reiterated this charge, remarking, 'je ne ferai pas grande dépense en paroles pour faire évanouir tout ce qui paroît s'opposer à mes principes dans le résultat de ses essais' (Spallanzani 1769, pt.1:216). Needham's principal response was that, by boiling his sealed flasks for an hour, Spallanzani had affected the air trapped in the flasks and had weakened or destroyed the vegetative force present in the infused substances. That no organisms subsequently appeared in the infusions was not due, as Spallanzani had maintained, to all their eggs' having been destroyed but rather because vegetation could not proceed after such excessive heat had been used. Spallanzani had in fact admitted the possibility in the *Saggio* that the air might have been affected. Thus, Needham concluded, 'il n'est pas étonnant par-conséquent que ses infusions, ainsi traitées, n'aient donné aucun signe de vie; & il en devoit être ainsi, comme il le soupçonne lui-même, en me suggérant la vraie réponse qu'il semble attendre de ma part à son objection' (Spallanzani 1769, pt.1:217). Needham proposed a repetition of these experiments, using only enough heat to kill any existing eggs in the infusion. The result, he predicted, would confirm his system; and if it did not, Needham offered, he would abandon his ideas.

Such a repetition was not carried out by Needham nor exactly on Needham's terms, but in the early 1770s Spallanzani performed a series of experiments on the effects of heat and cold on infusion organisms. As one would expect, Bonnet was delighted with Spallanzani's renewed efforts to refute Needham. He wrote to Needham on 17 February 1770 in a very critical letter that Spallanzani's reading of Needham's edition 'a produit un grand effet sur son Esprit, et que vous n'aviés peut être pas prévu: ça été de l'affermir plus que jamais dans ses Principes et dans les miens. Vous pouvés compter qu'il vous refutera publiquement, solidement et fortement' (letter 41). Spallanzani described his proposed experiments in several letters to Bonnet in 1770, and Bonnet responded with sustained encouragement. On 5 May 1770, for example, Bonnet wrote, 'Les expériences que vous projetez pour réfuter solidement notre obstiné épigenésiste, me paraissent très propres à décider entre lui et nous: je ne puis trop vous exhort[er] à les tenter le plus tôt possible' (Castellani 1971:128). And again, on 15 September, Bonnet commented, 'Je ne doute pas que vous ne parveniez par vos expériences à écraser notre bon Abbé épigenésiste: ses visions contredisent trop la Nature elle même, pour que vos nouveaux procedés conduisent à des résultats qui leur soyent tant soit peu favorables' (Castellani 1971:136). During the remainder of 1770 and during 1771, Spallanzani reported the results of his experiments to Bonnet and described a new treatise he proposed to write on infusions. Bonnet was delighted with Spallanzani's success, remarking elatedly, 'voilà le pauvre épigenésiste reduit en poudre impalpable' (16 October 1771; Castellani 1971:223).

Spallanzani continued to work on this treatise, and on several others, during the next few years. During this period, there was only one exchange of letters between Bonnet and Needham, in which Bonnet simply remarked, 'Notre estimable Ami l'Abbé Spallanzani va publier un Ouvrage sur les *Animalcules des Infusions*, qui vous étonnera beaucoup et n'étonnera pas moins l'illustre Inventeur des *Molécules organiques*' (18 September 1773, letter 47). Spallanzani wrote to Bonnet at the end of 1774 that he was sending his treatise on infusion animalcules to the printer, yet the work did not appear until March of 1776. Bonnet received a copy in May; and, after having portions of it read to him because he could not read Italian, he wrote to Spallanzani, 'Tout ce que j'ai vu jusqu'ici de cet ouvrage m'a fait le plus grand plaisir; et il m'a paru aussi bien dit que bien pensé.' Referring specifically to a long note in which Spallanzani had described the history of his relationship with Needham, where he claimed that he had never supported Needham's views, Bonnet commented, 'Je suis très impatient de savoir ce qu'il vous répondra: vous le mettez au pied du mur. Je ne crois pas qu'il saute par dessus: je préfère de penser qu'il reconnaîtra sa précipitation et ses erreurs' (15 May 1776; Castellani 1971:304).

Spallanzani's book, titled *Opuscoli di fisica animale, e vegetabile*, consisted of two volumes. The first volume contained his treatise on infusion animalcules, which covered such topics as the effects of heat and cold on eggs, seed, animals, and plants; the reactions of these to various odours and liquids, to electricity, and to a vacuum; Needham's arguments concerning the interconversion of microscopic plants and animals; multiplication of animalcules by division; and the true animality of infusion organisms. Throughout the work, Spallanzani's overriding purpose was to demonstrate, beyond the shadow of a doubt, that infusion animalcules were true animals that developed from eggs deposited in the infusion from the air, and consequently that all notions of vital beings, vegetative forces, and the like were unnecessary to explain the origin and life cycles of microscopic beings. Spallanzani also appended to this treatise two lengthy letters Bonnet had written to him in 1770 and 1771 concerning his experiments. The *Opuscoli* was quickly translated into French by Jean Senebier, appearing in 1777 as *Opuscules de physique animale et végétale*.

Spallanzani began his discussion of Needham's views with an examination of Needham's accusation that heating the infusions as much as Spallanzani had done in his earlier experiments had destroyed the vegetative force and corrupted the air. This had also been the subject of a lecture Spallanzani gave at the University of Pavia in 1770 (see Spallanzani 1770 and 1978a:353-72). In order to test Needham's claim that boiling infusions for a lengthy period of time weakened or destroyed the vegetative force, Spallanzani compared infusions of various seeds that had been boiled for differing amounts of time. He found that the number of animalcules present in the infusions was not diminished by the amount of boiling, as one would expect if the vegetative force were affected, but, on the contrary, that many of the longer-boiled infusions exhibited more animalcules than those boiled only briefly. From these observations Spallanzani concluded, 'Ces faits me persuadérent pleinement que les infusions faites avec des graines exposées à une intensité quelconque du feu, produisent toujours des Animalcules; d'où il résulte par une conséquence rigoureuse & incontestable, non-seulement que la premiére objection du Naturaliste Anglois est fausse, mais encore que la *force végétatrice*, dont il fait un si grand usage, n'est autre chose qu'un ouvrage de pure imagination' (Spallanzani 1776, 1:24; 1777, 1:27).[26]

To test Needham's claim that by heating sealed infusions too long one affected the elasticity of the air trapped in the flask, Spallanzani heated several sealed infusions for various lengths of time. He found that the air pressure (elasticity) inside the flasks was not less than atmospheric air (and often greater); and he also found that larger animalcules were absent from sealed infusions heated for only a short period of time, whereas the smallest organisms required three-quarters of an hour's boiling time to be prevented from appearing in infusions. On the basis of these experiments, Spallanzani reasoned, 'je ne verrois pas qu'il fut possible d'attribuer la naissance des Animalcules à d'autres choses qu'à de petits œufs, ou à des semences, ou à des corpuscules préorganisés, que je veux appeler & que j'appellerai du nom générique de *Germes*. Au reste je prouverai dans la suite de cet ouvrage, par des faits nombreux & incontestables, que c'est là véritablement l'origine de ces Animalcules' (Spallanzani 1776, 1:40; 1777, 1:48).

In one chapter of this treatise, Spallanzani dealt again with the appearance of filaments and globules in infusions and with Needham's contention that filaments produced globules. With seeming disregard for Needham's new class of vital beings, Spallanzani continued to describe this phenomenon as a meta-morphosis of plants into animals. Having repeated Needham's infusion obser-vations with several new variations, Spallanzani again reported that, although he saw both filaments and globules, he never saw the latter produced by the

---

26. All quotations will be from the French translation, *Opuscules de physique animale et végétale* (Spallanzani 1777).

former. He concluded by attributing Needham's claims to optical illusions and to too great a love for his theory. Spallanzani also reported numerous observations on division in animalcules, which he found to be a normal means of reproduction among many animalcules, and on viviparous and oviparous animalcules. He included the letter that Saussure had written to Bonnet in 1769 on division, discussed earlier, which Bonnet had also published (see letter 41, n.26). Spallanzani welcomed Saussure's claim that Needham had misinterpreted his original observations and cited them as evidence in support of his own explanation of division rather than of Needham's. Finally, in a concluding chapter, Spallanzani reasserted his belief in the true animality of infusion organisms, thus denying Needham's distinction between vital beings and true animals.

Spallanzani had sent Needham a copy of his *Opuscoli* in the summer of 1776; but, as he was later to learn, this copy never reached Needham. During this period Needham and Bonnet had ceased to correspond as well, and letters did not pass between them again until 1779, after a six-year gap. In his first letter to Bonnet after this lapse, Needham explained that the interruption in his letters was not due to their differences of opinion, for he had in fact grown tired of their seemingly endless controversy: 'je suis las jusqu'à l'excés de toutes ces recherches inutiles, et tous ces debats interminables. Bref, il y a bien du tems, que jetté par terre mon bouclier, et mes armes offensives en tournant mon dos à mes adversaires, et Spalanzani, comme vous le sçavés, est resté maitre du champ de bataille' (28 October [September] 1779, letter 48). Bonnet pressed Needham further in his reply for Needham's reaction to Spallanzani's book, claiming, 'Le sage Auteur vous a suivi pas à pas, et partout il a interrogé la Nature comme vous le desiriés et comme elle demandoit à l'être' (8 November 1779, letter 49). Bonnet also informed Needham that he was adding new footnotes to the edition of his *Corps organisés*, soon to be published in his *Œuvres*, in which he was summarising Spallanzani's critique of Needham's views and the new discoveries he had made on animalcules. But Needham was apparently not impressed with either Spallanzani's *Opuscoli* or Bonnet's opinion, commenting in reply, 'j'ai consideré suffisamment toutes les experiences de notre ami Spalanzani [...]; cependant loin de changer de sentiment à cet égard, j'ai cru pouvoir meme sans blesser le respect, et l'amitie, que je vous dois à tant de titres, vous accuser d'un peu trop de predilection en faveur de votre systeme' (25 November 1779, letter 50). Explaining to Bonnet that he had never received the copy of the *Opuscoli* that Spallanzani had sent him but had obtained the work on his own, Needham concluded simply, 'Il est inutile de dire davantage par raport à nos differentes façons de voir en Physique certains objets.' But Bonnet added a further comment in his next letter, writing, 'Vous sçavés tout ce que notre celèbre Ami Spallanzani vous oppose et qu'il tient des mains de la Nature elle même' ([8] March 1780, letter 51).

As he had informed Needham in 1779, Bonnet did add several notes to the edition of his *Corps organisés* published in his *Œuvres* that same year (see letter 49, n.2). Several of these discussed Spallanzani's work on infusions, on spermatic animalcules, on regeneration, and on fecundation. The most extensive discussion of the Needham-Spallanzani controversy occurred in a long note Bonnet appended to the chapter he had devoted to Needham's microscopical observations (discussed earlier). Here Bonnet reviewed the events of their debate, beginning with his own confirmed prediction that the 'professor from Reggio' would discover results opposed to Needham's system, and proceeding to a detailed analysis of Spallanzani's experiments in the *Opuscoli*. After reviewing Spallanzani's new infusion observations and the conclusions he had drawn from them concerning the origins of animalcules from eggs deposited from the air, Bonnet remarked, 'Notre Observateur Philosophe conclut de toutes ses recherches sur la génération des Animalcules des infusions, *que MM. de* BUFFON *&* NEEDHAM *se sont trompés*, en bâtissant leurs systèmes sur les phénomenes que présentent ces Etres microscopiques. "Leur origine, dit-il [quoting from Spallanzani], étant entiérement différente de celle que ces deux Auteurs leur assignent, il résulte de là, qu'un des plus forts argumens de M. de BUFFON est anéanti, & que les idées de M. NEEDHAM sont entiérement ruinées, &c."' (B.O., 3:423-24 n.1/6:334 n.1). Bonnet concluded, as had Spallanzani, that infusion organisms are true animals that reproduce in fashions consistent with larger organisms, that is, from an animal of the same species through development from a preformed germ or by division from an identical organism. Thus for Bonnet, the extensive observations made by Spallanzani served to confirm the objections that he had initially outlined against the views of Needham and Buffon and to reaffirm the universality of preformation.

Spallanzani's role in the controversy with Needham over generation was discussed once more in the final two Bonnet-Needham letters, and the acrimonious nature of this last exchange was very probably responsible for the termination of the correspondence. In his letter of 17 March 1780, Needham pointed once again to Spallanzani's initially favourable attitude toward Needham's views and accused Spallanzani of having switched his support to preformation because he thought an allegiance with Bonnet would do more for his career than would one with Needham: 'C'est donc un homme', Needham wrote, 'qui souffle froid et chaud, et sa conduite à cet égard est l'inverse precisement de ce que tout Philosophe, qui aime le vrai, doit tenir pour maxime, *amicus Plato, sed magis amica veritas*' (letter 52). Claiming that he could have published, but did not, Spallanzani's first letter to him in which he supported Needham's ideas, Needham concluded, 'j'abandonne pour toujours un homme, en qui il m'est impossible d'avoir pour l'avenir la moindre confiance'. As one would expect, Bonnet was in complete disagreement with Needham over his account of the origins of Spallanzani's ideas on generation and took particular offense at the motives Needham had imputed to Spallanzani: 'je vous avouerai, que je ne sçaurois me persuader que M.ʳ Spallanzani aît pu être inspiré par le motif si peu philosophique que vous lui supposés. Il m'a paru trop honnête et trop vrai dans tout le cours de ma propre correspondance qui dure sans interruption depuis quinze ans' (18 April 1780, letter 53). Accepting Spallanzani's claim that Needham had misinterpreted Spallanzani's initial letter to him, Bonnet remarked that, in any case, the results presented in the *Opuscoli* were what really counted. 'Soufrés que j'ajoute', Bonnet concluded, 'que je n'ai pas prôné le Naturaliste de Reggio; je n'ai fait que rendre justice aux grandes Vérités dont il a enrichi l'Histoire naturelle, et que vous êtes bien capable d'apprécier.' On this note the correspondence between Needham and Bonnet ended.

Although Bonnet and Spallanzani continued to write letters to one another for several more years, they ceased to discuss Needham or his theory of generation, apparently believing that their side had been victorious. After Needham's death in 1781, which Bonnet did not learn of for some time, he wrote to Spallanzani, 'Nous lui devons de bonnes observations, mais sa métaphysique gâtait souvent ce que la Nature lui montrait' (25 February 1784; Castellani 1971:509). This was perhaps the most charitable thing Bonnet could say about Needham, after so many years of disagreement on such fundamental issues.

3. Metaphysics and epistemology

THE subject of metaphysics is not discussed at length in the Bonnet-Needham letters, yet the important role that metaphysical questions played in each of their overall scientific systems warrants highlighting here those discussions that do occur. In the eighteenth century, the term 'metaphysics' had a wider meaning than it does today, encompassing not only questions concerning the first principles of substance and being but also several epistemological and religious issues. Bonnet and Needham agreed on many metaphysical questions, such as the existence of an incorporeal soul and the dependence of the universe and its operations on the laws established by its divine Creator. Yet they diverged on their beliefs concerning the nature of matter and concerning epistemology, and they viewed the relationship between science and metaphysics from completely different perspectives.

The question of what role metaphysics should play in science was broached in the first few letters between Bonnet and Needham. In letter 1, Needham remarked that many scientists seemed to limit themselves to dealing with physical questions while ignoring, often intentionally, the more difficult metaphysical issues that are necessarily involved. Both Newton and Descartes, he explained, simply assumed for the sake of their physical systems that matter was either indivisible or divisible, without further discussing the problem. Yet Needham felt that this was a mistake, and that science must necessarily address itself to the metaphysical questions to which it inevitably leads. As he remarked to Bonnet, 'On croit communement, que les phenomenes physiques ne menent pas necessairement à la metaphysique, mais qu'on examine sans prejugé toutes vos observations, et celles de Mr Trembley sur le Polype, et qu'on fixe, s'il est possible, les principes de la generation en deça de la metaphysique' (28 August 1760, letter 1). The issues involved in generation, in other words, like the regenerative capabilities of the polyp, required a metaphysical approach. Needham also gave three examples of people he had encountered who had unusual visual abilities, maintaining that only metaphysical explanations could account for such phenomena.

Bonnet's more cautious attitude toward metaphysics and science is evident in his reply. Claiming that he did not scorn metaphysics, he nevertheless felt that too many people attempted to pursue it without possessing the necessary 'Esprit Geometrique' that enabled them to properly generalise from the facts available to them. 'La Metaphysique est fille de la Physique,' Bonnet maintained; 'elle doit donc comme sa Mere tenir à l'observation, et l'Art d'observer est trop peu connu encore. Il ne faut donc pas se presser trop de recourir aux explications Metaphysiques; il faut n'y recourir que lorsque les explications Phisiques sont evidamment insuffisantes' (16 September 1760, letter 2). There was no need, Bonnet stated, to have any recourse to metaphysics to explain the optical puzzles Needham had mentioned, for they could all be handled on physical grounds. To this Needham responded that, although he agreed that metaphysics if poorly pursued led to a labyrinth of errors, and although he himself had perhaps resorted to metaphysics more quickly than he needed to, 'mais tot ou tard, il faut que la science la plus étendue se termine à ce point' (26 September 1760, letter 3).

These differing attitudes toward the use of metaphysics in science are reflected in Bonnet's and Needham's published works. Whereas Needham discussed his own views on the nature of matter and on epistemology as a necessary part of his theory of generation in both his *Nouvelles observations microscopiques* (1750) and his notes in the *Nouvelles recherches sur les découvertes microscopiques* (Spallanzani 1769), Bonnet ventured into metaphysical territory only in limited and carefully defined ways. Bonnet was frequently critical of Needham's overzealous attitude toward metaphysical issues, and he often complained about this in his letters to Haller and Spallanzani, both of whom agreed with Bonnet. To Haller, for example, Bonnet wrote after receiving Needham's first letter, 'Mr Needham est certainement du petit nombre de ces Hommes rares à qui la Nature se plait à dévoiler ses secrèts. Ses *observations Microscopiques* l'ont rendu célèbre, et sa reputation est bien meritée. [...] mais l'on peut reprocher avec raison à Mr Needham d'aimer trop à se perdre dans la Metaphysique.' Bonnet added that he would write to Needham and tell him his own views on 'l'application de la Metaphysique a la Physique', since Needham's letter had been 'plein de conséquences Metaphysiques qui ne me paroissent pas de la plus grande justesse' (3 September 1760; Sonntag 1983: 218-19). Several years later, after receiving Needham's edition of the *Nouvelles recherches*, Bonnet again complained to Haller and Spallanzani about Needham's obscure metaphysics (see section 2.iv of this Introduction). Perhaps if Needham's views on metaphysical issues had been more in accord with Bonnet's, Bonnet would not have been quite so critical.

In the Preface to his *Nouvelles observations microscopiques* (1750), Needham claimed that the paper he had published on generation in the *Philosophical transactions* in 1748 had been unduly criticised because he had been interpreted from the wrong metaphysical viewpoint.[1] In particular, Needham noted, if one did not understand his views on the first principles of matter, one could easily misinterpret his biological theory. As he explained, 'On regarde communément la matiere comme une substance composée, continuellement étendue, continuel-lement divisible, c'est là sa définition, & j'avoue qu'une telle idée contredit toutes les conséquences immédiates qui suivent mes observations' (Needham 1750: vii-viii). Needham thus rejected the still popular Cartesian definition of matter as an extended, infinitely divisible substance.

In the text of this book, Needham presented his own theory on the nature of matter. His principal thesis was that matter does not exist in itself as we perceive that it does. Rather, our ideas of extension, solidity, and impenetrability are only relative, for they are the product of perception alone just as are secondary qualities like colour. As he explained, 'les *qualités* que nous appellons *premiéres*, ne sont précisément, comme les secondaires, que de purs effets rélatifs, dont le modele d'évaluation ne se trouve que dans les sensations' (Needham 1750: 267-

---

1. For further discussion of Needham's metaphysical views, see Roger (1963:494-520) and Roe (1983).

68). The reason for Needham's contention was two-fold. First, Needham believed that the world beyond our senses consisted of simple active agents rather than extended matter. Second, he thought that everything that we perceive in the world as existing or occurring, such as matter, movement, and sensation, was due solely to interactions among these active agents. We are like the men in Plato's cave, Needham asserted, whose knowledge of the world is based only on shadows. Thus, to be misled into thinking that matter as we perceive it is identical with matter as it exists was, Needham contended, 'non-seulement réaliser un phantôme & transformer en Etre, ce qui n'est qu'un point de vuë particulier à l'état, dans lequel il a plu à la divine Providence de nous placer, mais c'est faire naître une source de difficultés insurmontables' (Needham 1750: 269). Yet, he also argued, although we can never know in themselves these active agents that produce our idea of matter, we can investigate our relationship to them and thereby gain an understanding of their actions.

One example of these simple agents was the active and resistive forces Needham claimed were responsible for all vital activity. When decomposition of living matter produced active microscopic beings, this was due to the active forces becoming freed from the resistive ones. In the same way, he contended, all physical matter and all interactions in the physical realm were due to the relative proportions and reactions among active and resistive agents. '[T]ous les effets produits dans l'Univers', he proclaimed, 'ne sont que le résultat de l'action & de la réaction soit simple ou complexe' (Needham 1750:322). Needham also believed that one could construct a continuous scale of natural activity, in which all types of matter and all processes could be ranked with regard to the proportions of these agents that are combined together. This scale included not only vital activity but also chemical processes, electricity, light, and so forth.

Needham outlined these metaphysical and epistemological views in letter 11, written to Bonnet on 11 July 1761.[2] There he presented his views on primary and secondary qualities, on the essential unknowability of matter and the soul in themselves, and on the scale of active agents. He further argued that his position made a strong case for proving the existence of the soul and of God. As he remarked, 'comme il ne se trouve pas aucun materialiste si insensé, de nier, ou de douter de l'existence de matiere, parce que c'est une substance inconnue en elle meme, et connue seulement par les effets produits en nous, de meme tout homme est egalement insensé, qui doute sous ce pretexte ou de l'existence de la divinite ou de [celle] de son ame immaterielle' (letter 11).

Bonnet did not respond directly to this letter from Needham, yet we know from his own views on perception and on the nature of matter that he disagreed with some of Needham's opinions. Letter 11 was in fact written by Needham in response to his having received Bonnet's *Essai analytique sur les facultés de l'ame* (1760) and having read its Preface. There Bonnet outlined his method for studying the 'faculties of the soul', in particular the nature of sensation and the formation of ideas. Bonnet's method was straightforward: to examine the human being from the point of view of the naturalist. As he declared in the opening

2. Extensive discussions of Needham's views on matter and on epistemology may also be found in his letters to Joseph Berington of 2 December 1771 and 2 January 1772 (BDA, C.685) and of 12 February 1772 and 1 May 1772 (WCRO, Throckmorton MSS, CR 1998/Gate box, folder 8).

sentences of his Preface, 'J'ai entrepris d'étudier l'Homme, comme j'ai étudié les Insectes & les Plantes. L'Esprit d'observation n'est point borné à un seul Genre: il est l'Esprit universel des Sciences & des Arts' (Bonnet 1760: i; B.O., 6:vii/13:vii). Reiterating this point in a letter to Needham, Bonnet described his method as 'une route nouvelle ou presque nouvelle', which would open a way for others to pursue such investigations even further (letter 10). The reason Bonnet felt that one should begin by observing human beings as a naturalist, he further explained in his Preface, was that all abstract ideas, even those concerning the nature of the soul, must ultimately be derived from sensations, that is, from observation. 'Ainsi la Physique est, en quelque sorte, la Mere de la Métaphysique, & l'Art d'observer est l'Art du Métaphysicien, comme il est celui du Physicien' (Bonnet 1760: ii; B.O., 6:vii/13:viii). Furthermore, Bonnet maintained, since it is the body on which the soul acts and from which it receives sensations, it is to the bodily processes and mechanisms of sensation that one must first turn to study the faculties of the soul. Thus, Bonnet explained, 'J'ai mis dans mon Livre beaucoup de Physique & assez peu de Métaphysique: mais, en vérité, que pouvois-je dire de l'Ame considérée en elle-même?' (Bonnet 1760:xiii; B.O., 6:xv-xvi/13:xxi). Humans are mixed beings, who have ideas only through the intervention of sensations: 'C'est sur son [human] Corps & par son Corps que l'Ame agit. Il faut donc toujours en revenir au physique comme à la premiere origine de tout ce que l'Ame éprouve' (Bonnet 1760:xiii; B.O., 6:xvi/13:xxi).

Bonnet carried out this programme in the *Essai analytique*, as he had in his anonymously published *Essai de psychologie* (1756). In both works, attention is paid to the system of nerve fibres that connect the sense organs with the brain, and to the mechanical process that is initiated by an external object impinging on a sense organ and that results in an idea arising in the soul. In the *Essai analytique*, Bonnet used the artificial notion of a statue (see fig. 10), which he claimed he had conceived of independently of Condillac, to examine the effect of a single sensation on the soul. Building upon this, Bonnet then dealt with the interaction among several sensations and with memory, the association of ideas, attention, imagination, and the will. The entire analysis was thus constructed on this mechanistic and observational basis. His approach was apparently well received by several of his contemporaries, judging from the favourable comments he reported to Needham (see letter 14).

Bonnet's views on matter were diametrically opposed to Needham's. Although he admitted in the *Essai analytique* that the real essence of matter was unknowable by us and that our idea of matter is relative to our perceptions, he argued that the effects matter produces on our senses must be caused ultimately by matter in itself (see Bonnet 1760:xiv-xvii; B.O., 6:xvi-xix/13:xxiii-xxvi).[3] From our perceptions, that is, we can assert that there is something outside of us that causes the ideas of extension and solidity to arise in our minds. Thus Bonnet believed that even if extension as we perceive it is not an attribute of matter in itself, there must be some (unknowable) attribute of matter that, by acting on

---

3. For further discussions of Bonnet's views on the nature of matter, see Bonnet (1769a, 2:32-35), Bonnet (1771a:50-92), and B.O., 7:351-52, 437-49/16:33-36, 160-78; 8:437-42/18:288-95. See also Sonntag (1983:890-906).

Fig. 10. Bonnet's statue, receiving its first sensory stimulation through the sense of smell. (From Bonnet, *Œuvres d'histoire naturelle et de philosophie*, 1779-1783, 4° ed., vol.vi, pt. 1. Courtesy of the Taylor Institution Library, Oxford.)

our perceptual faculties, gives rise to this idea in us. Although this position could be viewed as being consistent with Needham's, Bonnet did not accept Needham's metaphysical conclusion that the cause of our perceptions of matter is active agents.

In his *Considérations sur les corps organisés* (1762), Bonnet explicitly addressed the question of active forces in matter (see Bonnet 1762, 1:63-65; B.O., 3:46-47/5:157-60). Speaking of attraction as a force that is evidenced by the effects that it produces, Bonnet argued that it should be considered as being separate from the essential attributes of matter. Extension, solidity, and inertia are essential to, that is, inseparable from matter, he claimed, whereas attraction is not. This was a common Newtonian position in the eighteenth century – that forces are not essential to matter – and one that Bonnet adopted, as did many others, because of the materialist implications of attributing active powers to matter. Forces, he believed, are given to matter by God and are the agency of material interaction while not being material in their origins.

The influences in metaphysics on Needham and Bonnet were also diverse. In his notes in the *Nouvelles recherches sur les découvertes microscopiques*, Needham drew an explicit parallel between his own views and Leibniz's, remarking, 'Que l'on examine bien ce système, on lui trouvera de la conformité avec la bonne métaphysique; j'entends celle de *Leibnitz*, qui traite l'essence primitive de la matiere, & la nature de ses principes' (Spallanzani 1769, pt. 1:146). Needham had also earlier listed Leibniz, along with Plato, Cudworth, Grew, Malebranche, Berkeley, and Pope, as philosophers whose views had elements in common with his own, although he was quick to point out that his system coincided with none of theirs in its entirety (see Needham 1750:260-64). What Needham approved of in Leibniz's metaphysics were his rejection of Cartesian ideas of matter in favour of a system of active agents, and his theories of simple substances and of action and reaction. It is difficult to determine exactly when Needham became exposed to Leibniz's philosophy and in what manner it influenced the development of his own metaphysical views.[4] Yet Needham saw in Leibniz a kindred spirit and used the similarities between their views to bolster the credibility of his own ideas. Bonnet found all of this somewhat two-faced, because Leibniz was also a preformationist. As he wrote to Needham regarding Leibniz, 'cette Métaphysique qui vous plait tant la possedés-vous assés? [...] Vous êtes Epigénésiste: Leibnitz regardoit tout *Epigénèse* comme une *absurdité*. [...] Eh bien! Mon Ami, qu'en dites vous?' (17 February 1770, Letter 41).[5] Although Needham's reply to this letter is missing, he would undoubtedly have responded, as he did

4. Needham later wrote to Joseph Berington that he had not yet read Leibniz when he began his microscopical investigations with Buffon and formulated his system (letter of 12 February 1772; WCRO, Throckmorton MSS, CR 1998/Gate box, folder 8). Needham referred favourably to the abbé Sigorgne's *Institutions léibnitiennes, ou, précis de la monadologie* (Lyon 1767) in Spallanzani (1769, pt.1:147) and in his letters to Berington of 12 February 1772 and 1 May 1772 (WCRO, Throckmorton MSS, CR 1998/Gate box, folder 8). Yet Needham was certainly exposed to Leibniz's thought, at least in a general manner, before 1767. For further discussion of this question, see Roe (1983:168-71).

5. See also Bonnet's similar comments in letter 36 and in his letters to Haller (29 November 1769; Sonntag 1983:844) and to Spallanzani (18 [29] January 1769 and 17 January 1771; Castellani 1971:98, 188). Needham had also been criticised by Roffredi for not fully understanding Leibniz and for making inconsistent use of his views (see Roffredi 1769).

in print, that he followed Leibniz only in his views on the first principles of matter and that he had not adopted all of Leibniz's system (see Needham 1775a:227).[6]

Part of the reason Bonnet was critical of Needham's reliance on Leibniz was that he himself had been strongly influenced by Leibniz, although in a different way. Bonnet first read Leibniz's *Théodicée* (1710) in 1748, an occasion that he later described as 'une des principales époques de ma vie pensante. [...] La *Théodicée* fut pour mon esprit une espèce de télescope, qui me découvrit un autre univers, dont la vue me parut une perspective enchantée, je dirais presque magique' (Savioz 1948b:100). Leibniz's influence on Bonnet is most evident in one of Bonnet's later works, *La Palingénésie philosophique* (1769), which will be discussed more fully in section 4 of this Introduction. Among the principal areas of Leibniz's influence must be listed Leibniz's law of continuity and belief in a scale of being in nature, his support for preformation, and his views on the survival of the soul (and the body) after death. In the areas of epistemology and theory of matter, however, Bonnet did not adopt Leibniz's ideas. Rather, one can discern a strong influence of English philosophers, especially Newton and Locke, both of whose ideas Bonnet was exposed to as a student (see Savioz 1948a:39-42). Certainly Bonnet's sensationalist psychology and his view of matter as passive extension with forces added by God had much stronger affinities with English thought of the period than with Leibniz's. Thus, although both Bonnet and Needham found Leibniz to be a stimulating guide, their reactions to Leibniz took completely different routes.

Needham further discussed his metaphysical views in letter 48, one of his last letters to Bonnet, written in September 1779. Here he explained the motives that had led him to oppose both preformation and Cartesian metaphysics. Both the hypothesis of preexistent germs and that of innate ideas served well to prove the existence of God as creator of the universe and to support the moral foundations of society. Yet the difficulty was, in Needham's opinion, that both of these theories were false and, because of this, that once they were overthrown, the way would be open to materialism and irreligion. Thus Needham felt the only way to stop this consequence was to offer a new metaphysics as well as a new theory of generation. Although this letter to Bonnet will be more thoroughly discussed in section 4 of this Introduction, it serves here to illustrate Needham's commitment to his metaphysical system as well as his belief that his reform of biology was intimately tied to his revision of metaphysics. Bonnet also believed that he had something new to offer in metaphysics and was united with Needham in opposing the spread of materialism. Yet Bonnet's reform consisted in a different approach to metaphysical questions – to study man as a naturalist would – and in an eschewal of anything but analytic reasoning based on observations in dealing with such questions. He was adamantly opposed to Needham's metaphysics not only because it contradicted his own sensationalist epistemology and Newtonian matter theory but also because he believed that adopting a metaphysics based on active agents would not ward off, but rather lead directly

6. For further discussions of Leibniz in Needham's works, see Spallanzani (1769, pt.1:232, 291; pt.2:35, 48-49) and Needham (1781:14).

to, materialism. In metaphysics as in generation theory, Bonnet and Needham shared ultimate goals but diverged widely on how to attain them.

4. Revealed religion, materialism, and unbelievers

THROUGHOUT the Bonnet-Needham letters, there are frequent references to revealed religion, materialism, and unbelievers, and to the problem of preserving the moral foundations of society. In an early letter, for instance, Bonnet wrote to Needham, 'Je déplore avec vous, mon cher Confrère, l'esprit d'Irréligion par lequel divers Autheurs entreprennent aujourd'hui de se faire une reputation brillante. Il est bien evident que leurs ecarts sont le fruit d'un amour propre mal ordonné, et si le gros des Hommes étoit Deïste ou Athée, ces Gens-là seroient Chrétiens. Je les regarde comme des ennemis nès du genre Humain, puis qu'ils cherchent à lui enlever la plus solide baze de son bonheur' (31 October 1760, letter 4). To this comment, Needham replied, 'Le monde croit assés communement, que les noms de Philosophe, et d'incredule sont synonimes, il nous importe beaucoup, que les vrais Philosophes se declarent ouvertement pour la Religion pour le desabuser' (15 November 1760, letter 5). By proclaiming the truth of revealed religion through their scientific and philosophical works, Bonnet and Needham hoped to counter the use of science and philosophy by unbelievers to undermine religion. This was the only way, they thought, that one could halt the spread of incredulity. As Needham remarked to Bonnet a few years later, 'Mais malgré tout ce que j'ai pu faire, si je ne me flatte pas trop, meme en vous ayant pour associé, que nous fassions entendre raison à nos incredules, j'espere toujours que nous arreterons en quelque façon la contagion, en l'ecartant de ceux, qui ne sont pas encore touchés' (25 August 1768, letter 31). This common goal – to stop the contagion of irreligion – underlay nearly all of Bonnet's and Needham's scientific and philosophical work.

There were several elements that contributed to their concern over unbelievers. Philosophically, both Needham and Bonnet were opposed to materialism, although each was accused (for different reasons) of supporting this doctrine. Yet neither allowed matter to have totally independent self-active powers, for this would have threatened the role of God in the material world. Bonnet, as we have seen, completely denied material activity, while Needham tied active material powers to a divine origin and plan. Second, both Needham and Bonnet believed, although in slightly different fashions, not only that science should be consistent with revealed religion but that it should provide proofs for it as well. Both consequently sought in their publications to offer accounts of revelation, miracles, and the like that had a rational, and often even scientific, basis. They were opposed to deism as much as they were to atheism; for by removing from religion the Christian tenets of revelation, one took away, they argued, its moral force. This was tied to the third principal element of their concern over unbelievers, their worries about the social effects of the spread of atheism and materialism. Both Bonnet and Needham believed that the cohesive structure of society rested on morality, which in turn was founded on revealed religion. This was really the principal motivating force behind their campaigns against the unbelievers. Adopting different, and sometimes conflicting, strategies, Bonnet and Needham were nevertheless united in their efforts to use science and philosophy to promote Christianity and morality and thereby to preserve the social fabric.

Bonnet's religious beliefs were formulated in the climate of liberal protestant-ism extant in eighteenth-century Geneva (see Marx 1976:98-99 and S. Taylor 1981). The rigid Calvinism of the sixteenth and early seventeenth centuries had given way to a less dogmatic and more tolerant religious establishment. Although Bonnet was never closely allied with the Genevan protestant ministry, his own attitudes toward religious issues reflected the more liberal atmosphere of his day. Opposed to deism as well as to atheism, Bonnet sought to preserve the principal tenets of revealed religion, but in a rational, rather than dogmatic manner. By demonstrating how the concepts of revelation and a future life could be understood and explained through philosophical analysis, Bonnet hoped to return the doubtful to the fold of revealed religion. Thus Bonnet's apologetics were written principally for the deists and the unbelievers, rather than for the already religious (Marx 1976:101-102). His motivation was based in part on his own religious convictions, but even more on his firm belief that, without the spectre of future judgement, mankind would lose all morality and thus society would collapse. A common concern of the Enlightenment period, Bonnet's fears reflected as well his own experience in opposing the reform movement of the Genevan constitutional crisis in the mid-1760s (see section 8 of this Intro-duction).

Bonnet's principal work of Christian apologetics was his *La Palingénésie philoso-phique, ou idées sur l'état passé et sur l'état futur des êtres vivans* (1769). Several chapters of this work, together with an additional new chapter, were also separately published in 1770 as *Recherches philosophiques sur les preuves du christianisme*. A second edition of the *Palingénésie* appeared in 1770 and one of the *Recherches* in 1771, with a further chapter added to the latter on proofs for the existence of God, written in response to d'Holbach's *Système de la nature* (1770; see Savioz 1948b:239). In the *Palingénésie*, Bonnet presented a global theory of the survival and restitution of all living things after death, together with a mechanism for their perfection in a future life. This theory incorporated contemporary notions of progress and optimism as well as the Christian concept of general resurrection. Bonnet also presented an explanation of miracles that served to provide a basis for belief in his doctrine of a future life. Bonnet's intent was to offer a philosophically sound explanation of these two fundamental concepts of revealed religion that would appeal to the rational thinkers of his day.

Bonnet outlined his method and goals in the Preface to the *Palingénésie*. Claiming that the work grew from an initial idea for a short sketch applying to animals his ideas on the future happiness of man, Bonnet commented, 'J'ai donc été conduit par une marche aussi neuve que philosophique à m'occuper des fondemens de ce bonheur; & parce qu'ils reposent principalement sur la RÉVÉLA-TION, l'examen logique de ses preuves est devenu la partie la plus importante de mon travail' (Bonnet 1769a, 1:xi; B.O., 7:iv/15:viii-ix). This philosophical approach to the proof of revelation consisted in building his analysis only on constant facts, on immediate consequences, and on an uninterrupted chain of logical reasoning. Rather than claiming certain demonstration, Bonnet would offer only probabilities. By this means, he hoped to avoid both polemics and religious dogma. The readers he particularly had in mind, Bonnet explained, were those who had doubted their faith and who had not yet succeeded in resolving their doubts. As he wrote to Needham, 'J'ai eu uniquement en vuë dans cette belle Recherche de dissiper les doutes de l'Incrédule Philosophe et vertueux. J'ai essayé d'éclairer son Entendement, de toucher son Coeur; de l'intèresser à méditer avec moi sur les Preuves si nombreuses, si variées, si frappantes de cette REVELATION, qu'il admettroit probablement si elle lui avoit été présentée d'une manière assortie à sa manière de voir et de philosopher' (8 July 1769, letter 37). Needham and other philosophers would be the judges of whether his method was preferable to those of other Apologists.

Three principal topics of the *Palingénésie* will be highlighted here in relation to Bonnet's professed goals: his notion of a future life for animals, his explanation of the resurrection of all mankind, and his discussion of miracles. Bonnet's ideas on the future life of man and on how one can explain the Christian doctrine of general resurrection by means of philosophical principles grew out of his psychological research and were in fact first presented in chapter 24 of his *Essai analytique sur les facultés de l'ame* (1760). In the *Palingénésie*, Bonnet extended these ideas to encompass the perfectibility and future existence of animals, turning to human beings in Parts VIII, XVI, and XXII of this work. We shall begin, as did Bonnet in the *Palingénésie*, with animals.

Bonnet believed that all animals possess a soul, which although not intellectual as in humans, is immaterial and is the source of the animal's sensibility and 'personality'. The seat of the animal's soul Bonnet located in a 'petits Corps organique & indestructible' lodged from the beginning of the world in the larger, destructible body. Bonnet had previously argued as a preformationist that all future animals had been formed by God in one act of creation. Now he extended this idea to include God's having preordained and preorganised these 'small organic bodies' in animals as well. The reason for this was tied both to Bonnet's geological ideas and to his notion of perfectibility. He believed that the Earth and physical universe had undergone a series of 'revolutions' in which all life forms of the period were destroyed.[1] In the new world after each revolution, organisms emerged not from a new creation but from the indestructible 'small organic bodies' contained in the grosser corporeal bodies of the organisms in the previous world. These 'germs of restitution', as Bonnet also termed them, contained, in a material, but ether-like form all of the preformed elements necessary for the development of the new organisms. Yet these new organisms after the revolution would not be the same ones that preceded it, but rather were preordained to be both suitable to the new geological conditions and also, even more importantly for Bonnet, more perfect than their previous form. They would be more perfect by possessing new and better organs, especially for sensation. Each organism, each rung in the chain of being, would eventually thus reach the most perfect state it is capable of attaining.

Although there are several elements of Bonnet's theory that could be explored,

---

1. For further discussion of Bonnet's views on cosmogony and the history of living organisms, see Whitman (1895b:251-55), Gould (1977:22-28), and section 7 of this Introduction.

suffice it to say here that this theory allowed Bonnet to combine his ideas on organic preformation, on animal psychology, on geological change, on perfectibility and God's goodness, and on the resurrection of all creatures, including man, in a future life of eternal happiness. No wonder he expressed at times his feelings of being overwhelmed by such an enormous task. His global vision of tying natural history, metaphysics, and religion together hearkened back to his reading of Leibniz's *Theodicée* in 1748 and to his personal goal of wanting to work out his own system of equal scope. Leibniz's many influences on the particulars of Bonnet's ideas are also apparent, and Bonnet himself discussed some of the similarities and differences between their two views in Part VII of the *Palingénésie*.[2] One of the principal distinctions one can point to is that Leibniz's theory on the survival of germs after death was not nearly as detailed as Bonnet's, for Leibniz did not propose the notion that the future germ is lodged in the present body nor any mechanism like Bonnet's for perfectibility.

Bonnet's ideas on the future life of human beings were based in part on his psychological theories of brain fibres and memory, partly on his wish to preserve a concept of future judgement for mankind, and finally on his adherence to saint Paul's description of the final resurrection in his letters to the Corinthians.[3] In Paul's first letter, it is written that each human being will be resurrected in an incorruptible, glorious, and spiritual body (I Corinthians xv.35-56). Bonnet saw in this the idea that even at the resurrection, humans would still be mixed beings, possessing a soul and a body, albeit a body of a completely different form. This new body, composed, he postulated, of an ether-like substance, must exist already in the present corruptible body and, after death, survives as an imperishable germ until its resurrection. There, each human will be judged according to the past actions performed while in his corruptible body (II Corinthians v.10). Bonnet believed that this judgement would be possible because the ethereal incorruptible body lodged in each person's seat of the soul possessed its own brain fibres that would retain memories of its past actions. Each person is thus, in essence, indestructible and fully accountable for all actions good or bad. Thus Bonnet felt that he was able to offer an explanation for the resurrection based on scientific fact and on philosophical reasoning. Moreover, this explanation, he felt, offered a sound basis for the importance of morality in the present life.

But could one be certain that Bonnet's explanation was correct? Admitting that our own reasoning powers are not sufficient to assure us of the certainty of a future life, Bonnet turned to a discussion of miracles as God's signs to man evidencing this future state.[4] But Bonnet presented a nontraditional view of

2. See also Bonnet's 'Recueil de divers passages de Leibniz sur la survivance de l'animal, pour servir de supplément à la partie VII. de la Palingénésie philosophique, et réflexions sur ces passages', B.O., 8:245-68/18:3-39; and his 'Vue du Leibnitianisme', B.O., 8:277-314/18:52-107. For Leibniz's influence on Bonnet, see Savioz (1948a:19-21) and Marx (1976:79-86). For Bonnet's priority dispute with the abbé Sigorgne over his ideas on the future life of organisms, see his 'Lettre aux auteurs de la Bibliotheque des sciences, au sujet des Institutions Leibnitiennes', B.O., 8:269-76/18:40-51; Savioz (1948b:309-24); and Marx (1976:604-605).

3. See Bonnet (1769a, 1:308-19, 2:127-56) and B.O., 7:228-38, 413-34/15:334-47, 16:124-56; see also Bonnet (1760:473-88) and B.O., 6:350-63/14:229-49.

4. See Bonnet (1769a, 2:157-201) and B.O., 7:435-79/16:157-224.

miracles, explaining them as the natural result of a preordained system of events. Since God does not multiply actions unnecessarily, Bonnet argued, why could he not have preorganised in the world he created all of the future events that we would later view as miraculous? Postulating two systems of laws in nature, one governing ordinary events and the other giving rise to extraordinary events, Bonnet claimed that miracles are produced through physical, albeit extraordinary means, as, for instance, by the suspension of gravitation on an object, the accumulation of electrical matter (aura) around a person, or the removal of an obstruction to a person's sight. Moreover, God could have preordained in certain individuals brain fibres that, at the appropriate moment, would give rise to a prophetic vision. God also sent his messenger, that is, Christ, to aid mankind in interpreting miraculous events as evidence of immortal life and future judgement. In one unique act of Creation, God produced not only all living things with their indestructible germs but also a predetermined set of extraordinary physical events to convince humans of their future life. Thus, by explaining the origin and purpose of miracles, Bonnet thought he could produce the final step in a chain of philosophical reasoning that would convince even the most doubtful of the goodness of God, the accountability of actions, and the certainty of a future life of eternal happiness.

Bonnet sent Needham a copy of his *Palingénésie* in July of 1769 (see letter 37). Still not having received it in late August, Needham wrote Bonnet of his impatience to read 'sur tout cette partie, qui traite de la revelation; tous les systemes de philosophes passés et à venir ne sont rien en fait d'importance vis à vis de ce seul sujet' (21 August 1769, letter 38). In the next few months, however, Needham did receive the *Palingénésie*; and he wrote Bonnet a lengthy letter discussing the work on 1 January 1770 (letter 40). Needham's general reaction was highly favourable. Praising Bonnet's strong support for religion and the good that should result for humankind from his book, Needham commented that Bonnet's arguments might have more impact on the unbelievers because Bonnet was not an ecclesiastic but rather a philosopher. However, Needham also remarked that he was not in agreement with Bonnet on several specific theological and metaphysical points. One must remember that Needham was a Catholic priest and well versed in the doctrines of the Catholic church, even if he was not himself always an outspoken proponent of these articles of faith.

Needham's principal criticism of Bonnet's discussions of religion was that he had gone too far in shrinking metaphysics and lowering religion to the level of physics so as to make them easy to grasp. Needham argued in response that, 'il est plus convenable, et plus philosophique à mon avis d'exalter la physique avec Leibnitz, et Mallebranche pour la faire atteindre à la foi' (letter 40). Needham disliked Bonnet's emphasis on physical explanations for resurrection, miracles, and the like and recommended instead that one build faith on physics rather than reduce faith to physics. The mysteries of religion, Needham maintained, should not be watered down to conform to our weak conceptions; otherwise faith would be destroyed. Needham also objected that Bonnet did not support the doctrine of the eternity of punishment, that Bonnet's explanation of miracles denied that God could ever operate immediately, and that Bonnet was wrong

Fig. 11. Bonnet's chain of being, depicted here as a series of ascending steps, with man at the top. (From Bonnet, *Œuvres d'histoire naturelle et de philosophie*, 1779-1783, 4° ed., vol.iv, pt. 1. Courtesy of the Taylor Institution Library, Oxford.)

to claim that the soul could not think without the body. God is free to act to produce local exceptions in nature, Needham claimed, which are all part of a larger plan that is beyond our level of understanding. 'C'est ainsi qu'au lieu de restraindre les vües de la divinité, je cherche plûtot à les étendre, et loin de la croire assujettie à une pure necessité materielle indigne de sa toute puissance, je me persuade qu'elle se perd pour moi bien au de la du palpable dans le moral, et l'intellectuel' (letter 40).

Bonnet's reply (letter 41) to Needham's letter, dated 17 February 1770, indicates the fundamental differences between their conceptions of metaphysics and their attitudes toward religious dogma. To Needham's claim that Bonnet had lowered religion to the level of physics, Bonnet replied that his main purpose was to convert unbelievers and that he thought he would be more successful in this by rendering religion intelligible than by writing a lot of gibberish about matters that exceed all understanding. To each of Needham's specific objections, Bonnet replied that Needham had misunderstood his views and that he had offered untenable opposing explanations. In particular, he objected to Needham's several mentions of Leibniz in support of his own views, for Bonnet pointed out that Leibniz's doctrines agreed with Bonnet's on the unity of soul and body, and especially on preformation.

Bonnet's comments on Needham's criticism serve to underscore the fact that, although they had similar goals in promoting religion, they diverged on how to attain these and on the particulars of faith. Bonnet seems to have recognised this incompatibility when he wrote, 'Nos Principes sur la FOI doivent differer autant que nos Principes sur la Génération' (letter 41). Arguing for faith without understanding, Bonnet maintained, was the surest way of destroying it. Needham wrote in reply (letter 43) that even though their differences in matters of religion were serious ones, Catholic doctrine held that God would pardon Bonnet for his involuntary errors.

Needham's own views on religion and its relationship to science were expressed most clearly in his *Nouvelles recherches physiques et métaphysiques sur la nature et la religion* (1769), which formed the second part of his French edition of Spallanzani's *Saggio* (Spallanzani 1769). One of Needham's principal motivations both for publishing his commentary on Spallanzani's research as well as for including his own treatise on religion and cosmogony was to further his campaign to defend science against irreligion. He also wanted to counter misinterpretations that had arisen over his earlier biological work with regard to materialism. To Paolo Frisi he wrote, after sending him several copies of the book, that perhaps an Italian translation might be a good idea 'sans autre vüe quelconque, que celle de faire connoitre mes sentimens en fait de Religion. C'est presque la seule raison, qui m'a engagé à faire paroitre mon ouvrage' (10 July 1769, BAM, Y 153. Sup., lett. 49). To Sabatier de Cabre, he wrote similarly, 'Vous verrez, tel qu'en eu être le succes, que mes intentions sont pures, et que je n'écris pas pour me faire une vaine reputation, mais uniquement pour defendre la morale, et la religion sans nuire à la bonne physique' (2 December 1768, BLUL).

The religion Needham was referring to was of course revealed religion, and one of his major arguments was that the truths science discovers about the natural world and those made known through revealed religion can never be in contradiction. As he explained, 'aucune conséquence physique, bâtie sur des hypothéses humaines, ne peut tenir contre les vérités révélées, de même qu'aucune conséquence théologique, tirée directement des simples paroles de l'Ecriture Sainte [...] ne doit être regardée comme concluante dans la classe des vérités philosophiques' (Spallanzani 1769, pt.2:xiv). Needham sought thus to avoid the two extremes of those who wanted to use scientific arguments to contradict revealed religion and of those wishing to interpret religious dogma too narrowly to allow for proper scientific inquiry. His solution was to base his own philosophical inquiries on two tenets: that the natural world could not be understood without recalling its divine origins and that the truths of revealed religion could best be interpreted in harmony with the natural world. As he wrote to Bonnet, 'dieu avec le monde est un miracle, un mystere, dont la realité est constatée par le fait; le monde sans dieu est une absurdité pleine de contradiction, dont l'impossibilité saut aux yeux' (8 June 1768, letter 29).

Needham offered his treatise as an illustration of this approach to religion and nature, that is, of 'la Physique dirigée par la révélation' (Spallanzani 1769, pt.2:27). The subject matter to which he devoted himself was cosmogony, the origins and history of the Earth and its inhabitants.[5] His goal was to show that the account of Creation provided by Moses in the book of Genesis could be given a sound scientific interpretation, so that both the revealed word of God and the facts presented by the natural world could be harmonised into one coherent and self-substantiating system. Neither the objects of faith nor the first principles of science, Needham argued, can be known *a priori* but rather are discovered and proved through self-evident facts. Complaining to Bonnet about those who would accept abstract scientific truths derived from facts but who rejected religious truths, which were equally grounded, Needham declared, 'La Trinité, l'incarnation, la redemption, la chute de l'homme, le peché originel, la liberté humaine, le mal moral sont-ils ces mysteres plus in-intelligibles, que la doctrine des infinis, à laquelle la Geometrie nous mene par des routes assurées, l'existence, et l'essence de la matiere, l'identité personelle, la nature de la divinité, la production de l'univers, et mille autres verités tres physiques, et tres in-intelligibles' (30 June 1764, letter 17).

One can cite several examples of religious events or doctrines for which Needham strove to give physical explanations. In his treatise on cosmogony, he offered a natural explanation for the Deluge, a developmental sequence for the appearance of life on Earth through his system of active principles, and even an account of the formation of Eve from Adam's body as a vital propagation, operating through the same principles that Needham believed governed all generation. In his dispute with Voltaire over miracles, Needham attempted to counter Voltaire's ridicule of various miracles with a physical explanation of their occurrence (see section 5 of this Introduction). For example, he explained the prolongation of the day for Joshua by a temporary suspension of the rotation of the Earth; he proposed that the new star heralding the birth of Jesus Christ was a comet; and he described the multiplication of two fish and five loaves of bread into food for thousands as a simple conversion of other matter into fish

5. Needham's views on cosmogony are presented in detail in section 7 of this Introduction.

and bread (Needham [1765a]:4-8; 1769b:34-39). In 1765 Needham also wrote a defence of the Athanasian Creed for James Boswell and John Wilkes.[6] In this document, he likened the Trinity to a plant, which is composed of three parts: root, stalk, and branch. Each part proceeds from the previous part, each possesses individual differences, yet all form the unity of one plant. As a further example of his attempts to reconcile religious doctrines with natural explanations, Needham wrote to Joseph Berington that his theory of matter as active agents allowed one to account for the reality of transubstantiation and numerous other scriptural paradoxes, such as a camel fitting through the eye of a needle.[7] One should not misinterpret Needham as explaining away such religious doctrines by offering physical interpretations. Rather his purpose was always to make them intelligible to the doubter and to counter the unbeliever's ridicule of miracles and other revealed truths by showing how they could have happened through natural causes, under the direction of God's intervention.

In his own scientific work, Needham continually sought to promote the kind of science within a framework of revealed religion that he thought would counter the rising tide of materialism and atheism. In proposing a theory of generation that opposed preformation, which had a clear religious basis, Needham hoped to replace what he saw as a faulty theory with one that would offer just as firm a foundation for religion but that would be biologically sound. Unfortunately, because he proposed an epigenetic system based on active agents, he found his views both attacked as being materialist and endorsed by materialists.[8] Needham was walking a thin line, allowing material self-activity (which the preformation-ists always denied) while retaining a necessary role for God in generation.

Needham seems to have been aware of the possibility that his views might be misinterpreted as early as 1748, when he first outlined his system of generation in the paper he sent to the Royal Society. Near the conclusion of his paper, he remarked that in speaking of a productive force in nature, he was in no way dealing with the human soul, which had a separate, spiritual existence. Adding that he was sure the members of the Royal Society would not misinterpret his views, he nevertheless felt it necessary to clearly separate them from materialism, 'from which no one can be more distant or averse than myself', in case his paper might be read by 'others less acquainted with Matters of this sort' (Needham 1748:665). His fears were apparently well founded, for in the preface to the expanded French version of this paper, published in the *Nouvelles observations microscopiques* (1750), Needham stated that he had been accused of attacking the foundations of religion. His principal reason for adding so much material to the French version, he explained, was to outline his metaphysical and epistemologi-cal views and to show that they in no way supported materialism or atheism (see section 3 of this Introduction).

6. Needham and Boswell met in Turin in 1765 when Boswell was there on his Grand Tour. Needham read Boswell his defence of the Athanasian Creed in January 1765, which Boswell apparently mentioned to John Wilkes, who was then in Italy as well. Needham sent Boswell a copy of his explanation of the creed for Boswell to send on to Wilkes (see Brady and Pottle 1955:11-12, 35-36, 52 n.3, 74-76). A copy of Needham's defence in Boswell's hand is in the YUL (Boswell Papers); see also Needham's letter to Boswell of 13 March 1765 in the same collection.
7. See Needham's letter to Joseph Berington of 2 December 1771 (BDA, C.685).
8. For further discussion of Needham and materialism, see Roe (1983).

Needham's concern over being misinterpreted as a materialist is evident also in an early letter to Spallanzani, written when he thought Spallanzani agreed with his views. He cautioned his fellow experimenter: 'j'ajoute un autre [opinion] de plus grande importance; c'est surtout de ne pas donner prise par vos observations aux materialistes, et aux demi-philosophes [...] pour les precipiter encore d'avantage dans l'autre extreme, je veux dire le materialisme, et la generation equivoque. [...] Nous ne cherchons pas nous autres à faire rentrer le monde dans son chaos primitif en l'abandonnant au pur hazard, mais nous cherchons à établir solidement la providence en decouvrant les loix generales par lesquelle il gouverne un systeme, qui n'appartient qu'à lui seul' (29 August 1761; Castellani 1973:80). To Haller, to whom he had sent a 'metaphysical memoir' demonstrating that his system 'could be of no use to the modern materialists', Needham maintained that neither his theory of epigenesis nor Haller's theory of preformation could 'be of any service to the cause of materialism', since in both cases God had preordained the general laws governing the process of generation (27 September 1760, Mazzolini 1976:71-72; see also letter 1, n.4). And to Bonnet Needham wrote, after learning of Spallanzani's experiments in refutation of his theory, 'J'ai pourtant eu soin de ne jamais donner dans l'absurdité de la generation equivoque; en augmentant les puissances de la matiere, je les presente toujours, et vous le sçavés, meme par des consequences necessaires tirées des observations, comme subordonnées au dieu, et astreintes à des loix invariables. C'est à tort que le materialiste voudrait se prevaloir de mon systeme' (3 August 1765, letter 19).

Needham was accused of supporting atheism and materialism both because his theory was seen as one of equivocal generation and because he attributed self-active powers to matter. He responded to both accusations by claiming that his theory explained generation as a lawful, regular process entirely governed by divine law. Thus, the self-active capabilities of matter were carefully limited and provided no basis for accidental, equivocal generation (see section 2.ii of this Introduction). He also made further attempts to clearly delineate the sphere of activity of material causation from the operations of the sensitive principle in animals and the human soul in human beings. One of his goals in the notes he added to the French translation of Spallanzani's *Saggio* was to make this distinction perfectly clear. He commented to Bonnet, while working on this edition, that 'dans mes notes j'ai fait un resumé de mon système, en demontrant qu'il n'est nullement favorable au materialisme, mais conforme en tout, et par tout à la bonne morale, comme à la bonne physique' (8 June 1768, letter 29). To Sabatier de Cabre, Needham wrote that he had sequestered himself from the outside world to work on these notes 'that will, as I hope, not only demonstrate from matters of fact the truth of our doctrine, but illustrate it, and vindicate it from the cavils of half-witted philosophers, such as the illustrious proprietor of the Castle of Fernex [Voltaire], and others of the same depth, whose wits, according to an English proverb, outrun, or outweigh their judgements' (27 December 1767, BLUL). Voltaire had in fact been one of Needham's most outspoken critics, accusing him of atheism and materialism at every opportunity (see section 5 of this Introduction).

Needham took great pains in his notes in the *Nouvelles recherches sur les découvertes microscopiques* (1769) to demonstrate that the possession of active powers by matter did not threaten the existence of a divine Creator. '[E]n donnant à la matiere un principe de mouvement intérieur, & des forces vitales comme les phénomenes l'exigent,' he argued, '& en détaillant les opérations de la nature, qui n'agit qu'en vertu de la puissance qu'elle a reçue de la Divinité, personne n'ignore que la matiere & l'être le plus spirituel ne posséderont ni force ni existence, que sous la dépendance du Créateur, & ne l'exerceront que selon les loix qu'il a librement établies' (Spallanzani 1769, pt.1:149). Furthermore, with his new class of vital beings,[9] Needham was able to add both a biological and a metaphysical defence against materialism. He argued that microscopical vital beings are completely separate from true animals, which possess a sensitive principle. Thus, even though vital beings generate through active forces by division, true animals and human beings retain further immaterial principles.

Yet Needham's hopes that he had successfully defended his theory against misuse by materialists were soon dashed. In 1770 there appeared the most infamous materialist manifesto of the period, d'Holbach's *Système de la nature*, in which Needham's work was cited as evidence for materialism. In an early chapter in which d'Holbach was arguing for the existence of active matter, he claimed that matter possesses many abilities of its own without the need of external forces. One example he gave was chemical reactions, in which seemingly inert ingredients often combine to produce violent explosions. Similarly, d'Holbach commented, 'En humectant de la farine avec de l'eau & renfermant ce mélange, on trouve au bout de quelque tems à l'aide du microscope qu'il a produit des êtres organisés qui jouissent d'une vie dont on croyoit la farine & l'eau incapables. C'est ainsi que la matiere inanimée peut passer à la vie qui n'est elle-même qu'un assemblage de mouvemens.' Thus, even more dramatically than in chemical combinations, inanimate matter can be observed to organise itself into moving, living organisms. D'Holbach continued in a footnote, 'Voyez les *Observations microscopiques* de M. Néedham, qui confirment pleinement ce sentiment. Pour un homme qui réfléchit, la production d'un homme, indépendamment des voies ordinaires, seroit-elle donc plus merveilleuse que celle d'un insecte avec de la farine & de l'eau? La fermentation & la putréfaction produisent visiblement des animaux vivans. La génération que l'on a nommée *Equivoque*, ne l'est que pour ce qui ne se sont pas permis d'observer attentivement la nature' ([Holbach] 1770, 1:23 and n.5). Since it had been demonstrated, especially by Needham, d'Holbach claimed, that living creatures can arise from fermentation and decomposition, why could one not argue that even a human being might be able to originate from matter as well? D'Holbach drew from this argument the obvious implications about the existence of the human soul.

Needham was understandably incensed by d'Holbach's comments. In December 1770 he wrote a letter to the *Journal encyclopédique*, in which he condemned the *Système de la nature* as a 'triste & sombre' book, an 'ouvrage ténébreux' that was full of 'sophismes éblouissans'. The reader should not be taken in by the eloquent style and lengthy arguments of the work, Needham cautioned; for it represented an attempt 'a séduire la partie foible du genre humain, en représen-

9. See section 2.iv of this Introduction.

tant le côté obscur de l'objet, & en cachant, ou en obscurcissant tout ce qu'il a de clair & de lumineux' (Needham 1771a:296). Needham did not respond to the misuse of his biological ideas in this letter, but rather in a lengthy note he added to a book he had edited, *La Vraie philosophie* (1774, 1775) by the abbé Monestier (see also Needham 1774b and letter 50, n.5). Needham republished this note, along with his letter to the *Journal encyclopédique*, as a separate work, titled *Idée sommaire, ou vüe générale du systeme physique, et metaphysique de Monsieur Needham sur la génération des corps organisés* (1776, 1781), which he described as the 'common center' toward which all his previous works had tended.[10] Needham sent a copy of his *Idée sommaire* to Bonnet, asking him, if the opportunity presented itself in any future publications, to support Needham in defending him 'contre la fausse idée, que le malheureux auteur du système de la nature a donné de mes observations microscopiques' (25 November 1779, letter 50).

In the *Idée sommaire*, Needham admitted that his early statements on the origins of eels in blighted wheat and in flour paste might have misled the inattentive reader into thinking he supported equivocal generation. But, he commented with regard to d'Holbach, 'c'est en vain qu'on espére qu'un écrivain tel que l'Auteur du *Système de la Nature* rende justice aux autres, & je ne suis point surpris, que pour couvrir l'absurdité de son hypothese il confonde le Ciel & la terre en mêlant mes expériences sur les parties vitales, qui se détachoient continuellement dans mes infusions des corps organisés, avec celles que j'avois faites autrefois sur les anguilles de la farine' (Needham 1781:13). D'Holbach had indeed confused Needham's two sorts of observations when he described eels arising from flour and water in a sealed vessel, as in an infusion. But Needham's principal response to d'Holbach was to restate his views on vital matter and sensitive beings, offering now a four-part division of the natural world. The most basic level, the '*minéro-végétal*' which included minerals that form by condensation and cohesion, was followed by the '*végéto-végétal*' level, that is, plants that nourish by intussusception. Then came the '*végéto-vital*' level, the zoophytes that possess the ability to move but are purely vital, followed finally by the '*sensitif*' level, true animals that possess a sensitive soul and man who has an intellectual soul. This latter distinction, between material vitality and the sensitive principle was, once again, where Needham defended himself against materialism. Allying himself with Leibnizian philosophy, Needham declared, 'L'espece d'activité que [I and] ces Philosophes donnent aux élémens de la matiere, en la réduisant dans ses prémiers principes aux agens simples [...] est purement matérielle: elle ne s'étend pas plus loin que la vitalité la plus exaltée, [...] & ne sauroit jamais arriver à la sensibilité, encore moins à la puissance intellectuelle' (Needham 1781:14). To use Needham's observations on vital beings to bolster a materialist explanation for the origin of human beings was, Needham concluded, a gross misinterpretation of his views.

One could perhaps ask the question, why, if by arguing for active matter Needham could so easily be misunderstood as a materialist, did he support this view at all? Would it not have been better to accept passive matter and

---

10. See Needham's letter to Joseph Berington of 28 January 1774 (WCRO, Throckmorton MSS, CR 1998/Gate box, folder 8).

preformation, as so many of his contemporaries had, than to provide a possible foundation for materialism? Needham addressed the question of the motivations behind his views in a lengthy letter to Bonnet written in September 1779 (letter 48). 'Voulés vous que je vous dise un secret, qui me régarde, et que je n'ai dit encore à personne?', he began. Having been taught from his youth that the moral science was the most important of all, he found the philosophical climate in Paris when he first arrived there in 1746 too carefree and frivolous. The then-popular hypothesis of preexistant germs, Needham continued, did as much or more than any other hypothesis to assure morality and the creative powers of God. In metaphysics the Cartesian hypothesis of innate ideas, though false, served likewise to convince people of the presence of God and the immutability of morals. 'Le seul malheur étoit, qu'en prenant ces deux hypotheses [...] pour la vraie, et l'unique base de la morale, les faux Philosophes, qui en voyoient la foiblesse, ou pour le moins l'incertitude, ont conçu la folle esperance en les renversant de pouvoir sapper les fondemens de toute religion tant naturelle, que révelée, et de la detruire radicalement.' Thus, if the hypotheses of preexistent germs and innate ideas were to be shown to be untenable, as Needham believed would inevitably be the case, the way would be open for the destruction of religion and morality. 'Voyant par consequent du commencement meme de ma carriere Philosophique, et prevoyant que ces differentes resources cartesiennes, et autres en faveur de la religion pouvoient fort aisement nous manquer, en meme tems que la morale, sans laquelle la société ne peut subsister, periclitoit, si on ne prenoit pas les precautions de la pourvoir d'un second retranchement plus fort que le premier, j'ai voulu en prevenir les suites funestes.' Needham proposed his own system on the active forces of matter and on the scale of vital, sensitive, and intellectual beings as this new foundation. And so, he concluded, 'Maintenant, mon cher ami, vous voyez complettement mon but, et la parfaite unité de mon plan dans toutes mes entreprises' (letter 48).

Bonnet's reply to Needham's letter was somewhat curious (letter 49). Claiming that he had never doubted Needham's good intentions and reminding Needham that he himself had never either privately or in his published works portrayed Needham's views as materialist, Bonnet interpreted Needham as saying that he had adopted epigenesis *only* because it seemed to be less attacked by the unbelievers. 'Au fond,' Bonnet wrote, 'il ne s'agit pas de sçavoir quelle est l'hypothèse qui nous met le plus à l'aise ou la chaussure qui convient le mieux à notre pied. Il s'agit uniquement de sçavoir quelle est l'hypothese que la Nature paroit avouer' (8 November 1779, letter 49). Bonnet related Needham's comments to Spallanzani, calling Needham's account an 'apologie' (23 October 1779; Castellani 1971:387). Needham's reply to Bonnet's misinterpretation of his remarks was to reiterate his belief in the truth of epigenesis as the system that conformed the best *both* with good morals and with good science (letter 50).

Needham made a number of other comments that indicate how concerned he was that the moral foundations of society were crumbling under the new wave of materialism and atheism sweeping the intellectual circles of Europe. He wrote to Sabatier de Cabre in 1767 describing with what little regard religion seemed to be held in Paris: 'Society decays apace in the great world, not only revealed religion, but even the law of nature is become an object of ridicule; materialism, and a metaphysical kind of atheism is substituted. [...] man in his present situation abandoned by faith, reason, and morality without any fixed mechanical principle whatsoever to restrain him; what is left but Luxury, libertinism, caprice in the midst of gaiety, and passion in their most serious moments variable as the wind?' (9 January 1767, BLUL). In a similar vein he wrote from Paris to Da Costa, 'I know no philosophy going forward here, that I can either learn from books or conversation, but that which they call by that name, irreligion. This they are led into by aiming at what is termed an inlarged way of thinking, and no man is supposed to have acquired the desired latitude, but those who refuse to be confined within the bounds of morality, and have effaced every sentiment, that may serve to allay, or circumscribe their passions' (12 February 1767; BL, Add. 28540). Needham was struck when he returned to live in Paris in 1766, even more than he seems to have been when he was there in the late 1740s, with how decadent society had become as it turned away from religious morals. One of the reasons he spent so much time on his edition of Spallanzani's *Saggio* that he published in 1769 trying to show how his own views were not materialist was in fact to fulfil the ambition he described to Bonnet. He wanted to offer a new foundation for society that would retain the morality provided by religion. At the close of his book, he even apologised for discussing so extensively how his views did not support materialism, that 'doctrine importante qui touche de si près le bien-être moral de la Société' (Spallanzani 1769, pt.2:219). No wonder Needham was so dismayed when his views were adopted and promulgated by materialists – the very people whose success he had hoped to undercut. Misunderstood by materialists and rejected by the preformationists, Needham was in an unenviable position.

Bonnet and Needham were thus in agreement about the dangers facing society, and they both sought a return to morality based on revealed religion as the proper solution. They also agreed that, to counter the spread of irreligion, it was essential to present firm accounts of generation and cosmogony that necessarily involved the divinity. For it was in these two areas of scientific inquiry that the unbelievers had made their most serious challenges to orthodoxy. Yet Bonnet and Needham disagreed on the kinds of generation and cosmogony theories that would best promote religion, as well as on the epistemological and metaphysical bases on which they rested. As Needham expressed to Bonnet, 'je ne pouvois pas ignorer, que nous tendions de meme, quoique par des routes differentes dans le cours de nos récherches Philosophiques, au seul bien solide, l'affermissement de la morale Evangelique' (28 October [September] 1779, letter 48). The spectre of social disorder, buttressed by materialism and atheism, was in large measure the principal motivating factor behind both of their endeavours in philosophical and scientific inquiry.

5. Needham's controversy with Voltaire

IN August 1765, Needham wrote to Bonnet that he was sending him 'deux brochures de ma façon contre Voltaire' (letter 21). He explained that these were part of 'une petite guerre' that he had been waging against Voltaire on the subject of miracles and that the pamphlets he had written were 'ce que la partialité d'un ami pourra regarder comme mes trophées'. Needham then remarked, 'Il est vrai que la gloire qui resulte d'une victoire si aisée, contre un ennemi affaibli par l'âge, et engagé dans une si mauvaise cause n'est rien moin qu'un sujet de triomphe pour moi: mais n'importe, je n'ai pas travaillé pour la gloire, mais pour le bien de la societé en dessillant les yeux du peuple, offusqués par le moindre nuage.' To the receipt of Needham's pamphlets Bonnet replied, 'Vos Brochures contre Voltaire m'auroient prouvé vôtre Zèle pour la Réligion et vos talens, si j'avois eu besoin de preuves en ce genre. Vous l'avés mis au pié du mur; il la sauté. Vous lui avés poussé des Argumens; il les a repoussés par des Injures' (10 September 1765, letter 22). Voltaire, Bonnet continued, had no basis for accusing Needham of atheism, since Needham was such a devout defender of Christianity. Bonnet concluded by remarking that if Voltaire were really convinced of the falsity of religion, he would not spend so much time trying to refute it.

The two pamphlets that Needham sent to Bonnet were his anonymously published *Reponse d'un theologien au docte proposant des autres questions* and *Parodie de la troisieme lettre du proposant, adressée à un philosophe*, which were both written and published in Geneva in August 1765.[1] These had been composed in response to a series of pamphlets written by Voltaire that had begun to appear in Geneva in July,[2] beginning with the anonymously published *Questions sur les miracles à Monsieur le professeur Cl ... par un proposant* (V.O., 25:358-71). Needham's *Reponse* was a reply to Voltaire's second pamphlet, *Autres questions d'un proposant à M. le professeur en théologie, sur les miracles* (V.O., 25:371-78); and the *Parodie* was issued in response to Voltaire's *Troisième lettre du proposant à Monsieur le professeur en théologie* (V.O., 25:378-86). Needham later published a third pamphlet, *Projet de notes instructives*, véridiques, *théologiques, historiques & critiques sur certaines brochures polémiques du tems, adressées aux dignes editeurs des doctes ouvrages du proposant*, which responded to Voltaire's *Sixième lettre sur les miracles, laquelle n'est pas d'un proposant* (V.O., 25:431-37),[3] which had appeared in November 1765. Voltaire's pamphlets eventually grew to twenty by January 1766, but Needham wrote no new pamphlets in reply.

What was this pamphlet war all about and how did Needham become

1. Needham sent a copy of his first pamphlet to Sabatier de Cabre with a letter dated 13 August 1765 (BLUL).
2. For the dates of publication of Voltaire's pamphlets on miracles, see Bengesco (1882-1890, 2:153-59) and V.O., 25:357-58. See also Gargett (1980:226-28).
3. In the edition of Voltaire's pamphlets published in V.O., the nineteenth letter is mistakenly included as the fifteenth, so that the subsequent letters (sixteen to nineteen) are actually, in the original, letters fifteen to eighteen.

embroiled in a controversy that, as it turned out, was to plague him for more than a decade? Needham had moved to Geneva in August 1765 with Charles Dillon, his pupil, and he remained there for ten months. Soon after arriving he wrote to Sabatier de Cabre, 'Voltaire, et Rousseau occupent toute la conversation de cette ville remuante, et la brochure [Needham's *Reponse*], que je vous envoye, est un produit du climat, comme il se trouve actuellement' (13 August 1765, BLUL). The previous year Rousseau had published his *Lettres écrites de la montagne*, in which he had discussed (in letters 2 and 3) the subject of miracles. Rousseau's *Lettres* were written in the midst of a political crisis in the Republic of Geneva that had been sparked by the condemnation in 1762 of his *Emile* and *Contrat social* (see section 8 of this Introduction). In addition to containing a defence of his doctrine of political rights and a critique of the Genevan governing institutions, Rousseau's *Lettres écrites de la montagne* offered a defence against the charge that his books were impious and encouraged irreligion. The topic Rousseau took his stand on was miracles; and after maintaining that the true essence of Protestantism was the right of each person to interpret the Scriptures for himself and the promulgation of faith through reason alone, he claimed that miracles were not a necessary part of religion. Furthermore, by defining a miracle as an exception to the laws of nature, laws that we can never know in their entirety, Rousseau concluded that one could never know for certain if any occurrence was miraculous, since one could never know if it violated all of the laws of nature. Yet Rousseau also proclaimed his own personal belief in Jesus Christ and in natural religion (see R.O., 3:cxcii).

Rousseau's *Lettres écrites de la montagne* had an immediate effect on the Genevan political situation, catalysing the attempts by the burghers to promote institutional reform. It also prompted a theological reply by David Claparède, a Genevan pastor and professor of theology, whose *Considerations sur les miracles de l'evangile* represented one of the principal responses of the Genevan clergy (see also Vernes 1765). Claparède confined himself to responding to the theological issues raised in Rousseau's third letter and to defending the existence and necessity of miracles as attested to in the Gospels. He countered Rousseau's claim that we cannot know for certain if any event is miraculous by maintaining that all one needs is a working familiarity with the regularity of natural phenomena to recognise miraculous exceptions. Claparède's work is not distinguished for its theological argumentation but rather for its having provoked Voltaire to begin writing his own series of pamphlets on miracles, which served as a forum for satirical attacks on Calvinism, on the Genevan political hierarchy, and, most importantly for our purposes, on Needham.

Voltaire's first pamphlet, written under the guise of a *proposant*, was ostensibly a series of questions put to a professor (Claparède) by a theology student confused by all of the rhetoric of the modern unbelievers. Through this device, Voltaire was able to satirise and attack points of Christian dogma and generally to make a stronger case for the unbelievers than for the Christians. Claiming that the early Christians forged documents and exaggerated events, Voltaire ironically admitted that miracles might be needed in the present day, since the Church was in such a state of disarray. Yet, as a deist, his main point was that one did not need to believe in miracles or in any other doctrines based on revelation to lead a virtuous life.

In his second letter, Voltaire turned to the question how does the philosopher, familiar with the natural laws of the universe, make sense of miracles, the same issue to which Rousseau had addressed himself. Here Voltaire asked, if God had established a universe based on immutable laws, why would he upset the entire system for a local exception, such as stopping the Earth and the moon so that Joshua could massacre the Amorites? If one considered, for example, the star that supposedly guided the wise men, its movement through the heavens would have totally disturbed the celestial system – but why? The only conceivable reason, Voltaire claimed, was, 'Pour que dans ce petit tas de boue appelé la terre, les papes s'emparassent enfin de Rome, que les bénédictins fussent trop riches, qu'Anne Dubourg fût pendu à Paris, et Servet brûlé vif à Genève' (V.O., 25:372-73). Still in the role of the *proposant*, Voltaire declared, 'Le cœur me saigne quand je vois des hommes remplis de science, de bon sens et de probité, rejeter nos miracles, et dire qu'on peut remplir tous ses devoirs sans croire que Jonas ait vécu trois jours et trois nuits dans le ventre d'une baleine' (V.O., 25:378).

It was principally to Voltaire's discussion of science and miracles in his second pamphlet that Needham directed his *Réponse*. Needham knew that Voltaire was the author of the pamphlets, yet he attempted to answer Voltaire's ridicule with a serious discussion, a circumstance that served only to fan the flames in Voltaire's subsequent attacks on Needham. Needham began his pamphlet by arguing that one should not subjugate morals to physics but rather vice versa and that miracles are only local exceptions to the natural system. Furthermore, they had served the important function of furnishing human beings with a basis for morality and thus for society. Turning to the specific miracles objected to by Voltaire, Needham attempted to give explanations consistent with science for the prolongation of the day for Joshua, for the new star (which Needham suggested was a comet), and for the conversion of two fish and five loaves of bread into food for thousands of people. Defending the possibility of Jonah having lived for three days and nights in the belly of a large fish, Needham declared, 'C'est un évenement prophétique, qui regarde directement le Messie, comme tant d'autres dans la Bible, rejetté par l'incrédule, qui ne voit que la singularité du fait, sans voir ni les moyens, ni la fin; mais il est très intelligible, & très croyable au fidèle Chrétien, qui, connaissant la voix de Dieu, se repose sur sa puissance, sa sagesse, & sa véracité' (Needham [1765a]:14; 1769b:45).[4] In an added 'Observation', Needham declared that the *Incrédules* could not really be 'esprits forts', as commonly alleged, unless Christianity were really true; for to reject a mere fable was only an act of weakness.

Although Voltaire answered Needham's *Réponse* in his fourth pamphlet, he did not yet know that Needham had been the author. He soon learned, however, and, in his fifth pamphlet, began a series of personal attacks on Needham that were to run through the remaining fifteen letters he wrote. What apparently

4. Page references will be given both to the originals of Needham's pamphlets ([1765a], [1765b], [1765c]) and to his published collection of them (1769b).

piqued Voltaire's ire even more than Needham's specific arguments was that Needham had mentioned Voltaire by name in his *Reponse*.[5] Voltaire pointed angrily in his fifth letter to the insolence and crudeness 'de nommer des gens qui ne devaient pas s'y attendre' (V.O., 25:395), the impropriety of which was noted as well in the *Correspondance littéraire* (*C.L.*, 6:408). Anonymous skirmishes, even when everyone knew who the interlocutors were, were apparently fully acceptable to Voltaire, but crossing the line into named conflict, thereby revealing the identity of one's adversary, was not.

In order to further understand both Voltaire's motivations and the substance of his satire of Needham, it is necessary to discuss Voltaire's biological poësie views and his previous knowledge of Needham's work. Needham became a symbol for Voltaire of all of the dangers he saw in recent materialist tendencies in biology. Ironically, both Voltaire and Needham opposed biological materialism for many of the same fundamental reasons, yet Voltaire never understood Needham's views well enough to be able to recognise this. He found Needham to be far too useful as a butt for ridicule to deserve any serious consideration.

Although Voltaire indicated his preference for the theory of preformation as early as 1740, in his *Métaphysique de Newton* (V.O., 22:429), his preoccupation with topics in the life sciences did not really begin until the mid-1760s.[6] In 1764, he explicitly endorsed preexistence of germs in a review he published of Bonnet's *Considérations sur les corps organisés* (V.O., 25:153-58), where he also criticised the views of Buffon and Maupertuis. Voltaire found in the theory of preformation an account of the generation of life that was consistent with his own Newtonian and deistic conception of nature. Believing that matter is a passive substance, which is incapable of self-organisation, Voltaire attributed the diversity and design of the natural world to an intelligent first cause. He also, especially after the mid-1760s, saw in preformation a defence against atheism and materialism, which he felt had received new support from the epigenetic theories of Mauper-

---

5. Needham made two references to Voltaire in the *Reponse*, neither of which stated *directly* that Voltaire was the *proposant*. In the first, Needham was commenting on the passage (cited earlier) where miracles were claimed to exist for the benefit of popes and Benedictines. Needham responded, 'C'est précisément comme si l'on disait, qu'il ne valait pas la peine d'avoir une législation en France, pour que deux cent maltotiers s'enrichissent aux dépens du peuple, ou d'encourager la poësie, pour que la Pucelle d'Orleans fût mise au jour au grand scandale de tous les gens de bien' (Needham [1765a]:6; 1769b:37). To this a note was appended, explaining, 'Je raisonne ici *ad hominem*, selon sa façon d'envisager les objets, pour le frapper avec plus de force, & faire sentir vivement au Lecteur le fiel & la faiblesse de ses paralogismes; *Répondez*, dit Salomon, *à un insensé selon sa folie*' ([1765a]:6n; 1769b:37n). Needham later apologised for this note, claiming, in an 'Avis' added at the end of his *Parodie* ([1765b]:25), that the footnote asterisk had been misplaced by the printer, giving the misimpression that Needham was referring to the author of *La Pucelle d'Orléans* (Voltaire), rather than to the *proposant*. (The note was not moved, however, in the 1769 edition.)

The second reference to Voltaire occurred a few pages later, when Needham was accusing the *proposant* of having erroneously viewed individual miracles in too much isolation from their divine causal chains. 'Pour tout remède à la bassesse de sa vuë, je lui [the *proposant*] conseille la lecture de l'Histoire universelle de [Jacques Bénigne] Bossuet, qui vaut bien celle de Voltaire pour le moins; parce que Bossuet ne choisit pas les événemens, en les isolant, pour les présenter ensuite selon la petitesse de certaines vuës particuliéres, sous tel coloris faux qu'il plait à l'amour propre de leur donner; mais il les enchaine ensemble dans leur ordre naturel, pour faire paraître les desseins de la Divinité' (Needham [1765a]:9; 1769b:39-40).

6. For Voltaire's biological views, see Roger (1963:732-48), Perkins (1965), Marx (1975), and Roe (1985).

tuis, Buffon, and Needham. The principal motivation for Voltaire's attacks on these theories was his opposition to atheism and his concern over the social consequences of its spread. Especially in his later years, Voltaire explicitly endorsed the need for belief in a rewarding and vengeful God as a basis for morality.[7] Rejecting the possibility of a virtuous society of atheists, Voltaire offered his own deistic and preformationist views as a foundation for a tolerant and moral social order.

Voltaire first learned of Needham's biological views by reading Maupertuis's *Lettres*, published in 1752. There Maupertuis briefly alluded to Needham's observations on eels in blighted wheat and in flour paste (see Maupertuis 1756, 2:281, and Hoffheimer 1982). In a series of pamphlets written in 1752 and 1753, collectively titled *Histoire du docteur Akakia et du natif de Saint-Malo*, in which Voltaire satirised Maupertuis, partly because of a priority dispute Maupertuis was then engaged in with König over the law of least action, Voltaire used Needham's work to ridicule Maupertuis. In one section, where he was poking fun at the Berlin Academy of Sciences, of which Maupertuis was then president, Voltaire had the 'galant' president serve the ladies present 'une superbe collation, composée de pâtés d'anguilles, toutes les unes dans les autres, et nées subitement par un mélange de farine délayée' and also 'grand plats de poissons qui se formaient sur-le-champ de grains de blé germé' (V.O., 23:573). At this point in Voltaire's thinking, he was not yet particularly worried by the biological ideas of either Maupertuis or Needham; and he found in Needham's work simply further grist for the mill in his attack on Maupertuis.

By the time of the miracles episode in 1765, however, Voltaire had begun to find the new biological ideas worrisome. When he finally learned that Needham was the author of the *Reponse* to his second pamphlet, Voltaire began a concerted attack on Needham, on dangerous biological ideas, and on atheism. Claiming in his fifth pamphlet that Needham was no more a theologian than he was an astronomer, Voltaire added, 'Vous vous étiez fait une petite réputation parmi les athées pour avoir fait des anguilles avec de la farine, et de là vous avez conclu que si de la farine produit des anguilles, tous les animaux, à commencer par l'homme, avaient pu naître à peu près de la même façon' (V.O., 25:394). In the 'Avertissement' that Voltaire later added to this pamphlet, he made his worries over the implications of Needham's biological work even more explicit. Falsely characterising Needham as an Irish Jesuit, who roamed the countryside disguised in secular clothing, spreading papist dogma, Voltaire continued, 'mais ce qui étonna davantage, c'est que ce prêtre déguisé était celui-là même qui, plusieurs années auparavant, se mêla de faire des expériences sur les insectes, et qui crut avoir découvert, avec son microscope, que de la farine de blé ergoté, délayée dans de l'eau, se changeait incontinent en de petits animaux ressemblant à des anguilles. Le fait était faux, comme un savant italien l'a démontré' (V.O., 25:393). Voltaire was referring here to Spallanzani's refutation of Needham's work in the *Saggio di osservazioni microscopiche* (1765), of which Voltaire had just received an anonymous copy. But, Voltaire then continued, Needham's claim

7. See especially Best.D15189 and 16736; and V.O., 10:402-405, 17:472-76, and 18:376-81. See also Besterman (1965 and 1967), Mason (1963:78-89), Pomeau (1969:391-427), Jacob (1981:101-106), and Roe (1985).

'était faux par une autre raison bien supérieure, c'est que le fait est impossible. Si des animaux naissaient sans germe, il n'y aurait plus de cause de la génération: un homme pourrait naître d'une motte de terre tout aussi bien qu'une anguille d'un morceau de pâte. Ce système ridicule mènerait d'ailleurs visiblement à l'athéisme. Il arriva en effet que quelques philosophes, croyant à l'expérience de Needham sans l'avoir vue, prétendirent que la matière pouvait s'organiser d'elle-même; et le microscope de Needham passa pour être le laboratoire des athées' (V.O., 25:393-94).

Voltaire lashed out at Needham in this fifth pamphlet and in the next three, for insincerely entering a debate over miracles on the side of the theologians, when in fact, Voltaire claimed, Needham was himself an atheist, for his impolite attack on such a well-meaning *proposant*, and for his self-aggrandisement. 'Si on dit que Jésus-Christ a changé l'eau en vin,' Voltaire charged, 'aussitôt M. Needham pense à sa farine qu'il a changée en anguilles' (V.O., 25:395).

Voltaire's first eight pamphlets had appeared by 4 September, and he claimed in a later republication of all the pamphlets together that Needham's second pamphlet, the *Parodie de la troisieme lettre du proposant, adressée à un philosophe*, was published after his own eighth pamphlet. Needham had in fact sent a copy of his *Parodie* to Bonnet on 28 August (letter 21). The *Parodie* was written in imitation of Voltaire's third pamphlet, in which the *proposant* was called on to defend the existence of miracles against the questions and critical comments of 'un grand seigneur allemand' (probably meant to be Frederick II). The *proposant*'s rather weak defence and naive faith in miracles did not compare well with Voltaire's 'seigneur', whose own deistic moral beliefs, which were not based on miracles and revealed religion, appeared all the more reasonable. Needham decided to parody this by substituting for the German lord a giant Patagonian from Tierra del Fuego and for the *proposant* a character sympathetic to deism and to the philosophes. Needham declared in an 'Avis préliminaire' that he had changed neither the form of the dialogue nor the ideas expressed but rather that, 'On n'a changé simplement que les interlocuteurs, & les objets qu'on discute, pour faire sentir, que les ténèbres répandues par les Incrédules sur la Religion, aménent en même tems des ténèbres universelles sur toutes les autres vérités. L'Infidéle se verra comme dans un miroir, & ses propres argumens sont tournés directement contre lui-même' (Needham [1765b]:1; 1769b:59). By caricaturing Voltaire's virtuous lord as an uncivilised savage and by switching from a discussion where deism challenged revealed religion to one where deism was called upon to defend itself against the mores (or lack thereof) of unbridled nature, Needham hoped to drive home the message that religion based only on reason and not on faith was powerless against the destructive powers of immorality. '[I]l suffit de montrer aux clair-voyans', he declared in his preliminary remarks, 'l'abime où ces Messieurs veulent nous précipiter; les faux principes qu'on employe contre la Religion sont par leur nature même destructifs de la société; comme nous avons demontré dans ce court imprimé' (Needham [1765b]:2; 1769b:60).

The only acknowledgement Needham gave in the *Parodie* to Voltaire's attacks on him was in a brief 'P.S.', later titled 'Post-Scriptum en Réponse à la cinquième Lettre du Proposant'. Here Needham stated simply that if Voltaire had wanted polite replies to his attacks on religion, he should have written politely himself. 'Le genre de l'attaque décide de celui de la défense' (Needham [1765b]:23; 1769b:87). Needham remarked as well that he was not even going to mention the 'mille autres erreurs' of the *proposant* in the other pamphlets.

Needham's correspondence with Sabatier de Cabre during these months contains a number of discussions of the miracles controversy. Sabatier seems to have been concerned about the abuse Needham was taking at the hands of Voltaire and to have cautioned him against writing anything further. Responding to these worries in a letter of 1 October 1765, Needham reassured Sabatier, 'que l'artillerie de Fernex, tonne en vain, et que mon aneantissement ne depend pas de la volonté de mon adversaire. La fortune a fait plus pour ma reputation de bravoure, que vos craintes, et elle m'a forcé malgré moi, non seulement de tenir le champ de bataille sans branler, mais aussi de camper ici non obstant la proximité du Geant Patagon, qui me menace toujours.' Remarking that the Republic of Geneva had permitted him to remain there even though he was a Catholic, Needham claimed to Sabatier that 'Monsieur Voltaire en m'Irlandai-sant, atheisant, et Jesuisant par une suite de brochures à six deniers, qui n'ont cessé de sortir sans aucun interval, n'a pas meme reussi à me rendre ou odieux, ou ridicule aux yeux des Genevois' (BLUL). He then quoted from a letter he had received from someone else in Paris, who had assured him that Voltaire's libels had done more on Needham's behalf than any defence of him by honest people could do. Needham reassured Sabatier that he would write no more against Voltaire.

Although Voltaire satirised Needham again in letter nine, it was not until his sixteenth pamphlet that he responded to the *Parodie*, the intervening pamphlets having been devoted to Genevan politics and the clergy. Needham re-emerged in the sixteenth letter as a dinner guest of a count and countess; the conversation is reported by the *proposant*, who was also present. 'Admirez, je vous prie,' he remarked, 'la politesse de monseigneur et de madame: il y avait un pâté d'anguilles délicieux; ils ordonnèrent qu'on ne le servît point parce que, depuis quelque temps, M. Needham se trouve en peu mal toutes les fois qu'on parle d'anguilles' (V.O., 25:431). The count proceeded to read aloud a letter he had received from America that reported that, after a peace had been signed with an Indian tribe, all the previously captured boys and girls were returned by the Indians to the English. In a speech the Indian chief pleaded with the Englishmen to treat the children with kindness and understanding, since they had been taught Indian ways. The dinner guests all marvelled at the humanity of the chief, but the character Needham claimed that the chief must have been a disguised Irish Jesuit, because savages could not have morals without having been instructed by a Christian missionary. Voltaire poked further fun at Need-ham when, after calling him 'l'anguillard' and having him defend the massacre of heretics, criticise Protestantism, and make some ridiculous comments concerning Jesus and the devil, the *proposant* reported, 'Il y avait là un Anglais qui n'avait encore ni parlé ni ri; il mesura d'un coup d'œil la figure du petit Needham avec un air d'étonnement et de mépris, mêlé d'un peu de colère, et lui dit en anglais: "Do you come from Bedlam, you, booby!"' (V.O., 25:437).

Although Needham had promised Sabatier that he would publish nothing more against Voltaire, he did write one last pamphlet, the *Projet de notes instructives*, probably composed in November 1765.[8] Perhaps the least inspired of his three pamphlets, Needham's *Projet* took on issues of Biblical dating and answered the claim (made by the fictional Needham) that savages are all condemned because they have no knowledge of Jesus Christ. Following saint Paul, Needham argued in reply that each individual is judged according to the law that he knows. Leaving the question open of whether the truly noble savage could ever exist, he quoted from a report on American Indian customs that described the torture and execution of prisoners at celebrations after battles. 'D'après ce tableau,' he proclaimed, 'regrette qui voudra la vie animale, les forces physiques des Sauvages, & qu'on nous dise que les sciences acquises ne sont que des maladies de l'ame destructives de son vrai bonheur' (Needham [1765c]:14; 1769b:113). Needham also defended himself in this pamphlet against Voltaire's fictional Needham, declaring, 'Pauvre *Anguillard*! quoique tu ne sois point, pour le malheur de ton adversaire, ni *Athée*, ni Irlandais, ni Jésuite, ni même *éléve des Jésuites*, la réputation que tu procures en vain, dit-on, parmi les Athées, par tes découvertes mal-entendues, ne te sauvera jamais du grand ridicule, dont ton adversaire te couvre aux yeux de toutes les Ravaudeuses de Genève, en substituant dans sa Lettre ses paroles aux tiennes' (Needham [1765c]:8-9; 1769b:105-106). This was Needham's only direct reference in these pamphlets to Voltaire's ridicule of his biological views and his attribution of an atheistic foundation to them.

Voltaire responded to some of the issues raised in Needham's *Projet* in his nineteenth letter, but it was in letter twenty, the last, that Voltaire had his final say. There the fictional Needham was arrested in Neufchâtel and tried for spreading heretical beliefs about the fallibility of the Holy Scriptures. The interrogator asked if he was a papist, to which 'Il avoue hardiment qu'il l'était, qu'il célébrait sa synaxe tous les dimanches, qu'il faisait l'*hocus pocus* avec une dextérité merveilleuse' (V.O., 25:446). Asked if he was a Jesuit, the fictional Needham replied ambiguously that he was not what they believed he was. Yet then a letter fell from his pocket addressed 'Al reverendo, reverendo padre Needham, della Società di Giesù'. After being questioned about various scriptural inconsistencies, the priest Needham attempted to reconcile them by absurd suggestions, such as that one should read in Matthew, Nazareth for Egypt and in Luke, Egypt for Nazareth. After the trial, Needham was 'condamné tout d'une voix à faire amende honorable, une anguille à la main, et ensuite à être lapidé hors la porte de la ville, selon la coutume' (V.O., 25:448). A brief defence of Needham was put forward by a 'M. du Peyrou', who argued that the sentence of stoning was too severe for a visitor and that it would hinder Englishmen from visiting their town, to which it was replied that Michael Servetus, a Spaniard, had been a stranger too but had been burned for the love of God. The sentence stood, yet no one could decide who would have the honour of throwing the first stone, and the prisoner escaped.

Needham and Sabatier continued to discuss the Voltaire episode in their

8. On 11 December 1765, Needham wrote to Paolo Frisi and enclosed a pamphlet (the *Projet*) 'que je viens d'imprimer en reponse à Voltaire depuis très peu de jours' (BAM, Y 153. Sup., lett. 48). Handwritten on the copy of the *Projet* at the BPUG is 'donnée par Mr Needham le 29 9bre 1765'.

letters, with Sabatier apparently warning that Needham was the subject of ridicule among some people in Paris, and Needham claiming again that he would write no more. Yet in February 1766, Needham wrote to say that he was sending Sabatier a new edition of the *Parodie*. The pages he had added, Needham wrote, 'Vaillent qu'elles vaillent, il etait necessaire de toute nécessité de donner quelques signes de vie, pour prouver que je n'étais pas ni abattu, ni emporté par le torrent des injures, que le vieux dragon a vomi contre moi dans une suite de vingt lettres' (11 February 1766, BLUL; see also letter of 18 February).

In his new edition of the *Parodie*, Needham made only slight alterations in the text. But he added a new section at the end, entitled 'Réponse en peu de mots aux dix-sept dernières Lettres du Proposant', which was followed by two epigrams 'Imitée de J. B. Rousseau' and an extract from Rousseau that was critical of Voltaire. Needham's very brief 'Réponse' claimed simply that although those who defend religion may not always write as well as the unbelievers, 'je n'appelle point bien écrire de dire des sottises en beau langage' (Needham [1766]:27; 1769b:88). He saw no reason to respond in detail to all of the 'Ecrits impies' of the *proposant* (Voltaire).

In May, Needham announced to Sabatier that Voltaire had just published a new edition of all the letters on miracles, which was apparently being printed in Geneva and then smuggled into Germany for distribution to the rest of Europe, so that no one in Geneva would be able to see it and respond before it had been circulated. 'Il n'est plus une affaire, qui me regarde, celle de lui repondre, supposé que son libelle merite une reponse,' Needham remarked, 'c'est l'affaire de tout le monde, et je me perds dans la foule' (2 May 1766, BLUL).

Voltaire's edition, the *Collection des lettres sur les miracles*, did not appear until early 1766, although it had a publication date of 1765 (see Bengesco 1882-1890, 2:158). In addition to republishing all of his own pamphlets, Voltaire included the three by Needham, annotated with numerous notes further ridiculing him. Calling him 'Jésuite calomniteur', 'pauvre Néedham', and 'mon pauvre Anguillard', Voltaire retitled the *Parodie* to include 'Par le Sieur Néedham, Irlandois, Prêtre Jésuite, transformateur de farine en anguilles. Il fait parler un Patagon dans cette Parodie. Et le Patagon raisonne comme Néedham' ([Voltaire] 1765:95; V.O., 25:401). Revealing once again his underlying worries over the implications of what he understood to be Needham's biological views, Voltaire commented in a note, 'celui qui écrit que les animaux viennent sans germe, écrit contre Dieu' ([Voltaire] 1765:119n; V.O., 25:403 n.2).

Although Needham did not discuss Voltaire's edition any further in his letters to Sabatier, he did react to another of Voltaire's publications in which he was named, *La Guerre civile de Genève ou les amours de Robert Covelle*. This was a mock epic poem in five cantos that characterised the Genevan political situation as a confrontation between the clergy and the people. Composed during the first half of 1767, the separate cantos circulated in manuscript form in Paris before they were published together in 1768 (see Bengesco 1882-1890, 1:175-77; V.O., 9:507 n.1). In the first canto, the main character, Robert Covelle, is summoned before the Consistoire, a tribunal of Genevan pastors, to be tried for fathering a child out of wedlock. When ordered to kneel before the tribunal to receive his sentence,

Covelle replied that he kneeled only before God, not men. Based on a true character and incident, Voltaire's account of the trial portrayed Jacob Vernet, one of Geneva's leading theologians who was satirised by Voltaire in a number of works, as the head of the tribunal. He was described thus (V.O., 9:518):

> Du noir sénat le grave directeur
> Est Jean Vernet, de maint volume auteur,
> Le vieux Vernet, ignoré du lecteur,
> Mais trop connu des malheureux libraires;
> Dans sa jeunesse il a lu les saints pères,
> Se croit savant, affecte un air dévot:
> Broun est moins fat, et Needham est moins sot.

In a note, Voltaire continued on Needham, 'Needham est un jésuite irlandais, imbécile qui a cru faire des anguilles avec de la farine. On a donné quelque temps dans sa chimère, et quelques philosophes même ont bâti un système sur cette prétendue expérience, aussi fausse que ridicule' (V.O., 9:518 n.3).[9]

Needham must have seen Voltaire's poem in manuscript form, for he wrote to Sabatier on 14 July 1767, 'Avez vous vu un poeme manuscrit, qui coure le monde ici, ou Voltaire se moque des malheurs de la ville de Geneve? Magistrat, clergé, Bourgeoisie, Jean Jacques Rousseau, milord abington, tout ce enfin, qui tient, ou qui a tenu depuis quelque tems à cette malheureuse ville devient sujet à ses railleries atrabilaires.' Referring specifically to the verse quoted above, Needham continued, 'J'entre aussi comme anneau dans cette chaine Ideale, qui roule dans sa tête, et il m'a fouri par nom comme *sot*, dans un vers, et comme *jesuite irlandais* dans une note.' Because of this, Needham explained, he had decided to take action: 'Je lui reponds par l'avis de mes amis en donnant un precis au publique de notre querelle, et en publiant les lettres, qu'il m'a ecrit autre fois sans un nom emprunté. Je vous en verrai un exemplaire par quelque occasion favorable' (BLUL).

Needham's edition of the miracles pamphlets and 'précis' of the controversy did not actually appear until 1769, with the title *Questions sur les miracles, à M. Claparede [...] par un proposant: ou extrait de diverses lettres de M. de Voltaire, avec des réponses par M. Needham.*[10] In his 'Avis au lecteur' he explained that he was including only those portions of Voltaire's pamphlets that were necessary to understand Needham's responses, claiming that 'le reste n'est qu'un tissu des lieux communs ou des impertinences folles & dégoûtantes' (Needham 1769b:3). What better way to respond to insults and blasphemy than by scorn and silence, he added? Included by Needham were extracts from Voltaire's second and sixteenth pamphlets, and the third and fifth letters in full. Needham then

9. For the Covelle incident and for Voltaire's relationship with Vernet and Brown, see Gargett (1980:173-77, 216); letter 14, n.15; and letter 28, n.28 and n.29. Covelle figures as well as one of Voltaire's spokesmen in the miracles pamphlets.

10. An edition of the first sixteen of Voltaire's pamphlets plus Needham's *Projet* was published in 1767 with the title *Questions sur les miracles, en forme de lettres. A Monsieur le professeur Cl. . . . Par un proposant* [Genève]. However, Needham was not responsible for this edition, since he would certainly have included his two other pamphlets. It is unlikely that the edition was Voltaire's either, since the pamphlets contain none of the changes and additions that Voltaire made in his *Collections des lettres sur les miracles* (1765) nor his annotations on Needham's pamphlet.

reprinted his own pamphlets in their entirety, adding occasional phrases and a few new notes.

Following the *Parodie*, Needham added a 'Note generale sur cette nouvelle Edition', in which he explained that he had not intended to answer all of Voltaire's slurs against the Bible and religion, something he would leave to the theologians. Rather, 'M. Néedham fait voir en général, comme Philosophe, l'absurdité de sa façon de raisonner dans les écrits précédens contre la Religion' (Needham 1769b:92). All of Voltaire's discussions of religious dogma should be treated with distrust, he further claimed, as they are full of mistakes, only a few of which Needham had space to point out. Needham also warned, with regard to his own *Parodie*, that one should remember that it was written to show the absurdities of Voltaire's attacks on religion in his third pamphlet by imitation and exaggeration. Thus, one should not interpret the arguments against God and society presented by Needham's Patagonian as anything but an ironic exposé of the pernicious implications of Voltaire's line of reasoning, not to be believed. '[T]out homme sensé', Needham proclaimed, 'sera forcé dorénavant de regarder l'Auteur de l'original contre le Christianisme [...] comme un misérable Sophiste digne du mépris de tous les siécles' (Needham 1769b:94-95). And in an addition to a concluding 'Avis au lecteur', Needham remarked that reading the absurd works of Voltaire would only serve to strengthen peoples' religious faith. 'Plût à Dieu,' he wrote, 'que la partie foible du genre humain fût en état d'en profiter, & de ne puiser dans ces sources infectes, que l'horreur qu'elles doivent inspirer, à tous ceux qui respectent quelques principes de la croyance ou des mœurs!' (Needham 1769b:115).

Voltaire's attacks on Needham were not confined to these pamphlets on miracles, nor did they cease when the pamphlets had all been published. Having drawn in 1765 a connection (erroneous as it may have been) between Needham's biological work and atheism, Voltaire continued to pillory Needham at every opportunity. Writing a congratulatory letter to Spallanzani after having received a copy of the *Saggio*, Voltaire declared, 'Vous avez très grand raison de combattre les prétendues expériences de Mr Needham. On l'a attaqué depuis peu à Genêve sur les miracles. Il pourait se vanter en éffet d'avoir fait des miracles s'il avait pu produire des anguilles sans germe. Il faut se défier de toutes ces expériences hazardées, qui contredisent les loix de la nature' (17 February 1766, Best. D13177; see also *Epistolario*, 1:57 n.3).

After the miracles episode, two events rekindled Voltaire's attacks on Needham: his reading of Buffon's *Histoire naturelle* in 1767[11] and of Lagrange's translation of Lucretius's *De rerum natura* in 1768. Needham's observations figured prominently in both works, and Voltaire was once again prompted to attack some of the more dangerous materialist tendencies that he saw emerging from contemporary biology. In his copy of the second volume of Buffon's *Histoire naturelle*, Voltaire made numerous marginal comments indicating his distaste for the theory being propounded. To a mention of Needham's observations on eels in blighted wheat, Voltaire remarked, 'est il possible que vous ayez pu répeter

11. For evidence that Voltaire did not read any volumes of the *Histoire naturelle* before 1767 and for his marginal comments in this work, see *Corpus* (1979-, 1:559-612, 655 n.413) and Roe (1985).

après maupertuis cette enorme sottise de l'embécile needham!' (*Corpus* 1979-, 1:604). Further comments reiterated Voltaire's rejection of organic molecules and his support for preformation.

In Lagrange's anonymous translation of *De rerum natura*, Needham's work was discussed in a footnote. Lagrange reported that most people believed that all organisms were preformed in eggs, even those that appeared to come from putrefaction. 'Mais ce principe de physique,' he remarked, 'ainsi que bien d'autres qu'on regarde comme aussi sûrs, est démenti par l'expérience. Tout le monde connaît celle de M. Néedham, qui découvrit, à l'aide du microscope, des anguilles dans la farine délayée avec de l'eau' (Lucretius 1768, 1:407n). Lagrange was now added, although Voltaire was never aware of his name, to Maupertuis, Buffon, and Needham as dangerous biological thinkers who must be combated.

Voltaire responded to Buffon and Lagrange in several works published during this period, including *La Défense de mon oncle* (1767), *Les singularités de la nature* (1768), *Les Colimaçons du révérend père l'Escarbotier* (1768), and *L'Homme aux quarante écus* (1768).[12] In all of these, Needham, Buffon, Maupertuis, and the anonymous translator of Lucretius figured as the villains of the story. Not having read Needham's work directly, Voltaire completely confused Needham's observations on the viviparous eels of flour paste with those on the eels of blighted wheat and on microorganisms found in infusions, erroneously referring to heated and sealed infusions of blighted wheat that yielded viviparous eels. In *La Défense de mon oncle*, he repeated his equation of the formation of eels with the formation of man, resulting in no further use for God (V.O., 26:408-409). This was reiterated in *Les singularités de la nature*, where, after describing Needham's experiments, he remarked, 'Aussitôt plusieurs philosophes s'efforcèrent de crier merveille, et de dire: Il n'y a point de germe; tout se fait, tout se régénère par une force vive de la nature. C'est l'attraction, disait l'un [Maupertuis]; c'est la matière organisée, disait l'autre [Buffon]; ce sont des molécules organiques vivantes qui ont trouvé leurs moules. De bons physiciens furent trompés par un jésuite' (V.O., 27:159). Voltaire referred also to Lagrange's approval of Needham's observations and to Spallanzani's disproof, and concluded with a firm espousal of the theory of preexistence. Finally, in *Les Colimaçons du révérend père l'Escarbotier*, which was written in response to Spallanzani's experiments on regeneration in snails' heads (see letter 29, n.11), Voltaire turned again to Needham's observations. Criticising Buffon for forming a universe on the basis of a chimerical experiment, Voltaire praised Spallanzani's refutation. 'A peine le père des molécules organiques était à moitié chemin de sa création,' he wrote, 'que voilà les anguilles mères et filles qui disparaissent. M. Spallanzani, excellent observateur, fait voir à l'œil la chimère de ces prétendus animaux, nés de la corruption, comme la raison la démontrait à l'esprit. Les molécules organiques s'enfuient avec les anguilles dans le néant dont elles sont sorties. [...] Dieu rentre dans ses droits; il dit à tous les architectes de systèmes, comme à la mer: *Procedes huc, et non ibis amplius.*' And so, Voltaire concluded, 'Il est donné à l'homme de voir, de mesurer, de compter, et de peser les œuvres de Dieu; mais il ne lui est pas donné de les faire' (V.O., 27:220-21).

---

12. See also Best.D15189, D15199, D15210, D15413, and D15582.

During 1767 and 1768, Voltaire's position on Needham solidified into an often repeated argument. Needham's observations provided grounds for atheism and materialism, Voltaire claimed; and, even though they were erroneous, they had seduced other good philosophers, notably Buffon, Maupertuis, and the translator of Lucretius, into falling into the trap of believing that matter can form life. All of this reinforced Voltaire's own leanings toward preformation into an inflexible and almost fanatic defence of preexistent germs against epigenesis. Ironically, since he never read Needham's work himself, relying only on the descriptions he encountered in the works of Maupertuis, Buffon, and Lagrange, Voltaire never knew that he and Needham actually shared similar concerns about the implications of biology for materialism.

After a brief respite of two years, Needham was once again brought to Voltaire's attention when in the infamous *Système de la nature*, published in 1770, the disguised author, d'Holbach, claimed an intellectual kinship with Needham. As discussed previously (see section 4 of this Introduction), d'Holbach pointed to Needham's observations on eels in flour paste as providing evidence for the material production of life. 'Pour un homme qui réfléchit,' d'Holbach declared, 'la production d'un homme, indépendamment des voies ordinaires, seroit-elle donc plus merveilleuse que celle d'un insecte avec de la farine & de l'eau?' ([Holbach] 1770, 1:23 n.5). Voltaire, as one might expect, was incensed by this work. His letters and subsequent publications are full of complaints about the *Système*, not the least of which was its reliance on Needham.[13] The culmination of Voltaire's reaction was his article 'Dieu, Dieux', written during the summer of 1770 and published in the *Questions sur l'encyclopédie* in 1771 (see Voltaire 1770-1772). In the third and fourth sections of this article, parts of which had been separately published in 1770,[14] Voltaire objected to d'Holbach's views on matter and his attack on the existence of God. In a special subsection Voltaire devoted himself to the 'Histoire des anguilles sur lesquelles est fondé le système'. Here Voltaire presented the now familiar argument that if flour could produce eels, men could originate this way also (as d'Holbach had claimed), and there would no longer be a need for God. He proceeded through the same list of duped philosophers and pointed again to Spallanzani's refutation. Against d'Holbach, Voltaire claimed that matter was incapable of producing life and intelligence, thus affirming the necessity for God.

Voltaire continued to ridicule Needham in his works, notably in *Les Cabales* (1772), *Histoire de Jenni, ou l'athée et le sage* (1775), and finally *Dialogues d'Evhèmere* (1777), published the year before Voltaire's death. The theme remained the same, and d'Holbach was simply added to the list of those misled into materialism by the false experiments of the Irish Jesuit. In 1776 Voltaire received Spallanzani's *Opuscoli di fisica animale, e vegetabile*, which contained even further experiments made in refutation of Needham (see section 2.iv of this Introduction). To Spallanzani Voltaire wrote gratefully, 'Vous donnez le dernier coup, Monsieur, aux anguilles du jesuite Need'ham. Elles ont beau frétiller, elles sont mortes. [...] Des animaux nés sans germe ne pouvaient pas vivre longtems. Ce

---

13. See Best.D16602, D16666, D16673, D16693, D16736, D16786, and D17066.
14. *Dieu. Réponse de Mr. de Voltaire au Système de la nature* (Château de Ferney 1770).

sera vôtre livre qui vivra, parce qu'il est fondé sur l'expérience et sur la raison' (20 May 1776, Best.D20133).

Needham mentioned Voltaire's attacks on him only once in the annotated French edition he published of Spallanzani's *Saggio* in 1769. Claiming, in reference to the letters on miracles, that 'cet Auteur n'omet rien pour égaier le public à mes dépens par des plaisanteries ingénieuses', he said he would not respond. 'MM. *de Voltaire* & *de Lignac* [another critic] ne nous entendent pas ou ne veulent pas nous entendre,' Needham concluded; 'tout ce qu'ils lisent chez nous, ils l'expliquent à leur façon, & ils le critiquent ensuite selon leurs idées' (Spallanzani 1769, pt.1:213).

After the publication of d'Holbach's *Système de la nature*, Needham decided he had to respond to the double challenge of d'Holbach's misuse of his ideas and Voltaire's critique of d'Holbach via Needham. The long note that he added to Monestier's *La Vraie philosophie* in 1774, which he separately published as the *Idée sommaire* (1776, 1781), discussed earlier (see section 4 of this Introduction), was the result. Altering the first sentence of this note when republished to include Voltaire's name, Needham explained that he had felt it necessary to present a précis of his views because 'Certains Auteurs modernes, & sur-tout le soi-disant philosophe Voltaire, semblent confondre les anguilles du Blé Rachiti-que avec celles de la colle de farine que j'ai décrites dans mes nouvelles découvertes microscopiques' (Needham 1781:3). Adding as well to the *Idée sommaire* a 'Remarque sur la réponse de M. de Voltaire au Système de la Nature', he claimed that in all of Voltaire's works one found 'le même esprit faux, la même manie'. Objecting in particular to Voltaire's misuse of his ideas, Needham continued, 'S'il vouloit une seule fois sortir de chez lui pour interroger la vérité des choses à la lumiere du jour, il pourrait peut-être se convaincre, qui ni lui, ni l'Auteur du Système de la Nature, n'ont aucun droit de citer mes expériences, comme favorables au matérialisme.' Concerning Voltaire's ridicule of him, he commented, 'Son très-petit artifice, & l'imposture à laquelle il s'acharne depuis ma querelle avec lui à Geneve, de me faire passer pour Jésuite, & pour Irlandois, on ne sait pas trop pourquoi, ne servira jamais qu'à faire retomber sur sa tête le faux ridicule, qu'il dirige contre son adversaire' (Needham 1781:27-28). Those who wished to know Needham's true ideas, he concluded, would do better to consult his works.

There was really very little else Needham could say in response to Voltaire, after having been so badly misunderstood and misrepresented. Yet apparently he took Voltaire's ridicule with something of a sense of humour, for, as Bonnet later reported to Haller: 'Il me lisoit lui même tous les *Sarcasmes* que Voltaire lui avoit lachés dans ses *Lettres sur les Miracles*, et il en rioit de la meilleure grace du monde' (20 September 1768; Sonntag 1983:774). Bonnet, Spallanzani, and Haller were all quite sympathetic to Needham's plight. A few months earlier Bonnet had written to Spallanzani, '[Needham's] intentions sont les meilleures du monde, et Voltaire est inexcusable de l'avoir tant de fois crimisé. Combien les siennes sont moins pures! Il s'est servi contre notre ami des plus grossières injures et du langage des crocheteurs' (22 June 1768, Castellani 1971:77; see also letter 21, n.2). To this Spallanzani replied, 'J'étois aussi au fait de la façon très-impolie dont il a été attaqué par M.r de Voltaire. Voltaire même n'eût difficultè de me l'apprendre par ses lettres. Ce Savant François semble né pour tourner tout en ridicule' (15 July 1768; *Epistolario*, 1:160). Even though Voltaire was in many ways on the same side as Bonnet and Spallanzani, they found his treatment of Needham to be far too scandalous to condone, not to mention his beliefs on religion. Neither Bonnet, Spallanzani, nor Haller ever viewed Voltaire as any kind of ally in their struggles to promote preformation against epigenesis.[15]

Needham made one other attempt to strike back at Voltaire when in 1770 he published anonymously an *Extrait d'un discours prononcé a Pekin cent ans après la mort d'un poete historiographe et celle d'un orateur-philosophe ou le parallele.* Sent by Needham to Bonnet in 1770 (letter 43), Needham's *Extrait* was published in *Les Vrais quakers*, an anonymous work of which Needham was the editor ([Colmont de Vaulgrenand] 1770; see letter 43, n.6). The *Extrait* was purportedly the prize-winning discourse delivered before the '*Hio*' or 'Salle d'Assemblée des Lettres' of Peking and was intended to be a comparative eulogy of the most famous poet and the greatest orator of the previous century. Thinly disguised as Tévilaor and Suasoure, Voltaire and Rousseau are subjected to a critical and candid scrutiny, in which the vain poet, filled with scorn and envy, does not fare well against the virtuous orator-philosopher, who is too sensitive to the injustices of the world to be anything but a misanthrope. Born to rank and fortune, educated by a Mandarin, Tévilaor wrote only to ridicule: 'fait pour son siecle comme le siecle pour lui il se moqua toujours des hommes Religieux, quelquefois des pauvres & des infortunés, & ne respecta que les Comédiens & les Athées' ([Colmont de Vaulgrenand] 1770:86). Suasoure on the other hand shunned glory for poverty and persecution, and wrote only against the evils of the time. Summarising their similarities and differences, Needham concluded that 'si l'un eut le défaut de ne trouver aucun ami digne de son ame, l'autre n'eut jamais l'ame digne d'aucun ami; que l'un égara nos esprits sous la dictée de son cœur, ainsi que l'autre corrompit nos cœurs sous la dictée de son esprit; & qu'en tout il eut peut-être mieux valu que l'un & l'autre n'eussent jamais illustré leur Nation' ([Colmont de Vaulgrenand] 1770:103).

Needham was quite proud of his portraits of Voltaire and Rousseau. When announcing the *Extrait* to Bonnet in 1770, he described it, without revealing his identity as the author, as a piece 'qui part d'une main de maitre' (26 June 1770, letter 43). Bonnet's opinion was not nearly so high. Remarking that Needham must have had too much of an attachment for the author, Bonnet said that the *Extrait* was weakly written in rather poor English-style French and was quite unoriginal in content. Quoting a number of phrases and indicating in what way the French was in error, Bonnet dismissed Needham's arguments as 'trop dépourvues d'interet' and the *Extrait* as not being of a high enough quality to do battle with such skilful writers as Voltaire and Rousseau (29 September 1770, letter 44). To Haller, Bonnet wrote even more critically that Needham had announced the work to him as 'un Ouvrage de *main de Maître*. Remarqués ces expressions. Au style lâche, embarassé et incorrect de l'*Imprimé*, il ne me fut

15. See Haller's *Briefe über einige Einwürfe nochlebender Freygeister wieder die Offenbarung* (Bern 1775-1777), which was directed against Voltaire's *Questions sur l'encyclopédie* (1770-1772) and his *Nouveaux mélanges* (1765-1775), and in which Haller defended Needham's observations on the phenomenon of revivification in eels in blighted wheat as bona fide (see 1:120-21, 2:225, and 3:178, 297-98).

pas difficile de reconnoître l'Abbé lui même' (18 December 1770; Sonntag 1983:911-12). Bonnet stated that he had replied to Needham giving his frank opinion of the piece but not letting on that he recognised Needham as its author. Needham, however, was upset by Bonnet's reaction. In a rather angry letter (letter 45) in reply to Bonnet's critique of the *Extrait*, Needham accused Bonnet of having acquired an excessively narrow sense of stylistic taste that had led him to prefer colour to substance. No one else to whom he had shown the piece had objected to the style or had thought it to be unoriginal in content. Perhaps what piqued Needham's ire the most was that Bonnet had stated in his letter that had he been with Needham when he had been composing his pamphlets on miracles in reply to Voltaire's, he would have 'fait les plus grands efforts pour vous arracher la Plume de la main', since Needham's pamphlets simply provoked Voltaire into writing a dozen more (letter 44). Attributing this comment to Bonnet's too great a love for style, Needham rejoined, 'Sans cela comment peut il arriver, que vous preferez les vingt satyres indecentes, et ridicules de Voltaire remplies d'absurdites, d'inepties, d'ordure, et de blasphemes aux trois lettres, ou hors d'œuvres, pour ainsi dire, qui m'ont échappés à Geneve, sur tout à la parodie de sa troisieme lettre sur les miracles, dont la justesse et la vérité a été par tout estimée, et meme à Geneve' (28 October 1770, letter 45).

The result of Needham's angry reply to Bonnet was a break in their correspondence that lasted nearly three years and that was ended only by Needham's sending Bonnet a work he had edited in 1773 on the 'bust of Isis' controversy (see letter 46 and section 6 of this Introduction). Bonnet admitted in his reply (letter 47) that he had been reluctant to write to Needham because of the 'tirade' contained in Needham's previous letter. Needham had in part been quite justified in reacting as he had to Bonnet's critique of his *Extrait*, which Bonnet had expressed in rather spiteful terms. One can only surmise that Bonnet was still exceedingly angry with Needham over his edition of the French translation of Spallanzani's *Saggio* (see section 2.iv of this Introduction), which he had repeatedly complained about in letters to Spallanzani and Haller during 1769 and 1770. Bonnet had also not reacted well to much of Needham's critique of his *Palingénésie* (see letters 40 and 41). Needham's *Extrait* certainly contained nothing with which Bonnet would have disagreed, as his own opinions of Voltaire and Rousseau were decidedly negative. He may indeed have wanted to spare Needham the kind of ridicule that had resulted from his earlier attack on Voltaire, yet the way in which he chose to do this understandably upset Needham.

Bonnet's own relationship with Voltaire was less acrimonious than Needham's but not without some ill-feeling. In his *Mémoires autobiographiques* Bonnet recounted the one and only personal meeting he had had with Voltaire. When the latter moved to Geneva at the end of 1754, everyone rushed to see him as they would 'à voir un animal très rare' (Savioz 1948b:178). Bonnet, however, held off until one of his friends told him that Voltaire had asked where Bonnet lived and would very likely pay a call on him soon. Preferring to avoid this eventuality, Bonnet went with two friends one day to Voltaire's house. They arrived at nine in the morning and were greeted by Voltaire in his robe and night cap. Spotting a book on a table, Bonnet opened it and was surprised to see that it was a copy of Condillac's *Traité des sensations* (1754), a work that he had recently read. Remarking this to Voltaire, Bonnet asked him what he thought of it and offered to discuss it with him. To this Voltaire reportedly replied, 'Non, Monsieur, [...] je ne me mêle point de cela; je fais quelques mauvais vers et c'est tout' (Savioz 1948b:178). Not long after this, Bonnet followed Voltaire into another room, leaving his friends seated on a sofa outside an open connecting door. Voltaire then began to talk quite perceptively about Condillac's book and the advantages and disadvantages of using his method of analysis. Somewhat surprised at Voltaire's sudden change of attitude and apparent knowledge of Condillac's views, Bonnet only later learned from his friend that Voltaire had been simply repeating word for word to Bonnet what his friends had been discussing about the book when seated outside the room Voltaire and Bonnet were in. Knowing that Bonnet was hard of hearing, Voltaire had taken advantage of the situation to try to impress Bonnet. 'Vous conviendrez, mon bon ami,' Bonnet wrote in his autobiographical letters, 'que ce plagiat est d'une espèce bien nouvelle et qu'un écrivain qui savait piller ainsi, ne se refusait pas, sans doute, à piller d'une manière plus commune' (Savioz 1948b:179). Needless to say, Bonnet did not visit Voltaire again.

Although Bonnet was extremely critical of Voltaire and his writings in private, especially in his letters to Haller and to Spallanzani, he never attacked him publicly in his works. Yet he still found himself the butt of Voltaire's ridicule after he published *La Palingénésie philosophique* in 1769.[16] In this work, Bonnet had discussed the future state of human beings and of other living organisms after death (see section 4 of this Introduction). He hypothesised that all animals possess a soul and that this soul survives as a 'petit corps indestructible', which was contained during the animal's life in its body. Closely tied to Bonnet's belief in the preexistence of germs and to his theory of geological revolutions (see section 7 of this Introduction), the concept of 'palingenesis' was given a new and precise meaning by Bonnet. With regard to human beings, Bonnet explained the doctrine of resurrection and judgement by arguing that the human soul continues to exist as an indestructible entity without its present body and that it eventually will become united to a new more perfect corporeal structure.

Voltaire found this doctrine to be exceedingly hilarious and took the opportunity, in several discussions of the absurdity of resurrection, to poke fun at it. In the manuscript version of *Dieu et les hommes* Voltaire apparently wrote: 'Je ne sais quel rêveur nommé Bonnet, dans un recueil de facéties appelées par lui *Palingénésie*, paraît persuadé que nos corps ressusciteront sans estomac, et sans les parties de devant et de derrière, mais avec des *fibres intellectuelles*, et d'excellentes têtes. Celle de Bonnet me paraît un peu fêlée [...]: je lui conseille, quand il ressuscitera, de demander un peu plus de bon sens, et des fibres un peu plus intellectuelles que celles qu'il eut en partage de son vivant' (V.O., 28:218-19). Bonnet reported in his autobiography that he was shown this passage while the

---

16. Bonnet had also been mentioned in Voltaire's *La Guerre civile de Genève* (1767) as a physician from Lausanne whose principal prescription was wine (V.O., 9:536-37, 538). Apparently Bonnet's name was used here as a substitute for Tissot (see Best.D14963n). Bonnet, however, seems not to have been aware of this reference to him (see Sonntag 1983:747, 749).

work was being printed. Having never attacked Voltaire or the other *Incrédules* openly in print, he felt that he was the last person to deserve such insults. Apparently, unbeknown at the time to Bonnet, someone else made this same point to Voltaire, after seeing the work in manuscript, and when the first edition was printed in 1769, the passage was altered to be almost flattering to Bonnet (see Savioz 1948b:252-53).[17] In later editions beginning in 1770 with Voltaire's *Nouveaux mélanges*, the original passage was restored.[18]

Yet this was not Voltaire's only ridicule of the *Palingénésie*. Briefly mentioning in the *Fragments sur l'Inde, sur l'histoire générale et sur la France* (1774), a philosopher 'qui a dit que nous ressusciterions sans derrière' (V.O., 29:178), Voltaire found one further opportunity to make fun of Bonnet. When he published several of his own letters at the end of his *Commentaire historique sur les œuvres de l'auteur de la Henriade* (1776), Voltaire included a letter he had written to Spallanzani on 6 June 1776. Voltaire and Spallanzani had exchanged four letters in 1776 concerning Spallanzani's *Opuscoli* and his earlier work on snail regeneration (Spallanzani 1768a). In the letter that Voltaire published, he discussed animals than can be ressuscitated after being apparently dead (a subject that Spallanzani had experimented on and had treated in the *Opuscoli*). In particular, Voltaire raised the question of what happens to the animal's soul. In one of the last paragraphs of his letter, Voltaire stated that if anyone could penetrate the mysteries of revivification, Spallanzani could, and that the secret of resurrection known by the Greeks had been lost. He then added a sentence to the published version that had not been in the original letter: 'Je crois que c'est Mr. Bonnet, grand observateur, qui a prétendu que nous ressusciterions avec notre devant, mais sans derrière. C'est là le fin du fin, &c.' ([Voltaire] 1776:273; see also Best. D20158 n.*c*).

Bonnet saw this published version and immediately wrote to Spallanzani, angry that Spallanzani had not warned him about this passage in Voltaire's letter. Claiming that he had always said he would never respond to Voltaire, Bonnet declared, 'Je déplore son aveuglement et ses écarts; mais je déplore bien davantage encore les maux sans nombre que ses écrits ne cessent de produire, et qu'ils produiront longtemps après sa mort. [...] Il parle sans cesse de tolérance, et il est le plus intolérant des hommes envers ceux qui ne pensent pas comme lui' (18 September 1776, Castellani 1971:313-14; see also Best.D20300). Surprised by Bonnet's letter and the phrase he quoted from the published version of Voltaire's letter, Spallanzani wrote back explaining that the sentence about Bonnet was not in fact in the letter that he had received. Including a copy of Voltaire's original letter, Spallanzani apologised to Bonnet, remarking, 'Je n'aurois jamais pensé que ce Bouffon vous eüt melé dans les lettres qu'il écrivoit à moi même autrement je m'abstenois bien volontiers de lui envoyer mon Livre. C'est qu'il me deplait que le Public sache qu'un de mes Amis si respectable, et

17. The altered version opened with 'Monsieur Bonnet d'ailleurs très estimable, dans un recueil de facéties'. In place of 'Celle de Bonnet me paraît un peu fêlée' was the sentence 'Je crois celle de Monsieur Bonnet fort bonne'. The remainder of the passage was unchanged (see Voltaire 1769:201).

18. The original version may be found in the editions of *Dieu et les hommes* published in the *Nouveaux mélanges philosophiques, historiques, critiques, &c. &c.* ([Genève] 1765-1775, 9[1770]:151-52); in *Pièces détachées, attribuées à divers hommes célèbres* ([Genève] 1775, 1:125); and in V.O., 28:218-19.

si cher, tel que vous l'êtes, et pour le quel je dois prendre le plus grand interet, soit critique hors de propos dans une lettre [a]dressée à moi même' (16 October 1776; *Epistolario*, 2:137; see also Best.D20351). Bonnet replied that there was really nothing to do but laugh about the incident and deplore Voltaire's indifference to the truth. Finally understanding the situation, Bonnet said he held Spallanzani in no way responsible for what had happened (see Castellani 1971: 315-16; see also Savioz 1948b:253-54).

Although Bonnet and Voltaire shared the common ground of believing in preformation and although Voltaire had written favourably about Bonnet's biological views in his review of the *Corps organisés* (V.O., 25:153-58), there was little further agreement between the two. In religious matters Voltaire was a deist, and in politics he was opposed to the powerful rule Bonnet's aristocratic class held over the Genevan republic (see section 8 of this Introduction). For his part, Bonnet had little respect for Voltaire's manner of criticising and ridiculing everything with which he came in contact, even when Voltaire's attention was focused on someone with whom Bonnet also disagreed, like Needham. It was the injustice and virulence of Voltaire's attacks that disturbed Bonnet and his contemporaries, Haller and Spallanzani.

Needham felt he had come out the moral victor in his controversies with Voltaire. Although he was repeatedly called upon to disclaim any connection between his own biological views and materialism, Needham believed that he had met Voltaire's challenge on the miracles issue and had succeeded in staving off some of the 'contagion' of atheism and materialism that had been prompted by Voltaire. Ironically, Voltaire was deeply concerned about many of the same connections Needham saw between atheism, morality, and biological materialism. Voltaire's response had been to fanatically defend preformation, while Needham's was to propose a new non-materialist biology. Neither ever really understood how close their motives really were. Yet in rejecting revealed religion, Voltaire crossed a line that Needham felt would inevitably lead to atheism and the collapse of society. It was here that the two diverged irrevocably. From Needham's defence of the sacred chronology against Voltaire in the 'bust of Isis' affair, to his parody of Voltaire the deist in the miracles episode, to his final 'portrait' of the petty, vainglorious, and destructive Tévaloir, Needham combated as best he could the misguided tendencies and dangerous influence of the 'Geant Patagon' of Ferney.

6. The 'bust of Isis' and the sacred chronology

THE possible connections between the ancient Chinese and Egyptians constitute a topic of discussion in two groups of letters in the Bonnet-Needham correspondence. The topic was first discussed in 1761 and early 1762 (letters 11-15) in connection with Needham's publication of the pamphlet *De inscriptione quadam Aegyptiaca Taurini inventa*, which appeared in Rome in September 1761; and the subject was taken up again much later, when Needham edited in 1773 the *Lettre de Pekin, sur le génie de la langue Chinoise*, which he sent to his Genevan correspondent (letters 46-47). At first sight, *De inscriptione* is Needham's most uncharacteristic literary production. Needham, who was neither a philologist nor an orientalist, claimed to have demonstrated beyond a shadow of doubt that the ancient Chinese script was related to the ancient Egyptian. This theory gave rise to a dispute that aroused considerable interest among the antiquaries in Europe and that was finally resolved by the *Lettre de Pekin*. The aim of this introductory section is twofold: to suggest the motivations that might have led Needham to tackle this particular question, and to delineate some aspects of the dispute that followed the publication of the *De inscriptione*.

In late 1760 and early 1761 Needham was in Turin and visited the University Museum where a number of Egyptian artifacts were housed. He had visited it before, ten years earlier (Needham 1761:8), but now he was looking at the ancient monuments with new interest. In the forefront of his mind were two works that he had been reading recently: a paper by the French orientalist Joseph de Guignes and the first volume of the *Histoire de l'empire de Russie sous Pierre le Grand* (1759) by Voltaire. Guignes had put forward the idea that the Chinese were an Egyptian colony and that they had derived their culture from the Egyptians. This idea was not new and had been suggested in the past by such authors as Athanasius Kircher, Pierre-Daniel Huet, and, more recently, Dortous de Mairan.[1] What was new was the kind of proof offered. Guignes claimed that the Chinese characters could be decomposed into basic elements, which he called 'radicals'. He then noticed that a number of these 'radicals' were similar to the letters of the Phœnician alphabet, which had recently been deciphered by his friend and colleague Jean-Jacques Barthélemy (David 1961). As it was assumed that the Phœnician alphabet was based upon ancient Egyptian characters, Guignes came to the conclusion that the Chinese derived their characters from the Egyptians not as alphabetical signs, but as hieroglyphs (Guignes 1759a:67-68). The following is an example of Guignes's method of analysis: 'Je pris les trois racines du mot *Iada* qui en Phénicien signifioit, *sçavoir, connoître*; ces racines sont un *Iod*, un *Daleth* & un *Ain*. La première quant à sa

---

1. At times this idea had been put forward in conjunction with speculations about the superior wisdom contained in the Egyptian mysteries. For the artistic popularity of hieroglyphs during the Renaissance, see Wittkower (1977:113-28, 210-13); for seventeenth- and eighteenth-century attempts to decipher hieroglyphs, see Hartleben (1906, 1:352-70), Iversen (1961), David (1965), and Dieckmann (1970); and for a short general survey of interest in Egypt during the eighteenth century, see Pevsner and Lang (1956).

dénomination grammaticale signifie, comme je l'ai dit, la *main*; la seconde une *porte*, & la troisiéme un *œil*. Je choisis les trois anciens caractères Chinois qui désignent l'œil, la porte & la main; je les réunis, & je vis paroître un Hiéroglyphe en usage parmi les Chinois, & qui signifie *examiner, sçavoir*' (Guignes 1759a:67). According to Guignes's researches, the names of the Chinese emperors, Yu and Ki, were the same as those of the Egyptian kings, Menes and Athoes; and he concluded that ancient Chinese historical records actually related to Egyptian history.

In a letter to Dortous de Mairan, Voltaire confessed that while he was reading Guignes's paper, 'j'éclattai de rire en voyant que le Roy Yu était précisément le roy d'Egipte Menès, comme Platon était chez Scarron l'anagramme de Chopine, en changeant seulement *Pla* en *Cho*, et *ton* en *Pine*' (Best.D9126). As this suggests, Voltaire considered Guignes's theory absurd and ridiculous. In a letter to the comte d'Argental he wrote: 'je n'aime pas que l'histoire soit traittée comme les mille et une nuit' (Best.D9372). In his preface to the *Histoire de l'empire de Russie sous Pierre le Grand*, Voltaire had poured scorn on Guignes's theory and had dismissed it entirely (see letter 11, n.5). Needham was disgusted by Voltaire's behaviour, and so was Bonnet (see letter 14), who had welcomed Guignes's alleged discovery with enthusiasm and had no doubts as to its validity. In a letter of 16 January 1759 to Carl de Geer, Bonnet wrote: 'Mr de Guignes vient de faire une découverte qui embarassera davantage notre sceptique: il a découvert que les Caractères Chinois sont composés de Caractères Egyptiens, et que les Noms des Rois des premières Dynasties de la Chine reviennent à ceux des anciens Rois de Thèbes en Egypte. Ainsi, cette antiquité si vantée de la Chine n'est qu'une fable; & ses Inventions & ses Arts ne sont, suivant Mr de Guignes, qu'une émanation de l'ancienne Egypte' (Best.D8049). To Bonnet, as well as to Needham, it was clear that if, as they believed, Guignes's theory was correct, Voltaire's conception of universal history and his dismissal of sacred chronology were wrong. Thus Bonnet and Needham, as well as others, saw support for Guignes's hypothesis as a weapon against the philosophes.

It was with this in mind that Needham examined the ancient Egyptian artifacts in the University Museum at Turin. He took particular notice of a black marble bust, the so-called 'bust of Isis', depicting a woman with two long plaits of hair joined three times on her chest, first by a clasp and then by knots (see figs. 12, 13). He was intrigued by strange signs carved on the forehead, cheeks, nose, and chest. He believed the statue to be an ancient Egyptian bust and was struck by what seemed to him to be a great similarity between these characters and the ancient Chinese script. He felt that he was on the verge of a great discovery. He had a drawing of the bust and characters made, collected information about the bust, and left Turin for Rome in early 1761. There he contacted a Chinese scholar with whose help he hoped to establish the similarity of the characters on the 'bust of Isis' to ancient Chinese characters contained in a Chinese dictionary in the Vatican Library. In July 1761 he communicated his supposed discovery to Bonnet, to Vallisneri, and to Guignes himself.[2] In the

---

2. See respectively letter 11, n.3; Paravia (1842:155-56); and Needham's letter to Guignes of 8 July 1761 in the BL (Add. 21416).

meanwhile he also started collecting, with his friend Joseph Wilcocks, what he regarded to be even more conclusive evidence from Egyptian monuments in Rome. On 22 September 1761, one thousand copies of Needham's pamphlet *De inscriptione* were printed in Rome and published at his own expense. In late September he began sending copies of the book all over Europe. Thomas Jenkins forwarded a copy to the London Society of Antiquaries;[3] Needham himself sent 205 copies to Guignes to be distributed in France;[4] and Joseph Wilcocks, on the way to Switzerland, took copies to be distributed to Needham's friends there (see letter 13). Needham also arranged for copies to be distributed among his correspondents in Italy.

In *De inscriptione* Needham put forward the view that the 'bust of Isis' was a very ancient Egyptian statue and that the signs inscribed on it were ancient Egyptian hieroglyphs. He expressed his belief in the similarity of these signs to characters in the Vatican's Chinese dictionary and the possibility that, because of this similarity, they could be deciphered and translated. By way of such reasoning, Needham came to the conclusion that the Chinese must have had contacts with the Egyptians and that they must have learned from the Egyptians not only their method of writing, but also their arts, sciences, morals, customs, and mode of government (Needham 1761:51-52). Needham's apparent aim in this work was to provide what he believed to be a definitive proof of Guignes's theory. However, behind this lay the true motivation, which was his desire to show that the sacred chronology was correct and that Voltaire's views on universal history were erroneous.[5] In a letter to Haller of 28 December 1760, Needham disclosed (Mazzolini 1976: 75-76):

What you mention concerning the materialists inclines me to confide to you, what I intend as a secret to the world in general, that I am actually employed in writing an essay against this species of mad men: as it attacks many, who have honored me in appearance with as much friendship, as such persons are capable of, my design is, that it shall be anonymous, and therefore I beg that what I say to you concerning my intentions may not be communicated. They intrench themselves first behind egyptian fables, or a far-fetched chinese chronology of no credit: and when they are drove from that, they bury themselves in the eternity of the world. I have a strong physical argument against the pretended antiquity of the Egyptians, and if your countryman Mr. Smidt's arguments, [as] well as those of Mr. Guignes prove, the chinese to be a colony of Egyptians, there is an end of the chinese antiquity.

In September 1761 Needham believed that he had conclusively proved this last point, and Bonnet's immediate grasp of the implications is shown by his letter to Needham of 31 December 1761: 'J'aime a voir cette Antiquité si vantée des Chinois rabaissée au niveau de celle des Egyptiens, qui se mésure elle même

3. See SAL, *Minutes*, viii:352-54; Jenkin's letter to William Norris of 23 September 1761 (SAL, Correspondence, Thomas Jenkins F.S.A. Nine Letters to Norris 1758-1772); and Pierce (1965:212).

4. See Needham's letters to Guignes of 23 and 30 September 1761 in the BL (Add. 21416).

5. For secondary sources on Needham's pamphlet *De inscriptione*, and on the dispute that followed its publication, see Paravia (1842:35-39), Gauthier (1906:82-83), Dawson (1932 and 1935-1938), Appleton (1951:149-51), Iversen (1961:106-107), Curto (1962-1963), Guy (1963:390), and Pierce (1965:212-15). None of these authors seems to be aware of Needham's anti-Voltairean motivation, which was however perceived by Needham's contemporary reviewers; see *Journal des sçavans* (December 1761, p.806) and *The Monthly review* (July 1763, 29:31-36).

Fig. 12. The head (38 cm in height) of the 'bust of Isis', now in the Museo Egizio, Turin. The torso to which the head was attached is now lost.

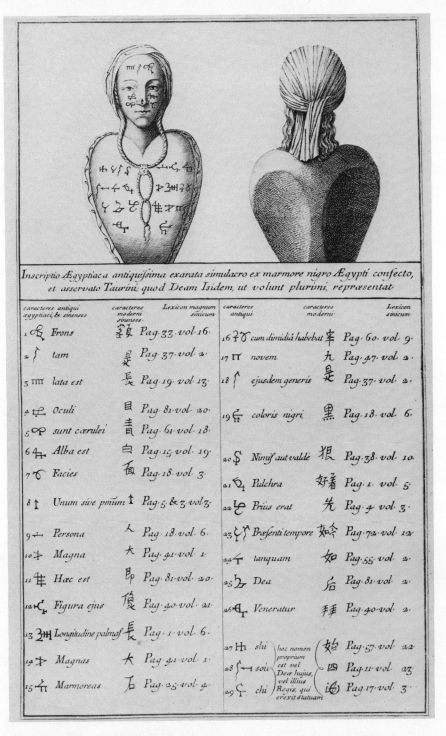

Fig. 13. Needham's illustration of the 'bust of Isis' and its thirty-two characters. The table shows (for twenty-nine of them) their supposed translation into Latin, and what Needham regarded as their equivalents in Chinese, with the page numbers of the Chinese Dictionary in the Vatican on which they could be found. (From Needham, *De inscriptione quadam Aegyptiaca Taurini inventa*, 1761. Courtesy of the Bodleian Library, Oxford.)

par notre Chronologie sacrée. Ce n'étoit pas le compte de Voltaire, et je vous sais gré d'avoir si bien repoussé ses insultes et ses railleries [to Guignes]. Vous avés tiré de vôtre Statue le meilleur parti possible, et vous n'avés assurement rien négligé pour arriver a la découverte du vrai' (letter 14).

In his *Essai sur les moeurs* of 1757, Voltaire had emphasised the great antiquity of China, its large population, its excellent form of government, the high standard of its morality and laws, and its early development of all the sciences and arts. Furthermore he had stressed the superiority of its historiography based upon astronomical observations and noted with approval the absence of fables from its chronicles (V.O., 11: 165-81). Simultaneously he had challenged the idea of both the chronological and cultural primacy of Egypt. He argued that the floods of the Nile would have impeded the habitation and cultivation of the surrounding areas and that epidemics would have debilitated and decimated the population (V.O., 11:59-60). He considered Egyptian monuments devoid of taste and proportion, and wrote that the pyramids 'furent élevés par le despotisme, la vanité, la servitude, et la superstition' (V.O., 11:65). By adopting a comparative approach that enabled him to contrast the Chinese with the discredited Egyptians, and by stressing the antiquity of China and its autonomous and independent cultural and religious traditions, Voltaire was in fact producing an image of the past that was entirely different from that usually provided by universal histories.[6] By stating that the Chinese empire had remained practically unaltered for over four thousand years and that no Chinese chronicle had ever mentioned the flood, Voltaire was in fact attacking the Christian exegesis of the Bible, according to which the flood had taken place in 2,300 B.C. The implications of Voltaire's views of the past thus had wide philosophical repercussions. The unity of the historic past as seen within the late Christian syncretic conception of history, in which profane and sacred elements as well as Greco-Roman and Judeo-Christian traditions coexisted, was replaced, in Voltaire's account, by a geographically and chronologically expanded and multicentred world view.

It was this, the core of Voltaire's new conception of history, that Needham was hoping to demolish by deciphering the inscription on the 'bust of Isis'. He clearly believed that he had made an important discovery and was also hoping to profit from it financially. When in late September 1761 Needham wrote to Guignes, sending him 205 copies of *De inscriptione*, he asked Guignes to distribute copies to Barthélemy, Buffon, the king, the Dauphin, the duc de Choiseul, and the Academy, and to give all the other copies to a bookseller to be sold in Paris (BL, Add.21416). In addition, Needham mentioned that cardinal Spinola was in the process of writing to the duc de Choiseul in order to sound out the prospects of a pension for him, and asked whether Barthélemy could put any pressure on the duc de Choiseul on his behalf. Guignes's reply was apparently a very unpleasant letter. We know of its contents only indirectly, through Needham's response of 4 November 1761 (BL, Add. 21416). Guignes refused

6. For secondary sources on Voltaire's conception of history, see Diaz (1958), Rihs (1962), and Brumfitt (1968); for the role played by Voltaire's image of China in shaping his conception of the past and for its theological implications, see especially Kaegi (1942) and Löwith (1949:104-14); and for Voltaire's lasting interest in and admiration for Chinese history and culture, see Guy (1963), Pitou (1972), and Maggs (1974).

to forward any copies of Needham's pamphlet and must have accused Needham of not knowing Chinese, of vanity, of having rushed into print, and of having purloined his own research project.

Needham was clearly upset by Guignes's reaction and wrote that while he might have not deserved praise he surely did not deserve reproach. Not only was Guignes unwilling to help Needham, but he was also the first to criticise his work in an anonymous review published in the December issue of the *Journal des sçavans* (see letter 15, n.1). First of all Guignes claimed that 'son travail, qu'il annonce comme la plus grande découverte, n'est que l'exécution du projet de l'Académicien de Paris [Guignes himself], ou plutôt un essai & une tentative' (*Journal des sçavans*, December 1761, p.808). Then he listed his criticisms. According to Guignes, Needham had not completely understood Guignes's theory, he seemed more concerned to show that the unbelievers were wrong than to prove his point, and he had provided a false translation of the inscription, because there was no resemblance between its characters and those of the Chinese. It seems that Guignes wanted to differentiate his own work decisively from Needham's, fearing that the latter's treatment of the subject might discredit his own theory.

The subject of the 'bust of Isis', however, was stirring considerable interest in different learned circles. Needham was, as a result, elected an Honorary Fellow of the London Society of Antiquaries on 10 December 1761.[7] The astronomer George Parker, second Earl of Macclesfield and President of the Royal Society, asked Edward Wortley Montagu to stop off in Turin and verify Needham's account of the bust. Montagu was a man well versed in oriental languages and was about to travel through Italy on his way to Egypt. In the middle of April 1762 he arrived in Turin, there meeting Giuseppe Bartoli, Antiquary to the king of Sardinia and Director of the University Museum. It must be noted that when Needham had visited the Museum, Bartoli had been away on a visit to his native Veneto (Paravia 1842:35) and that the two men had therefore never had the opportunity to discuss the authenticity of the bust. During Montagu's visit, Bartoli addressed two letters to him, dated 14 April and 24 April 1762, which were published as two separate pamphlets (Bartoli 1762a and 1762b). Together they represented the most shattering criticism of Needham's theory. According to Bartoli, Needham's theory could be regarded as correct only if all the following points were proven: that the 'bust of Isis' was ancient, that the inscription was also ancient, that the bust was Egyptian, that the inscription was also Egyptian, and finally that the Egyptian characters on the bust were similar to ancient Chinese characters. Bartoli criticised the first point and claimed that the bust was not in fact ancient. He supported his claim by identifying the black marble with local Italian stone and suggested that it came from a quarry at Laveggio, near the Lake of Chiavenna (Bartoli 1762a:7). He criticised the second point by noting that there was absolutely no stylistic similarity between the bust and ancient Egyptian sculptures. He denied that there was any resemblance between the characters inscribed on the bust and

---

7. See SAL, *Minutes*, viii:353-54, 371-72, and 422. See also Needham's letter of appreciation to the Society, dated 13 February 1762 (SAL, Correspondence 1761-1770).

either Egyptian or Chinese characters, and finally stated that Needham had not even reproduced the characters faithfully in the plate representing the 'bust of Isis' (see fig. 13). He substantiated this statement in his second pamphlet in which he published a plate containing an exact copy of the characters in all their dimensions and reproduced those given by Needham.

Bartoli sent both pamphlets to Guignes, who received them favourably, and also to the Secretary of the Académie des inscriptions, Charles Le Beau, who thanked him for having clarified an issue that could have been detrimental to the study of the Chinese language (Curto 1962-1963:9). In reply to Bartoli's criticisms, Needham published a pamphlet dated 8 May 1762, containing various certificates (Needham 1762). One was from the draughtsman Giuseppe Alberti, who had copied the bust and inscription. He declared he had followed Needham's instruction 'de ne pas se soucier de prendre la forme exacte du dit Bust, mais seulement de faire une copie fidéle des Caractères avec leur situation' (Needham 1762:4). Another declaration was by a group of scholars in Turin, friends of Needham who had accompanied Montagu on his visit to the Museum. They admitted differences between the copy of the bust and inscription and the original, but emphasised the fact that they did not claim to be able to judge whether such differences could substantially alter the meaning of the characters. Finally Needham added the following *Certificat*, which was the most important and which was signed by several of his friends in Rome (Needham 1762:8-9):

Caractères Egyptiens pris des monumens publics à Rome & ailleurs, & confrontés avec des Caractères pareils dans le grand Dictionnaire Chinois au Vatican gravé à Pekin en vingt-six volumes. Le tître Chinois du Dictionnaire est Ching-Zu-Tung.

Primo. Vingt-neuf Caractères, dont quelques uns sont composés, sur le Buste qu'on trouve à Turin, dans le Cabinet Royal des Antiquités, publiés par Monsieur NEEDHAM.

2.° *Deux-cens & deux Caractères pris d'un moule fait à Venise par ordre de M.^r* JENINGS *Gentilhomme Anglois, & actuellement en sa possession, sur un marbre noir quarré, qui contient outre ces caractères plusieurs figures Hiéroglyphiques.*

3.° *Soixante & dix Caractères pris des Obelisques* Barbérien *&* Latéran, *les deux Lions aux* Thermes Diocletiennes, *les deux Sphinx dans la* Villa Borghese, *les deux Statues Egyptiennes dans la* Villa Albani, *& de la Table d'*Isis *à Turin.*

Nous soussignés attestons & certifions, qu'une grande partie des dits Caractères cités ci-dessus nous ont été montrés dans le Dictionaire Chinois, & que nous n'en avons point trouvés, qui ne fussent conformes à l'Original particuliérement ceux du Buste, qui ont été gravés dans la dissertation de Mr NEEDHAM *que nous avons examinés avec plus d'attention.*

Fait à Rome le 25. Mars 1762.

Le Chev. LYTTELTON.	Le Duc de GRAFTON.
Le Bailli de BRETEUIL.	Milord TAVISTOCH.
Ambassadeur de Malte à Rome.	Le Duc de ROXBURGHE.
	H. JAMES.
	R. SMITH.

THOMAS LE SEUR   }   Professeurs au College
FRANÇOIS JACQUIER }   de la Sapienza.
RIDOLFINO VENUTI Antiquaire de SA SAINTETÉ.[8]

8. Manuscript copies of this *Certificat*, in Needham's hand and signed by the attestees, were sent to Guignes (see BL, Add. 21416) and to the London Society of Antiquaries (see Thomas Jenkin's letter to William Norris dated 7 April 1762 (SAL, Correspondence, Thomas Jenkins F.S.A. Nine Letters to Norris 1758-1772; and *Minutes*, viii:437-39); see also Pierce 1965:213-15).

Needham completely dismissed Bartoli's criticism based on the material and style of the bust. He claimed to have seen other Egyptian statues of the same material in Rome and added that two artists who had been in Egypt confirmed the existence of statues stylistically similar to the bust in Turin. Altogether Needham had very little esteem for Bartoli, whom he later dismissed as an ignorant pedant who meddled in matters beyond his comprehension.[9]

When Montagu was in Turin he wrote a letter to the President of the Royal Society, dated 17 April 1762, in which he put forward Bartoli's observations. He then left for Rome, and there he sought the opinions of three learned scholars: the art historian Georg Winckelmann, his patron the connoisseur cardinal Alessandro Albani, and the orientalist Giuseppe Assemani. They all agreed that Needham was wrong and put forward the opinion that the statue was a forgery. Montagu enclosed their judgement in a second letter to the President of the Royal Society dated 2 October 1762. Both letters were read to the Society on 25 November and published as a pamphlet the following year (Montagu 1763).[10]

The dispute had reached its peak. The antiquary William Stukeley denied that it was possible 'to read the Egyptian hieroglyphics, by means of the Chinese lexicon' (Dawson 1932:470) and dismissed as absurd any idea of contact between the Egyptians and the Chinese.[11] The Secretary of the Royal Society, Charles Morton, on the other hand, wrote to Guignes suggesting that, although Needham did not know Chinese, he might have been, for this very reason, unprejudiced in the matter of judging the superficial likenesses of the characters.[12] Contemporary periodicals paid considerable attention to the whole question, while some authors made satirical comments on Needham's theory.[13] For foreigners in Turin it became *de rigueur* to see the 'bust of Isis'. Gibbon noted in his diary: 'Nous sommes retournès au Cabinet du Roi avec M. Bartoli. C'etoit principalement pour voir ce fameux buste qui a occasionè la dispute entre M.M. Needham et Bartoli, et qui a interessè M.M. le Cardinal Albani, de Guignes et tous les grands antiquaires de l'Europe. La societè du Comte de Saluces qui est composèè des amis de Needham se dispute avec Bartoli le plaisir de me remettre toutes les pieces du procès' (Bonnard 1961:35-36).

Needham's friends in Turin were completely confused by the debate, and the count of Saluzzo wrote to the abbé Barthélemy in order to find out his opinion. Barthélemy wanted to keep out of the dispute; but when Needham was in Paris in late May and again in early June 1762, Barthélemy acted as a mediator between Needham and Guignes. In his reply[14] to Saluzzo's letter, Barthélemy described his meeting with Needham and Guignes and pointed out that the

9. See Needham's letters of 15 October 1765 and 3 January 1766 to Sabatier de Cabre in the BLUL.

10. According to Montagu (1763), the two letters were read on 25 December, but according to William Stukeley they were read on 9 December 1762 (see Dawson 1932:472-73).

11. See also Stukeley's discussion of Needham's theory in the SAL, *Minutes*, viii:399-400, 404-406.

12. See Morton's letter to Guignes of 12 July 1763 in the BL (Add. 21461).

13. See Appleton (1951:149-51) and *W.C.* (23:551).

14. Barthélemy's letter is undated, but it was probably written at the end of December 1762 or at the beginning of January 1763 (see Barthélemy 1797, 2:397-406). A manuscript copy of this letter, in Bartoli's handwriting, is preserved in the BNT (Ris. 46. 8/6).

main issue consisted in finding the characters of the 'bust of Isis' in the Chinese dictionary and in distinguishing between ancient and modern Chinese characters. His own account of the meeting with Guignes and Needham was as follows (Barthélemy 1797, 2:400-401):

Ce dernier vint à Paris, il y a cinq à six mois. Je fus ravi de le connoître, et sur ce que je démêlai de son caractère je crus qu'il seroit facile de le lier avec M. de Guignes, et d'éclaircir entre nous l'étrange problême que j'ai l'honneur de vous exposer. Nous nous assemblâmes chez M. de Guignes. Nous avions le dictionnaire chinois sous nos yeux. M. Needham y trouva sans peine deux ou trois des caractères qui sont sur votre buste, et que M. de Guignes avoit reconnu dès le commencement pour des caractères égyptiens et chinois; mais il étoit question du reste de l'inscription. Comme M. Needham n'avoit pas beaucoup de tems à donner à cet objet, et que l'examplaire du dictionnaire que nous avons est distribué dans les volumes d'une manière toute différente de celui du Vatican, M. Needham renvoya cette recherche à un tems plus convenable, et je restai dans mes doutes.

The same meeting was described by Needham in a letter dated 5 June 1762 and addressed to Wilcocks:

The whole of Turin, as well Court as City, even those, who at first were declared Protectors of my Adversaries, were all at last on my side of y.ᵉ Question. I have not had less success at Paris with relation to Abbé Barthelemy, & M.ʳ de Guignes. The Abbé at the least prepossessed, & the most reasonable of the two, was first convinced, & then acted as a Mediator. M.ʳ de Guignes was more obstinate, but we fortunately met with the same Chinese Dictionary in the King's Library, as that of the Vatican; & after two or three Interviews, when I had shewed to him & the Abbé a certain number of our Egyptian Characters, mostly Obeliscal, or of other undoubted publick monuments at Rome, he agreed not only, that they were all to be found in the Chinese dictionary, but in the hurry of our Conversation wrote down upon a paper several other ancient Chinese Characters, which I knew immediately to be Obeliscal Characters. His only difficulty at last was this, that as the Chinese distinguish between modern Characters, & ancient, for their Historians say, that about 200 years after our Era, their Characters were considerably altered, I should, to evince the Truth, have made use of the Dictionary called *Chouven*, which is a Dictionary of ancient Characters explained by modern ones, & not the *Ching-zu-Tung*, where the ancient & modern Characters are confounded together without distinction.[15]

At this point in the dispute Needham was counting entirely on the outcome of the enquiry being made by the Royal Society with the assistance of Joseph Wilcocks and the East India Company. Copies of Needham's pamphlet together with a letter setting out the matter in question had been sent to the Jesuits in Peking, who were considered as being in a position to resolve the question. The Royal Society wanted to know from the Jesuits whether the characters on the 'bust of Isis' were indeed Chinese and, if so, what their meaning was; whether there was any historical evidence that they were derived from a foreign source; and, finally, whether there was any monument or custom extant in China suggesting that the Chinese had had communications with the Egyptians.[16] The exact dates on which the letter was sent and reached the Jesuits in Peking are

15. See Wilcocks's extract of Needham's letter in the SAL, Correspondence 1761-1770; see also SAL, *Minutes*, ix:10-11, and Pierce (1965:213-14 n.5).

16. See C. Morton (1769:490-91) and Needham's preface to [Cibot] (1773: iv).

unknown. The reply, however, written anonymously, was dated 20 October 1764 and entitled *Lettre sur les caractères chinois* (see letter 46, n.1, and letter 47, n.6). In October 1765 the ships of the East India Company were back in London; and in December 1765 Needham, who at the time was in Geneva, received the news that the Jesuits' answer was unfavourable to his theory. With admirable honesty he communicated the news to some of his correspondents,[17] asking them to forward it to those who were interested in the matter. To Paolo Frisi he wrote that the Jesuits' answer 'n'est pas du tout favorable ni à mes idées, ni à celles de Mr de Guignes, mais n'importe; c'est toujours un tribut que je dois à la verité; et que j'embrasse par devoir en vous la communiquant' (BAM, Y 153. Sup., lett. 48).

There was some delay before the contents of the Jesuits' reply were made publicly known. Charles Morton provided an extract on 23 June 1768, which was published in the *Philosophical transactions* (Morton 1769). The full account was edited by Needham himself in 1773 under the title *Lettre de Pekin, sur le génie de la langue chinoise, et la nature de leur écriture symbolique, comparée avec celle des anciens Egyptiens* (see [Cibot] 1773 and letter 46, n.1). As far as the characters on the 'bust of Isis' were concerned, the Jesuit scholar, father Cibot, had written from Peking that they were not genuine Chinese characters, with the possible exception of four or five that bore some resemblance and that the inscription as a whole was completely unconnected with China. He did, however, put forward an interpretation that implied some doubts as to the antiquity of the Chinese, and Bonnet was ready to concentrate on this aspect in order to discredit the critics of sacred chronology (see letter 47). Voltaire, on the other hand, commented in 1773, with his customary sarcasm toward Needham (V.O., 29:10):

Cette puérile idée que les Egyptiens allèrent enseigner aux Chinois à lire et à écrire vient de se renouveler encore; et par qui? par ce même jésuite Needham qui croyait avoir fait des anguilles avec du jus de mouton et du seigle ergoté. Il induisit en erreur de grands philosophes; ceux-ci trouvèrent, par leurs calculs, que si de mauvais seigle produisait des anguilles, de beau froment produirait infailliblement des hommes.

Le jésuite Needham, qui connaît tous les dialectes égyptiens et chinois comme il connaît la nature, vient de faire encore un petit livre pour répéter que les Chinois descendent des Egyptiens comme les Persans descendent de Persée, les Français de Francus, et les Bretons de Britannicus.[18]

The disrepute into which Needham's theory had fallen did not at once dispel interest in the 'bust of Isis', and scholars went on discussing the possible meaning of the inscription,[19] which, to this day, remains completely mysterious.[20] On 8

17. See Needham's letters to Sabatier de Cabre of 10 December 1765 in the BLUL, and to Paolo Frisi of 11 December 1765 in the BAM (Y 153. Sup., lett. 48).

18. Voltaire owned a copy of the *Lettre de Pekin* (see *Biblioteka* 1961: 256) but not Needham's *De inscriptione* of 1761, of which, however, he received a detailed account from the orientalist and critic of Guignes's theory, Michel-Ange-André Le Roux Deshautesrayes (see Best.D10246).

19. See Guasco (1768:296), Pauw (1773, 1:24-25), Cetto (1776:105-15), and Poinsinet de Sivry (1778:164-85). The latter denied that the bust was a forgery, but did not agree with Needham's translation of the inscription and provided one of his own.

20. Current scholarly opinion is that the bust probably dates from the seventeenth century and that the characters belong to that 'dottrina dei grani di beltà' (Curto 1962-1963:13), which was developed at the end of the sixteenth and during the seventeenth century. But apart from Bartoli's suggestion as to the provenance of the stone, we know nothing about the origins of the bust, neither

June 1824, the day after his arrival in Turin, a young Frenchman who in his early youth had toyed with the idea of deriving Egyptian hieroglyphs from Chinese characters (Hartleben 1906, 1:40) and was firmly dissuaded by his master, visited the Turin Museum and wrote to his brother, 'Je saluai une ancienne connaissance, la *Table Isiaque*, et ne trouvai dans les morceaux Egyptiens que des drogues, telles que le fameux *buste d'Isis* couvert de *caractères chinois*, – celui sur lequel le chevalier Needham a publié un in-4° que nous avons' (Hartleben 1909, 1:11). The young Frenchman was the distinguished egyptologist Jean-François Champollion.

the sculptor nor by whom it was first acquired; and the meaning of the characters themselves remains impenetrable.

7. Cosmogony and theory of the Earth

IN letter 29 Needham announced to Bonnet that he was adding a second treatise to his edition of Spallanzani's *Saggio*, which would be devoted to his own views on cosmogony. Needham explained that he would discuss the Mosaic account of Creation, Buffon's theory of the Earth, and his own explanation of the Deluge, which he regarded as a natural event. Bonnet replied in letter 30 that he was very curious to see Needham's '*Cosmogonie Sacrée*' because he had himself recently written an account of his own views on this subject. The two works referred to here were Needham's *Nouvelles recherches physiques et métaphysiques sur la nature et la religion, avec une nouvelle théorie de la terre, et une mesure de la hauteur des Alpes* (1769) and Bonnet's *La Palingénésie philosophique* (1769), the sixth part of which was devoted to the origins and history of the Earth.

At first glance, one might think it surprising that Bonnet and Needham should be interested in geological subjects. Yet in the seventeenth and eighteenth centuries, when geology as such was not yet a distinct scientific speciality, interest in the formation and history of the Earth was widespread. Most naturalists and natural philosophers turned to the subject at one point or another in their intellectual careers. One need only think of such figures as Descartes, Leibniz, Hooke, Ray, Buffon, and Kant to realise how important theory of the Earth had become during this period. As Jacques Roger has remarked, 'l'histoire de la terre passionnait le monde savant' (Buffon 1962:xvi).

Even more important for Bonnet and Needham, the subject of cosmogony, like generation, had become a battleground with the unbelievers, who were using Earth history to make serious inroads into the Christian account of Creation.[1] If one could explain the origin and subsequent development of the Earth and the solar system through natural causes alone, or if one could prove that the universe was eternal, then the power of God's creative act, revealed to humankind through Moses, lost all sway over human society. Thus, in his initial letter to Bonnet on cosmogony, Needham declared, 'En tout cela je crois avoir rendu service à la religion révelée, comme toute personne aussi clairvoyant, que vous meme, Monsieur, sentira facilement sans entrer dans un detail inutile' (8 June 1768, letter 29). To this Bonnet replied, after remarking on the coincidence of their both having turned to cosmogony at the same time, 'Nous avons donc travaillé tous deux, chacun à nôtre manière, à déffendre le Texte Sacré de la Genèse, contre les Assauts redoublés de nos Incrédules Modernes. Je ne me flatte pas trop que nous leur fassions entendre raison: leurs Oreilles ne sont pas faites pour nôtre *Harmonie*' (13 July 1768, letter 30). Both Bonnet and Needham approached their defence of cosmogony against the unbelievers in characteristic ways: Needham, by offering physical explanations for the development of the

---

1. Needham directly addressed Diderot's materialist vision of the origins of the universe by chance, as presented in the *Lettre sur les aveugles* (1749); see Spallanzani (1769, pt.2:32-38). At mid-century, the most atheistic account of the Earth's origins was the *Telliamed* (1748), discussed below. For materialism and theories of the Earth, see Palmer (1961:155-66).

Earth and its inhabitants that supported both revealed religion and his own metaphysical views of the universe; Bonnet, by interweaving the history and future state of the physical Earth with his account of the palingenesis of all living creatures in past and future worlds (see section 4 of this Introduction). Both were thus attempting to meet the unbelievers on their own terms, that is, to offer rational, physical accounts of the creation and history of the world that would also be consistent with, rather than contradictory to, the revealed word of the Bible.

It is important to note at the outset, however, that neither Needham nor Bonnet believed in a strictly literal interpretation of the Mosaic account of the Creation and Deluge as presented in Genesis. By the mid-eighteenth century, many strategies had been adopted to save the story of Moses while also offering an explanation of natural events (see Rappaport 1978). From the Renaissance period, when rational explanations were sought with increasing frequency for the literal descriptions of the Bible (see Allen 1945:25-40), through to the late seventeenth century, when theories of the Earth's history blossomed, the Mosaic account became adapted to different ends. Some argued that Moses was simply describing the origin of our Earth rather than the entire universe, and thus had depicted the Creation from an Earth-centred point of view. This allowed one to argue that Moses was describing *appearances* rather than actual events. Others took this line a step further, claiming that Moses was offering merely a story or parable to his people, using language and simple concepts they would understand, so that God's goodness and power would be revealed to them. The scientific content of Moses's account could then be interpreted to be negligible. Another tack taken was to loosen the physical strictures of the Mosaic chronology, by arguing that the Mosaic 'day' was not in fact equivalent to the twenty-four-hour day based on the rotation of the Earth. Needham and Bonnet found all of these approaches of some use, with Bonnet relying most on the appearances argument and Needham on the reinterpretation of the length of the Mosaic day. In neither case was the reconciliation of physical theory with the Mosaic account mere window-dressing, for both Needham and Bonnet recognised the vital importance of not giving any ground on this point to the unbelievers.

Before discussing the cosmogonies of Needham and Bonnet in detail, it may be useful to review the state of theories of the Earth in the late seventeenth and early eighteenth centuries.[2] During the 1680s and 1690s, the subject of cosmogony received considerable attention in England, through the publications of Thomas Burnet, John Ray, John Woodward, and William Whiston. All sought to offer Cartesian or Newtonian physical explanations of the origin of the Earth, and all paid particular attention to the Deluge as a major cause of the present state of the Earth's features. Burnet, who wanted to account not only for the creation but also for the final conflagration of the Earth and its inhabitants, maintained that the Earth had originally been a smooth sphere which had enjoyed perpetual spring since its orbit was circular and its axis not oblique. Yet as the heat of the sun dried the Earth's crust, it cracked and

2. For the seventeenth- and eighteenth-century cosmogonies and theories of the Earth discussed below, see Geike (1905:66-97), Collier (1934), Allen (1949:92-112), Haber (1959:36-136), Rappaport (1964, 1974:8-37, and 1978), Stokes (1969), Rudwick (1972:49-100), and Porter (1977:70-90).

weakened; and, at the appointed time, the surface caved in and the waters of
the abyss covered the Earth in the universal Deluge. The final catastrophe of
the Earth, Burnet predicted, would be a consummation by fire, as foretold in
the Bible. Burnet presented these views in his *Telluris theoria sacra* (1681), which
appeared in a fuller English version as *The Theory of the Earth* (1684) and in many
later editions. In a further work, the *Archaeologiae philosophicae* (1692), he rejected
most of the literal narrative of Genesis, arguing that Moses spoke in ways that
would be understandable to his people and that the story of the Creation
pertained only to the formation of the Earth about 6000 years previously and
not to the rest of the universe, which was much older.

Burnet's theory drew many critics (see Collier 1934:81-91; Allen 1949:100-
101) and inspired the cosmogonies of Ray, Woodward, and Whiston. John Ray,
in his *Three physico-theological discourses* (1693), on the Creation, the Deluge, and
the final conflagration, rejected Burnet's notion that the antediluvian Earth had
been without mountains. Although Ray believed in the universality of the Flood
and offered his own explanation for its production, his special interest was in
fossils. He was one of the major proponents of the idea that fossils were the
remains of organisms and not products of the Earth's 'plastic virtue', although
he was uncomfortable with the possibility that some fossils might be from species
no longer in existence.

The question of fossils formed a central core in the theory proposed by John
Woodward in his *Essay toward a natural history of the Earth* (1695).The most
experienced of these early cosmogonists in field collecting, Woodward was aware
of the presence of marine fossils on even the highest mountains. He attributed
the locations of fossils to the Deluge, when the Earth's crust was dissolved in
the floodwaters. After the Flood, he maintained, everything settled in layers
according to specific gravities, producing the fossiliferous strata observed on
Earth today. Woodward's theory also faced criticism, not the least difficulty
being the fact that the strata are not layered in order of specific gravity.

Woodward had not attempted to offer a mechanism for the production of the
Flood, a defect that was remedied by his contemporary William Whiston. In
his *A new theory of the Earth, from its original, to the consummation of all things* (1696),
Whiston offered yet another account of the Creation, Flood, and conflagration
but this time with a new twist. He argued that the Earth had been formed from
a comet, and also that the Deluge had been precipitated by the approach of a
large comet. The Earth passed through the comet's tail, producing great tides
in the seas and enormous rains from the condensation of the comet's atmosphere.
He explained the final conflagration by the approach of a comet as well, which
would draw the Earth so far out of its orbit that it would be burned by the sun.

Whiston's system had the blessing of Isaac Newton, having been submitted
to him prior to publication. Woodward's theory also rested on the Newtonian
conception of gravity. On the Continent, however, other cosmogonies were
proposed on the Cartesian model. In his *Principia philosophiae* (1644) and his
posthumously published *Le Monde* (1664), Descartes had presented an account
of the formation of the universe based on his principles of matter and motion
and his theory of vortices. Claiming that the planets had all been originally
molten masses like the sun, Descartes presented a history of the Earth based on

the melting and cooling of its constituent elements and the separation of land, water, and air into distinct layers. He completely ignored the Mosaic account of Creation, declaring that he was offering an explanation only of how God *could* have created the universe through secondary causes.

The other major cosmogonist prior to the mid-eighteenth century, even though his views were not fully known until that time, was Leibniz. Having composed a treatise on the theory of the Earth in 1690, titled the *Protogaea*, he published only a very brief summary of it in the *Acta eruditorum* in 1693. It was not until 1749, long after his death, that the treatise was published in its entirety. Like Descartes, Leibniz believed that the Earth had once been a molten globe and that the original hardened substance of the Earth was a form of glass. As cooling progressed, vapours condensed into water, and the crust cooled unevenly into mountains and valleys. Unlike many of his contemporaries and successors, Leibniz attributed both an igneous and an aqueous origin to rocks and strata, some having been formed as the first cooled masses of the Earth and others by sedimentation from water. He offered an explanation for the source of the Deluge waters, and he was especially concerned to account for fossils, which he believed had an organic origin.

By the mid-eighteenth century, the principal issues that occupied naturalists treating the origins and history of the Earth were not really very different from those discussed by the cosmogonists of the 1690s. The extent of fossil distribution was much better known, due to avid fossil collecting; and the continuity and universality of strata were more widely recognised. Yet most still viewed the Deluge as the major geological event of the past, serving to explain the present features of the Earth and the location of fossils. And the Mosaic story of the Creation still formed the foundation, even though not as a literal account, of many cosmogonies. But in 1749 a theory of the Earth appeared that challenged these commonly held assumptions about its origin and history. Opening the first volume of the *Histoire naturelle* was Buffon's *Histoire et théorie de la terre*, which contained a cosmogony based not on Moses and the Deluge but, at least purportedly, on everyday natural causes.[3]

In Buffon's cosmogony, the planets were all created when a comet struck the sun, projecting into space a mass of liquids and gases that coalesced into spheres all rotating around the sun in concentric orbits. Adopting from Leibniz the idea of an originally molten Earth, Buffon believed that the cooled Earth was homogeneous throughout and that its surface features were the result of the actions of water. Buffon's neptunian views were based on two facts: the existence of parallel layers of different materials composing the surface of the Earth, and the presence of shells and marine fossils far from the sea, even on mountain tops. The extent of fossil distribution he took on Woodward's authority, even though he rejected Woodward's own explanation for their locations. He argued that all parts of the Earth had at one time been covered by water – not all at the same time but rather by the successive submersion and emergence of different land masses. Refusing to grant the reality of a universal Deluge, Buffon claimed that he did not wish to conflate scripture and natural history. Yet the effects of

3. For Buffon's geological ideas, see especially Roger's analysis in Buffon (1962:xv-lxxxi).

submersion under water were, on Buffon's theory, not unlike those that others attributed to a single Deluge; for he explained sedimentation and fossil distribution by the sea's presence on all land. But the major role for the ocean, according to Buffon, was to sculpt the mountains and valleys of the Earth through the flux and reflux of sea currents and the tides.

Buffon directly criticised the views of Burnet, Woodward, and Whiston, discussing as well Leibniz, Bourguet, and Scheuchzer. He presented his own theory as a completely new system that relied on known causes and eschewed inexplicable past catastrophes to account for the present state of the Earth. Yet Buffon's attempt to offer a natural cosmogony, independent from religious orthodoxy, led to his theory's being condemned by the theologians at the Sorbonne. Four of the fourteen propositions cited by the Sorbonne from the first two volumes of the *Histoire naturelle* pertained to Buffon's theories of mountain-building and of the formation of the Earth from the sun. Buffon attempted to placate the Theology Faculty at the Sorbonne by declaring that he had had no intention of going against the Holy Scriptures and that he would abandon anything in his cosmogony that contradicted the story of Moses. Taking an escape route similar to Descartes's, Buffon professed that his hypothesis on the formation of the planets was only 'une pure supposition philosophique'.[4] Yet he continued to develop and refine his ideas on the origin and history of the Earth, offering thirty years later an even more daring account of the development of the Earth in seven epochs in his *Epoques de la nature* (1779).

The final theory to briefly mention before turning to Needham's work was the most speculative, and potentially the most dangerous, of all. In 1748, an anonymous work appeared titled *Telliamed*, which was the posthumous publication of Benoît de Maillet. Presenting a totally naturalistic and materialistic view of the history of the Earth, the *Telliamed* was widely criticised, and even ridiculed. De Maillet accounted for the formation of mountains and continents by the action of retreating waters (in a manner that clearly influenced Buffon). He also envisaged a developmental history of life that was overtly transformist, explaining the origins of all land animals and plants from sea forms, including the origin of human beings from mermen and mermaids.

Buffon's theory, and even more so de Maillet's, presented a disturbing challenge to the status quo of eighteenth-century cosmogony. Although naturalistic theories of the origin of the universe and history of the Earth had been presented earlier in, for instance, Descartes's work, the impact of Buffon's system was far greater, probably because it seemed to bring together a large amount of empirical observations about the features of the Earth's surface within a coherent framework. Yet its independence from the revealed account of the Creation in the book of Genesis and its reliance on known, everyday causes to account for the development of the Earth were disturbing to those who sought to curtail the spread of materialism and atheism. Buffon's views were thus criticised by Needham and Bonnet, and ridiculed by Voltaire. Yet their impact was unavoidable; and the extended time scale implied by his ideas, along with

---

4. For the text of the Sorbonne's condemnation and of Buffon's reply, see Buffon (1749-89, 4:v-xvi).

Fig. 14. The forming Earth, as depicted in Buffon's *Histoire et théorie de la terre*. (From Buffon, *Histoire naturelle*, 1749-1789, vol.i. Courtesy of the Wellcome Institute Library, London.)

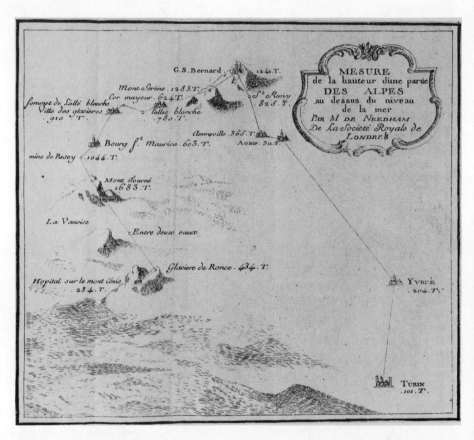

Fig. 15. Needham's illustrations of the heights of several mountains in the Alps of Savoy and the Duchy of Aosta. The altitudes were measured with a barometer and then converted into heights (in toises, equal to fathoms). The expedition took place in August 1751, setting out from Turin, with Needham accompanying the Earl of Rochford, who was then the British envoy extraordinary to the King of Sardinia. The results were published in Needham 1752, Needham 1760a, and Spallanzani 1769, pt. 2 (From Needham, *Nouvelles recherches physiques et métaphysiques sur la nature de la religion, avec une nouvelle théorie de la terre, et une mesure de la hauteur des Alpes*, in Spallanzani 1769, pt. 2.)

his denial of the universal Deluge, irrevocably altered the course of mid-eighteenth-century geological thinking.

Needham turned to cosmogony and the theory of the Earth well versed in the literature of his day on the subject and with experience in fossil collecting and field observation. In the early 1740s, when he taught at an English school at Twyford, he studied petrified shells and the structure of malm, a chalky soil found in a nearby valley. This work formed the basis for his first letter to the Royal Society and his first scientific publication.[5] When Needham was in Paris in 1747-1749 and in Turin in 1751-1752, he collected numerous fossils and crystals, principally to send to his friend Emanuel Mendez Da Costa but also for his own cabinet.[6] He apparently also visited mines and peat strata in the English countryside to observe the various depths of fossil deposits (see Spallanzani 1769, pt.2:118, 122). Thus Needham was no stranger to the geological evidence presented by fossillised shells and organisms in England and on the Continent.

Needham's principal goal in writing his book on cosmogony was to present a physical account of the creation and early history of the Earth that would be consistent both with Genesis and with his own principles of physics. He squared his explanation with Genesis by arguing that the six days of the Creation were really six periods of indefinite length, thus allowing sufficient time for the natural operation of physical forces. He also utilised the Deluge as a major cause of present geological and palaeontological phenomena. In this way, Needham hoped to counter the unbelievers by offering a credible natural explanation of the creation and present state of the Earth that necessarily entailed the six-'day' Creation, the Deluge, and the revealed word of God. As he explained, his account was based on principles drawn from 'la Physique dirigée par la révélation' (Spallanzani 1769, pt.2:27).

Needham opened the *Nouvelles recherches physiques et métaphysiques sur la nature et la religion* with a letter addressed to Buffon, the theme of which was how to interpret the description of the Creation as presented in Genesis. Remarking that he and Buffon had often puzzled together over the meaning of the phrase 'le soir & le matin firent un jour' (Genesis i.5), Needham proceeded to discuss the relationship between the Deist and the Christian, that is, between natural and revealed religion. His basic argument was that the Christian philosopher had the best of both positions, for he possessed all of the truths based on the natural world plus those that could only be known by God's having revealed them to man.[7] Having established the necessity of revealed wisdom for understanding both nature and God, however, Needham then claimed that one was

5. See Needham's letters at the Royal Society of 24 February 1743 and 11 August 1743 (L&P. I. 167, 244) and Needham (1743).

6. See Needham's letters to Paolo Frisi of 10 December 1751 (BAM, Y 153. Sup., lett. 45); to Ferdinando Bassi of 12 January 1752 and 25 March 1752 (BUB, Cod. 233, vol.ii); and to Emanuel Mendez Da Costa of 24 March 1747, 29 December 1747, 22 October 1749, 21 March 1752, and 25 March 1752 (BL, Add. 28540). The inventory of Needham's belongings after his death lists a large fossil collection (see WDA, series A, vol. 42, no. 183).

7. For further discussion of Needham's views on revealed and natural religion, see section 4 of this Introduction.

not tied to a completely literal interpretation of the Scriptures. Although inspired by God, the original authors of the books of the Bible, Needham explained, possessed individual styles and capabilities; and in matters not essential to faith they differed and even erred sometimes in their accounts. Even theologians and commentators on the Bible had offered only opinions on matters of interpretation that did not impinge on the Church's articles of faith. Thus, Needham claimed, when the Church had not declared that a particular mode of interpretation was an article of faith, one was free to interpret Scriptural passages on whatever reasoned basis one wanted. Citing the authority of saint Augustine on this point, he concluded, 'à l'égard du sens littéral de l'Ecriture, si vos raisons tirées de la nature des choses mêmes, sont fortes & urgentes, vous pouvez vous écarter de la lettre dans l'explication de l'histoire de la création par *Moyse*' (Spallanzani 1769, pt.2:15-16). On this basis Needham claimed that he was fully justified in interpreting the six days of Moses as six periods of time, not six rotations of the Earth each lasting twenty-four hours. As a corroborating argument, he cited numerous Biblical passages in which the word 'day' had been used to signify an indefinite period of time (Spallanzani 1769, pt.2:67-76).

Needham was not being entirely novel in either his comments on Biblical interpretation or his liberalising of the Mosaic days to longer periods of time. Within the Catholic Church there was not only a long history of allegorical interpretations of Genesis, but also a tradition of considering the word 'day' as used in the Creation story to be something other than the twenty-four-hour day (see Vigouroux 1889:11-122). Needham's solution thus fell well within his religious tradition. Furthermore, 'liberal' interpretations of the Mosaic Creation were quite common in the geological literature of the late seventeenth and early eighteenth centuries, and the lengthening of the days of Creation was suggested in some form or other by such figures as Burnet, Ray, and Whiston. Yet Needham viewed his conception of the six periods of creation and his cosmogonical system in general as highly original and as providing a unique synthesis of religious and physical truths.

Much of the main body of Needham's book that followed his letter to Buffon is devoted to a presentation and critique of Buffon's cosmogony, as outlined in the first volume of the *Histoire naturelle* (1749), as well as to a discussion and adoption of Linnaeus's ideas on the structure of Paradise and the dispersal of organisms. Needham moulded together parts of Buffon's theory with Linnaeus's views; and by adding his own conception of a central expansive heat, he presented a coherent theory of the Earth that encompassed the Creation and Deluge and that accounted for mountains, strata, and fossil distribution. These were the principal features of the present-day Earth that eighteenth-century naturalists felt one had to explain.

From Buffon, Needham adopted the idea that every part of the Earth had at one time been covered with water, although he identified this event with our original universal ocean, whereas Buffon had believed in successive, piecemeal inundations. Both used the covering of the Earth by water to account for the laying down of strata on the Earth's surface and the existence of marine fossils on even the highest mountains. But where Needham differed from Buffon was in not accepting the latter's explanation for the formation of mountains by the action of water currents. Rather, he thought that mountains had arisen from the actions of an expansive force interior to the Earth. 'Si M. *de Buffon*', he declared, 'veut admettre avec moi une force intérieure expansive, modifiée par la gravitation, un feu central qui se répand jusqu'à la superficie du globe, & dont lui-même trouve par-tout avec les Naturalistes modernes les traces les plus évidentes, pour pousser au dehors toutes les grandes chaînes des montagnes, [...] il s'approchera de si près de la Cosmogonie de *Moyse* & des phénomenes' (Spallanzani 1769, pt.2:131-32). Needham allowed currents to act only as modifying agents once mountains had been pushed up under the water. For evidence of the interior expansive force, he pointed to the existence of active and extinct volcanoes in mountain chains in South America, France, Scotland, Italy, and on numerous volcanic islands (Spallanzani 1769, pt.2:160-67; see also letter 48, n.5).

Needham also rejected in Buffon's theory the excessively long time that it appeared his process of Earth-formation would have taken. Although Buffon did not hazard a guess at the age of the Earth in the first volume of the *Histoire naturelle* (1749), it was clear to Needham and to others that the formation of mountains and continents by the action of the sea would have required an extremely long time (see Buffon 1962:lx-lxi). Needham estimated that such an operation would have taken a minimum of three million years. Yet he rejected this figure for the age of the Earth on the grounds that, at present sedimentation rates, the Earth would have to be covered by an enormously thick layer of shells[8] and should moreover contain far more petrified formations than it does. Needham certainly did not hold to the date of 4004 B.C. for the Creation, as promulgated by archbishop Ussher; yet he was also unwilling to allow millions of years to have passed. This would have given far too much ground to the unbelievers and their hypotheses of an Earth formed randomly from chaos.

Needham's own view was that the chronology described by Moses was not that of the Earth but only that of human beings. Needham's six periods of Creation allowed him to extend the pre-human parts far beyond the twenty-four-hour Mosaic days. Yet the physical appearance presented by the Earth (mountains, strata, and fossils) did not, Needham believed, 'prouve nécessairement la très-grande antiquité de la terre, & ne demande pas que les six périodes de *Moyse* soient d'une plus grande durée que la simple nature des élémens amalgamés ensemble qui se séparent successivement en occupant leurs places respectives, & que le tempéramment des différentes productions qui se développent ensuite pour remplir & peupler toutes les parties de la terre, peuvent le requérir' (Spallanzani 1769, pt.2:81-82). Attempting to retain the advantages of an extended chronology while avoiding the dangers of Buffon's theory, he proposed an age for the Earth of an indefinite time, yet one that would not be so absurdly old that it would threaten revealed religion.

Needham's account of the initial state of the Earth as it rose from the universal sea on the third 'day' of Creation was based heavily on Linnaeus's description of Paradise. In an address given in 1743 titled 'Oratio de telluris habitabilis

---

8. According to Rappaport (1964:68), Needham was the only figure of this period who used sedimentation rates in discussing the possible age of the Earth.

incremento', Linnaeus had proposed that God initially created only one small island with a large mountain on it.[9] Here the first individual or pair of each species of plant and animal found their first home, and it was here that Adam gave each animal its name. Since all climatic zones were represented at the different altitudes on the mountain, from tropical at the bottom to alpine at the summit, all organisms existed in this Garden of Eden in proper harmony. As more and more land emerged from the sea (and Linnaeus thought this process was still going on in his day), plants and animals spread into new regions until the present distribution was reached. Locating Paradise somewhere in Africa, below the equator, Linnaeus viewed the original Earth as a perfect Creation.

Needham devoted several sections of his treatise to a discussion of Linnaeus's ideas, as taken directly from the 'Oratio'. Adopting the notion that the original Earth was a mountain on which lived the first individuals or pairs of all organisms, he added the idea that this mountain was a volcano. Its eruption, which occurred when Adam and Eve were expelled from the Garden of Eden, destroyed all trace of Paradise. He also argued that between the Creation and the Deluge all animals and man had been vegetarians, a not uncommon notion, stemming from Renaissance discussions of the particulars of the antediluvian Earth (see Allen 1949:72-73).

Needham synthesised these various ideas drawn from Linnaeus and Buffon with his own principles of expansive and resistive forces to explain the events of the six periods of Creation. Central to his account was the notion that God had planned the entire sequence of events by organising the necessary physical forces in advance. 'La matiere premiere, dont le ciel & la terre sont composés dans l'état où nous les voyons,' he claimed, 'contenoit en elle-même les principes nécessaires pour produire la forme présente des choses' (Spallanzani 1769, pt.2:56). Likening the Earth to an egg, which develops into an animal through vegetative principles operating as planned by God, just so the Earth had developed by degrees from a mass of primitive matter to its present state. 'Dieu,' Needham declared, 'dont la puissance, selon l'Ecriture Sainte, fait tout *par nombre, poids & mesure*, avoit tout combiné d'avance relativement à ses desseins' (Spallanzani 1769, pt.2:168). With this argument Needham freed himself to discuss a purely physical explanation of the events of Creation, just as he had in discussing the generation of organisms, while still retaining a necessary role for God.

According to Moses, the first thing created was light (Genesis i.3). Needham interpreted this initial light as a subtle 'electrical' matter, claiming that this most universal and powerful agent pervades even today all matter. Existing before the sun, this 'feu électrique' permeated the first matter of the Earth and, by expansion, caused the first land to push out above the sea (Spallanzani 1769, pt.2:158-60). This first mountain was located in Asia, according to Needham; and it began to acquire green plants toward the end of the third period, which were illuminated by the sun at the beginning of the fourth period. The Earth and sea were then warmed by the sun, and in the fifth period the fish and fowls

9. See Linnaeus (1744, 1749-1769:430-78, and 1781). For Linnaeus's views on cosmogony and on geographical distribution, see Nathorst (1909), Browne (1983:16-23), and Frängsmyr (1983).

were produced. Needham envisaged this as a natural generation, for 'La présence du soleil avoit échauffé la terre & les eaux, pendant tout l'espace du quatrième période, pour les disposer à devenir prolifiques, quand les eaux émues intérieurement par l'esprit de la Divinité toûjours agissant sous le voile de causes secondes, se fécondent & produisent les poissons & les oiseaux' (Spallanzani 1769, pt.2:188). The Earth proceeded to gradually perfect itself, and in the sixth period the quadrupeds and finally human beings appeared.

In the first part of his book, which consisted of his letter to Buffon, Needham characterised this process of creation as the continued operation of action and reaction, of movement and repose. Describing all physical activity in the present universe as the alternation of the positive and negative, he claimed that, if ever they came into perfect equilibrium, the world would stagnate. In the scale of exaltation on which Needham believed all types of matter could be ordered, from the most brute to the most exalted (electrical matter), Needham portrayed each level as positive or negative in relation to the others. The emergence of this scale during the periods of Creation, culminating in vitality, the sensitive principle, and finally the intelligent principle of humans, was for Needham a natural process (Spallanzani 1769, pt.2:20-21):

En examinant l'histoire de la création dans les livres de *Moyse*, il est aisé d'y observer cette échelle si conforme à la Philosophie & à la nature des choses. On voit d'abord la séparation du chaos & l'éduction des quatre principaux élémens, aussi-bien que leur disposition successive; ensuite les quatre élémens, ainsi distribués & prolifiquement dispersés, retournent une seconde fois en eux-mêmes partiellement, & se mêlent ensemble dans certaines portions pour produire les corps sublunaires moins considérables, & recommencer encore une nouvelle échelle, qui monte graduellement de l'imparfait au parfait, de la simple *apposition* réguliere à l'économie vitale & *l'intus-susception* organique; & de la simple vitalité à l'organisation la plus complette, parcourant chaque classe de la vie distinctement, avec une addition vers le milieu du terme d'un principe sensitif, jusqu'à ce que l'échelle finisse à l'homme auquel, dit l'Ecrivain Sacré, Dieu inspira d'en haut une ame spirituelle & immortelle.

This entire development Needham described as the continual interaction of the positive and the negative, beginning with the night preceding the first day and each period thereafter following in a dialectical fashion from the previous one.

Needham characterised the forming world as 'une espéce de globe vital & organisé' and the initial chaos from which it developed as a 'masse vitale de la matiere' (Spallanzani 1769, pt.2:169, 77). Envisaging the six periods of Creation as six developmental stages, during which the scale of nature increasingly advanced upward, Needham attempted to synthesise his metaphysical and biological ideas with a history of the Earth. Wishing to encompass every aspect of the Mosaic Creation within his system, he even described the formation of Eve from Adam as a vital generation from Adam's body, occurring while he slept (Spallanzani 1769, pt.1:291-97, pt.2:204). Throughout the presentation of his cosmogony, Needham remained loyal to his principal goal of offering a physical explanation for creation within a framework of the Mosaic description and the revealed word of God.

Like most other eighteenth-century naturalists who discussed the theory of the Earth, Needham encompassed the Deluge within his system as well. Having accounted for the formation of mountains by the action of subterranean expansive heat and for the deposition of regular strata by the gradual emergence of land from a universal ocean, he still needed to explain the disruptions one finds in these strata and the unusual locations that had been discovered for fossils and marine shells. For this purpose, he, like many of his predecessors, turned to the Deluge.[10] That a major disruption had occurred on the Earth's surface, of short duration, rapid action, and universal extent, was clearly evidenced, Needham argued, by fossil distributions (Spallanzani 1769, pt.2:81, 117-21, 195-96). The Scriptures testified that the Flood had been universal, covering even the highest points on the Earth; and Needham rejected the idea that some parts of the globe, for instance, America, had been spared because no humans lived there. He also argued against those who claimed that the Deluge had been produced through supernatural, miraculous causes alone. Rather, he countered, one should view the Flood as the result of natural causes, preordained by God to operate at the proper time, as well as a moral event designed to punish mankind.

One of the principal problems encountered by those who wanted to claim that the Flood had been universal was to account for the source of the vast quantities of water needed as well as for their diminution after the floodwaters began to subside. If, as Moses claimed (Genesis vii.20), the water covering the Earth was at least fifteen cubits deep (over twenty feet), then how could so much water have been produced in forty days and nights? Burnet had proposed in his *Theory of the Earth* that it would have taken eight oceans of water to cover the Earth, and he envisaged a layer of subterranean water under a thin crust that had ruptured to produce the floodwaters. Interconnected underground channels of water were suggested by Ray, whereas Whiston thought that the condensed vapours of a comet would have produced enough water. These explanations were all debated during the late seventeenth and early eighteenth centuries.

In order to demonstrate that both the source of the water that had covered the Earth and its amount could be explained by manageable, natural causes, Needham suggested an ingenious model. Let us suppose, he proposed, that the Earth is a globe seven and a half feet in diameter. On this scale, the highest mountains (the Cordilleras of Peru) would be only one half a line (about 1/24 inch) high. The volume of such a globe would be 7931 pints of Paris (nearly 7000 litres). To cover the entire surface of this globe to a height of 1/24th of an inch would require 24 pints of water, or less than 1/360th of its interior capacity. Thus the quantity of water required, when reduced to an imaginable scale, turned out to be a relatively small amount, Needham concluded. By an increase in the interior heat of the Earth, the expansive force could have suddenly caused the floodwaters to appear from ruptures in the Earth, as described by Moses (Genesis vii.11). At the close of the Deluge, the waters could again have receded into the caverns from which they had come (see Spallanzani 1769, pt.2:175-80). Needham even envisaged a machine that one could construct on this scale model

10. For the use of the Deluge in eighteenth-century theories of the Earth, see the sources listed in note 2 above.

to demonstrate the Flood, but apparently he never actually built it.

In the Preface to his book, Needham discussed Edmund Halley's ideas on the interior structure of the Earth, which had been proposed some years earlier (see Halley 1692). In order to explain the variations encountered in the directions of the magnetic poles on the Earth, Halley had suggested that the Earth was composed of an interior core and an exterior crust, separated by a fluid medium. This allowed Halley to identify four magnetic poles and thereby to explain magnetic variation. Needham adopted this general model of the Earth's structure and argued that, when extended to include the idea of an interior heat, Halley's model provided the best structure to explain the Deluge. Thus, in something of a roundabout way, Needham came to the conclusion of several of his contemporaries, that the water for the Flood came principally from a subterranean layer of water under the Earth's crust. Needham's originality perhaps lay more in the scale model he proposed and the resulting conclusion that the amount of water needed did not exceed imaginable physical causes.

When Needham described his treatise on cosmogony to Bonnet in June of 1768, he discussed his model globe. He reiterated that he had wanted to explain the Deluge on simple physical terms principally to counter the unbelievers. 'Les incredules,' he wrote, 'sans ôser nier ouvertement le deluge cherchent à le faire passer pour un miracle immediat, on sçait bien pourquoi, sans considerer, que ce n'est pas la maniere, dont Moyse le represente. Mes idées la dessus sont plus conformes à l'esprit de l'ecriture sainte; dieu n'opere jamais inutilement des miracles, la physique est assujettie à la morale, parce que dieu, qui a tout prevu la voulut ainsi du commencement' (8 June 1768, letter 29). With this Bonnet was evidently in full agreement, as he replied, 'J'aime à vous voir représenter le Déluge par une petite Machine: c'étoit un bon moyen de ne s'y noyer point, et d'y noyer les Incrédules' (13 July 1768, letter 30).

Needham believed that his theory of the Earth accounted for all of the principal geological features of the present Earth (mountains, strata, and fossils) within a cosmogony consistent with the Mosaic Creation. He further maintained that his system obviated all of the difficulties his predecessors' and contemporaries' theories had encountered. With his interior expansive force and model for the structure of the Earth, he claimed, he did not need Burnet's total destruction of the world, nor Whiston's comet, nor Woodward's dissolution of the solid parts of the Earth, nor the author of the *Telliamed*'s confusion of the mountains on continents with the islands in the sea, nor finally Voltaire's pilgrims dropping shells in the mountains (Spallanzani 1769, pt.2:173-75). Admittedly influenced to a great extent by Buffon and Linnaeus, and clearly aware of the theories of the other major cosmogonists of his time, Needham offered his own unique synthesis of physical, metaphysical, and religious ideas. And all was designed to counter the foothold gained by the unbelievers in the theory of the Earth.

When Needham first described his treatise on cosmogony to Bonnet, Bonnet replied that he was looking forward to reading it since, as was mentioned earlier, he had recently written down his own thoughts on the subject (see letters 29 and 30). After having received Needham's book in December 1768, Bonnet reported (letter 33) that he had only glanced at it but that he was concerned that Voltaire and other unbelievers would seize on Needham's explanation of the formation of Eve from Adam as a new source for ridicule. Would it not have been better to have interpreted Moses's account of Eve's origin allegorically? To this Needham replied (letter 34) that Bonnet should not have begun his perusal with the section on Adam and Eve, since this explanation came after he had presented the rest of his theory and had to be understood in relation to the whole. Rather than resort to allegory, Needham said that he preferred to offer physical explanations whenever possible for the various parts of the story of Moses. If one said that the formation of Eve was an allegory, he argued, wouldn't one then have to say the same about the production of all of the animals and plants from the Earth and of Adam from vitalised clay? On none of these points was Needham willing to concede to allegory, since he felt that his developing scale of matter offered a good basis for explaining these aspects of the Creation.

Bonnet mentioned Needham's views on cosmogony only once more in their correspondence when Needham, after having heard nothing further from Bonnet about his book for several months, asked him for his reaction (letter 35). He replied that he did not want to give Needham a detailed critique of the book, since they differed so much in their opinions, especially on generation (letter 36). They were closer in their views on cosmogony, Bonnet conceded, but he did not elaborate. We can recall that Bonnet had reacted quite strongly against the first part of Needham's book in his letters to Spallanzani and to Haller (see section 2.iv of this Introduction). Not wanting to deal with Needham any further in the area of generation, he seems simply to have let Needham's theory of the Earth pass with little comment. Had he discussed Needham's views in any detail, there is no doubt that he would have rejected Needham's reliance on epigenetic-style development in his account of the appearance of the different groups of organisms on Earth, as well as his metaphysical description of material action and reaction. But perhaps the main reason why Bonnet was not very interested in Needham's cosmogony was that he had himself only recently worked out his own views on the subject within a completely different framework. Very little in Needham's account of the history of the Earth would have been relevant to his own, and it is even likely that he never really read Needham's treatise in any detail.

Bonnet's views on cosmogony were presented as part of his panoramic account of the past, present, and future state of the Earth and its inhabitants that he outlined in *La Palingénésie philosophique* (1769). Far less knowledgeable than Needham about contemporary theories of the Earth, or at least far less interested in them, judging from the lack of references in his book, he was also not as intimately involved with fossil collecting as Needham had been. Rather, cosmogony was for Bonnet one further aspect, albeit a major one, of his grand vision of the history of the world; and his theory of the Earth was consequently moulded in such a way as to provide a basis for his ideas on the future perfection of all organisms on Earth.

Bonnet believed that, since its original creation, our globe had undergone a series of 'revolutions' that had completely destroyed all existing organisms and had radically altered the geological features of the Earth. It was just such a revolution that Moses had described in the first book of Genesis. 'Comme les

Corps organisés ont leurs phases ou leurs révolutions particulieres,' Bonnet explained, 'les Mondes ont aussi les leurs. Nos lunettes paroissent nous en avoir découvert dans quelques-uns de ces grands Corps qui pendent au Firmament. Notre Terre a donc eu aussi ses révolutions.' Stating that he was not referring to the limited and local effects of the sea, volcanoes, and earthquakes, Bonnet continued, 'Je parle de ces révolutions générales d'un Monde, qui en changent entiérement la face & qui lui donnent un nouvel être. Telle a été cette révolution de notre Planete que Moyse a consacrée dans ses Annales' (Bonnet 1769a, 1:247; B.O., 7:182/15:266-67). As evidence for the existence of revolutions preceding the one Moses described, Bonnet pointed to, without elaborating on, the 'amas immenses de ruines, qui paroissent être celles d'un ancien Monde' that one finds on the surface and in the depths of the Earth (Bonnet 1769a, 1:237; B.O., 7:174/15:255; see also 1769a, 1:173; B.O., 7:121/15:179). Presumably, he meant fossil evidence indicating that creatures had once existed that were different from present-day organisms, as well as geological features that recorded previous upheavals in the Earth's surface.

Although such revolutions had wiped out all existing flora and fauna, Bonnet claimed that germs from these organisms survived into the next world. After the destructive events ceased, these germs developed into new organisms to people the new Earth. The plants and animals that Moses described as appearing on the third and fifth day thus originated not *de novo* but rather from the indestructible minute germs of their predecessors. '[L]es Plantes & les Animaux qui existent aujourd'hui', he maintained, 'sont provenus par une sorte d'évolution naturelle des Etres organisés qui peuploient ce premier Monde sorti immédiatement des mains du créateur' (Bonnet 1769a, 1:250; B.O., 7:184/15:269). At the original Creation, Bonnet explained, God not only preformed the germs of all the organisms that would people that initial world, but he also created all the germs for each future world in a determined relationship to what each world would be like. If, he suggested, there were to be three great revolutions, the germs of the first organisms would contain within them the proper organs and structures for three successive organisms that would be called into being after each revolution. There could, of course, he admitted, have been several revolutions (although not an infinite number) before the one the Mosaic account pertained to. But Bonnet very clearly separated the Mosaic Creation (revolution) from the original creation of the Earth and universe.

As part of his grand scheme for global perfection of organisms through time, Bonnet suggested that the organisms arising from the same germ series would not necessarily be identical. Since after each revolution the Earth might be very different geologically and climatically, the organisms that would people it ought to differ as well. Thus both the Earth and the organised beings upon it would have been greatly modified by each revolution – so much so, that we would not necessarily recognise the ancestors of our present organisms. '[J]e me persuade facilement,' Bonnet remarked, 'que si nous pouvions voir un Cheval, une Poule, un Serpant sous leur premiere forme, sous la forme qu'ils avoient au tems de la Création, il nous seroit impossible de les reconnoître' (Bonnet 1769a, 1:258; B.O., 7:190/15:278). As evidence for the changes organisms had undergone since their original creation, he cited the enveloping of seeds and germs revealed by the microscope and the metamorphoses insects undergo during their lifetimes. Regarding the astronomical and organic systems as having parallel and interlocking histories, Bonnet even suggested, in a passage presaging later notions of recapitulation, that the stages one observes the embryonic chick undergoing during development might indicate the revolutions that it had undergone before becoming the organism that we know (Bonnet 1769a, 1:178-79; B.O., 7:125-26/15:186-87).[11]

Bonnet's cosmogony required an age for the Earth that was much greater than that suggested by the Bible. Yet this did not invalidate the sacred chronology, according to Bonnet, for he simply claimed that the Earth had existed, in different forms, prior to the events depicted by Moses. 'Je suis infiniment éloigné de vouloir infirmer le moins du monde cette Chronologie,' he remarked; 'Je sais qu'elle est la base la plus solide de l'Histoire Ancienne: mais, l'infirmerois-je en avançant qu'elle n'est que celle d'une révolution particuliere de notre Monde, & qu'elle ne pouvoit s'étendre au-delà?' (Bonnet 1769a, 1:259-60; B.O., 7:192/15:281). If there had been astronomers on Venus or Mars before the revolution of Moses, he suggested, they would have known something about the previous revolutions. Using a calculation for the age of the Earth based on the alleged gradual diminution of the obliquity of the ecliptic, Bonnet claimed that the ecliptic would have taken 2,160,000 years to make one complete rotation through the poles and might have already made several rotations around the Earth.[12] Yet he also argued that the age of the Earth could not be infinite. Revelation had established, he claimed, the existence of a First Cause who preordained the entire future history of our globe.

Bonnet's attribution of the Mosaic account of the Creation to the most recent revolution of our globe allowed him to dispense as well with a literal reading of the events of the six days. When Genesis proclaimed that God made the sun, the moon, and the stars on the fourth day for the purpose of lighting the Earth (Genesis i.14-19), he declared, this was simply what *appeared* to be the case from the Earth's perspective. Moses was not describing the creation of the heavens along with the Earth, but only the events of the renewal of our globe as it emerged from its revolution. Since our planet is such a tiny speck among the myriad of stars, one could not believe that God would have created them only for our light. We should not criticise Moses for not speaking the language of Copernicus, Bonnet declared, for his mission was simply to teach man about God. 'Cet Historien n'étoit pas appellé à dicter au Genre humain des Cahiers d'Astronomie,' he explained, 'mais il étoit appellé à lui tracer en grand les premiers Principes de cette Théologie sublime, que l'Astronomie devoit enrichir un jour, & dont il étoit réservé à la Métaphysique de démontrer les grandes vérités' (Bonnet 1796a, 1:241; B.O., 7:176/15:259). Bonnet's theory represented thus simply a further exploration of these 'great truths'.

The past revolutions of the globe, including the Mosaic Creation, were all designed to lead to that future revolution predicted in the Bible that would

11. See also Whitman (1895b:251-55) and Gould (1977:17-28).

12. Bonnet did not clarify how the rotation of the ecliptic could prove the age of the world (see Bonnet 1769a, 1:258-59; B.O., 7:191/15:279-80). He based his calculations on a discussion of the obliquity question in Dortous de Mairan's *Lettres de M. de Mairan, au R.P. Parrenin* (1759:112-13).

culminate in the final Day of Judgement. Bonnet cited the Second Epistle of Peter, in which the future destruction of the Earth by fire is foretold (II Peter iii.7 and 10-13; Bonnet 1769a, 1:175, 257; B.O., 7:122, 189/15:181, 277).[13] Such a revolution, he maintained, would bring forth a new order of life on Earth, one in which each type of living organism would be more perfect than it had been in its previous form. Human beings would emerge in their 'glorious and spiritual body' and would be judged for their past actions.

Bonnet's geological ideas concerning the history of the Earth were thus closely tied to his palingenetic vision of the world. One can argue that he was more interested in providing a physical basis for his notion of the future perfectability of germs and their ultimate resurrection than he was in offering an empirical theory of the Earth. He needed to show how, in one unique act, God could have preformed the cosmos and all of its inhabitants to evolve slowly and inexorably to the future revolution that would bring the final resurrection. Bonnet thus could counter the unbelievers by offering a natural explanation for the truths of revealed religion as well as a physical basis for morality. He did not enter into any of the geological controversies of his day because they were in some sense irrelevant to his purposes. His grand vision of the universe was thus an *a priori* synthesis of natural history, geology, psychology, and revealed religion – and his ultimate goal was to ward off social immorality.

Although Needham read Bonnet's *Palingénésie* with great interest and commented on it extensively in letter 40, he did not discuss Bonnet's cosmogony, criticising rather his metaphysics and explanation of miracles (see section 4 of this Introduction). Nor did Bonnet discuss Needham's views on cosmogony any further in his letters. Both had turned to cosmogony for the same reasons – to combat the unbelievers – and both developed explanations for the history of the Earth that dovetailed with their own religious, metaphysical, and biological beliefs. Perhaps this is the reason they commented so little on each other's cosmogonies, for their differences in biology and metaphysics had already been so clearly manifested. To criticise each other's views on the history of the Earth would have been to reopen the metaphysical and biological debate that had resulted in a stalemate. As Bonnet put it with regard to generation, they differed so markedly in their views that he saw no reason to continue discussing them (letter 36).

Needham mentioned his own views on the theory of the Earth once more, in letter 48, when he was explaining to Bonnet the rationale that had underlain his work on generation and on metaphysics. Remarking that his cosmogony differed from Buffon's as much as his theory of generation did, Needham explained that he had set forth his own theory of the Earth 'pour obvier aux mauvaises consequences, que les Impies tirent tous les jours de la sienne contre la chronologie de Moyse'. The theory that he had presented had been well received by the better naturalists of the day, he claimed, and it had profoundly influenced Buffon as well. 'Non seulement il adopte dans ses ouvrages posterieurs,' Needham explained, 'mes idées sur la force expansive developpant la terre par degrés, et sur l'activité du feu comme agent universel depuis le

---

13. See also section 4 of this Introduction.

commencement du monde, mais il s'accorde avec moi sur l'explication, que j'ai donnée de six jours de la generation du ciel, et de la terre pris pour six periodes d'un tems inconnu' (28 October [September] 1779, letter 48). What Needham was claiming here was that in Buffon's most recent geological work, the *Epoques de la nature* (1779),[14] the addition of the concept of central heat and the organisation of the formation of the Earth into seven epochs were the direct result of Needham's book on cosmogony.

Although Needham's claim may have some validity, it is not easy to verify. We know that Needham and Buffon discussed cosmogony together, for in the opening paragraph of his letter to Buffon in his treatise on cosmogony, Needham stated that, 'Vous pouvez vous rappeller, Monsieur, qu'il y a quelque tems qu'examinant ensemble dans les Livres de *Moyse* l'histoire de la création, nous cherchâmes à développer le sens caché de cette phrase obscure & remarquable, le soir & le matin firent un jour' (Spallanzani 1769, pt.2:1). This letter was dated 27 March 1767, after Needham had been living in Paris for nine months; and it is very likely that the discussions he referred to took place during this period.[15]

The principal changes that Buffon made in his theory of the Earth for the *Epoques* were the addition of a concept of a central heat that is continually cooling and the division of the history of the globe into seven epochs. Buffon outlined a dynamic developmental sequence of events on Earth, beginning with an initial molten globe, then passing from an Earth covered with water to the emergence of land and the separation of the continents, and culminating in the emergence of human societies. As in Buffon's earlier theory of the Earth, the actions of the sea played the major role in the shaping of the Earth's features, with the addition of a greater role for volcanic activity and the influence of a slowly cooling central heat.

Roger (Buffon 1962:xxvii-xxviii) has argued that it was in 1766 or, at the latest, in the early months of 1767 that Buffon developed his notion of a progressively cooling Earth, stimulated in part by his encountering Jean-Jacques Dortous de Mairan's ideas on the central heat of the Earth.[16] In the spring of 1767, Buffon began his own experiments on the heating and cooling of globes of varying diameters and materials. We know that Buffon and Needham were in contact during this period, at least in February 1767, when Needham contacted Buffon concerning the Royal Society's request to receive volumes of the *Histoire naturelle* (see letter 6, n.5). The question is, then, did Needham influence to any extent the development of Buffon's new ideas on cosmogony and theory of the Earth? Needham claimed in particular that Buffon had 'adopted' his own ideas on the influence of the interior expansive force in the development of the Earth and also his account of the six days of Creation and six periods of unknown length.

14. See letter 48, n.4.

15. Needham and Buffon were in personal contact during at least three periods (and possibly more): in the late 1740s, in 1764, and in 1767 (see letter 6, n.5).

16. Buffon referred in the *Epoques* to the fourth edition of Mairan's *Dissertation sur la glace* (1749), which was the first edition to contain the theory of central heat. Roger (Buffon 1962:xxvii n.2) has suggested that Buffon learned of this work through a mémoire Mairan read to the Académie des sciences in 1765 (see Mairan 1767 and 1768).

First of all, since we know that the major components of Buffon's theory of the Earth as presented in the *Epoques* were formulated during 1766 and 1767 (Buffon 1962:xxvii-xxx), then it could not have been by reading Needham's treatise on cosmogony that Buffon could have been influenced by Needham's ideas, since this work was not published until 1769 (althouth it was available by December 1768; see letter 32). Thus, only personal contact between them in 1766 or 1767 could have played any role in the development of Buffon's new views. But is there any internal evidence in the *Epoques* itself to support Needham's claims?

It would seem unlikely that Needham's views on the interior expansive force influenced Buffon's ideas on central heat to any great degree. Not only has a different stimulus been identified in the work of Dortous de Mairan, but there is also a great deal of difference between Needham's force and Buffon's cooling central heat. Thus, even if Buffon was somehow made aware of Needham's ideas on this subject in 1767, there is no evidence to suggest that they influenced him in the fundamental way that Needham claimed.

With regard to Buffon's division of the development of the Earth into seven epochs, this again may be more of a coincidental similarity than any direct influence of Needham. In the seventeenth and eighteenth centuries, as we have already mentioned, the idea that the six 'days' were not twenty-four-hour days was quite common. So Buffon could have come across the notion in any number of places. Furthermore, although Buffon included a discussion of Genesis in the *Epoques*, in which he argued that his account of the development of the Earth did not threaten the truth of the Mosaic account (Buffon 1749-1789, *Supplément*, 5:28-39), the points that Buffon made bear no obvious similarity to the arguments Needham advanced on the same topic. Buffon rested his case on two principal claims: that there was a long period of time between God's initial creation of matter and its being organised and formed into the Earth that we know, and that the Bible is a book of religion and morals that made use of common language and beliefs to express its intent. Thus one should not take its wording literally on scientific issues. The first of these arguments was never advanced by Needham, and the second was articulated by him in a somewhat different fashion. It may well be that he and Buffon conferred on the interpretation of the days of Creation in their discussions of the Mosaic story. Yet since Buffon's expressed attempt to reconcile his scientific views with Genesis was so different from Needham's, one cannot conclude that there was too close an influence on this point either.

We also have Needham's own testimony that their discussions on cosmogony were probably not very extensive. In his letter to Buffon in his treatise on cosmogony, Needham also remarked, 'J'aurois pû vous répondre sur le champ à la question qui occasionne cette lettre, car il y a long-tems que j'ai une opinion sur ce sujet; mais j'ai jugé que la matiere étoit trop délicate pour être traitée par la voie de la conversation, & j'ai imaginé que la correspondance seule du cabinet pourroit l'éclaircir' (Spallanzani 1769, pt.2:5). When he claimed to Bonnet that he had been responsible for the changes in Buffon's views, the impression given is that Needham thought it was through reading this letter and the remainder of his treatise that Buffon had been influenced. He could well have thought this was the case, since Buffon's *Epoques* did not appear until ten years after Needham's treatise was published, even though Buffon's new theory was formulated much earlier (something Needham was not necessarily aware of). In sum, then, both internal and circumstantial evidence suggests that Needham's boast to Bonnet would seem to be more wishful thinking on Needham's part than actual fact.

The general question remains, however, did the geological views of Needham or Bonnet have any impact on their contemporaries and successors at all? It would seem not. None of the major geological figures of the late eighteenth century that one might expect to have discussed either of them made any mention of their theories.[17] One might have expected that Needham's theory, being more geological than Bonnet's, would have received some attention.[18] But it apparently did not. One might also have expected Bonnet's view of the Earth's successive revolutions to have influenced later catastrophists. But even though figures like Georges Cuvier and Louis Agassiz were aware of Bonnet's work in general, they did not acknowledge his notion of revolution, perhaps because his views were simply too speculative to be mentioned at all.[19] It is useful here to reiterate Roger's point about why Buffon's *Epoques* had so little impact on his contemporaries (Buffon 1962:lix-lx). By the time this work was published in the early 1770s, geology was taking a turn away from grand syntheses and toward empirical investigations of limited scope. Needham's and Bonnet's cosmogonical systems, both published in 1769, would seem to have encountered this difficulty as well. The universal visions of Buffon, Needham, and Bonnet were no longer the guiding rubric in theories of the Earth. Nor were Bonnet and Needham successful in rescuing cosmogony from the materialists, for in d'Holbach's *Système de la nature* (1770), geological arguments concerning the origin of the universe from matter played a key role. Yet within each of their own viewpoints, Needham and Bonnet both accomplished what they set out to do when they turned to cosmogony: to offer an explanation for the origin and history of the Earth that would complement their biological views and that would at the same time further, rather than threaten, the promotion of revealed religion and a moral social order.

17. We have been unable to find any discussion of the geological ideas of either Bonnet or Needham in the published works of Guettard, Desmarest, de Luc, or Lamétherie (see also letter 50, n.12). We are grateful to Rhoda Rappaport, Kenneth Taylor, and Clarissa Campbell-Orr for their assistance on this question.

18. Needham's treatise was certainly not unknown, since it formed the second part of a book that was widely circulated (Spallanzani 1769). Reviews of this work contained discussions not only of Spallanzani's treatise and Needham's notes but also of Needham's treatise on cosmogony; see the favourable summaries in Fréron's *L'Année littéraire* (1768, 8:238-44) and in the *Journal encyclopédique* (1 July 1769, 5, pt.1:52-63). Haller's review in the *Göttingische Anzeigen von gelehrten Sachen* (7 July 1770, pp.699-704) contained a brief discussion of Needham's views on mountain-building.

19. Cuvier wrote an éloge on Bonnet, but his geological ideas were not mentioned (Cuvier 1819-27:383-409). Nor are they referred to in Cuvier's published writings on the revolutions of the Earth. Agassiz referred to Bonnet in his *Essay on classification* but only to his concept of a chain of being and to his work on parthenogenesis (Agassiz 1859:36 n.2, 139 n.2). For a discussion of the concept of 'revolution' in eighteenth-century geology (but not including Bonnet's views), see Rappaport (1982).

8. Bonnet and the Genevan political crisis, 1765-1768

THE Bonnet-Needham correspondence contains a number of references both to political events in Geneva during the years 1765 to 1768 and to the political activity Bonnet engaged in during that period (letters 23-24, 26-30). With one exception (Gaullieur 1855), neither the historical literature on Bonnet nor that on eighteenth-century Genevan politics[1] has investigated either Bonnet's political ideas or his political involvement. This omission can probably be attributed to the reticence of his early biographers, who, writing during the period of the French revolutionary occupation of Geneva, deliberately glossed over his political leanings.[2] In the politically revolutionary climate of the 1790s his image became the object of partisan popular historiographic distortion. In Geneva both Rousseau and Bonnet were raised to the level of 'Pères de la Patrie', and their portraits were placed side by side in the streets (see fig.16).[3] The only justification for such an association was the European reputation of both men and Genevan patriotic pride, but it was to prove misleading in view of their consistently divergent opinions on both the cultural and political planes.

It is the aim of this introductory section to delineate some aspects of Bonnet's political activity, following the chronological sequence of events that occurred in the years 1765 to 1768. As far as his own political ideas are concerned, it seems sufficient to recall that he was strongly influenced by his early reading of Montesquieu's *De l'esprit des lois* (see letter 24, n.19), whose political tenets he tried to apply to the political situation in Geneva, where he had been active as a member of the Council of Two Hundred since 1752. It should also be remembered, at a general level, that the constitutional conflict in which he took part marked the high point of a prolonged struggle between the ruling patriciate and the burghers and saw the beginning of the slow political emergence of the social group known as the Natives (*Natifs*), that is, the three-quarters of Geneva's population who were not citizens and had no political rights. Although this constitutional conflict was local and outwardly appeared no more than 'a teapot tempest' (Palmer 1959-1964, 1:112), it had a vast international resonance, in addition to some more immediate political repercussions. This resulted from a combination of factors: the peculiar political, geographic, and religious position of the Republic of Geneva; the presence in Geneva of the major international watch-making trade; the large number of publications that accompanied every development in the dispute; the earlier polemics that had been aroused by d'Alembert's article on Geneva in the *Encyclopédie*; the part played in the conflict

---

1. For secondary literature on Geneva's constitutional crisis of 1765-1768, see letter 24, n.1.

2. See, for example, Saussure [1793], [J. Trembley] (1794), and [Lévesque de Pouilly] (1794). Another reason is, of course, that Bonnet did not publish his political speeches in his *Œuvres* and that his autobiography was not published until 1948 (Savioz 1948b).

3. For a parallel of Bonnet and Rousseau, see Anspach (1793) and the anonymous *Abrégé de l'histoire de Geneve* (Neuchâtel 1798).

by men of international reputation such as Rousseau and Voltaire; and the fact that Geneva was one of the obligatory stopping-places on the Grand Tour.

Geneva was a cosmopolitan city, one of the capitals of the Protestant world, almost completely surrounded by Catholic countries, with a population of about twenty thousand people and a territory of about seventy square miles. From the Edict of 1738 up to the early 1760s, Geneva enjoyed a period of internal peace and flourishing economy. The Edict had put an end, by the mediation of the Kingdom of France and the Republics of Bern and Zürich, to the conflict that had arisen between burghers and patricians. It should be remembered that originally the population enjoying political rights and economic privileges was formed exclusively by *Citoyens et Bourgeois*. However, during the seventeenth and early eighteenth centuries, a group of families of *Citoyens et Bourgeois* using the mechanism of reciprocal election in the Small and Great Councils, had assured that the greatest concentration of power rested in their hands. The election of new members to the Great Council (or Council of Two Hundred) was made by members of the Small Council (or Council of Twenty-five), and the election of members of the Small Council, by those of the Great Council. This is the origin of the distinction between these powerful families (the Patriciate), who built a small organised oligarchy, and the remaining burghers, whose political involvement was relegated mainly to attending the General Council once a year and to electing the Syndics and other magistrates whose names were presented to them by the Small Council. Thus, while both patricians and burghers were *Citoyens et Bourgeois* and were therefore *de iure* politically equal, the patricians in fact enjoyed greater power, as they occupied almost all the seats on the Small and Great Councils, which between them determined policy.

The social peace that followed the Edict of 1738 favoured a period of economic expansion, prosperity, and urban renovation. The Edict brought about some alteration in the ancient republican institutions of Calvin's city, and became the major constitutional charter of the new political and social order of the Genevan territory. Furthermore the Edict was guaranteed by the three foreign powers that had been instrumental as arbitrators, thus ensuring its acceptance by the *Citoyens et Bourgeois*. One of the main points in the Edict related to the rights attributed to the General Council, that is, the assembly attended by all *Citoyens et Bourgeois*, which was numerically dominated by the burghers. The General Council was empowered to either accept or reject the laws presented by the two other councils; and it alone had the right of voting taxes and of electing or rejecting the Syndics, the Attorney General, and other magistrates, all of whom, however, had to be chosen from lists of names presented by the other two councils. The General Council was also asked to approve treaties with foreign countries, war declarations, and any alienation of parts of the Genevan territory (Art. III of the Edict). Its legislative power was however very limited. Members had the right to make 'representations' to the Syndics and the Small Council (Art. VII), but these could not be discussed directly by the General Council. Such representations generally consisted of remonstrations and petitions but could also contain proposals for new regulations. They were presented to the Syndics and the Small Council (the true centre both of legislative and executive power and the stonghold of the Patriciate), which, after examining them, could

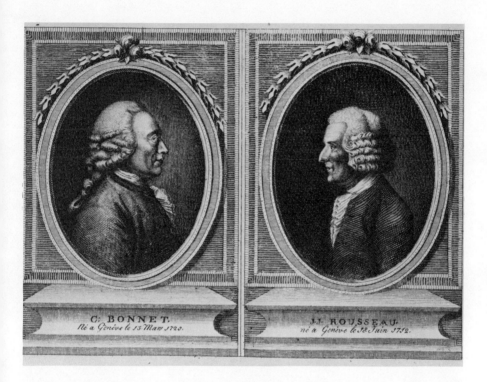

Fig. 16. Bonnet and Rousseau, 'Pères de la Patrie'. (From *Abrégé de l'histoire de Geneve*, 1798. Courtesy of the Bibliothèque Publique et Universitaire, Geneva.)

either accept or reject them. In the case of rejection, the legislative process initiated by members of the General Council came to an end. In the case of acceptance, however, the representations were then put forward to the Great Council. Only if the latter approved them were they presented to the General Council for their definitive approval or rejection.

The social peace gained with the Edict of 1738 and the unchallenged political predominance of the Patriciate, which as time passed grew increasingly dependent on Versailles, was threatened by an event that seemed superficially a small incident, but that in fact catalysed the burgher's resentment against the social and political hegemony of the patricians and marked the beginning of a deep-seated constitutional conflict between the two groups. On 19 June 1762, on the basis of a report by the Attorney General, the mathematician Jean-Robert Tronchin, the Small Council condemned Rousseau's *Emile* and *Contrat social* to be torn up and burned, and put Rousseau himself under threat of arrest should he attempt to enter Genevan territory. Although this decision elicited some adverse comment from a few burghers, it did not produce any significant immediate reaction (see Candaux in R.O., 3:clxiii). The only criticism to appear in print was a letter written by colonel Charles Pictet, a member of the Council of Two Hundred (the Great Council), who condemned the action of the Small Council, alleging that it had acted under pressure from Voltaire and with an eye to pleasing the Court of Versailles. As a result, Pictet was deprived of his membership in the Council of Two Hundred and sentenced to jail after a formally irregular trial. On 12 May 1763, after the Small Council forbade the reprinting of his *Lettre à Christophe de Beaumont*, Rousseau resigned his citizenship (Leigh, 2686). A few days later on 26 May he wrote to some of his Genevan supporters, such as Marc Chappuis (Leigh, 2726), lamenting their lack of protest in the face of the action undertaken against him by his own country. Rousseau's ideas on the voluntary participation of the people in all acts of the political community, and on the possibility of changing the form of government and removing public officers, were now beginning to be more widely shared by some of his compatriots. It was at this point that, on 18 June 1763, a delegation of about forty citizens and burghers submitted representations[4] to the first Syndic concerning the condemnation of Rousseau's books in 1762 and the legal action taken against Pictet. On 25 June the Small Council rejected the representations. During the summer the same representations were again submitted and again rejected. On 20 August a letter signed by 480 citizens demanded that both questions be submitted to the General Council. On 31 August Jean-Robert Tronchin answered that this was not in conformity with the Edict of 1738, and that the Small Council alone had the right to establish whether the representations were legally well founded, thus asserting its power of veto, which soon came to be known as *droit négatif*. Meanwhile, two parties were forming: one favourable to the government, consisting of patricians, who were named *Négatifs*; the other opposed to the government and formed by burghers, who became known as *Représentants*.

---

4. *Representations des Citoyens et Bourgeois de Geneve au Premier Sindic de cette république; avec les réponses du Conseil à ces representations* (1763).

Between the end of September and the end of October 1763, an anonymous pamphlet entitled *Lettres écrites de la campagne* was published on two separate occasions. It was the work of the patrician Jean-Robert Tronchin, the Attorney General, and contained an apology for the conduct of the Small Council. While this work silenced the *Représentants*, it provoked the polemic vigour of Rousseau, who at once set to work to provide an answer. In November 1764 Rousseau's reply was published at Amsterdam, and copies of it were already circulating in Geneva in early December. A personal defence and a defence of his own works and of the theories he had expounded, the *Lettres écrites de la montagne* were also an analysis of Genevan political conflicts, in which the Genevan refugee showed a deep understanding of both the political and institutional history of his own country (see Candaux in R.O., 3:clxxxii-cxcviii).

In Geneva the effects of the publication of Rousseau's book were impressive. A year of political lethargy suddenly came to an end. The younger burghers all supported Rousseau. The Small Council did not even dare to condemn the work in which Rousseau argued that since the Small Council had the legal right of vetoing proposals for new legislation, it could not sit in judgement on itself when accused of violating the law. Furthermore Rousseau showed that, while the citizens of Geneva were theoretically sovereign, they were in fact impotent (R.O., 3:813-15):

En Conseil général vous êtes Législateurs, Souverains, indépendans de toute puissance humaine; vous ratifiez les traités, vous décidez de la paix et de la guerre; vos Magistrats eux-mêmes vous traitent de *Magnifiques, très honorés et souverains Seigneurs*. Voila votre liberté: voici votre servitude. [...]

En Conseil général votre Souveraine puissance est enchaînée: vous ne pouvez agir que quand il plait à vos Magistrats, ni parler que quand ils vous interrogent. S'ils veulent même ne point assembler de Conseil général, votre autorité, votre existence est anéantie, sans que vous puissiez leur opposer que de vains murmures qu'ils sont en possession de mépriser.

Enfin si vous êtes Souverains Seigneurs dans l'assemblée, en sortant de-là vous n'êtes plus rien. Quatre heures par an Souverains subordonnés, vous êtes sujets le reste de la vie et livrés sans réserve à la discrétion d'autrui.

A number of pamphlets both for and against Rousseau's views were published by the *Représentants* and the *Négatifs*. The Small Council was driven to the point of considering mass resignation. On 7 February 1765 the burghers, while asserting their loyalty to the constitution, reiterated their representations and asked that a meeting of the General Council be called in order to interpret article 88 of Calvin's *Ordonnances ecclésiastiques*, which regulated the procedures for the inquisition of those suspected of erring in matters of faith. It was the failure to observe these procedures that, according to the *Représentants*, invalidated the condemnation of Rousseau's works.[5] In the same month, Rousseau wrote to his correspondents in Geneva that he was withdrawing from the dispute (Leigh, 4052, 4075). The representations of the burghers were rejected by the Small Council with the exception of one regarding regulations of wine imports. At this point Voltaire proposed his own mediation in the controversy, but his offer was turned down (Gay 1965:210-14). The patricians, on the other hand, after the

5. *Representation des Citoyens & Bourgeois remise à Messieurs les Sindics le 7 Février 1765.*

shock caused by Rousseau's answer, started to organise themselves and mounted a counter-offensive. It was in this context that Bonnet, like many other *Négatifs*, entered actively upon the scene.

On 1 April 1765 Bonnet, fearing the spectre of democratic reform, made a speech in the Great Council, of which he was a member, that was on the one hand a defence of the government and, on the other, a criticism of its excessive caution and insufficient rigour. He attacked Rousseau fiercely, condemning his *Lettres écrites de la montagne* as an 'Ouvrage de ténèbres, qu'on ne lisoit d'abord que dans les ténèbres', a 'production monstrueuse', and a 'Libelle abominable'.[6] He also attacked those burghers who were guilty, in his eyes, of having published a representation in which they had voiced indecent and scandalous remarks, which were injurious to the honour and dignity of the government. In addition he criticised the government for its feeble actions, for not having condemned 'au feu un Livre fait pour le feu' (f.4), and for not having reacted with vigour and unity to the intemperate demands of the burghers. It was his conviction that such feebleness strengthened the opposition instead of weakening it. He therefore called for firmness and resolution, and added four pieces of practical advice. First, he suggested that the laws of the fatherland should be studied more than the laws of the Ancients, and that such study should be directed toward understanding the spirit rather than the letter of the law. Secondly, he recommended that the government should not only observe the laws itself, but should also enforce others to observe them by means of reinforcing the police. Thirdly, he expressed his belief that any representation altering the constitution should be firmly rejected; and fourthly, he called for a greater unity between the members of the Small and Great Councils, because it was their unity that provided 'le salut de la République' (f.9). It is clear that Bonnet regarded all the actions of the *Représentants* as an attack on the oligarchical hegemony, and thus he would not accept any kind of compromise.

It was traditional in the Great Council to devote the first Monday of May to questions relating to the *Bien public*. On this occasion (6 May 1765), Bonnet made a new speech, devoted this time to 'la Liberté et l'Amour de la Patrie'. His intention was to discredit the reiterated declarations of *amor patriae* made by the burghers, and their statement that the representations 'n'ont eu d'autre but que le maintien de notre heureuse constitution'.[7] He argued:

Comment donc s'est-il trouvé parmi nous des Citoyens, qui faisant profession du respect le plus profond pour cette Loi, ont été assés inconsiderés, assés ennemis du repos public ou assés peu éclairés pour élever et soutenir avec opiniatreté des Prétentions qui attaquoient la Constitution jusques dans son Principe? Comment est-il arrivé, que quelques idées folles qui n'étoient dabord que dans la Tête d'un Seul Citoyen [Rousseau], ont passé avec tant de rapidité dans la Tête d'un si grand nombre de Citoyens, et leur ont persuadé que le Gouvernement le plus débonnaire qui soit sur la Terre, étoit le plus tyrannique? C'est que l'ambition ou le mécontentement dans le Chef de Parti se sert des Loix contre les Loix mêmes: c'est que le Peuple a plus de passions que de lumières: c'est qu'il est en general plus fait pour sentir que pour penser; c'est qu'il n'est rien qui le remuë plus fortement que la Liberté, & sur quoi il soit plus facile de lui en imposer.

---

6. 'Ecrits politiques', II: 'Discours prononcé au Grand Conseil le lundi 1.er Avril 1765 sur les circonstances actuelles de la République', BPUG, MS Bonnet 16:3, 4.

7. *Representation des Citoyens & Bourgeois remise à Messieurs les Sindics le 7 Février 1765*, p.1.

Donnés moi une demi douzaine de Citoyens qui ayent de bons Poûmons, & qui crient du matin au Soir *Tyrannie! Tyrannie!* le Peuple repetera aussi tot *Tyrannie*; il la verra par tout, & jusqu'au sein de la prosperité & dans les Actes les plus paterneles: il cherchera la Liberté où elle n'est point; il ne la découvrira point où elle est, et les Chefs de Parti profitant habilement de ses méprises, les feront servir à leurs fins.[8]

Liberty, according to Bonnet, was neither a feeling nor a sensation, but a science: the science of laws. If the people intended to judge their own legitimate magistrates, he claimed, they should first of all judge their own party leaders. But how could such an aim be achieved if, as in the present circumstances, the people were under the effects of an 'enchantement politique, aidé de la dangereuse Magie du Sophiste [Rousseau] le plus artificieux' (f.7), who stirred up spurious, not genuine patriotism. With strong anti-Rousseauist emphasis Bonnet declared (ff.8-9):

Souveraines Seigneures! c'est dans la Science de la Liberté, qu'il faut chercher les vrayes sources de l'Amour de la Patrie. Les Peuples Esclaves ont des demeures ou plutôt des Prisons, & point de Patrie. Les Peuples Sauvages ont des retraites & sont sans Patrie: c'est que des Maisons & des Bois ne font pas une Patrie. Le Peuple Libre a seul une Patrie; il connoit seul toute la valeur de ce mot si doux à prononcer, *la Patrie*. La Patrie est donc une moralité; elle resulte de la réunion des Volontés & des Forces d'un certain nombre d'Homme qui s'opère par le ministère des Loix pour leur bonheur commun. L'Amour de la Patrie est donc *l'Amour des Loix*, et cet amour n'est autre chose que l'attachement le plus vif & le plus éclairé pour la Constitution. Il conduit nécessairement à l'amour & au respect dus aux Ministres des Loix & aux Dépositaires de la Constitution. Il est le germe précieux de toutes les Vertus Patriotiques, & le Patriotisme embrasse dans ses heureux effets tous les Ordres tous les Individus. Le vrai Patriotte est l'Esclave volontaire des Loix; il porte dans son Cœur ses Concitoyens, comme il y porte la Patrie, dont ils sont les Enfans, le Soutien & l'esperance. Son respect pour les Loix est si vrai, si profond, qu'il ose à peine fixer la pensée d'y faire des changemens utiles. Il jouit du bien, sans oser chercher le mieux, par la crainte raisonnable du pire. Il ne nourrit dans son Ame qu'une Seule passion, celle du Bien Public. Débiteur éternel de la Patrie, il ne croit pas de pouvoir jamais s'acquiter auprès d'elle.

By opposing true to false liberty, true to false patriotism, Bonnet managed to characterise the political activity of the burghers as a form of despotism, and that of the patricians as enlightened and paternal administration. While the former would destroy the state and the country, the latter maintained it.

The political struggle continued throughout 1765. In the autumn the General Council was called on five occasions to elect the magistrates. Each time they were rejected. The burghers in the General Council had adopted a tactic, technically correct, that was known as 'ligne de nouvelle élection'. It consisted in the unlimited use of the right of refusing to elect the candidates proposed by the Small Council (Ivernois 1782:223-28). As a result, normal administration came to a standstill in the absence of newly elected magistrates, and the government felt compelled, on 31 December, to appeal to the foreign powers that had guaranteed the Edict of 1738 for a new arbitration in the internal conflict. On 22 March 1766 the Ministers Plenipotentiary of the Kingdom of France and of the Republics of Bern and Zürich entered the city of Geneva. As

8. 'Ecrits politiques', III: 'Discours prononcé au Grand Conseil le lundi 6.ᵉ de Mai 1765, sur la Liberté & l'Amour de la Patrie', BPUG, MS Bonnet 16:5-6.

head of a delegation of members of the Great Council, Bonnet made three speeches of welcome, one for each minister, in which he underlined the fact that he had been a witness to the regularity of the administration carried out by the Genevan magistrates and defended them against any possible criticism.[9] The *Négatifs* exerted considerable pressure to ensure that the only interlocutor of the Guarantors was the government itself and that all contact with delegations of burghers was avoided. At first, however, each of the Ministers Plenipotentiary appeared to be open-minded and tolerant; but the attitude of the French Minister, the chevalier de Beauteville, soon changed. He was influenced by several factors: the hard line assumed by the French Foreign Minister, the duc de Choiseul; the sympathy for the Patriciate evinced by his personal secretary; and a petition he received from Genevan patricians. The patricians insisted that the first public act of the Guarantors should be a declaration stating that all charges made against the Genevan magistrates were unsubstantiated, insulting, and unjustified. This was in fact the content of the Declaration made by the Ministers Plenipotentiary on 25 July 1766, which thus represented a true triumph for the *Négatifs* (Ivernois 1782:255). It was this same Declaration that Bonnet hastily sent to Needham and to Adam Smith (letter 23, n.23).

At this point it is interesting to note Needham's changing attitudes toward the development of the political struggle in Geneva, which he had been observing as a temporary resident there from August 1765 to May 1766. Needham was a good witness, since he knew a number of patricians personally and occasionally sat at the tables of Jean-Robert Tronchin and of the chevalier de Beauteville. He relayed much of the information gleaned from these contacts to his friend Honoré-Auguste Sabatier de Cabre, Secretary to the French Ambassador at the Court of Turin, to whom he also sent all the major pamphlets concerning the dispute.[10] After his arrival in Geneva, Needham soon became pessimistic and wrote bluntly that 'la ville de Geneve se trouve à present assise sur les ruines de l'evangile, grace à Calvin, à Rousseau, et à notre ami Voltaire' (letter to Sabatier of 13 August 1765, BLUL). He regarded Tronchin's *Lettres écrites de la campagne* as a masterpiece, but believed that the arguments put forward were far too rational to be accepted by the burghers. As time passed, however, his attitude changed. He realised that the radicalisation of the conflict had resulted from the magistrates' apparent refusal to accept that the General Council was 'the legislative power, sole Law-giver, and sole interpreter of the code' (letter of 8 April 1766, BLUL). Furthermore he foresaw that the burghers would be enraged by the magistrates' appeal to foreign powers for arbitration, because the burghers considered it their right to settle grievances without foreign intervention. It was, however, the conduct of the burghers that caused Needham's change of heart. Contrary to his initial fears, he saw no sign of anarchism and admired both their orderly procedures and the rational principles upon which they based their discussions. A few weeks before leaving Geneva, he felt, unlike Bonnet, that in the long run it was the unlimited use of the *droit négatif* on the

9. The welcome speech for the Minister Plenipotentiary of the Kingdom of France, 'Ecrits politiques', III (BPUG, MS Bonnet 16) was inserted by Bonnet in his autobiography (Savioz 1948b:222-23).
10. See Needham's letters to Sabatier de Cabre in the BLUL.

part of the Small Council that might well lead to real despotism. Needham left Geneva in the hope that the mediation would produce a result favourable to the burghers (letter of 15 April 1766, BLUL).

Between the end of March 1766 and June of the same year, Bonnet, together with his friend the naturalist Abraham Trembley, met the Ministers Plenipotentiary several times and furnished them with two manuscript reports of his own. He also exerted active pressure through his almost daily correspondence with Albrecht von Haller, who had been charged by the government of the Republic of Bern to follow Geneva's constitutional crisis closely. The unanimity of Bonnet's and Haller's political opinions, their common horror of any greater democratic participation in the administration of the State, their deep religious feelings, their hatred of Rousseau's ideas, and their mistrust of the philosophes made them both the natural allies of the more conservative elements in the Patriciate.

Bonnet's first report was delivered to the Ministers Plenipotentiary on 5 May 1766, and was entitled 'Vuës politiques'. It set forth the most recent political events and urged that the Guarantors make a solemn declaration in favour of the conduct of the magistrates during the crisis. As Bonnet himself recalled in his autobiography, his report was inspired by 'l'admirable tableau que Montesquieu trace de la Constitution anglaise' (Savioz 1948b:224). It also contained one of Bonnet's most deep-rooted convictions. The people, a term by which he meant only the burghers and neither the *Natifs* nor the peasants, were capable, according to the Genevan scientist, only of 'sentir, désirer et s'agiter'.[11] They had no 'head' and for this reason were often swayed by demagogues, who became their unnatural 'head', their clandestine leaders. The danger was that if 'une sorte d'inspection generale' was granted to the people, this might well be used solely by the 'Chefs secrets du Peuple' (f.2) to increase their personal power to the detriment of the *Bien Public*.

On 19 May 1766 Bonnet handed over to the Ministers Plenipotentiary a second report entitled 'Questions sur le Droit Négatif'. By employing Montesquieu's method of political analysis, Bonnet tried to clarify the major topic under discussion. He did allow the people 'une sorte d'inspection generale'[12] over the government, because he believed that the executive power should be subject to some kind of public accountability operating through the people's 'droit de représentation'. At the same time, however, he granted to the executive power a moral defensive force, which took the form of the 'droit négatif', which he considered might more appropriately be called 'droit défensif' (f.3). If the executive (the Small Council), which had no physical powers of enforcement, did not have the right to reject without possibility of appeal the representations made by some members of the General Council, it would, according to Bonnet, soon be deprived of its executive power. The result of this would be that legislative power would take over the executive function. Bonnet considered the *droit négatif* and the *droit de représentation* as two moral forces that always had to be kept in balance. This report by Bonnet also illustrates his political tactics.

11. 'Ecrits politiques', v: 'Vuës Politiques', BPUG, MS Bonnet 16:1.
12. 'Ecrits politiques', vi: 'Questions sur le Droit Négatif', BPUG, MS Bonnet 16:1.

If, as he wished, the Guarantors were to make a solemn statement that the executive had not misused its power, it would be sufficient to restate the constitutional validity of the use of the *droit négatif* by the executive to bring the disputes to an end, at least on the legal level. However, Bonnet was quite aware that it was the unlimited use of the *droit négatif* that had exasperated the burghers. He therefore suggested not that it should be modified, but that it should be transferred from the Small Council to an intermediate body, the Council of Sixty (which already existed but which at the time had no constitutional power). This was Bonnet's only concession to the demands of the burghers.

After the Guarantors published their Declaration on 25 July 1766, Bonnet made a speech on 4 August in which he thanked them profusely for their impartiality and their scrupulous attention in handling the problem. He rejoiced in the title of 'Pères de la Patrie' they had bestowed on the magistrates of Geneva,[13] and exhorted his fellow citizens to eradicate any despotic attitudes from their hearts and to be true patriots, this being a precondition of their accepting the results of the new mediation: 'Travaillons donc à devenir plus indépendans de nos Idées, de nos Gouts, de nos Préjugés, de nos Habitudes. Préparons nous à recevoir avec une raisonnable docilité tout ce qui sera proposé pour le plus grand Bien general. Faisons passer la Charruë dans nôtre Cerveau pour le disposer à recevoir de nouvelles semences. Et plaise au Ciel qu'elle extirpe en même tems toutes les Semences qui pourroient nuire à cette heureuse reconciliation, qui doit être l'Objet de nos Vœux les plus ardens!'[14] When a rift developed between the Small and Great Councils in August 1766, Bonnet once more called for unity of action and intention on the part of the two bodies and asked them to abandon 'l'Esprit de Corps', which he saw as antithetical to true patriotism.[15] He was in fact afraid that division among patricians would weaken their cause. While the Ministers Plenipotentiary were undertaking their laborious investigations prior to putting forward their project of pacification, which included some constitutional modifications, Bonnet exerted himself to convince them that these should only be minor changes, such as enlarging the membership of the Great Council. He made critical annotations to his colleagues' reports that were later to be handed to the Ministers, and incessantly warned his colleagues that a political constitution had to be conceived as an integral set of relations, customs, institutions, and traditions, as 'la chose du monde la plus composée',[16] sustained by an internal harmony that could easily be upset by the most trivial alteration.

13. 'Ecrits politiques', VII: 'Discours prononcé au Grand Conseil le Lundi 4.ᵉ d'Aoust 1766. à l'occasion de la Déclaration des Seig.ʳˢ Médiateurs du 25.ᵉ de Juillet et de l'Ouverture de la nouvelle Médiation', BPUG, MS Bonnet 16:2. In the Declaration this title was not actually given to the magistrates, but it was stated that their administration 'a été légale, intégre, modérée & paternelle: qu'il s'est montré constamment animé du desir le plus sincére de procurer le bien public & particulier; ce qui est évidemment prouvé par la prospérité & l'état florissant dans lequel nous avons trouvé cette République' (*Nous soussignés* 1766:2). See also letter 23, n.23.

14. 'Ecrits politiques' VII, BPUG, MS Bonnet 16:8.

15. 'Ecrits politiques' VIII: 'Discours prononcé au Grand Conseil le Vendredi 29.ᵉ Aoust 1766. sur quelques concessions du Petit Conseil au Grand Conseil et sur l'Esprit de Corps', BPUG, MS Bonnet 16:4.

16. 'Ecrits politiques' IX: 'Remarques sur un Mémoire remis à l'Auteur pour l'éxaminer, et qui concernoit certains changemens à faire à la Constitution. Aoust 1766', BPUG, MS Bonnet 16:7.

On 23 November 1766 the Guarantors finally published their *Projet de Règlement* (see letter 26, n.2). It was based on the regulations set forth in the Edict of 1738, 'également réclamé par tous les Ordres de l'Etat, comme une Loi salutaire & fondamentale', and suggested some emendations (*Projet* 1766:3). Such emendations were designed to avoid possible abuses either by the patricians or by the burghers. Article I of the project proscribed the tactic of indefinite rejection in the election of the magistrates (*Projet* 1766:9-12), while Article V regulated the right of making representations and proposed the establishment of a special tribunal to evaluate possible irregular procedures of the Small Council (*Projet* 1766:16-27). The members of this tribunal were to be elected only from among those of the Small and Great Councils.

In the days following the publication of the *Projet*, the *Négatifs* did all they could to influence the voting population. The voting date itself was changed from 11 to 15 December in order to allow the Compagnie des Pasteurs to recommend the acceptance of the *Projet*. During the same period, letters were written by Genevan watch-sellers working in Paris, who were alarmed by talk of possible economic retaliation in the event that the *Projet* was rejected by the General Council. Bonnet himself prepared a speech in favour of the *Projet*, but circumstances prevented him from delivering it. However, all these efforts were destined to be fruitless. The *Projet* was turned down by 1095 votes to 515. This was a serious defeat for the Patriciate. On the same day, 15 December, under direct orders from the duc de Choiseul, the chevalier de Beauteville announced that commerce with France was forbidden to all *Représentants*. Fifteen Genevan watch-sellers who supported the *Représentants* were expelled from Paris. Fearing an uprising, many patricians left Geneva. Three days after the voting had taken place, Bonnet, his wife, and his father-in-law left Geneva for Genthod, a nearby community on Lac Léman, which became his permanent home. The Small Council was reduced to eight members, and the Great Council to half of its former membership. The massive exodus from Geneva was partly due to fear, but mainly to political calculation. The patricians did not want to hinder the operation of the ban on commerce declared by France, and at the same time wanted the responsibility for the political situation and for the expected economic crisis to fall on the burghers alone.

On 30 December the Ministers Plenipotentiary also left Geneva for Solothurn. French troops formed a cordon around Geneva to prevent any food supplies from getting through. Applauding the military initiative of the French, Bonnet wrote to Haller on 30 December 1766: 'le but secrêt du Ministére de France est de frapper le Peuple & ses Conducteurs par un démarche qui les fasse rentrer en eux-mêmes. Si les deux Républiques [Bern and Zürich] secondent ses vües, nous pouvons espérer un succès heureux' (Sonntag 1983:562). Some days later, on 17 January 1767, he wrote to a French correspondent:

L'interdiction de commerce le fera peut-être rentrer en lui même [the people of Geneva]. Il a des fortunes bonnes à conserver et je ne pense pas qu'il veuille les sacrifier à son héroïsme fanatique. Plût au Ciel qu'il rentrât en lui-même pour les motifs que je voudrais lui inspirer!

Vous n'imaginez pas, Monsieur, l'excès de confiance de ce peuple pour ses 24 députés ou commissaires. Jamais la foi n'a produit de néophytes plus convaincus. L'apôtre

Rousseau les a tous inspirés. 'Demeurez unis, leur a-t-il dit, quand le parti que vous auriez pris serait mauvais votre union le rendra bon.' Ce conseil perfide aurait fait venir la peau de poule à Machiavel lui-même.

Peut-être néanmoins que cette fatale union ne tiendra pas contre un accroissement de maux et ceux que le Roi nous fait et nous ferait encore sont et seraient des biens déguisés. Une scission dans le parti amènerait tout à une heureuse fin.[17]

However the military blockade of Geneva failed as food supplies could reach the city directly from Savoy, across the lake. The attempt thus backfired on France, while the merchants of Lyon saw their trade come to a halt, and the export of foodstuffs from the Pays de Gex to Geneva was blocked. A new French plan was therefore developed, that of founding a town at Versoix, to rival and supplant Geneva as a centre of trade, finance, and industry. Had this plan succeeded, Geneva would indeed have been punished. Voltaire himself applauded the project, which he had been instrumental in initiating, and exerted himself to persuade a number of *Natifs* to move from Geneva to Versoix (see letter 28, n.2.). During the entire course of the constitutional conflict in Geneva, Voltaire had increasingly sympathised with the lower orders of society. At first he had sided with the Patriciate, among whom he counted a number of friends and admirers; then he transferred his support to the *Représentants*; and finally he became a fervent advocate and adviser of the disinherited *Natifs*. He himself was hoping, not without some tinge of utopian enthusiasm, to establish at Versoix a true haven of tolerance.[18]

The Versoix project was widely publicised in the papers of the day and constituted a concrete threat to Geneva. It represented a threat not only to the economic interests of the burghers, but also to those of the patricians. In the first months of 1767 the Patriciate split into two main factions. One was formed by intransigent patricians who, like Bonnet, were loyal to Versailles and hoped to break down the resistance and unity of the burghers by adopting an inflexible political line. The other was formed by the moderates, who believed that the time had come to negotiate with the burghers. On more than one occasion they attempted to do so secretly (see letter 27, n.1.). It was during this period, for instance, that Gédéon Turrettini contacted members of the opposition such as Jean-André de Luc. When the patricians of the hard line faction discovered these manoeuvres, they succeeded in putting an end to them.

The failure of the French blockade, the limited success encountered by the Versoix project, the total standstill of normal administrative activity in Geneva, the firmness of the burghers, the internal division among the patricians, and the exodus of most of the uncompromising faction from Geneva were all factors that, at the end of 1767, compelled the Small Council to moderate its politics. On 18 December 1767, the first Syndic informed the Great Council that a new plan of pacification was being formulated. It contained on the one hand a proposal that the burghers should give up their 'ligne de nouvelle élection' and, on the other, that this should be compensated by an increased proportion of membership and hence increased participation in the Great Council. Among

17. Quoted by Ferrier 1926:90.
18. For Voltaire's changing attitudes, see Ceitac (1956a), Gay (1958 and 1965:185-238), and Gargett (1980:219-24).

the moderate patricians the maxim 'vouloir conserver la Constitution c'est vouloir perdre l'Etat' became something of a catchword. They now felt it necessary to test the attitudes of the most influential burghers by establishing a joint committee to discuss the new plan of pacification. It was after this initiative by the Small Council that Bonnet went to Geneva and, on 30 December 1767, gave a speech to the Great Council in which he summarised his political viewpoint. With his usual eloquence and directness, he recapitulated the history of recent events and expressed his conviction that the old constitution of 1738 should not be abandoned. He firmly opposed the idea of establishing a committee to hold conferences with the *Représentants* because this would endanger both the constitution and the status of the Guarantors. He dissociated himself from steps taken by the moderate patricians, exhorted them to unity, and emphasised that a single constitutional change would inevitably lead to more changes, until the entire constitution would be abandoned. He conceded nothing to the *Représentants*, not even those points that he had been ready to agree to a year and a half previously, and, maintaining his habitual stern paternalistic attitude, prayed that they would repent. He called on the patricians to emulate the 'inébranlable fermeté'[19] of the burghers, and to place themselves entirely in the hands of Providence. Providence, in this context, evidently meant the policies promulgated by Versailles. For this reason, he opposed the establishment of a committee, which he feared might compromise the work of the Guarantors. At the same time he clearly sensed, as did most of the right-wing patricians, that if a settlement of the conflict was to be reached by the burghers and patricians alone, without the endorsement of the Guarantors, it would be unstable.

The day after Bonnet made this speech, he was offered the candidature for Councillor of State, a position that had been vacant since the retirement of his father-in-law Horace-Bénédict de La Rive. Bonnet did not accept, refusing on the grounds of ill-health and his sense of having already paid his debt to society. However he did not intend to retreat into a 'honteuse oisiveté' (Savioz 1948b:229), but to devote his time to an activity that would be even more profitable to his country than direct participation in affairs of state: the investigation of that religion 'dont le sentiment s'affaiblit trop parmi nous' (Savioz 1948b:230). Consequently the Great Council did not put forward Bonnet's candidature. Notwithstanding his resolute opposition to the establishment of formal consultations between the burghers and the patricians, Bonnet's refusal to engage more actively in political affairs suggests an awareness that the political battle of the last few months had already been lost (Sonntag 1983:710). His refusal to accept this offer of a greater political responsibility is otherwise inexplicable. Having withdrawn from day-to-day politics, he set out to formulate a kind of testament based on the principles for which he had fought and that he saw evaporating, thus transferring the political battle to the level of philosophical debate. The resulting works, *La Palingénésie philosophique* (1769) and the *Recherches philosophiques sur les preuves du christianisme* (1770), to the composition of which he devoted himself passionately in those years, have their

19. 'Ecrits politiques' XI: 'Discours prononcé au Grand Conseil le 30.ᵉ de Décembre 1767, sur le *Projet de Conciliation* du Petit Conseil', BPUG, MS Bonnet 16:7. This speech was reproduced in full by Bonnet in his autobiograhy (Savioz 1948b:226-29).

most immediate roots in the preceding constitutional conflicts of his town and in his intention to present, resurrect, and diffuse those principles for which he had also stood politically.

Although on 13 January 1768 the *Représentants* refused to participate with the patricians in 'des conférences réglées', members of the two groups met informally, and moderate patricians began to draw up a new constitutional project. In February 1768 Bonnet made his last political speech to the Great Council.[20] It was both a testament of faith and a condemnation of the government's political conduct, which he saw as being responsible for the imminent collapse of the constitution, for the almost certain submission of the Patriciate to the burghers, and for the victory of a democracy that would ultimately reveal itself as dangerous and destructive. Bonnet predicted that a new constitution would come into being and that because of the concessions that the patricians were ready to make, it would not be guaranteed as had that of 1738 and therefore would be subject to pressure from any popular movement. He also pointed out that, paradoxically, those very chimerical Rousseauist principles that had been condemned in 1762 and that had given birth to the entire constitutional conflict were on the point of prevailing. He concluded his passionate address by professing his devotion to the old constitution and by declaring that he 'a cru de son devoir d'élever aujourdhui sa foible voix pour reclamer cette Constitution qui va périr, et c'est probablement pour la dernière fois qu'il à l'honneur de parler céans; car de quelle utilité ses foibles efforts pourroient ils être, quand ce Gouvernement qu'il respectoit & chérissoit ne sera plus?' (f.11).

By sampling opinion among some of the burghers, the government discovered that, within the opposition as well, divergent factions had emerged. The burghers were not as united as they had been only a few months earlier. This made an immediate settlement impossible. The government itself adopted delaying tactics, which on the one hand exacerbated its relations with some of the burghers, and on the other revived hopes of a hard-line solution among the uncompromising patricians. The whole situation was now inflammable. On 29 January 1768 Turrettini wrote to Sinner, 'Ces gens [the burghers] commencent à parler de bayonnettes' (Gür 1967:190-91). It was in fact under the growing threat and fear of violence that a compromise was finally reached on 11 March 1768, and an Edict of conciliation was voted on and accepted by the General Council by a majority of 1204 to 37. Most of the right-wing patricians did not even participate in the voting procedure. By comparison with the Edict of 1738, the new Edict sanctioned a different balance of power which, as Bonnet had foretold, was eventually unstable. The burghers gave up their 'ligne de nouvelle élection' and were given increased participation in the Great Council, greater guarantees in matters relating to individual freedoms and judicial procedures, and changes in the procedures for the election of magistrates, thus re-establishing the principle of popular election of magistrates (Gay 1965:231). The *Natifs*, who had played a lesser role in the entire conflict, were given some trading rights and granted admission to the liberal professions. They were, however, excluded from political

20. 'Ecrits politiques' XIII: 'Discours prononcé au Grand Conseil en Fevrier 1768; sur les malheurs actuels de la République et les nouvelles Concessions faites au Peuple', BPUG, MS Bonnet 16.

rights, with the exception of five who were every year allowed to purchase citizenship.[21] In view of this, it is hardly surprising that both the constitutional conflicts following 1768 and the revolution of 1782 were to originate among the *Natifs*.[22]

The hard-line patricians claimed that the Edict of 1768 had been extorted by force and referred to it as the 'Edit des pistolets'. They did not see any role for themselves in the new establishment and resigned *en masse* from their posts. Bonnet resigned from the Great Council in a letter dated 1 January 1769, addressed to the Small Council. He based his resignation ostensibly on ill-health, but also gave the true reason (Savioz 1948b:232):

Que les grands changemens survenus à cette heureuse Constitution, les moyens qui les ont operés; la naissance, l'accroissement et l'affermissement d'une puissance secrette, que la Loi méconnoit et qu'elle réprouve: que tout cela entraînant naturellement la chute des Principes dont l'Exposant avoit fait une profession si sincère, si constante, si ouverte; il seroit obligé aujourd'hui de reconnoître, qu'il n'est plus propre à participer à une Administration où il auroit, même à redouter le peu de bien qu'il pourroit faire: elle sera, sans doute mieux exercée par ceux qui possèdent ou qui ont su revêtir l'esprit & les maximes de la nouvelle Constitution, à l'établissement de laquelle il a du moins la satisfaction de n'avoir point concouru.

The resignation of Bonnet and other patricians from the Great Council marks the decline of the patricians as the only ruling group in Genevan politics. From 1768 onwards, Bonnet kept himself informed of political developments in Geneva, following events there with a pessimistic detachment from his retreat in Genthod. It was only after the revolution and counter-revolution of 1782 that, persuaded by the pressing invitation extended by sympathisers among the patricians, he once more became a member of the Great Council.

21. See Art. xi of the *Edit du 11. Mars 1768* (1768:24-27).
22. For a review of recent research on the 1782 revolution, see Candaux (1980); and for its repercussions, see Venturi (1982).

9. Needham and the Brussels Academy of Sciences

On 25 August 1768 Needham announced to Bonnet that he had been invited to Brussels by the Austrian Court to help in the creation of a new society 'des gens des lettres' (letter 31). On 14 March 1769 he wrote from Paris saying that he was on the point of leaving for Brussels and that he had been granted a pension by empress Maria Theresa (letter 35). Bonnet congratulated him on his new appointment (letter 36) and subsequently inquired from time to time about the progress of the Academy (letters 39, 49). Needham, although generally reticent about his activities in Brussels, did on one occasion write optimistically on the future of the Academy and revealed that he had been asked by the new Minister Plenipotentiary to write a memoir 'sur les moyens les plus prompts et les plus efficaces pour son avancement' (letter 45). But on the whole, Needham's letters to Bonnet do not provide much information about his activities at the Academy. Nevertheless, it is not unreasonable to suppose that his appointment as Director first of the Société littéraire and then of the Académie impériale et royale des sciences et belles-lettres marked a turning-point in his career. The following pages provide an attempt to fill in the background to Needham's Brussels appointment, and to summarise his activities during the first years of the Société littéraire and the Academy within the context of the academic movement of the eighteenth century and of Theresian cultural policy in the Austrian Netherlands.

It should be noted that scientific academies and mixed academies, that is literary and scientific societies such as the early Academy of Brussels, were just two of the many different types of societies that were being formed in increasing numbers during the eighteenth century. To abstract the scientific academies from the larger family of institutions to which they belonged, as is usually done, is to isolate them from their historical context and to create unnecessary difficulties in understanding the role they played. Academies, scientific societies, literary and archeological societies, societies with economic or philanthropic aims, *Lesegesellschaften*, secret societies, social clubs, and early political clubs are all part of that society-building movement which, from the sixteenth to the eighteenth centuries, reveals at the institutional level some of the most fundamental features of historic change in early modern Europe.[1] As institutions, such societies represented new forms of social aggregation. On the one hand they were a result of historic change, on the other they produced even greater historic change by their diversified activities. Although, particularly in the late sixteenth and early seventeenth centuries, they were generally structured on medieval or idealised classical models, the new societies differed greatly from these both in the projects they set themselves and in the commitments of their individual members. In the course of the eighteenth century the number and scope of these societies increased enormously all over Europe. Light-hearted conversation on

---

1. For a general analysis of these institutions, see Im Hof (1982:105-75); and for lists of eighteenth-century societies, see H.-H. Müller (1975:276-86) and Im Hof (1982:259-63).

subjects of contemporary interest dominated in these societies, often leading to more serious discussion, which in turn prompted investigation. But such discussion was also about the world external to the societies, and about the ways in which it could be understood, modified, and enjoyed. It was through such societies – their projects, investigations, discussions, and activities – that people of the eighteenth century tried to translate utopias into reforms, began to look more to the future than to the past, and gave a wider audience to scientific research.

Societies did not have an easy life in the early modern period. Some were proscribed, many lasted for only a few years. In order to survive and eventually flourish, such societies were often forced to seek protection and recognition from the two main powers structuring social life: the secular and the religious. To do so they adopted different strategies such as, for instance, repeatedly declaring the utility of the sciences, thus hoping to gain recognition and support. But the process of legitimation was not as simple as this, so that members of societies were often forced to adopt dissimulating procedures so as to ensure the survival of their societies. It was mainly, however, by exploiting opportunities offered by the friction existing between the secular and religious powers, or among the ruling groups within the secular power, that societies first emerged and established themselves. While organised religion either opposed or tried to assimilate into its own social structures such new forms of social aggregation, it was the secular power that slowly realised the profit it could gain by a controlled support of societies' activities. A mutual process of legitimation then took place between the secular power and societies, whose members often became what we would now call civil servants. However, when such societies did gain protection they also conditioned secular power by creating needs and an audience that, without their help, neither the secular nor the religious power could satisfy. Often societies in the eighteenth century were of private origins, seeking official recognition only after their foundation. There are, however, many cases in which academies were founded directly by states as a means of enforcing plans of modernisation. The Academy of Brussels was founded with this end in view. Before describing this it will be useful to recall some general aspects of Maria Theresa's politics after 1745.

The two Silesian wars, which ended in 1745 with the peace of Dresden, convinced Maria Theresa of the precarious organisation of her hereditary states. The military confrontation with her 'faithless enemy', as she used to call Frederick II, had clearly shown her that courage and determination alone were insufficient to preserve and strengthen her States. To bring back the House of Austria to its ancient dignity, a substantial transformation of domestic affairs was now felt to be necessary. This had to be carried out by processes of modernisation (in different areas) which, either by reforming old structures or creating new ones, would make it possible to develop, as count Kaunitz insisted in 1745, a foreign policy that could successfully oppose and isolate the Prussian neighbour who had dared to offend Habsburg honour.

Reforms enacted in the organisation of the armed forces, administration, finance, agriculture, education, as well as new social measures had often been connected to sporadic attempts either partially put into practice or projected in previous years. But it was only after 1745, following the humiliating defeats in military confrontation and in foreign policy, that such reforms constituted a coherent network of measures that ultimately aimed at attaining a bureaucratic centralised absolutism. Maria Theresa's politics and her reforms became the focal point of small groups of discontented intellectuals, of enlightened Catholics advocating greater public welfare, of small numbers of scattered bourgeoisie hoping for some form of greater freedom in commerce, and of enterprising patrician families. All these groups recognised that the only way to achieve their own aspirations, at least in part, was by strengthening the Crown and by enabling it to assume the functions of centralised coordination. Opposition to such aspirations and to Maria Theresa's politics originated mainly among the aristocracy, the high clergy (both of which classes now had to pay taxes for the first time), and the powerful guilds, which by their regulations often inhibited private initiative. These groups witnessed the reduction of their own power in local and provincial government, as well as the takeover by civil servants of functions that they had been exercising for a long time.

The new alliance established between the Crown and its subjects brought about a new relationship between the State and the Church, that strong and active centre of social, political, and economic organisation. It was, ironically, under the pious and devoted Maria Theresa that the process of secularisation, culminating in a great reduction of the power of the Church and in the formation of a centralised and centralising bureaucracy, had its origins in the Habsburg States. Not only did Maria Theresa found a new school for nobles, the Theresi-anum in 1749, and the military Academy of Wiener Neustadt in 1752, two institutions that were designed to provide a more efficient governing elite, but she also carried out an impressive reform of the educational system at the primary and secondary level by removing education from the control of the clergy and by placing it under State control.[2] The new university system created in Vienna by Maria Theresa and advisers such as van Swieten, Martini, and von Sonnenfels, was of functional value to the new State. Its purpose was to provide well-trained professionals and a system of recruitment of and training for civil servants. Unlike other reforms of the Theresian era, which were first tried out in the periphery of the Empire and, only if successful, later extended to other provinces, the university reform was first carried out in the centre, at Vienna; and only after it appeared to be successful was it introduced into other universities. The reason for this was that a major upheaval like wresting higher education from the monopoly of the clergy and placing it in the hands of civil servants had to be carefully engineered: it required the concentrated effort of all of the State's apparatus and the constant and direct protection of the Crown. Furthermore the Crown itself needed to create a vital intellectual centre, from which it could draw competent advisers, as well as to avoid any disparity that might have arisen had the periphery developed more advanced cultural centres than Vienna itself.

It is interesting to note that in most of the states under Austrian rule the

---

2. For the history of the university educational system under Maria Theresa, see Klingenstein (1974:812, 1976, and 1978).

society-building movement was far behind in comparison with other European States. Vienna itself had no academy of science; and when a project for establishing one was presented, it was rejected first on financial grounds, secondly because there were far too few eminent scholars who could have entered it, and finally because priority had been given to reforming the university. However in those provinces without a university, measures were taken to enhance cultural life by patronising or founding learned societies such as the Accademia degli Agiati of Rovereto, the Accademia Virgiliana of Mantua, the Società patriottica of Milan, the Societas incognitorum of Olmütz, and the Société littéraire of Brussels.[3] Evidently the consequence of support for such societies was political control and their use as instruments of a politics of modernisation.

Count Charles de Cobenzl (see letter 31, n.4), a cultivated aristocrat and hardworking enlightened bureaucrat, who was from 1753 Minister Plenipotentiary of the Austrian Netherlands, was the chief promoter of the idea of founding a learned society in Brussels. The project itself was part of his more general strategy of economic, agricultural, and cultural reforms, which encountered opposition and obstruction from the narrow self-interests and privileges of the nobility, the clergy, and the guilds. At times Cobenzl's programmes also came up against resistance from the Governor General, Charles of Lorraine, who stood as the major spokesman for the autonomist privileges of the upper class in the Lowlands, and who perceived Cobenzl as the *longa manus* of Maria Theresa's State Chancellor, prince Kaunitz. However, as a highly cultivated man, a lover of the arts and sciences, and an ingenious constructor of machines, Charles of Lorraine was not likely to impede the proposal for a new academy. Although he favoured the project, he did not provide any great assistance in its realisation. The records of the foundation of the first society in Brussels clearly prove that it was strongly advocated not so much by the Court as by the bureaucratic State machinery, which saw it as a potential aid for modernisation. Count Cobenzl regarded the Lowlands as a cultural desert and found the teaching at Louvain University, the only oasis, backward and unproductive. He could perceive no private cultural activity of any significance and no intellectual ferment; and he hoped that the creation of an academy would simultaneously stimulate taste for the arts and new ideas in the useful sciences, and would provide new technology for developing industries and expertise for his agricultural plans. When the abbé Corneille de Nelis, Librarian of Louvain University, suggested in 1764 the creation of a small academy to stimulate the intellectual life of the University, Cobenzl stated that he did not want it to be located in Louvain, but at the centre of the Austrian Netherlands, in Brussels.[4] Late in 1766 Cobenzl invited to Brussels an old acquaintance, the historian Johann Daniel Schöpflin, founder of the flourishing Academy of Mannheim, from whom

3. There is no general history of eighteenth-century scientific and literary societies in territories under Austrian rule. For the history of attempts to create an academy of sciences in Vienna, see Feil (1861) and Meister (1947:14-17); for the Academy of Rovereto, see Garbari (1981); for the Academy of Mantua, see Baldi (1979:3-9); for that in Olmütz, see Hemmerle (1957); for those in Innsbruck, see Grass (1948); and for the Academy in Brussels, see Mailly (1883), *L'Académie* (1973), Lavalleye (1973), Pirenne (1972-1975, 3:371-72), Voss (1976), and Marx (1977).

4. See Lavalleye (1973:15) and Voss (1976:327).

he sought expert advice on teaching at the university level and on the internal organisation of scientific institutions. During his stay in Brussels in the summer of 1767 and after having visited the University of Louvain, Schöpflin agreed that, as there was no immediate possibility of reforming this old and glorious institution, the only alternative was to create an independent academy (Voss 1976:329). He submitted to Cobenzl a memoir entitled 'Réflexions sur le rétablissement des bonnes études dans les Pays-Bas',[5] recommending the foundation of an academy modelled on the one in Mannheim, with an emphasis on the historical and juridical fields of enquiry, rather than the scientific. He suggested that, to start with, six members should be elected, considering this to be a sufficient number for carrying out all the necessary procedures connected with the examination of papers and awarding of prizes.

The abbé Nelis was subsequently asked to comment on Schöpflin's proposals. While praising the general structure of the academy as envisaged by Schöpflin, Nelis thought it wiser to start with a less ambitious society and see how this would function. If this proved successful, the foundation of an Academy proper could then go ahead. He also made a list of scholars who might be considered for membership and put forward the name of Needham as possible Director: 'Si on pouvait avoir M. Needham, on aurait un homme qui a fait beaucoup de recherches dans sa vie, et qui serait bien capable de diriger celles des autres, surtout en fait de physique.'[6] Cobenzl passed on both Schöpflin's memoir and the abbé de Nelis's report to count Patrice-François de Neny, the influential President of the Austrian Privy Council. Count de Neny agreed with the abbé Nelis as to the form the society should take: 'Le projet de M. Schöpflin est aussi bon que les vues qui l'ont dicté sont justes. Je pense néanmoins avec M. l'abbé Nelis, qu'au lieu d'établir tout de suite l'académie en titre et par lettres-patentes, il est de la prudence de commencer par former cette société de gens de lettres qu'il propose.'[7] He also supported Needham's candidacy for the Directorship, bearing in mind the fact that an opportunity for employing Needham in 1759 had been missed: 'pour ce qui concerne M. Needham, il jouit dans toute l'Europe de la juste considération que méritent ses talens, ses mœurs et ses profondes connaissances. J'ai exposé par un mémoire du 17 mars 1759, qui a été remis à S.M., le parti que nous espérions tirer alors de ce sujet, pour l'avancement des bonnes études; si nous pouvions encore aujourd'hui en faire l'acquisition, personne ne serait plus en état que lui de se charger de la principale direction de l'établissement qu'on médite' (Gachard 1838:177).

With considerable assistance from the abbé Nelis, Needham had tried in 1759 to have a chair of experimental physics and a cabinet of natural history established for himself at the University of Louvain. Although supported by count de Neny and by count Cobenzl, his proposal had encountered opposition from Kaunitz in Vienna. In a period of war and financial difficulty, the latter had other priorities than innovation in teaching and improvement in research at the University. He remarked, with characteristic cynical realism, 'ce n'est que pour trouver une niche au prêtre Needham que l'on a songé au nouvel

---

5. Published in Gachard (1838:169-73).
6. Quoted from the report by Nelis published in Gachard (1838:176).
7. Quoted from the report by Neny published in Gachard (1838:176).

établissement' (De Boom 1932:236 n.3). However, this affair to some extent paved the way for Needham's candidacy in 1768. Other factors in his favour were a first-hand knowledge of the scientific environment in England and in parts of the Continent and his being a Fellow of several learned societies, which both assured a competent grasp of the workings of scientific institutions and made possible the creation of links with them. Last, but not least, as a devoted Catholic and opponent of the unbelievers, he represented no threat to the Lowlands religious establishment. In view of his eminent suitability, both Neny and Nelis established contacts with Needham (see letter 31, n.5), and his consent to move to Brussels was obtained.

When the dossier on the proposed new society was ready, it was sent from Brussels to Vienna, where Kaunitz prepared his own report for the empress (see letter 35, n.1) and summarised his proposals in the following four points (Gachard 1838:165):

1°   D'agréer l'établissement d'une société de gens de lettres, sur le pied du projet de l'abbé Nelis;

2°   D'autoriser le gouvernement-général à conférer tous les ans deux pris consistant en des médailles d'or du poids de 25 ducats chacune, aux meilleurs des ouvrages qui auront concouru sur les sujets proposés;

3°   D'autoriser S.A.R. [Charles of Lorraine] à nommer l'abbé Needham à un des canonicats qui sont à sa collation;

4°   De lui assigner, en attendant qu'il entre en jouissance des fruits de cette prébende, une pension de 1,000 florins de Brabant.

All these points were approved by the empress and later carried out. The importance of Kaunitz's report lies in its delineation of the province within which the society should operate. First, there was the question of the relationship of the new society with the University of Louvain. He clearly perceived that this would be a delicate one and therefore stressed the fact that the two institutions had different functions (Gachard 1838:160-61):

Une institution pareille [Société littéraire] n'est point superflue dans un pays où il existe déjà des universités, puisque leur but et leur opérations sont différentes, et que les sociétés littéraires contribuent beaucoup plus à l'instruction générale que ne le peut faire une université quelque parfait qu'elle soit d'ailleurs. [...] Obligés par état de revenir toujours sur les élémens pour les expliquer et les mettre à la portée de la plupart de leurs élèves, les professeurs et les régens n'ont guère le temps de s'élever au-dessus des premiers principes de la science qu'ils enseignent, ni de franchir les bornes étroites des élémens. [...] C'est pourquoi, dans les pays les plus cultivés de l'Europe, on a laissé l'éducation des enfans aux colléges et aux universités, mais on a établi des académies et des sociétés pour les faire travailler aux progrès des arts et des sciences, et pour instruire, par leur moyen, le corps de la nation.

He also stressed (Gachard 1838:159-60) the importance of the useful sciences in comparison with literary disciplines, which, he believed, should not be cultivated for themselves, but should be subordinated

aux sciences utiles, pour éviter l'inconvénient où sont tombées tant d'académies de belles-lettres en Italie, qui, au lieu d'éclairer et instruire la nation, lui ont imprimé un esprit de bagatelle et de frivolité si nuisible aux progrès de la raison. Il faudra donc pour rendre un établissement pareil utile à la culture de la nation, écarter de l'institution tout ce qui pourrait faire penser que c'est pour l'exercice et l'avancement des seuls belles-lettres qu'on l'aurait adopté. Il faudra de plus, ainsi que le remarque fort judicieusement l'abbé Nelis, inviter le public à tourner ses vues et ses recherches vers les sciences utiles à l'humanité et nécessaires à l'industrie.

Kaunitz thus laid down the guidelines for the activities of the new society, which both attempted to forestall any possible ill-feeling on the part of Louvain's scholars and directed the society's investigations mainly toward the useful sciences.

On 1 February 1769 count Cobenzl wrote to Needham and to nine other scholars formally asking them to be founding members of a Société littéraire to be located in Brussels. These scholars included three members of the University of Louvain, the anatomist Adrien-Charles-Joseph van Rossum, the chemist Josse-Jean-Hubert Vounck, and the botanist Jean-Joseph Michaud; three historians, Luc-Joseph vander Vynckt, Jean-Noël Paquot, and Jean-Baptiste Verdussen; the instrument-maker Henri-Joseph de Seumony; the civil servant Georges-Joseph Gerard, who was to act as Secretary of the Society; and Corneille-François de Nelis. As the Society had no fixed address, its first meeting on 5 May 1769 was held at count de Neny's. On that occasion Needham was officially elected Director, new members were co-opted, and the questions for the prize awards were set.

The Society was slowly taking shape when on 27 January 1770 count Cobenzl died, leaving it bereft of patronage. In the period between Cobenzl's death and the arrival on 9 June 1770 of Georg Adam Starhemberg, the new Minister Plenipotentiary (see letter 45, n.3), the Society met only once. The fact that the Society survived at all can be attributed to Needham's presence and efforts. Defections among the early members of the Society were frequent. Michaud had never actually accepted membership; van Rossum only turned up at the first few sessions; Vounck did indeed attend more assemblies but made little contribution; and count de Neny claimed he was too busy to follow the Society's proceedings. Without any headquarters, with no patronage, library, or scientific instruments, with travel expenses to be paid directly by those who lived outside Brussels, and with no financial reward, the Society's members had no particular incentive to play the part envisaged for them by Cobenzl. At the first opportunity Needham made this clear to count Starhemberg, who asked him to formulate a project for reorganising the Society. The resulting scheme, together with Starhemberg's personal interest, set the entire bureaucratic machinery in motion. In his 'Mémoire sur la Société littéraire de Bruxelles' (see letter 45, n.4), probably written in late summer 1770, Needham set out a number of points, some of which were taken up in the establishment of the Académie royale, others remaining as *desiderata*, which Needham devoted the rest of his life to realising. Needham lamented the total absence of active governmental protection for the Society and proposed that it should be elevated to a Royal Academy by patent letters of the empress, thus attaining an indisputable legitimacy through the actual involvement of the Crown. He also asked for a headquarters and for a library. As plans were being made for the creation of a public Royal Library, he suggested that the Academy be located there. He argued in favour of granting pensions to at least six members of the Academy, providing evidence that this was the common practice in other scientific institutions on the Continent. He further requested that travel expenses incurred by members of the Academy in attending its meetings should be covered by the academic endowment, and that special scientific journeys undertaken by members of the Academy in the Austrian Netherlands should also be covered. He stressed the importance of establishing a chair in experimental physics and a laboratory at Brussels with public lectures. Finally he asked that a President 'distinguée par sa naissance ou par son rang' be appointed. The function of the latter would be to legitimate the activities of the Academy, to keep necessary contacts with the different branches of the civil service, and to act as mediator in the case of conflicts among the academicians.

Before finally arriving on Maria Theresa's desk, Needham's views were analysed and commented upon in written reports by count de Neny, by Gerard, by the Chancellor of Brabant Joseph de Crumpipen (the future President of the Academy), by Charles of Lorraine, and by Kaunitz. At its final stage Needham's project was somewhat reduced, but it indeed forced the Austrian Government to face the consequences of its initial encouragement of the Society. Kaunitz clearly perceived the situation: 'il semble qu'on est réduit à opter entre ces deux partis, de laisser crouler l'établissement dont il s'agit, et d'abandonner ainsi le projet de former une académie aux Pays-Bas, ou de réaliser dès à présent ce projet, en donnant à la société littéraire la forme d'une académie stable' (Gachard 1840:95-96). The second course was taken and, on 16 December 1772, Maria Theresa signed the 'Lettres-patentes d'érection de l'Académie Impériale et Royale des Sciences et Belles-Lettres de Bruxelles'.[8] A few months after the new Academy started its activities, Needham wrote to Bonnet: 'Notre nouvelle academie des sciences, et belles lettres, dont j'ai l'honneur d'etre le directeur, vient d'etre fondée radicalement par des lettres patentes de sa Majesté Imperiale sous le titre *d'Imperiale et Royale*, qui conferent en meme tems aux membres jusqu'a des titres, et des prerogatifs de Noblesse. [...] jusqu'à present tout paroit promettre assés bien pour l'avenir' (letter 46).

Needham retained this optimism, in spite of the fact that the Academy, caught in the web of Habsburg bureaucracy, did not flourish as he had hoped. On 22 March 1776 he wrote to his friend the astronomer and Fellow of the Royal Society, Nathaniel Pigott: 'appearances begin to be favorable, and there is now a real prospect that our academy will at last be placed upon solid foundation'.[9] Over a year later he wrote again to Pigott: 'I have reason to hope now, that this our academy will at last acquire the desired stability.'[10] The growth of the Academy was stunted by excessive bureaucratic control and lack of funding, a combination that rendered its existence precarious. However, some aims were achieved. From the first session of the new Academy on 13 April 1773, during which Needham was elected Director, up to 19 May 1780, which marked the end of his tenure, ninety-eight sessions were held with great regularity. Under Needham's directorship membership was expanded, a good number of awards were given, and three large volumes of papers were published as the Academy's *Mémoires*. However, Needham felt that scientific equipment was needed, and

8. See Gachard (1840:107-109) and letter 46, n.6.
9. See Needham's letter to Pigott of 22 March 1776 in the VF.
10. See Needham's letter to Pigott of 27 May 1777 in the VF.

Fig. 17. Frontispiece from the *Mémoires de l'Académie impériale et royale des sciences et belles-lettres de Bruxelles*, 5 vols., 1777-1788. Drawn by Guillaume Herreyns and engraved by Antoine Cardon, the plate was originally intended to appear in the Jesuit *Analecta Belgica*. There is some evidence to suggest that the physical and mathematical instruments were added to the original design for the *Mémoires* (see Mailly 1883, 1:150).

unsuccessfully petitioned the government for an experimental physics laboratory, an observatory, a *salle électrique* in which to carry out investigations in
medical electricity, and a cabinet of natural history. The parsimony of the
government was not his only source of frustration and opposition: some of the
academicians themselves proved hostile, possibly as a result of Needham's habit
of making unsolicited additions and corrections to the mémoires presented to
the Academy. On one occasion Needham even went so far as to publish a paper
by Jean-Louis Launay on geology, with the addition of a series of comments on
materialism and incredulity that Launay had never envisaged.[11] Such procedures compromised his position within the Academy and favoured the growth
of opposition, which was also fostered by his diminishing scientific authority
among his colleagues.

True to the spirit of the new Academy, Needham devoted himself to tackling
practical problems. His investigations diverged from his usual scientific interests
and included the study of minerals in the Austrian Netherlands, new methods
in apiculture, the process of iron smelting, the barrenness of the soil in the
province of Luxemburg, diseases in cattle, and practical problems in electromag-
netism. He also attempted to bring under scientific scrutiny current opinions
on the behaviour of ants and popular beliefs on the tolling of bells during
thunderstorms.[12] The results were not always satisfactory, and most of his
papers were heavily criticised for being superficial or for relying on 'theological'
arguments.[13] The academicians had explicitly decided against employing such
arguments, in order to avoid the censorship of theologians who suspected some
of them of supporting principles of contemporary philosophy.

The opposition to Needham expressed itself in various ways. On one occasion
Needham strongly supported the candidacy for membership of the metallurgist
Jean-Baptiste Marquart, stressing the fact that his expertise would be essential
to the development of useful knowledge, to which the Academy was committed.
However, Marquart was not elected because most of the academicians regarded
him as only a specialist and not a complete *homme des lettres* (Mailly 1883, 1:101-
104). More importantly, Needham encountered strong opposition to his plan
for making the Bollandists associates of the Academy. These were four ex-Jesuits
who had been publishing the *Acta sanctorum*, and Needham's scheme, which
would have helped them in their critical situation after 1773, would also have
strongly reinforced the historical research section within the Academy itself.
Needham again encountered opposition when he sponsored the election of the
engineer and mathematician Rombaut Bournons. On 31 August 1775, he wrote
to the abbé Mann enumerating all the reasons in favour of Bournons and
concluded: 'je continue à rencontrer une opposition perpétuelle à toutes mes
propositions, soit de la part du président [Joseph-Ambroise de Crumpipen] ou
du secrétaire [Georges-Joseph Gerard], comme cela m'est presque toujours
arrivé jusqu'à présent, si les Bollandistes avec leurs biens ne sont pas annexés
à l'Académie, etc., etc., je quitterai certainement Bruxelles l'année prochaine,

---

11. This paper was not published in the Academy's *Mémoires*, which had not yet begun to appear,
but rather in Rozier's *Observations sur la physique*; see Launay (1775) and Mailly (1883, 1:125).
12. See Needham (1770a, 1777, 1780a, 1780b, 1780c, 1783a, 1783b, and 1788).
13. See Mailly (1883, 1:130, 254-55, and 2:1-5, 11, 13-14, 55-57, 63-65, 116-17).

et j'abandonnerai pension, bénéfices et Académie, pour vivre dans un état de complète indépendance, comme je le faisais avant de venir à Bruxelles' (Mailly 1883, 1:129-30). Notwithstanding Needham's threat, the Bollandists did not become affiliated to the Academy, because both its President and the Minister Plenipotentiary feared that such a step would have turned the Academy into a body dominated exclusively by ecclesiastics (Mailly 1883, 1:138-39).

However, not all of Needham's projects were unsuccessful. On one occasion he was able to obtain, by overcoming both bureaucratic resistance and suspicion, the necessary permission and assistance for Nathaniel Pigott to carry out astronomical observations in the Austrian Netherlands. The aim of the project was to establish with greater accuracy the latitudes and longitudes of all the major towns in the Austrian Netherlands and thus to improve the cartography of the area. Needham accompanied Pigott on his journey, which lasted from September 1772 to January 1773. The observations were carried out with Pigott's own scientific instruments, and he paid all his own expenses; but Needham at least succeeded in persuading the government to meet the expenses incurred in transporting the instruments. Pigott's results were first published in summary form in the *Philosophical transactions* for 1776 and then as a memoir in the first volume of the *Mémoires* of the Academy of Brussels in 1777. Later Needham repeatedly tried to convince the government to buy Pigott's astronomical equipment, but without success.[14]

Although Needham did not enjoy the full confidence of all of his colleagues and although his authority was undermined by the scientific output of his later years, his lack of organising ability, and his credulity, he repeatedly pointed out with great clarity of vision, which he owed to his internal knowledge of several European academies, the necessary steps the Austrian government had to take if it were to create an active scientific institution.[15] Unfortunately Austrian patronage turned out to be excessively parsimonious (Lavalleye 1973:31), especially as far as scientific equipment was concerned. Notwithstanding these limitations, and in spite of the apparent scientific conservatism that colours many of the papers published by the Academy (Marx 1977:58), the Austrian bureaucracy was able with Needham's help to create an institution that marked the beginning in the Austrian Netherlands of a 'culture scientifique laique' (Pirenne 1972-1975, 3:320).

14. For Pigott's astronomical observations, see Pigott (1776 and 1777); and for historical documents related to Pigott's journey of 1772-1773, see Mailly (1883, 1:80-81, 251-64).
15. See Gachard (1840:58-65) and Mailly (1883, 1:37-38, 111-20, 193-203, 206-208, 335-37).

10. The controversy over Schirach's experiments on bees

LETTERS 51, 52, and 53 are not readily accessible on first reading. They are concerned with the interpretation of certain experiments, now mostly forgotten, undertaken by Adam Gottlob Schirach, to discover a new method of producing 'artificial hives' to increase honey and wax production. These experiments had led Schirach to the conclusion that young worker honeybees' larvae could develop into queen's larvae and finally into queens if they were suitably housed and fed. At the time this was a new and daring interpretation; and, as is often the case in the history of science, *ad hoc* theories were produced to account for a newly discovered phenomenon. Letters 51 to 53 deal mainly with such theories. However, before exploring the significance of Schirach's experiments, it seems appropriate to outline the general state of the literature on bees in the seventeenth and eighteenth centuries.

Until well into the nineteenth century many new phenomena regarding bees were first noted by expert beekeepers and not by professional scientists. This disproportion is easily explainable given the number of skilled beekeepers, who were involved in what was, owing to the commercial importance of honey and wax in the period, a financially rewarding enterprise.

Bees were not only the subject of commercial and scientific interest but were also invested with symbolic significance. Many diverse symbols and metaphorical meanings were attached to bees in different ages and countries. For example, the Ancients had used the working of bees as an image for poetic activity, whereas medieval theologians had seen it as an apt metaphor for ecclesiastic activity: *apis est ecclesia*. French peasant legend saw bees as the work of God and wasps as a bad imitation created by Satan. In the seventeenth and eighteenth centuries the 'industrious' bee became a commonplace in moralising and didactic poetry. The analogy with the kingdom of bees was also often used in works of political theory and in satirical political pamphlets.[1]

Another aspect of this analogical tradition was the frequent use made by naturalists and expert beekeepers, in their descriptions of bee colonies, of a highly anthropomorphic terminology. Naturalists seem to have been looking for the natural laws of well-organised political coexistence in nature itself, while in fact projecting their own, either existing or coveted, political forms of government onto the hive. The government of bees was for many 'le parfait modèle d'un gouvernement monarchique' (Réaumur 1734-1742, 5:xiv). The resulting literature, although overtly aimed at promoting useful knowledge, in fact had the effect of legitimising existing political structures by promulgating rules of conduct,

---

1. For bibliographies of literature on bees, see De Keller (1881) and Harding (1979); for historical literature on both research on bees and their symbolism, see Glock (1891), Müller-Graupa (1938), Fraser (1951a and 1958), Théodoridès (1968), Misch ([1974]), Waszink (1974), and Marchenay (1979).

apparently deduced from natural observations, which were to be applied by the potential reader. This literature was thus not confined to education on the subject of beekeeping alone, but bordered on social and prescriptive writing. A few examples may serve to illustrate this point.

In 1657, a significant year in English politics, Samuel Purchas the younger, pastor at Sutton in Essex, published a book with the title *A theatre of politicall flying-insects*, which contained the following passage (Purchas 1657:16-17):

Bees are political creatures, and destinate all their actions to one common end; they have one common habitation, one common work, all work for all, and one common care and love towards all their young, and that under one Commander, who is not elected Governour; for the vulgar often want judgement, raising the worst and wickedest to the Throne; nor hath hee his power by lot, for the chances of lots are absurd, and ridiculous, conferring command often upon the meanest: Nor is hee by hereditary succession placed in the Throne; for often through pleasures and flatteries are they rude and ignorant of true vertue, but by nature hath hee the Sovereignty over all, excelling all in goodliness, and goodness, in mildness, and majesty.

It should be noted that during the seventeenth century what we now call the queen bee was generally considered to be a king. However, when the French translation of Swammerdam's work *Histoire generale des insectes* appeared in 1682 and his contention that 'le Roi [...] est la femelle' (1682:96) became generally known, opinions on the subject changed rapidly. In 1713 Joseph Warder, then a practising physician at Croydon, dedicated the second edition of his very popular book *The True Amazons: or the monarchy of bees* to queen Anne.[2] In his Preface he wrote: 'Indeed, no Monarch in the World is so absolute as the Queen of the Bees; (which pleads very much with me, that Monarchy is founded in Nature, and approv'd by the great Ruler of Princes.) But oh, what Harmony, what lovely Order is there in the Government of the Bees. The Queen-Bee Governs with Clemency and Sweetness, so doth Your Majesty; she is Obey'd and Defended, out of Choice and Inclination by her Subjects, so is Your Majesty. And here I cannot but wish that all Your Majesty's Subjects were as unanimously Loyal as the Subjects of the Queen-Bee' (Warder 1713:v-vi). In much of the literature on bees written by non-naturalists, one comes across, quite unexpectedly, sentences like the following, written by Schirach (1771:35): 'Le vrai bonheur d'une monarchie consiste dans le nombre de sujets laborieux'. Are such passages merely projections of human political society on the hive, or do they have a prescriptive intention? One also finds a number of scientists who tried to avoid using anthropomorphic terminology, especially those who shared the Cartesian view of insects as machines.

The major single advance in the history of entomology during the seventeenth and eighteenth centuries resulted from the application of the microscope to the study of insects. This made possible a superior knowledge of their anatomy, and its impact may still be vividly perceived in the very high artistic and scientific quality of book illustrations of the period (Lehmann-Haupt 1973:479-88). Bees were, in fact, the first subjects to be actually investigated with a microscope and to be drawn and engraved from microscopical observations. In 1625 prince

2. The first edition of this book had no dedication and appeared in 1712. The 9th edition appeared in 1765; see Fraser (1958:47).

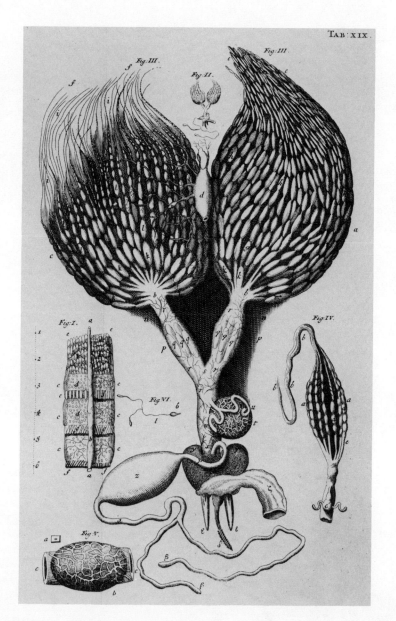

Fig. 18. Anatomical illustrations of parts of the queen bee, according to Swammerdam. *Fig. I*: The bee's heart and appended parts. *Fig. II*: The reproductive organs of the queen bee, without magnification. *Fig. III*: The reproductive organs of the queen bee as seen with a microscope, including the venom sac (*z*) and the sting (*δ*). Swammerdam noted with regard to the ovaries (*a* and *c*): 'This double ovary is composed of parts extracted from two different female Bees, *viz.* The part *a* from a full-grown impregnated Bee; and part *c* from another Bee less perfect, and not as yet impregnated. This I did to avoid the necessity of two figures, where I thought one might be made to answer' (Swammerdam 1758: xxi). *Fig. IV*: The ovary of a wasp. *Fig. V*: The egg of a bee, with (*b*) and without (*a*) magnification. *Fig. VI*: The venom sac of the bee, without magnification. (From Swammerdam, *Biblia naturae*, 1737-1738, vol.ii, plate XIX. Courtesy of the Wellcome Institute Library, London.)

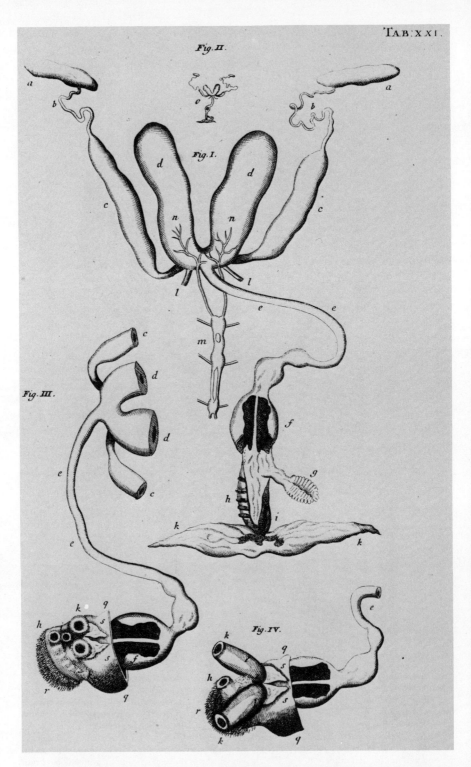

Fig. 19. Swammerdam's illustrations of the reproductive organs of the drone, as seen with (*Figs. I, III, IV*) and without (*Fig. II*) a microscope. (From Swammerdam, *Biblia naturae*, 1737-1738, vol.ii, plate XXI. Courtesy of the Wellcome Institute Library, London.)

Federico Cesi, head of the Accademia dei Lincei, and Francesco Stelluti, a distinguished member of the same learned society, presented to the newly elected pope, Urban VIII of the Barberini family, the *Apiarium* (Belloni 1969: 180-84), which contained engravings showing the external anatomy of bees 'magnified about twenty diameters' (Singer 1953:201). The gift was both symbolic and political: symbolic because the arms of the Barberini family was a shield with three bees, political because Cesi was hoping to gain patronage and support for the cultural policy of his Academy. His hopes were destined to be disappointed (Olmi 1981).

A mid-eighteenth-century scholar interested in the natural history of bees would have turned for information mainly to two outstanding works. The first of these was the treatise on bees contained in Swammerdam's two-volume masterpiece, the *Biblia naturae*, published in 1737-1738, over fifty years after his death; and the second was Réaumur's series of nine memoirs devoted to bees in the fifth volume of his *Mémoires pour servir à l'histoire des insectes*, which appeared in 1740 (see letter 49, n.7). In order to understand the significance of Schirach's experiments, discussed by Bonnet and Needham, it is necessary to recall a few of Swammerdam's and Réaumur's conclusions on the problem of the generation of bees. As he had done in his other investigations on insects, Swammerdam refuted the idea of metamorphosis or transformation of bees as understood by some of the Ancients, and he demonstrated their gradual growth and development. Exceptionally skilled at microdissection, Swammerdam was also able to prove, contrary to an ancient and still current opinion, that insects, and therefore also bees, had a complex internal anatomy. Using a microscope, he described the daily changes of external structures as well as of internal organs and compared analogous organs in different species. In keeping with his Cartesian outlook, he regarded insects as machines made by God and always sought laws of regularity. Unlike most of his contemporaries and successors, Swammerdam appears to have denied the validity of both political and social analogies in the description of the behaviour of bees, as he wrote that, 'the whole society of Bees regard not any thing else but only propagation and rearing of their young; nor is there any other government whatsoever, nor any election, or any politic or economical discipline or order among them'. On the contrary he believed that bees 'make nests, and nourish their young, being compelled thereto by such laws as they cannot avoid nor suppress by any rational principle; because they are impressed on them by the eternal law of nature' (Swammerdam 1758:170).[3] Swammerdam stated that in the hive the queen alone lays all of the eggs, an assumption that is correct in so far as the normal process is concerned, but to which there are, as we shall see, some exceptions.

By dissecting a great number of queens and examining their abdomens with a microscope (see fig. 18), Swammerdam was able to describe the two large ovaries (III, *a*), each of which is made up of egg tubes or ovarioles containing maturing eggs (III, *h, g, k*), which run into the oviducts (III, *b*). He was also able to observe a *particula sphaerica*, the exterior tissue of which was interwoven with *innumeris fistulis*, and which later was to be identified as the spermatheca

---

3. For the original Dutch version and the Latin translation, see Swammerdam (1737-1738, 1:393).

(III, *t*). He also delineated what we now denote as the spermathecal gland (III, *u*) and accurately described both the *exitus uteri* (III, *x*), now called *bursa copulatrix*, and the vagina. Swammerdam provided the decisive anatomical demonstration that drones were males (see fig. 19). He showed, in fact, the two flat testes (I, *a*), the vasa deferens (I, *b*), and the vesicula seminalis (I, *c*), each of which terminates in a big mucus gland (I, *d*). He also saw and described the long slender tube of the ductus ejaculatorius (I, *e*) and the highly complex intromittent organ (I, *f-k*). More generally he noted that drones have no sting and therefore no defensive apparatus. Swammerdam considered the worker honeybees to be neuters, as 'natural eunuchs', but perceived that they 'approach nearer to the nature and disposition of the females than of the males' (Swammerdam 1758:169).[4] He reached this conclusion on the basis of an observation and an analogy, which seems at first sight to conflict with his expressed dislike of using anthropomorphic analogies, but which has primarily an illustrative function. First, he could not observe any ovaries in workers, and he concluded from their behaviour that they were like women who having 'lived virgins till they are past child-bearing, serve only the purpose of labour in the economy of the whole body' (Swammerdam 1758:169).[5] Furthermore, he believed that the queen laid three sorts of eggs: a queen egg, a drone egg, and a worker egg. (The modern view is that there are either fertilised eggs, which develop into females, or unfertilised eggs, which develop into drones.)

In 1740 Réaumur published his nine memoirs on bees, which constituted a veritable treatise on the subject. They were the result of many years of systematic investigation and combined a high level of morphological and ecological observations with physiological experimentation. To carry out his observations, Réaumur built different kinds of experimental glass hives, some of which contained only two combs, in order to facilitate viewing the queen in the process of laying eggs (see fig. 20). His achievements were numerous. He observed and described the method used by workers in collecting pollen and propolis. He saw the eviction of the drones from the hive and how workers attacked and often killed them. He studied the venom produced by workers and identified the venom gland, its sac, and the bulb of the sting, using the technique of self-inoculation. He analysed the way in which bees build their own hive and combs; and he studied and measured the structure of the hexagonal cells, their septum, and the fineness of their walls and pyramidal base (Réaumur 1734-1742, 5:379-460). According to Bonnet (1775a:329-30), Réaumur's greatest discoveries were those regarding 'la police des Abeilles'. In order to study the reactions of workers when presented with more than one queen in a hive, Réaumur marked the latter with blue and yellow colours. He observed that when a swarm was newly placed in a hive, and, at the same time, deprived of its queen, the workers would be totally inactive although they would start working again as soon as they were presented with a queen. By this and similar experiments he demonstrated that the queen is indispensable to the life of the community and stated that she was the 'âme de la ruche', responsible for putting everything into action (Réaumur 1734-1742, 5:256).

4. For the original Dutch version and Latin translation, see Swammerdam (1737-1738, 1:391).
5. For the original Dutch version and Latin translation, see Swammerdam (1737-1738, 1:391).

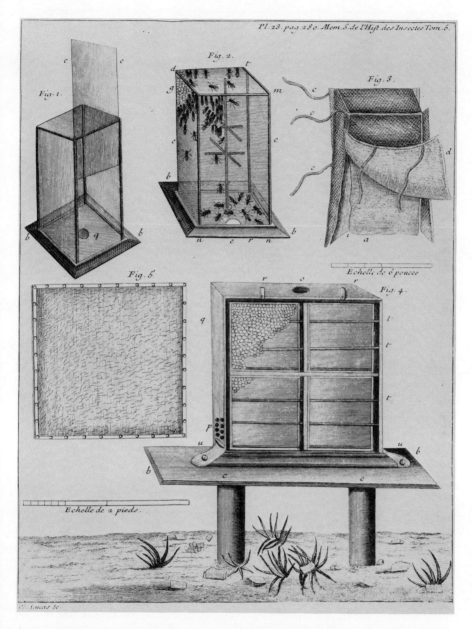

Pl. 23. pag. 280. Mem. 5. de l'Hist. des Insectes Tom. 5.

Fig. 20. Réaumur's methods for constructing beehives suitable for making observations. *Figs. 1, 2, 3*: A small beehive made with glass windowpanes, and its cloth cover. *Figs. 4, 5*: A larger beehive, with a glass front and lined wooden cover. Réaumur used this hive especially to observe the activities of the queen bee, since its thinness forced the bees to construct honeycombs spread out on the glass. (From Réaumur, *Mémoires pour servir à l'histoire des insectes*, 1734-1742, vol.v, plate 23. Courtesy of the Wellcome Institute Library, London.)

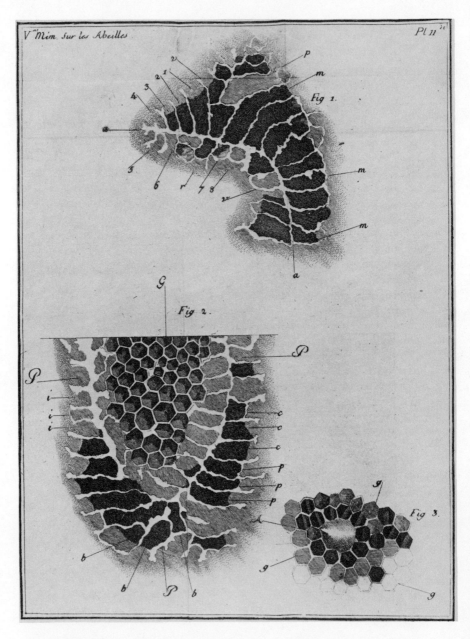

Fig 21. Three honeycombs examined by Bonnet. (From Bonnet, *Œuvres d'histoire naturelle et de philosophie*, 1779-1783, vol.v [pt.1]/10.)

Although Réaumur seems to have rejected anthropomorphic explanations in his study of ants (Théodoridès 1959:66), he constantly made use of political and social analogies in describing the behaviour of bees and the structure of the hive. In some cases such analogies played a heuristic role in his explanation of certain aspects of the behaviour of bees (Réaumur 1734-1742, 5:473). Réaumur affirmed that under normal conditions there is only one queen in a hive, laying from thirty to fifty thousand eggs every year, and he called her the 'Mere de tout son Peuple'. He considered drones to be males, counted from six to seven hundred in a single hive, and related the numbers obtained to different seasonal periods. He also noticed that drones did not work, stating that their only function was to fertilise the queen, and that the great majority of the population were worker bees. Réaumur counted from forty to fifty-five thousand worker bees in one hive. He considered them to be neuters and observed that they did all the work, collecting pollen and propolis, building the combs, and feeding the larvae. As already noted in classical sources, Réaumur observed that queen, drones, and workers were of different sizes, but correlated this fact with the three different kinds of cells that are to be seen in a comb: the queen's cell, the drones' cells, and the workers' cells. He calculated that the wax necessary to build a queen's cell would have been sufficient to build one hundred to one hundred and fifty ordinary cells. Like Swammerdam, he believed that the queen laid three different kinds of eggs in the three different kinds of cells and that, in so doing, she was never mistaken. He studied the feeding techniques of bees carefully and noticed that the larvae received different amounts of food according to their larval stage. Furthermore, he noticed, quite correctly, that the queen larvae received special food, which was both quantitatively more than that received by other larvae, and qualitatively different (the 'royal jelly'). By observing the behaviour of the queen and drones in the hive, Réaumur conjectured that they actually copulated, and he described the queen as a Messalina. He believed that the period of fecundation must logically occur when there were many drones, and therefore he could not understand how queens went on laying eggs in winter when no drones were to be seen in the hive.

Réaumur's observations and reflections on bees became quite popular among natural historians and beekeepers in the mid-eighteenth century. They were translated into German in a book published in 1759, and were the basis of the article 'Abeille' published in the *Encyclopédie* (Diderot and d'Alembert 1751-1765, 1:18-23). Bazin provided an elementary account of Réaumur's work in his *Histoire naturelle des abeilles* (1744), which was also translated into English; and Bonnet disseminated Réaumur's ideas in his own *Contemplation de la nature* (1764, 2:119-33). There he maintained, like his mentor, that worker honeybees were neuters and explained their devotion to the queen and especially to the larvae by assuming that the *police* of the hive was regulated by the principle of the conservation of species. By invoking this principle, Bonnet was apparently able to avoid any hint of anthropomorphism in his discussion of behaviour in the hive. In order to arrive at a better understanding of the behaviour of worker bees in the absence of a queen, Bonnet (1764, 2:128), with typical ingenuity, proposed a new experiment. He recommended that a flourishing hive, with all of its population, larvae, and honey well distributed, should be divided into two completely separate parts, and attention should be concentrated on the behaviour of the worker bees in the part without a queen. This experiment had actually already been carried out in 1760, before Bonnet's suggestion, by the German divine Adam Gottlob Schirach. His results were to throw new light not only on the bees' behaviour, but also on their complex system of reproduction.

Schirach was a remarkable man. In a period marked by growing interest in the foundation of learned and ever more specialised societies dedicated to the pursuit and propagation of useful knowledge, he founded a Society of Apiculture that attracted bee amateurs of both sexes. Its ideological base was physico-theology, and its aims were pragmatic. Because of the highly satisfactory results obtained by the rationalisation of beekeeping, publicised in its journal, the Society received the financial support of a number of reigning Sovereigns, some of whom sent their beekeepers to learn the new methods developed at Kleinbautzen, the headquarters of the Society. These techniques were very quickly adopted by many beekeepers in several German-speaking countries. Schirach himself wrote a *Melitto-theologia* (1767) and published all of the major results of his investigations in the journal of the Society during the 1760s. It was, however, partly through Bonnet's accounts (1770c, 1775a, 1775b, and 1775c) and even more through the French translation of Schirach's papers in a book entitled *Histoire naturelle de la reine des abeilles* (1771) that his lasting contribution to bee research was made available to French-speaking countries. This book was translated into Italian in 1774 (see letter 46, n.2) and discussed in at least one English periodical.

Schirach's investigations were aimed principally at solving a practical problem, that of increasing the number of swarms and consequently of colonies. He regarded the normal process of forming new colonies by swarming as not productive enough and looked for a method by which he could obtain 'artificial swarms'. He discovered such a method and first publicised it in 1760 (see Schirach 1771:xxxvi, 17-38). It consisted in placing a good number of worker honeybees and a large piece of comb containing larvae and honey, but no queen, in an empty hive. By keeping the hive closed for a few days, Schirach was able to observe that bees would start building a queen's cell, that as days passed they would become more and more active, and that after about twenty days a new queen would appear in the hive. Schirach's observations caused something of a stir and were confirmed by many beekeepers who adopted his method for obtaining 'artificial swarms'. Yet the phenomenon by which a new queen was produced remained mysterious to all beekeepers; and some stated that, although Schirach's observations were truthfully reported, they could not believe them. Schirach came to two main conclusions. The first was that any two to three day-old worker's larva, given the right conditions of housing (in a queen's cell) and of feeding ('royal jelly'), would develop into a queen. Second, there was, according to Schirach, no difference between a queen's egg and a worker's egg, which meant that the workers also were originally females and that it was only their upbringing that turned them into 'vestals' (Schirach 1771:189-98).

Both conclusions reached by Schirach were correct, in so far as modern research has shown that the genetic constitution of queens' eggs and workers' eggs is the same, and that very young larvae turn into either queens or workers depending upon how they are housed and fed. However both statements, as well as the evidence produced by Schirach, seemed to his contemporaries – as in fact they did – to overthrow the authoritative claims made by Swammerdam and Réaumur that there were three kinds of eggs and that the workers were neuters. Schirach also envisaged the possibility of a parthenogenetic reproductive system in bees, and erroneously conjectured that drones did not play any specific role in fertilisation. Perplexed by these new and striking observations and results, some beekeepers turned to Bonnet for advice and illumination. Among them were Schirach himself, Wilhelmi, and Riem. They all corresponded extensively on the subject of bees with Bonnet, who, either quoting at length from their letters or summarising them, composed three memoirs first published in Schirach's book (1771:181-254) and later separately (Bonnet 1775a, 1775b, and 1775c). Bonnet compiled two additional memoirs on the same subject and published them in his collected works (B.O., 5:123-77/10:196-281) in 1781. One of them, the fourth, reported new experiments made by Riem, while the fifth was mainly devoted to a critical analysis of the paper Needham sent Bonnet in 1780, which he had read at the Brussels Academy of Sciences on 9 December 1777 and had published in the Academy's *Mémoires* (Needham 1780c).

In the course of time, Bonnet modified his attitude toward Schirach's experiments and conclusions. At first he was unwilling to believe that workers' larvae if properly housed could develop into queens, influenced, as he admitted, by the great authorities of Swammerdam and Réaumur. But later, as more and more evidence accumulated, he passed from mild scepticism to cautious acceptance (Bonnet 1775b:427; B.O., 5:106/10:169):

Il y a [...] aujourd'hui beaucoup à changer dans les idées que Mr. de REAUMUR s'étoit faites sur le gouvernement ou la police des Abeilles. La Reine est bien toujours la Mere de tout son Peuple, & l'Ame de tous les travaux de la petite République. Mais la vie du Peuple a été mieux assurée. Par un moyen très-simple, & qu'aucun Naturaliste n'avoit soupçonné, les Abeilles peuvent en tout tems se donner une ou plusieurs Reines, & perpétuer ainsi la durée de leur République.

Les Abeilles ouvrieres ou les Neutres ne sont donc plus de vrais *Neutres*: elles sont toutes originairement de vraies Femelles, mais d'un genre fort singulier; des Femelles qui n'engendrent point, & qui ne peuvent engendrer; des Femelles condamnées à une virginité ou plutôt à une stérilité perpétuelle; des Femelles en un mot, qui ne sont point actuellement *Femelles*, mais qui auroient pu le devenir, si sous leur premiere forme, elles avoient été autrement logées & nourries.

This last statement, however, was to be challenged and modified by Riem. An indefatigable man and keen observer, Riem repeated and varied Schirach's experiments. In one such experiment he placed a comb with honey in a closed box, making certain that it contained no eggs, larvae, queen, or drones, but only a good number of worker bees. The result was that after several days he found eggs. He believed that the so-called neuters were actually females and that, given special circumstances, they could lay eggs. He also reported, after Bonnet had pressed him to do so, that in the dissection of some workers he had seen very small ovaries. Riem had indeed made a completely new observation. It is now well-known that workers also have rudimentary ovaries and that they can lay eggs several days after a colony has become queenless. But at the time Riem described his observations in a letter to Bonnet, this notion appeared incredible. On 13 July 1771 Bonnet replied to Riem: 'Ce fait, le plus remarquable de tous ceux que vous raportez, est aussi celui qui choque le plus ce que les Swammerdam, les Maraldi, les Réaumur, nous avoient enseigné sur la Théorie des Abeilles' (Schirach 1771:249; B.O., 5:117/10:187). Bonnet was very sceptical and urged Riem to repeat and verify his own observations.

These were the main lines of research on the problem of generation in bees when in 1773 Needham and Bonnet first mentioned the topic briefly in their correspondence (see letters 46 and 47). It was, however, not until 1780 that they really exchanged opinions on the subject (see letters 51, 52, and 53). The occasion was provided by Needham's sending to Bonnet his own recent paper on bees, which Bonnet severely criticised. The two scientists diverged completely on their opinions of Schirach's experiment and on their explanations of generation in bees.

Needham was well aware of the interest shown by various states in the rationalisation of beekeeping, an activity that constituted a remarkable economic resource. As Director of the Brussels Academy, which was dedicated 'par institution au progrès de toutes les connoissances utiles', he felt obliged to direct his own investigations to that end, thus hoping to help in the promotion of practical beekeeping, especially in the Ardennes (Needham 1780c:327). In his paper, Needham reviewed most of the literature on the subject of generation in bees, put forward his own explanation, and finally provided practical advice for the improvement of beekeeping. Needham regarded Schirach's experiments as 'contraires à nos idées reçues' and a 'mélange monstrueux de peu de vérités avec beaucoup de faussetés' (1780c:332, 334). He contested all of the statements made by Schirach, using the doubts raised by Wilhelmi and the observations made by Riem; and he resolutely denied the validity of Schirach's claim that, given adequate housing and food, a very young worker's larva could become a queen's larva. He then presented a theory of generation in bees, the essential points of which were based on the works of Swammerdam and Réaumur, on new observations published in 1777 by John Debraw (see letter 51, n.8), who claimed that drones impregnated the queen's eggs in the hive in the manner of fish, and on a few observations of his own. According to Needham, there existed two queens of different sizes, a large one and one the same size as common bees. The queens were the only females in the hive. The drones were males and were also of two sizes. He argued that the smaller ones were not evicted from the hive and would survive during the winter in order to impregnate the queen's eggs in the coming spring. Worker honeybees he thought were neuters. Three kinds of eggs thus existed according to Needham, the queen's, the drone's, and the worker's. They were distributed in combs with no discrimination, first by the queen and then by the workers. Because Needham assumed the existence of two different sizes of queens and because he believed in the existence of three kinds of eggs arbitrarily distributed in the different types of cells, he was able to provide an explanation of all the curious phenomena related by Schirach. The problem was, however, that he provided no observational evidence for his assumptions, an omission that was at once taken up by Bonnet.

In his letter of 8 March 1780 (letter 51) Bonnet listed all of the major topics on which he disagreed with Needham and accused him of not having undertaken experiments of his own (neither did Bonnet) and of making statements without providing evidence. 'Si donc vous avés fait vous même de nombreuses expériences sur ce sujet intéressant,' Bonnet queried, 'comment est il arrivé que vous ne les ayés point détaillées dans votre Mémoire? Comment n'avés-vous point indiqué votre marche, vos procedés, les précautions que vous avés prisés pour n'être point trompé, les divers faits qui se sont présentés sur votre route &c &c?' (letter 51). Commenting that he expected more from Needham, Bonnet further reproached him: 'Ce n'est pas ainsi que vous avés traité d'autres sujets d'Histoire naturelle qui ont rendu votre nom célèbre.' Needham answered (letter 52) by reiterating what he had previously written in his paper and by claiming that he had in fact offered proofs for all of his assertions. Because the subject of the generation of bees had already been discussed by so many people, Needham explained, he had to treat it somewhat differently than he had other topics in natural history so that he could separate the true observations and theories of others from the false. He also pointed out that he *had* included a report of his own observations on bees at the end of his memoir. Bonnet's reply (letter 53) briefly repeated his critical remarks on Needham's lack of experimental proof and criticised Needham's rejection of Riem's observation of ovaries in worker bees. Clearly, Bonnet and Needham possessed completely incompatible views on the nature of generation in bees and on the methods of investigation one ought to pursue on the subject.

Needham died in Brussels on 30 December 1781, but his controversy with Bonnet on bees continued even after his death. Bonnet published in 1781 in his collected works a new memoir on bees partly dedicated to a critical investigation of two statements made by Needham. Bonnet began in an ironic vein: 'M̂R. NEEDHAM, qui avoit cru assez facilement à la prétendue conversion du Végétal en Animal, ne s'étoit point pressé de croire à celle d'un Ver d'Abeille commune en Ver de Reine' (B.O., 5:143/10:227). In response to Needham's claim that in Schirach's experiments the larva of the queen developed from a misplaced queen's egg and not from a worker's egg he opposed a new and negative statement by Wilhelmi, to whom he had expressly written (B.O., 5:147/10:233). On this occasion Wilhelmi also gave Bonnet confirmation of a new observation made by Riem, that when worker honeybees did lay eggs, these developed *only* into drones (which is quite correct, because they are unfertilised eggs). Second, to Needham's claim that queens existed of exactly the same size as worker honeybees, he opposed Wilhelmi's competent and resolute denial (B.O., 5:159/10:253).

The problem of generation in bees continued to occupy Bonnet for the remaining years of his life. A year before his death in 1793 he had the pleasure of seeing in print the *Nouvelles observations sur les abeilles, adressées à Charles Bonnet* (1792). This classic account was the work of his pupil, the blind Genevan, François Huber. Aided by his assistant François Burnens and by his wife Maria Aimée, Huber was able to demonstrate with searching logic the mating flight of drones and virgin queens.[6]

6. It should be noted that Fraser (1951b) has shown that the beekeeper Anton Janscha, appointed Imperial and Royal Beekeeper by Maria Theresa in 1770, had published twenty years before Huber an exact account of the fertilisation of the queen, but that it had passed unnoticed.

The letters

Note on the text

In our transcription of the Bonnet-Needham letters, we have attempted to provide as faithful a copy as possible, preserving original spellings, capitalisations, and punctuation. The principal exception to this policy is that in Needham's letters, we have capitalised the first letter of the first word of each sentence beginning after a full stop, where Needham generally used lower-case letters. We have, however, followed Needham's own capitalisations (or lack thereof) of proper names and his tendency to capitalise '*Je*'. The reader should also be alerted that, as an Englishman, Needham wrote French in a somewhat idiosyncratic style and that his French spellings and grammar were frequently inconsistent and often incorrect. Rather than littering the text with *sic*s or correcting Needham's errors, we have chosen to present his letters exactly as Bonnet would have received them (see fig. 22). In a few instances, especially in letter 11, we have used square brackets [ ] to indicate words or phrases that have a tentative reading due to an obscured text. In both the Needham and Bonnet letters, we have not included crossed-out words nor have we identified interlinear words or phrases. The latter are incorporated into the text at their appropriate points of insertion. Finally, in the Bonnet letters we have spelled out '&' as '*et*'.

In the case of Bonnet's letters, the originals that Needham received seem no longer to be in existence. In the BPUG, however, are preserved two sets of Bonnet's letters to Needham. One is the draft copy (which we shall designate as copy A) that was made by Bonnet's secretary from his dictation and from which the letters sent to Needham were then made (see fig. 23). The second set (which we shall designate as copy B) is a copy that was made under Bonnet's direction after 1780, most probably intended for publication (see fig. 24). Copy A was produced by a succession of secretaries working for Bonnet and presents numerous differences in orthography, whereas in copy B (which is all in one hand), the spellings have been standardised. We have based our transcription on copy A, which is clearly more faithful to the originals, even though this has necessitated preserving the secretarial inconsistencies and spelling mistakes that exist in these letters, especially in the earlier ones.

Several words and phrases present in copy A were changed or omitted in copy B. Such passages are indicated in the text by a footnote letter that either follows the word or, in the case of a phrase, both precedes and follows the relevant passage. Where a word or phrase was changed in copy B, the text note reads 'B:', followed by the substitute passage. Where a word or phrase was added, the note repeats the word in the text, followed by the new material. Where a word or phrase was omitted in copy B, the text note reads simply 'B: *omitted*'. Some of the letters in copy A were not included by Bonnet in copy B; where appropriate this is indicated in the manuscript location notes. Our intent has been to present not only the letters as Needham would have received them, but also the alterations that Bonnet considered necessary to make in them for publication.

Each letter is followed by the manuscript location (in the BPUG), references to any previous publications of the letter or extracts from it, and text notes (where necessary). The footnotes at the bottom of each page provide identifications of the personalities, books, letters, disputes, and scientific questions mentioned or alluded to in the letters. The aim of the footnotes is to provide the principal bibliographical references relating to an individual or a topic. For well-known individuals we have not given biographical details, but simply referred to an authoritative biography or entry in a standard reference work (such as the *D.S.B.*), to the main primary and secondary bibliographies, and, where possible, to reviews of recent scholarship. In the case of less well-known individuals, we provide a short biographical sketch, followed by bibliographical information as outlined above. In the interests of avoiding needless repetition, we have generally not cited secondary literature that is included in the bibliographies of the works we cite. Finally, we have included references whenever possible to indicate when a person mentioned in the letters was in contact with Bonnet or Needham.

I

Needham to Bonnet – Turin, 28 August 1760

Mon cher Monsieur,

Voulant m'eclaircir sur un fait assés interessant de l'histoire naturelle J'ai pris la liberté par cette lettre de m'adresser à vous, et je me persuade tant pour l'amitie, que vous me portés, que pour le liaison, que ce fait bien eclairci doit avoir avec les premiers principes, aussi bien que pour les consequences importantes, qu'on peut tirer, que vous ne negligeriés rien, qui dependra de vous, dans la recherche, que Je vous prie de faire. Voila de quoi il s'agit; il y a aux environs quatre ans que Je fait connoissance avec le chevalier Worsley[1] à Spaa; ce seigneur a des grandes possessions dans l'isle de Wight, et entre autres des salines tres considerables. Il m'assura d'avoir observé, quand toute l'humidite étoit evaporée, par la force du feu, et quand le sel étoit au plus haut periode de sa chaleur, naitre de tres petits vers rouges à peine visibles aux yeux sans microscope, qui vivoient pendant qu'un certain degré considerable de chaleur duroit, et qui devenoient languissants à proportion, que la chaleur diminuoit jusqu'a mourir, quand le sel étoit quasi refroidi. La chose, il me semble, merite d'etre examinée de près, en tant qu'elle etend nos idées extremement, et prolonge l'echelle de la vie animale à perte de vûe; tous les elemens deviennent par ce moyen en quelque sens habitables, au moins n'aurons nous aucune difficulté d'imaginer tel temperament qu'on voudra propre à peupler des planettes à la plus petite distance possible du soleil. En un mot les consequences m'ont paru si etendues, et en même tems si contraires à nos idées ordinaires, resserrées comme elles sont, que J'aurai été tres disposé à croire, quelque illusion de la part de l'observateur, s'il m'avoit pas assuré, qu'il avoit envoyé à la societé Royale de Londres un certain nombre de ces vers,[2] qui, quoique morts, paroissoient à l'examen des corps autant organisés, que tout autre ver. J'aurai pû ecrire à M[r.] Haller[3] en droiture, qui est à la tête des salines de son Pais, pour

---

1. Sir Thomas Worsley, sixth baronet of Appuldurcombe, Isle of Wight, died in 1768. Little is known about him; he was the father of Richard Worsley (1751-1805), an antiquary and traveller (see Worsley 1781:218). At the time when Needham wrote this letter, Worsley was Lieutenant Colonel Commandant of the south battalion of the Hampshire militia, the same battalion in which the historian Edward Gibbon (1737-1794) was a captain. Gibbon (1966:116) described him thus: 'Sir Thomas Worsley was an easy good-humoured man fond of the table and of his bed: our conferences were marked by every stroke of the midnight and morning hours, and the same drum which invited him to rest has often summoned me to the parade. His example encouraged the daily practise of hard and even excessive drinking'.

2. No letters of Sir Thomas Worsley are to be found at the Royal Society, London.

3. For a short but accurate biography of Albrecht von Haller (1708-1777), Bern's most famous scholar and physiologist, see Erich Hintzsche, *D.S.B.*, 6 (1972) 61-67. A bibliography of Haller's writings may be found in Lundsgaard-Hansen-von Fischer (1959). An excellent list of secondary literature up to 1970 is provided by Toellner (1971:203-28); for books and papers on Haller published after that date see Fontana (1980:18) and Roe (1981:184-204). At the time when Needham wrote this letter to Bonnet, Haller was living at Roche as director of the Bern saltworks; on his diverse

m'eclaircir, mais soit qu'il a été effraié de ma metaphysique, soit qu'il la meprisé, comme creuse, illusoire, et fantastique, il n'a pas encore daigné de repondre à une asses longue lettre, et un memoire, que Je lui a envoyé, il y a present pres des neuf mois.[4] En effet Je ne dois pas trop m'ettonner, car c'est rare qu'un Physicien de son merite, et de son grand sçavoir sort de la physique pour entrer dans ce qu'on croit communement les espaces imaginaires de la metaphysique. Le champ de la physique est si etendu, et en même tems les objets, qu'il contient, si sensibles à tout le monde, que les decouvertes semblent donner une reputation, et fournir des plaisirs beaucoup plus solides. On commence par poser des bornes imaginaires à la science, et on espere moyennant ces bornes de pouvoir l'epuiser, c'est ainsi que descartes[5] a cherché à ecarter les difficultés, qui le pressoient sur la divisibilité infinie de la matiere par sa division en parties indefinies,[6] aussi bien que le chevalier Newton,[7] en posant pour principe, que les parties primitives physiques des corps étoient naturellement indivisibles par les forces ordinaires de la nature;[8] laissant entierement à coté la partie metaphysique de la question; lui il avoit besoin des principes pour les corps physiques fixes, et inalterables naturellement afin de soutenir le systeme, qu'il avoit etabli; et le systeme de descartes au contraire demandoit des principes toujours divisibles pour

activities there see Valceschini (1977) and Balmer (1977:26-29). The extant correspondence between Needham and Haller has been edited by Mazzolini (1976), and the momentous correspondence of Bonnet and Haller has been edited by Sonntag (1983).

4. Needham's letter cannot be traced. It was dated 12 November 1759; see 'Bestandtheile des Hallerschen Briefwechsels', BB, Mss. Hist. Helv. XVIII., vol.68. See also Mazzolini (1976:70 n.13). Needham's mémoire, entitled 'Ideae quaedam generales de mundi systemate', is preserved in the BNM, B. II.3151/19. A very short and slightly altered section of it was published by Needham in Spallanzani (1769, pt.1:289-91); the entire mémoire has been published by Monti (1985).

5. For an authoritative biography of René Descartes (1596-1650), see Charles Adam, 'Vie et œuvres de Descartes: étude historique', published as vol.xii of Descartes's works (Descartes 1897-1910). For a bibliography of Descartes's works published in the seventeenth century, see Guibert (1976); for an annotated bibliography of works on Descartes published in the years 1800-1960, see Sebba (1964); for secondary sources on Descartes's mathematical works, see May (1973:123-26); and for more recent literature on Descartes, see Doney (1978) and the serial publication *Studia Cartesiana*. For Descartes's works owned by Needham, see *Catalogue* (1782, pt.1:14 and pt.2:62, 63, 88, 92).

6. Needham probably had in mind the following passage from the *Principia philosophiae*, I, §26: 'Nos autem illa omnia, in quibus sub aliquâ consideratione nullum finem poterimus invenire, non quidem affirmabimus esse infinita, sed ut indefinita spectabimus. Ita, quia non possumus imaginari extensionem tam magnam, quin intelligamus adhuc majorem esse posse, dicemus magnitudinem rerum possibilium esse indefinitam. Et quia non potest dividi aliquod corpus in tot partes, quin singulae adhuc ex his partibus divisibiles intelligantur, putabimus quantitatem esse indefinitè divisibilem. Et quia non potest fingi tantus stellarum numerus, quin plures adhuc à Deo creari potuisse credamus, illarum etiam numerum indefinitum supponemus; atque ita de reliquis' (Descartes 1897-1910, 8, pt.1:15). Other references to the problem of the infinite divisibility of matter in Descartes's works include *Principia philosophiae*, II, §34 (Descartes 1897-1910, 8, pt.1:59-60); *Meditationes de prima philosophia*, VI (Descartes 1897-1910, 7:85-86); and *Les Météores*, II (Descartes 1897-1910, 6:238-39).

7. For an introduction to the life and work of Isaac Newton (1643-1727), see I. Bernard Cohen, *D.S.B.*, 10 (1974) 42-101; the major intellectual biography of Newton is Westfall (1980). For a bibliography of Newton's works and works on Newton, see Wallis (1977); and for reviews of recent literature on Newton, see Pighetti (1960), Whiteside (1962), Westfall (1976), and A. R. Hall (1982). For Newton's works owned by Needham, see *Catalogue* (1782, pt.1:61-62).

8. Isaac Newton, *Philosophiae naturalis principia mathematica*, editio secunda auctior et emendatior, Bk. III, rule III, pp.357-58 (Cambridge 1713).

59.

Mon cher Monsieur,

voulant m'eclaircir sur un fait assés interessant de l'histoire naturelle J'ai pris la liberté par cette lettre de m'adresser à vous, et je me persuade tant pour l'amitié, que vous me portés, que pour le liaison, que ce fait bien eclairci doit avoir avec les premiers principes, aussi bien que pour les consequences importantes, qu'on peut tirer, que vous ne negligerés rien, qui dependra de vous, dans la recherche, que je vous prie de faire. voilà de quoi il s'agit : il y a aux environs quatre ans que je fais connoissance avec le chevalier Worsley à Spaa; ce seigneur a des grandes possessions dans l'isle de Wight, et entre autres des salines très considerables; il m'assura d'avoir observées, quand toute l'humidité étoit evaporée, par la force de feu, et quand le sel au plus haut periode de sa chaleur, naitre de très petits vers rouges à peine visibles aux yeux sans microscope, qui vivoient pendant qu'un certain degré de chaleur duroit, et qui devenoient languissants à proportion, que la chaleur diminuoit jusqu'à mourir, quand le sel étoit quasi refroidi. la chose, il me semble, merite d'être exa= =minée de près, en nous quelle etend nos idées anciennement, et prolonge l'echelle de la vie animale à peine de vûe, vous les valeurs deviennent par ce moyen en quelque peu habitables, au moins n'aurons nous aucune difficulté d'imaginer tel temperament qu'on voudra propre à peupler des planetes à la plus petite distance possible du soleil, en un mot les consequences nous paroissent si etendues, et en même tems si contraires à nos idées ordinaires, resserrées comme elles sont, que j'aurai été très disposé à croire, quelque illusion de la part de l'observateur, s'il n'avoit pas assuré, qu'il avoit envoyé à la société Royale de Londres un certain nombre de ces vers, qui quoique morts, paroissoient à l'examen des corps autant organisés, que tout autre vers.

s'accomoder en tout sens à remplir toute l'espace, et neanmoins ni l'un ni l'autre vouloit s'embarquer dans les difficultés metaphysiques de la question. En effet cette façon de repondre peut servir à eluder, mais jamais à resoudre la question, qui demeure toujours en son entier, et qui touche de tres pres pourtant à la nature de la matiere en tant que substance productive de tous les phenomenes physiques, que nous voyons. On croit communement, que les phenomenes physiques ne menent pas necessairement à la metaphysique, mais qu'on examine sans prejugé toutes vos observations, et celles de M[r.] Trembley[9] sur le Polype,[10] et qu'on fixe, s'il est possible, les principes de la generation en deça de la metaphysique. Mais Je n'ai guere besoin de prendre un si grand champ, Je ne voudrai que leur proposer trois phenomens, qui regardent le seul organe de la vûe pour me dire apres, s'ils ne menent pas beaucoup plus loin, que la mechanique connue, et la physique ordinaire. Nous avons actuellement deux exemples connus de deux personnes, d'une dame en Ecosse, et d'un marchand drapier à Birmingham en angleterre, qui voient parfaitment tous les objets, qui connoissoient les personnes d'aussi loin, q'un autre, et qui neanmoins ne sçavent pas distinguer une couleur d'un autre; apparemment que pour eux tout est blanc, et noir, ombre, et lumiere, et qu'ils connoissoient les personnes, comme nous autres nous distinguons les portraits en estampe. Le second phenomene extraordinaire regarde une femme à Lyons, qui m'a été communique par M[r.] Bertrandi[11] chirurgien du Roi de Sardaigne, qui a fait l'experience lui même avec trois

---

9. For a biography of the well-known Genevan naturalist Abraham Trembley (1710-1784), see J. Baker (1952), who lists all of his works. For a shorter biography, see John R. Baker, *D.S.B.*, 13 (1976) 457-58. A valuable source for Trembley's early intellectual development and scientific investigations is provided by his correspondence with Réaumur, edited by M. Trembley (1943). A close friend of Bonnet for over thirty years and one of his most assiduous correspondents (sixtynine letters from Trembley to Bonnet are in the BPUG), Trembley is often mentioned in Bonnet's autobiography, which was composed of letters originally addressed to Haller, Trembley, and Saussure (see Savioz 1948b:217-19). Needham and Trembley met when Trembley visited England from June to November 1745. The two observed polyps and the milt vessels of calamary together; and Needham gave Trembley some blighted wheat grains, which Trembley later shared with Allamand (see Needham 1745:8 and 1748:648; see also letter 6, n.4).

10. Experiments on the freshwater polyp, or hydra (*Chlorohydra viridissima*), the strange aquatic 'plant-animal' whose parts could regenerate into new hydra when cut, and observations on its normal reproductive method by budding were reported by Trembley in his classic account, *Mémoires pour servir à l'histoire d'un genre de polypes d'eau douce, à bras en forme de cornes* (Leide 1744). As noted by Vartanian (1953:388), 'Trembley's contemporaries had the startling spectacle of Nature caught, as it were, *in flagrante* with the creation of life out of its own substance without prior design.' For secondary literature on Trembley's discoveries and on their impact, see especially Vartanian (1950), Moeschlin-Krieg (1953), Roger (1963:384-95), Ritterbush (1964:122-25), Bodemer (1964), Gasking (1967:64-65), Schazmann (1976:55-61), and Delaporte (1977:55-57).

11. Giovanni Ambrogio Bertrandi (1723-1765) was born in Turin of very poor parents. A scholarship enabled him to study surgery at the Real Collegio delle Provincie. In 1749 he became affiliated with the Turin College of Surgeons and began practising surgery. In 1752 he was sent with a Royal stipend to specialise in surgery both in Paris and in London. On his return to Turin in 1754 he was first made Professore straordinario of Surgery and Anatomy at the Royal University and in 1758, Professor of Practical Surgery. A member of the Academy of Turin, Bertrandi made great innovations in the teaching of surgery in the Kingdom of Sardinia. The best biography of Bertrandi is provided by G. A. Penchienati and G. Brugnone in Bertrandi (1786-1799, 1:11-96); see also Bonino (1824-1825, 2:244-64) and Domenico Celestino, *D.B.I.*, 6 (1967) 637-39. All of Bertrandi's published and posthumous works are included in Bertrandi (1786-1799). Bertrandi did not describe the case reported by Needham in any of his works dealing with the anatomy or the surgery of the eye.

autres chirurgiens: elle voit parfaitment bien les deux yeux ouverts, mais soit qu'elle ferme ou l'un, ou l'autre, c'est la même chose, elle ne voit absolument rien avec un seul œil. Le troisieme phenomene est encore plus extraordinaire, s'il est possible, et cela m'a été communiqué depuis peu par Milord Tichfield[12] fils de duc de dorset[13] actuellement ici à Turin: il regarde Madame la duchesse de dorset sa mere;[14] cette dame l'assuré plusieurs fois, et lui même a vû des preuves sensibles en differens tems; que quand elle est agitée par quelque nouvelle imprevue, ou quelque accident triste, qui arrive, elle ne voit pour quelque tems, pendant que l'agitation dure quelquefois plusieurs jours de suite, que la moitie de tout objet pris selon sa longueur, qui se presente, et cela non pas d'une maniere confuse, mais claire, et distincte. Je pourai ajouter quantité des autres phenomenes, qui regardent la seule vision, et qu'on trouvera à la fin de l'optique de Smith,[15] mais ceux ci suffisent pour prouver la necessité malgré nous de sortir hors de la physique, et la mechanique ordinaire. Enfin pour finir cette lettre deja trop longue, que Je vous ecris selon ma façon en assés mauvais françois; Je vous prie de vous informer, ce que Je n'ose pas faire moi meme, aupres de M[r.] Haller[16] de la verité de cette premiere observation du chevalier

12. As Needham later clarified in his letter of 26 September 1760 (here letter 3), he did not mean the son of the duke of Dorset but rather William Henry Cavendish Bentinck, marquess of Titchfield (1738-1809), who was the son of the Duke of Portland and who later himself became the third Duke of Portland. Head of the Rockingham whigs for a number of years and Home Secretary from 1794 to 1801, Portland was twice appointed Prime Minister in 1783 and in 1807. For a short biography see H. Morse Stephens, *D.N.B.*, 4 (1885) 302-304; and for his political career, see Feiling (1959) and Turberville (1958). In December 1757, after taking his M.A. at Oxford, Titchfield was sent abroad to make the Grand Tour. He spent three years on the Continent, apparently mainly in Italy (see Turberville 1938-1939, 2:33-52).

13. William Cavendish Bentinck, second Duke of Portland (1709-1762), succeeded to the dukedom when he was still a boy. He owed most of his education to a Swiss tutor, John Achard, who later became his loyal friend. In 1739 he was elected a Fellow of the Royal Society. He lived a quiet domestic life at Bulstrode and Welbeck; and, according to his only biographer, 'he did not engage in politics, and the only public functions in which we hear of his taking part were chapters of the Garter' (Turberville 1938-1939, 2:18; see also pp.17-20, 27-28). For Portland's relation to Achard, see Goulding (1913).

14. Margaret Cavendish Holles Harley, Duchess of Portland (1715-1785), only daughter and heiress of Edward, second Earl of Oxford, married the second Duke of Portland on 11 July 1734 at Oxford Chapel, Marylebone. More active than her husband, the Duchess loved collecting, as did most of her Harley ancestors; and she collected books, coins, pictures, busts, bronzes, miniatures, and many objects of natural history such as corals, fossils, and fish. She also purchased the famous Barberini vase (now known as the Portland vase). She had an interest in botany and entomology, saw much of the society of the day, and was in contact with literary circles. She corresponded with Rousseau who, on one occasion, adopted the title of 'l'herboriste de Madame la Duchesse de Portland' (Leigh, 5971). According to Horace Walpole (1717-1797), who was among the purchasers, she ordered that her entire collection should be sold after her death for the benefit of her second son and her daughters. The collection was indeed sold in May and June 1786 (see Walpole 1936). An account of her circle of friends is given by Mary Delany (1700-1788), who spent many summers with the Duchess at Bulstrode (Delany 1861-1862); for a biography, see Turberville (1938-1939, 2:20-30) and Schazmann (1976:173-82).

15. Needham is alluding to 'An essay upon distinct and indistinct vision' by the London physician James Jurin (1684-1750), who was from 1721 to 1727 Secretary of the Royal Society. The essay was published as an appendix to the 2nd volume (pp.115-71) of Robert Smith's *A complete system of opticks* (Cambridge 1738) and provided an excellent account of contemporary physiological optics and especially of accommodation. On Jurin, see G. T. Bettany, *D.N.B.*, 30 (1892) 229-30.

16. Lengthy quotations from Needham's letter were included by Bonnet in his letter to Haller of 3 September 1760; see Sonntag (1983:216-19).

Worsley, et de me communiquer la reponse, si elle vous vient, avant mon depart pour l'Italie au commencement du mois de Janvier de l'année prochaine. Vous adresserés votre lettre, s'il vous plait, pour moi à l'academie Royale à Turin, ou je serai en tout tems charmé d'avoir de vos nouvelles, aussi bien que de Mr Trembley, et Je vous prie en même tems de le saluer de ma part de la maniere la plus respectueuse. M.[r] de voltaire[17] serait-il malade, ou s'il lui a survenu quelque accident qui auroit donné occasion au bruit, qui couroit ici de sa mort? Comment va la vûe?[18] Ecrivés moi quatre mots de reponse à votre loisir, et me croyés toujours, mon cher Monsieur, avec estime, et respect,

                    votre tres sincere ami, et tres obeissant serviteur,

                                                            Needham.

à Turin, ce 28. de Aoust 1760.

MANUSCRIPT
    BPUG, MS Bonnet 26:119r-120v.

2

Bonnet to Needham – Geneva, 16 September 1760

                              a Geneve le 16.e 7.bre 1760
    Vôtre Lettre, Monsieur mon cher Confrere, m'a fait un très grand plaisir, et je recevrai toûjours avec beaucoup de reconnoissance tout ce que vous voudrés-bien me communiquer. Vous ne pouviés-pas mieux vous adresser qu'à-moi pour aller à Mr de Haller: il y a long-tems que nous avons ensemble une etroitte correspondance.[1] Dès que j'eus rèçeu vôtre Lettre je m'empressai à lui écrire[2] et a lui expimer tout le cas que je fais de votre merite, de vos Talens et de vos Decouvertes. Je ne le croiois pas dans le tort vis-à-vis de vous; je le connois trop bien et je sçais trop combien il apprécie les Talens. Voiés, mon cher Confrére par l'extrait cy-joint de sa Reponse si je me suis trompé.
    Vous avès ici la Lettre que vous écrit Mr de Haller.[3] J'avois bien présumé

17. For a biography of François-Marie Arouet de Voltaire (1694-1778), see Besterman (1976). For a bibliography of his writings, see Bengesco (1882-1890); and for lists of studies on Voltaire, see Barr (1929) and Barr and Spear (1968). A review of recent scholarship on Voltaire is given by Candaux (1979). Voltaire owned several books by Bonnet (1760, 1762, 1764, 1769a); he also owned Needham's edition of Spallanzani (1769), together with Needham's pamphlets on miracles (see Havens and Torrey 1959:113, 233; *Bibliotheka* 1961:194, 648-49; and Roe 1985). For Voltaire's work owned by Needham, see *Catalogue* (1782, pt.1:52-53, 87, 93-94, and pt.2:75, 92, 120). For Needham's controversies with Voltaire, see sections 5 and 6 of the Introduction; and on Bonnet and Voltaire, see Marx (1976:514-33) and section 5 of the Introduction.
18. On Bonnet's sight problems, see Savioz (1948b:324-39) and Soleto (1968).

1. Bonnet's correspondence with Haller began in 1754 and continued until Haller's death in 1777; see Sonntag (1983).
2. See letter 1, n.16.
3. Haller had first sent his reply to Needham in Paris, but it was returned to him because Needham was no longer there; see Sonntag (1983:219). The letter was dated 29 July 1760, but it cannot be traced; see Mazzolini (1976:70).

qu'il revoqueroit en doute l'existence de ces Vers. Vous sçavés aussi bien que moi, les soins, les précautions, le travail qu'exigent des Faits de ce genre pour être bien constatés. Le témoignage de la Societé Roiale, quoi que très respectable, ne me suffit point: ce ne seroit pas la premiére fois qu'un Corps éclairé s'en seroit laissé imposer. Un pareil Corps ni aucun Corps ne peut assés approfondir; il faut toûjours en revenir à quelque Observateur infatigable qui, comme moi, veuille bien se crever les deux[a] yeux pour le service de la verité. Vous sçavés, mon cher Confrere, tout ce que les *Pucerons*[4] m'ont couté; vous n'ignorés pas à quel point ils ont maltraité ma vüe, et pourtant vous allés me proposer d'observer ces infinimens petits du Sel? Y songés-vous, je vous en conjure? Gardés-vous bien vous même de les observer, et menagés-enfin ces yeux qui nous ont valu tant de belles connoissances.

Je suis bien eloigné d'être du nombre de ceux qui meprisent la Metaphysique; j'en fais au contraire le plus grand cas: elle est, à mon avis, une espéce de Geometrie, aussi précieuse que la Geometrie même. Mais il faut convenir que tous ceux qui ont manié la Metaphysique n'etoient pas doüés de cet Esprit Geometrique qui sçait comparer, combiner, généraliser, et qui ne tire des Faits que les conséquences qui en découlent immédiatement. La Metaphysique est fille de la Physique; elle doit donc comme sa Mere tenir à l'observation, et l'Art d'observer est trop peu connu encore. Il ne faut donc pas se presser trop de recourir aux explications Metaphysiques; il faut n'y recourir que lorsque les explications Phisiques sont evidamment insuffisantes. Je ne recourrois donc point à la Metaphysique pour rendre raison des Faits singuliers que vous me communiqués dans vôtre Lettre. Ils ne m'ont point du tout surpris et l'un deux m'etoit très connu pour l'avoir moi-même observé plusieurs fois. J'en sçais encore de plus singulier et dont j'ai aussi été temoin. Vous en verrés bien tôt une explication qui vous satisfera, je pense, et que je n'ai puisée que dans la comparaison exacte des Faits. Je n'espere pas de pouvoir vous l'envoyer avant le Mois de Decembre prochain, et comme vous partés de Turin en Janvier, dites-moi où et comment il faudra que je vous la fasse parvenir. Vous verrés-ici ce que peut une Analyse rigoureuse en Matière de Metaphysique, et vous trouverés que cette Science a été bien mal traittée par la plupart des Auteurs qui m'ont precedés.

Mr de Voltaire peut dire comme nôtre Rousseau,[5] qu'on l'a accusé de tout

4. Bonnet's 'Observations sur les pucerons' are contained in the first part of his *Traité d'insectologie* (Paris 1745). See also B.O., 1:1-113/1:1-154.

5. Courtois's (1923) chronology is still a valuable guide to the biography of Jean-Jacques Rousseau (1712-1778). For bibliographies of Rousseau's works, see Dufour (1925) and Sénelier (1950); and for works in French on Rousseau published during the eighteenth century, see Conlon (1981). Bibliographies of works on Rousseau are contained in the serial publication *Annales de la Société Jean-Jacques Rousseau*; and reviews of recent scholarship on Rousseau are presented in Trousson (1977) and Wirz (1979). Bonnet's opposition to Rousseau's ideas first manifested itself in his refutation of Rousseau's *Discours sur l'origine et les fondemens de l'inégalité parmi les hommes* (R.O., 3:109-223), which took the form of an anonymous and apparently polite letter, signed 'Philopolis, Citoyen de Genève', and was published in the *Mercure de France* (October 1755:71-77; see also Leigh, 316; R.O., 3:1383-86; and B.O., 8:331-37/18:133-42). In this letter, Bonnet pointed out, in a somewhat patronising fashion, the paradoxes inherent in Rousseau's thinking. Rousseau's answer was published posthumously in 1782 (see Leigh, 328, and R.O., 3:230-36). Bonnet once even went so far as to express regret in a letter to Haller that disapprobation of Rousseau could only be expressed by burning his

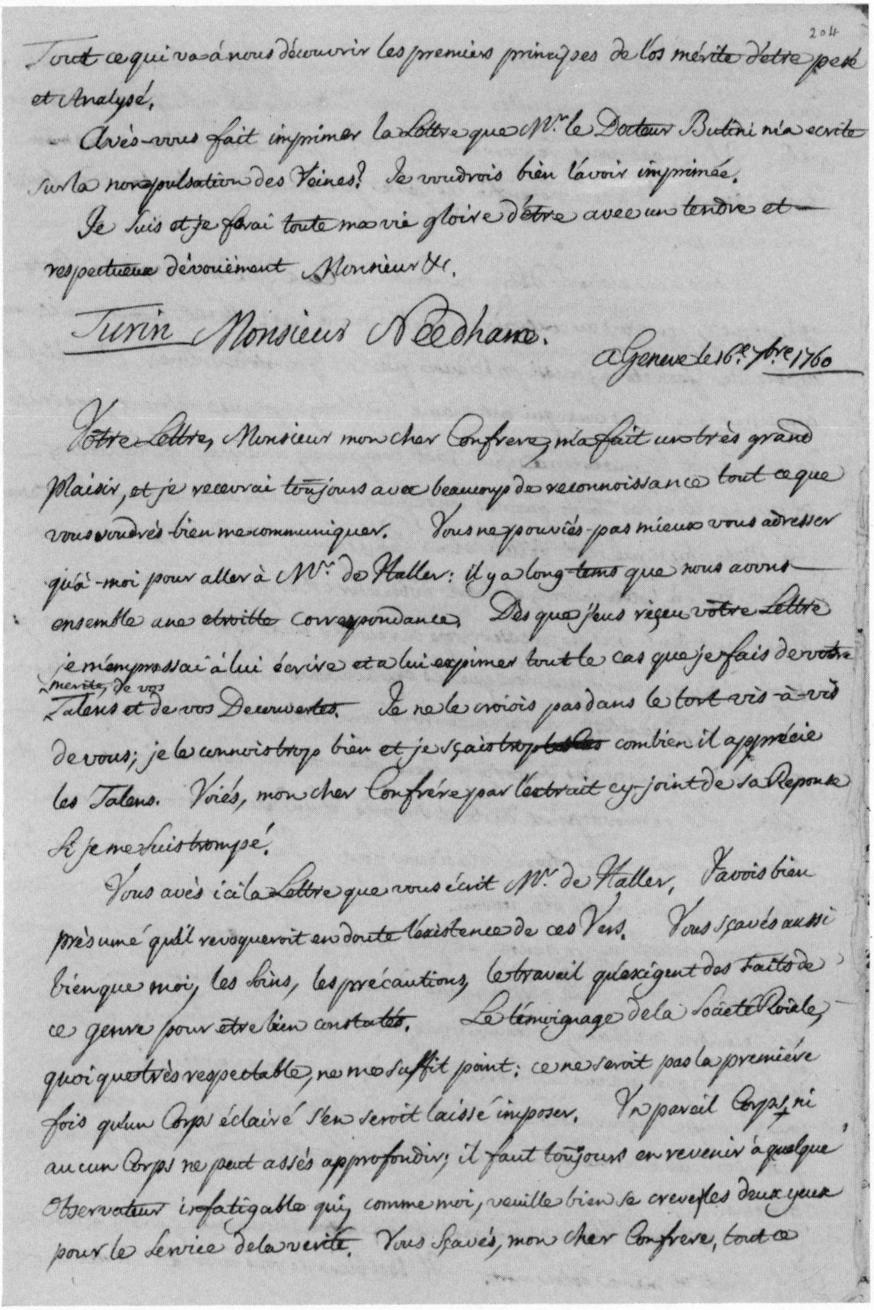

Tout ce qui va à nous découvrir les premiers principes de los mérite d'être pesé et Analysé.

— Avés-vous fait imprimer la Lettre que Mr le Docteur Butini m'a écrite sur la non-pulsation des Veines? Je voudrois bien l'avoir imprimée.

Je suis et je ferai toute ma vie gloire d'être avec un tendre et respectueux dévoüement Monsieur &c.

Turin Monsieur Needham.   à Genève le 16.e 7bre 1760

Votre Lettre, Monsieur mon cher Confrere, m'a fait un très grand plaisir, et je recevrai toujours avec beaucoup de reconnoissance tout ce que vous voudrés bien me communiquer. Vous ne pouviés pas mieux vous adresser qu'à moi pour aller à Mr de Haller: il y a long-tems que nous avons ensemble une étroitte Correspondance. Dès que j'eus reçu votre Lettre je m'empressai à lui écrire et à lui exprimer tout le cas que je fais de votre mérite, de vos Talens et de vos Decouvertes. Je ne le croiois pas dans le tort vis-à-vis de vous; je le connoirois trop bien et je sçaois trop bien combien il apprécie les Talens. Voiés, mon cher Confrère par l'extrait cy-joint de sa Reponse si je ne me suis trompé.

Vous avés ici la Lettre que vous écrit Mr de Haller, j'avois bien prés une qu'il revoqueroit en doute l'existence de ces Vers. Vous sçavés aussi bien que moi, les soins, les précautions, le travail qu'exigent des faits de ce genre pour être bien constatés. Le témoignage de la Société Roiale, quoique très respectable, ne me suffit point; ce ne seroit pas la première fois qu'un Corps éclairé s'en seroit laissé imposer. Un pareil Corps, ni aucun Corps ne peut assés approfondir; il faut toujours en revenir à quelque Observateur infatigable qui, comme moi, veuille bien se crever les deux yeux pour le service de la verité. Vous sçavés, mon cher Confrere, tout ce

Fig. 23. Bonnet's secretary's draft (copy A) of his first letter to Needham, dated 16 September 1760. (Courtesy of the Bibliothèque Publique et Universitaire, Geneva.)

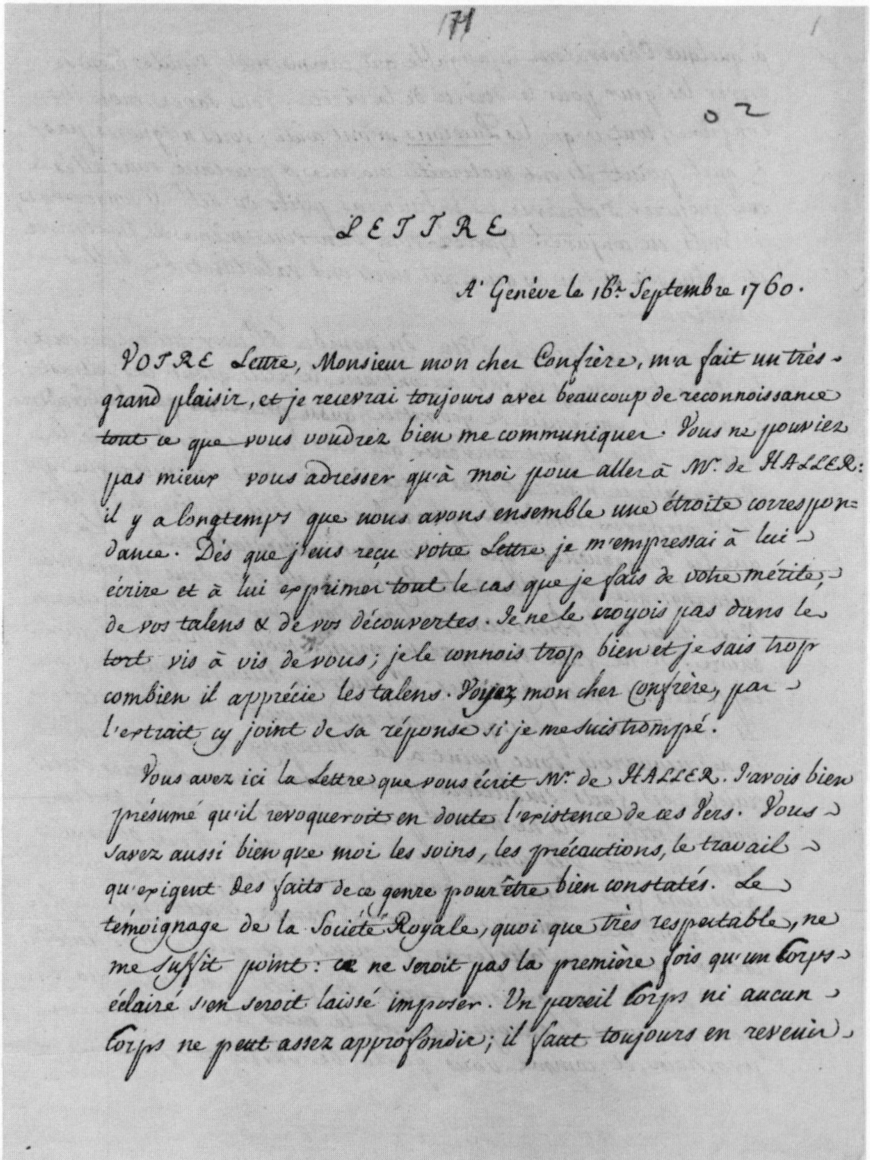

o 2

L E T T R E

A' Genéve le 16.e Septembre 1760.

VOTRE Lettre, Monsieur mon cher Confrère, m'a fait un très-
grand plaisir, et je recevrai toujours avec beaucoup de reconnoissance
tout ce que vous voudrez bien me communiquer. Vous ne pouviez
pas mieux vous adresser qu'à moi pour aller à Mr. de HALLER:
il y a longtemps que nous avons ensemble une étroite correspondance. Dès que j'eus reçu votre Lettre je m'empressai à lui
écrire et à lui exprimer tout le cas que je fais de votre mérite,
de vos talens & de vos découvertes. Je ne le croyois pas dans le
tort vis à vis de vous; je le connois trop bien et je sais trop
combien il apprécie les talens. Voyez mon cher Confrère, par
l'extrait cy joint de sa réponse si je me suis trompé.

Vous avez ici la Lettre que vous écrit Mr. de HALLER. J'avois bien
présumé qu'il revoqueroit en doute l'existence de ces Vers. Vous
Savez aussi bien que moi les soins, les précautions, le travail
qu'exigent des faits de ce genre pour être bien constatés. Le
témoignage de la Société Royale, quoi que très respectable, ne
me suffit point: ce ne seroit pas la première fois qu'un Corps
éclairé s'en seroit laissé imposer. Un pareil Corps ni aucun
Corps ne peut assez approfondir; il faut toujours en revenir

Fig. 24. The first page of the copy Bonnet had made (copy B) of his letters to Needham. (Courtesy of the Bibliothèque Publique et Universitaire, Geneva.)

et même d'etre mort. Il l'est bien si vous le voulés relativement au vrai bonheur; mais il est très vivant relativement à la composition; il enfante chaque jour quelque Brochure, qui loin d'ajouter à sa gloire la diminue.

Quand j'eus le plaisir de vous voir,[6] mon cher Monsieur, vous m'annonçates un Ouvrage que vous deviés m'envoyer de Turin, et dont vous ne me parlés point. J'ai été très content de vos *Alpes*.[7]

Nôtre cher ami M.[r] Trembley a été fort sensible aux assurances obligeantes de vôtre souvenir, et me prie de vous présenter ses plus sincères compliments.

Recevés les témoignages de la grande[b] estime et du parfait attachement avec les quels je serai toujours

[a]Monsieur mon cher Confrere[a]

[ADDRESS] Turin Monsieur Needham.

MANUSCRIPTS
  BPUG, MS Bonnet 70:204r-205r; MS Bonnet 85:171r-172r.

TEXT NOTES
  a. B: *omitted* *b*. sincère

3

Needham to Bonnet – Turin, 26 September 1760

Je vous remercie, mon cher Monsieur, des attentions, que vous avés pour moi, et de ce, que vous avés bien voulû faire parvenir mes desirs à M[r.] Haller: Je ne le croiois pas, non plus que vous, absolument dans le tort vis à vis de moi, mais n'ayant reçu de lui aucune reponse à ma lettre, qu'on lui avoit remise entre ses mains au commencement de l'année, et ne sçachant pas trop bien la raison, Je n'ai pas voulu l'importuner par des nouvelles demandes. Je lui ecris[1] par cette même poste pour le remercier de sa bonté, et pour lui temoigner toute ma reconnaissance; bien loin d'avoir rien à lui reprocher, Je l'estime, et Je l'estimerai toujours infiniment, comme l'homme du siecle, qui a travaillé le plus utilement et le plus efficacement pour l'avancement des lettres, et pour le bien de l'humanité en general, pendant que tant d'autres sçavans, ou de soi-disants tels, ne sont

works, and not the man himself (Ritter 1916-1917b:171; Sonntag 1983:290). On the complex relationship between Bonnet and Rousseau, see Ritter (1916-1917b), who published numerous passages from Bonnet's correspondence showing his constant and increasing hostility; Savioz (1948a:42-45 and 1948b:360-61); Rocci (1975:94); and especially Marx (1976:485-513). For Bonnet's opposition to Rousseau's political views, see also section 8 of the Introduction. For the works by Rousseau owned by Needham, see *Catalogue* (1782, pt.1:94-95 and pt.2:22, 32). See also Needham's fictional comparison of Rousseau and Voltaire, anonymously published in 1770 (see letter 43, n.6; letter 44, n.6 and n.7; and section 5 of the Introduction).

6. Needham apparently visited Bonnet in June or July 1760. Bonnet wrote to Haller on 3 September 1760, 'Il [Needham] me vint voir il y a deux mois' (Sonntag 1983:219).

7. John Turberville Needham, *Observations des hauteurs, faites avec le baromètre, au mois d'Août 1751, sur une partie des Alpes, en presence, et sous les auspices de Milord Comte de Rochford* (Berne 1760).

1. For Needham's letter to Haller, dated 27 September 1760, see Mazzolini (1976:71-73).

employés, que pour satisfaire leur vanité, et pour acquerir une vaine reputation au depens de la verité en faisant leur cour aux plus honteux dereglemens. Je doute aussi bien, que vous, et M^r. Haller de l'existence de ces vers amateurs du feu, mais comme même en doutant, il faut que les faits se decident toujours par l'experience, sur tout dans un siecle, qui nous a valu la decouverte du Polype, J'ai pris, il me semble, le moyen le plus sur d'eclaircir la verité en la mettant entre les mains de M^r. Haller. Quant'aux sentimens de la Societé Royale sur cette maniere, Je les ignore absolument ne me trouvant plus à portée depuis quelques années, ni de consulter les membres, ni les transactions immediate-ment; tout ce que J'ai sçu, et que Je vous a ecris Je le tenois du chevalier Worsley même auteur de la decouverte; Je serai faché de compromettre en aucune façon l'autorité d'un corps si respectable.

Je pense entierement comme vous sur la metaphysique, et Je suis tres persuadé par ce que Je vois tous les jours, que cette science mal maniée nous jette dans une labyrinthe d'erreurs, d'ou nous sortons rarement; toute la difference, qui pourra se trouver entre vous, et moi sera, qu'ayant la vûe en physique plus racourcie peutêtre que vous, J'aurai quelquesfois recours à la metaphysique plûtot que vous; et J'aurai en cela tort, mais tot ou tard, il faut que la science la plus étendue se termine à ce point. Je vous a cité trois ou quatre faits singuliers, qui regardent l'optique, les premiers, qui se sont presentés à moi dans cette occasion *currente calamo*; du premier même Je vous a donné une explication physique à ma façon; mais tout ce que j'ai voulu en les citant étoit de vous indiquer une suite des pareils faits, qui menent ou directement, ou indirectement à la metaphysique; la suite se trouvera sur tout à la fin de l'optique de Smith,[2] ou on voit certains faits, qui dependent pour leur explication de la nature de nos idées, et de nos connoissances, qui ne sont qu'autant des relations, et par consequent de la nature du principe immateriel comparant, autant que de la physique, et de la nature du corps mechanique. L'exemple, d'ou part M^r. Lock[3] pour etablir ses principes sur la nature des qualités secondaires, tiré de l'action de la même eau tiede, qui paroit chaude et froide à nos deux mains differemment disposées,[4] explique suffisamment mes idées sur cette matiere. Je verrai avec la plus grande satisfaction vos explications, et vous ne pourrés pas mes faire un plus grand plaisir, qu'en me les envoyant au plûtot; Je resterai à Turin jusqu'au quinze pour le moins du mois de janvier, et peutêtre jusqu'au mois de mars; je crois, que la meilleure façon sera de me les adresser directement à l'academie par quelque voiturier, ou roulier, de ceux qui passent communement pour le transport des marchandises, ou des voyageurs entre Geneve, et Turin; je payerai les frais du transport avec plaisir. Si vous avés quelquefois occasion de citer les faits, dont J'ai parlé, dans ma lettre, vous aurés, s'il vous plait, l'attention de ne pas nommer Milord Titchefield,[5] ni sa famille, peutêtre n'auroit-il-pas pour

---

2. See letter 1, n.15.

3. For a biography of John Locke (1632-1704), see Cranston (1957); for a bibliography of his writings and lists of studies on Locke, see Christophersen (1930), Hall and Woolhouse (1970), and Sina (1982:157-99). Reviews of recent literature on Locke can be found in De Dominicis (1978) and Sina (1980).

4. John Locke, *An essay concerning human understanding*, Bk. II, ch.VIII, §21.

5. See letter 1, n.12.

agreable, qu'on le cite; Je me souvienne de plus, que J'ai fait une petite faute en ecrivant un peu trop precipitamment; J'ai dit Milord Titchefield fils ainé du duc de dorset; c'est le duc de Portland, qui est son Pere, et c'est la duchesse de Portland, qui se trouve quelquefois affectée de la maniere decrite dans ma lettre.

J'ai honte de vous dire, que j'ai oublié totalement le titre même de l'ouvrage, que J'ai promis de vous envoyer de Turin; fait moi le plaisir de me faire resouvenir; si c'est un ouvrage de ma façon, ce n'est peut être, que la derniere edition de mes observations microscopiques,[6] dont Je ne trouve plus d'exemplaires ici; ou si c'est quelque autre ouvrage, mandés moi au plûtot, afin que Je repond, comme Je dois, à vos desirs. Je vous prie de presenter mes respects à Mr. Trembley, et de recevoir en même tems les temoignages de la grande estime, et du parfait attachement avec les quels je serai toujours

Mon cher Monsieur, et confrere,

à Turin, Le 26. de Septembre
1760.

votre tres humble
et tres obeissant ami,
et serviteur
Needham.

[ADDRESS] A Monsieur / Monsieur Charles Bonnet / de la societé Royale de Londres, / correspondant de l'academie Royale / des sciences &c. / à Geneve.

MANUSCRIPT
    BPUG, MS Bonnet 26:121r-122v.

4

Bonnet to Needham – Geneva, 31 October 1760

Geneve 31. 8.bre 1760.

^aTranquilisés vous, Monsieur mon Cher Confrere; je ne nomme personne dans l'Ouvrage dont ma derniere Lettre faisoit mention, et pour lequel vous me montrés une impatience obligeante. Je ne pourrois pas vous l'envoyer avant le mois de Decembre prochain. Je profiterai de l'avis que vous me donnés pour cet envoi; c'etoit bien aussi le Canal auquel j'avois pensé. Je connois un Mulletier de confiance qui est en habitude de faire le voyage de Turin, et auquel je le recommanderai. Mais tout git à sçavoir, s'il vous arrivera avant le 15 de Janvier, jour où vous me dittes que vous pourriés bien partir. J'aurai bien au moins une de vos Lettres avant ce tems-la, et vous voudrés bien m'informer de vos Resolutions ultérieures. Je ne trouverai pas beaucoup de Juges aussi éclairés que vous l'etes; et je recevrai vôtre jugement avec autant de plaisir que de reconnoissance.^a

---

6. John Turberville Needham, *Nouvelles observations microscopiques, avec des découvertes intéressantes sur la composition & la décomposition des corps organisés* (Paris 1750).

Je déplore avec vous, mon cher Confrere, l'esprit d'Irréligion par lequel divers
Autheurs entreprennent aujourd'hui de se faire une reputation brillante. Il est
bien evident que leurs ecarts sont le fruit d'un amour propre mal ordonné, et si
le gros des Hommes étoit Deïste ou Athée, ces Gens-là seroient Chrétiens. Je
les regarde comme des ennemis nès du genre Humain, puis qu'ils cherchent à
lui enlever la plus solide baze de son bonheur. Vous avés raison d'opposer à ces
Enthousiastes de l'Incredulité, car comme la Superstition elle a aussi les Siens,
vous avés dis-je raison de leur opposer l'excellent M.ʳ De Haller. Il fait partie
de ce Sel que la Providence à menagé pour preserver la Masse de la Corruption.
C'est un Homme qui auroit figuré dans le premier Siecle comme un Pere de
l'Eglise, et qui figure dans le nôtre comme un parfait Philosophe Chrétien.

Je crois me rapeller que l'Ouvrage dont vous me parlâtes, et que vous
m'offrittes obligeamment de m'envoyer, rouloit sur la Theorie de la Terre: Sujet
si fécond et si interessant, et sur lequel nous avons plutôt des Romans que des
Histoires. Je ne connois pas la nouvelle Edition de vos observations
michroscopiques.[1] J'en fais grand usage dans le Livre que je compose actuellement sur les Corps organisés,[2] et ou je tache de déduire des Faits les conséquences
naturelles qui peuvent nous éclairer sur les causes. S'il y a de nouvelles découvertes dans vôtre Seconde Edition, elles me seroient bien utiles.

Un Chimiste de nôtre Voisinage à trouvé par hazard, un Dissolvant du
Verre.[3] Il ne dit pas encore son secret: mais il m'a envoié le Verre, que j'ai vû
rongé, creusé et percé. Je vous en dirai d'avantage un autre jour si vous le
souhaittés.

Passerés-vous à Bologne et quand à peu près? Vous voudrés-bien y dire
quelque chose pour moi à M.ʳ Zanotti,[4] mon ancien et sçavant Correspondant:
mais je crains qu'il ne soit mort, car il étoit bien vieux.

Ne mourés que le plustard que vous le pourrés pour vous, pour moi et pour

---

1. See letter 3, n.6.

2. Bonnet's book appeared in 1762 with the title *Considérations sur les corps organisés* (Amsterdam).
See also B.O., 3:1-579/5:57-468 and 6:1-550. For the difficulties Bonnet experienced in getting this
work approved by the Paris censors, see Perkins (1981).

3. Bonnet wrote to Duhamel Du Monceau (1700-1782) on 18 October 1760: 'M.r Vasserot de
Dardagni [Dardagny] qui se plait aux recherches Chimiques, m'a fait communiquer le Memoire
cy-joint que j'ai apostillé en témoignage du fait singulier qu'il renferme. Il est digne de l'attention
de l'Academie, à qui vous voudrés bien le communiquer de ma part' (BPUG, MS Bonnet 70:206*v*).
On 27 October 1760 Duhamel answered, 'A l'egard de la dissolution du verre par les acides rien
est mieux connu. On sait meme que de touts les acides c'est celui du sel marin qui agit le plus
efficacement. M. Geoffroi dans les memoires de l'academie a meme prouvé que le vin dissolvoit
certaines verres. Enfin M. Cadet apotiquaire de Paris a communiqué à l'academie des Experiences
qui prouvent que toutes les especes de verres sont dissolubles par toutes les especes d'acides'
(BPUG, MS Bonnet 26: 67*r*-67*v*).

4. On Francesco Maria Zanotti (1692-1777), Bolognese philosopher, polymath, and an early
proponent of Newtonian science in Italy, who was from 1723 Secretary and from 1766 President of
the Istituto dell' Accademia delle Scienze of Bologna, see Fantuzzi (1778), where all of his published
works are listed, and Fabroni (1778-1805, 5:326-68). Volume 9 of Zanotti's collected works (Zanotti
1779-1802) contains interesting letters addressed to him, and his important correspondence with
Morgagni edited by Rocchi (1875) sheds light on much of his activity at the Bolognese academy.
For more recent works on Zanotti, see Bosdari (1928), Ambri Berselli (1955), and Casini (1978:95).
Eleven letters from Zanotti to Bonnet are preserved in the BPUG.

tous les Etres qui pensent. L'estime et l'attachement que je vous ai voüés ne finiront qu'avec la vie de celui qui est. &c.

[ADDRESS] Turin, M. Needham.

MANUSCRIPTS
BPUG, MS Bonnet 70:207r-207v; MS Bonnet 85:172r-172v.

TEXT NOTES
   a. B: *omitted*

5

Needham to Bonnet – Turin, 15 November 1760

Mon cher Monsieur, et Confrere

   Plûtot que j'aurai votre ouvrage, plûtot j'aurai un tres grand plaisir, que Je desire avec empressement. Je comptois de pouvoir partir de Turin vers le 15. du janvier, mais je prevois à present, que nous passerons ici l'hyver entiere: à mesure que le nombre des anglois augmente ici, le sejour paroit plaire d'avantage au seigneur que j'accompagne, ainsi je compte non seulement de me fêter, et me nourir tranquillement des pensées contenues dans votre livre, mais de vous ecrire les idées, qui me naitront en consequence, et recevoir encore de vos lettres. Cette decouverte physique, dont vous me parlés, d'une menstrue propre à dissoudre le verre est assés particuliere, et si l'auteur communique son secret, Je vous serai même obligé, si vous voulés me le transmettre. Le monde croit assés communement, que les noms de Philosophe, et d'incredule sont synonimes, il nous importe beaucoup, que les vrais Philosophes se declarent ouvertement pour la Religion pour le desabuser, ce seroit en tout tems et votre devoir, et cel de Mr Haller; on l'attaque sans menagement, ne doit on pas la defendre de même? Je voudrois avoir et la reputation, et la force necessaire pour cela, il me semble, que Je traiterai le sujet tout autrement, que certaines philosophes François, quoique sincerement chretiens, dont la politesse paroit presque degene-rer en lacheté. Je vous aurai peutêtre, quand j'eu le plaisir de vous voire à Geneve, dit quelque chose sur la Theorie de la terre, et même que je meditois quelque chose sur ce sujet, mais je me souviens pas de vous avoir parlé de quelque ouvrage, qui paroit actuellement digne de votre attention, d'autant plus, que je ne connois aucune, dont Je peu me resouvenir pour le present. Je vous suis tres obligé du cas, que vous faites de mes observations microscopiques, et Je suis tres persuadé que vous tirerés meilleur parti de mes experiences, que j'ai pû faire jusqu'à present faute du loisir; ma vie toujours errante m'est un grand obstacle en tout ce, que j'entreprends. Si vous écrivés à Mr Haller Je vous prie de lui temoigner mes respects, aussi bien qu'à Mr Trembley. On me demande ici douze livres de Piemont pour votre ouvrage sur les feuilles[1] etc.

---

1. Charles Bonnet, *Recherches sur l'usage des feuilles dans les plantes, et sur quelques autres sujets relatifs à l'histoire de la vegetation* (Gottingue, Leide 1754); republished in B.O., 2:179-459/4:1-438.

Mandés moi, je vous en prie, si c'est un prix convenable, et si Je pû l'avoir de Geneve à meillieur compte, ayés la bonté de me faire parvenir un exemplaire par le même muletier, à qui j'ai tiendrai compte de tout ce qu'il auroit à depenser. Je le lû deja avec tres grand plaisir, et j'admire la clarté de vos observations, et la justesse de vos consequences; il falloit un esprit juste, comme le votre, pour avoir imaginé des experiences si lumineuses, et j'ai vu absolument avoir votre ouvrage aupres de moi, même au prix, qu'on le vende ici, si j'ai ne reçois pas de Geneve par votre moyen. J'appelle la seconde, ou la nouvelle edition de mes observations[2] celle, qui a été faite à Paris apres celle d'hollande l'année 1750. C'est celle que vous aures deja vu, et je n'ai ajouté rien de nouveau depuis cette date. Comment vont les yeux? Vous me ne dites rien sur cet article, Je m'interesse pourtant autant que personne, menagés votre vûe et pour vous même, et pour vos amis, aussi bien que la santé, que Je vous souhaite de tout mon coeur. Je suis avec un parfaite estime, et attachement

Monsieur, et tres cher confrere

votre tres humble, et tres obeissant
ami, et serviteur

Needham.

à Turin, Le 15. de Nov: 1760.

Je passerai surement à Bologne, s'il plait à dieu, et Je ne manquerai pas de voir M[r.] Zanotti de votre part, s'il vit encore; Je le connois assés, et je l'estime infiniment apres l'avoir frequenté suffisamment la derniere fois, que j'ai passé par cette ville.[3] Voyés pour toute autre chose quelqueconque en quoi je pu vous être utile pendant mes voyages, et donnés moi vos ordres avec toute la liberté possible.

[ADDRESS] A Monsieur / Monsieur Charles Bonnet / de la societé Royale de Londres, / correspondant de l'academie Royale de Paris, / &c. / à Geneve.

MANUSCRIPT
BPUG, MS Bonnet 26:123r-124v.

6

Bonnet to Needham – Geneva, 20 December 1760

Geneve le 20. X.[e] 1760

J'ai été un peu incommodé, Monsieur mon Cher ami et Confrere: je n'ai pu repondre plutot à votre obligeante Lettre du 15e. 9bre. Vous ne poures avoir le Paquet que je vous destine que dans le Courant de janvier: mandes moi donc s'il vous plait s'il vous trouvera encore à Turin; car il seroit possible que vous eussies changé de resolution.

---

2. See letter 3, n.6.

3. Needham met Zanotti and other scientists in Bologna in 1751; see Needham's two letters of 1752 to Ferdinando Bassi (1714-1774) preserved in the BUB, Cod. 233, vol.ii.

Je n'ai qu'un seul exemplaire de mon Livre sur les Plantes.[1] Le Libraire ne m'en avoit donné que 30 et j'ai été obligé d'en acheter pour donner à des Amis. Il n'y en avoit plus ici. C'est ce qui me prive du plaisir que j'aurois eut à vous en faire present, comme une legère marque de mes sentimens pour vous: mais je puis vous dire que le prix qu'on vous en demande à Turin est raisonnable. J'avois fait un Errata: aprenes moi s'il se trouve à la fin de l'exemplaire qu'on vous offre sinon je vous l'envoyerai.

Vous me demandes, mon Cher ami, des nouvelles de mes yeux: ils se ressentent et se ressentiront toute ma vie des Observations. Je suis un martyr de l'Histoire Naturelle: vous l'etes aussi; dittes moy à votre tour comment va vôtre vuë, et si vous pouves encore observer la Nature. Si vous le pouves faites le, je vous en conjure avec la plus grande sobrieté. Je suis forcé à me servir de Lecteur et de Secretaire.

On me lisoit l'autre jour la critique de vos observations par Lignac, auteur des *Lettres a un Americain*[2]: je vous avoue que plusieurs de ses remarques m'ont paru fondées; mais avant que de prononcer, je voudrois savoir votre jugement. Vous vous etes *ᵃpeut-etreᵃ* un peu trop ecarté de ce que nous connoissons de plus certain sur la Generation des Insectes, et vous aves quelques fois tiré des consequences plus generales que les Faits qui vous servoient de premisses. Votre traducteur,[3] un de mes meilleurs amis, vous avoit ouvert une bonne Route dans

---

1. See letter 5, n.1.

2. Joseph-Adrien Lelarge de Lignac (1710-1762), a member of the congrégation de l'Oratoire and a friend of Réaumur, on two occasions criticised the ideas Needham had expressed in his book of 1750. His criticism is contained in letters 11 and 12 of his *Lettres à un Amériquain sur l'histoire naturelle, générale et particuliere de monsieur de Buffon* (Hambourg [Paris] 1751) and in the *Suite des lettres à un Amériquain* (Hambourg [Paris] 1756). Lignac expanded the subtitle of vols.iv and v of the *Lettres à un Amériquain*, adding *et sur les observations microscopiques de m'. Néedham*. Inspired in his criticism by Réaumur (see Roger 1963:696-99), in whose house at Poitou he spent several summers, Lignac scrutinised Needham's microscopical observations, which he and Réaumur tried to repeat, claiming that Needham had not sufficiently clarified his experimental techniques (Lelarge de Lignac 1751, 5:91). He did not accept Needham's concept of a productive force and, as an orthodox Catholic, feared the implications of Needham's views with regard to materialism. He did point out, however, that Needham was not a materialist but rather an idealist attempting to combat materialism (Lelarge de Lignac 1756, 1:13-14). For an intellectual biography of Lignac, see Le Goff (1863); for a summary of his philosophical views and a list of his publications, see Bouillier (1868, 2:621-31); for his collaboration with Réaumur and his ideas on natural history, see M. Trembley (1943: 361-62, 362-63 n.1), Torlais (1961:237-40), Roger (1963:691-704), and Roe (1983:178); and for Lignac's criticism of Bonnet's optimism, see Le Goff (1863:199-220), Starobinski (1975), and Marx (1976:601-604).

3. Jean-Nicolas-Sébastien Allamand (1713-1787) was born in Lausanne and studied at Leiden University. There he became a pupil and friend of Willem Jacob 'sGravesande (1688-1742) and, later, tutor to his children. In 1749 he was appointed to the chair of mathematics and philosophy at Leiden and, some years later, also to that of natural history. Short biographies are given by Paquot (1763-1770, 13:445-48); *B.U.* (1:490-91); and C. de Waard, in *N.N.B.W.*, 1 (1911) 75-77. The most complete list of his publications is that provided by Suringar (1867). For Allamand's botanical studies, see Markgraf and Steiger (1969); for those on electricity, see Heilbron (1979:299, 313); and for his opposition to Rousseau, see Ritter (1916-1917b:183-85). Allamand conducted an extensive correspondence with Bonnet (sixty-four letters addressed to Bonnet are preserved in the BPUG) and assisted him in the publication of some of his works in Holland (see Savioz 1948b:210, 220; and B.O., 2:183/4:5). He translated into French Needham's *New microscopical discoveries* (see Needham 1747a).

ses judicieuses Nottes[4] sur le Bled nielé. Je doute que vous soyes resté dans vos premieres idées sur l'origine des Corps organizés: vous etes trop capable de reflechir, et vous aimes trop le Vrai. [a]M.[r] De Buffon[5] à fait bien pis; mais en verité on ne sauroit le prendre pour guide en matiere d'observation et de

---

4. Allamand's note runs as follows: 'Un de mes Amis [Trembley] aiant eu l'avantage de voir à Londres Mr. Needham, en a reçu quelques grains de ce Blé dont il s'agit ici, & il a eu la bonté de les partager avec moi. J'ai vu avec admiration les Anguilles qui sont dans leur intérieur; & comme ce spectacle m'a paru fort surprenant, j'y suis revenu plusieurs fois, toujours avec le même plaisir. Quoique le mouvement de ces Anguilles soit très sensible, je n'oserois cependant pas assurer positivement que ce sont des Animaux. Peut-être ne sont-elles que des Etuis qui renferment d'autres petits Animalcules. Ce qui me le feroit croire c'est un phénomène dont j'ai été témoin plusieurs fois, & dont je dois la découverte à une personne à qui j'avois donné quelques grains de ce Blé. Voici le fait. *Il arrive assez souvent à ces Anguilles de se rompre, & alors on voit sortir de leur Corps plusieurs petits globules, noiratres; enveloppés dans une fine membrane; or j'ai observé plusieurs fois que de ces paquets de globules, il sortoit de petits Corps qui nageoient dans l'eau avec beaucoup de vitesse. Ces globules, qu'on peut même découvrir dans le Corps de l'Anguille à cause de sa transparence, sont-ils donc de petits animaux, renfermés dans l'Anguille, comme dans un Etui? Pour être en état de resoudre la question, il faut observer de suite une Anguille jusqu'à ce qu'on ait vu tous les globules en sortir; examiner ce qu'elle devient alors, & suivre les progrès de ces derniers.* Mais quoi qu'il en soit, le merveilleux de la chose subsistera toujours dans son entier' (Needham 1747a:102-103n). In the *Considérations sur les corps organisés*, Bonnet (1762, 2:220; B.O., 3:404/6:307) reproduced the section in the above quotation we have italicised and suggested that the eels observed by Needham in blighted wheat were not 'zoophytes', but 'probablement des especes de fourreaux habités par des Animalcules, ou pleins de globules mouvans' (Bonnet 1762, 2:221; B.O., 3:405/6:309). In 1775 Maurizio Roffredi (1711-1805), by demonstrating the existence of female eels in blighted wheat that were larger than males and that produced a great number of eggs, was able to show that the white mass of dried eels discovered by Needham in blighted wheat was actually composed of larvae produced by sexually mature eels that had contaminated the grain (Roffredi 1775a and 1775b). As a result of Roffredi's observations Needham (1775a) acknowledged both the animal nature of the filaments (eels) he had seen and their origin by eggs. Bonnet was delighted with Roffredi's observations and later retracted his views on these eels as expressed above (see B.O., 3:404-405 n.2/6:307-308 n.1; see also B.O., 3:345-55 n.2, 407-409 n.2/6:215-29 n.2, 312-15 n.1). For Needham's observations on eels in blighted wheat, see letter 14, n.8; letter 49, n.3; and section 2.ii of the Introduction.

5. For the life and work of Georges-Louis Leclerc, comte de Buffon (1707-1788) up to 1749, see Hanks (1966); and for a short biography, see Jacques Roger, *D.S.B.*, 2 (1970) 576-82. Some important aspects of his personality are elucidated in Roger's introduction to Buffon (1962: ix-cxlix). For a bibliography of works by and on Buffon, see E. Genet-Varcin and J. Roger, 'Bibliographie de Buffon', published in Buffon (1954:513-75). Among numerous recent publications on Buffon, see especially Roger (1963:527-84), Fellows and Milliken (1972), Farber (1975), Sloan (1979), Dougherty (1980), and Raitières (1981). Bonnet wrote once to Buffon, but received no reply; see Savioz (1948b:303-309) and Marx (1976:344-45). For a comparison of their theories of generation, see Castellani (1972) and Bowler (1973). It is not known when Needham first met Buffon, but he was certainly in contact with him in 1746 (Needham 1746a:258). In 1747 he reported to the Royal Society on experiments carried out in Paris 'with a new-constructed reflecting Mirror' and said that Buffon had acquainted him with the technical procedures (Needham 1747b:493). He also helped Buffon to obtain, via England, 'fossils from the East and West Indies' (see Needham's correspondence with Da Costa of 1747-1748 preserved in the BL, Add. 28540). Buffon and Needham undertook joint microscopical investigations from March to May 1748 (see Needham 1748:640 and Roger 1963:498). On this collaboration, see Fellows and Milliken (1972:100-102), Roe (1983), and section 2.ii of the Introduction. It is usually assumed that after their collaboration their relationship came to an end, but they met when Needham was in Paris in 1764 (see Sonntag 1983:380) and again on at least two occasions when Needham returned to Paris to live from 1766 to 1769 – once to settle a small problem that had arisen between Buffon and the Royal Society (see Needham's letter to Da Costa of 12 February 1767 preserved in the BL, Add. 28540) and again to discuss cosmogony (see letter 29, n.5). We also know that Needham wrote to Buffon at least once in 1765 (see Needham's letter to Spallanzani of 24 September 1765 in Castellani 1973:87).

Philosophie. Son imagination l'emporte, et il ne sait pas analiser, moins encore observer: je vous en parle comme à mon ami.[a]

La dissolution du Verre est tres connue de l'Academie de Paris. Un Apoticaire lui à demontré que toute sortes d'acides dissolvent toute sortes de Verres.[6]

Je sui et serai toute ma vie avec la plus parfaite estime &c.

[ADDRESS] Turin; M. Needham d. l. Soc. Roy:

MANUSCRIPTS
BPUG, MS Bonnet 70:212*r*-213*r*; MS Bonnet 85:173*r*-173*v*.

TEXT NOTES
a. B: *omitted*

7

Needham to Bonnet – Turin, 10 January 1761

Voila la quatrieme fois, mon cher Monsieur, ami, et confrere, que Je m'assis pour repondre à votre lettre obligeante du 20. X[bre]. Les trois derniers jours de poste m'ont été quasi entierement enlevés par des affaires inattendues, enfin me voila rendu à moi-même pour vous remercier de toutes vos bontés. Je ne quitterai pas surement la ville de Turin avant le mois d'avril, ainsi le paquet, que vous me destinés, m'arrivera entre les mains, quand il vous plaira de me l'adresser, sans vous trop gêner pour le tems de son depart. Je vous suis tres obligé de vos bonnes intentions en ma faveur par raport à l'exemplaire de votre ouvrage, dont vous m'aures fait un present tres agreable, si vous aviés encore quelques uns à distribuer; mais ce n'étoit pas du tout mon dessein, Je ne regretterai jamais les douze livres, que je depense pour me le procurer, mais Je suis en garde toujours contre les libraires, ceux sur tout de Turin, et j'ai voulu sçavoir d'avance, si le prix, qu'on me faisoit, étoit raisonable. Pour les *errata*, vous me ferés plaisir, si cela ne vous coute pas trop de peine, de me les envoyer. Vous me ne pouvés presque rien dire de plus facheux, que ce que vous me dites de l'état de vos yeux; pour les miens ils ont de vicissitudes bonnes et mauvaises alternativement, mais Je ne les fatigue pas trop, et Je ne sent guere aucun mal, sinon après avoir ecris trois, ou quatre heures de suite à la lumiere des bougies, comme cela m'arrive quelquefois. Je ne connois pas cette critique, dont vous me parlés, de mes observations par l'abbé de Lignac,[1] si ce n'est ce, qu'il a donné, il y a quelques années, dans ses lettres ameriquaines. Je ne crains aucune metaphysique, que celle, qui est fondée sur la physique, ou plûtot, Je ne la crains pas, mais je la souhaite, même au depens de tout ce, que j'ai donné au public, de telle main, qu'elle peut partir. On sçait assés, et on y voit, il me semble clairement par sa façon de raisonner, que l'abbé de Lignac, bien loin d'être un observateur,

6. See letter 4, n.3.

1. See letter 6, n.2.

n'est pas même assés avancé dans la physique ordinaire pour m'entendre, comme j'ai voulu être entendu: mais quand vous me paroissés approuver plusieures de ses remarques, il faut avouer, que me faites recûler un peu des idées, que j'ai établi; je ferai cent fois plus de cas de la simple opinion d'un observateur, tel qui vous étes surement, que de toute la metaphysique de l'abbé de Lignac. Cependant je viens de recevoir une lettre de Mr de Haller,[2] qui me marque, que Mr Wolff[3] un jeune observateur à Berlin vient nouvellement de faire des observations assés interessantes,[4] et pareilles à plusieures, que j'ai fait à Paris, qui lui paroissent decisives pour l'Epigenese. Mr Haller lui meme, en me marquant, qu'il me rendra toute la justice, qui m'est due, du coté de la morale de mon systême, et qu'il m'a deja rendue en partie de son chef dans sa sçavante preface, qui precede la traduction allemande de l'histoire naturelle de Mr de Buffon;[5] J'ai dis, Mr Haller lui-même ne s'eloigne pas beaucoup du systême de l'épigenese. Il tient, comme il me dit, un milieu entre l'ancienne, et la nouvelle opinion, parce que toutes les observations, qu'il a fait jusqu'à present ne les portent pas, comme il croit, plus loin, mais en-bien envisageant son systême qu'il me decrit, Je crains beaucoup, qu'il ne peut pas se tenir la; Je me suis expliqué la dessus à lui dans ma reponse,[6] et Je ne vois pas aucun milieu stable entre les deux systêmes. Du reste pour un philosophe raisonable, il doit suffire, que l'une de deux opinion ne donne dans la generation equivoque, la plus folle de toutes les folles idées, pas plus que l'autre; le reste doit suivre

2. Haller's letter to Needham cannot be traced; see Mazzolini (1976:71).

3. Caspar Friedrich Wolff (1734-1794) first studied at the Collegium Medico-Chirurgicum in Berlin, and in 1755 he moved to the University of Halle where he defended his doctoral dissertation in 1759. He then became a military physician in Breslau during the Seven Years War. In 1763 he returned to Berlin and gave public lectures on physiology. In 1764 he applied for a professorship at the Collegium, but was unsuccessful. In 1767 he moved from Berlin to St Petersburg where, upon the recommendation of Leonhard Euler (1707-1783), he became Professor of Anatomy and Physiology at the Academy of Sciences. For biographical information on Wolff, see A. E. Gaissinovitch, *D.S.B.*, 15 (1978) 525-26; Gaissinovitch (1961); Lukina (1975); Roe (1979) and the literature cited therein. Apparently Needham never read Wolff's book, *Theoria generationis* (Halle 1759).

4. In his letter to Needham (see n.2 above), Haller must have referred to Wolff's doctoral dissertation *Theoria generationis* (1759), which Wolff sent to Haller in 1759 and which was reviewed by Haller in the *Göttingische Anzeigen von gelehrten Sachen* (29 November 1760, pp.1226-31). For the debate over embryology originated by Wolff's book and Haller's review, see Schuster (1941), Herrlinger (1959), and Roe (1981).

5. Haller's preface to the second volume of the German translation of Buffon's *Histoire naturelle* (see Buffon 1750-1772), published in 1752, actually contained a critical analysis of both Buffon's and Needham's theories, the latter of which seems to have appeared to Haller to be even more dangerous than that of Buffon. Before this preface appeared in German it was translated into French and published as a pamphlet entitled *Réflexions sur le système de la génération, de M. de Buffon* (Genève 1751). Needham's statement here suggests that he had not yet read Haller's preface. However, by 1769 he had seen it, as he quoted from the French edition in his notes in Spallanzani (1769, pt.1:141-42). Haller's preface was republished in German in his *Sammlung kleiner Hallerischer Schrifften* (1756; 2nd ed., 1772) without any alterations except for the addition, in the second edition, of footnote references to Spallanzani's refutation of Needham's infusion experiments (see Haller 1772:93n, 94n). When Haller republished this preface in Latin in the third volume of his *Opera minora*, which appeared in 1768 (see Haller 1762-1768, 3:174-90), he made several changes and eliminated many references to Needham. Compare Haller (1751:52, 54, 55, 65, 66-67) with Haller (1762-1768, 3:187, 188, 189, 190). For Haller's opinion of Needham's views on generation, see Duchesneau (1979) and Roe (1983).

6. For Needham's letter to Haller of 28 December 1760, see Mazzolini (1976:73-77).

absolument le sort des observations. Vous me faites un procés sur mes idées principalement, celles qui regardent la generation des insectes, et vous ne pensés pas, mon cher confrere, que vous, et notre bon ami Mʳ Trembley, ont plus contribués que personne par vos observations sur les polypes, et sur les pucerons, à nous faire étendre nos idées sur cet article. Je ne veu, que les seuls polypes pour aneantir l'ancien systême de germes preexistans, et la generation extraordinaire des pucerons pour nous faire voir, que la nature s'ecarte et s'echappe des bornes, que les philosophes lui avoient prescrits, sans pourtant se precipiter dans aucune irregularité, qui menera la generation equivoque. Et s'il y est une classe des êtres, comme j'ai lieu de croire par plusieures observations, intermediare entre le sensitive, et le vegetal, dont la constitution, et le temperament seroit purement irritable, sans être sensitive en partant d'après les experiences[7] de Mʳ Haller, ne pourroit elle pas, la divinité, conduire par la pure physique tels êtres à leur destination, et les diriger par des regles mecaniques sans aucune puissance sensitive; comme elle conduit les bêtes, qui n'ont en elles aucun principe de la raison, par des causes finales, dont la raison n'est pas dans ces mêmes animaux, mais en lui, qui a tout combiné d'avance pour les faire arriver, ou elle veut, qu'ils arrivent? Cela posé, de quelle absurdité peut on me charger en metaphysique, pour avoir dit, après l'avoir vu plusieures fois en compagnie de tant d'autres philosophes dans la production presqu'instantanée des animaux spermatiques et d'autres du même genre, qu'il se trouve dans la nature une classe des êtres, qui sort de certaines matieres, sans pere et sans mere proprément dits, mais avec autant de regularité, et de specification même tant du coté de la semence productive, que du coté de leur forme constante, que les christaux de toute espece. Surement personne ne s'avisera jamais de tirer des consequences en faveur du sot systême d'hasard de ces procedés de [sa] nature dans la formation, ou de la neige, ou des crystaux; encore moins doit on se prevaloir de ce, que nous avons observés sur la generation de certains êtres de cette espece inferieure, dont il s'agit dans mes observations microscopiques. Quant à Mʳ de Buffons, j'étois du commencement de notre connoissance tres éloigné de sa façon de penser sur ce sujet, d'autant plus, que je ne voyois pas, ce qu'il pouvoit esperer de gagner pour resoudre toutes les difficultés, qui

---

7. Needham is alluding to Haller's famous physiological experiments on the irritability and sensibility of parts of the body. Haller read his results on 22 April and 6 March 1752 during two sessions of the Royal Academy of Göttingen and published them in a paper entitled 'De partibus corporis humani sensilibus et irritabilibus', *Commentarii Societatis Regiae Scientiarum Gottingensis. Ad annum MDCCLII*, 2 (1753) 114-58. Lundsgaard-Hansen-von Fischer (1959:30-32) lists nineteen editions and translations of Haller's work published in the eighteenth century. It became the manifesto for a new experimental physiology and had a vast influence both on medicine and on related disciplines. Haller regarded irritability, i.e. muscular contractility, as completely separate from sensibility, i.e. sensation, and ascribed the former to muscles, and the latter to nerves. Historical literature on Haller's theory of irritability is vast. For the concept of irritability before Haller, see Buess (1942) and Temkin (1964); for the philosophical background to Haller's concept and for its implications, see Irsay (1928:192-93, 196), Toellner (1967 and 1971:173-82), and Roe (1984). Haller's point of view is discussed in Rothschuh (1953:77-79) and Rudolph (1964); and the controversies that followed Haller's publication of 1753 are treated in Lesky (1959) and Fontana (1980:17-36). For the use of the theory of irritability in Haller's embryological research, see Roe (1981:32-44); for its use in the study of microorganisms, see Mazzolini (1972:74-75); and for its use as a method of investigating the working of the iris, see Mazzolini (1980:70-78), where further literature is cited.

pressoient contre l'opinion des germes preexistans. Qu'on prend un germe preexistant tout entier, ou qu'on les partage en des millions de molecules organiques, c'est la même chose, vous ne faites rien, les mêmes difficultés subsistent dans leur entier. Mais le malheur de M^r· de Buffon étoit d'avoir formé sa theorie avant de faire aucune observation, et il ne voyoit par tout, que des molecules organiques.[8] Faits bien de complimens de ma part à M^r· Trembley avec tous les souhaits d'une amitie, et d'un respect inviolable, qui sont trop étendus pour se borner au commencement de la nouvelle année, et acceptés les mêmes avec la même ardeur de la part de celui, qui est toujours a vous

> L'ami, et le confrere le plus attaché
> pour toujours

Needham.

à Turin, Le 10. de janvier 1761.

[ADDRESS] A Monsieur / Monsieur Charles Bonnet / de la societé royales de Londres, / correspondant de l'academie des sciences / à Paris &c. / à Geneve.

MANUSCRIPT
  BPUG, MS Bonnet 26:125*r*-126*v*.

8

Bonnet to Needham – Geneva, 20 February 1761

Geneve 20. Fev. 1761

Quand vous ne recevres pas de mes Lettres, aussi promptement que vous aves droit de les attendre, n'en concludes point, Monsieur mon Cher ami et Confrere que je vous oublie; mais conclues[a] en seulement que des circonstances survenues m'ont enpeché de vous repondre plutot. Votre obligeante lettre du 10e. Janvier, à laquelle je reponds si tard, m'a fait un vrai plaisir. Il s'en faut bien que vos yeux ayent été aussi maltraités que les miens. Vous n'y sentes aucune douleur, et vous n'eprouvés de la fatigue, que lors que vous aves ecrit, dittes vous, trois ou quatres heures à la lumiere d'une bougie: et vous appelles cela ne pas fatiguer ses yeux? Vous etes un ingrat et ils ont droit de se plaindre du peu d'egars que vous aves pour eux. Il faut bien que j'en use autrement; car les miens ne peuvent ecrire demi heure à la lumiere du jour sans etre fatigués. Il predisent, comme des Barrometres les changemens de temps, par un sentiment

---

8. Buffon put forward his ideas on 'molécules organiques' in the second volume of his *Histoire naturelle, générale et particulière* (Paris 1749-1789), published in 1749. Buffon's theory of generation was based on a distinction between two kinds of matter, organic and brute, and on an identification of the reproductive process with nutrition. Buffon believed that organic particles are taken up in the organism's food and used by each part of the body for growth and maintenance, and that, in the adult, surplus organic particles are collected in reservoirs to become the seminal liquid. During reproduction, these particles come together under the influence of an 'internal mould' to form the new organism, which, in the case of sexual reproduction, results from a mixing of seminal material from both parents. Among the vast literature on this topic some of the more recent works are Roger (1963:542-58), Gasking (1967:87-91), Castellani (1972), Duchesneau (1979), and Roe (1981:15-18).

douloureux, qu'ils me font eprouver alors. J'aurois bien d'autres choses à vous en dire, mais c'est avoir assez parle de ces pauvres infirmes. L'etat où ils se trouvent depuis bien des années, m'a valu une grande compensation; celle de pouvoir mediter longtems sur des sujets abstraits, et de pouvoir retenir dans ma tête *b*30 ou 40*b* pages sans les ecrire. Aussi mes manuscrits sont-ils exenpts de rature. Je fais les ratures dans mon cerveau. C'est ainsi que j'ai composé ce livre sur *l'usage des Feuilles*,[1] dont vous faites un eloge qui me flatte d'autant plus qu'il part d'un grand*c* maitre dans l'art d'observer. Voici l'*errata* de ce livre que vous me demandies. Quand je pourai vous envoyer l'autre Ouvrage que je vous destine, vous jugeres mieux encore de ma maniere de mediter et de composer. En attendant je vais *d*remettre au Muletier *Pierre Grisat*,*d* un Esai de Psychologie qui m'a paru interressant par les matieres tres variées qu'il renferme et par l'art avec Lequel elles sont exposées.[2] Je fais cas de l'Esprit Philosophique et de la Candeur de cet Anonyme: je lui sais gré d'avoir taché à concilier avec la Revelation des principes rigoureux que des Incredules avoient entrepris de tourner contr-elle. Mais je ne saurois admettre *e*toutes les expressions de ce Philosophe Vertueux*e*. Un de mes amis qui m'en avoit donné deux Exemplaires,*f* m'avois remis un *Errata* dont je joint ici la copie, et qui est absolument neccessaire. L'Abbe de Lignac vient d'essayer de refuter[3] ce Livre, et de lui substituer une metaphisique qui n'engendre point d'idées claires, mais ou il y à bien des invectives contre tous ceux qui ne pensent pas comme lui. C'est un Theologien qui se scandalise aisément et qui voit partout des poisons.

Vous me dirés, s'il vous plait, mon digne ami, votre jugement sur cette *Psychologie*, et vous ne me repondres qu'apres que vous aurez achévé de la lire. Vous trouveres dans les principes philosophiques[4] qui sont à la fin, bien des verités presentées avec tant de precision, qu'elles fourniront un vaste champ à vos meditations. Je respecte les Philosophes Anglois; mais c'est grand domage qu'ils ne s'attachent pas plus à repandre de la netteté et de l'ordre dans leurs Ecrits. *g*Compares je vous prie, Locke avec notre Anonyme sur l'*immaterialité* de l'Ame et sur la *liberté*,[5] et dittes moi lequel à votre avis à le mieux frapé au but?*g*

1. See letter 5, n.1.

2. The anonymous *Essai de psychologie* (Londres [Leyde] 1755) was Bonnet's own work. In the 'avertissement' prefixed to the last volume of his collected works, Bonnet wrote: 'Me voici enfin arrivé au moment où je suis, en quelque sorte, forcé de faire l'aveu public de cet Ouvrage de ma jeunesse, que j'ai cité assez fréquemment dans mes Ecrits, critiqué plus d'une fois, plus souvent encore commenté & éclairci, & pour lequel j'ai presque toujours laissé transpirer un penchant secret qui déceloit trop aux yeux d'un Lecteur pénétrant cet amour paternel que je paroissois pourtant vouloir lui cacher, & que je n'étois peut-être pas fâché qu'il soupçonnât. L'*Essai de Psychologie* parut à Leyde en Hollande, dans l'Eté de 1754, quoiqu'il portât au Titre 1755' (B.O., 8:v/17:v). See also Starobinski (1975).

3. Joseph-Adrien Lelarge de Lignac, *Le Témoignage du sens intime et de l'expérience, opposé à la foi profane et ridicule des fatalistes modernes* (Auxerre 1760). On Lignac's refutation of Bonnet's *Essai de psychologie*, which he claimed led to materialism, see Marx (1976:601-604).

4. The 'principes philosophiques' refer to a separate work published as the second half of the *Essai de psychologie* (1755:271-390): 'Principes philosophiques sur la cause premiere et sur son effet'. See also B.O., 8:163-242/17:237-341.

5. Bonnet (1755:108-22, 157-79); B.O., 8:65-70, 93-107/17:93-101, 136-55. In *An essay concerning human understanding*, Locke discussed the question of the immateriality of the soul mainly in Bk.IV, ch.III, §6, and that of liberty in Bk.II, ch.XXI, §§7-27 and §§49-54. For the problem of liberty in Bonnet, see G. Bonnet (1930:189-247).

Pope dans son admirable *Essai*[6] ne me paroit pas non plus avoir assés creusé dans le fondement des actions *Morales*; il entrevoit plus qu'il ne voit. D'un autre coté l'Anonyme merite des reproches pour avoir trop pressé la *Neccessité*; il est trop crud, et beaucoup de Lecteurs ne pouront le digerer; mais un plus grand nombre encore ne l'entendront pas, et le critiqueront pourtant comme l'a fait le bon Pere Lignac. Je releve cette Psychologie en plusieurs endroits de l'Ouvrage que vous recevrés, j'espere le mois prochain, et vous jugerés si ma critique est juste. La refutation de Lignac à pour titre le *Temoignage du sens intime* &c. 3 Tome 1760. J'ai ecrit a Paris pour l'avoir; je ne le connois que par les journeaux, qui declarent sa Metaphysique la plus tenebreuse du monde[7]: lors que je l'aurai lû je vous en dirai mon sentiment.

C'etoit bien dans la 4.[c] Partie des *Lettres à un americain* que j'avois vû la Critique des consequences que vous aves tirées de vos curieuses Observations.[8] Si j'acheve jamais mon Livre sur les *Corps organizes*[9] vous verres ce que je pense de ces faits.

Je suis et serai toute ma vie avec la plus parfaite estime et le plus sincere attachement ꞌmon Cher ami et Confrereꞌ &c.

[ADDRESS] Turin M. Needham.

MANUSCRIPTS
   BPUG, MS Bonnet 70:222r-223r; MS Bonnet 85:173v-174v.

TEXT NOTES
   a. B: inférez *b*. B: vingt à trente *c*. B: *omitted* *d*. B: vous envoyer *e*. B: certaines expressions de cet hardi Pensant *f*. B: Exemplaires de ce Livre,

human understanding, Locke discussed the question of the immateriality of the soul mainly in Bk.IV, ch.III, §6, and that of liberty in Bk.II, ch.XXI, §§7-27 and §§49-54. For the problem of liberty in Bonnet, see G. Bonnet (1930:189-247).
   6. The first three epistles of *An essay on Man. In Epistles to a friend. Epistle III.* (Dublin 1733) were published anonymously. The fourth epistle appeared in 1734 as *An essay on Man. In Epistles to a friend. Epistle IV* (London 1734). Alexander Pope (1688-1744) acknowledged authorship in 1735. For a list of Pope's works, see Griffith (1922-1927); and for bibliographies of studies on Pope, see Tobin (1945) and Lopez (1970). The reception of Pope's works during the eighteenth century is discussed in Guerinot (1969), Barnard (1973), and Reeves (1976). Bonnet commented on Pope in Bonnet (1770a, 2:43-44; B.O., 7:358/16:43-44). For Needham's opinion of Pope's *Essay*, see Needham (1750:260-62n, 506-10); and for works by Pope in Needham's possession, see *Catalogue* (1782, pt.1:108 and pt.2:9).
   7. Bonnet is probably alluding to the review of Lignac's work *Le Témoignage du sens intime* (see n.3 above) that appeared in the *Journal encyclopédique* (15 November 1760, 8, pt.3:3-22). In summarising his criticism, the author wrote: 'En un mot le grand principe de la Métaphysique de l'Auteur, c'est-à-dire, le sens intime considéré comme indépendant des pensées, des sensations & des actions de l'ame, n'est qu'un mot vuide de sens: il a été probablement imaginé pour imiter la théorie de Locke, & donner, à l'exemple de ce grand homme, une Métaphysique expérimentale, pour ainsi dire: mais quelque bonne opinion que Mr de Lignac ait de sa pénétration, nous doutons qu'il vienne jamais à bout de flétrir la réputation de ce célèbre Philosophe' (pp.21-22). However not all reviews of Lignac's book were unfavourable. The one that appeared in the Jesuit *Journal de Trévoux* (June and July 1761, 61:1459-75, 1563-74) was favourable and applauded Lignac's metaphysics as 'vrai Métaphysique' (p.1475) and his reasoning as 'logique tranchante' (p.1467).
   8. See letter 6, n.2.
   9. See letter 4, n.2.

9

Bonnet to Needham – Geneva, 29 May 1761

Geneve 29. Mai 1761.

Je vous fais mille remerciemens, Monsieur mon cher ami et Confrere, de toutes les remarques que vous aves bien voulu me communiquer[1] sur le Livre[2] que je vous envoyai il y a quelques tems. Lors que je le lus pour la premiere fois, la plupart de ces remarques s'offrirent à mon esprit. Il me paru tres evident que l'Auteur avoit été trop loin dans ses consequences, et qu'on pouvoit lui reprocher d'avoir confondu quelquefois le Moral avec le Physique. Je souscrit donc volontier, mon Cher ami, à plusieurs de vos reflexions et surtout à celles qui concernent la Religion. Ce n'est pas neantmoins que je suspecte le moins du monde celle de l'Auteur; il ne me paroit point du tout un incredule; mais ses principes pouroient devenir tres dangereux pour ceux qui ne sauroient pas en faire la Correction; Il y a plus; quand les principes de cet auteur seroient vrais, ce qu'on peut justement lui contester, il auroit été mieux sans doute, de ne les publier pas. Il est vrai aussi, que plusieurs avoient été tournés contre la Religion, et que l'Auteur paroit etre sincere quand il tache de les concilier avec elle. Lors que je pourai vous envoyer mon *Essai Analytique* sur l'Ame, vous verres la critique que je faix çà et là de cet auteur; je ne l'attaque pas dans tous ses principes; mon Plan ne m'y conduisoit pas; mais je le releve sur des sujets qui font une partie essentielle de celui que j'ai entrepris d'Analiser. Cest Ovrage est imprimé à Copenhague[3] depuis le mois d'octobre dernier. Les malheurs de la Guerre ne m'ont pas encore permis de le recevoir ici: le sejour des Troupes dans la Hesse à retenu à Hambourg les Exemplaires qui m'etoient destinés, mais il y a deja du temps qu'il se vend en Allemagne, en Hollande et en Angleterre. Il a obtenu dans l'etranger des suffrages illustres et que je ne vous nommerai point afin de ne pas prevenir votre jugement. Il est actuellement en route pour notre Ville: des qu'il me sera parvenu j'en ferai partir un Exemplaire pour Turin a votre adresse, que je recommanderai aux Correspondans que vous m'indiqués. Ce ne sera gueres qu'a la fin de juin prochain que je l'aurai en main et ce retard n'est pas agreable.

Je viens de lire une petite Brochure Latine[4] de P. De la Torre, qui demeure

1. This letter from Needham to Bonnet cannot be traced.
2. See letter 8, n.2.
3. Charles Bonnet, *Essai analytique sur les facultés de l'ame* (Copenhague 1760); republished in B.O., 6:1-427/13:1-319 and 14:1-338.
4. Bonnet is alluding to Della Torre's observations of blood corpuscles described in a short publication entitled *Praeclarissimo viro Abbati Noleto publico physicae professori*, which was printed in 1760 (see Della Torre 1776:166). Della Torre wrote letters to a number of scholars, giving them a detailed description of his observations, and sent copies of his pamphlet to others (see his letter to Haller published in Haller 1773-1775, 4:237-42, and his letter to Paolo Frisi, BAM, Y.151. Sup.39). He also showed his observations to several scholars, who in turn described them to others, as did for example, Raimondo Cocchi (1735-1775) to Felice Fontana (1730-1805). The shape of the red corpuscles was at the time a much debated topic. Sénac (1749, 2:654-70), for instance, believed they had a 'lenticular' form, whereas Haller (1756a:15-31, 178-90) held the older view that they

à Naples:[5] elle renferme ses decouvertes microscopes sur les Globules du sang. Il dit avoir observé qu'ils sont formés de six Globules plus petits, lies les uns aux autres et qui forment des anneaux Circulaires ou Elyptiques. Chaque Globule constituant d'un anneau, est selon lui, un petit sac plein d'une Lymphe subtile. Cela e[s]t extremement curieux et fait beaucoup d'honneur à la sagacité de l'inventeur. Mais je voudrois bien qu'il se trouvat un autre Needham qui verifia ces observations. Vous verrés apparemment ce Père et vous le mettres à la question. Il a envoyé ici quelques exemplaires de sa Brochure, qu'il a adressé à quelques uns de nos*a* gens de Lettres et qui ont été bien reçus. Si vous avies encore ces yeux qui ont decouvert les Globules infiniment petits des Etamines, j'aurois bien du plaisir à aprendre qu'ils s'exercent sur les Globules du sang. J'aime a contempler l'Esprit Humain faisant des incursions dans les provinces les plus reculées de l'Univers sensible. Mais combien de precautions, combien de retenues, combien d'exactitudes n'exigent pas de pareils objets pour etre bien vûs et bien decrits! Vous le saves, mon cher ami, vous à qui nous devons tout en ce Genre. Pour moi je n'ai observé que des Elephans en comparaison; et ces Elephans m'ont pourtant fatigué les yeux au point qu'il à falu renoncer au microscope. *b*Aprenes moi je vous prie, s'il ne se sera point trouvé en Italie de Physicien qui ait repeté mes experiences *sur l'usage des feuilles*, sur les *Pucerons* et sur les *Vers qui peuvent etre multipliés de Bouture*. Vous aures passé à Boulogne et vous vous seres souvenu de moi aupres de M. Zanotti. J'ai faits vos Complimens a notre Cher Trembley qui vous fait les siens.*b*

Je vous embrasse de tout mon Coeur, mon Cher Confrere, et vous assure de l'attachement sincere et de la parfaite estime de &c.

[ADDRESS] Turin. M. l'Abbé Needham.

MANUSCRIPTS
  BPUG, MS Bonnet 70:232*v*-233*r*; MS Bonnet 85:175*r*-175*v*.

TEXT NOTES
  a. B: vos *b.* B: *omitted*

were 'spherical'. In 1760 Della Torre denied that they were spherical and described them as tiny membranaceous bags of a ring-like shape, filled with lymph, and pierced in the middle. His observations generated much sensation, scepticism, and controversy. In response, Della Torre refined his arguments and provided longer descriptions of them in what are probably his two most original works as a microscopist: Della Torre (1763:95-130) and Della Torre (1776:83-88, 116-28). For secondary literature on Della Torre's observations on red blood corpuscles, see Zanobio (1961), Fontana (1980:36-39, 165-66), and the literature cited therein.

  5. Giovanni Maria Della Torre (1710-1782) was born in Rome, where he studied at the Collegio Clementino of the Somaschi Fathers, whose order he joined in 1730. He first taught mathematics and philosophy at various Italian colleges and then settled in Naples as a lecturer at the Seminario Arcivescovile. In 1743 Charles III of Bourbon (1716-1788) appointed him as his personal Librarian, Superintendent of the Stamperia Reale, and Keeper of the Museum of Capodimonte. Della Torre was a man of great learning, but his main research fields were microscopy and vulcanology. Apart from the bibliographical references given by Pietro Franceschini in *D.S.B.*, 4 (1971) 25-26, see those provided in Fontana (1980:161-62). For Della Torre's microscopical investigations on the structure of nerves, ses Zanobio (1959:309-10); for those on the iris, see Mazzolini (1980:105-107, 146-47); and for his contributions to vulcanology, see Massa Piacentini (1941). Needham certainly met Della Torre in Naples, because he is mentioned among the visiting scholars to whom Della Torre had shown his preparations revealing the structure of the red blood corpuscles (see Della Torre 1763:95-97).

10

Bonnet to Needham – Geneva, 16 June 1761

Genève ce 16.ᵉ Juin 1761.

Enfin, Monsieur mon cher ami et Confrère, j'ai reçu mon *Essai Analytique sur les facultés de l'Ame*,[1] et un de mes premiers soins a été d'en faire partir un Exemplaire à Vôtre adresse, pour Turin: ᵃje l'ai recommandé aux Banquiers que vous m'aviés indiqués dans vôtre derniere Lettre, savoir Mess.ʳˢ Long, Barde et Haldiman. Ce Paquet partit hier, et si ces Mess.ʳˢ sont diligens vous l'aurés bien-tôt.ᵃ Je me hâte de vous en donner avis, afin que vous pourvoyés au necessaire.

Lisés avec attention ma Preface[2]: elle vous aprendra la manière dont je veuxᵇ être lû, entendu et medité. Vous y verrés la marche de mon Esprit, le Plan que j'ai suivi, les Ecueils que j'ai tâché d'eviter, et tout ce que j'ai à craindre de la precipitation et des prejugés d'un certain ordre de Lecteurs.

La Chaine est longue; pour la bien saisir il faut tenir tous les Chainons. Je n'ai raisonné que d'aprés les Faits; et leurs Conséquences naturelles ont été mes Principes.

J'ai ᶜosé le premierᶜ appliquer l'Analyse à l'examen des operations de nôtre Etre, et j'ai été etonné moi-même de la fecondité et de la simplicité de mes principes.

Si j'ai erré, je le reconnoitrai sans peine; mais je ne repondrai à aucune Critique virulente. Mon Coeur me rend temoignage de la pureté de mes intentions.

Je n'annonce point des Demonstrations; je n'ai cherché que le plus probable, et j'ai dit souvent, *il me paroit, il me semble, on peut inferer*, &c.

J'ai pourtant lieu de croire que j'ai suivi une Methode plus rigoureuse que ᵈtous ceuxᵈ qui m'avoient precedés: au moins toutes mes propositions paroissent-elles bien enchainées les unes aux autres.

Quoi que je sois entré dans des détails où personne n'etoit entré avant moi, j'espere que je ne me serai pas egaré. Je n'ai rien negligé pour être toûjours aussi netᵉ et aussi precis que la Nature de chaque sujet le comportoit.

J'ai eu le bonheur de decouvrir une route nouvelle ou presque nouvelle: des Genies plus heureux et plus habiles iront plus loing que moi dans cette route. J'ai observé l'Homme comme une Plante ou une Insecte, et j'ai dit ce que j'ai vû ou crû voir.

Vous ne gouterés peut être pas mes Principes, mon cher Confrere, et je ne vous en serai pas moins attaché: Vous donnés plus que moi dans le pur Metaphisique: mais vous gouterés probablement ma Methode.

J'aurai bien des Lecteurs, et fort peu de bons Lecteurs. Le siècle est trop accoutumé aux lectures frivoles, et le prejugé vâ toûjours son train.

Vous serés surpris quand je vous dirai que le Manuscript Original de mon

---

1. See letter 9, n.3.
2. Bonnet (1760:i-xxiv) and B.O., 6:vii-xxiv/13:vii-xxxvi.

Livre n'a pas une rature. J'ai retenu dans mon Cerveau un grand nombre de Paragraphes des jours et des semaines, et je ne les ai ecrit ou fait ecrire qu'aprés les avoir reduits à leurs plus petits termes. C'est la seule*f* maniere de bien composer; ce n'est pourtant pas celle dont on compose ordinairement. Voiés là-dessus mon Chap. XXV.[3]

Lisés et relisés et dites moi vôtre Jugement: ne me condamnés point sans m'avoir bien entendu: ne me loüés point non-plus qu'à bonnes enseignes. Si vous n'avés pas la patience d'aller jusqu'aù bout, ne me dites rien; vous ne pourriés pas juger de l'ensemble.

Je vous embrasse de tout mon Coeur et suis avec le plus sincère attachement, mon cher Confrère, tout à vous.

[ADDRESS] Rome M.*r* Needham.

MANUSCRIPTS
    BPUG, MS Bonnet 70:238*r*-238*v*; MS Bonnet 85:176*r*-176*v*.

TEXT NOTES
    a. B: *omitted b.* B: désire *c.* B: essayé d' *d.* B: celle des Auteurs *e.* B: clair *f.* B: meilleure

I I

Needham to Bonnet – Rome, 11 July 1761

Le present agreable, que je viens de recevoir, de votre livre[1] est une preuve bien assurée, mon cher Monsieur, de votre amitié pour moi, et un gage precieux de votre estime, qui m'est bien plus chere, et plus agreable, que la voix de la multitude, dont tant de soi-disans philosophes paroissent enchantés dans ce siecle. Je n'ai le reçu que ce matin, et je n'ai lu encore que la preface, dont Je suis parfaitment content. Elle me promette avec la sagesse, et la penetration, dont Je vous connois doue, une lecture tres agreable, tres satisfaisante, et tres utile. Je vous ne ferai pas assurement la guerre de ce que vous ne penetrés pas, comme vous me dit dans votre lettre, si avant dans le pur metaphysique, comme j'ai voulu faire, si la route s'étend vraiment au de la de vos recherches, ou si celle, que j'ai pris pour un route n'est q'un passage, ou une breche qui nous detourne du vrai chemin en nous menant à des precipices n'importe; nous serons pas moins, comme je prevois deja, d'accord sur tous les objets, qui se presentent en chemin jusqu'à ce point, ou vous vous arretés, et moi je tache d'avancer. J'avois mes raisons pour faire, comme je fais, et comme vous me jugerés non selon le succes de mon travail, qui ne depend pas toujours de nous, mais selon mes intentions; J'ai voulu en premier lieu prouver à Messieurs les philosophes modernes, ce que vous dit assés clairement dans votre preface, que l'essence

---

3. Bonnet (1760:494-523) subtitled one section of chapter 25, 'Du physique de la composition en matière d'ouvrages d'esprit'. See also B.O., 6:369-94/14:257-96.

1. See letter 9, n.3.

reelle des substances etant par sa nature meme et par la nature de nos connoissances, qui ne sont qu'autant de relations, entierement inconnue, nous savons tout
aussi peu, ce qui fait que la matiere est etendue, et solide, que nous savons ce
qui fait que l'ame pense, et agit. Les effets neanmoins prouvent au de la de la
moindre doute, malgre cette ignorance de la nature absolue de la cause, l'existence de la matiere; de meme les effets prouvent egalement l'existence de l'ame
immaterielle, et celle de la divinité, d'ou elle emane. Pour reussir en cela, et
arriver à ce point, ou tout philosophe, qui avance dans ses recherches doit
arriver, il falloit developper la nature de nos connoissances, et traiter les qualites
primaires de la matiere, comme on les nomme, tout comme Lock a traité les
qualités secondaires,[2] c'est à dire, les reduire, en tant que senties, et connues de
nous, à des purs effets, ou des idees produites en nous, dont cette substance
inconnue, par elle meme que nous appellons matiere, est la cause. Il ne m'est
resté donc pour attribut primaire, et absolu de la matiere que l'idee d'une
multitude d'agens, et une certaine coactivité, ou l'action simultanée de plusieurs
étres agissans sur mon ame selon certaines loix prescrites par la divinité, d'ou
proviennent les idees en moi de figure, et d'etendue solide. Enfin J'ai conclu,
que si le raisonnement de Lock est juste, comme il est indubitablement par
raport aux qualites secondaires de couleur, chaleur, etc. il est egalement juste
par raport aux qualités primaires d'etendue solide, figure etc. à lesquelles il ne
s'etende pas moins en les embrassant egalement, qu'aux qualites secondaires.
J'ai été deja pleinement convaincu de la simplicité de notre ame, quoique je ne
conçois pas la nature absolue d'un etre simple; mais la possibilité, et la realité
un fois etablie, Je ne vois pas pourquoi je dois m'arreter à ne vouloir pas
appliquer la meme idée aux premiers principes de la matiere, puisque d'un
autre cote tous les argumens dont les Philosophes s'en servent par [rapport][a]
aux qualités secondaires etendus aux qualities primaires, comme ils doivent
etre, me portent à cette conclusion, aussi bien que mes idées sur le fini, et sur
l'infini. Il me paroit de plus, que par cette maniere d'envisager la nature, Je
rend les preuves de l'existence de la divinité et celle de mon ame immaterielle
aussi fortes, que sont celles de l'existence de la matiere; puisque tout est reduit
au meme niveau, et comme il ne se trouve pas aucun materialiste si insensé, de
nier, ou de douter de l'existence de matiere, parce que c'est une substance
inconnue en elle meme, et connue seulement par les effets produits en nous, de
meme tout homme est egalement insensé, qui doute sous ce pretexte ou de
l'existence de la divinite ou de [celle] de son ame immaterielle. De plus dans
une echelle des êtres simples dont toute la nature est composée à ma façon de
penser, J'ecarte et le systeme des causes occasionelles, et cel d'une harmonie
preetablie, qui m'ont paru toujours des pures hypotheses inventées pour calmer
nos doutes, a peu pres comme celle autrefois des anges, qui faisoient rouler les
planetes. Dans une echelle des êtres simples, qui ne different, que par le plus,
par le moins des attributs dont ils sont doués dans leur origine par la divinité,
mais pourtant qui different essentiellement, il me semble que l'union systematique, [pour faire] des êtres mixtes, tels que l'homme, et l'animal [est plus
naturelle], en meme tems que la subordination du [composé] à un seul etre

---

2. John Locke, *An essay concerning human understanding*, Bk.II, ch.VIII, §§ 7-26.

simple [principale] telle que l'ame intelligente, et sentante dans l'homme, ou simplement, si vous voulés, sentante dans le brut n'est pas ni moins forte, ni moins certaine que dans toute autre systeme, qu'on peut imaginer. Mais passons à d'autres choses en attendant, que je trouve le tems necessaire de bien mediter votre essai analytyque, Je vous dirai alors mes sentimens; je prevois deja que Je n'aurai qu'à vous louer, mais je ne vous louerai jamais qu'a bonnes enseignes. Depuis, que je suis à Rome, Je m'amuse beaucoup avec les antiquités, et Je profite de l'occasion, comme j'ai coutume par tout, pour m'avancer dans cette espece de connoissance, qui est propre au climat. A Turin en faisant quelques recherches de cette espece J'ai trouvé, et j'ai fait dessiner un bust tres ancien, qui represente une Isis egyptienne,[3] et qui est tout garni des caracteres sur la front, le nés, les joues, et les mammelles au nombre de trent deux en touts. Ils avoient tout l'air non des [mots] composes des lettres alphabetiques, mais des caracteres à la façon des chinois, et meme un certain tour de resemblance avec ceux actuellement en usage à la chine. Vous savés les recherches, qui ont été fait[es] par Messieurs de Guignes, Barthelemy, et Smidt[4] à Paris, et à Bernes sur la connection autrefois, probable, entre ces deux nations de l'egypte, et de la chine. Vous connoissés leur façon de penser sur la realité de ce liaison, et la force de leurs preuves. Vous avés lû sans doute la sotte preface de Voltaire à le premier volume de Pierre le Grand,[5] ou l'auteur joue le role d'un bouffon assés

3. In Needham's time this bust was kept in the Museo d'Antichità dell' Università in the Palace of via Po (see Curto 1962-1963:6). It is now in the Museo Egizio of Turin. See fig.12.

4. Joseph de Guignes (1721-1800), the famous French Orientalist, was born at Pontoise and died in Paris. After the death of his teacher Etienne Fourmont (1683-1745), he was appointed in his place as 'secrétaire interprète pour les langues orientales' at the Bibliothèque royale. In 1752 he became Royal Censor. He was a lifelong contributor to the *Journal des sçavans*. In 1757 he was appointed to the chair of Syrian at the Collège royal but resigned when this was amalgamated with the University in 1773. In the same year he was appointed pensionnaire of the Académie des inscriptions. For a short biography and list of his publications, see *B.U.* (18:126-29). Five letters from Needham to Guignes, written in 1761, are preserved in the BL, Add.21416. For Needham's relationship with Guignes, see section 6 of the Introduction.

For biographies of the famous French numismatist and antiquarian abbé Jean-Jacques Barthélemy (1716-1795), Keeper of the Royal Collection of Medals from 1753 and the author of the *Voyage du jeune Anacharsis*, see *B.U.* (3:179-81), the éloge prefixed to Barthélemy (1797, 1:xiii-cxxii), and Boufflers (1806). Barthélemy frequented the salon of Anne-Marie Du Boccage for fifty years. Gibbon found him 'fort aimable' (Gibbon 1966:301), and Alessandro Verri (1741-1816) considered him 'il primo medaglista non pedante che forse sia mai esistito al mondo' (Gaspari 1980:50). For his relationship with Needham, see section 6 of the Introduction. Although he was acquainted with Needham's pamphlet *De inscriptione quadam Aegyptiaca* (1761), he did not have a copy in his own library (see *Catalogue* 1800).

Friedrich Samuel Schmidt (1737-1796), antiquarian, Orientalist, and librarian, was born in Bern and, at a fairly young age, gained a reputation as an Egyptologist (see F. Schmidt 1765 and 1768). In 1757 he was awarded the annual prize of the Académie des inscriptions of Paris, where he spent the winter of 1758-1759. In 1762, not having obtained an appointment in Bern as he had hoped, he moved to the University of Basel. In 1764 he was appointed Hofrat, Librarian, and Director of the Art Gallery of the Markgraf von Baden in Karlsruhe. He later also worked in Frankfurt am Main. His MSS are preserved in the Badische Landesbibliothek of Karlsruhe, but none of Needham's letters directed to him are included. For his biography, see *B.U.* (38:379) and Dübi (1893).

5. The first volume of Voltaire's *Histoire de l'empire de Russie sous Pierre le Grand* appeared in 1759. Needham alludes particularly to the following passage: 'On ne s'est point fatigué dans cette histoire de PIERRE LE GRAND à rechercher vainement l'origine de la plupart des peuples qui composent l'Empire immense de Russie, depuis le Kamshatka jusqu'à la mer Baltique. C'est une étrange entreprise de vouloir prouver par des piéces authentiques que les Huns vinrent autrefois du Nord

platement à mon avis, mais n'importe ce n'est pas la seule fois, ou le bon sens lui manque totalement quand il s'acharne contre tout ce, qui paroit favoriser la religion. Enfin par le moyen d'un chinois sçavant[6] natif de Pekin, qui est ici employé dans le Vatican Je suis parvenu à decyphrer douze de trent deux caracteres dont l'inscription est composée, qui font un sens complet, et relatif parfaitment à son objet le buste. J'ai deja par le moyen de M[r.] Haller fait parvenir une copie de l'inscription à M[r.] Smidt à Bernes.[7] Il m'a recrit, et il soupçonnoit alors, que cette inscription pouvoit être Coptique, et faite en forme de Talisman par quelques heretiques Basilidiens ou autres enthusiastes en astrologie. J'ai consulté ici de Copthes, et J'ai le fait avant, que de consulter mon chinois, mais ils n'entendoient rien, et meme il ny est pas la moindre apparence d'aucun ordre alphabetique dans toute l'inscription, puisque il ne [se trouve] pas deux caracteres, qui se resemblent. Enfin le nœud est delié par le chinois, qui pour decypher ces douze [caracteres] etoit obligé de consulter des livres tres anciens; et ces caracteres, dont il n'est pas un seul en usage à present à la chine, sont d'une antiquité de plus, que dix sept cens ans avant J. Xt, Je vous prie de faire parvenir cette decouverte à M[r.] Smidt avec mes complimens à tous les deux par M[r.] Haller,[8] en attendant que Je lui pu ecrire plus au long, aussitot que Je recevrai une reponse de Naples, ou j'ai envoyé l'inscription pour la montrer à d'autres chinois, qui sont la dans un college etabli par le Roi. J'espere, que par leur moyen Je pourrai peutetre decyphrer le reste de la dite inscription. Fait bien des complimens de ma part à M[r.] Trembley; recevés mes remercimens, et me croyés toujours, cher ami, et confrere

votre tres humble, et tres obeissant serviteur

Needham.

à Rome Le 11. de Juillet 1761.

MANUSCRIPT
  BPUG, MS Bonnet 26:127r-128v.

TEXT NOTES

de la Chine en Sibérie, & que les Chinois eux-mêmes sont une colonie d'Egyptiens. Je sçai que des philosophes d'un grand mérite ont cru voir quelques conformités entre ces peuples: mais on a trop abusé de leurs doutes; on a voulu convertir en certitude leurs conjectures.

'Voici, par exemple, comme on s'y prend aujourd'hui pour prouver que les Egyptiens sont les pères des Chinois. Un ancien a conté que l'Egyptien *Sésostris* alla jusqu'au Gange; or s'il alla vers le Gange, il put aller à la Chine, qui est très loin du Gange; donc il y alla, donc alors la Chine n'était point peuplée; il est donc clair que *Sésostris* la peupla. Les Egyptiens dans leurs fêtes allumaient des chandèles; les Chinois ont des lanternes; donc on ne peut douter que les Chinois ne soient une colonie d'Egypte. De plus, les Egyptiens ont un grand fleuve, les Chinois en ont un; enfin, il est évident que les premiers Rois de la Chine ont porté les noms des anciens Rois d'Egypte: car dans le nom de la famille *Yu*, on peut trouver les caractères qui arrangés d'une autre façon forment le mot *Menès*. Il est donc incontestable que l'Empereur *Yu* prit son nom de *Menès* Roi d'Egypte, & l'Empereur *Ki* est évidemment le Roi *Atoës*, en changeant *k* en *a* & *i* en *toës*' (Voltaire 1759-1763, 1:xv-xvii; see also V.O., 16:381-82).

  6. Needham (1761:14 n.1) referred to him as 'Josephus Lucius Vu in Bibliotheca Vaticana Scriptor Sinensis, & Codicibus Sinensibus tam manuscriptis, quam exaratis praepositus'.

  7. This was confirmed by Needham (1762:12n).

  8. Needham must have previously sent Haller a drawing of the characters, because the latter wrote to Bonnet on 16 March 1761, 'M Needham m'a envoyé je ne sais quels caracteres qu'il croit Chinois' (see Sonntag 1983:235). For Haller's interest in Needham's pamphlet of 1761, see Hintzsche (1965:81, 83).

a. This letter was written on very thin paper, causing several passages to be obscured by the writing on the reverse side. We have indicated with brackets [ ] those words having a tentative reading.

12

Needham to Bonnet – Rome, 21 September 1761

J'ai pris la plume, mon cher Monsieur, et confrere, pour recommander à vos attentions, et à votre politesse mon tres estimé ami M[r.] Wilcocks,[1] un cavalier anglois qui voyage moins pour son plaisir, que pour l'utilité publique, et celle de ses amis sçavans. Par tout ou il va, il fait entre autre choses des recherches tres exactes après des manuscrits anciens de la bible hebraique pour cooperer autant qu'il est possible à son ami M[r.] Kennicot[2] d'oxford, qui travaille actuellement à nous donner le *variantes* de ce livre sacré avec un applaudissement general, et avec le concours de toute l'europe. Il est en effet tres inutile, que je vous le recommande pour ce propos, l'importance de l'ouvrage, et le merite particulier de M[r.] Wilcocks auprès d'une personne de votre esprit vous porteront naturellement à lui prêter toute l'assistance possible. Il vous presentera de ma part une petite ouvrage[3] de ma façon, et il vous expliquera plus au long le commencement, et le progres, dont il a été temoin, d'une decouverte assés singuliere, et à la perfection de la quelle il a beaucoup contribué par tous les moyens possibles. Il vous dira de plus, verité que je dois avouer pour me ne pas

1. Joseph Wilcocks (1723-1791), the only son of Joseph, bishop of Gloucester and later of Rochester, matriculated at Christ Church Oxford in 1740, receiving his B.A. in 1744 and M.A. in 1747. In 1765 he was elected a Fellow of the London Society of Antiquaries. His major work, *Roman conversations* (London 1792), was published after his death. For a short biography, see E. Irving Carlyle, *D.N.B.*, 61 (1900) 218-19. According to the biography of Wilcocks prefixed to the second edition of his *Roman conversations* (1797:xxx), Wilcocks met Needham in Rome and helped him in his investigations on the inscription of the 'bust of Isis' (see section 6 of the Introduction). It was Wilcocks who later sent the specimens of the inscription to Peking 'to be there examined by learned Jesuits' (Wilcocks 1797:xxx). An extract of a letter from Needham to Wilcocks, dated 5 June 1762, which concerns the controversy over the 'bust of Isis', is in the SAL, Correspondence 1761-1770; see also SAL, *Minutes*, ix:10-12, and Pierce (1965:213-14 n.5).

2. At the time of this letter, the biblical scholar Benjamin Kennicott (1718-1783), a Fellow of Exeter College, Oxford, was engaged in collating the Hebrew manuscripts of the Old Testament. His enterprise had considerable backing. Subscriptions were raised in England; and ancient manuscripts were sent to him from the king of Denmark, the king of Sardinia, and all parts of England. The Stadtholder of Holland made a yearly donation of thirty guineas available, and help was provided by a number of private scholars. Both cardinal Passionei in Rome and the Vénérable Compagnie des Pasteurs et des Professeurs de l'Eglise de Genève warmly recommended that the work should be undertaken and gave access to the manuscripts preserved in Rome and Geneva. From 1762 Kennicott published a yearly report in English and Latin on *The State of the collection of the Hebrew manuscripts of the Old Testament* (Kennicott 1770), and these were given widespread publicity in the periodicals of the time (see, for example, *The Annual register*, 1768, fifth ed., pp.146-57). The first volume of his work *Vetus Testamentum Hebraicum, cum variis lectionibus* appeared in 1776, and the second in 1780.

3. *De inscriptione quadam Aegyptiaca Taurini inventa et characteribus Aegyptiis olim et Sinis communibus exarata idolo cuidam antiquo in Regia Universitate servato* (Romae 1761). For an account of this work by Needham, see Dawson (1932:467-68), Curto (1962-1963:6-7), and section 6 of the Introduction.

attribuer plus que m'appartient en droit, que l'hazard va plus loin souvent, que la raison ou la penetration. Je dois cette decouverte à une heureuse combinaison des circomstances totalement imprevues, dont Je suis moi meme encore tout étonné, et qui me paroit comme une songe. Vous sentez bien q'une pareille distraction m'a empeché de finir la lecture de votre livre, dans lequel j'avois fait quelque progrés. Vous me defendez avec raison de vous donner mon sentiment la dessus avant de l'avoir fini entierement. C'est un livre, que quoique tres clair par la maniere, qu'il est traité, ne se lit pas, comme la nouvelle Heloise de votre compatriote.[4]Vous me permettrés neanmoins de vous dire, que je suis tres content de cette partie, que j'ai deja lû, et qui fait un bon tiers du total; sur tout vous me plaisez en profitant de tant des bonnes choses, qu'on trouve dans l'essai de psychologie, en meme tems que vous ecartez les erreurs de cet auteur si dangereuses à la societé. J'ai ecris par la meme occasion à notre ami M[r.] Trembley pour lui recommander la meme personne. Je connois son bon coeur, et le votre, et je suis avec une tres grande estime

et un attachement inviolable
votre tres bon ami, et confrere
Needham.

A Rome: le 21. de Sept: 1761.

Saluez, si vous plait, notre ami M[r.] Haller, quand vous lui ecriverés, et assurez le de mon estime, et de mes tres humbles respects. Je vous envoye pour lui et M[r.] Smidt en meme tems deux exemplaires de mon ouvrage, que vous aurez la bonte de faire passer à Bernes.

[ADDRESS] A Monsieur / Monsieur Charles Bonnet / de la societé Royale de Londres, / correspondant de l'academie des sciences / de Paris &c. / A Geneve.

MANUSCRIPT
BPUG, MS Bonnet 26:129r-130v.

13

Needham to Bonnet – Rome, 30 September 1761

Monsieur Mon ami, et tres cher confrere,

Je viens de vous ecrire par mon ami Monsieur Wilcocks un sçavant anglois, qui va à Geneve, et à qui J'ai remis un exemplaire d'une brochure,[1] que j'ai fait imprimer ici, pour vous, et un autre pour notre ami M[r.] Trembley. Je ne vous dira rien de plus, si non que c'est la prosecution d'une decouverte, dont j'ai vous a deja marqué l'heureux commencement, et à la quelle j'ai mis la derniere main: la dissertation doit parler pour elle meme. Je ne sçai de quelle façon

4. Jean-Jacques Rousseau.

1. See letter 12, n.3.

bonne, ou mauvaise, Mr. de Voltaire prendra la critique, que j'ai fait en peu des mots de sa façon de traiter le sujet dans sa preface à son Pierre le grand;[2] tout ce que je peu vous dire est, que j'ai me suis tenu loin, et tres loin de toute personalité, c'est à sa façon de traiter souvent des sujets de la derniere importance, que je veu, et non pas à lui. Ici par exemple il ne faut pas de l'esprit, dont il n'a pour son malheur, que trop, et que je goute assés, quand il est bien placé, il nous faut des recherches, et des raisonnemens, dont les moindres ne sont pas souvent meprisables; parce que souvent il nous faut q'une etincelle pour produire une tres grande lumiere. C'est sa faute, s'il a voulu mal a propos eteindre ces etincelles. Du reste, s'il me reponde et me reponde solidement, Je lui pardonnerai tout, et Je ne me plaindera plus de sa façon d'ecrire dans des sujets trop graves pour admettre badinerie. C'est ainsi que je vous previent sur mon ouvrage, parce que je vois, que Mr. Wilcocks n'arrivera pas à Geneve avant la fin du mois d'octobre. Vous prevoiés deja par ce que Je vous annonce sur mes occupations, que je ne suis pas beaucoup avancé dans la lecture de votre ouvrage, qui demande une lecture posée, et lente. J'ai lu pourtant aux environs un tiers de votre livre,[3] et Je suis content, mais tres content; vous ne differés rien jusqu'à present de ma maniere de penser, et ce que vous avés si bien detaillé est clair, net, et precis. Je vous felicite sur le beau present, que vous venés de faire au public; c'est tout ce, que je peut vous dire pour le present. Quant à ce que je vous a marqué sur Mr. de Voltaire, Je ne serai pas faché, que vos amis le sçachent, meme jusqu'à le faire parvenir aux oreilles de Mr. de Voltaire; il sera toujours ma justification par raport au public, s'il n'est trouve aucun accés auprès de lui car s'il veut étendre ma critique au dela de sa façon burlesque d'ecrire contre ses adversaires jusqu'à des personalités il aura tres grand tort, et il ne m'entend nullement. Les generalités que j'ai laché par ici, par la contre un tas des auteurs modernes, il ne doit nullement appliquer à lui même s'il ne se sent pas coupable; les vices du siecle ne sont jamais des personalités, si personne ne l'applique à des individus, et moi moins que personne. Je vous prie

---

2. In his *De inscriptione quadam Aegyptiaca*, alluding to Voltaire's preface (see letter 11, n.5), Needham wrote: 'Animum mihi non parum commovit nuperrima praefatio operi, quod jam jam in lucem prodiit praefixa. Quis non indignaretur rem tanti momenti facetiis, nullius penè saporis, scurrarum, & mimorum more tractari. Mendaciis Sinensium a nobis longo maris, terraeque tractu dissitorum per fas, & nefas utcumque litandum est, ut proteratur Sacrorum Codicum auctoritas, & historia fabulosa prorsus, vel ipsis Sinensibus fatentibus, ubi agitur de illius Imperii principio, & antiquitate, observationibus astronomicis, ipsum anteuntibus diluvium, muniri falso dicitur, cum prima ab ipsis Sinensibus eclypsis designata coaeva solum sit circa circiter vocationi Abraham. Qui contra sentit, imbecillitatis illi nota inuritur, miserum aliquod in triviis plebi disperditur carmen, vanitatis arguitur, & dicteriis imperitur, quorum in dies erumpens ad nauseam usque crescit mulitudo; nec solus Scurra Pantolabus, irrisoribus scatet Europa, et locustis Asia, & scomma pro omni argumento est; peccatum non infrequens hoc, ne dicam Saeculi, quantumvis fastuose incedat, & philosophiam praetexet turba hominum ratione furens, & mentem pasta deliriis. Luditur in nomine, dicteriis, & epigrammatibus res agitur, Salus Populi, suprema lex, Pharmacopolis, Mimis, Nepotibus dijudicanda, & definienda traditur, omne breve dictum sale aliquo conditum pro oraculo est, ipsaque Religio condemnatur more insolito, quo non cuperet vel absolvi. Caeterum si vapor sit horum Virorum halitus, qui scientiam sibi arrogant universalem, flores, & fructus nobilissimos rubigine inficiens, melius sanè omninò erit pauca rectè, & firmiter scire, quam multa fatalibus mixta erroribus' (Needham 1761:5-7).

3. See letter 9, n.3.

de saluer, Monsieur Trembley de ma part, et de me croire toujours

mon cher ami, et confrere

votre tres humble, et tres

obeissant serviteur

Needham.

A Rome Le 30. de sept:
1761.

Mʳ· Wilcocks doit vous remettre deux exemplaires de mon ouvrage pour Messieurs Haller, et Smidt à Berne.

[ADDRESS] A Monsieur / Monsieur Charles Bonnet / de la societé Royale de Londres &c. / à Geneve.

MANUSCRIPT
BPUG, MS Bonnet 26:131*r*-132*v*.

14

Bonnet to Needham – Geneva, 31 December 1761

à Genève le 31.ᵉ Xᵇʳᵉ 1761.

La mort de mon excellent et respectable Père[1] ne m'a pas permis, Monsieur mon cher Ami et Confrère, de rendre a vôtre estimable Ami M.ʳ Wilcoks les services auxquels j'étois si porté, par l'Interet que je prends à l'objet de ses recherches et par le plaisir de vous obliger. Il a reçu tous les secours qu'il pouvoit attendre du Zèle éclaire de nos gens de Lettres, et nôtre cher Trembley m'a remplacé auprès de lui.

Je regarde vôtre Dissertation comme très propre a étayer l'ingenieux systême de M.ʳ de Guignes.[2] J'aime a voir cette Antiquité si vantée des Chinois rabaissée

1. Pierre Bonnet became a member of the Council of Two Hundred in 1709 and was suspended for four years for debts in 1722. In 1719 he married Anne-Marie Lullin. In his autobiography, Bonnet wrote that his father 'ne négligea rien pour mon éducation' (Savioz 1948b:41); and in a letter to Haller of 22 December 1761, he expressed a great affection for him (see Sonntag 1983:247-48).

2. Guignes first formulated the hypothesis that the Chinese were an Egyptian colony in a paper read at the Académie des inscriptions on 18 April 1758. The full work was not published until 1764 (see Guignes 1764), but a summary by Guignes himself was published in 1759 with the title *Mémoire dans lequel on prouve, que les Chinois sont une colonie Egyptienne* (Paris 1759). Guignes's basic thesis was that 'les caracteres Chinois, ne sont que des espéces de Monogrammes formés de trois Lettres Phéniciennes; & que la lecture qui en résulte, produit des sons Phéniciens ou Egyptiens' (Guignes 1759a:5). A new edition of Guignes's summary appeared in 1760 (see Guignes 1760). The pamphlet aroused great interest but also provoked criticism from his former colleague Michel-Ange Deshautesrayes (1724-1795) and started a bitter controversy between the two (see Deshautesrayes 1759 and Guignes 1759b). Guignes was also criticised by Corneille de Pauw (1739-1799) (see Pauw 1773 and Guignes 1774). In order to demonstrate his hypothesis, Guignes later engaged in a comparative study of Egyptian and Chinese religion. He intended to publish a treatise establishing that 'les Chinois ont été policés & instruits par les Egyptiens' (Guignes 1780:163), but this remained only in manuscript form (see *B.U.*, 18:129). See also letter 11, n.4, and letter 15, n.1.

au niveau de celle des Egyptiens, qui se mésure elle même par notre Chronologie sacrée. Ce n'étoit pas le compte de Voltaire, et je vous sais gré d'avoir si bien repoussé ses insultes et ses railleries.[3] Vous avés tiré de vôtre Statue[4] le meilleur parti possible, et vous n'avés assurement rien négligé pour arriver a la découverte du vrai. Je suis très flaté du présent que vous m'avés fait de vôtre savant écrit et je vous en remercie *de tout mon coeur*.

Je souhaiterois d'avoir autant aproché du vrai en travaillant sur cette Statue Philosophique,[5] qui commencoit a vous plaire, et dont vous n'aviés pu voir encore que quelques traits quand vous m'écriviés vôtre dernière Lettre. Avés vous achevé de la parcourir et trouvés vous que la métode que j'ai choisie soit aussi feconde et aussi lumineuse qu'elle me l'avoit paru? J'ai taché de concentrer dans ma Théorie generale des Idées tout ce que nous connoissons de plus certain sur nos perceptions et sur les Notions qui en dérivent. Je ne[a] puis vous dire combien[b] M.[r] Trembley a été[c] satisfait de ce Livre, et vous [d]sçavés aussi bien que[d] moi tout le poids de son jugement. MM de Bentinck, Allamand, Gaubius, Albinus, Haller, Formey[a][6] &c. m'en ont écrit des choses qui me feroient oublier

3. See letter 11, n.7, and letter 13, n.2.

4. See letter 11, n.3.

5. Both Etienne Bonnot de Condillac (1714-1780), in his *Traité des sensations* (Londres, Paris 1754), and Bonnet used the image of the statue in order to describe the origin of ideas. 'Imaginons un Homme dont tous les sens sont en bon état, mais qui n'a point encore commencé à en faire usage. Supposons que nous avons le pouvoir de tenir les sens de cet Homme enchaînés, ou de les mettre en liberté dans l'ordre, dans le temps, & de la manière qu'il nous plaira. Offrons successivement à chaque sens, & ensuite à différens sens à la fois, les Objets propres à les affecter: voyons ce qui doit résulter de ces impressions: suivons, pour ainsi dire, à l'oeil le développement de l'ame de cet Homme, ou plutôt faisons-la développer à nôtre gré: Cet homme sera une espéce de *Statue*, & nous lui en donnerons le nom. La Philosophie sera la Divinité qui animera cette Statue, & qui nous aidera à l'élever par degrés, au rang d'*Etre pensant*' (Bonnet 1760:8-9; B.O., 6:6/13:9-10). Bonnet claimed that his idea of the statue was conceived independently from Condillac's (Savioz 1948b:176).

6. Bonnet sent his book to count Willem Bentinck (1704-1774), curator of Leiden University and an influential figure in Dutch politics (Schazmann 1976:162). Bonnet first came into contact with Bentinck through Trembley, who was tutor to Bentinck's sons, and later through Allamand. His brother, Charles John Bentinck (1708-1779) also admired Bonnet's book (Schazmann 1976:163). It was principally with the latter that Bonnet corresponded (Leigh 2929, 3010, 3163) and debated Rousseau's ideas, of which Bentinck was a fervent advocate. Twenty-two letters from Charles Bentinck to Bonnet are preserved in the BPUG. On the two Bentincks, see C.H.Th. Bussemaker, *N.N.B.W.*, 1 (1911) 297-98 and 301-303; Schazmann (1976:125-72); and Jacob (1981;198-201).

Allamand congratulated Bonnet on his book in a letter dated 16 January 1761 (BPUG, MS Bonnet 26:139r-140v).

The most complete biography of Hieronimus David Gaub (also Gaubius) (1705-1780), a pupil of Hermann Boerhaave (1668-1738) and from 1713 professor at Leiden University, is that by Hamers-van Duynen (1978:5-59), which also contains a good bibliography. For a shorter biographical note, see W. P. Jorissen, *N.N.B.W.*, 3 (1914) 431-32. On Gaub's medical theories, which were also very influential on psychological theories of the time, see Meyer-Steineg (1923) and Rather (1965:1-30). On 16 July 1760 Bonnet wrote to Gaub and sent him his book (BPUG, MS Bonnet 70:188). On 10 April 1761, Allamand (BPUG, MS Bonnet 26:141v) sent Gaub's answer to Bonnet, who later included it in full in his autobiography (Savioz 1948b:194). Gaub stated that, 'comme je regarde votre analyse pour un développement mathématique de ce que j'ai avancé, ainsi je pourrais en fournir des preuves innombrables et des plus frappantes, soit de ma propre expérience, soit des observations d'autres médecins tant anciens que modernes. C'est principalement la médecine, dont la physique de l'âme peut puiser ses lumières. Des esprits malins en tirent des conséquences irréligieuses. M. de La Mettrie était assis sur les degrés de la chaire fort attentif, quand je prononçais ce discours à la fin de mon rectorat, et peu après il publia son *Homme Machine*.'

Bernard Siegfried Albinus (1697-1770), one of the greatest anatomists of the eighteenth century

les imperfections de mon travail, si le sentiment vrai que j'ai de la médiocrité de mes Talens et de mes Lumières pouvoient m'abandonner un instant. J'attribue donc les Eloges de ces grands Maitres plutot a la difficulté de l'entreprise, qu'a la manière dont je l'ai exécutée. Mais; si j'essuye des Critiques amères, je me consolerai par l'Idée d'avoir plu à ce petit nombre d'hommes rares dont l'approbation est si respectable. Si vous m'accordés la vôtre, mon Celebre Confrère, j'y serai assurement très sensible, et si vous me critiqués, je recevrai vos remarques avec reconnoissance et j'en profiterai de mon mieux. Nous avons tous deux un amour égal pour le vrai.

N'avés vous rien découvert de nouveau sur les *Animalcules Microscopiques* depuis les observations que vous avés publiées dans les *Transactions Philosophiques*?[7] Etés vous toujours dans les mêmes Idées sur l'origine de ces Animalcules? Pensés vous qu'ils la doivent toujours a ces filamens que vous avés regardé comme des *Zoophytes*? Admettes vous encore cette dégradation continuelle des filamens et des Animalcules, et cette conversion des filamens en Animalcules, et des Animalcules en filamens qui décroissent graduellement jusques a ce qu'ils soyent devenus invisibles au Microscope? Avés vous repeté de nouveau vos curieuses

and a very influential teacher, was born at Frankfurt an der Oder. In 1702 he was taken to Leiden by his father Bernard Albinus (1653-1721), who had been appointed to teach theoretical and practical medicine at the University. Later he studied there and began teaching medicine even before he was awarded his M.D. In 1718 he spent several months studying in Paris. In 1721 he was appointed to the chair of anatomy and surgery at Leiden, which he relinquished in 1745 for that of general medicine and physiology. The main biographical source is still Allamand (1771), which also contains a list of Albinus's publications. See also E.D. Baumann, *N.N.B.W.*, 4 (1918) 22-24; Peter W. van der Pas, *D.S.B.*, 15 (1978) 4-5; and, for further references, Punt (1977 and 1983), Mazzolini (1980:33-34), and Fontana (1980). Albinus did not write directly to Bonnet, but his judgement was passed on to Bonnet by Allamand in his letter of 10 April 1761 (BPUG, MS Bonnet 26:141*v*).

For Haller's reaction, see his letters to Bonnet of 31 July 1761, 5 October 1761, and 28 December 1761 (Sonntag 1983:242, 246, 250).

There is no significant secondary study on the polymath Jean-Henri-Samuel Formey (1711-1797), a Protestant pastor of French origin, who was from 1744 Perpetual Secretary of the Royal Academy in Berlin. He was well known both as editor of the *Bibliothèque germanique* and the *Bibliothèque impartiale*, and for his controversies with Rousseau and Voltaire. The main source on his life is his autobiography, *Souvenirs d'un citoyen* (Berlin 1789); see also *B.U.* (14:401-403) and Roman d'Amat, *D.B.F.*, 14 (1979) 489-91. The most complete list of his published works is still Meusel (1802-1816, 3:409-18). For his contributions to the *Encyclopédie*, see Marcu (1953); and for a list of some of his correspondents, see Krauss (1963). Formey and Bonnet had a considerable correspondence (not mentioned by Krauss 1963); twenty-five letters from Formey to Bonnet are preserved in the BPUG. Although in his autobiography Formey published an interesting selection of letters addressed to him, none of Bonnet's were included as the latter was still alive. Formey did however include a tribute to Bonnet in the Conclusion: 'M. *Bonnet* m'a écrit quantité de lettres remplies de cette philosophie qui lui a fait tant d'honneur, & qui le place aujourd'hui à la tête des plus profonds penseurs du siècle' (Formey 1789, 2:394-95). On Bonnet and Formey, see Savioz (1948b:198-99) and Marx (1976:425-26). Formey expressed his appreciation of Bonnet's book in two letters dated 23 December 1760 and 13 May 1761 (BPUG, MS Bonnet 26:241-242, 243-244) and told Bonnet he was going to publish an extensive review (see letter 16, n.2).

7. 'A summary of some late observations upon the generation, composition, and decomposition of animal and vegetable substances', *Philosophical transactions*, 45 (1748) 615-66. This and Needham (1747a) were extensively discussed by Bonnet in chap.6 of volume ii of his *Considérations sur les corps organisés* (1762), which was heavily annotated in the republication of the same work in B.O. (3:391-427/6:286-339). For a historical evaluation, see Roger (1963:499-501), Roe (1983), and section 2.ii of the Introduction.

Expériences sur le Blé niellé,[8] je veux dire sur ces filamens animés que présente la poudre corrompue qu'il renferme? Je ne vous demande qu'un mot sur tout cela; je respecte trop vos occupations pour en éxiger d'avantage. Mais écrivés moi en caractères un peu plus gros que les derniers pour ménager mes yeux et les vôtres.

[a]Mr Brown Ministre Anglois vient de publier contre MM. d'Alembert[9] et Voltaire une petite brochure[10] qui fait du bruit, et qui plait beaucoup a tous ceux qui ont été choqués du ton de leurs Ecrits. Le dernier est certainement bien plus coupable que le premier, et je ne me rappelle pas d'avoir rien trouvé dans celui ci qui combatte le Christianisme. A cet égard, il a été surement plus avisé et plus prudent que tous ses Confrères.[a]

Recevés tous les voeux que je ne cesserai de faire pour vous et les assurances de la très parfaite estime et du sincere attachement avec lesquels je serai toute

8. Needham first described these observations in 'A letter [...] concerning certain chalky tubulous concretions, called malm: with some microscopical observations on the farina of the red lily, and of worms discovered in smutty corn', *Philosophical transactions*, 42 (1742-1743) 634-41, and later in Needham (1745:85-89), which was translated into French as Needham (1747a). This work contains probably Needham's most significant contribution, because it brought to the fore the phenomenon which was later to be called latent life or criptobiosis. For historical literature on this topic, see Keilin (1959) and Mazzolini (1972:70-72). See also letter 6, n.4, and letter 49, n.3.

9. For biographies of the French mathematician, philosopher, and encyclopedist Jean Le Rond d'Alembert (1717-1783), see Grimsley (1963) and Hankins (1970), which also provides a list of d'Alembert's mathematical papers.

10. Bonnet is alluding to the pamphlet *Lettres critiques d'un voyageur anglois sur l'Article Genève du Dictionaire encyclopédique; et sur la Lettre de Mr. D'Alembert à Mr. Rousseau. Publiées avec une Preface par R. Brown Ministre Anglois à Utrecht* (Utrecht [1761]), which contained two anonymous letters and a preface, signed '28 July 1767 Utrecht', written by the pastor of the Scottish Church at Utrecht, Robert Brown (1728-1777). A second edition appeared at Utrecht in 1763 containing six letters; and a third edition in two volumes, of seven and six letters respectively, bearing for the first time the name of the author Jacob Vernet (1698-1789), was published at Copenhagen in 1766. One of the accusations levelled at d'Alembert in the first edition of Vernet's pamphlet was that of religious 'indifference' and of d'Alembert's having been bewitched by Voltaire. The hostility of the Encyclopedists to religion is also illustrated by the following example, which must have been provided to Vernet by Bonnet: 'On m'a aussi fait observer à Geneve une chose presqu' imperceptible, qui aide à deceler leur tour d'Esprit. Dans l'Article *Feuilles* ils ont copié mot à mot plusieurs pages du livre de Mr. *Bonnet* Genevois, en le citant avec honneur, mais avec l'affectation de substituer au mot *Dieu* celui de *Nature*, au mot *Providence* celui de *Loix Generales* &c' ([Vernet] 1761:22). In a review of the pamphlet published in the *Journal encyclopédique* (15 March 1762, 2, pt.3:73-77), it is stated that the author was a 'Ministre Génevois très-connu'. Voltaire, however, who was well aware of this review, continued to attribute the book to Brown and, in a letter to d'Alembert, said that the 'sot libelle de ce misérable était si méprisé, si inconnu à Genève que je ne vous en avais point parlé. [...] Vous voyez que les presbitériens ne valent pas mieux que les Jesuites, et que ceux cy ne sont pas plus dignes du carcan que les Jansenistes' (Best.D10394). After Voltaire's letter was published, Brown replied in an anonymous letter addressed to the editors of the *Bibliothèque des sciences et des beaux arts* (January-March 1763, 19, pt.1:205-10) and stated that he had only been the editor of the *Lettres critiques*. He also provided autobiographical references that form the main part of our limited information about him: 'M. Brown est un homme de lettres & un homme de bien. [...] C'est un homme, qui, pendant un séjour de plus de douze ans à Utrecht, revêtu d'un ministère destiné à l'avancement de la piété & de la vertu, s'est acquis la considération des personnes les plus distinguées par leurs qualités personnelles, aussi bien que par le rang illustre qu'elles tiennent dans la société' (p.208; see also Ritter 1904:158 and Best.D11077). Voltaire seems to have been unaware of Vernet's authorship of the book until the third edition of 1766 appeared (see letter 23, n.27). On the Voltaire-Brown controversy see Desnoiresterres (1875:70-71), Ritter (1904), Spink (1934:151-52, 157-58), Grimsley (1963:75-76), de Beer and Rousseau (1967:49-50), and Lough (1968:385-86). For a critical evaluation of the contents of the *Lettres critiques*, see Matteucci (1953:731-33).

ma vie; *ª*Monsieur mon cher Ami et Confrère, Vôtre*ª* &c.

[ADDRESS] Rome, M.ʳ Néedham.

MANUSCRIPTS
BPUG, MS Bonnet 71:6r-7r; MS Bonnet 85:177r-178r.

EDITIONS
'N'avez-vous [...] qu'il renferme?' published in Bonnet (1762, 2:225) and B.O., 3:410/6:316.

TEXT NOTES
a. B: *omitted* *b*. B: que *c*. B: été bien *d*. B: connoissez comme

15

Needham to Bonnet – Rome, 13 February 1762

Je vous remercie de tout mon coeur, mon cher ami et confrere, de toutes les choses obligeantes, que vous me dites, dans votre derniere de Geneve. Je ne crains aucune mauvaise critique, ni meme celle, qu'on vient de lacher contre moi dans le Journal des sçavans du mois de decembre passé,[1] quand J'ai pour moi les suffrages de mes amis de Geneve, et tant d'autres en angleterre, qui m'ont repondus sur le meme ton. Je ne sçai pas trop si vous étes informé de la maladie, qui m'a tenue au lit à Rome dans le mois de Novembre pendant vingt cinq jours, et qui m'a reduit à la derniere extremité. C'est pour le retablissement de ma santé, qui Je suis parti pour Naples dans le courant du mois de decembre, ou j'ai passé six semaines. Les medecins m'ont defendus toute sorte d'application, et c'est à cause de cela, que Je n'ai pas pû finir la Lecture de votre livre, que je désire avec ardeur. Je viens en attendant de le prêter au Pere Jaquier,[2] mais

1. This anonymous review of Needham's work *De inscriptione quadam Aegyptiaca* appeared in the December issue of the *Journal des sçavans* (December 1761, pp.806-10) The author was Joseph de Guignes himself (for this identification see Curto 1962-1963:8 n.9). He denied that the characters inscribed on the so-called 'bust of Isis' (see figs. 12, 13) resembled either Chinese or Egyptian ones, regarded Needham's work as useless, and strongly recommended that he should not continue with such a method of investigation. Guignes commented: 'Nous exhortons M. Néedham à ne point aller si vîte pour les autres monumens Egyptiens sur lesquels il dit avoir déjà jetté les yeux dans le dessein de les expliquer; qu'il examine lui-même plus à fond le sujet qu'il veut traiter, puisque sa Dissertation n'est dans quelques endroits qu'une répétition de ce qui a été dit, & que dans d'autres elle est aussi peu fondée que la Traduction Chinoise. Il seroit à desirer que l'on pût expliquer les monumens Egyptiens par les caractères Chinois; mais une tentative de l'espèce que nous venons d'annoncer, loin d'être utile, ne serviroit qu'à faire croire qu'il est impossible d'y parvenir' (*Journal des sçavans*, December 1761, p.810). For Needham's reaction to this review, see section 6 of the Introduction.

2. François Jacquier (1711-1788), French friar and mathematician, was the editor, with Thomas Le Seur (1703-1770), of the three-volume annotated Latin edition of Newton's *Philosophiae naturalis principia mathematica* (Genevae 1739-1742). Jacquier met Needham while he was professor at La Sapienza in Rome. In 1763 he was appointed tutor to the heir of the Dukedom of Parma, and in 1773 he returned to Rome where he taught mathematics in the reformed Collegio Romano. For a short biography, see *B.U.* (20:513-14), and for additional material, see Mazzolini (1974:386 n.43). One of Needham's closest acquaintances in Rome, Jacquier was among the signatories of the *Certificat* dated 25 March 1762, which attested to the similarity between several of the characters on the 'bust of Isis' and those found in the Chinese Dictionary kept at the Vatican. The *Certificat* was published in Needham (1762:8-9) and [Cibot] (1773:v-vi); it is reproduced in section 6 of the Introduction.

vous pouvés être sur d'avance, que ni lui ni moi nous ne pourrons jamais être d'autre sentiment par rapport à son merite, que cel de tant des autres grands hommes dont vous avés reçus deja les suffrages. Je vous ecrirai neanmoins la dessus mes sentimens plus en detail, quand j'aurai le bonheur de le pouvoir étudier avec l'application, que cela merite. En attendant, aux questions, que vous me faites, J'ai l'honneur de vous repondre, que Je n'ai pas trouvé encore aucune raison de changer mes sentimens sur l'origine des animalcules en question; j'ai souvent depuis repeté les memes experiences toujours avec le meme succès, et encore depuis peu un professeur de Reggio[3] me vient d'ecrire,[4] qu'il a fait precisement les memes observations à lesquelles il a ajouté plusieures autres pour confirmer mes sentimens la dessus. Il va publier incessamment ses observations en forme de lettres, et vous les verrés bientot, comme je crois. Je vous prie de saluer M[r.] Trembley de ma part, et tous mes autres amis de Geneve, qui ont fait tant des politesses à mon ami M[r.] Wilcoks. Ma santé n'est pas encore totalement retablie, excusés la brieveté de cette lettre, et me croiés toujours, Monsieur, et tres cher confrere,

> votre tres humble, et tres obeissant
> ami, et serviteur
> Needham.

à Rome, Le 13. Fevrier 1762.
Reçue le 23 Fevrier[a]

[ADDRESS] A Monsieur / Monsieur Charles Bonnet / de la Societé Royale de Londres &c. / à Geneve.

MANUSCRIPT
  BPUG, MS Bonnet 26:133r-134v.

EDITIONS
  'Je n'ai pas trouvé [...] verrés bientot' (slightly altered) published in Bonnet (1762, 2:225-26), Bonnet (1770a, 1:425), and B.O. 3:411/6:317 and 7:321/15:470-71. 'En attendant [...] comme je crois' published in Castellani (1973:81).

TEXT NOTES
  a. Written in another hand.

3. Needham is alluding here to Lazzaro Spallanzani (1729-1799). For a biography of the great naturalist of Scandiano, from 1757 Professor of Physics in Reggio Emilia, from 1763 at the Collegio di San Carlo in Modena, and from 1769 Professor of Natural History at the University of Pavia, see Claude E. Dolman, *D.S.B.*, 12 (1975) 553–67, and especially Di Pietro (1979:15-107). For a bibliography of Spallanzani's writings and of secondary literature on him up to 1952, see Prandi (1952); for a list of studies on Spallanzani after 1952, see Di Pietro (1979:304-11). A catalogue of his manuscripts preserved in the BCRE is given in Manzini (1981), and a list of his correspondents in Di Pietro (1977). Spallanzani's letters to Bonnet are published in *Epistolario*, and Bonnet's letters to Spallanzani in Castellani (1971). Spallanzani's extant letters to Needham are published in *Epistolario* (1:132-33, 136-37, 152, and 2:92); and Needham's letters to Spallanzani have been edited by Castellani (1973), who described the progressive deterioration of the relationship between the two scientists. For the controversy between Spallanzani and Needham over generation, see the bibliographical note appended to Needham's biographical notice and section 2.iv of the Introduction.
  4. This letter cannot be traced. Needham's reply is dated 29 August 1761 (see Castellani 1973:79-80).

16

Bonnet to Needham – Geneva, 2 March 1762

A Geneve le 2.e Mars 1762.

Je n'ai apris que fort tard, Monsieur mon cher Ami et Confrère, la maladie dangereuse dont vous avés été attaqué à Rome, et dont je vois par vôtre Lettre du 13.e de fevrier que vous n'êtes pas encore parfaitement rétabli. Recevés tous les voeux que je fais pour vôtre guerison, et veuillés par amour pour vos amis, user sobrement du plaisir que vous goutés à augmenter vos connoissances et les nôtres. Sur tout n'allés pas fatiguer trop tôt vôtre tête en méditant sur mon Analyse de l'Ame. Vôtre sufrage me sera toujours précieux^a, et quand vous ne me ^{b}le donneriés^b que dans quelques mois, je ne vous en sçaurois pas moins de gré. Vous m'avés fait plaisir en prêtant cet Ouvrage au P. Jacquier dont le mérite et le sçavoir me sont si connus. Je n'ose espérer qu'il se soit donné la peine de me suivre d'un bout à l'autre, comme il auroit fait une Analyse Géometrique. Mais, s'il achève cette lecture, et s'il vous en communique son jugement, vous m'obligerés beaucoup de me le faire parvenir. M.^{r} ^{c}le Baron^c de Haller à sçu malgré ses grandes occupations, trouver des momens pour les consacrer^d à ce Livre, il en a fait un extrait qu'il m'a envoyé,[1] et qui me prouve le cas ^{c}tout particulier^c qu'il veut bien faire de mon travail. Un autre Homme Célèbre, M.^{r} le Professeur Formey, s'en est ^{e}amouraché au point de vouloir en donner un abregé[2] dans le gout de celui de Locke.^{e} D'un autre côte quelques Journalistes m'ont estropiés, plus encore que je ne m'y étois attendu, et ils m'ont fait des objections qui démontrent rigoureusement^e qu'ils ne m'ont point du tout saisi.[3] Quelques unes même prouvent une ignorance de la matière qui m'a surpris. Qu'y faire? J'ai un meilleur emploi à faire de mon temps que de le perdre à repéter de nouveau ce que j'ai tant développé en divers endroits de mon Livre, je ne crois pas que je me laisse jamais entrainer à repondre à aucune critique. Les écrits polémiques ne plaisent qu'a l'amour propre; mais si l'on me prouve que j'ai erré, je le reconnoitrai publiquement et sans peine.

1. Bonnet was very anxious to know Haller's opinion of his *Essai analytique*. As soon as Haller told him that he had written a review in German, Bonnet asked him to send it to him before publication, saying that he would have it translated; see Sonntag (1983:258-60). Haller's anonymous review appeared in 1763 in the *Göttingische Anzeigen von gelehrten Sachen* (8 January 1763, pp.25-32). It was an excellent summary of Bonnet's book, described as 'ein sehr wichtiges Werk', but contained no other evaluative comments.

2. On 28 February 1762 Bonnet wrote to Haller, 'Mr Formey en a fait huit Extraits qu'il avoit envoyés l'année derniére au *Journal Encyclopédique*, et que l'Auteur de ce Journal n'a pas publié, nous ne sçavons pourquoi' (Sonntag 1983:261). Formey's work appeared later as a book with the title *Entretiens psychologiques, tirés de l'Essai analytique sur les facultés de l'ame de Mr. Bonnet* (Berlin 1769).

3. Bonnet is alluding to the review of the *Essai analytique* that appeared in the October-November 1761 issue of the *Excerptum totius italicae nec non helveticae literaturae* (pp.61-81). The review was the work of Fortunato Bartolomeo de Felice (1723-1789), the well-known Italian publisher who was later active in Yverdon. De Felice criticised Bonnet for being far too hypothetical in his investigations, and Bonnet never forgave him for this criticism. He complained bitterly about it to Haller (Sonntag 1983:258-59, 261, 268, 279). For Bonnet's reaction to de Felice's review, see Maccabez (1903:183-85) and Marx (1976:208-209).

Si vous allés à Bologne, mon cher Confrère, souvenés vous de mon venerable Ami M.ʳ Zanotti. Je le croyois mort, lors que j'en reçu, il y a environ ⁵4 à 5ʲ mois, une Lettre⁴ la plus obligeante, qui me sembla venir des Champs élisées. Il me témoignoit sa satisfaction et celle de l'Institut sur mon Essai. Vous ne pouvés lui dire assés de choses pour moi.

J'ai été cet hyver fort travaillé de maux de yeux qui m'ont retenu en Chambre. Vous voyés combien ces Insectes qui nous ont été si chers m'ont maltraité. L'habitude que j'ai contractée de dicter est venue au secours de mon Esprit actif, et je puis continuer à composer sur differentes matières. Je viens d'en traiter une qui vous interessera plus que l'Analyse de l'ame: c'est l'importante matière des *Corps organisés.* Je vous en entretiendrai plus au long dans une autre Lettre.

ᶜVous verrés à Naples M.ʳ de la Torre,⁵ bon Observateur, et dont j'ai fort gouté les recherches sur les globules du sang,⁶ qu'il avoit envoyé ici à quelques uns de nos Professeurs. Demandés lui de ma part, s'il ne les a point reprises. Il étoit en beau chemin, et j'attend beaucoup de sa sagacité. Vous me dirés bien aussi un mot d'Herculanum.ᶜ

M.ʳ de Haller continue sa grande *Physiologie.* Le 4.ᵐᵉ Tome va paroitre.⁷ Il m'a communiqué de belles observations sur les yeux des Poissons.⁸ Vous savés qu'il est un excellent observateur.

M.ʳ Schaeffer⁹ de Ratisbonne, grand Naturaliste, m'a envoyé sa Dissertation

---

4. In his letter to Bonnet, dated 2 August 1761, Francesco Maria Zanotti wrote, 'Il libro dottissimo scritto con rara eleganza e profondità da V.S. Il.ma sopra la facoltà del nostro essere, non potrà mai parere lontano da ciò, che l'Accademia nostra delle Scienze professa, essendo composta e da un'Accademico de' più distinti, che essa abbia, e con un metodo così ingegnoso' (BPUG, MS Bonnet 27:25r).

5. See letter 9, n.5.

6. See letter 9, n.4.

7. Volume iv of Haller's 8-volume *Elementa physiologiae corporis humani* (1757-1766) appeared in 1762. For the editorial history of the *Elementa*, see Buess (1958:24-28, 32-34); and for an analysis of the scientific and philosophical problems in Haller's masterpiece, see Toellner (1971:128-88).

8. Haller mentioned his observations on the eyes of fish to Bonnet several times; see Sonntag (1983:250, 253, 256). These observations were published by Haller with the title 'Mémoire sur les yeux de quelques poissons', in *Histoire de l'Académie royale des sciences. Année MDCCLXII. Avec les Mémoires,* 1764:76-95. A Latin version also appeared in Haller's *Opera minora* (see Haller 1762-1768, 3:250-62).

9. Jacob Christian Schaeffer (1718-1790) was born in Querfurt in Thuringia. He studied theology at Halle University and in 1741 obtained a position as preacher at Regensburg where he remained, later becoming Superintendent of the Evangelical community. In 1763 he received a doctorate in theology from the University of Tübingen. A versatile and prolific writer, Schaeffer made contributions to several different fields: he tried out a new method for making paper, built and improved some scientific instruments, carried out investigations in botany and zoology, and collected objects in natural history. In his own time he was best known for his illustrations of plants and animals. There is no significant contemporary study on this important and neglected scholar; see *B.U.* (38:233-35) and *A.D.B.* (30:530-31). The most complete bibliography of Schaeffer's works is still that contained in Meusel (1802-1816, 12:71-79); for a bibliography of his illustrated zoological works, see Nissen (1969-1978, 1:362-64). Schaeffer corresponded with Bonnet and sent him most of his zoological publications. (Eleven of his letters to Bonnet are preserved in the BPUG). In a letter to Haller, Bonnet characterised Schaeffer as a 'bon Observateur [...] mais, son point de vuë n'est pas philosophique' (Sonntag 1983:491).

sur les Poissons,[10] et ses premiers essais sur les Champignons.[11] Les Planches en sont très bien enluminées, et les Figures me paroissent éxactes. Je souhaitois depuis longtemps qu'on aprofondit l'Histoire des Champignons. Il travaille utilement à les renger en Classe et en Genre. Michéli[12] n'avoit pas assés creusé cela; ses Observations m'ont cependant beaucoup plu. Les Champignons sont dans le Règne Végétal, ce que nos Insectes sont dans le Règne Animal.

'Je vous annonce une importante nouvelle, qui changera bien la face du Nord. Le Roi de Prusse s'est arrengé avec le nouveau Czar, et les Prisonniers ont déja été mis en liberté. On ignore encore les conditions. Mais le traité est certain. Sans doute que la Reine d'Hongrie traitera à son tour, et voila la paix qui s'aproche enfin.'

Recevés, Monsieur mon cher Ami et Confrère, le renouvellement des assurances de l'attachement cordial et plein d'estime &c.

'Notre digne Ami M.ʳ Trembley vous présente ses complimens.'

[ADDRESS] Rome; M.ʳ Néédham.

MANUSCRIPTS
BPUG, MS Bonnet 71:18r-18v; MS Bonnet 85:178r-179r.

TEXT NOTES
a. B: bien agréable *b*. B: donneriez votre jugement *c*. B: *omitted* *d*. B: donner *e*. B: occupé au point d'en composer un Abrégé qu'il destine au Public *f*. B: quatre à cinq

17

Needham to Bonnet – Turin, 30 June 1764

Mon cher Monsieur, ami, et confrere.

J'ai reflechis depuis mon depart[1] de Geneve sur ce, que nous avons resolus ensemble par raport à la publication des lettres, et autres écrits relatifs à ma decouverte, et je crois, que, tout bien pesé, nous serons d'accord, qu'il conviendra

10. Jacob Christian Schaeffer, *Piscium Bavarico-Ratisbonensium pentas. Cum tabulis IV. aeri incisis icones coloribus suis distinctas exhibentibus* (Ratisbonae 1761).

11. Jacob Christian Schaeffer, *Fungorum qui in Bavaria et Palatinatu circa Ratisbonam nascuntur icones nativis coloribus expraessae* (Ratisbonae 1762-1763).

12. On the famous Florentine botanist and collector Pietro Antonio Micheli (1679-1737), see Cocchi (1737), Fabroni (1778-1805, 4:105-69), *B.U.* (28;250-51), and especially Targioni-Tozzetti (1858), which lists all of Micheli's published works, his manuscripts, and the main items of his private collection. Bonnet is alluding to pp.133-200 of Micheli's masterpiece *Nova plantarum genera iuxta Tournefortii methodum disposita* (Florentiae 1729). This work was completed for publication in 1720; but, given the cost of the 108 plates, Micheli applied in vain for a subsidy to the Grand-Duke of Tuscany Cosimo III (1639-1723). He was then forced to turn to subscriptions from both Italian and foreign friends and admirers. For the editorial history of this work, see Targioni-Tozzetti (1858:144-45, 248-52).

1. Needham visited Bonnet while he was in Geneva in May 1764. On 28 May 1764 Bonnet wrote to Haller, 'Mʳ Néédham est ici en passant. Il me surprit beaucoup hier au soir en entrant dans ma Chambre: je le croyois au fond de l'Angleterre. Il revenoit de Paris. Il part Mardi pour Turin, où il séjournera' (Sonntag 1983:380).

de differer la dite publication pour quelques mois en attendant la reponse de Canton.[2] Aussitot qu'elle arrive, je vous mettrai exactement au fait de tout, et nous agirons en consequence. Avec tels adversaires, dont vous connaisses si bien le caractere, prêts à faire sacrifice de mille faits incontestables à leurs hypotheses cheries, il me faut une lance de la trempe de celle d'Ithuriel en Milton,[3] qui les obligera par la simple touche de se montrer, tels qu'ils sont, ou faute de cette arme celeste la massue materielle d'Hercule; on ne les abattra jamais, que par des coups fermes, et bien medités. La Philosophie Neutonienne, dont la metaphysique est in-intelligible, c'est à dire, hors de portée de la raison ne subsiste, que par des faits. O! que les soi-disans philosophes du dixhuitieme siecle sçavent bien raisonner, quand il s'agit des verités sêches, et presque steriles, qui servent à exalter l'esprit, dont ils sont bienaises de faire parade, pourvu qu'elles ne choquent pas leurs passions. Mais le moment, qu'on entreprend de demontrer, que la Religion, et tout ce, qui soutient la religion est également bati sur des faits, dont personne de sang froid ne peut contester la verité, ces messieurs habiles à saisir le baton par l'autre bout ne hesitent pas un instant de jouer le rolle tant meprisé des Cartesiens. Ils detournent la vue, parce que la lumiere creée toujours limitée se perd à la fin dans les ombres, ou ils se plongent dans les tenebres exterieures, qui l'environnent, afin de contester sa realité. Nulle science en elle meme est bornée; c'est un courant, qui va se perdre dans le sein de la divinité; mais toute science en nous mene à des mysteres, ou autrement dit, à une metaphysique, que nous ne faisons qu'entrevoir, se repandant bien au de la de notre entendement, precisement parce qu'illimitée en elle meme, une partie seulement se transvase en nous, dont la capacité est tres bornée. Mysteres pour mysteres que m'importe, s'ils tiennent à la religion, ou à la nature, pourvu qu'ils soient également batis sur des faits certains. La Trinité, l'incarnation, la redemption, la chute de l'homme, le peché originel, la liberté humaine, le mal moral sont-ils ces mysteres plus in-intelligibles, que la doctrine des infinis, à laquelle la Geometrie nous mene par des routes assurées, l'existence, et l'essence de la matiere, l'identité personelle, la nature de la divinité, la production de l'univers, et mille autres verités tres physiques, et tres in-intelligibles. En nous debarassant, comme ils pretendent, des mysteres de la religion, s'ils pouvaient en meme tems nous debarasser de tout autre mystere, ils auraient au moins quelque lueur de raison: mais je ne connais pas d'autres moyens, puisqu'il ne suffit pas avec Rousseau de se reduire aux courtes connaissances des sauvages, que de pouvoir produire par quelque miracle chymique la metamorphose si ardemment desirée de l'homme en bête, et de se borner ensuite au pur sensitif. Plaisirs momentanés, si vous voulés, pleins d'ivresse à l'exclusion de toute intelligence, mais les seuls biens compatibles avec la vraie santé de l'ame à leur façon de penser, puisque science selon l'auteur d'Emile n'est qu'une maladie de plus, que nous nous donnons. Mais je me perd à vous dire une verité tres palpable en elle meme, que l'intelligible étant par tout, et par sa nature necessairement lié à l'in-intelligible, ces messieurs, qui raisonnent si bien, comme

---

2. This refers to the enquiries being made by Needham and Wilcocks of Jesuit missionaries living in China about the inscriptions on the so called 'bust of Isis'.

3. Milton, *Paradise lost*, IV, 810-14.

astronomes, ne sont que des sophistes volontaires en fait de Religion. Par tout aillieurs les faits établissent les mysteres metaphysiques sans contradiction, et quand il s'agit de Religion, les mysteres établis aneantissent selon eux les faits les plus incontestables. Ce beau portrait, que le meme auteur d'Emile fait de J. Christ après l'evangile,[4] forcé malgre lui par l'éclat de la verité, ne parait un instant, que pour nous eblouir; les mysteres de la religion, que nul mortel ne peut separer de la morale evangelique, frappent ensuite son esprit altier, il recule aussitot, et tout est effacé. Philosophe à demi! Vos écrits pleins de contradictions seront-ils donc plus intelligibles, que les mysteres, que vous rejettés, et vous meme plus croyable, que le Docteur, dont vous venés de declarer la divinité? L'obscurité d'une chose n'empeche pas sa realité, la lumiere existe en depit des aveugles; mais le *Oui*, et le *Non* ne peuvent jamais subsister ensemble. Pour revenir d'ou je suis parti; un philosophe Neutonien, qui aurait pour auditeurs mille paysans goguenards ne fera-t-il pas une plus sotte figure, que vous ou moi entourés de tous nos sceptiques modernes armés à la legere de bons mots, et d'antitheses? Quel remede prescrira-t-il notre philosophe dans un pareil cas? Ou le mepris, ou la compassion. Eh bien! Tenons nous, si nous nous trouvons assis à coté de nos Voltaires, de nos Helvetius,[5] et de nos Rousseaux à cel de deux mouvemens, qui tient plus à l'humanité, je veu dire, la compassion. il est tems de finir ma lettre; en me souvenant de nos amis Messieurs Trembley, et Jallabert[6] je vous prie de les saluer de ma part, et de me croire avec la plus grande estime, et sincerité

Monsieur tres cher ami, et confrere,

votre tres humble, et tres obeissant serviteur

Needham.

à Turin, Le 30. Juin 1764.

4. As already noted by Leigh, 3370, this is an allusion to the famous passage in Rousseau's 'Profession de foi': 'Je vous avoüe aussi que la majesté des Ecritures m'étonne, la sainteté de l'Evangile parle à mon cœur. Voyez les livres des Philosophes avec toute leur pompe, qu'ils sont petits près de celui-là! Se peut-il qu'un livre à la fois si sublime et si simple soit l'ouvrage des hommes? Se peut-il que celui dont il fait l'histoire ne soit qu'un homme lui-même? Est-ce là le ton d'un enthousiaste ou d'un ambitieux sectaire? Quelle douceur, quelle pureté dans ses mœurs! quelle grace touchante dans ses instructions! quelle élevation dans ses maximes! quelle profonde sagesse dans ses discours! quelle présence d'esprit, quelle finesse et quelle justesse dans ses réponses! quel empire sur ses passions! Où est l'homme, où est le sage qui sait agir, souffrir et mourir sans foiblesse et sans ostentation? Quand Platon peint son juste imaginaire couvert de tout l'opprobre du crime et digne de tous les prix de la vertu, il peint trait pour trait Jesus-Christ; la ressemblance est si frapante que tous les Péres l'ont sentie et qu'il n'est pas possible. de s'y tromper' (R.O., 4:625-26).

5. For a biography of Claude-Adrien Helvétius (1715-1771), see Keim (1907); and for a guide to primary and secondary literature, see Cioranescu (1969, 2:934-37). A provisional list of Helvétius's correspondence is provided by D. Smith (1973); and a partial list of books owned by Helvétius, of which there is no catalogue, may be found in D. Smith (1971). For recent literature on Helvétius, see D. Smith (1965) and Gianformaggio (1979).

6. Jean Jallabert (1712-1768) was born in Geneva of a patrician family. He studied the exact sciences at Geneva's Académie under Gabriel Cramer (1704-1752) and Jean-Louis Calandrini (1703-1758), who were instrumental in establishing a chair in Experimental Physics, which Jallabert held from 1737. In 1750 he was appointed Professor of Mathematics and in 1752 Professor of Philosophy. Jallabert travelled extensively in France, England, and Holland. In 1746 he was elected a member of the Council of Two Hundred, and in 1757 he entered the Small Council. From 1765 to 1768 he was a Syndic. His major scientific research was in elecricity, and his book *Experiences sur l'électricité* (Genève 1748) aroused considerable interest especially because of its medical implications. He was a correspondent of Rousseau. The main source for Jallabert's life is the éloge published by

MANUSCRIPT
   BPUG, MS Bonnet 28:11r-12v.

EDITIONS
   'En nous debarassant [...] la divinité' and 'Tenons nous [...] la compassion' published in Leigh,
3370.

18

Bonnet to Needham – Genthod, July 1764

[Juillet 1764][a]

J'ai à vous remercier, Monsieur mon estimable et celèbre Confrère, de vôtre
bonne Lettre du 30.e de Juin. Nous attendrons donc les réponses de la Chine,[1]
et vôtre ouvrage déjà très bon, en deviendra meilleur. Il servira la Societé comme
j'aime qu'elle le soit, et il sera *cette massuë d'Hercules* dont vous parlés, *avec laquelle
vous terrassés les Monstres qui en veulent au bonheur du Genre-humain.* Il est certain que
ces Ennemis-nés de la Société sont pour le moins très injustes. Ils ne peuvent
souffrir qu'on aplique à la Réligion les Règles de critique dont ils sçavent si bien
faire usage dans toutes les matières Historiques, comme si l'Evangile n'étoit pas
dans l'ordre des Faits. Pourquoi admettent-ils l'éxistence d'un Ninus, d'un
Aléxandre, d'un César, qu'ils n'ont jamais vus, et dont ils ne peuvent s'assurer
par la Geométrie? Ils les croyent sur le témoignage d'autrui, et ils évaluent ce
témoignage à l'aide d'une Logique plus ou moins éxacte. Qu'ils apliquent donc
cette même Logique au témoignage des Apôtres, qu'ils éxaminent s'ils ont pû
être trompés ou s'ils ont voulû tromper, et après cet éxamen refléchi, ils seront
admis à nous apporter leurs Objections. Mais où sont les Incrédules qui prennent
cette peine? Vous l'avés judicieusement remarqué; ils tirent leur coup de Pistolet,
et s'enfuyent. Jamais ou presque jamais ils n'osent se batre en bataille rangée.
Vôtre malicieux Correspondant a tiré plus de dix mille coups de Pistolet en sa
vie, qui ont blessé à mort plus d'un ignorant, et qui n'ont pu entamer la cuirasse
des vrais sçavans. Si ces prétendus Philosophes admettent l'éxistence d'un
Aléxandre ou d'un César, c'est qu'Aléxandre et César ne choquent pas le moins
du monde leurs passions favorites. Si l'on pouvoit être Chrétien, présisément
comme l'on est Cartésien ou Neuvtonnien, je veux dire, s'il ne falloit pas plus
de gène et de sacrifices, ces Philosophes [b]du bel air[b] seroient facilement Chrétiens.
Peut-être qu'ils le seroient encore si le gros des gens qui pensent étoit athée:
c'est qu'il y a bien de la vanité dans leur fait. Vos remarques sur les Mystères
reviennent à celles qui se sont offertes plus d'une fois à mon Esprit. Autre preuve
d'injustice et de partialité. Il seroit facile de prouver à ces petits-maîtres en

Ratte (1774); for shorter biographies, see *B.U.* (20:535-36), Wolf (1858-1862, 4:149-60), and Leigh's
commentary to letter 257. For Jallabert's contributions to medical electricity, see Cramer (1962),
Rudolph (1964:24), and Heilbron (1979:353-54). For thirty years Bonnet and Jallabert were close
friends and often discussed scientific matters; however in the last months of Jallabert's life they
diverged on political questions (see Savioz 1948b:117 and Sonntag 1983:745).

   1. See letter 17, n.2.

Philosophie qu'il y a plus de Mystères dans la Nature que dans la Grace. Et encore les Théologiens ont ils grossi le nombre des Mystères de la Grace. Je consentirois volontiers que les Incrédules missent dans le Creuzet la Théologie scholastique et la Réligion: l'une en sortiroit très alterée où plutôt elle s'evapore- roit toute, tandis que l'autre y demeureroit fixe et inalterable.

[ADDRESS] Turin. M.ʳ Néedham de la Societé Royale de Londres.

MANUSCRIPTS
    BPUG, MS Bonnet 71:155*v*-156*r*; MS Bonnet 85:179*r*-179*v*.

TEXT NOTES
    a. Although this letter is not dated in Copy A, it falls between letters of 9 July and 18 July in Bonnet's secretary's book of letter drafts. *b.* B: de la nouvelle Ecole

19

Needham to Bonnet – Geneva, 3 August 1765

Mon cher ami, et confrere,
    Je me trouve à Geneve pour quelques jours, et j'ai le desagrement par votre absence d'etre privé du plaisir de vous revoir. Je veux neanmoins me consoler en renouvellant une correspondance, qui m'est chere, et je vous envoye une livre,[1] qui vient de paraitre, qui vous interessera indubitablement. L'auteur est mon ami, et je l'estime, quoique sa façon de philosopher, et de raisonner sur les memes phenomenes differe beaucoup de celle, que j'ai donné au public dans mes observations microscopiques. Je tiens pour fanatique en Philosophie tout homme, qui s'obstine dans ses notions sur des sujets, ou il est si facile de se tromper, et je prevois quasi deja, que je pourrais fort bien revenir sur mes pas en me rapprochant de lui, aussi bien que de vous jusqu'à un certain point, sur l'article de la generation. Ses observations m'ont données des lumieres nouvelles, et je commence à croire, que j'ai trop étendu mes idées, en donnant des puissances à la matiere, qui ne sont pas necessaires pour expliquer les Phenomenes du monde microscopique. J'ai pourtant eu soin de ne jamais donner dans l'absurdité de la generation equivoque; en augmentant les puissances de la matiere, je les presente toujours, et vous le sçavés, meme par des consequences necessaires tirées des observations, comme subordonnées au dieu, et astreintes à des loix invariables. C'est à tort que le materialiste voudrait se prevaloir de mon systeme. Voici ou mes vües actuellement plus éclairées par mon ami Spalanzani me portent à present. Je crois l'epigenese, et je ne puis jamais me reconcilier avec

    1. Lazzaro Spallanzani, *Dissertazioni due* (Modena 1765). This publication contains two works, one in Italian entitled *Saggio di osservazioni microscopiche concernenti il sistema della generazione de' Signori di Needham, e Buffon*, and the other in Latin entitled *De lapidibus ab aqua resilientibus dissertatio*. For the history of the complex origin of the *Saggio* and of its different drafts and final form, see Pancaldi (1972) and Castellani's edition of Spallanzani (1978a:59-352). For the impact of Spallanzani's *Saggio* on Needham, see section 2.iv of the Introduction.

le developpement des êtres, qui sont censés d'exister depuis la creation, mais je crois, que tout procede d'un individu parent, ou dès individus generateurs specifiques, n'importe quant' à la mode de generation soit par male, et femelle, soit par melange de deux sexes dans le meme individu, par accouplement, ou sans accouplement, soit par semence, oeufs, ou division de parties; tout cela me parait indifferent, et ne doit se determiner que selon les classes, et les especes par observation. De la je suis très porté à croire, à bien considerer le resultat des observations de Spalanzani en combinaison avec les miennes, que la generation des êtres microscopiques en general se fait non par des œufs proprement dits, comme il affirme, mais par division à la façon des Polypes, en parties attenuées au dela de toute conception. Dans cette vue chaque partie infiniment petite sera prolifique de son espece, transportable par tout, se trouvant par tout, et s'insinuant par tout tellement, qu'il sera toujours tres difficile à les exclure totalement des infusions tellement preparées qu'on voudra, et avec toutes les precautions presque imaginables. Lisés Spalanzani, et dites moi ensuite ce que vous pensés sur mes sentimens presents. J'ai dessein neanmoins de reconsiderer toute cette matiere plus murement à mon arrivée à Paris cet hyver, de donner les observations de Spalanzani en François,[2] et d'ajouter une dissertation à ma façon en presentant mes observations, et les siennes dans un point de vüe totalement differente de mes vües anciennes. J'ai l'honneur d'etre, mon cher ami, et confrere

votre très humble, et très obeissant serviteur
Needham.

à Geneve, Le 3. d'aoust 1765.

Je vous prie de me renvoyer ces observations, quand vous les aurais lues, dans la huitaine, s'il est possible, car je n'ai que ce seul exemplaire.

[ADDRESS] A Monsieur / Monsieur Charles Bonnet / de La Societé Royale de Londres, &c. / à Rolle.

MANUSCRIPT
    BPUG, MS Bonnet 28:13*r*-14*v*.

EDITIONS
    '[J]e vous envoye […] monde microscopique' and 'Voici ou […] vües anciennes' published in Castellani (1973:84-85).

2. The French translation of the *Saggio di osservazioni microscopiche* (see preceding note) appeared in 1769 as pp.1-138 of *Nouvelles recherches sur les découvertes microscopiques, et la génération des corps organisés. Ouvrage traduit de l'Italien de M. l'Abbé Spalanzani par M. l'Abbé Regley. […] Avec des notes, des recherches physiques et métaphysiques sur la nature et la religion, et une nouvelle théorie de la terre. Par M. De Needham* (Londres, Paris 1769).

20

Bonnet to Needham – Perroy, 5 August 1765

Perroy près de Rolle le 5.ᵉ d'Aoust 1765.
Je suis faché, mon cher et célèbre Ami et Confrère, de ne pouvoir jouir de vôtre Séjour à Genève. Je suis ici encore pour quelque tems. Les Eaux Minerales me font quelque bien. Ma Santé, dérangée par le travail avoit besoin de cette sorte de remède. Celle de ma Femme en avoit un plus grand besoin encore.

J'étois très persuadé que vous modifieriés vos Idées dès que de nouvelles lumières vous apparoitroient. Vous êtes trop bon Philosophe pour n'être pas Ami sincère du Vrai. Vous verrés que nous-nous rapprocherons de plus en plus, et j'en serai très flatté.

Je vous renvoye tres promptement vôtre Livre: c'est Lettre close pour moi. Je n'entend pas L'Italien. J'attendrai donc la Traduction Françoise que vous vous proposés d'en donner. Je ne suis pas moins curieux de vos nouvelles méditations sur un sujet si intéressant; car pour de nouvelles Observations je sçai que vos yeux vous les interdisent. La Conjecture que vous preferés à présent sur la Generation des Animalcules, je l'avois indiquée dans mon Livre sur les *Corps Organisés*. J'y comparois expressément cette Generation à celle des differens Polypes *à Bouquet* qui se fait *par Division*.[1] Cela vous auroit-il échappé en me lisant? Je le soupconnerois puis que vous ne m'en dites rien. Vous ne me dites rien non plus de ce Livre dont je souhaitois fort de scavoir vôtre Jugement.

J'ai regret que vôtre Ami Spalanzani ne laye pas vû: il parut en 1762, et il est étrange qu'il ne soit pas encore parvenu à Modène.[2] Ne lui en avés-vous point parlé? Il a obtenu des sufrages bien respectables. Le vôtre mon digne Ami, seroit d'un grand poids.

Depuis j'ai publié ma *Contemplation de la Nature*.[3] Je vous en dois un Exemplaire, comme une legère marque de mon estime et de mon amitié. Envoyés chés le S.ʳ Chirol, Libraire au Grand-Mézel et demandés-le lui de ma part en lui montrant cette Lettre. J'ai remanié dans cet Ouvrage la grande Matière de la *Generation* et de la *Reproduction*. Je souhaite qu'il vous plaise.

Entretenés-vous de tout ceci avec nôtre cher Ami et Confrère M.ʳ Trembley. Il est tout près de vous à Saconex. Il me rendra vos entretiens.

1. Bonnet (1762, 1:114-16) and B.O., 3:83-84/5:219-21. See also Bonnet's discussion of his priority on this point and of Saussure's confirmation of division in animalcules in Bonnet (1770a, 1:426-31) and B.O., 7:323-28/15:473-80.
2. According to Spallanzani (*Epistolario*, 1:63), the *Considérations sur les corps organisés* was unknown to him when he was writing the *Saggio di osservazioni microscopiche* (see letter 19, n.1). An error in the transcription of the dates of two letters (*Epistolario*, 1:37-38, where 1765 is given as 1763) has led to the hypothesis that Spallanzani was familiar with the work in 1763-1764 (see Pancaldi 1972:33 n.60); but for evidence that this is not the case, see Mazzolini (1974:378). It is interesting to note that on two occasions John Turton wrote to Bonnet that his work was practically unknown in Italy. (See his letters to Bonnet from Turin in November 1763 and from Venice in July 1764 in BPUG, MS Bonnet 27:148r and 154v.)
3. Charles Bonnet, *Contemplation de la nature* (Amsterdam 1764); republished in B.O., 4, pt.1:1-396 and pt.2:1-502/7:1-364, 8:1-464, and 9:1-539.

Je vous embrasse cordialement, mon cher Ami; mon attachement pour vous est inviolable.

P.S. Ma Lettre écrite, j'ai jetté un coup d'Oeil sur les Théses Latines[4] de vôtre Ami. J'y ai vû avec le plus grand plaisir, qu'il confirme sans le sçavoir, mes petites Opinions sur l'origine des Animalcules. J'en ait d'autant plus de regrêt qu'il n'ait pas connu mes *Corps Organisés*. J'ai soutenu dans cet Ouvrage que vos *Zoophytes* étoient de vrais *Animaux*[5] et j'ai fortifié mes divers Argumens des Observations[6] de M.ʳ de Réaumur.[7] Je souhaiterois fort que vous en écrivissiés à vôtre Ami. Il n'y seroit pas indifferent.

Je vous assure qu'il en coutoit beaucoup à mon amitié de vous relever. Vôtre Amour pour le Vrai me l'a pardonné, comme le mien vous pardonneroit en cas

4. We have been unable to identify what Bonnet meant by these 'Théses Latines'. No copy of Spallanzani's *Saggio* that we have examined includes any printed or handwritten Latin summary. It may be that either the copy of the *Saggio* that Needham first loaned to Bonnet or the one that Spallanzani sent to him contained, possibly in handwritten form, these additional 'Théses Latines'. See also Bonnet's letter to Spallanzani of 27 December 1765 (Castellani 1971:8 and n.8).

5. Bonnet (1762, 2:216-24) and B.O., 3:400-407/6:301-12.

6. 'Je suis donc fort dispensé d'examiner d'où provient cette dégradation continuelle des filamens & des Animalcules, ou pour suivre l'idée de notre Auteur, cette conversion graduelle des Zoophytes en Animalcules, & des Animalcules en Zoophytes toujours décroissans. Ce ne sont là que de pures apparences, & M. NEEDHAM l'auroit sans doute reconnu, si ses yeux, qui nous ont découvert tant de choses, lui avoient permis de reprendre des observations qui auroient exigé de leur part de nouveaux efforts. M. de REAUMUR n'avoit point été trompé par ces apparences. On peut se rappeler ce qu'il en écrivoit à M. TREMBLEY, & qu'il m'avoit confirmé à moi-même dans ses Lettres. *Il est très-faux*, disoit ce grand Observateur, qui ne voyoit dans la Nature que ce qui y étoit; *il est très-faux que les générations de ces Animalcules soient d'Animaux de plus en plus petits, comme l'ont avancé MM.* NEEDHAM *& de* BUFFON; *tout va ici comme à l'ordinaire, les petits deviennent grands à leur tour*' (Bonnet 1762, 2:221-22; and B.O., 3:406/6:309-10; see also 1762, 1:117-18n, 173-75, and B.O., 3:85-86 n.3, 139-40, 426 n.1/5:224-25 n.1, 310-12, and 6:337 n.1). Réaumur had reported to Bonnet in 1751 that he and Lignac had jointly repeated the microscopical observations of Buffon and Needham, which Réaumur described as 'observations mal faites, souvent fausses' (letter of 10 December 1751, BPUG, MS Bonnet 42:131r-132v; see also M. Trembley 1943:362-63 n.1 and Réaumur's letter to A. Trembley of 31 December 1751 in M. Trembley 1943:361-62). Lignac's critique of Needham (see letter 6, n.2) was inspired in part by these observations and by Réaumur's opposition to the views of Needham and Buffon (see also section 2.iii of the Introduction).

7. For a biography of René-Antoine Ferchault de Réaumur (1683-1757), see Torlais (1961) and J. B. Gough, *D.S.B.*, 11 (1975) 327-35, to whose bibliographies may be added Bodenheimer (1928-1929, 1:415-48), Courtheoux (1957), and, for more recent years, Gens (1978). For a list of Réaumur's original works, see Torlais (1958a). It was reading the first volume of Reaumur's *Mémoires pour servir à l'histoire des insectes* (Paris 1734-1742) that awakened Bonnet's interest in natural history. After confirming for himself some of Réaumur's observations, young Bonnet started a correspondence with the famous academician, who became his mentor in scientific questions. The correspondence lasted until Réaumur's death, and his letters to Bonnet were collected by the latter in a single volume and provided with a subject index (BPUG, MS Bonnet 42). Bonnet's original letters to Réaumur are preserved in the AASP, Dossier Réaumur. For an evaluation of this correspondence, see Torlais (1932); and for Réaumur's influence on young Bonnet, see Savioz (1948b). When Needham moved to Paris in 1746, he met Réaumur, probably through their mutual friend Trembley. Réaumur wrote to Trembley on 28 January 1747, concerning two French translations of Needham's *New microscopical discoveries* that had been independently done, 'Monsieur Needham qui est à Paris depuis six à sept mois ne savait rien de tout cela, je le lui ai appris, il me fait l'amitié de venir me voir de temps en temps. Nous avons parlé de vous ensemble bien des fois' (M. Trembley 1943:290). Needham also procured fossils for Réaumur from England (see Needham's letter to Da Costa of 22 October 1749; BL, Add. 28540).

pareil. L'Homme de Reggio[8] se sera donc trompé, comme je l'avois présumé.

[ADDRESS] Genève, M.ʳ Néedham.

MANUSCRIPT
  BPUG, MS Bonnet 71:225*r*-225*v* (not included in Copy B).

EDITIONS
  'J'etois très persuadé [...] dites rien'; 'J'ai regret [...] point parlé?'; 'P.S. Ma Lettre [...] Réaumur'; and 'L'Homme de Reggio [...] présumé' published in Castellani (1973:85).

21

Needham to Bonnet – Geneva, 28 August 1765

à Geneve Le 28 d'aoust
1765.

Mon cher ami, et confrere

J'ai différé de repondre à votre obligeante lettre tant pour finir une petite guerre, que j'ai entrepris en passant contre M.ʳ de Voltaire, que pour vous envoyer ce que la partialité d'un ami pourra regarder comme mes trophées. Il est vrai que la gloire qui resulte d'une victoire si aisée, contre un ennemi affaibli par l'âge, et engagé dans une si mauvaise cause n'est rien moin qu'un sujet de triomphe pour moi: mais n'importe, je n'ai pas travaillé pour la gloire, mais pour le bien de la societé en dessillant les yeux du peuple, offusqués par le moindre nuage.

Je suis faché, que vous n'entendez pas l'Italien, mais notre bon ami M.ʳ Trembley pourra vous dedommager de cet inconvenient en vous rendant compte d'un livre, qu'il vient de lire avec grand plaisir. Je vous remercie de tout mon cœur du present, que vous venez de me faire, et que j'attend encore de votre libraire; comme il n'avait aucun exemplaire prête à me remettre. J'ai parcouru seulement jusqu'à present assés rapidement vos *corps organisés*, mais ce coup d'œil rapide me suffit pour bien sentir son grand merite: vous avez bien dit, que la generation de ces êtres se faisait *par division*, et c'etait une conjecture heureuse, mais il me fallait une suite d'observations, telle que je trouve en Spalanzani pour me convaincre. Encore il m'en reste de doutes, qui probablement disparaitront en meditant le sujet plus à mon aise. J'attend avec impatience le terme d'affranchissement de mon emploi present, et c'est alors que je m'occuperai serieusement tant à discuter de nouveau ces matieres, qu'à lire avec attention vos ouvrages physiologiques.

  8. Bonnet had not realised at this point that 'l'homme de Reggio' (see letter 15, n.3) was Spallanzani.

Je vous envoye les deux brochures de ma façon contre Voltaire,[1] vous m'en dires votre sentiment[2] à loisir. En attendant je suis tout à vous, et avec la plus grande sincerité, amitie, et estime, mon cher Monsieur,

> votre très humble, et très obeissant
>
> serviteur, confrere, et ami
>
> Needham.

MANUSCRIPT
    BPUG, MS Bonnet 28:15*r*-15*v*.

EDITIONS
    'Je suis faché [...] grand plaisir' and 'J'ai parcouru [...] à mon aise' published in Castellani (1973:89).

22

Bonnet to Needham – Genthod, 10 September 1765

Genthod le 10.e 7bre 1765.

Ce fut inutilement, mon digne Ami et Confrère que j'allai vous chercher l'autre jour *a*à aux Balances*a*. Je n'ai pu y retourner depuis, et j'aprens que vous partés aujourd'hui.[1] Recevés mes voeux les plus sincères, et donnés moi de tems en tems de vos nouvelles. Je voudrois sçavoir en particulier, si vous allés en droiture à Paris et quelle est vôtre Adresse dans cette Capitale.

Vos Brochures contre Voltaire*b* m'auroient prouvé vôtre Zèle pour la Réligion et *c*vos talens*c*, si j'avois eu*d* besoin de preuves en ce genre. Vous l'avés mis au pié du mur; il la sauté. Vous lui avés poussé des Argumens; il les a repoussés par des Injures. Cet Homme qui a tant crié contre l'accusation d'Athéisme

---

1. Needham is alluding to *Reponse d'un theologien au docte proposant des autres questions* and *Parodie de la troisieme lettre du proposant, adressée à un philosophe*, which were published anonymously in 1765, along with a third pamphlet by Needham, entitled *Projet de notes instructives*, véridiques, *théologiques, historiques & critiques sur certaines brochures polémiques du tems, adressées aux dignes editeurs des doctes ouvrages du proposant*. These were later published together, with some additions, and along with extracts from four of the anonymous pamphlets of Voltaire that had inspired them (see Needham 1769b). Voltaire also published an annotated edition of Needham's pamphlets, along with all twenty of his own (see Voltaire 1765 and V.O., 25:357-450, where unfortunately only abridgements of Needham's pamphlets are included). For the Needham-Voltaire controversy, see Roger (1963:732-48), Perkins (1965), Roe (1985), and section 5 of the Introduction. See also Bonnet's later statement on Needham's pamphlets in letter 44.
2. Bonnet wrote to Formey on 7 September 1765: 'Voltaire nous inonde de Brochures contre la Réligion: jamais on ne vit un Homme plus acharné contr'elle. Mr Néédham dans son Passage par nôtre Ville, s'est mis à rompre une Lance avec ce Chef des Incrédules en répondant à ses Brochures par d'autres. Voltaire a riposté par des injures grossières. Il va jusqu'à accuser son adversaire d'Athéisme, *pour avoir fait des Anguilles avec de la Farine* &c. &c. Que dites-vous de ces Hommes qui se piquent de Philosophie?' (BPUG, MS Bonnet 71:232r).

1. Needham apparently did not depart or, if he did, he soon returned, since Bonnet wrote to Haller on 17 September 1765 'J'eu[s] samedi dernier un long entretien avec lui [Needham] sur ce sujet [generation] dont je fus très satisfait' (Sonntag 1983;439). From Needham's letters to Sabatier de Cabre (in the BLUL) we know that he lived in Geneva from August 1765 to May 1766.

intentée à quelque Philosophe ne rougit point de vous l'intenter, à vous qui êtes Chrétien, qui faites gloire de l'être et qui consacrés vôtre Plume à établir la Vérité. Et puis quel fondement donne-t-il à son infame[e] accusation? Aviés-vous jamais prétendu que la Matière possedat par elle même la faculté d'organiser? Si cet Ecrivain s'étoit persuadé la fausseté de la Religion, il n'écriroit pas tant contr'elle; mais, plus il vieillit et plus ses craintes s'accroissent. Jamais Homme n'eut une si grande frayeur de la mort.

J'ai été agréablement surpris de recevoir une Lettre[2] de vôtre bon Ami Mr Spallanzani. Il me dit les choses les plus obligeantes sur mon Livre des *Corps Organisés*; il se félicite de nôtre accord dans la manière de penser sur vos *Etres microscopiques* et de la prédiction que je faisois à la page 226 du Tom. II.[3] Il m'aprend que le Chevalier Wallisniéri,[4] Professeur de Padouë s'est chargé de me faire tenir de sa part un Exemplaire de la Dissertation Italienne[5] que vous m'envoyates à Perroy. Je vai écrire en réponse à Mr Spallanzani et lui témoigner combien je m'aplaudis de la conformité de mes sentimens avec les siens. Je joindrai à ma Lettre[6] un Exemplaire de ma *Contemplation de la Nature*.

Au reste; il me confirme ce que j'avois pensé, qu'il n'avoit point lû mon Livre avant que de publier sa Dissertation.[7]

Je ne vous comprens pas bien, mon bon Ami, quand vous me dites; *je crois l'Epigénèse, et je ne puis jamais me reconcilier avec le Développement des Etres qui sont sensés exister depuis la création.* Vous voulés dire apparemment que vous rejettés l'*Emboitement des Germes*: je ne l'ai pas donné pour certain; mais par combien de Faits et de Faits très divers n'ai je pas combattu cette *Epigenèse* que vous semblés

2. Letter of 24 August 1765; see *Epistolario* (1:63-64).

3. After quoting the passage 'Je n'ai pas trouvé ... vous les verrez bientôt' from Needham's letter of 13 February 1762 (see letter 15) in his *Considérations sur les corps organisés*, Bonnet added the following prediction concerning the 'Professeur de Reggio': 'En attendant la publication de ces nouvelles observations, j'oserois bien prédire qu'elles ne *démontreront* pas que les Animalcules dont il s'agit, ayent une origine aussi étrange que l'a pensé & que le pense encore mon célèbre Confrère [Needham]' (Bonnet 1762, 2:226 and B.O., 3:411/6:317).

4. Antonio Vallisneri the younger (1708-1777) was born in Scandiano, near Reggio Emilia, the son of the great naturalist Antonio Vallisneri (1661-1730). He donated his father's museum, which he had inherited, to the University of Padua; and in gratitude the Venetian Republic established for him the chair of natural history, which he held until his death. His major contribution was the splendid edition of his father's works, *Opere fisico-mediche stampate e manoscritte del kavalier Antonio Vallisneri raccolte da Antonio suo figliuolo* (Venezia 1733), to which he added a short paper of his own. He published nothing more; and his own manuscripts, preserved in the BCL, which are difficult to decipher, do not really show any special talent as a naturalist. In many ways he was a superficial scholar who did not keep in touch with current research; but because of his position he had several influential acquaintances. He helped young Spallanzani (also born in Scandiano) by lending him books from his personal library. A short biography of Vallisneri may be found in Tiraboschi (1781-1786, 5:336-37); more references are given by Badaloni (1967), Ongaro (1973), and Mazzolini (1974). Much information about his personality may be inferred from the forty-one letters addressed to him by Spallanzani and published in *Epistolario*. Needham was acquainted with Vallisneri and corresponded with him both on his microscopical observations and on the so-called 'bust of Isis'; see Paravia (1842:152-60).

5. See letter 19, n.1.

6. Bonnet's first letter to Spallanzani is dated 14 September 1765 (see Castellani 1971:1-6).

7. In the letter mentioned above (see n.2) Spallanzani wrote, 'nella lettera che [...] riceverà [...] non ho fatto punto parola dell'aureo suo libro circa i corpi organizzati, per essermi questo allora ignoto, così mi permetta che adesso, che fortunatamente mi è giunto nelle mani, me ne rallegri, quanto so e posso con Lei' (*Epistolario*, 1:63). See also letter 20, n.2.

croire. Combien les Observations de mon Illustre Ami M.ʳ de Haller *Sur la Formation du Poulet*,[8] sont elles contraires à cette Opinion? Mais j'ignore si vous en avés lû l'exposition dans le Chap: IX du Tom: 1 de mes *Corps Organ.*[9] Je vous remis moi même cet Ouvrage au Printems de l'année dernière à vôtre départ pour Turin, et vous me marqués dans vôtre Lettre du 28.ᵉ d'Aoust dernier, *que vous ne l'avés que parcourû* et *assés rapidement*: je m'en étonne un peu, parce que le tems qui s'est écoulé est long, et que la Matière vous interessoit beaucoup. J'ai bien des petites affaires; mais surement je ne resterois pas deux mois sans dévorerᶠ une de vos Productions. Passés-moi ce petit reproche que je fai à l'amitié que je vous connois pour moi.

Vous ne me dissimulés pas, qu'il vous reste encore des doutes sur les Observations de vôtre Ami Spallanzani et sur les Remarques par lesquelles j'ai refuté vos Conséquences. J'en suis bien aise; ces doutes vous engageront à nous éplucher, et la vérité que nous chérissons tous trois y gagnera. Je ne puis assés vous repeter combien je desire que vous puissiés bientôt remanier ce Sujet intéressant et nous donner la Traduction Françoise de la Dissertation de M.ʳ Spallanzani.

Pensés-vous que M.ʳ de ᵍBuffon soit fort tenté d'imiterᵍ le bel éxemple que vous lui donnés, en avouant avec tant de candeur, *que vous avés trop étendu vos Idées en accordant une force productrice à la Matière*? S'il le faisoit, il se couvriroit de gloire, et cette gloire seroit plus vraye encore que celle qu'il tient de ses talens et de son genie. ᵈIl n'a pû croire que le seul Amour du Vrai m'eut inspiré la Critique[10] que j'ai faite de lui.ᵈ Il a imaginéʰ du *personnel* et s'est persuadé que je ne l'avois critiqué que parce qu'il avoit donné a Lewenhoëck la Découverte des *Pucerons*. Or, vous remarquerés, que j'ignorois profondément cela, lors que je critiquoisⁱ ce celebre Academicien. Ce traitʲ m'avoit échappé, et vous sçavés si de pareils motifs peuvent agir sur moi. Vous sçavés aussi, mon estimable et celebre Ami, que vous pourrés toûjours compter sur l'inviolable attachement de

[ADDRESS] Genève, M.ʳ Néédham

MANUSCRIPTS
    BPUG, MS Bonnet 71:233v-234r; MS Bonnet 85:180r-181r.

EDITIONS
    'J'ai été […] sa Dissertation' and 'Vous ne me dissimulés […] de M.ʳ Spallanzani' published in Castellani (1973:90).

TEXT NOTES
    a. B: dans vôtre Logis *b.* B: V.*** *c.* B: votre sçavoir *d.* B: *omitted* *e.* B: odieuse *f.* B: lire *g.* B: B*** imite bientôt *h.* B: soupçonné *i.* B: combattois *j.* B: trait de son bel Ouvrage

8. Haller presented his observations on the development of incubated chicken embryos and his theory of preformation based upon them in *Sur la formation du cœur dans le poulet* (Lausanne 1758). For historiographical discussion of this work see Roe (1975), Mazzolini (1977), Roe (1981), and the literature cited therein. On Haller's observations and their influence on Bonnet, see also section 2.iii of the Introduction.
    9. Bonnet (1762, 1:124-49) and B.O., 3:91-118/5:233-76.
    10. Bonnet (1762, 1:77-123, 172-76) and B.O., 3:56-90, 136-40/5:174-232, 308-13.

23

Needham to Bonnet – Mesnil le Roi, 16 August 1766

Mesnil le Roi, près St. Germain en Laye
Le 16. d'aoust 1766.

Je vous dois une lettre, mon très cher ami, et confrere, depuis long tems; mais j'ai voulu toujours, sans jamais vous oublier, differer de vous écrire, pour en avoir matiere suffisante, et pour rendre ma lettre un peu plus interessante, que celles qui courent ordinairement entre les hommes sans en laisser aucune trace. Je commence par vous annoncer, que j'ai donné les observations de Spalanzani à mon libraire pour les faire traduire, à lesquelles je travaillerai incessamment pour ajouter la dissertation, dont je vous ai parlé à Geneve. Actuellement je me trouve, comme vous voyez cy dessus, à la campagne à l'entrée de la forest de St. Germain, ou je compte de rester jusqu'à la fin de l'été; mais vous m'écrirez, quand vous êtes dans la disposition de me faire ce plaisir, à mon adresse *à Paris dans la rüe des Postes près l'estrapade.* Marqués moi, si vous plait, l'état de votre santé, celle de Madame[1] de M[r.] Le Conseiller[2] votre beaupere, vos occupations, vos amusements, les nouvelles litteraires, qui vous viennent de dehors, tout ce qui peut regarder mes amis à Geneve, particulierement M[r.] Trembley, et sa famille, M[r.] de Sausure[3] &c. l'état present de vos disputes politiques, enfin

1. Jeanne-Marie de La Rive (1728-1796), daughter of Horace-Bénédict de La Rive (see n.2 below) and of Jeanne-Marie Franconis (1693-1762), married Charles Bonnet in 1756. Jean Trembley (1794:74-76) provided the following information about their marriage; 'M. Bonnet n'était pas fait pour éprouver les convulsions de l'amour, présage souvent trompeur; il se présenta à Mlle. de la Rive comme un Ami tendre & vrai, qui mettait tout son bonheur à la posseder. Mlle. de la Rive avait trop de sentiment & de sagacité pour ne pas apprécier M. Bonnet; elle s'unit à lui avec cette satisfaction douce que cause la réunion de deux ames sensibles & vertueuses. Dès ce moment, elle lui consacra tous ses soins, pour ainsi dire son existence, & cette existence aurait été delicieuse, si des maux longs & cruels n'étaient venus la troubler. Une année était à peine écoulée, qu'un accident qui ne paraissait pas dangereux entraina les suites les plus graves; la constitution de Madame Bonnet, vigoureuse mais affaiblie par des remedes administrés mal à propos, ne put surmonter la maladie; des années de langueur & d'angoisse succederent à des maux plus violens; un état de convalescence plus ou moins favorable donna souvent des espérances qui ne se réaliserent jamais entierement.' For Bonnet's own description, see Savioz (1948b:180-82).

2. The Genevan patrician Horace-Bénédict de La Rive (1687-1773), who became a member of the Council of Two Hundred in 1714 and of the Small Council in 1731, played a significant role in the mediation of the conflicts between burghers and patricians in 1738, and occupied influential positions in Geneva's government until he retired from his position as Councillor of State in 1768.

3. For a biography of the Genevan scientist and patrician Horace-Bénédict de Saussure (1740-1799), from 1762 Professor at Geneva's Académie, see Freshfield (1920) and Albert V. Carozzi, *D.S.B.*, 12 (1975) 119-23, both of which list the major primary and secondary literature by and on Saussure. See also the bibliographical information provided by Geisendorf (1966:470-72). For recent works on Saussure's investigations on the hygrometer, see Archinard (1977:367-80); and on his chemical research, see Smeaton (1978). Saussure was Bonnet's nephew and was very much influenced by him in his early studies, keeping always in close contact with his uncle, of whom he also wrote a biography (Saussure 1793). From 26 August 1765 to 9 October 1765 and again in December 1765, Saussure carried out microscopical investigations on infusions, which he also discussed with Needham (BPUG, MS Saussure 63, 64). In his notebook 'Observations sur les Animalcules des Infusions', he noted under the heading 30 August 1765, 'Ce même matin Mr. Needham est venu me voir' (BPUG, MS Saussure 63:32). Later in the same notebook (f.100),

tout ce, qui vous interesse; c'est le vrai moyen de hausser la valeur de votre lettre à mes yeux, car tout ce qui vous fait ou peine, ou plaisir, comptez que cela m'interessera pareillement. Vous n'ignorez pas sans-doute la decouverte, que vient de faire le chef d'escadre Biron[4] à la terre des Patagons. La race des Geans, dont la taille ordinaire passe les huits pieds, est constatée; il a penetré assés avant dans le pais pour les decouvrir, et il a vu de cette espece plusieurs centaines. C'est M[r.] Maty,[5] qui vient d'ecrire à ce sujet à M[r.] de la

Saussure reported that Needham and Bonnet had come to view his experiments. Needham also wrote to Spallanzani from Geneva on 24 September 1765 about 'phenomenes, que nous venons de decouvrir depuis peu dans un cours d'observations, qu'un jeune professeur [Saussure] vient d'instituer ici sous mes yeux' (Castellani 1973:87). The results of such observations were later reported by Bonnet (see letter 41, n.26, and section 2.iv of the Introduction).

4. For a biography of Commodore, later Vice-Admiral, John Byron (1723-1786), the second son of the fourth Lord Byron, see John Knox Laughton, *D.N.B.*, 8 (1886) 161-63. For a vivid description of the wreck of the Wager on the southern coast of Chile in 1741, and of the hardships suffered by Byron and a group of survivors who managed to get back to England in 1746, see his often republished book, Byron (1768); see also Shankland (1975). In 1764 Byron was appointed to the Dolphin for a voyage to the South Seas. On his return to England in 1766, many periodicals reported the news that giants had been seen in Patagonia. The belief in the existence of giants in South America can be traced back to the sixteenth century (Gerbi 1955:93-97), but scholars of the early eighteenth century were sceptical. Oral and written statements by officers of the Dolphin, made before the official journal of the voyage was published (Hawkesworth 1773, 1:1-522), provided ample material for a revival of that belief. For example, the *Gentleman's magazine* of 9 May 1766 (36:245) reported that, 'Commodor Biron, in his Majesty's ship *Dolphin*, arrived in the Downs from the East Indies. She has been out upon discoveries and the papers say, has found out a new country in the East, the inhabitants of which are eight feet and half high.' *The London magazine* for June 1766 (35:323) wrote that the inhabitants were of 'great stature'; and *The Scots magazine* for June 1766 (28:329) first stated that the inhabitants were 'nine feet', but then added that the report concerning the stature of the inhabitants was later 'said to be fictitious'. On 20 October 1766, Alessandro Verri wrote to his father from Paris, not without a trace of irony: 'Qui se ne parla come cosa sicura. Si dicono alti fino a dieci piedi; sarebbe il doppio di noi altri poveri nani' (Gaspari 1980:45). He wrote from London to his brother Pietro (1728-1797) on 8 January 1767: 'Anche qui come a Parigi si credono i Pattagoni. Il Segretario e secondo Segretario, Dottor Morton e Dottor Mattys [Maty], lo credono, come credono ch'esista il sole' (Gaspari 1980:220). For the story of the Patagonian giants, see Adams (1962:19-43).

5. Matthew Maty (1718-1776) was born in Montfoort, near Utrecht. His father was a Huguenot who had left France and settled in Holland. He studied at Leiden University and obtained his doctorate in both philosophy and medicine in 1740. He went to England in 1741 and practised as a physician in London. Elected a Fellow of the Royal Society in 1751, he was appointed Foreign Secretary of the Society in 1762 and finally Secretary in 1765. In 1753 he was named Under-librarian and in 1772 Principal Librarian of the British Museum. He was involved in several contemporary controversies, such as that on methods of inoculation. He wrote biographies of some of the leading physicians of his day and translated many foreign works into English, such as Spallanzani's *Prodromo* in 1769. However, as Gibbon (1966:100), who was one of his many friends, wrote, his 'reputation was justly founded on the eighteen volumes of the *Journal britannique* which he had supported almost alone with perseverance and success'. His appointments led him to have a very wide circle of correspondents in Britain and on the continent; but no list of them is available, because in his will he requested his wife to burn all of his papers. Some of his correspondents have been mentioned by Janssens-Knorsch (1975), but the following may be added: Spallanzani (whose letters to Maty are published in *Epistolario*, 1:150-51, 157, 223-24, whereas Maty's letters to him are preserved in the BCRE, 213.2), Frisi (BAM, 154. Sup., cc.165-168), Bonnet (BPUG), and Haller (BB). Needham was among the contributors to the *Journal britannique* (see Needham 1752); and Maty had in his own library two of Needham's works (Needham 1745 and Needham 1747a; see *Catalogue* 1777:142, 144). Maty also reviewed Needham's *Philosophical transactions* paper of 1748 in the *Journal britannique* (January 1751, 4:54-64). Maty's review was later described by Needham as 'un précis juste' (Spallanzani 1769, pt.1:267). For biographies of Maty, see Thomas Seccombe, *D.N.B.*, 37 (1894) 76-78; Janssens-Knorsch (1975:7-42, 195-97), who also provides the most

Condamine.[6] Le vrai esprit de la philosophie est de s'elever au dessus de ce que nous voyons, et de ne vouloir jamais concentrer les œuvres de dieu, ni sa puissance, ni sa volonté dans le petit cercle de nos connoissances; tout ce qui est concevable, et possible, et encore plus, mille faits se realisent tous les jours, qui ne sont pas concevables; ai je tout dit? Non. Mille millions de faits existent dans la creation, qui ne sont ni concevables, ne se realiseront jamais à nos yeux dans l'état present. Vous connaissés parfaitment aussi bien que moi le caractere de nos menus philosophes; ils ont le mot du jour, comme Crambé remarque dans le Martinus Scriblerus de Swift,[7] qui les gouverne, et les conduit despotique-

complete list of his publications; and J. Patrick Lee in Sgard (1976:265-68).

6. For a biography of the famous French mathematician, natural historian, traveller, and member of the Académie des sciences, Charles-Marie de La Condamine (1701-1774), see Yves Laissus, *D.S.B.*, 15 (1978) 269-73, to whose references may be added Conlon (1967). *The London chronicle* for 10-12 July 1766 (20:46) quotes, under the heading Paris, June 30, a letter written by Maty to La Condamine, which contains the statement that 'The existence of giants [...] is here confirmed. Between four and five hundred Patagonians of at least eight or nine feet in height, have been seen and examined.' Maty also wrote to the editors of the *Journal des sçavans* (July 1766, p.506), who remarked, 'Les Philosophes qui ont pensé que la puissance génératrice étoit encore dans son enfance en Amérique, trouveront dans ce fait-là une nouvelle objection. Il est singulier de voir le contraste des Lapons à l'extrémité boréale d'un continent, & des Patagons à l'extrémité australe de l'autre.' The *Journal encyclopédique* (15 July 1766, 5, pt.2:135-36) also contained the news; but in this case Maty's letter, dated 13 June, was addressed to Joseph Jérôme Lefrançais de Lalande (1732-1807) 'pour être communiquée à l'académie des Sciences'. The next issue of the same journal (1 August 1766, 5, pt.3:130-33) contained 'Fragmens d'une lettre de M. de La Condamine aux Auteurs de ce Journal', in which it was stated, among other things: 'J'ai appris aujourd'hui que l'histoire de la découverte des Géans Patagons est une fable, & que les Anglois ont fait courir le bruit pour dissimuler le motif de l'armement de quatre vaisseaux qu'ils envoyent en ce pays pour y exploiter une mine qu'ils y ont découverte. Je suis fâché que mon ami le Docteur Maty ait donné dans ce panneau. [...] Notre ministère a rayé cet article qu'on vouloit mettre dans la *Gazette de France*; il s'est fondé sur ce que M. de Bougainville qui a relâché sur cette côte, a communiqué avec les Patagons, & fait des échanges avec eux; ils sont de la taille ordinaire: il est vrai que M. de Bougainville n'a abordé qu'à un endroit de la côte; mais aussi une race entière, une nation de Géans de 9 pieds de haut, est bien difficile à croire.' The story of the Patagonians did not come to an end after the publication of La Condamine's letter. A period of tension ensued between the Royal Society and the Académie des sciences. In 1767 an anonymous midshipman on board the Dolphin published an account of the voyage. His book attained a wide circulation by means of translations into French, German, Dutch, and Spanish, and by the many abstracts that were given by journals of the time (e.g. *The London magazine*, 1767, 35:181-84; *The Scots magazine*, 1767, 39:258-62). In it he stated that the Patagonians 'were about ten feet high' and that there was a 'prodigious disproportion [...] between their size and ours' (*A journal* 1767:24). Also in 1767, the abbé Gabriel-François Coyer (1707-1782) published a polite but ironical letter to Maty in which he stated, 'j'admire combien ma nation, que la vôtre accuse encore de credulité, est changée' (quoted from Coyer 1782-1783, 2:453). Ironical remarks were made also by some of the philosophes. Maty himself pressed officers of the Dolphin for more accurate accounts. In reply, Charles Clarke, an officer on board the Dolphin, published a letter in *The Annual register* (1768, fifth ed., 11:68-70) stating that among the Patagonians, 'there was hardly a man there less than eight feet'. Returning from a new voyage to South America, captain Philip Carteret (d. 1796) reported: 'We measured the heights of many of these people; they were in general all from six feet to six feet five inches, although there were some who came to six feet seven inches, but none above that' (*The Annual register*, 1771, fifth ed., 14:11). Byron himself wrote in his official journal that the chief of the Patagonians 'could not be much less than seven feet' and described him as a 'frightful Colossus', (Hawkesworth 1773, 1:28). From the first accounts it may well be understood why scientists like Maty, James Douglas (1702-1768), Bonnet, Needham, and Frisi (1771:xviii-xix) could easily have been led to believe in the existence of giants.

7. Needham is alluding to the following passage: 'Every day I am under the dominion of a certain Word', *Memoirs of the extraordinary life, works, and discoveries of Martin Scriblerus* (Kerby-Miller 1950:128). Although Needham attributed the *Memoirs* to Jonathan Swift (1667-1745), they were in fact written

ment dans leurs conclusions. *Geant, revenant, miracle, mystere, Foi, magie &c.* voila des mots, qui font rire dans l'instant, et qui rit non seulement ne raisonne plus, lui meme, mais empêche par une espece de mauvaise honte tous les autres de raisonner. 'Comment? Vous croyez donc aux geans, aux revenans, aux miracles, à la magie?—Vous avez donc demonstré l'impossibilité absolue des toutes ces choses?[¹] Commencez par me donner votre demonstration, mais pour la faire il vous faut de la reflection, et la reflection, dont la force est en raison inverse du ris, demande du serieux. Pour moi je ne connais en toute chose aucune autre philosophie, que celle des faits; christianisme, Neutonianisme, physique, rien n'est solide, si non en tant qu'il se pose sur cette base inebranlable.—Est-il vrai, comme on nous annonce ici, que M[r·] Voltaire se retire en Prusse; vous sçavez que certaines jeunes gens de famille ont été executés depuis peu à amiens pour avoir insulté d'une maniere inoüie la religion; mais enfin pour vous mettre au fait, Je vous envoye l'arret du Parliament, qui les condamne à la mort,[8] et ordonne en meme tems le dictionaire philosophique d'être brulé avec leur corps publiquement. On pretend que ce procedé a tellement frappé Voltaire, que la crainte, dont il est très susceptible, l'ait determiné à se refugier chez le Roi de Prusse.[9] Fanatique pour fanatique; le chretien vaut bien l'incredule. *Quis tulerit gracchos de seditione querentes?*[10]

Autre aventure encore, qui regarde Rousseau,[11] et qui ne lui fait pas grand

by various members of the Scriblerus Club. For the authorship, composition, and publication of the *Memoirs*, see Kerby-Miller (1950:57-67).

8. The chevalier Jean-François Le Fèvre de La Barre (1747-1766) and his friend d'Etallonde de Morival had been accused in Abbeville by the judge Nicolas-Pierre Duval de Saucourt of not having taken their hats off while passing in front of a procession, and of having sung anti-religious songs at the end of a dinner. Both were also suspected of having mutilated the wooden crucifix on the Pont-Neuf of Abbeville. Furthermore Voltaire's *Dictionnaire philosophique* had been found among La Barre's possessions. The judge condemned them to be burned alive, having had their tongues cut out and their right hands cut off. D'Etallonde escaped and found asylum in Prussia. La Barre appealed to the Parlement in Paris, which mitigated the judge's sentence by condemning them to be beheaded first and burned afterwards. The sentence, which was carried out on 1 July 1766 at Abbeville, caused an enormous sensation. Voltaire was deeply shocked and wrote, under the pseudonym of Casen, the *Relation de la mort du chevalier de La Barre* (V.O., 25:503-16), in which he described the final moments of the execution thus: 'Tout ce que je sais par les lettres d'Abbeville, c'est qu'il monta sur l'échafaud avec un courage tranquille, sans plainte, sans colère, et sans ostentation: tout ce qu'il dit au religieux qui l'assistait se réduit à ces paroles: *Je ne croyais pas qu'on pût faire mourir un gentilhomme pour si peu de chose*' (V.O., 25:514). Voltaire tried in this pamphlet and on other subsequent occasions to rehabilitate the memory of young La Barre, but without success. It is interesting to note that neither Needham nor Bonnet (see letter 24) was moved by the execution of this young man.

9. The rumour that Voltaire had written to Frederick II asking for asylum at Wessel near Düsseldorf spread rapidly, but was subsequently denied by Voltaire himself (see Best.D13538 and D13539).

10. Juvenal, II, 24.

11. In the following paragraphs Needham informs Bonnet of the final stages of what Guillemin (1942) has called the *affaire infernal*, i.e. the notorious relationship between Hume and Rousseau in the years 1765-1766. The events leading up to this affair are as follows. After the publication of his *Lettres écrites de la montagne* (Amsterdam 1764), Rousseau found himself severely criticised. On 8 September 1765, his house at L'Ile Saint-Pierre on the Lake of Bienne was stoned: and a few weeks later the Great Council of Bern expelled him. Rousseau intended to join his protector Georg Keith, tenth Earl Marischal (1693?-1778) in Berlin; but when he stopped at Strasbourg during his journey, a letter from David Hume reached him. The Scottish philosopher tactfully offered him hospitality in England, assuring him that he 'would find absolute security against all persecutions' and would

honneur dans notre Pais. Son très grand ami, patron, et protecteur Hume[12] vient de le peindre dans differentes lettres au Baron de Holbach,[13] comme le plus noir, le plus atroce, et le dernier des hommes. On pretend ici, que dalembert, diderot,[14] et autres sçavans, qui le connaissaient dit on d'avance, avaient avertis Hume avant son depart, qu'il nourrissait un serpent dans son sein,[15] qui ne manquerait pas de le mordre, aussitot qu'il ressentirait la chaleur. Si cela est vrai, leur prediction a été verifiée. En peu de mots, Hume l'avait engagé à accepter une pension de la part du Roi d'angleterre sous secret, pour se conformer

'have no difficullty to live frugaly in that country, on the fruits of [his] own industry', because English booksellers could afford to pay higher prices to authors than those in Paris (see the English draft of Hume's letter of 22 October 1765 in Hume 1932, 1:526). Hume (1932, 1:364-65) had once before offered hospitality to Rousseau, but the latter refused, though not without some hesitation. Now, pressed both by circumstances and by his friends, he accepted. He left Strasbourg on 9 December and joined Hume in Paris on 16 December (*C.L.*, 6:434, 436). After some time there, Hume and Rousseau departed on 4 January 1766 and reached London on 13 January. Hume found Rousseau a residence at Wootton and was in the process of obtaining a pension from the king for his protégé when Rousseau accused him, in a long letter written to Hume dated 10 July 1766, of being part of a plot, headed by Voltaire and d'Alembert, the aim of which was to dishonour and ruin him (Leigh, 5274). Hume (1954:144) himself dismissed this as a 'cabale'. Most of the documents concerning the dispute between Rousseau and Hume may be found in volume ii of Hume's (1932) correspondence, and especially in the volumes for the years 1765-1766 of Rousseau's correspondence edited by Leigh (see also *C.L.*, 7:139-46, 162-64, 204-206). Most historians interpret these documents as evidence of Rousseau's 'persecution mania', but they seem to forget that Rousseau was indeed a persecuted man. Guillemin's (1942) treatment of the subject is biased in favour of Rousseau. More balanced are Roddier (1950:259-306) and Mossner (1980:507-32). See also Boiteux (1950-1952), Meyer (1952), and Cranston (1962).

12. An authoritative biography of David Hume (1711-1776) has been provided by Mossner (1980). For a bibliography of his writings and a list of works on him up to 1937, see Jessop (1938). For writings on Hume from 1925 to 1976, see R. Hall (1978), which also contains a list of the main literature for the period 1900-1924.

13. For an intellectual biography of Paul Henri Thiry, baron d'Holbach (1723-1789), see Naville (1967:481-85), who also provides a list of secondary literature on d'Holbach. For a bibliography of d'Holbach's own works, see Vercruysse (1971). D'Holbach owned several books by Bonnet (1760, 1764, 1769, and the 1768 ed. of the *Considérations sur les corps organisés*), but none by Needham; see *Catalogue* (1789:58, 59, 65, 68). In June-July 1766, Hume wrote two important letters (possibly three; see n.21 below) to the baron d'Holbach, which have not been preserved. It was through d'Holbach that the news of Rousseau's accusations against Hume first spread in Paris (Meyer 1952:341). On 15 and 25 July 1766, Hume (1954:136-41, 144-48) also wrote two letters to d'Alembert, giving extracts from Rousseau's letter of 10 July 1766. He also sent a lengthy account of the affair to the comtesse de Boufflers (1725-1800); see Hume (1932, 2:59-63, 77-80).

14. For a biography of Denis Diderot (1713-1784), see Wilson (1972). As a preliminary guide to Diderot's own works, see Cioranescu (1969; 1:668-75); and for a bibliography on Diderot, see Spear (1980). For scholarship on Diderot, see Casini (1958) and Chouillet (1979 and 1980). For books by Diderot owned by Needham, see *Catalogue* (1782, pt.1:108). Needham refuted the *Lettres sur les aveugles*, which had appeared in 1749 (see Needham 1750:345-47n and Spallanzani 1769, pt.2:32-38). There is also some evidence suggesting that Needham and Diderot might have met (Rogers 1876:234). Although Diderot (1964:305) found Needham's style obscure, he had certainly read Needham's book of 1750 and was influenced by it in his own later speculations on matter and generation. Neither author believed in the theory of preformed germs. In his *Rêve de d'Alembert*, Diderot (1971:34-38) alluded to Needham's experiments on eels; and in his *Eléments de physiologie*, he made use of Needham's experiments to support his own views about living matter (Diderot 1964:12-13, 44-45). For Diderot's biological views, see Roger (1963:585-682); and for Bonnet's influence on Diderot, see Marx (1976:545-58).

15. According to Morellet (1822, 2:109), who was with Hume at the time, it was the baron d'Holbach who told Hume, on the eve of the latter's departure from Paris: 'Vous ne connaissez pas l'homme. Je vous le dis franchement, vous allez réchauffer un serpent dans votre sein.'

à son orgueil, et comme il desirait lui meme; quelque tems après, comme vous sçavez, la petite lettre sous le nom du Roi de Prusse[16] parut dans les gazettes anglaises;[17] nous l'avions en manuscrit à Geneve,[18] il y a present quatre mois. Rousseau se mit en tête, qu'elle avait été composée à Paris pour le rendre ridicule à son arrivée en angleterre par dalembert, Hume, et M[r.] Walpole.[19] Sur cette idée non seulement il rejette la pension, qu'on avait obtenu du Roi pour lui, mais il écrit une lettre[20] de dixhuit pages à M[r.] Hume remplie d'injures, et d'invectives. On m'a recité à Paris une partie, à moins de l'entendre jamais on concevra le fiel, et la mechancété, dont elle regorge. Il semble, qu'il somme toutes ses forces, et vous les connaissés assés par ses autres écrits, pour aneantir Hume, et ses amis. Enfin le voila en guerre avec tout le monde,[21] comme Esau, et ses descendans autrefois, *manus ejus contra omnes, et manus omnium contra eum.*[22] Avant de finir ma lettre je dois vous feliciter, et tous mes amis sur la declaration

16. The notorious 'King-of-Prussia' letter had actually been written by Horace Walpole (1717-1797) with the aid of an unnamed friend. It poured derision on Rousseau's decision to turn down a pension from the king of Prussia, and was ironic about his constant feelings of persecution. Walpole read it out at various dinners and distributed some copies. Since its original appearance it has often been published; see *A concise* (1766:21), *C.L.*, 6:458-59, Mossner (1980:513-14), and especially Leigh, A 431.

17. The letter appeared only in *St James's chronicle* (1-3 April 1766, p.4); see Leigh, A 431. It has been republished by Pottle in W. Smith (1967:258-59).

18. See Leigh, A 431, MS 6.

19. For a biography of Horace Walpole, see Lewis (1961) and the volume edited by W. Smith (1967). For a bibliography of his works, see Hazen (1973).

20. For the definitive edition of Rousseau's famous letter to Hume dated 10 July 1766, see Leigh, 5274. During late July and early August, Hume wrote a short narrative of his relations with Rousseau, including transcripts of their letters, and sent the manuscript to d'Alembert sometime before 12 August (Hume 1932, 2:79). The manuscript was translated into French by Jean-Baptiste-Antoine Suard (1723-1817), and alterations were later made by d'Alembert and d'Holbach. The result was a pamphlet that appeared in late October (Meyer 1952:342), entitled *Exposé succinct de la contestation qui s'est élevée entre M. Hume et M. Rousseau, avec les pieces justificatives* (Londres [Paris] 1766), in which Rousseau's letter was first published (pp.46-110). Soon an English translation appeared, based upon the French edition and not on Hume's manuscript: *A concise and genuine account of the dispute between Mr. Hume and Mr. Rousseau: with the letters that passed between them during their controversy* (London 1766). Contemporary journals devoted much space to the dispute (e.g. *The London magazine*, 1766, 35:557-60, 620-21, 670-76; *The Scots magazine*, 1766, 28:599-601, 648-54, 695-99). Walpole's conduct was attacked in an anonymous pamphlet ([Greene] 1766), but he was later defended by another writer ([Heathcote] 1767).

21. Needham seems to have obtained some of his information on the Hume-Rousseau affair from his friend and correspondent John Wilkes (1727-1797). In a letter to Sabatier de Cabre, Needham included the following passage from a letter he had just received from Wilkes: 'I am sorry, that I cannot fully gratifie your curiosity about J.J. Rousseau. Monsieur d'Holbach has been a week at Voré with Mr Helvetius, and continues there *another* fortnight, as Swift says. He shewed me three letters from Hume, in which Rousseau is stiled the most black, and atrocious villain on earth, a monster, a disgrace to human nature &c. &c. The dispute is about a pension, which Hume says J. J. Rousseau employed him to sollicit from the King of England, and Rousseau absolutely denies. The pension, as it is said, had been obtained for him in consequence of his request, but this whim of rejecting it together with his denial of any application for it on his part has irritated Hume above measure: as it compromises him with his majesty. Hume has written a long pamphlet, which is inscribed by permission to M.[r] Secretary Conway, and is soon to be published. Thus the war between these litterary potentats is declared. We shall soon be overrun with manifestoes, declarations, replies, rejoinders &c. Both parties are more animated, than becomes philosophers, or men of common sense, and the impartial publick will turn them both to ridicule. I have no copies of Hume's letters or I should most willingly have sent them' (24 July 1766, BLUL).

22. Genesis xvi.12.

publique des mediateurs en faveur du magistrat.[23] Ils n'ont rien fait en cela que de rendre justice à la vertu. Mais le tems n'est pas peutetre favorable ni à l'un, ni à l'autre. Dieu veuille, que cet acte de justice vous donne la paix, mais les hommes d'aujourdhui ne sont pas faits pour la recevoir. *Summa ratio summa injuria.*[24] Je vous prie de saluer Madame de ma part, et d'être très persuadé, que personne ne vous aime, ni vous estime plus, que, mon très cher ami, et confrere

votre très humble, et très obeissant serviteur

Needham.

P.S. Après toutes mes recherches si inutiles à Geneve je trouve en depaquetant mes livres ici votre addison.[25] Je vous demande mille pardons, et je vous le renverrai par Messieurs Trant, et Hely[26] deux de mes amis, qui doivent partir au commencement du mois prochain.

J'ai vu la lettre de Voltaire contre notre ami Vernet.[27] Il a promis, m'at'on

23. Needham was well aware of the constitutional crisis that had been developing in Geneva since 1763 (see section 8 of the Introduction and letter 24, n.1). The number of accusations lodged by the burghers against the magistrates had increased; and during 1765, normal governing procedures were blocked by the fact that the Small Council (dominated by the Patriciate) could not get any candidate elected as Syndic by the General Council (dominated by the burghers). The Genevan Patriciate was thus forced to appeal to the Guarantors of the Edict of 1738, namely to the Kingdom of France and the Republics of Bern and Zürich. The Plenipotentiares of the Guarantors arrived in Geneva at the end of March 1766 and set to work at once. On 25 July 1766, they produced a declaration in favour of the magistrates (*Nous soussignés Ministres Plenipotentiaires*) consisting of four printed pages and signed by le chevalier de Beauteville, Escher de Keffiken, Heidegger, Ougspourguer, and Sinner (see also Rivoire 1897, nr.942). In it they stated that 'toutes les imputations injurieuses faites aux Magnifiques Conseils, tant des Vingt-cinq que des Deux Cent, dans les différentes brochures; & notamment dans le livre intitulé *Réponse aux lettres écrites de la Campagne*, sont injustes, dictées par la prévention & la passion; & que ledit Conseil, n'ayant rien fait qui dût le priver de la confiance de ses Concitoyens, c'est à tort & sans raison qu'ils ont refusé de choisir dans le Corps du Magnifique Conseil les Chefs de la République' (pp.2-3). On 4 August 1766, Bonnet gave a speech in the Great Council and, referring to the Declaration, stated, 'Les Puissances respectables qui veillent si genereusement à nôtre conservation et à nôtre bonheur, viennent de confirmer solemnellement à nos Sages Magistrats, le Titre le plus cher à leurs Coeurs, celui de *Peres de la Patrie*. Elles viennent de déclarer à la face de la Patrie et de l'Europe entière, que les Magistrats de Geneve, si injustement & si publiquement accusés, avoient été de fidèles dépositaires des Loix *que leur administration avoit été légale, intègre, moderée, paternelle*, et qu'ils n'avoient jamais cessé de mériter la confiance de ceux que la Loi les appelloit à gouverner' ('Ecrits politiques', VII. 'Discours prononcé au Grand Conseil le Lundi 4.ᵉ d'Aoust 1766. à l'occasion de la Déclaration des Seig.ʳˢ Médiateurs du 25.ᵉ de Juillet et de l'Ouverture de la nouvelle Médiation', BPUG, MS Bonnet 16:2-3). See also section 8, n.13, of the Introduction.

24. Reminiscent of Cicero's 'summum ius, summa injuria': *De officiis*, I, 10. 33.

25. It is impossible to identify for certain which book by Joseph Addison (1672-1719) Bonnet had lent to Needham. As no book by Addison appears in the catalogue of Needham's library, it seems that he must have returned the book, in spite of Bonnet's offering to let him keep it (letter 24). Given Needham's and Bonnet's taste for religious controversy, it might have been an edition of *The Evidence of the Christian religion*, first published in Addison (1721, 4:559-94).

26. We were unable to identify Trant and Hely. At Trinity College, Dublin, a John Hely matriculated in 1754, and a Dominick Trant in 1756.

27. When the third enlarged edition of the *Lettres critiques* appeared in 1766 with the name of the author (see letter 14, n.10), Voltaire was determined to punish and publicly mortify Jacob Vernet. On 26 May 1766, he wrote to Paul Claude Moultou, 'Mon cher philosophe, il faudrait être aussi sot que Vernet pour lire tout son livre. Mais le peu qu'on en lit excite l'indignation. Il mériterait d'être puni publiquement de ce qu'il a écrit très obscurément' (Best.D13320). In another letter he stated, 'Je sais fort bien qu'il ne mérite pas qu'on lui réponde, mais il mérite qu'on le punisse' (Best. D13329); and again, 'Je suis en droit de le punir de plus d'une façon' (Best.D13334). To d'Alembert he wrote on 13 June 1766, 'je me dispose à faire une justice exemplaire de la personne dudit

dit ici, sa reponse, et sa justification.[28] Ayez la bonté de me la communiquer.

[ADDRESS] A Monsieur / Monsieur Charles Bonnet / de la Societé Royale de Londres &c. / au chateau / à Geneve.

MANUSCRIPT
BPUG, MS Bonnet 28:17r-18v.

EDITIONS
'Je commence [...] à Genève' published in Castellani (1973:91). 'Est-il vrai [...] Needham [end of letter]' published in Leigh, 5371.

24

Bonnet to Needham – Genthod, 5 September 1766

À Genthod près de Genève le 5.e de 7bre 1766.
[a]Je vous doi bien des remercimens, mon cher Ami et Confrère, de vôtre obligeante Lettre du 16 du mois dernier. Je me seroi fait un plaisir de vous prévenir si mes occupations me l'avoient permis. Vous connoissés le tourbillon politique ou je nage actuellement[1] et qui m'emporteroit malgré moi, si les liens

huguenot, lorsqu'il viendra sur mes terres catholiques. Je ne souffrirai pas qu'il attaque impunément notre saint père le pape, et vous et frère Hume, et frère Marmontel, et même faux frère Rousseau, et la comédie' (Best.D13345). The result of all this was Voltaire's *Lettre curieuse de M. Robert Covelle, célèbre citoyen de Genève, à la louange de M. V..., professeur en théologie dans ladite ville*, published in June 1766 (Dijon; reprinted in V.O., 25:491-96).

The Genevan apologist, historian, and theologian Jacob Vernet (1698-1789) was one of the most influential personalities in the religious life of his town. He studied in Paris for eight years; and in Geneva he was the most prominent of Jean-Alphonse Turrettini's (1671-1737) pupils, of whose theological reform of Calvinism he was both a disciple and a promulgator. Pastor from 1734 and Professor of Theology and History at the Académie from 1739, he was the first editor of Montesquieu's *De l'esprit des loix* ([1748]) and of Turrettini's *Traité de la vérité de la religion chrétienne* (1750). He attempted to see the papers concerning Servetus's case (see Vernet's letters edited by Galiffe 1877:86-97), but was unsuccessful. For some time he was both a correspondent and friend of Rousseau, whose concern about Voltaire's negative influence in Geneva he entirely shared. For a biography, list of publications, and information on his theological activities, see Saladin (1790), Falletti (1885), and Budé (1893); for his relations with Rousseau, see Ritter (1916-1917a); for the striking similarity between his religious convictions and Rousseau's, see Masson (1916, 1:200-202, 283-84); and for his influence in Geneva, see Spink (1934:121-47). Two letters of Vernet to Bonnet are preserved in the BPUG.

28. See letter 24, n.15.

1. Bonnet is alluding to the constitutional crisis developing in Geneva at this time, in which he consistently supported the Patriciate. An old but excellent chronicle of the events is provided by [Ivernois] (1782:159-400). The political pamphlets published in the period 1763-1768 are listed by Rivoire (1897). For the general political history of the crisis, see Karmin (1920:3-31), Ferrier (1951:446-56), Palmer (1959-1964, 1:111-39), Piuz (1974:241), Venturi (1969-1979, 3:343-53), and Im Hof (1980:709-11). For the part played by Rousseau, see Candaux's introduction to the *Lettres écrites de la montagne* in R.O. (3:clix-cxcviii); for that played by Voltaire, see Gay (1965:185-238) and Ceitac (1956a). Specific aspects of the crisis are dealt with by Ferrier (1926 and 1927), Rovillain (1927), and Gagnebin (1955). The diplomatic efforts leading to the Edict of 1768 are reconstructed by Ceitac (1956b) and Gür (1967). For Bonnet's political activities in those years, see Savioz (1948b:221-33), Gaullieur (1855), and section 8 of the Introduction.

qui nous attachent à la Patrie n'étoient pas toûjours volontaires. Mais; je vous avouë, que je rentrerai avec empressement dans mes fonctions de Philosophe, des que la paix nous sera renduë. La vie que je mène n'est point du tout celle qui me plait le plus ni celle pour laquelle je suis le plus fait. Cependant vous n'ignorés pas que la première Loi de la Philosophie que nous aimons, est de se soumètre aux circonstances dans lesquelles le SOUVERAIN ARBITRE de nôtre sort juge à propos de nous placer.[a]

[a]Vous avés donc lu cette Déclaration[2] solemnelle que nos Médiateurs ont rendu dans leur Sagesse, en faveur d'un Gouvernement si publiquement et si injustement accusé. Vous n'avés pas oublié, mon bon ami, que je n'avois jamais eu la moindre inquietude sur le jugement que porteroient les Puissances respectables[3] qui veillent si genereusement à nôtre bonheur. Nos Representans[4] ont commencé par murmurer dans leurs Cercles et ont fini par se soumetre. Vous comprenés que des Moucherons n'auroient pas bonne grace à lutter contre des Elephants. D'un autre côté nous aurions méconnu les vrais interets de nôtre Patrie, si nous[5] avions tiré vanité d'un acte de Justice. Nous devions tacher d'en adoucir l'amertume à nos Frères les Opposans, et leur montrer par nôtre moderation et par nôtre modestie que nous ne sommes pas indignes de l'estime et de la confiance qu'ils s'obstinent à nous refuser. Nous n'avons donc rien négligé pour atteindre à ce but si cher à nôtre Coeur; mais, je ne vous dis pas que nous ayons eu la consolation d'y parvenir. Le retour de la confiance sera l'Ouvrage du tems et des modifications que la Constitution recevra.[a]

[a]Le travail des Médiateurs est très avancé, et nous ne sommes pas éloignés de ce denouement que nos voeux appellent depuis si longtems. Tout se traite dans un profond secret. Vous comprenés combien la nature des Affaires l'exige. Nos Médiateurs doivent élever leur Edifice derrière un Rideau épais, et quand l'Edifice sera achevé, ils tireront le Rideau. Ce moment sera interessant et peut être critique.[a]

Je suis charmé[b] que vous ayés donné à traduire en François nôtre estimable Ami Spallanzani. Je jouirai donc enfin du plaisir de le lire. Il a la complaisance de m'ecrire en François, et je vous assure qu'il ne s'exprime point mal dans cette Langue. Il veut bien me rendre compte de ses Recherches; je l'encourage et je lui fait part de mes vuës. Je l'ai surtout exhorté à suivre les *Reproductions animales*, et en particulier celle du *Ver-de-Terre*, si dignes d'être aprofondis.[6] Je n'avois qu'ébauché ce sujet dans le Traité[7] que je publiai en 1745; mais j'en vis alors assés pour être en droit de prononcer sur la Reproduction et pour en indiquer les premiers progrès. C'est aussi de cet Objet que Mr Spallanzani est

2. See letter 23, n.23.

3. That is, the Guarantors of the Edict of 1738.

4. The members of the burgher's faction referred to themselves as *Représentans*, from the 'represen-tations' they submitted to the Syndics.

5. That is, the members of the government party who were called *Négatifs*, because they claimed the right of refusing to transmit any burgher representation to the General Council. They all belonged to old Genevan patrician families.

6. Bonnet had suggested the study of 'reproductions animales' to Spallanzani in his letter of 27 December 1765 (Castellani 1971:6-15). He continued to provide suggestions on the subject throughout 1766.

7. In the second volume of his *Traité d'insectologie* (1745); B.O., 1:115-258/1:167-352.

le plus occupé à présent. Vous avés la Copie de la Lettre[8] que je lui écrivis en Décembre dernier, en réponse aux instructions qu'il m'avoit demandées et dont ses lumières et ses talens pouvoient aisément se passer. Il me marque[9] qu'il suit les Directions de cette Lettre. J'attends ses résultats.

J'aurois fort souhaité, mon estimable Ami, qu'en même tems que vous avés donné à traduire la Dissertation de nôtre Observateur de Modène, vous eussiés pû m'aprendre que vous lui avés remis vos Remarques sur cet Ecrit. Vous sçavés combien je suis impatient d'en juger et 'tout le cas que j'en fais'. Nos entretiens là dessus accroissent mon impatience. J'aime à penser que vous consacrerés le repos dont vous jouissés à étendre et à perfectionner nos Connoissances sur une des plus belles Parties de l'Histoire Naturelle.

La Découverte des Patagons[10] interesse les Observateurs de la Nature. J'ai du plaisir à voir l'echelle de nôtre Espèce se prolonger et à contempler depuis le Lapon jusqu'au Patagon. J'ay essayé de crayonner cette Echelle dans le Chapitre X de la Partie IV de ma *Contemplation de la Nature*.[11]

Vos refléxions sur nos Incrédules ne sont malheureusement que trop vrayes. Plaignons leur aveuglement, faisons des voeux ardens pour leur conversion et félicitons nous *d'avoir choisi la bonne part qui ne nous sera point ôtée*. Toute la Nature est pour eux un Enigme, le Passé un tourment, le Présent une vapeur, l'Avenir un Goufre.

L'Arrêt que vous m'avés envoyé m'a fait frissonner: mais je n'ignore pas que les Juges humains ont dans vôtre Communion des Loix dont ils ne peuvent s'écarter sans manquer à l'Eglise.

Quel compte n'aura point à rendre le malheureux Auteur[12] du Dictionaire Philosophique. Il n'est pas vrai qu'il se retire en Prusse;[13] mais on assure fort qu'il a écrit au Roi pour lui demander une retraite en cas de besoin. Son Libelle[14] contre Mr Vernet a été reduit en poudre impalpable par celui-ci.[15] Il n'est pas possible de répondre plus victorieusement ni avec plus de moderation. Je voulois, ainsi que ses vrais Amis, qu'il rendit sa réponse publique; mais des considerations étrangères ne lui ont pas permis de ceder encore à nos désirs. Je ne puis donc vous communiquer cette Refutation,[16] dont il ne laisse pas prendre des Copies.

8. Letter of 27 December 1765 (Castellani 1971:6-15). Bonnet probably gave Needham a copy of this letter during one of their meetings while Needham was living in Geneva in 1765-1766. (There are no letters between Bonnet and Needham from September 1765 to August 1766.)

9. Letter of 18 November 1765 (*Epistolario*, 1:68-70).

10. See letter 23, n.4 and n.6.

11. Bonnet (1764:81-83). In the *Contemplation de la nature* Bonnet had mentioned the 'Géant des Terres Magellaniques' and in the republication of this work in B.O., he added the following note: 'On comprend que je parle des *Patagons*, sur la haute stature desquels les Voyageurs sont si peu d'accord. On n'avoit pas moins exagéré leur grandeur que la petitesse des Lappons. Il est des relations où on leur donne jusqu'à douze ou treize pieds de hauteur; mais les Voyageurs les plus modernes & les plus éclairés, ne portent pas leur stature à plus de six à sept pieds. Ils sont gros à proportion, assez bien faits, & leur visage, quoiqu'un peu plat, présente des traits assez réguliers' (B.O., 4, pt.1:131 n.3/7:198 n.3).

12. Voltaire.

13. See letter 23, n.9.

14. See letter 23, n.27.

15. Jacob Vernet, *Memoire présenté à M.[r] le Premier Sindic* (1766). Vernet presented this mémoire on 30 June 1766; see also Rivoire (1897, nr.937).

16. As of the date of Bonnet's letter to Needham, Vernet's *Mémoire* had not yet been published.

Les Conducteurs de l'Etat et de l'Eglize l'ont luë et éxaminée *juridiquement* et après l'éxamen en forme de differentes Pièces relatives à cette affaire; ils ont donné à M.ʳ Vernet une Déclaration authentique la plus tranchante et la plus honorable.[17]

A force d'Esprit, de Malheurs et d'orgueil Rousseau paroit avoir perdu le sens. Sa conduite à l'egard de son Bienfaiteur le celebre Hume est une extravagance continue avec des redoublemens. C'est pourtant ce même Homme que ses aveugles[a] Partisans osoient élever au rang des Grotius[18] et des Montesquieu.[19] Ne voila-t-il pas un admirable Précepteur du Genre-Humain! On écrit de Londres qu'il est devenu fou, et qu'on le garde à vuë dans le Compté de Derby.[20] Si cela est, il ne mérite plus que de la compassion.[d]

[a]Ma Femme est très sensible à vôtre obligeant Souvenir, et vous présente ses honneurs et ses voeux les plus sincères. Elle est toûjours travaillée de sa cruelle insomnie. M.ʳˢ Trembley et de Saussure vous font mille complimens. Ils se portent très bien et sont très occupés. Le dernier suit actuellement ses Recherches sur l'Electricité.[21] Il va présider à des Thèses publiques sur cette matière

It is interesting to note that Vernet, while defending himself against the sarcasms of Voltaire, gave the following as an example of the latter's behaviour: 'on pût tout attendre de lui [Voltaire], après la maniére dont il a déchiré depuis peu Mr. NEDHAM, homme aussi estimable par son bon caractère que par son savoir' (Vernet 1766b:52). For Needham's controversy with Voltaire, see section 5 of the Introduction.

17. Vernet's personal defence is followed by the 'Extrait des Registres du Conseil', the 'Extrait des Registres de la V. Compagnie', and the 'Extrait des Registres du V. Concistoire', all of which declared their satisfaction with his justification (Vernet 1766b:54-62).

18. For a biography of the famous political theorist Hugo Grotius (1583-1645), see Knight (1925); for a complete bibliography of his works, see Meulen and Diermanse (1950); and for works on Grotius published during the seventeenth century, see Meulen and Diermanse (1961). The popularity of Grotius during the eighteenth century was partly due to the growing interest in the concept of natural law.

19. For a biography of Charles-Louis de Secondat, baron de la Brède et de Montesquieu (1689-1755), see Shackleton (1961). A list of his works is given in Vian (1872) and Marchand (1960); and, for bibliographies of works on Montesquieu, see Cabeen (1947 and 1955). For a review of recent studies, see Rosso (1976). Parts of *De l'esprit des lois* were read to Bonnet from the manuscript copy in the possession of Pierre Mussard (1690-1767), before the book was actually published. Recalling this event in his autobiography, Bonnet wrote that he was seized by enthusiasm: 'Il me sembla que j'écoutais les instructions d'une intelligence supérieure à l'homme et qui me faisaient passer tout d'un coup de l'état d'enfance à celui d'homme fait. [...] je me mis à prédire que cet ouvrage étonnant causerait une grande révolution dans le monde pensant' (Savioz 1948b:139). He noted with particular admiration Montesquieu's literary quality, erudition, and elevated principles. In 1753-1754 he corresponded with Montesquieu and suggested to him a slightly different definition of law, which was not accepted by Montesquieu (see Montesquieu 1914, 2:489-91, 510-11, 514-19, 525-26; and Savioz 1950). In 1760 Bonnet discussed his own view in the final chapter of his *Essai analytique*, entitled 'Observations sur quelques endroits de *l'Esprit des Loix* rélatifs à cette Analyse' (1760:541-52 and B.O., 6:409-17/14:318-31). Needham owned the 1750 Genève edition of *De l'esprit des lois* (*Catalogue* 1782:87). For Bonnet's relations with Montesquieu, see Humbert (1858), Savioz (1950), and Postigliola (1978).

20. Rousseau was living at Wootton, near the border of Derbyshire. The day before, Bonnet had written a similar remark to John Turton (see Leigh, 5406).

21. In his biography of Saussure, Senebier (1801:37-39) reported: 'Lorsque Desaussure commençait ses études de philosophie, l'électricité occupait tous les physiciens. Franklin faisait en Amérique ses grandes découvertes; Nollet les contestait à Paris. Desaussure voulut que l'expérience et la raison jugeassent pour lui entre ces deux hommes célèbres, qui s'opposaient des expériences et des raisonnemens; l'examen de cette controverse lui fit faire des découvertes qu'il publia en 1766, dans sa *Dissertatio physica de electricitate* [this dissertation was actually written by Amadeus Lullin under

interessante, qui lui a valu de nouvelles Découvertes. Quand vous m'écrivés n'oubliés pas les *Chinois* et leurs Auteurs les *Egyptiens*. C'est peut être à eux qu'il a été reservé de confondre l'incrédulité. Je vous embrasse, mon très cher Ami, du fond de ce Coeur qui vous est bien connu et où vous aurés toûjours une bonne place.[a]

[a]Addisson étoit fait pour voyager avec vous.[a] [22]

[ADDRESS] Paris Mr Néédham, de la Societé Royale d'Angleterre

MANUSCRIPTS
BPUG, MS Bonnet 72:59*v*-6o*r*; MS Bonnet 85:181*v*-182*r*.

EDITIONS
'A force d'Esprit [...] compassion' published in Leigh, 5406.

TEXT NOTES
    a. B: *omitted b*. B: charmé, mon cher Ami, *c*. B: l'attention que je leur donnerai *d*. B: compassion. Je vous embrasse &c

25

Bonnet to Needham – Geneva, 28 November 1766

à Genève le 28.e 9bre 1766.

Je vous remercie[a] de vôtre Abbé *Poncelet*.[1] Je vous avouerai que je prefère de beaucoup vos Principes et même ceux de Mr de Buffon aux siens. Il ne vous rend pas même la Justice qui vous étoit duë à l'un et à l'autre.[2] Il employe

the supervision of Saussure (Genevae 1766)]. Il paraît ici comme le rapporteur impartial des opinions de Franklin et de Nollet; mais peu content de rapporter leurs expériences, et de les comparer avec les conséquences qu'ils en tiraient; il en imagina de nouvelles pour estimer la solidité de celles qui sont l'objet de son examen; on y remarque sa pénétration pour discerner le noeud des difficultés, et trouver des moyens sûrs pour le dénouer. Il établit partout, d'une manière originale, la théorie de Franklin, et démontre la faiblesse des objections de Nollet; comme celui-ci vivait encore, il laisse tirer les conclusions de ses expériences, sans se permettre de les énoncer.'
    22. See letter 23, n.25.

    1. There is evidence (Sonntag 1983:548) to suggest that Needham may have accompanied Poncelet's book with a letter to Bonnet, which we have been unable to trace. Very little is known of the life of the abbé Polycarpe Poncelet, an agronomist mainly remembered for his *Histoire naturelle du froment* (Paris 1779). A list of his published works is provided in *B.U.* (34:45). Bonnet is referring to *La nature dans la reproduction des êtres vivans, des animaux, des végétaux; mais particulierement du froment* (Paris 1766) which was published as the second part of Poncelet (1766a) with a different title page and different pagination. The following brief mention of this work appeared in *C.L.* (7:60-61): 'Tout ce qu'on peut dire de plus certain, c'est que M. l'abbé Poncelet de Paris et M. Robinet d'Amsterdam écrivent sur la nature d'une manière très-différente.' A long laudatory review of Poncelet (1766a and 1766b) appeared in *L'Année littéraire* (1766, 4:289-305), but most of it was devoted to the first part of the volume.
    2. Poncelet (1766b:iii-iv) wrote in his 'Avertissement' that he had read many dissertations in scientific journals in addition to 'Loewenhoek, Swarmerdamm, Grew, Malpighi, Hartsoecker, mais plus attentivement que pas un MM. de Buffon & Needham; on s'en appercevra bien, si l'on se donne la peine de parcourir cet Ouvrage'. Needham's microscopical observations are mentioned only once by Poncelet (1766b:57), whereas Buffon is often referred to; see Poncelet (1766b:92, 119-21, 132-34, 138-39).

fréquemment vos Idées comme si elles étoient à lui. Il croit toûjours prouver ou démontrer, et il ne[b] démontre rien. Quest-ce, je vous prie, que cette *Force résistante* et cette *Force active* qui, suivant lui, forme le Germe en un instant?[3] Il semble n'avoir rien lû. Les Ouvrages de M.[r] de Haller, ʿles miens,ʿ ceux même de M.[r] de Réaumur paroissent lui être profondement inconnus. Il parle de la multiplication des Pucerons[4] comme si personne n'en avoit traité avant lui, et il y a 26 ans que je fis cette Découverte: Mr de Réaumur la publia en 1742,[5] et moi même en 1745.[6] Il estropie les Polypes de nôtre Ami comme il estropie son nom: il l'appelle *du Tremblay*,[7] preuve qu'il n'a pas beaucoup étudie cet Auteur. Il dit qu'aucun Physicien ne doute de la *circulation de la Sève*,[8] et il ne sait pas que Mr Duhamel[9] et moi[10] nous-nous sommes plus à creuser un peu le sujet, et que cet habile Homme cite des autorités pour et contre qui lui rendent la question très problêmatique. Il admet l'organization des Mineraux,[11] et il ne

3. Bonnet is alluding to the following passage: 'Cette union intime que les deux sexes desirent vient-elle à avoir lieu, les particules vivantes & brutes de la matière renfermées dans les organes sexuels, s'échappent, se rapprochent, s'unissent, se mêlent, les deux puissances active & résistante, qui en sont inséparables, développent au même instant toute leur force; ensorte que la puissance active du mâle est balancée par la puissance résistante de la femelle, & reciproquement la puissance active de la femelle par la puissance résistante du mâle' (Poncelet 1766b:34-35).

4. Poncelet (1766b:128-30).

5. 'Addition à l'histoire des Pucerons, donnée dans le troisième volume, sur la maniére dont ils se multiplient' in Réaumur (1734-1742, 6:523-68).

6. Bonnet (1745, vol.i) and B.O., 1:1-113/1:1-154.

7. Poncelet (1766b:121, 126). See also letter 1, n.10.

8. Poncelet (1766b:142) wrote: 'la circulation de la séve dans les plants, ignorée pendant longtems, découverte par M. Malpighi, & dont personne ne doute plus au-jourd'hui'.

9. Duhamel Du Monceau wrote at the end of a section of his book *La Physique des arbres* (Paris 1758), which was dedicated to an analysis of the question of whether sap circulated in trees: 'Je crois [...] le retour des liqueurs vers les racines bien prouvé; mais je n'ai garde d'en conclure affirmativement la circulation de la seve. Il me paroît que toutes les preuves qu'on a apportées pour établir cette circulation sont insuffisantes' (Duhamel Du Monceau 1758, 2:326). For short biographies of the influential agronomist, mechanical engineer, and natural historian Henri-Louis Duhamel Du Monceau (1700-1782), a member of the Parisian Académie and one of Bonnet's major correspondents, see St. Le Tourneur, *D.B.F.*, 12 (1970) 21-22, and Jon Eklund, *D.S.B.*, 4 (1971) 223-25, to whose lists of secondary bibliography should be added at least Bourde (1967, 1:253-76, 355-65) and Plantefol (1969). Bonnet and Duhamel Du Monceau corresponded for many years. Eighty-two letters from Duhamel Du Monceau to Bonnet are preserved in the BPUG; two of Bonnet's replies are published in B.O., 5, pt.2:403-10/12:484-96.

10. In the *Contemplation de la nature*, Bonnet wrote: 'Des expériences faites, par une main très-habile, démontrent que le mouvement de la Sève dépend uniquement des alternatives du chaud & du froid, des vicissitudes du jour & de la nuit. Ces expériences prouvent que ce mouvement est progressif pendant le jour, rétrograde pendant la nuit; que la Sève s'élève pendant le jour des Racines aux Feuilles, qu'elle descend pendant la nuit des Feuilles aux Racines. On voit cette Liqueur soulever, pendant le jour, le Mercure contenu dans un Tuyau de verre adapté à une Branche qui végète, & le laisser retomber à l'aproche de la nuit. En un mot, il en est de la marche de la Sève à peu près comme de celle de la Liqueur contenuë dans le Tuyau d'un Thermomètre. Tout se réduit à de simples balancemens' (Bonnet 1764, 2:48; and B.O., 4, pt.2:141/8:452).

11. Discussing the nature of minerals and 'la reproduction des individus du regne minéral', Poncelet (1766b:86-88) wrote: 'On ne peut donc raisonner sur cela que par analogie. Nous sommes assurés de la manière dont les animaux perpétuent leurs espèces. Nous savons que les végétaux ont beaucoup de rapport de ce côté avec les animaux; d'où vient ne conclurions-nous pas que les minéraux se reproduisent d'une façon approchante? [...] Nous avons établi dans le corps de cet Ouvrage, que la différence des animaux avec les végétaux ne provient que du plus ou du moins d'exaltation de la matière; n'en pourions-nous pas dire autant des mineraux, qui n'ont de matière exaltée, que ce qu'il en faut précisément pour dessiner une organisation très-brute, très-grossière,

scait pas que Bourguet et Robinet[12] ont fait des Livres pour la prouver. S'il ignore tout cela, il ignore beaucoup et il ne devroit pas écrire. S'il a feint de l'ignorer, il est exposé au reproche de *Plagiat*. Enfin, en parlant des Polypes des *Infusions*, dont vous connoissés la prodigieuse petitesse, il ajoute; *qu'il auroit fallu faire sur eux les mêmes Expériences que Mr du Trembley a faites sur les siens; mais qu'il n'a pas compté assés sur son adresse pour les tenter.*[13] Cela sent fort un Homme qui connoit peu les Polypes *à Bras*: étoit il nécessaire^d de dire une pareille chose? Il

très-imparfaite, suffisante cependant pour opérer la reproduction, la nutrition, & la conservation des espèces de ce regne?'

12. An accurate biography and list of the publications and manuscripts of the French Huguenot polymath Louis Bourguet (1678-1742), who first emigrated to Zürich from Nîmes and later settled in Neuchâtel, is provided by François Ellenberger in *D.S.B.*, 15 (1978) 52-59, which also lists secondary sources on Bourguet. See also the study by Crucitti Ullrich (1974) on the *Bibliothèque italique*, one of Bourguet's most important editorial enterprises. Bourguet expressed his views on the organisation of the mineral kingdom in many works in which he also recognised and documented the organic origin of fossils. See 'Lettre de Mr. L. B. P. à Monsieur Antoine Vallisnieri [...] sur la gradation & l'echelle des fossiles', in *Bibliothèque italique* (1728, 2:99-131); *Lettres philosophiques sur la formation des sels et des crystaux, et sur la génération & le mechanisme organique des plantes et des animaux* (Amsterdam 1729; 2nd ed., Amsterdam 1762); and *Traité des petrifications* (Paris 1742). Bourguet firmly opposed the idea of the 'vegetation' of minerals held by some previous authors; see Bourguet (1728:107-108 and 1729:79-80). For Bourguet's ideas on the process of crystallisation, see Metzger (1969:44-52, 151-55); for those on palaeontology, physical geology, and sedimentology, see Bork (1974:54-72); and for his views on the notion of organisation, see Schiller (1978:28-33). Some evidence suggests that Bouguet might have influenced the young Bonnet, not only because Bourguet spent most of his life trying to develop an interest in natural history in the French-speaking part of Switzerland, but also because his mechanistic conception of nature and his belief in the great chain of being and in preformation were later shared by Bonnet (see B.O., 4, pt.1:361 n.10/8:208 n.10). Bonnet listed him among those who had seen the phenomenon of parthenogenesis before he himself had observed it (Bonnet 1745:24; B.O., 1:11/1:17; Savioz 1948b:62; Bourguet 1729:77-79).

Short biographies of Jean-Baptiste-René Robinet (1733-1820), such as that in *B.U.* (36:184-85) and that by Jacques Roger, *D.S.B.*, 11 (1975) 492-93, have now been superceded by Murphy (1976a), who documents fully the different stages of Robinet's literary career and social commitments, from his early period, in which he justified a hierarchical order, to his advocacy of administrative, educational, and economic reform, and finally to his involvement in the French Revolution. Bonnet is alluding to the four-volume edition of Robinet's work *De la nature* (Amsterdam 1761-1766), in which a discussion of crystallisation is provided (1:285-334 and 4:176-96; see also 4:103-105, where Bourguet's ideas are acknowledged). Bonnet was acquainted with Robinet's work. When the first volume appeared anonymously, it could not be legally distributed in France; and in 1762 the Catholic church included the book in the *Index* (Murphy 1976a:191-92). Its authorship was much discussed: some attributed it to Helvétius, others to Diderot (*C.L.*, 4:490-91). Formey believed that Bonnet himself might have been the author and wrote to him asking whether this was the case (Marx 1976:353 n.70). In January 1762, Robinet revealed his authorship. In *De la nature* (1761-1766, 4:87-93), Robinet discussed at length Bonnet's ideas concerning the existence of brute matter. Robinet believed that stones, metals, and fossils, as well as fluids, were endowed with the faculties of nutrition, growth, and generation and therefore had an innate vital principle that made them similar to all living bodies in the 'échelle universelle des Etres'. Such ideas, leading as they did to a universal animalisation of the three kingdoms (Robinet 1761-1766, 4:115-16) were disliked and criticised by Bonnet (Marx 1976:353-56). For discussions of Robinet's work, see Gode-von Aesch (1941:140-48), Rosso (1954), Mayer (1954). Vernière (1954, 2:642-52), Mortier (1954:356-58), Metzger (1969:121), Roger (1963:642-53), and Rétat (1971:430-37). Information on his unpublished correspondence is given by Murphy (1976b).

13. Poncelet (1766b:126-27): 'J'apperçus quelque tems après de pareils Polypes dans une vieille infusion de feuilles de rose. Pour constater leur nature de vrais Polypes, il eût fallu faire subir à quelques-uns d'entre'eux les Expériences de M. du Tremblay; mais comment m'y serois-je pris pour cela? L'animal est si petit, que j'en regardai les essais comme impraticables, ne me sentant point assez d'adresse pour les entreprendre, j'y renonçai.'

rapporte encore des Expériences qu'il a faites sur les Feuilles des Plantes,[14] dont le seul énoncé me^c prouve qu'il n'est ni Observateur ni Logicien.

Toutes ces remarques ^cne sont que pour vous^c, mon cher Ami; je les écris très à la hate. Vous méritiés un sufrage plus instruit; je croi de tout mon Coeur à la Catholicité de Mr Poncelet[15]; mais un Ecrivain qui admet que les sensations des Animaux ne sont que des modifications de l'*organisation*, s'expose à de terribles conséquences.[16] Si vous scavés quelques détails sur cet Auteur veuillés me les aprendre.^e

[ADDRESS] Paris, Mr Néédham de la Societé Royale.

MANUSCRIPTS
  BPUG, MS Bonnet 72:78v-79r; MS Bonnet 85:182v.

TEXT NOTES
  a. B: remercie, mon cher Ami, *b.* B: ne prouve ni ne *c.* B: *omitted d.* B: raisonable *e.* B: apprendre. Tout à vous &c

26

Needham to Bonnet – Paris, 6 January 1767

à Paris, Le 6. janvier 1767.
rüe des Postes près l'estrapade.

Vous divinerés facilement la raison, mon cher ami, pourquoi j'ai tardé la reponse à votre lettre du 25. Novembre.[1] J'ai compté dans peu de jours après cette date de vous remercier du plaisir, que vous m'avez donné par la lecture

---

14. Poncelet (1766b:139-41).

15. In the 'Avertissement' of his book Poncelet (1766b:v) had stated: 'Une chose cependant m'embarrassoit beaucoup, c'étoit cette matière exaltée, toujours en mouvement, & remplie de corpuscules essentiellement doués d'un principe de vie, que j'etablissois comme base de tout mon systême. Je craignois que l'on n'abusât de cette découverte pour expliquer les actions de l'Homme dans le sens des Matérialistes; en un mot, je craignois de donner à la Foi Catholique, dont les intérêts m'ont toujours paru préférable à tout ce qu'il y a de plus avantageux dans le monde.' Poncelet believed that he had avoided possible criticism by placing man in both the animal and the intellectual worlds.

16. Poncelet believed there was a continuum extending through nature and the physical body of man and that the motion of particles could be transmitted from one to the other. He explained the sensation of touch in the following way: 'l'individu palpet-il un corps étranger tout-à-fait nuisible à l'accord qui regne dans sa constitution organique, un fer rouge par exemple; à l'instant les particules de matière exaltée, qui composent les houppes nerveuses, éprouvent une solution de continuité; elles subissent une altération violente, qui se communique bientôt aux organes du cerveau, où sont placées les particules les plus exaltées de la matière; ces particules éprouvent un choc dur, qui les étonne, qui les ébranle, qui trouble leur douce harmonie, & qui produit le mouvement discordant & desagréable, que l'on nomme douleur' (Poncelet 1766b:58-59).

1. The date given here by Needham seems to suggest that Bonnet wrote a letter to Needham on 25 November, but no copy of such a letter is preserved in the BPUG. As Bonnet kept drafts of all the letters he wrote, it seems more likely that Needham misread 28 as 25, and that Bonnet added a postscript to his letter of 28 November saying that he was enclosing a copy of the *Projet*, which had been distributed on 26 November (see n.2 below), for Needham to see and then send to Adam Smith (see n.7 below).

du projet de pacification,[2] en vous felicitant, et tous mes bons amis de Geneve sur le retablissement de la paix; mais *O! curas hominum! O quantum est in rebus inane!*[3] Vous avez vecu parmi les hommes en observateur pendant nombre d'années, et moi aussi, et cependant il nous faut avouer, que nous n'en connoissons rien. La raison est assés simple; ce que dans la pratique nous partons de nous memes pour en juger des autres malgré nos belles abstractions; et par ce moyen il arrive que, le sentiment present emportant toujours sur les speculations passées, les bons ne comprendront jamais les mauvais, et reciproquement, ni les gens raisonables ceux qui deraisonnent. Vous dites très bien, mon bon ami, que je m'interesse pour vous, vous en souffrés, tout comme l'ame d'un homme vertueux souffre dans cette vie mortelle par l'indisposition du corps; donnés moi donc quatre mots sur l'état present de Geneve, et s'il vous reste encore quelque lueur d'esperance dit moi tout ce que vous croyés prevoir. Quel abominable projet cel de vos demagogues[4] qu'on m'a raconté, il y a trois jours? Quelque peu de tems avant l'assemblée du Concile general du 15. decembre,[5] dit on, ils ont proposé entre eux dans les cercles l'approbation, ou la rejection de la pacification sous condition necessaire, et indispensable d'union de la part de la minorité à la majorité, quand il falloit voter en concile general. Par la il est arrivé que la minorité en effet a emportée sur la majorite dans le total de la republique. Car si les trois cens et quatre vingt voix, qui dans leur cercles ont votés en faveur de l'acceptation avaient gardé la liberté de s'unir selon leurs sentimens aux cinq cens et quinze acceptans dans le concile general, 895 contre 700 auraient donné la paix à leur patrie. Vous me sçaurés dire, si ce que je viens d'entendre est vrai, ou non; je souhaite qu'il soit faux de tout mon cœur pour l'honneur de l'humanité. J'ai vu hier Madame d'emville,[6] et je dois diner avec elle aujourdhui, nous nous ne voyons jamais sans parler de nos amis de Geneve, et très souvent de vous meme particulierement; elle m'a chargée de tout ce que l'estime la mieux fondée, et l'amitié la plus sensible peut se former en votre

---

2. *Projet de Règlement de l'Illustre Médiation, pour la pacification des dissentions de la République de Genève.* This pamphlet, consisting of 48 printed pages, is dated 23 November 1766, and is signed by le chevalier de Beauteville, Escher de Keffiken, J. C. Heidegger, B. Sigism. Ougspourguer, and F. Sinner. It was distributed to the electing body on Thursday 26 November and on the following days. It was rejected by the General Council on 15 December 1766 by 1095 votes to 515; see also Rivoire (1897, nr. 947).

3. Persius, *Saturae*, i, 1.

4. Among the *Représentants* were men of note, such as François-Henri d'Ivernois, Jean-André de Luc, Jacques-François de Luc, Jacques-Antoine Duroveray, Etienne Clavière, Flournois, Ami Melly, Jacques Vieusseux, and Jean Des Arts.

5. See n.2 above.

6. Marie-Louise-Nicole La Rochefoucauld, duchesse d'Enville (Anville) (1716-1794), was the grand-daughter of the duc François La Rochefoucauld (1613-1680). Hers was one of the brilliant Paris salons, and attendance was *de rigueur* for every foreigner of note. In a letter to Walpole, madame Du Deffand described her thus: 'elle n'a pas les grands airs de nos grandes dames, elle a le ton assez animé, elle est un peu entichée de la philosophie moderne: mais elle la pratique plus qu'elle ne la prêche' (*W.C.*, 4:47). While in Geneva in 1762, the duchesse d'Enville met Voltaire (Best.D10478, D10789) and Bonnet (Savioz 1948b:215), and, during a second visit in 1765, also Adam Smith (see A. Smith 1977:111). On two occasions she used her influence in favour of Bonnet: first, in 1762, by helping to prevent the censor's blocking the circulation of Bonnet's *Considérations sur les corps organisés* in France, and later by asking Buffon whether he would support the election of Bonnet as a foreign member of the Paris Académie des sciences (see Savioz 1948b:215, 303-305; and Marx 1976:343, 345).

faveur. Je n'ai pas manqué toute suite après avoir reçu votre lettre d'ecrire à M^r· Smith[7] en lui envoyant le meme plan de pacification, que j'ai reçu, après l'avoir bien étudié moi-meme, il est très sensible aux sentimens, que vous temoignés pour lui, et vous remercie de tout son cœur de vos bontés. Tout ce que vous me dites sur l'abbé Poncelet est trop juste pour pouvoir en disconvenir; mais je l'avais parcouru alors assés rapidement, et meme à present je ne regarde son ouvrage, que comme une esquisse de ce qu'il a envie de donner au public plus en detail. J'ai bien senti, qu'il avait adopté des idées, qui ne lui appartenaient pas sans rendre justice à ceux de qui il les avait empruntées. C'etait en effet le Geni de la fable. Mais s'il reprend son ouvrage, comme je crois, il pourra reparer tous ses torts, et meme corriger tous les autres defauts, dans une edition plus ample, ou les idées seront plus exactes, mieux liées ensemble, et suffisamment detaillées pour leur donner une certaine clarté, autant que l'obscurité naturelle du sujet lui permettra. Comme je n'avais jamais entendu parler de l'auteur avant la publication de son ouvrage, j'ecris une petite note à son libraire. Voici tout ce que j'appris de lui par ce moyen.—'M^r· l'abbé Poncelet est un homme de 42. à 45. ans; je crois qu'il se donne à l'education d'un seigneur en Lorraine; son caractere est doux; mais de la plus grande vivacité: il est actuellement à Bar-le-duc.' Presentés, s'il vous plait, mes respects à Madame, et mes complimens à M^r· de Sausure. M^r· Turton[8] est parti de Paris pour retourner à Londres, portant avec lui l'estime, et les regrets de tout le monde; jamais anglais a été si repandu que lui à Paris. Spalanzani avance, mais lentement.[9]

   Je vous embrasse, mon cher ami, de tout mon cœur,
   et j'ai le plasir d'etre avec estime
            votre affectionné Needham.

MANUSCRIPT
 BPUG, MS Bonnet 29:30*r*-30*v*.

7. For a biography of Adam Smith (1723-1790), see Rae (1895); for a list of his writings, see Vanderblue (1939); and for a bibliography of works on Smith, see Amano (1961:1-132). No letters from Needham to Adam Smith are published in Smith's correspondence (A. Smith 1977). Adam Smith met Bonnet during his visit to Geneva in late 1765. According to Rae (1895:191), Bonnet was one 'of the warmest of Smith's Swiss friends'. Bonar (1932:32, 151) lists three books by Bonnet (1745, 1755, and 1760) in Smith's library. When, in 1775, Patrick Clason (d.1811) was asked by Bonnet to forward two of his books (Bonnet 1754 and 1769a) to David Hume, he sent them via Smith. In the accompanying letter to Smith, Clason wrote that Bonnet's 'religious ideas are probably different from Mr. Hume's – mais qu'est que ça fait' (A. Smith 1977:181). Smith in turn, when sending the books to Hume, wrote: 'Mr. Bonnet [...] is one of the worthiest, and best hearted men in Geneva or indeed in the world; notwithstanding he is one of the most religious' (A. Smith 1977:181-82).

8. In 1752 John Turton (1735-1806) took a B.A. at Queen's College, Oxford. In 1761 he obtained a Radcliffe travelling fellowship from University College, Oxford, and studied in Leiden. There he became acquainted with Allamand, who wrote letters of introduction for him to Trembley and Bonnet when Turton visited Geneva (BPUG, MS Bonnet 27:17*r*). During his visit to Italy and Austria in 1763-1764, he often wrote to Bonnet, providing him with information on the reception of his works in those countries. Fifteen letters from Turton to Bonnet are preserved in the BPUG. Back in England he was made a Fellow of the Royal Society and of the College of Physicians. He assisted Saussure when the latter visited England in 1768 (Freshfield 1920:105). In 1782 he was appointed Physician in ordinary to the Queen and in 1797 to king George III. On Turton, see Norman Moore, *D.N.B.*, 57 (1899) 376-77, and Leigh, 3065 and 4073.

9. Needham is alluding to the translation and edition of Spallanzani's work *Saggio di osservazioni microscopiche*, on which he was working at the time; see letter 19, n.2.

27

Bonnet to Needham – Genthod, 7 March 1767

Genthod le 7.ᵉ Mars 1767.

J'ai sous les yeux vôtre bonne Lettre du 6.ᵉ de Janvier mon cher et digne Ami. J'y répons plus tard que je ne l'avois pensé: mais nos malheureuses affaires me dérobent trop de ce tems que j'aimerois à donner à mes Amis.

ᵃOn a travaillé et on travaille encore actuellement à engager nos fiers Tribuns à faire une démarche qui puisse fléchir le principal Garant. Jusqu'ici tous les efforts ont été vains. Un accomodement domestique, innocemment et très imprudemment conçu, clandestinement projetté par des Hommes en Place et dont tous les Principes sembloient s'y opposer, cet accomodement dis-je, a rendu les Chefs de l'Opposition plus opiniatres et moins traitables.ᵃ ¹

ᵃLa fermeté avec laquelle d'autres Hommes en Place se sont opposés à cette marche a forcé les Principaux Acteurs à abandonner leur Projet. Il étoit ruineux pour le Gouvernement: on le sacrifioit à la Paix, et je vous laisse à juger, si une Paix achettée a un tel prix auroit été durable.ᵃ

ᵃNous attendons patiemment le *Prononcé* ou le Jugement des Garans.² Le congrès de Soleure s'en occupe fréquemment, et vous pouvés compter qu'ils ne donneront pas gain de cause aux Représentans.³ Vous en avés pour caution la fameuse Déclaration du 24 Juillet, par laquelle les Médiateurs ont justifié pleinement le Gouvernement. Leur Prononcé ne scauroit contredire une Déclaration si forte et si précise.ᵃ

ᵃCe qu'on vous à rapporté de la manoeuvre des Tribuns dans leurs Conciles avant la journée du 15 de Décembre, m'a été donné pour très vrai. Il n'est pas douteux que cette manoeuvre a fait échouer le *Projet de Pacification.*ᵃ

Vous ne pouvés trop exprimer à M.ᵐᵉ la Duchesse d'Enville, combien je suis reconnoissant de son obligeant souvenir, et tous les voeux que je ne cesserai de faire pour son bonheur et pour celui de sa Famille. Je n'oublierai jamais les moments trop courts où cette respectable Emilie mêloit sa Philosophie avec la mienne. J'ai fort regretté de n'avoir pu lire avec elle tout cet *Essai Analytique* qu'elle saisissoit avec tant de pénétration ᵃet de justesseᵃ. Je sçais si elle aura trouvé à Paris quelcun qui ait pris auprès d'elle une place que j'aurois enviée.

Rafraichissés moi dans le souvenir de mon digne Confrère en Philosophie M.ʳ Smith, et aprenés-moi s'il a fait publier la nouvelle Traduction Françoise de sa *Métaphysique de l'Ame*. Le premier Traducteur⁴ ᵇl'avoit estropiéᵇ.

---

1. Bonnet also mentioned this 'plan clandestin' in two letters addressed to Haller on 4 and 11 March 1767; see Sonntag (1983:582-86).

2. The *Prononcé des Puissances garantes du Règlement de 1738*, consisting of 32 printed pages, finally appeared on 20 November 1767. It was signed by le chevalier de Beauteville, Escher de Keffiken, J. C. Heidegger, F. Sinner, and B. Sigism. Ougspourguer. It was read on 27 November 1767 in the Council of Two Hundred and distributed on 1 December; see also Rivoire (1897, nr. 1004).

3. Actually 25 July; see letter 23, n.23.

4. Adam Smith's first book, *The Theory of moral sentiments*, appeared in London in 1759. A French translation with the title *Métaphisique de l'ame, ou théorie des sentimens moraux, traduite de l'anglois de M. Adam Smith*, [...] *par M**** appeared in Paris in 1764 and was the work of Marc-Antoine Eidous

Grand merci de vôtre notice sur l'Abbé Poncelet. Je m'étois bien douté qu'il étoit très vif et qu'il voltigeoit comme un Papillon sur la superficie des Objets. Je ne reviens point de mon étonnement quand je vois un Ecrivain entreprendre de traiter la Matière la plus difficile, la plus composée, la plus profonde de toute la Physique, comme on traiteroit une avanture de Roman.

Quelle foule de faits et de Faits divers ne faut-il pas avoir présens à l'Esprit lorsqu'on écrit sur la *Reproduction des Etres vivans*! Avec quel art^c, avec quelle Logique, avec quelles précautions ne faut il pas analyser ces Faits, les comparer, les combiner et chercher leurs Résultats immédiats ou médiats et les Résultats de ces Résultats!

L'Abbé Poncelet n'a pas même le mérite d'avoir connu les Faits essentiels. Je ne connois point d'Ouvrage qui en soit plus apauvri^d, et le peu qu'il en employe, il l'expose mal. Il a crû qu'avec deux ou trois idées ^{e}d'assés mauvaise Métaphysique^e, il pourroit aisément faire un Livre. Il a tourné et retourné ces deux ou trois Idées; il les a souflées comme un Emailleur soufle le Verre, et il a appellé cela faire un *Traité de la Reproduction des Etres vivans*.

Si j'étois en liaison avec lui je ne lui conseillerois pas de perfectioner un travail dont les Principes sont si contraires à ceux de la bonne Physique. Il ne fera jamais rien de bon de sa *Force active* et de sa *Force résistante*. Ce ne sont là que des mots dont se payent des Lecteurs qui ne scavent pas les choses.

Je voudrois fort que vôtre Traduction de l'Abbé Spallanzani avançat un peu plus. Vos *Notes* vous retardent apparemment. Ne manqués pas de me dire où vous en êtes ^{f}d'un travail qui ne ressemble gueres à celui de Mr Poncelet.^{f}

J'ai passé le plus triste Hiver. ^{a}M.^{r} le Conseiller De la Rive a été tourmenté d'un dépot et d'un Ulcère à la jambe, qui l'a tenu sur le grabat, et ma pauvre Femme a eu un retour violent de ses anciens maux, dont elle est encore fort sécouée.^{a} Janvier a été terrible; un froid de 13 degrés et 2 pieds de Neige dans la Campagne. Nous n'avons pas quitté ^{g}ce lieu^g depuis le 18.e Décembre.^{h}

^{a}Notre ami de Saussure vous fait ses complimens et sa bonne tante y joint les siens.^{a}

Demeurés vous fixé à Paris? Y fréquentés-vous des gens de Lettres du Coeur et de l'Esprit desquels vous soyés content et sur? Êtes vous enfin indépendant et ne gouvernés-vous que vous même?

Vous sçavés, mon digne Ami, tous les sentimens que vous a voués vôtre fidèle Ami.

[ADDRESS] Paris, Mr Néedham de la Societé Royale

MANUSCRIPTS
BPUG, MS Bonnet 72:119v-120r; MS Bonnet 85:183r-183v.

(1727-1790). Bonnet's criticism of the quality of this translation is reminiscent of Grimm's (*C.L.*, 6:144) observation of 1764: 'ôtez à un livre métaphysique sa précision, et il ne reste plus qu'un jargon obscur et vague, qui est celui du traducteur de la *Théorie des sentimens moraux*.' Smith (1977:161) himself was very dissatisfied with it. Later, the son of the duchesse d'Anville, Louis-Alexandre, duc de La Rochefoucauld-d'Anville (1743-1792), began a new translation, but abandoned the task (A. Smith 1977:233-34) when he saw the translation produced by the abbé Jean-Louis Blavet (1719-1809), *Théorie des sentimens moraux. Traduction nouvelle de l'anglois de M. Smith* [...] *par M. l'Abbé Blavet* (Paris 1774-1775). For early reactions to and foreign translations of Smith's book, and for a selected list of works treating Smith's ethical thought, see A. Smith (1976:25-34).

TEXT NOTES
   a. B: *omitted b.* B: ne l'avoit pas bien rendue *c.* B: soin *d.* B: dépourvu *e.* B: d'une Métaphysique presque scholastique *f.* B: de ce travail. *g.* B: la Campagne *h.* B: Décembre de l'année dernière.

28

Needham to Bonnet – Paris, 14 December 1767

Paris, dec: 14. 1767.
rüe des Postes.

Je vous remercie, mon très cher ami, sincerement du *Prononcé* des Puissances garantes,[1] que vous avez eu la bonté de m'envoyer; vous me rendez justice en vous persuadant, que je m'interesse pour vous, et pour tous mes amis dans vos malheurs. Je m'interesse meme pour la bourgeoisie, qui se laisse seduire par la folie de certaines têtes échauffées, dont le foyer se trouve dans la personne de J. J. Rousseau; parce que la folie est contagieuse comme la peste, et opere presque malgré nous selon nos temperamens; dans la morale comme dans la physique les hommes sont bien à plaindre, et meritent très souvent plutot compassion, que colere. Quant' à moi je trouve le prononcé très juste, et très moderé de la part des puissances, qui sont en état de commander, et de contraindre. Dans un siecle moins doux on les aura pas menagé avec tant de sang froid, et de moderation. On y resiste cependant encore, et malgré cela on ne parle pas ici, comme si on voulait employer la force: que faire? Le seul remede, qu'on propose, et qui est, dit on, decidé en conseil est encore plus mauvais, que la force, qui ne pourra tomber que sur les chefs du parti. S'il s'execute, comme on pretend, il sera absolument destructif de la republique. C'est de batir un ville à versoy,[2] ou il y aura pleine liberté de conscience, et de commerce pour tous ceux qui

1. See letter 27, n.2.
2. The project of founding a town and a port at Versoix in the county of Gex, a few miles from Geneva, was first formulated by Voltaire in a letter of 10 February 1767 to the chevalier de Beauteville: 'Si on voulait effectivement rendre la vengeance utile, il faudrait établir un port au *pays de Gex*; ouvrir une grande route avec la Franche-Comté; commercer directement de Lyon avec la Suisse par Versoy; attirer à soi tout le commerce de Genève; entretenir seulement un corps de garde perpétuel dans trois villages entre Genève et le pays de Gex; cela coûterait beaucoup, mais Genève, qui fait pour deux millions de contrebande par an, serait anéantie dans peu d'années. Si on se borne à saisir quelques pintes de lait à nos paysannes, et à les empêcher d'acheter des souliers à Genève, on n'aura pas fait une campagne bien glorieuse' (Best.D13937). Having noticed that the blockade of Geneva was in fact having an adverse economic effect on France, the duc de Choiseul decided, in April 1767, to take up the suggestion. Voltaire was happy to help and hoped to create a true city of tolerance. The news spread at once in Geneva and caused alarm not only among the *Représentants* but also among those *Négatifs* who had supported the blockade. In his letter to Haller of 6 November 1767, Bonnet commented, 'V[oltaire] nous déteste et bâtiroit 20 maisons pour le plaisir de nous faire du mal. Il ne bâtiroit qu'en ce genre; partout ailleurs il tâche de démolir. La PROVIDENCE a permis les tremblemens de Terre, les inondations, les Hérésies et Arouet' (Sonntag 1983:684). Although some work was undertaken, the project failed because of its financial costs, because of the difficulty of obtaining toleration for Protestants in France, and because of the downfall of the duc de Choiseul in 1770. For secondary literature on the Versoix project, see Ferrier (1922 and 1926:96-98), Baldensperger (1931:602-603), Donvez (1955), Ceitac (1956a:184-97), Gay (1965:232-33), and Besterman (1976:514-15).

veulent s'etablir, et d'abandonner Geneve à son mauvais esprit, qui le minera infalliblement, et plus surement qu'une force militaire. On est si fort dans ce gout, qu'on propose de plus, dit on, d'avoir quatre villes dans le meme gout aux quatre extremités du Royaume, pour recueillir de pais étrangér tous les Protestans français, qui veulent revenir dans leur patrie, aussi bien que que[a] tous les juifs, ou autre forme de religion quelconque, qui desireront de s'y établir. Les nouveaux philosophes, qui tendent tous au materialisme par un vice essentiel à leur mauvaise façon de raisonner, et qui veulent tout raporter au climat, ont plus faits eux memes par leurs principes pour dementir leur systeme, que tous les croyans ensemble par leurs écrits, puisqu'en moins d'un demi siecle, ils ont operé plus de changements dans l'esprit humain par les causes morales mises en œuvre, que toutes les causes physiques auraient faites en mille ans. Par bonheur nous avons une providence, qui veille malgré nous sur nos actions, et qui sçaura nous reprimer dans nos extremes folies, quand il faut, comme il modere les causes physiques de plus furieux ouragans, qui sont passagers, et des tremblemens de terre, qui ne sont jamais universels en meme tems. Que la meme providence detourne les malheurs, qui vous menacent, ou qu'elle les fasse tomber sur les coupables en y retirant tous mes amis, dont vous étes le chef: il ne me restera alors qu'à souhaiter que vous soyez heureux par tout, ou vos pas vous conduiront, et *ibi patria ubi bene*.[3] En tout cas je vous prie de continuer à me donner de vos nouvelles de tems en tems, et de m'excuser de ce que j'ai differé si long tems à vous écrire; car j'etais à une certaine distance de Paris pendant toute l'été dans des endroits, d'ou je n'avais rien d'interessant à vous marquer. Ce n'est que depuis un mois environ, que je me trouve à Paris. Je travaille actuellement sur Spalanzani,[4] et je trouve beaucoup plus à faire, que j'avais prevu: il est extremement diffus; il n'ecrit pas avec une certaine precision; il s'epuise en descriptions; il donne très souvent pour des choses nouvelles, ce qui est très connu; il se trompe quelquefois dans ses observations; il établit des analogies, ou il n'y a aucune resemblance; il se meprend sur les sentimens, et la façon de raisonner de M[r.] de Buffon aussi bien que sur les miens; bref ses raisonnemens sont trop vagues, et par consequent nullement concluants. Dans les notes, que j'ajouterai à la fin de son livre[5] à cause de leur extreme longueur, je tacherai de bien developper notre systeme, de l'eclaircir, et de l'affranchir de toute ombre de materialisme, de prouver la necessité d'admettre l'epigenese par les meilleurs raisonnemens, et par les observations les plus decisives, qui se presenteront, et je conclurai par donner à nos adversaires tous les avantages, dont leur cause est capable, en établissant avec precision le pour et le contre de ces deux questions. Par ce moyen je presenterai avec franchise le côté faible de mon systeme, et tout ce qui reste à faire ou pour le demontrer sans replique, ou pour le detruire sans resource. C'est tout ce qui je puis faire pour la cause de la verité. Adieu, presentez mes respects à Madame Bonnet, à Messieurs Tremblay, et Saussure, et à tous nos amis. Soyez persuade de mon attachement, et que

---

3. Reminiscent of Cicero, *Tusculanae disputationes*, v, 37, 108: 'patria est ubicumque est bene'.

4. Needham is referring to his work on Spallanzani's *Saggio di osservazioni microscopiche*; see letter 19, n.2, and section 2.iv of the Introduction.

5. Needham's notes to the *Saggio* occupy 160 pages; see Spallanzani (1769, pt.1:139-298).

personne au monde n'est plus votre ami sincere, que, mon cher Monsieur,

votre très humble, et très obeissant serviteur

Needham.

[ADDRESS] A Monsieur / Monsieur Bonnet de la Société Royale / de Londres, de l'academie de Berlin, / correspondant de celle de Paris &c. / à Geneve. / Par Lyons.

MANUSCRIPT
BPUG, MS Bonnet 29:32r-33v.

EDITIONS
'Je vous remercie [...] J. J. Rousseau' published in Leigh, 6157. 'Je travaille [...] de la verité' published in Castellani (1973:95-96).

TEXT NOTES
a. Word repeated after page break.

29

Needham to Bonnet – Paris, 8 June 1768

à Paris Le 8. Juin 1768.

Vous étes étonné sans doute, mon cher Monsieur, de ce que vous n'entendés plus parler de moi, ni de ma traduction de Spalanzani; mais l'esprit voyage avec bien plus de vitesse, que le corps, et je me suis trompé moi-meme le premier en me flattant mal-a propos, que cet ouvrage m'aurait couté peu de tems, et de peine. Partie l'accroissement dans le nombre d'idées, à mesure que j'avançais, partie la lenteur de la Typographie m'ont mené insensiblement jusqu'à ce jour, et on vient seulement aujourdhui de finir à imprimer l'ouvrage de notre ami. On commence actuellement les notes, que j'ai ajouté pour chaque chapitre de l'original, qui sont copieuses, et se trouveront à la fin. Elles égalent pour le moins en masse l'ouvrage meme, et si elles ne sont pas absolument du gout de tout le monde, parce qu'elles ne sont pas conformes aux opinions courantes, elles pourront plaire par une certaine variété, et par le pouvoir, qu'elles auront peutetre d'exciter l'attention des autres, et d'echauffer des genies plus heureux. *Si je n'ai pas beaucoup d'esprit moi-meme*, dit un celebre Bouffon dans les comedies de Shakespear, *je fais naitre par tout l'esprit dans ceux, qui se donneront la peine de m'écouter*.[1] En pesant bien à loisir les observations, et les experiences de M^r· Spalanzani je trouve que nous marchons ensemble main en main jusqu'au dernier chapitre, exceptés de tems en tems certaines erreurs, que je suis obligé de relever, et qui proviennent de ce qu'il n'a pas trop bien compris par tout ni la force de mes termes, ni le tour de mes idées. Au dernier chapitre, après avoir dans les precedens sommé les preuves pour et contre, il conclut contre moi sur

---

1. Needham may have had in mind the following passage from Shakespeare's *Second Part of King Henry IV*, 1, 2, 12: 'I am not only witty in myself, but the cause that wit is in other men.'

le poids d'une seule espece d'experience,[2] que je trouve très equivoque, et point du tout concluante de la maniere, qu'il la conduit, dont j'ai raison de croire, qu'il était lui-meme sans dessein la dupe par trop de precautions. C'est pour cela que je reviens à mes principes, et que dans mes notes j'ai fait un resumé de mon système, en demontrant qu'il n'est nullement favorable au materialisme, mais conforme en tout, et par tout à la bonne morale, comme à la bonne physique. J'amene mes anciennes preuves, j'ajoute des nouvelles, je cherche à écarter l'obscurité, qui parait couvrir mes principes, et je propose en dernier lieu à M^r. Spalanzani une repetition de ses dernieres experiences, qu'il croit presque decisives contre l'epigenese, sur un autre plan plus equitable, et moins sujet aux exceptions. Enfin j'ai conclu, si apres avoir renouvellé ces experiences de la maniere à lui proposée, qui me parait juste pour pour^a les deux partis, il ne trouve rien de vital dans ses infusions, que je renoncerai à mes principes nouveaux en revenant de bonne foi aux anciens. J'ai traité tout ce que je viens de vous dire avec la liberté philosophique, que le desir, que j'ai de rencontrer la vérité me donne sans des complimens inutiles, de la façon de ceux, dont il m'accable, et sans l'amertume d'un critique, qui se fache contre ses adversaires, d'une maniere simple, mais energique, comme un homme qui cherche à percer vers ce qu'il croit vrai, par la ligne la plus droite. Comme dans mes notes j'entre dans la region des vérités generales, j'ai poursuit mon chemin après, et j'ai ajouté une seconde partie,[3] que j'appelle *recherches physiques, et metaphysiques sur la religion, et la nature.* Je commence cette partie par une nouvelle edition des hauteurs, que j'ai pris autrefois avec le barometre sur une partie des Alpes de la Savoye.[4] Après cela vient une lettre adressée à M^r. de Buffon[5] sur les six jours selon la cosmogonie mosaique, et je prouve par plus de soixante textes de l'écriture sainte, et par la raison, que nous devons les entendre, non pas de six jours naturels de 24. heures, mais de six periodes de tems indefinis pour nous, et abandonnés à la recherche des physiciens. Enfin je presente l'histoire sacrée de la creation dans un jour physique, et metaphysique entierement nouveau, et après avoir remarqué que la chronologie de Moyse n'est pas celle de la terre, encore moins celle du systême, dont elle ne fait qu'une partie peu considerable, mais celle uniquement du genre humain, je demontre que sa cosmogonie,

---

2. Needham is alluding to the experiments performed on sealed, heated infusions that Spallanzani presented in the final chapter of the *Saggio*. Spallanzani demonstrated that if one heated sealed infusions of seeds in boiling water for one hour, then no organisms would develop in them (Spallanzani 1765, pt.1:83-85; and 1769, pt.1:131-35). This result was contrary to Needham's earlier findings, which had been based on a shorter boiling time (see Needham 1748:637-39). In 1769, Needham responded to Spallanzani that his excessive heating had weakened or destroyed the vegetative force and had corrupted the air trapped in the flasks (see Needham's notes in Spallanzani 1769, pt.1:216-18). See also section 2.iv of the Introduction.

3. See letter 32, n.1.

4. See letter 2, n.7. Needham actually republished his essay on the height of the Alps at the end rather than at the beginning of this work (see Spallanzani 1769, pt.2:221-52).

5. The 'Lettre [...] à M. de Buffon', dated Paris, 27 March 1767, is published in the second part of Spallanzani (1769, pt.2:1-26). Needham also mentioned there that he had discussed cosmogony with Buffon: 'Vous pouvez vous rappeller, Monsieur, qu'il y a quelque tems qu'examinant ensemble dans les Livres de *Moyse* l'histoire de la création, nous cherchâmes à developper le sens caché de cette phrase obscure & remarquable, le soir & le matin firent un jour' (Spallanzani 1769, pt.2:1). See also section 7 of the Introduction.

quoique très simple est très conforme à la nature, et à la raison la plus rafinée, par l'ordre, et la chaine graduée, qui s'y trouve établie. Ensuite après avoir attaqué les athées et les materialistes je reviens à la Theorie de la terre par M^r· de Buffon, que je critique comme contraire aux phenomenes, au moins dans l'état, comme il nous la presente dans son histoire naturelle. Car s'il peut la reformer avec la liberté, que je lui accorde dans les six periodes de la creation, et la reduire, en la prouvant toujours exactement par les phenomenes, à un tems raisonable, je lui laisse le champ ouvert à repondre à mes objections. En tout cela je crois avoir rendu service à la religion révélée, comme toute personne aussi clairvoyant, que vous meme, Monsieur, sentira facilement sans entrer dans un detail inutile. Je donne après d'une maniere courte mes idées sur la formation des montagnes, sur l'*appareat aridum*[6] de Moyse, et sur le deluge, que j'explique d'une façon très naturelle, et très simple en reduisant l'échelle de notre globe à celle d'un globe de sept pieds et demi. Sur mon petit globe je trouve les plus hautes montagnes, celles des Cordelieres, égales à une demie ligne seulement; la capacité interieure de mon globe égale à peu près à huit mille pintes mesure de paris; et la quantité, qu'il me faut, d'eau, pour submerger ma montagne d'une demie ligne égale à vingt deux pintes, qui n'est pas la trois cent soixantieme partie du total; mon deluge par consequent n'est tout au plus, qu'une espece d'exsudation assés legere. J'ai imaginé meme une machine, pour le demontrer conformement à la description donnée par Moyse, qui outre la pluye de quarante jours dit positivement, que les *fontes magni abyssi rupti sunt*,[7] et c'est de cette machine, dont la surface plate representera une octante de la terre sur une échelle de sept pieds et demi de diametre, que je ferai sortir la quantité d'eau requise pour submerger mes cordelieres d'une demie ligne de hauteur, par une augmentation très legere d'une chaleur interieure. Les incredules, sans ôser nier ouvertement le deluge cherchent à le faire passer pour un miracle immediat, on sçait bien pourquoi, sans considerer, que ce n'est pas la maniere, dont Moyse le represente. Mes idées la dessus sont plus conformes à l'esprit de l'ecriture sainte; dieu n'opere jamais inutilement des miracles, la physique est assujettie à la morale, parce que dieu, qui a tout prevu la voulut ainsi du commencement; cela se peut entendre par une espece de harmonie preetablie, si on veut; de toute façon il est le maitre de la nature, il s'en sert librement, et comme nos auteurs sacrés s'expriment très philosophiquement, *pugnabit cum eo orbis terrarum contra insensatos*.[8] Enfin je raisonne sur l'existence de dieu; dieu avec le monde est un miracle, un mystere, dont la réalité est constatée par le fait; le monde sans dieu est une absurdité pleine de contradiction, dont l'impossibilité saut aux yeux; je demontre ensuite l'immortalité, et la spiritualite de l'ame, et je finis par diverses pensées sur diverses autres matieres; ainsi il y aura au moins de quoi vous amuser, s'il n'y a pas de quoi vous instruire.—Quel maheur, mon cher ami, cel

---

6. Genesis i.9: 'Dixit vero Deus: Congregentur aquae, quae sub caelo sunt, in locum unum: et appareat arida. Et factum est ita.'

7. Genesis vii.11: 'Anno sexcentesimo vitae Noe, mense secundo, septimo decimo die mensis, rupti sunt omnes fontes abyssi magnae, et cataractae caeli apertae sunt.'

8. Sapientia v.21: 'Acuet autem duram iram in lanceam, et pugnabit cum illo orbis terrarum contra insensatos.'

de la morte subite de Mr Jallabert,[9] dont je suis veritablement faché pour plusieurs raisons. On a parlé de ce terrible accident à la derniere seance de l'academie des sciences avec un vrai regret de la perte, que les lettres en general ont souffert par sa mort. Je suis en quelque façon consolé par la paix, que vous éprouvé maintenant à Geneve après toutes vos troubles; mieux l'avoir à des conditions les plus iniques, que d'avoir des dissensions civiles. Dieu conserve ma patrie dans la crise presente. Adieu mon cher ami, et confrere, et soyez persuadé toujours de la sincere amitié, et de la vraie estime,

de votre trés humble, et très obeissant serviteur

Needham

Tournez s.v.p.

P.S. Sans que j'ai la peine d'ecrire à Mr Spalanzani, dans ce moment, ou je suis le plus occupé voulés vous bien me faire le plaisir de faire passer à lui un extrait, ou un precis de cette lettre avec mille complimens de ma part.[10] Je le felicite sur sa nouvelle decouverte de la reparation de la tête du limaçon.[11] Elle vient d'etre communiquée à l'academie des sciences par le Pere Boscovich[12] l'ecrivant à Monsieur de la Condamine avec plusieurs autres nouvelles litteraires d'Italie.[13] Elle est d'autant plus interessante, qu'elle ajoute une nouvelle lumiere aux observations de notre ami M. Trembley sur les Polypes. En effet la tête du

9. On 12 April 1768, Bonnet reported to Haller the sudden death of Jean Jallabert, caused by a fall from a horse; see Sonntag (1983:745) and Ratte (1774:15-16).

10. Bonnet wrote to Spallanzani on 22 June 1768: 'Notre ami le célèbre Epigenèsiste, m'a écrit de Paris le 8 du courant, et m'a prié de vous envoyer l'extrait de sa lettre, en vous félicitant sur votre limaçon: vous trouverez donc cet extrait à la suite de ma lettre. Je n'ai pas grande opinion des arguments par lesquels il entreprendra de vous combattre: ce brave homme a bien peu de netteté dans l'esprit, et sa logique n'est guère exacte. Mais ses intentions sont les meilleures du monde, et Voltaire est inexcusable de l'avoir tant de fois crimisé' (Castellani 1971:77).

11. Spallanzani described the regeneration of the head of the snail in the *Prodromo di un opera da imprimersi sopra le riproduzioni animali* (Modena 1768). For historical comments on the discoveries documented in this work, see Belloni (1961 and 1976:104-105) and Di Pietro (1979:186-96).

12. For biographies of the famous Jesuit scientist Rudjer J. Bošković (Boscovich) (1711-1787), active in Rome, Milan, and later in Paris, see the volume edited by Whyte (1961); Željko Marković, *D.S.B.*, 2 (1970) 326-32; and Paolo Casini, *D.B.I.*, 13 (1971) 221-30, which include good bibliographies of and on Bošković (see also May 1973:86). For a complete bibliography of Bošković's works, see Sommervogel (1960, 1:1828-50). For works on Bošković published after 1971, see Casini (1980) and the volume of letters edited by Arrighi (Boscovich 1980).

13. The *Gazette de France* of 3 June 1768 reported the following news: 'Suivant une lettre écrite d'Italie par le Pere Boscovich, au sieur de la Condamine, de l'Académie Françoise & de celle des Sciences, le Docteur Spallanzani, Naturaliste résidant à Modene, a fait une découverte très-curieuse en Histoire Naturelle. Il prétend qu'ayant coupé la tête à des limaçons de terre, non-seulement ces animaux n'en sont point morts; mais, après s'être retirés pendant quelque temps dans leur coquille, ils en sont sortis de nouveau pour se promener sur les plantes qui leur servent de nourriture: il ajoute même qu'il leur est venu une nouvelle tête organisée comme la premiere. Ce fait est trop extraordinaire pour n'avoir pas besoin d'être confirmé par de nouvelles observations' (p.188). After Spallanzani read this report, he published an emendation in the *Foglio di notizie di Mantova* of 8 July 1768 in which he stated 'Quanto alla riproduzione della testa, il fatto è verissimo [...] ma che le lumache *andassero su per le piante, di cui esse si cibano*, l'Autore [Spallanzani] non lo ha mai sognato: e però lascia volentieri cotal giunta a chi [Bošković] ne ha scritta la lettera' (p.[4]). This resulted in friction between Bošković and Spallanzani, which was overcome only when the *Gazette de France* of 26 September 1768 admitted that 'on avoit annoncé cette découverte avec quelques circonstances qui n'étoient point énoncées dans la lettre du Pere Boscowich' (p.320). For the circumstances of this misunderstanding between Spallanzani and Bošković, see Costa (1967).

Limaçon est bien plus organisée, et plus compliquée que celle de ces êtres divisibles. Je crains que vous soyés reduit vous meme à la fin, aussi bien que lui de reconnaitre les forces plastiques, mais entendües sagement. Loin de vrai philosophe la generation equivoque: tout se conduit par des regles constantes, et par des loix invariables, qui supposent de toute necessité et un maitre de l'univers, et un sage legislateur. Mille complimens à tous nos amis de Geneve; mes respects à Madame.

*b*Reçue à Genthod, le 14. Juin, à 9.h. du Soir.*b*

MANUSCRIPT
    BPUG, MS Bonnet 29:34*r*-35*v*.

EDITIONS
    'Vous étes étonné [...] plus heureux'; 'En pesant [...] la plus droite'; and 'P.S. sans que [...] êtes divisibles' published in Castellani (1973:96-97).

TEXT NOTES
    a. Word repeated after page break. *b*. Written in another hand at the head of the letter.

30

Bonnet to Needham – Genthod, 13 July 1768

Genthod le 13.ᵉ de Juillet 1768.

Des affaires accumulées et bien de réponses arrièrées, Monsieur mon digne Ami, ne m'ont pas permis de répondre plutôt à vôtre bonne Lettre du 8.ᵉ de Juin.

Immédiatement après sa reception, je me hâtai d'en faire part selon vos désirs, à nôtre estimable Ami M.ʳ Spallanzani. Je lui en fis un Extrait relatif à sa Dissertation:[1] j'attens sa Réponse.

Il vous aura sans doute envoyé son *Prodrome* Italien.[2] Il m'avoit prié de le faire traduire en François:[3] je l'ai fait,[4] et j'ai chargé un Libraire de vous en remettre de ma part un Exemplaire.

Vous aurés été étonné de tant et de si grands Prodiges; si pourtant un Philosophe qui songe sans cesse à l'immensité de la Nature, peut être étonné.

Nôtre habile Observateur m'avoit dit tout cela très en détail dans ses Lettres

---

1. See letter 29, n.10.
2. See letter 29, n.11.
3. In his letter of 28 March 1768, accompanying two copies of his *Prodromo*, Spallanzani wrote to Bonnet: 'Il est vrai que ma brochure a le malheur d'être en italien et par consequent de n'être pas trop entendue hors de l'Italie, et vous prier de me trouver un Traducteur, ce seroit abuser de la bonté que vous avez pour moi. Mon amour prôpre m'inspireroit pourtant de vous faire cette prière' (*Epistolario*, 1:155).
4. As soon as Bonnet received the *Prodromo*, he wrote to Spallanzani that he had arranged for it to be translated into French; see Bonnet's letter of 25 May 1768 (Castellani 1971:69). The translation, entitled *Programme ou précis d'un ouvrage sur les réproductions animales* (Genève 1768), was soon finished; and Bonnet was able to send copies of it to Spallanzani on 11 July 1768 (Castellani 1971:78).

en 1765, 1766 &c[5] et je lui avois gardé le secret. Je voulois lui laisser le plaisir d'annoncer lui même au Public ses belles Découvertes. [a]Le P. Boskovitz n'a pas été si discret[6] que moi; vous êtes donc bien sûr que je garderai toûjours les secrets que vous me confierés.[a]

Je lirai avec le plus grand empressement l'Ouvrage que vous imprimés actuellement. Votre *Cosmogonie Sacrée* pique surtout ma curiosité. Il est bien singulier que nous-nous soyons tous deux occupés du même sujet à l'insçu l'un de l'autre. J'avois aussi composé quelque chose sur cette *Cosmogonie*[7] en Avril et Mai dernier, ou je supposois, comme vous, bien[a] des Révolutions de nôtre Planète antérieures à celles que Moyse a décrite: j'essayois de montrer la probabilité de cette supposition, et de la concilier avec le Texte. J'espère de vous mettre à portée de comparer nos Principes et notre Marche.

Nous avons donc travaillé tous deux, chacun à nôtre manière, à deffendre le Texte Sacré de la Genèse, contre les Assauts redoublés de nos Incrédules Modernes. Je ne me flatte pas trop que nous leur fassions entendre raison: leurs Oreilles ne sont pas faites pour nôtre *Harmonie*.

Je suis charmé que vous traitiés de l'Immatérialité de l'Ame: vous avés vû apparemment les preuves que j'en ai données dans la Préface de mon *Essai Analytique sur les Facultés de l'Ame*, et que j'ai rappellées en divers endroits du Livre. J'y suis encore revenu dans la Préface de ma *Contemplation de la Nature*. Il me semble que s'il est des *Démonstrations* en Psychologie, ces Preuves pourroient passer à bon droit pour telles. Et pourtant l'Auteur qui les a publiées, a été accusé de matérialisme. Il doit s'en consoler, puisque Descartes avoit été accusé d'athéisme et Montesquieu de Spinozisme.[8]

---

5. See especially Spallanzani's long letter to Bonnet of 21 September 1766 in *Epistolario* (1:101-24).

6. See letter 29, n.13.

7. Bonnet is referring to his 'Idées sur l'état passé des animaux: Et à cette occasion sur la Création & sur l'Harmonie de l'Univers', which was published as the sixth part of *La Palingénésie philosophique* (1769a, 1:236-62; and B.O., 7:173-94/15:254-84; see letter 37, n.1). For Bonnet's views on cosmogony, see section 7 of the Introduction.

8. The question of Descartes's supposed atheism had been raised as early as 1643 by the Dutch university professor Martin Schoock (1614-1669), who drew an analogy between Descartes and Giulio Cesare Vanini (1585-1619) in his *Admiranda methodus novae philosophiae Renati des Cartes* (Ultraiecti 1643), where he stated, 'Nulla [...] injuria Renato fit, quando cum subtilissimo Atheismi patrono Caesare Vaninio comparatur, iisdem enim artibus, quibus ille, in imperitorum animis Atheismi thronum erigere laborat' (p.265). In the life of Spinoza written by the publisher and free-thinker Jean Maximilien Lucas (1636?-1697) and first published in 1719, it is suggested that the Cartesians were worried by the accusation of atheism levelled against Descartes, and thus reacted against Spinoza: 'Mais quoiqu'il [Spinoza] ait pû dire à l'avantage de ce celebre autheur [Descartes], les partisans de ce grand homme etant accusés d'Atheïsme ont fait depuis tout ce qu'ils ont pu pour faire tomber la tempeste sur notre Philosophe' (A. Wolf 1927:110). It was however the French Jesuit Jean Hardouin (1646-1729) who formalised the suspicions into proper accusations by including Descartes and some of his followers in a very long section of his contentious 'Athei detecti' (Hardouin 1733:200-243).

In 1749, for instance, the Jansenist abbé Jacques Fontaine La Roche published two critical articles on Montesquieu's *L'Esprit des lois* in the *Nouvelles ecclésiastiques* (pp.161-64, 165-67; reprinted in Montesquieu 1875-1879, 6:115-37), and accused him of having a Spinozistic conception of law. Montesquieu himself felt obliged to respond to this criticism (Montesquieu 1875-1879, 6:209-37). In the anonymous pamphlet *Les Lettres persannes convaincues d'impiété* published in 1751 by Jean Baptiste Gaultier, one finds statements such as 'Spinoza est le modele que l'Auteur a voulu imiter', and 'Tout Spinoziste qu'il est, il a encore assez de pudeur pour ne vouloir pas passer pour tel'

J'aime à vous voir représenter le Déluge par une petite Machine: c'étoit un bon moyen de ne s'y noyer point, et d'y noyer les Incrédules.

Non, mon bon Ami; je n'aurai point besoin des *forces plastiques* pour expliquer les nouveaux Prodiges de Modène: si vous avés bien voulu me méditer un peu, vous *b*comprenés assés*b* comment j'essayerois d'y apliquer les Principes assés lumineux, que j'ai développés dans mes deux derniers Ouvrages.

Pour peu qu'on vous connoisse, mon cher Ami, on ne sçauroit suspecter le moins du monde votre Croyance philosophique, et bien moins encore vôtre Croyance théologique. Pour moi, qui vous connoit autant que vous mérités de l'être, je sçais combien vous êtes éloigné d'adopter les Conséquences que certains Libertins aimeroient fort à tirer de vôtre Doctrine physico-métaphysique. En un mot; je sçais très bien qu'en admettant l'*Epigenèse*, vous la subordonnés aux Loix de la SAGESSE ETERNELLE. Il ne s'agit donc entre nous deux que d'établir par des argumens solides les Loix de la SAGESSE dans la Formation des Etres vivans.

Mon Amour pour le Vrai vous est connu: si vous me rendés vôtre chère Epigenèse plus probable que la *Préformation Organique*, je renoncerai sans peine à mes petites Idées; j'embrasserai les vôtres, et je me declarerai publiquement vôtre Sectateur.

Il est vrai que nous jouissons de la Paix; mais il est fort à craindre qu'elle ne soit qu'une trêve. La nouvelle Constitution[9] est trop vicieuse, pour être durable. A dieu mon cher et digne Ami; je vous embrasse dans tous les sentimens de l'amitié la plus vraye.

*a*Ma Femme qui est très sensible à vôtre obligeant souvenir me prie de vous présenter beaucoup de complimens de sa part. Ses maux continuent à mettre à l'épreuve sa patience et sa résignation.*a*

[ADDRESS] Paris, M.*r* Néédham de la Societé Royale.

MANUSCRIPTS
BPUG, MS Bonnet 72:237*v*-238*r*; MS Bonnet 85:184*r*-185*r*.

TEXT NOTES
    a. B: *omitted* *b*. B: aurez assés compris

(Gaultier 1751:101-102). Bonnet resolutely denied that Montesquieu was a Spinozist (Savioz 1948b:155). Some modern scholars (Oudin 1911 and Vernière 1954, 2:447-66) also hold the view that Spinoza was a powerful influence on Montesquieu, but there does not seem to be any substantial evidence for stating that Montesquieu was a deliberate disciple of Spinoza, although they shared basic ideas on the *ius naturale* (see Shackleton 1961:261-64, and the literature cited in letter 41, n.6).
    9. The new constitution was enacted by the *Edit* of 11 March 1768, which was voted on by the General Council and accepted by a majority of 1204 to 37. For Bonnet's reaction to it, see section 8 of the Introduction.

31

Needham to Bonnet – Paris, 25 August 1768

Paris, Le 25. d'aoust 1768.

Je reponds, mon cher Monsieur, ami, et confrere, à votre lettre du 13. de Juillet, et je vois par toute sa teneur que vous allez prendre une idée trop exaltée de mon ouvrage. J'en souffrirai peutetre; mais n'importe, pourvu que dans le nombre de pensées, que j'ai assemblé, on en trouve quelques unes, dont un philosophe, qui travaillera avec les memes bonnes intentions, mais qui m'excedera en habilité peut profiter pour la defence de la religion. Je crois sans difficulté, que dans le choix, qu'on pourra faire d'un sujet de cette espece, le public se tournera de votre coté, comme presque le seul parmi les philosophes, qui en meritent le nom, dont le travail a été dirigé sans detour vers la cause de la revelation. Si vous l'entreprenez, ou je me suis arrété, certainement rien ne peut être plus heureux pour moi que d'avoir contribué au progres de cette science divine, quoique d'une maniere indirecte; et je ne puis rien desirer de plus favorable pour un ouvrage, au quel on peut appliquer à la lettre, sur tout si le style doit entrer en ballance, cette peinture de Martial

sunt bona, sunt quaedam mediocria sunt mala multa.[1]

N'allez pas le comparer avec ce que vous avez fait sur les memes sujets; pour rendre la stricte justice aux autres, il faut commencer par la rendre à vous meme. Mon ouvrage n'est guere plus qu'un repertoire; ni mes forces, qui s'abattent, ni le tems m'ont permis d'entrer dans des raisonnemens suivis sur tant de matieres interessantes, qui sont entrées comme d'elles memes, sans que j'ai pu les prevoir, dans mon plan, à mesure que j'ai voulu le tracer. Je ne touche pas souvent aux plus interessantes, qu'en passant; mes recherches, par exemple, pour prouver la spiritualité de l'ame, par ce que nous eprouvons en nous-memes, ne passent pas quatre ou cinq petites pages, et en les comprenant dans leur totalité mes plus grandes esperances n'excedent pas celles de notre ami Horace, qui ne s'attribue dans les choses élevées, que la triste qualité d'aiguiser quelque esprit plus tranchant, que le sien.[2] Mais malgré tout ce que j'ai pu faire, si je ne me flatte pas trop, meme en vous ayant pour associé, que nous fassions entendre raison à nos incredules, j'espere toujours que nous arreterons en quelque façon la contagion, en l'ecartant de ceux, qui ne sont pas encore touchés. Je vous remercie de vos bonnes intentions en chargeant votre libraire de me remettre de votre part un exemplaire françois du Prodrome de notre ami Spallanzani; il arrivera, quand il pourra, mais j'en ai reçu en attendant un en Italien, qui me vient de l'auteur en droiture, et dont j'ai fait une espece d'extrait, que je donnerai avec quelques remarques très courtes à la fin de la premiere partie de mon ouvrage.[3] On finira de l'imprimer dans la quinzaine, et je pourrai

---

1. Martial, *Epigrammata*, 1, 16: 'Sunt bona, sunt quaedam mediocria, sunt mala plura quae legis hic.'
2. Horace, *Ars poetica*, 301-308.
3. See Needham's notes in Spallanzani (1769, pt.1:275-91).

vous faire parvenir deux exemplaires, dont je destine un à M. Spallanzani, avant la fin de septembre, ou peutetre plutot, si vous avez quelque moyen de les attirer chez vous plus expeditif, et plus commode, que cel du messager ordinaire. Depuis que j'ai reçu votre derniere lettre, je me trouve appellé par la Cour à Bruxelles avec des offres d'un établissement avantageux. Le projet du ministere[4] dans ce pais est d'assembler une espece de société des gens des lettres, qu'on erigera ensuite en academie Royale, et imperiale des sciences.[5] Comme depuis vingt ans, que je courre le monde, j'acquis une grande indifference pour le local de ma demeure, et que je trouve la divinité, la nature, la société, les vertus, et les sciences plus, ou moins par tout, j'ai accepté sans hesiter les offres de la Cour, et je compte me transporter dans ce pais, que je connois deja, dans le mois d'octobre. Quand j'y me trouverai établi, je vous enverrai de mes nouvelles, afin de continuer notre correspondance; et vous me direz alors en retour *sans me flatter* vos sentimens sur mon ouvrage. Bien des respects, s'il vous plait de ma part à Madame Bonnet; je la plains plus, peutetre, qu'elle se plaint elle-meme tant pour les égards, que je vous dois, que pour l'estime qu'elle a merité personellement de tous ceux, qui ont le bonheur de la connoitre. Souvenez vous de moi, je vous en prie, auprès de notre ami respectable M. Tremblay, et mes autres amis de Geneve, que j'aime sincerement malgré le mur de separation, qui nous divise, posé par les malheurs du seizieme siecle. Quand vous recevrés mon ouvrage, commencés, je vous prie par corriger les erratas avec la plume, selon la table, que vous trouverés au commencement: il y en a plusieurs, qui font des contresens. Incluse vous trouverés une lettre pour M. Spallanzani,[6] que vous lui addresserés de chez vous plus directement, que je ne le pourrai faire de Paris; soyès toujours persuadé, mon cher, et digne ami, que personne ne vous aime, ni vous honore plus, que

> votre très humble, et très obeissant serviteur
> Needham.

J'avais quasi oublié Mr· Haller, que j'estime infiniment, il y aura un troisieme exemplaire de mon ouvrage pour lui, et peutetre un quatrieme pour Mr· Trembley, si je puis en tirer un nombre suffisant de mon libraire pour tous mes amis.

[ADDRESS] A Monsieur / Monsieur Bonnet de la Société / Royales de Londres,

4. For a short biography of count Jean-Charles-Philippe de Cobenzl (1712-1770), Minister Plenipotentiary in the Austrian Netherlands from 1753, see Wurzbach (2:389-90); for his political activities there, see especially de Boom (1932:63-319); for the part he played in the foundation of the Société littéraire, see Mailly (1883, 1:1-34), Lavalleye (1973:14-19), and Voss (1976:326-35); and for a general assessment of his personality and role in reforming institutional life in the Austrian Netherlands, see Davis (1974:36-38) and Moureaux (1974).

5. On 15 July 1768, count Patrice-François Neny (1716-1784), President of the Privy Council, wrote to Needham: 'Dans le dessein où Nous sommes de tacher de faire refleurir dans ces Païs le gout des bonnes études il a été jugé que rien ne pourroit y contribuer davantage, que l'établissement d'une Académie des Sciences et des belles-lettres: Mais avant que de prendre ce partie, nous voudrions commencer par une Societé d'un petit nombre de gens de Lettres, qui sous le titre d'Académie, pussent commencer à en jetter les foundemens' (AARB, Correspondance, for the years 1759-1769). Neny proposed that Needham should move to the Austrian Netherlands, where he would help to establish the new Society and would receive a Canonicat in return.

6. This, the last letter from Needham to Spallanzani, was written on 25 August 1768 (see Castellani 1973:98-99).

associé de l'academie / des Sciences à Berlin, et correspondent / de celle de Paris / à Geneve / Par Lyons.

MANUSCRIPT
BPUG, MS Bonnet 29:36r-37v.

32

Needham to Bonnet – Paris, 3 December 1768

Paris rüe des Postes, ce samedi le 3. dec: 1768.

Je viens de vous addresser, mon cher ami et confrere, par la diligence de Lyons, qui part demain, une caisse contenant douze exemplaires de mon ouvrage,[1] qui vient à la fin, et après bien de retardemens de paraitre. Vous aurez la bonté d'en tirer deux Exemplaires, dont un vous est destiné, et l'autre vous ferez remettre par la premiere occasion à M^r. Haller à Berne.[2] Mes premieres intentions étaient d'en ajouter quelques autres pour mes amis de Geneve, dont M^r. Trembley est un de premiers, mais le peu que j'ai reçu pour le present de mon libraire ne suffisent pas pour les differens envoyes indispensables, qui me pressent dans ce moment. Si vous ne desapprouvez pas entierement mon travail, vos sentimens favorables me determineront dans quelque tems ici de leur faire une seconde envoye: en attendant l'exemplaire, que je vous destine suffira pour satisfaire à leur curiosité. Les autres dix Exemplaires sont destinés pour differentes villes d'Italie, et je vous prie, quand vous aurez pris les deux, dont je viens de parler, d'envoyer la caisse avec ce qu'elle contient à l'adresse de Monsieur de Sabatiér[3] secretaire de l'ambassade

---

1. This book (here always referred to as Spallanzani 1769) is divided into two parts, each bearing a different title page. The first is *Nouvelles recherches sur les découvertes microscopiques, et la génération des corps organisés. Ouvrage traduit de l'Italien de M. l'abbé Spalanzani.* Premiere partie (Londres, Paris 1769). The second is *Nouvelles recherches physiques et métaphysiques sur la nature et la religion, avec une nouvelle théorie de la terre, et une mesure de la hauteur des Alpes.* Par M. de Needham [...] Seconde partie (Londres, Paris 1769).

2. Bonnet sent the book to Haller on 27 December 1768; see Sonntag (1983:792).

3. Honoré-Auguste Sabatier (Sabathié) de Cabre (1737-1802) was born in Aix. His father became a noble in 1757. In 1759 (or 1761) he was appointed Secretary to the French Ambassador at the Court of Turin, where he remained until early 1769. It seems that in Turin he was responsible for establishing a masonic lodge. He was known as a good chess-player (Best.D14542). Early in 1769 he was appointed Minister at Liège, but on 26 May 1769 he left Paris for St Petersburg ostensibly as *chargé d'affaires*, but actually as a government agent (*W.C.*, 23:127 n.15). He remained there until 1772, while his younger brother, the abbé Jean-Antoine replaced him at Liège. In 1772 he was back at his post at Liège where he remained until 1782. He was later appointed *Directeur des consulats* at the *Ministère de la Marine* in Paris. During the French Revolution he was involved in the defence of the Tuileries and later in a number of counter-revolutionary plots. For a short biography, see Roman d'Amat, *D.B.F.*, 7 (1956) 768-69, and especially Sirven (1934-1942, 2:139-42, 149-57, 170-81), who discusses Sabatier's important relationship with Vittorio Alfieri (1749-1803). The *B.U.* (37:175) confuses the two brothers. From 1765 until his death, Needham conducted a considerable correspondence with Sabatier. (Fifty-seven letters of his to Sabatier are preserved in the BLUL.) The most interesting letters are twenty-two written from Geneva in 1765-1766, which contain a detailed account of the political situation there (see section 8 of the Introduction).

chez S. E. L'ambassadeur de France à la cour de Turin par la premiere bonne occasion, messager, courier, ou autre. Vous aurez la bonté en meme tems de faire partir par la poste la lettre[4] contenüe dans celle-ci, avec un mot d'avis de votre part concernant le jour du depart de la caisse, et la personne, qui s'en charge. Cet ami à son arrivée en aura soin, et la distribution se fera selon les instructions, que je lui donne dans l'incluse.—Vous verrez, que je soutienne l'epigenese contre vos sentimens avec toutes mes forces, et vous en verrez bientot les raisons. Ce n'est pas certainement, que je m'interesse beaucoup, et l'ardeur qui parait dans mon ouvrage part d'un autre principe. Toutes les questions de cette espece en elles memes ne sont pour vous dire avec franchise ce que je pense, que des bagatelles difficiles, *difficiles nugae.* Mais comme j'ai remarqué depuis mon entrée dans le champ de bataille que les ennemis de la religion ont parus vouloir s'emparer des hauteurs metaphysiques pour elever leurs bateries, et la foudroyer en dominant sur les vallons, ou elle étoit assés bien retranchée par les soins de nos bons ancêtres selon la discipline militaire de ce tems, j'ai resolu de les deloger de bonheur, et de tourner leurs batteries contre eux. Je crois d'avoir assés bien reussi dans mes desseins, et soit que les Philosophes à venir s'avisent encore de grimper sur les memes hauteurs pour respirer l'air leger du pais, et pour prendre des nouveaux essors, soit qu'ils se contentent avec vous de s'arrêter plutot en s'appuyant et se reposant sur la cause universelle sous la voile des germes preexistans depuis la creation, ils ne seront pas au moins tentés de se plonger dans les tenebres du materialisme. Tot ou tard et dans votre systeme, et dans le mien dieu s'y trouvera, et le psalmiste a bien dit, *si ascendero in cælum, tu illic es.*[5] Le meme esprit domine dans la seconde partie de mon ouvrage, qui n'est que purement hypothetique, malgre les forces, que j'employe pour en étayer les sentimens, et provisionnaire contre le genre d'attaque de la part de nos adversaires. Vous me connoisses trop pour croire, que je donne trop de valeur aux opinions des hommes en fait de philosophie; et telle est ma façon d'envisager la plupart de ces objets, que, si on excepte les vérités révélées, je suis pret avec Newton d'avouer, que plus j'avance plus j'y trouve de l'incertitude. En un mot la forteresse que je viens d'eriger avec tant de frais n'est que locale, passagere, et provisionnaire contre les enemis, qui cherchent à nous detourner du chemin, qui mene à notre vraie patrie, ou la connoissance parfaite des sciences humaines n'est que la moindre part du prix de nos travaux dans la pratique de la vertu. Voila le clef de mon ouvrage, que je ne communique qu'à très peu de personnes, dont vous êtes un de premiers. Adieu, et me croyez toujours avec estime, et un veritable attachement, mon cher ami, et confrere,

votre très humble, et très obeissant serviteur
Needham.

Je vous prie de presenter mes respects à Madame, à Messieurs Trembley, Saussure, et à tous mes amis de Geneve.

P.S. Je ne parle pas du style de mon ouvrage; ce sont si vous voulez des

4. Needham's letter to Sabatier de Cabre is dated 2 December 1768 (BLUL) and contains instructions for delivering ten copies of Needham's work in Italy, one of which was destined for Spallanzani. The latter, however, never received this copy (see letter 39).

5. See Psalmi 138, 8: 'Si ascendero in caelum, tu illic es; se descendero in infernum, ades.'

pensées detachées sans suite, et sans presqu'autre liaison, que l'ideale: mais cela me suffit pour le present quelque autre viendra peutêtre après moi, qui me developpera mieux, que j'aurai pû faire avec mille peines, si j'avais entrepris de le faire.

MANUSCRIPT
BPUG, MS Bonnet 29:40*r*-40*v*.

33

Bonnet to Needham – Genthod, 26 December 1768

Genthod le 26.ᵉ de Décembre 1768.
J'ai reçu mon cher Ami et Confrère, cette Caisse que vous m'aviés annoncée par votre bonne Lettre du 3.ᵉ de ce mois. Elle est arrivée ici le 20. J'en ai tire deux Exemplaires, l'un pour mon Illustre Ami M.ʳ de Haller,[1] l'autre pour moi conformément à vos ordres.

La Caisse a été ensuite proprement et éxactement refermée et expediée Vendredi dernier 23.ᵉ du courant à M.ʳ Sabatier, par *André Travi*, Voiturier de Gènes qui alloit à Turin, et qui est un Voiturier très sur.

Cet Envoi a été en même tems annoncé à M.ʳ Sabatier par une Lettre d'avis. Il ne payera que 3 Sols par livres pesantes, monnoye de Turin. Et afin de prevenir toute difficulté pour l'entrée dans le Piémont, on a mis dans la *Lettre de Voiture* dont le Voiturier est Porteur, ces mots, *pour transit*.

Je n'avois pas manqué d'envoyer plusieurs jours auparavant à M.ʳ Sabatier la Lettre que vous m'aviés adressée pour lui[2] et qu'il aura surement reçuë.

Voila mon bon Ami comment votre Commission a été éxécutée. J'espère que vous serés content de mon éxactitude et de ma diligence.

J'expédie aujourdhui à M.ʳ de Haller l'Exemplaire qui lui est destiné et je vous remercie de celui que je tiens de votre amitié.

Vous comprenés assés que je n'ai pas eu le tems de lire votre Livre.[3] Je n'ai lu que le *Discours Préliminaire*.[4] Je parierois bien que l'Auteur n'est pas Observateur: j'en juge par la manière dont il rend les Observations d'autrui. Ses intentions sont au moins les plus louables.

Je parierois bien encore que M.ʳˢ de Haller et Trembley ne gouteront pas votre *Epigènese* et votre *Métaphysique*; mais, ils rendront justice, comme moi à votre amour pour la Vérité et pour la Religion.

1. A few days after sending Needham's book to Haller (on 27 December 1768), Bonnet wrote to Haller about it, strongly criticising its 'mauvaise Physique' and its 'Métaphysique plus mauvaise encore'; see Sonntag (1983:792).
2. See letter 32, n.4.
3. But on 24 December 1768 Bonnet had written to Turton: 'Le bon Needham vient de publier un asses gros livre en faveur de sa chère *Epigenèse*. Il est si mal fait, si obscurément écrit, si étrangement pensé, qu'il n'y a pas d'apparence qu'il fasse fortune auprès des vrais Adeptes' (BPUG, MS Bonnet 73:23*v*).
4. Published in Spallanzani (1769, pt.1:i-liv); see also letter 34, n.1.

Vous m'écrivés *que vous me combattés avec toutes vos forces*: je n'ai pas même trouvé mon nom dans la *Table des Matières*.[5] Je soupconne un peu que vous n'avés pas même pris la peine de lire mes deux derniers Ouvrages. Ils contenoient pourtant des *Faits*, qui vous auroient instruit et qu'il ne vous étoit pas permis d'ignorer. J'ai apperçu pourtant qu'ils vous étoient inconnus.

Je laisse au Public éclairé et impartial à juger entre vous et moi. Quand je vous aurai lu et médité, je vous dirai mon sentiment avec toute la franchise que vous aimés et que j'aime: peut être même le dirais-je au Public.[6]

Il est fort à craindre que Voltaire et les autres Incrédules ne trouvent une abondante matière à vous railler dans votre Formation d'Eve.[7] Avant que d'entreprendre d'expliquer physiquement un semblable Fait, n'auroit-il pas convenu de s'assurer, qu'il n'y a rien d'allégorique dans le recit de Moyse?

Vous n'etes donc pas allé à Bruxelles? Qu'est devenuë cette *Academie* que la Reine devoit y fonder.

M.ʳ le Conseiller De la Rive et ma Femme sont fort sensibles à votre bon souvenir, et me chargent de vous présenter leurs complimens et leurs voeux.

Adieu, mon cher et estimable Ami; comptés toujours sur l'inviolable attachement de

[ADDRESS] Paris, M.ʳ Néédham de la Societé Royale de Londres.

MANUSCRIPT
BPUG, MS Bonnet 73:24r (not included in copy B).

34

Needham to Bonnet – Paris, 31 December 1768

A Paris, Le 31. dec: 1768.

Je vous remercie, mon cher Monsieur, et confrere de votre exactitude, et de votre diligence dans la distribution, et l'expedition des livres, que j'ai confié à vos soins.

5. Published in Spallanzani (1769, pt.2:253-93).
6. Bonnet did not publicly respond to Needham's publication until he added new footnotes to the edition of his *Considérations sur les corps organisés* published in 1779 in his *Œuvres* (see especially B.O., 3:411-27 n.1/6:317-39 n.1).
7. See Needham's long note in Spallanzani (1769, pt.1:291-97), which was summarised by Needham himself thus: 'le corps de l'homme a été fait du limon organisé & vitalisé, & [...] la femme a été propagée ensuite par une espéce de génération, ou production vitale du corps de l'homme même pendant qu'il dormoit [...] conformément aux loix de la Physique moderne' (Spallanzani 1769, pt.2:204). Writing to Haller on 30 December 1768, Bonnet remarked, 'Néédham a les meilleures intentions du monde: mais, il est trop dépourvu de Logique *naturelle & artificielle*. Il compte de frapper sur les Incrédules, & ils frapperont sur lui: il ne fera que leur apprêter à rire à ses dépends. Voyés, je vous prie, sa *Formation d'Eve*, et cent autres traits tout aussi déplacés' (Sonntag 1983:792-93).

Vous avez bien raison de vouloir parier, que le compilateur[1] du discours preliminaire n'est pas observateur. C'est le Traducteur de Spalanzani, qui en est l'auteur, et c'est de Baker[2] en le feuilletant qu'il a tiré tout ce qu'il dit. Vous comprenes assés que Je ne m'interesse nullement, et que je le laissai faire à sa façon.

Vous pourrez encore peutetre parier avec sureté, que Messieurs de Haller, et Trembley ne gouteront pas ni mon *Epigenese*, ni ma *metaphysique*. Mais en revanche j'aurai peutetre raison de dire, qu'ils s'attachent trop à la façon des cartesiens au sensible, et au palpable. Qu'aurait devenu le beau systeme de Newton, en faveur de lequel tous les faits deposent journellement, s'il falloit le juger par les sens, et non par la raison? Si ma metaphysique de meme est batie sur des faits, qu'importe qu'elle ne peut être prouvée *à priori*, et qu'en philosophie tout ce que le genie humain peut faire soit de poser un principe, ou une idée abstraite et generale comprenant ensemble touts les faits, que la nature nous presente sur le sujet en question?

Ma metaphysique neanmoins me parait assés claire, et intelligible; J'en ai fait l'essai aupres de differentes personnes tant medecins, que Theologiens *Philosophes*, qui l'ont assés gouté, et qui ont été un peu étonné du nombre, et du choix des faits, que j'ai assemblé pour établir ma These. Mais ce qui leur a donné un surcroit de plaisir étoit de voir que tout était tellement assuré du coté de la morale, que le materialiste ne gagne rien, et qu'il étoit doresvenant libre de penser sur cet article, comme on voudra, sans faire tort ni à la raison, ni à la religion. En effet il aurait été assés triste pour les vrais philosophes, si leur sort dependoit d'un systeme, pour ne rien dire de plus, plein d'incertitude.

En attendant je m'etonne, que ni vous, mon cher Monsieur, ni Messieurs Haller, et Trembley ne voyent pas la convenance, et la necessité d'admettre la meme échellé montante, et graduée entre les parties insensibles de la matiere, qu'ils voyent si clairement entre les grandes pieces, qui composent ce monde visible. C'est sur cette échelle, que je crois parfaite dans toutes ces parties, et sur les faits, qui s'appliquent si bien en consequence, que ma Theorie est entierement batie.

Vous avez eu tort de chercher dans la Table, et de commencer, par la *formation d'Eve*[3] votre lecture de mon livre. Je la reservée exprès pour la fin, et ce n'est qu'après avoir tout lu que cette partie de ma Theorie paroitra très raisonable,

---

1. Very little is known of the abbé Régley, prieur of Estrechy, who translated Spallanzani's *Saggio* into French and provided an introductory discourse. He obtained the award for eloquence at the Academy of Amiens for his *Eloge historique du brave Crillon*, published in 1779. Régley sent a copy of his translation of Spallanzani's *Saggio* to Voltaire, who wrote to thank him (Best.D15582; see also Best.D15413). The *Histoire de Louis Mandrin* (Chambery 1755), which ran into many editions during the nineteenth century, is also attributed to Régley.

2. On Henry Baker (1698-1774), Fellow of the Royal Society, naturalist, populariser of science, and gifted speech therapist, see G. L'E. Turner, *D.S.B.*, 1 (1970) 410-12; New (1970); and Turner (1974). Needham is alluding to the second part of Baker's book *The Microscope made easy* (London 1742), where Baker presented microscopic observations on infusions, on blood, on seminal animalcules, on several kinds of insects, and on plants. In his *Employment for the microscope* (London 1753), Baker also discussed (pp.250-60) Needham's observations on eels in blighted wheat (see letter 14, n.8).

3. See letter 33, n.7.

et très consequente sans donner prise en aucune façon au ridicule des insensés, qui ne se connoissaient pas mieux en philosophie qu'en religion. S'il est permis à tout moment d'avoir recours au metaphorique pour se tirer de l'embaras, que causent certains passages de l'écriture sainte, un Iman ingenieux justifiera bien facilement toutes les absurdités d'alcoran. De plus s'il faut entendre l'histoire de la formation d'Eve metaphoriquement, ne faut il pas également entendre de la meme façon, la production des vegetaux et des animaux de la terre, celle des oyseaux, et des poissons de l'eau, et celle d'adam meme d'un limon organisé, et vitalisé? Tout cela se comprend très bien, et très litteralement dans mon systeme en partant de l'echelle que j'ai établie entre les parties insensibles de la matière; en quoi je crois ma Theorie beaucoup plus avantageuse, que celle de mes adversaires, et parfaitment conforme à l'esprit de la sainte écriture. L'échelle, dont je parle, est clairement marquée dans le livre de la sagesse, et le principe meme appliqué aux transmutations physiques de la matière tant celles de la cosmogonie, que celles operées par Moyse en Egypte, ou l'auteur sacré dit, qu'il est aussi facile au tout puissant d'operer ces changements substantiels dans la nature, qu'il est au musicien de donner un nouvelle relation au meme son en changeant seulement la clef musicale. *In se enim*, dit il, *elementa convertuntur, sicut in organo qualitatis sonus immutatur, et omnia suum sonum custodiunt*.[4]

Je vous ai marqué, mon cher Monsieur, il est vrai, dans ma lettre, que je vous ai combattu avec toutes mes forces, mais j'ai voulu dire votre systeme, mais non pas votre personne, dont je n'ai fait mention qu'une seule fois. C'est à la page 219. de la premiere partie.[5] Il est vrai que je n'avais pas devant moi, quand j'ai composé mon ouvrage ni votre livre, ni cel d'aucun autre auteur, comme c'est toujours ma coutume bonne ou mauvaise. Je ne sçai rien, mais je me suis souvenu très bien de deux faits observés par Mr. Haller,[6] et cités par vous, mon cher Monsieur, les seuls de tout le nombre, qui m'ont fait quelque impression, comme contraires à ma Theorie, et favorables à vos idées. J'ai taché de les expliquer, et de repondre aux difficultés, qu'ils paraissent faire naitre contre le systeme de l'epigenese. C'est une negligence de la part de l'abbe Regley,[7] qui a fait la table de vous n'avoir pas cité nommement.

---

4. Sapientia xix.17: 'In se enim elementa dum convertuntur, sicut in organo qualitatis sonus immutatur, et omnia suum sonum custodiunt; unde aestimari ex ipso visu certo potest.'

5. 'Les seuls faits physiques qui paroissent déposer, sinon en faveur des germes préexistans depuis le commencement du monde, du moins pour le développement des parties contenues dans d'autres parties, sont tous ceux qui ont été observés par le célèbre M. *Haller*, & cités par M. *Bonnet* de Geneve que j'ai l'honneur de connoître personnellement, & dont je respecte le sçavoir, la droiture, & l'honneteté au-delà de toute expression. Il est bon d'en faire part au Lecteur. Les voici: certaines parties, ou membranes des œufs avant qu'ils écloent sous la poule, deviennent des membranes & des parties substantielles du germe ou du poulet qui se développe. Quelques autres parties paroissent, avec le tems, pour la premiere fois sous des dimensions si considérables qu'à-moins d'avoir été invisibles auparavant par leur transparence naturelle, elles auroient paru bien plutôt aux yeux armés d'un microscope; d'où ces célèbres & sçavans Naturalistes concluent que le germe peut avoir vraiment préexisté depuis la création, & que la génération, dans la suite du tems, n'en est que le développement, quoique les parties paroissent à l'Observateur vraiment sortir l'une de l'autre par une nouvelle production, & que le développement positif ne soit pas toûjours visible' (Needham's note in Spallanzani 1769, pt.1:219). Bonnet was mentioned in one other note by Needham, with reference to the leaves of plants (Spallanzani 1769, pt.1:150).

6. See n.5 above.

7. See n.1 above.

En revoyant le passage precedent dans mon livre je remarque une negligence d'expression de ma part, ou une faute d'imprimeur page 219. ligne 7. *sont tous ceux lisés, sont ceux.*[8]

Du reste ayés la bonté de lire mon ouvrage avec les yeux d'un ami, et non pas ceux d'un critique trop exacte, et quand vous l'aurés lû et bien medité dit moi votre sentiment en grand sur le total pris ensemble, car Je ne pretends pas être exempt de fautes particulieres, et meme en assés grand nombre.

Sunt bona, sunt quaedam mediocria, sunt mala multa.[9]

Je finirai par les complimens de la saison, que je vous prie d'accepter de ma part, et de les presenter à votre chere famille, et à tous mes amis de Geneve.

J'ai l'honneur d'etre mon très cher ami, et confrere, avec estime, et un vrai attachement

votre très humble, et très obeissant serviteur,
et sincere ami,

Needham.

J'ai diné dimanche dernier chez Madame d'emville, nous avons parlé de vous, mon cher ami, et il s'en souvient toujours avec plaisir.

[ADDRESS] A Monsieur / Monsieur Bonnet de la Société / Royale des sciences à Londres, de l'academie / Royale de Berlin &c. correspondent de / celle de Paris, / à Geneve. / par Lyons.

MANUSCRIPT
BPUG, MS Bonnet 29:42r-43v.

35

Needham to Bonnet – Paris, 14 March 1769

à Paris, Le 14. de Mars 1769.

Je pars, mon cher Monsieur, et confrere, aujourdhui pour aller m'établir à Bruxelles avec une pension, que l'Imperatrice Reine me donne,[1] et pour aider

---

8. See n.5 above.

9. Martial, *Epigrammata*, 1, 16: 'Sunt bona, sunt quaedam mediocria, sunt mala plura quae legis hic.'

1. Prince Wenzel Anton von Kaunitz (1711-1794), Chancellor of Court and State in Vienna, wrote to Maria Theresa in his report of 24 October 1768 on the establishment of a new learned society in Brussels: 'Ce sérénissime prince [Charles of Lorraine] prévint au reste votre majesté qu'il avait fait écrire par le chef et président [Patrice-François de Neny] à l'abbé Needham, pour voir si la promesse d'un canonicat pourrait l'attirer aux Pays-Bas [see letter 31, n.5], et il résulte des réponses de cet ecclésiastique, qui m'ont été communiquées par un P.S. du comte de Cobenzl du 12 août dernier, qu'il comptait se rendre à Bruxelles vers la fin du mois de septembre, si, en attendant qu'il parvienne à la jouissance des fruits d'un canonicat, votre majesté lui accordait une pension annuelle de 1,000 florins de Brabant' (Gachard 1838:158). On 26 December 1768 prince Charles of Lorraine (1712-1780), Governor-General of the Austrian Netherlands, proposed, in his letter to Maria Theresa, to assign to Needham the vacant canonicate of the Eglise Collégiale et Royale de Soignies (AGR, Chancellerie autrichienne des Pays-Bas, nr.746, patentes ecclésiastiques).

à soutenir avec mes nouveaux confreres la société litteraire, qu'on forme actuellement, et dont la premiere seance se tiendra le six du mois prochain. Il y a
quelque tems sans doute, que vous aurez eu le loisir de parcourir au moins
rapidement mon ouvrage, mais vous ne me dites rien sur ce qu'il peut valoir ni
en bien, ni en mal. Je n'ai reçu non plus aucunes nouvelles à ce sujet ni de M^r·
Haller, ni de notre ami Spalanzani: est ce que j'aurai eu le malheur de degouter
une partie de mes Lecteurs, et de facher sans le vouloir, l'autre? Je n'ai jamais
pretendu autre chose toute ma vie, que de dire naivement mes sentimens bons,
ou mauvais, et je suis encore assés docile pour écouter mes amis, et pour me
prêter à leurs remontrances, pourvu que j'ai assés d'esprit pour sentir la force
de leurs raisonnemens; au moins je n'aurai jamais de l'humeur contre ceux, qui
ne pensent pas comme moi ni en fait de religion, ni en physique, dieu est notre
juge commun, en derniere instance, et la raison nous conduit malgré nous pour
finir sans replique nos controverses à son tribunal. Mais vous etes actuellement
peutetre trop occupé pour penser à moi, et à mes petites occupations, vous
imprimés, dit on, votre nouvelle cosmogonie, que je desire de voir le plutot
possible, et vous etes pour une partie considerable engagé dans la nouvelle
encyclopedie annoncée en Hollande,[2] à la quelle j'aurai deja souscrit, s'il y avoit
ici des libraires autorisés à prendre ma souscription. Si vous pourez le faire pour
moi à Geneve, je vous prie de le faire. Vous ne concevrez pas facilement le plasir
que cette annonce m'a fait munie de votre nom, de cel de Messieurs Haller,
Bernoulli, Tyssot,[3] et autres sçavans de vos climats. Non seulement la partie

When this was approved, count de Cobenzl wrote on 1 February 1769 to Needham and all the other
newly appointed members of the society: 'Sa Majesté notre auguste souveraine, pour relever les
belles-lettres de l'espèce d'engourdissement dans lequel elles se trouvent actuellement aux Pays-
Bas, a résolu d'y établir une Société littéraire, dont les membres, en s'attachant principalement à
l'histoire ancienne, ecclésiastique, civile et naturelle de ces pays, ainsi qu'aux arts et sciences, et en
se communiquant les fruits de leurs études, puissent faire revivre les belles-lettres dans ces provinces.
Elle vous a mis, monsieur, au nombre des membres destinés à composer cette Société.' Initially,
Cobenzl arranged that the first meeting of the new society would take place in his own residence
on 6 April 1769. This meeting was however later postponed to 5 May 1769 (AARB, Correspondance,
for the years 1759-1769; Cobenzl's letter is published by Mailly 1883, 1:21-22).

2. The *Gazette de Leyde* of 14 February 1769 contained an *Avis* announcing that Fortunato
Bartolomeo de Felice was in the process of publishing at Yverdon a revised and enlarged edition of
the *Encyclopédie*, naming as collaborators Bernoulli, Haller, Tissot, and Bonnet. A similar announce-
ment had appeared earlier, in late 1768 in the *Estratto della letteratura europea per l'anno MDCCLXVIII*
(3:241); see Hintzsche (1966:236). The 42 volumes containing the text of the Yverdon *Encyclopédie*
appeared between 1770 and 1775, the 10 volumes of plates between 1775 and 1780, and the 6
volumes of the *Supplément* in 1775 and 1776. On de Felice and the Yverdon *Encyclopédie*, see Maccabez
(1903), Guyot (1955:81-121), Hintzsche (1966), and Darnton (1979:19-21, 300-312).

3. The physician, mathematician, and physicist Daniel Bernoulli (1700-1782), one of the most
outstanding scientists of the eighteenth century, was born in Groningen. In 1721 he obtained his
medical doctorate at Basel University, and in 1723 he travelled to Italy where he continued his
studies in practical medicine at Venice. From 1725 to 1733 he worked at the Academy of Sciences
at St Petersburg. In 1733 he returned to Basel as Professor of Anatomy and Botany, and in 1750
he was appointed Professor of Physics. For a biography of Bernoulli, see Wolf (1858-1862, 3:151-
202); for a bibliography of his works, see Bernoulli (1787:26-32); for his physiological investigations,
see Fried. Huber (1959); and for secondary sources on his mathematical work, see May (1973:7).
An excellent bibliography of and on Bernoulli is provided by Hans Straub in *D.S.B.*, 2 (1970) 36-
46. For more recent works, see Delsedime (1971) and Sheynin (1972a). Daniel Bernoulli was
mentioned as a contributor to the Yverdon *Encyclopédie* in Haller's letter to de Felice of 22 August
1775 (Maccabez 1903:156-57).

Samuel-Auguste-André-David Tissot (1728-1797) was born at Grancey, near Lausanne. He first

medicinale du corps, qui est de la plus grande pauvreté, dit on, en profitera à l'avantage de la société, mais aussi celle de l'ame, qui est bien d'une autre importance, sera purifiée, rectifiée, et rendüe salutaire, d'empoisonnente, qu'elle étoit, au genre humain. Puisse le bon dieu vous recompenser amplement et dans cette vie, et dans l'autre pour avoir cooperé à un dessein si noble, et si plein de la vraie humanité! Je n'ai pas vu M[r.] de Saussure à son passage par Paris[4] pour retourner à Geneve, on me l'a dit après son depart; certainement je l'aurai été le voir à son Hotel, tout éloigné que je suis de cet quartier, si je l'avais sçu dans le tems. Faites lui bien de complimens de ma part, aussi bien, qu'à M[r.] Trembley, et à tous mes amis de Geneve. Il vient de paroitre ici un livre nouveau, dont le titre est, *singularités de la* nature,[5] qui a été enlevé en deux fois vingt quatre heures, avant meme qu'il fût affiché dans la gazette de Paris. Je sçais ce qu'il peut être encore, mais pour avoir été enlevé en si peu du tems il doit être ou bien mauvais, ou d'une excellence exquise. C'est un assés petit ouvrage compris dans un seul volume en douze, qui ne passera pas, supposé qu'il y passe, à la postérité par sa masse, comme l'encyclopedie de Paris pourait peutetre passer, si la votre moins massive, et plus spirituelle ne le consume pas avant l'incendie generale du globe. Adieu, mon cher Monsieur et confrere, saluez Madame de ma part, et me croyez toujours avec estime,

votre ami affectionné
Needham.

studied in Geneva, and from 1745 to 1749 he studied medicine at Montpellier under François Boissier de Sauvages (1706-1767). In 1749 he settled in Lausanne and devoted himself to medical practice, soon gaining a considerable reputation. While continuing the study of theoretical medicine, he always related it to practical experience. In 1755 he translated Haller's papers on irritability into French and became one of the main supporters of the theory. In the late 1750s he advocated preventive smallpox inoculation and entered into a long controversy with Anton de Haen (1704-1776). Later he made relevant contributions to popular hygiene and neurology. In 1766 he was made Professor at the Academy of Lausanne. At Joseph II's (1741-1790) second invitation to teach at the University of Pavia he accepted and taught clinical medicine there in 1781-1783. On his return to Lausanne he was made Director of the newly founded Collège de Médecine. The best-documented biography of Tissot, one of the major personalities of the Swiss medical Enlightenment, is still that by Eynard (1839), which also contains some of his correspondence with Bonnet (four letters from Tissot to Bonnet are preserved in the BPUG). Most of his published works were included in his *Œuvres completes* (1809-1813); and all the known letters of Haller to Tissot, which cast a fresh light on his medical practice, have been edited by Hintzsche (1977). For Tissot's ideas on psychology, see Harms (1956); for those on neurology, see Bucher (1958); for his theory of inoculation, see Giordani (1973); and for his contacts with Italian scientists, see Mazzolini (1973:318-19) and Fontana (1980:170-71).

4. In February 1768 Saussure set out for Paris with his wife. He lodged at the Hôtel de la Paix until 10 June and then departed for Holland and England. In Paris he met Bernard de Jussieu (1699-1777), spoke with Buffon and a few of the philosophes, frequented the salon of the duchesse d'Enville, and met madame Necker (1739-1794) several times. On 7 January 1769 he left England and was back in Geneva on 1 February. On his way he stopped in Paris, and it is probably to this second visit that Needham is alluding. For Saussure's tour, see Freshfield (1920:91-120).

5. *Les Singularités de la nature* (Basle [Genève] 1768). The anonymous author was Voltaire. Chapter 20 contains one of Voltaire's satirical accounts of Needham's observations on eels in flour paste and in blighted wheat (Voltaire 1768:65-68; see also Roe 1985 and section 5 of the Introduction). On 25 January 1769 Bonnet wrote to Haller, 'Les *Singularités de la Nature* ou plutôt celles de l'Ignorant Auteur, sont bien toutes entières de Fernex [Voltaire]. J'y ai trouvé beaucoup plus de bévues que de lignes. Jamais on ne vit une ignorance plus profonde, & une déraison plus continuë. Ce Garçon Naturaliste n'a rien lu ou n'a rien retenu ou n'a rien voulu retenir. Il traite la Nature comme la Bible' (Sonntag 1983:801).

Si vous m'ecrivés quelques fois, et si je peux vous être utile dans ce pais, addressés vos lettres pour moi de la société litteraire etc. à M^r· danoet Banquier, et negociant à Bruxelles.

[ADDRESS] A Monsieur / Monsieur Bonnet de la / Société de Londres, / de l'acade- mie de Berlin & c. / correspondant de celle de Paris. / à Geneve. / par Lyons

MANUSCRIPT
BPUG, MS Bonnet 29:44r-45v.

36

Bonnet to Needham – Genthod, 8 April 1769

Genthod le 8.e d'Avril 1769.
J'étois fort occupé, mon cher Ami: je le suis encore. J'achêve mon Ouvrage. Mais; ma *Cosmogonie* étoit finie six mois avant que je recusse la votre. J'en suis a present aux Preuves de la REVELATION. La Marche est toute^a à moi, et vous la jugerés nouvelle. Plusieurs Principes sont encore à moi. J'écris d'après mes propres Méditations: ^{a}ce sera, si vous voulés, un autre *Essai Analytique* & c^a

Soufrés que je n'entre point dans le détail sur votre Ouvrage. Vous sçavés que nous ne pensons point de même sur la Generation. Nous-nous rapprocherions un peu plus sur quelques Points de *Cosmogonie*.

Je ne sçaurois me faire aucune Idée d'une *Force végetatrice* qui *organise*. Vos *Feux d'Artifice* m'amusent et ne m'éclairent pas.[1] LEIBNITZ,[2] dont vous-vous

---

1. Bonnet is referring to the following passage in Needham's notes, in which Needham likened the predetermined manner in which the vegetative force operates in regeneration to the way the path of a projectile and the pattern of fireworks are determined by necessary physical laws: 'Or reprenons à présent l'idée générale qui doit résulter de ces idées particulieres, & nous concevrons sans difficulté qu'une force végétatrice, exactement distribuée, intérieure & déterminée en elle-même spécifiquement, doit donner par ces moyens, quand elle pousse au déhors, une figure toûjours déterminée, comme une force projectile quelconque déterminée, & combinée avec la gravitation, décrit nécessairement une certaine portion parabolique d'une forme déterminée, & s'arrête à un point mathématiquement fixé, ou comme un feu d'artifice dont des forces sont combinées avant que l'on applique le feu, se répand au déhors, & produit une figure déterminée d'avance par la volonté de l'Artificier' (Spallanzani 1769, pt.1:229). Bonnet quoted and criticised this passage in a letter to Spallanzani of 13 May 1769 (see Castellani 1971:102).

2. For a biography of Gottfried Wilhelm Leibniz (1646-1716), see Müller and Krönert (1969). For a bibliography of his writings, see Ravier (1937); and for writings on Leibniz, see K. Müller (1967) and the bibliographical supplements that appear regularly in *Studia Leibnitiana*. For the influence of Leibniz's thought on Needham, see Solinas (1967:85-91), Tega (1971:160), Roe (1983:168-71), and section 3 of the Introduction; and for his influence on Bonnet, see G. Bonnet (1930:87-92), Rocci (1975:67-76), Marx (1976:79-86), and section 4 of the Introduction. For Leibniz's biological views and his belief in preformation, see Roger (1968). Needham owned the Genevan edition of Leibniz's *Opera omnia* (Leibniz 1768) and other individual works (*Catalogue* 1782, pt.1:13, 61).

étayés,[3] posoit en Principe les Germes, et même l'Emboitement. Et vous traités de *monstrueuse* une telle Physique.

Je laisse à notre Ami Mr Spallanzani à vous répondre sur les Animalcules: plusieurs de vos Repliques me paroissent éxiger de nouvelles Expériences. Il sçaura les faire.[4]

Il vous est arrivé ce que j'avois prévu: vous m'avés cité de Tête,[5] et vous m'avés mal rendu. Vous avés estropié mon Poulet ou plutot celui de Mr de Haller.[6] Vous n'avés pas donné la moindre attention aux Conséquences immédiattes[a] &c. Vous avés passé à côté. Il falloit les analyser. Ce n'est point ainsi qu'on traite les Faits et de pareils Faits.

Vous allés jusqu'à tirer les Champignons de l'Animal. Ils ont des Graines comme l'Orme, le Frêne, &c. Pourquoi cette prétenduë *Clavaria* ne vient-elle que sur la Tête de la Nymphe? [a]Je l'y ai vue aussi, et ne l'ai point prise pour un *Végétal.*[a][7]

Je ne vous dis rien de votre Stile: vous êtes Anglois. Il nuit prodigieusement à vos Idées. Vos Phrases ne finissent point, et vos incidences se multiplient à l'infini. Vous n'émondés ni n'élagués. Il faut percer des Brossailles très épaisses pour arriver jusqu'à vous. N'auriés vous pas mieux fait d'Ecrire en Anglois? Vous ne frapperés pas les Incrédules; vous les amorcerés bien moins. Votre Antidote devoit être mis dans une autre Boite. Je crains qu'il ne trouvent ici de nouveaux Sujets de plaisanter.

Vous aimés la candeur en amitié: je l'aime aussi. Je vous écris donc comme à un Ami que j'aimerai toujours, et auquel je dirai toujours ce que je pense.

Je manquerois à la reconnoissance, si je ne vous remerciois point de la mention honnorable et si amicale que vous avés bien voulu faire de moi.

Mr de Haller a été très occupé: il ne vous a point lu encore et ne se flatte pas de vous entendre.[8] Vous deviés le lire lui même, et il ne me paroit point que

---

3. Needham cited Leibniz several times in his notes: 'Que l'on examine bien ce système, on lui trouvera de la conformité avec la bonne métaphysique; j'entends celle de *Leibnitz* [...]'; and 'Si dans mon essai sur la génération, j'avance, en raisonnant d'après *Leibnitz* [...]' (Spallanzani 1769, pt.1:146, 232; see also pt.1:147-48, 291, and pt.2:35, 48-49).

4. Spallanzani replied to Needham's criticism in the first volume of his *Opuscoli di fisica animale, e vegetabile*, which was published in 1776.

5. See letter 34, n.5.

6. See letter 22, n.8, and letter 34, n.5. See also Sonntag (1983:797).

7. In his notes in Spallanzani (1769), Needham discussed the 'mouche végétante des Caraibes', which was a type of fungus (*Clavaria sobolifera*, now *Cordyceps sobolifera*) that grew on the heads of dead nymphs of cicadas, reportedly found in the West Indies. Needham examined several specimens that had been sent to Paris and dissected one with Michel Adanson (1727-1806). Believing that fungi did not produce seeds and having found none in his dissection, Needham attributed the growth of this fungus on the nymphs to a vegetation of their animal substance. As he explained, 'Si cela n'indique pas un passage clair & manifeste du vital au végétal, & réciproquement, [...] il nous fournira néanmoins des preuves assez fortes par induction, pour croire que les plantes au moins subalternes, telles que les *fungi* en général, dont personne n'a jamais pû découvrir les semences avec certitude, peuvent se former par végétation de la substance morte des animaux' (Spallanzani 1769, pt.1:257; see also pp.249-54, 262-65). Bonnet disagreed and claimed that all 'champignons' (fungi) reproduce by seeds, although he admitted that their seeds were often invisible (see B.O., 4, pt.2:87-88 n.4/8:366-68 n.4; and Sonntag 1983:804).

8. On 3 January 1769 Haller, speaking about himself, wrote to Bonnet: 'Il a reçu le Needham; il est presque faché d'etre obligé de le lire'; and on 21 February, 'Je n'ai pas lu encore le tenebreux Needham. Je suis fort occupé, et j'ai des livres un peu anciens a lire' (Sonntag 1983:793, 805).

vous l'ayés lu. Votre méthode de ne point lire n'est pas applicable en matière de Faits.

M.ʳ Trembley ne vous lira pas: il connoit en general vos Principes, et ils ne peuvent se nicher dans sa Tête. Il connoit votre *Marche*, et elle n'est pas la sienne.

Je ne travaille point à cette Refonde de l'Encyclopédie. À peine ma santé suffit elle à mes propres Ecrits. L'Avis de la Gazette de Leide étoit faux.[9] Vous y verrés un Contre-Avis, que j'y ai fait insèrer.[10] M.ʳ de Haller étoit aussi annoncé faussement. Je m'en suis plaint à l'Editeur,[11] qui rejette la sottise sur des Amis de Hollande.

Dites-moi un mot de cette nouvelle Academie de Bruxelles. Je vous félicite de tout mon Coeur de cette marque distinguée d'estime que vous avés reçuë de cette grande Reine.

Recevés tous mes voeux, mon cher et bon Ami et les assurances de mon inviolable attachement. *ᵃNos Amis et ma Femme vous remercient de votre bon souvenir, et joignent leurs voeux aux miens.ᵃ*

[ADDRESS] Bruxelles, M.ʳ Néédham, de la Societé Royale d'Angleterre &c

MANUSCRIPTS
BPUG, MS Bonnet 73:37r-37v; MS Bonnet 85:185r-186r.

EDITIONS
'Je laisse [...] les faires' published in Castellani (1973:99).

TEXT NOTES
  a. B: *omitted*

9. See letter 35, n.2. Bonnet was furious with de Felice for including his name among the collaborators in the new revised edition of the *Encyclopédie*, without authorisation (see n.11 below). He had not forgotten de Felice's criticism of his *Essai analytique* (see letter 16, n.3) and strongly disapproved of de Felice's *Encyclopédie* project (Marx 1976:205-13).

10. On 22 March 1769 Bonnet wrote to his friend Allamand at Leiden asking him to insert in the *Gazette de Leyde* the following text: 'On fait savoir au public que c'est sans le moindre fondement qu'on a inséré dans un Avis, N° XIII de cette *Gazette*, 14 de février 1769, que M. Bonnet travaillait avec quelques savants à une nouvelle édition de l'*Encyclopédie*. Il déclare expressément qu'il n'a aucune part à cette édition, et que l'entrepreneur lui-même lui ayant proposé de s'y intéresser, il lui avait répondu que sa santé et ses occupations ne lui permettaient point de s'engager dans un semblable travail. M. Bonnet a donc lieu d'être fort surpris qu'après une réponse si positive, cet entrepreneur ait osé le donner au public pour un des auteurs de sa nouvelle édition' (BPUG, MS Bonnet 73:33; here quoted from Guyot 1955:88). According to Marx (1976:207) this text was never published.

11. On 25 March 1769 Bonnet wrote to de Felice: 'Je n'ai été informé que fort tard de cet *Avis*. Il ne peut guère partir que de vous, Monsieur; et si, en effet, vous l'avez fait insérer dans cette Gazette, comment est-il possible que vous m'ayez annoncé si expressément au public, avant même que d'avoir reçu ma réponse, qui n'était que sous la date du 21 de février? Comment, après avoir reçu cette réponse, ne vous êtes-vous point hâté de donner un contre-avis dans la même Gazette? J'ai donc écrit sur-le-champ à un ami célèbre que j'ai à Leyde, pour le prier de faire mettre dans la Gazette de cette ville un contre-avis si nécessaire, que je me devais à moi-même et que je devais à la vérité. Je le laisse le maître de la manière de le tourner, parce que je connais sa prudence et sa modération. Mon illustre ami, M. de Haller, est nommé le premier dans cet *Avis* dont j'ai à me plaindre. J'ai toutes les raisons du monde de douter qu'il soit nommé ici avec plus de fondement que moi. Vous êtes nommé le dernier, et ceci semblerait confirmer que vous êtes l'auteur de l'*Avis*. Ne prenez point, Monsieur, en mauvaise part le juste reproche que je suis forcé de vous faire; mais il ne serait pas bon que vous me fissiez contracter auprès du public une obligation que ma santé, mes occupations, et mes forces ne me permettraient point du tout de remplir. Je vous le répète: j'ai tout lieu de présumer qu'une si grande entreprise ne nuise beaucoup à votre santé et à vos affaires' (BPUG, MS Bonnet 73:34v; here quoted from Guyot 1955:89).

37

Bonnet to Needham – Genthod, 8 July 1769

À Genthod, près de Genève, le 8.ᵉ de Juillet 1769.

Ma Lettre du 8.ᵉ d'Avril vous sera, sans doute, parvenue à Bruxelles, mon digne Ami: je l'y avois adressée selon vos ordres. Je ne crains point que la franchise avec laquelle je vous ai parlé de votre dernier Ouvrage vous ait choqué. Je sçais que vous aimés la franchise en amitié, parce que votre Coeur cherche sincèrement le Vrai et le Bon.

Vous êtes bien sur que je ne me choquerois point non plus des remarques critiques que vous feriés sur mes Ouvrages. Nous sommes tous deux également amis du Vrai, et tous deux nous faisons plus de cas de la Philosophie *pratique* que de toutes les Spéculations les plus sublimes de la Philosophie Théorétique.

Ce nouvel Ouvrage, dont je vous entretenu dans mes Lettres, est sorti de dessous notre Presse à la fin de Mai ou au commencement de Juin.[1] Le Libraire qui l'a imprimé dans notre Ville s'est chargé de vous en faire parvenir un Exemplaire dans votre nouvelle résidence de Bruxelles. *Il doit y arriver par la voye ordinaire des Rouliers; cette voye est malheureusement un peu longue; mais je n'en connoissois point de plus prompte, qui fut aussi sure.*

Si vous prenés la peine, mon cher Ami, de lire ce Livre avec l'attention qu'il éxige, vous trouverés que j'y ai développé et éclairci la plupart de mes Principes fondamentaux sur l'Oeconomie de notre Etre, sur les Regenerations organiques, sur l'Accroissement des Corps organisés, &c &c. Cet Ouvrage contient donc tous les Supplémens nécessaires à l'intelligence de mes derniers Ecrits. Parce que ces Ecrits forment tous une Chaîne et une assés longue Chaîne, il peut facilement arriver que je ne sois pas bien saisi par des Lecteurs qui n'ont pas assés éxercé leur Attention: et combien le nombre de ces Lecteurs est-il grand! Il étoit donc très convenable que je m'interprêtasse moi même et que je prévinse ainsi les effets trop ordinaires de l'inattention, de la précipitation ou du préjugé.

J'ose me flatter, qu'il vous paroîtra, qu'aucun Ecrivain de Philosophie et d'Histoire Naturelle ne s'étoit plus appliqué que moi à mettre dans ses Pensés cet ordre, cette clarté, cette précision, cet enchainement qui ont tant d'influence sur l'acquisition et sur les progrès de nos Connoissances. Et parce que nos Idées tiennent indissolublement aux Mots qui en sont les Signes, j'ai du m'occuper autant des Mots que des Choses, et approprier mon Style aux divers Sujets que j'avois à manier.

Je n'ai pas entrepris l'éxamen critique de votre dernier Ouvrage[2]: je ne voulois pas donner au mien le caractère Polémique, qui ne pouvoit lui convenir, et qui n'a jamais été de mon gout. Je ne suis borné à établir mes Principes sur des

---

1. Charles Bonnet, *La Palingénésie philosophique, ou idées sur l'état passé et sur l'état futur des êtres vivans* [...] *et qui contient principalement le précis de ses Recherches sur le christianisme* (Genève 1769). See also B.O., 7:111-680/15:165-469 and 16:1-538.
2. This is an allusion to Needham's treatise in the second part of Spallanzani (1769). See letter 32, n.1.

fondemens que la Saine Philosophie put avouer. C'est ce que je crois avoir éxécuté dans mon *Tableau des Considerations*[3] et dans les Parties IX, X, XI, de la *Palingénésie.*[4]

J'ai taché d'esquisser dans cette *Palingénésie* ce ravissant Système de Bienveuillance universelle, qui s'étoit offert à ma contemplation, et qui m'a paru embrasser dans son immensité tout ce qui pense, sent ou respire. J'ai souhaité de pénétrer l'Ame de mes Lecteurs des hautes Idées que je m'étois moi même formées de cette BONTE ADORABLE qui enveloppe tous les Etres vivans.

Ces Méditations si propres à ennoblir toutes nos conceptions, m'ont conduit à des Méditations plus consolantes encore; et beaucoup plus importantes. Je parle de celles qui ont pour objet le Bonheur futur de l'Homme. J'ai donc été appellé à rechercher les Fondemens de nos plus chères Esperances ou ce qui revient au même, à m'occuper des Preuves du CHRISTIANISME.

J'ai eu uniquement en vuë dans cette belle Recherche de dissiper les doutes de l'Incrédule Philosophe et vertueux. J'ai essayé d'éclairer son Entendement, de toucher son Coeur; de l'intèresser à méditer avec moi sur les Preuves si nombreuses, si variées, si frappantes de cette REVELATION, qu'il admettroit probablement si elle lui avoit été présentée d'une manière assortie à sa manière de voir et de philosopher. La plupart des meilleurs[a] Apologistes ont pris un ton et une marche qui n'étoient point faits pour plaire à l'honnête[b] Incrédule. Je l'ai assés insinué dans ma Préface:[5] vous jugerés, mon bon Ami, si ma Méthode est préferable. J'aurai au moins fait l'essai d'une Méthode aussi nouvelle que philosophique. Veuille le PÈRE des Lumières répandre sa Bénédiction sur un Travail que je consacre à célèbrer ses Bienfaits, et à ramener à cette VÉRITÉ que nous chérissons, ceux qui ont eu le malheur de la méconnoitre!

Comptés, mon vertueux Ami, que je vous serai toujours inviolablement attaché.

[ADDRESS] Bruxelles, M.ʳ Néédham de la Societé Royale d'Angleterre

MANUSCRIPTS
    BPUG, MS Bonnet 73:60r-60v; MS Bonnet 85:186v-187v.

TEXT NOTES
    a. B: *omitted   b*. B: à l'Incrédule

3. 'Tableau des considérations sur les corps organisés; ou exposition succinte des principes de l'Auteur sur la génération et sur le développement, précédée de quelques remarques sur l'art de conjecturer en physique, &c.' (Bonnet 1769a, 1:59-113 and B.O., 7:39-75/15:59-112).
4. Bonnet (1769a, 1:320-423) and B.O., 7:239-320/15:351-469.
5. Bonnet (1769a, 1:xii-xv) and B.O., 7:iv-vi/15:ix-xii.

38

Needham to Bonnet – Brussels, 21 August 1769

à Bruxelles, Le 21. d'aoust, 1769.

Je vous remercie, mon très cher et respectable ami, de votre derniere lettre du 8. Juillet si convenable à votre caractere, et si digne de vous à tous égards par les sentimens qu'elle contient. Je vous dois encore de nouveaux remercimens pour le present, que vous m'avez destiné,[1] et que j'attends encore avec la derniere impatience. Je ne puis, ce qui me desole, former encore aucunes conjectures de temps, que votre ouvrage doit me parvenir; il me semble nean-moins qu'en trois mois depuis sa publication, il aura pû m'arriver du fond meme de l'amerique. Votre libraire assurément doit avoir quelque correspondant à Paris, et un certain nombre d'exemplaires. Ne pourra-t il pas lui donner ordre de m'en expedier un par le carosse, qui va regulierement deux fois la semaine de Paris à Bruxelles. Ce sera un paquet, qui me coutera quarante cinq sols de port; c'est peu de chose auprès de mon impatience de vous lire, et sur tout cette partie, qui traite de la revelation; tous les systemes de philosophes passés et à venir ne sont rien en fait d'importance vis à vis de ce seul sujet. Cette partie m'interesse d'autant plus, que j'attends de vous une certaine façon claire, lumineuse, et victorieuse de traiter les memes argumens si souvent deployés par tant d'autres, mais d'une maniere revoltante, ou lache, ou peu lumineuse. Tachez donc en parlant à votre libraire de me contenter aussitot, que cela se pourra, et de ne pas me laisser languir si long tems. J'ai d'autant plus de besoin des consolations, que je puis tirer de vos ouvrages, que je sort d'une maladie de langueur, d'une espece de Rheumatisme sourd, qui me tient depuis six semaines, et qui à la fin se decide de tomber sur mon œil gauche. Elle commence neanmoins à se dissiper, et dans peu de tems j'espere d'en être totalement delivré. Ayez la bonté de presenter mes respects à Madame, et à tous mes amis de Geneve. Soyez toujours persuadé de mon attachement parfait, et ne me rayez jamais du nombre de vos amis les plus fideles.

J'ai l'honneur, d'etre, mon très cher,
et très respectable ami et confrere,
votre très humble, et très obeissant serviteur
Needham.

Si je pouvois connoitre le nom du libraire, qui aura la distribution de votre ouvrage à Paris, j'engagerai le libraire françois Vasse établi ici d'en demander un certain nombre d'exemplaires. Il ne puis, il me semble, être trop connu pour l'interet de la religion. Adieu, et dieu vous recompense de vos travaux; ce qui vaudra plus, que tous les honneurs humains.

[ADDRESS] A Monsieur / Monsieur Bonnet de la Société / Royale de Londres, de l'academie de / Berlin &c. et correspondant de celle / de Paris / à Geneve

MANUSCRIPT
BPUG, MS Bonnet 29:46r-47v.

1. See letter 37, n.1.

39

Bonnet to Needham – Genthod, 16 September 1769

Genthod le 16.ᵉ 7.ᵇʳᵉ 1769.

Vous avés bien raison, mon vertueux Ami, de vous plaindre de l'extreme lenteur de la marche de ma Palingénésie. Çà été avec un vrai déplaisir que j'ai vu dans votre bonne Lettre du 21.ᵉ du mois dernier, que vous n'aviés point encore reçu l'Exemplaire que mon amitié s'étoit empressée à vous adresser. Les Associés Philibert et Chirol, mes Libraires de Genève, qui l'ont imprimé, en ont envoyé un bon nombre d'Exemplaires aux Libraires *Saillant et Nyon à Paris*, leurs Correspondans. Si vous n'avés pas en main celui que je vous destinois, prenés la peine d'écrire au S.ʳ Saillant et Nyon à Paris pour les prier de vous envoyer ce Livre par le Carosse de Bruxelles, et marqués leur que je leur en ferai rembourser la *valeur* et le Port. Croyés, mon digne Ami, que je ne suis pas moins impatient que vous, de voir ce Livre sur votre Table, et je ne serai pleinement satisfait, que lors que votre première Lettre m'apprendra l'impression qu'il aura produit sur vous. Je me refère là dessus à la Lettre que je vous ai écrite le 8.ᵉ de Juillet, et où je vous entretenois de mes vuës, de ma marche &c.

N'oubliés pas non plus de me parler de votre Santé. Elle m'intéresse sincérement. Vous me parliés d'un *Rhumatisme Sourd* qui s'étoit fixé sur votre Oeil gauche; apparemment sur celui qui a le plus observé et à qui nous devons des Vérités precieuses. Je fais mille voeux pour le rétablissement parfait d'une Santé à la conservation de laquelle un Ami de la Nature et de la RELIGION ne sçauroit être indifferent.

Etes vous content de votre nouvel établissement de Bruxelles? Cette nouvelle Académie que la grande Reine y a fondée, commence-t-elle à répondre au louable but de son Institution?

Vous n'avés pas oublié cette Caisse que vous m'aviés chargé d'expédier à Turin à M.ʳ Sabatier, et qui contenoit les Exemplaires de votre dernier Ouvrage destinés à vos Amis d'Italie. Cette Caisse est bien parvenue à M.ʳ Sabatier, et pourtant M.ʳ Spallanzani m'a mandé de Modène en datte du 26.ᵉ d'Aoust,[1] qu'il n'avoit point encore reçu votre Livre, et qu'il alloit en écrire à M.ʳ Sabatier. Ce dernier auroit-il été d'une si prodigieuse négligence, que de differer plus de *six mois* à rendre les Paquets à leur Adresse.

M.ʳ Spallanzani est toujours fort occupé de la Traduction Italienne de ma *Contemplation de la Nature* dont le Tome 1.ᵉʳ est sorti de dessous la Presse.[2] Il enrichit cette Traduction d'un assés grand nombre de Notes. Vous sçavés que ce Livre a aussi été Traduit en Allemand[3] et en Anglois.[4] On en a fait aussi

---

1. For Spallanzani's letter of 26 August 1769 to Bonnet, see *Epistolario* (1:201-203). See also letter 32, n.4.

2. Carlo Bonnet, *Contemplazione della natura* (Modena 1769-1770). This Italian translation went through many editions: Venezia 1773; Venezia 1781; Napoli 1787-1788; Venezia 1790; Catania 1791; Venezia 1797; and Venezia 1818 (see Prandi 1952:34).

3. *Betrachtung über die Natur* (Leipzig 1766). For further editions see Marx (1976:713).

4. *The Contemplation of nature* (London 1766).

quatre Editions Françoises.[5] Il y en a déjà trois de la *Palingénésie*,[6] et deux Traductions, l'une en Allemand,[7] l'autre en Italien[8] vont paroitre.

Je vous renouvelle, mon cher et bon Ami, les assurances les plus sincères d'un attachement qui ne finira qu'avec la vie de

[ADDRESS] Bruxelles, M.ʳ Néédham de la Societé Royale.

MANUSCRIPT
BPUG, MS Bonnet 73:81*v*-82*r* (not included in copy B).

40

Needham to Bonnet – 1 January 1770

à Bruxelles, Le 1. Janvier 1770.
chez Mʳ· danoot Banquier.

Mon cher Monsieur,
  ami, et confrere.

Vous étes également de toutes les saisons, ainsi ne mettez pas cette ressouvenance sur le compte de la nouvelle année, quoique je profite de la saison pour vous souhaiter, et à toute votre digne famille, non pas plusieurs années, mais une éternité de bonheur. Independamment neanmoins de tous ces devoirs d'amitie, et d'estime il est tems de vous remercier de votre ouvrage, que j'ai lû avec le double plaisir, d'un ami, qui se rejouit avec celui, qui'il aime, du bien, qui en doit resulter en faveur de l'humanité prise en general; et cel d'un chretien, qui reconnoit en votre personne un de plus puissants soutiens de ses plus chers interets. C'est un bonheur de plus pour l'avantage de la cause, que vous n'étes pas du nombre de ces ecclesiastiques, car les meilleurs ouvrages, qui partent de gens de cette classe, ne font gueres d'impression, vous le sçavez, sur les incredules qui en traitent les auteurs, comme des écrivains mercenaires, et comme des personnes aveuglés par leur interet present. Tels sont les sots préjugés dans une affaire de la plus grande importance de ce siecle puerile, qu'on nous presente comme cel de la Philosophie. C'est un exemple de la bonne espece encore, que vous donnez aux vrais philosophes en general, qui pendant qu'ils voient les interets de la société bouleversés par cette nouvelle irruption de barbares ne s'élevent pas contre eux pour repousser leurs attentats. Renfermés en eux memes, ils s'amusent avec leurs petits systemes, qui n'embrassent qu'une très petite partie de nos connoissances, pendant que le tout est en danger de perir par les mains destructives des nos Encelades modernes.[1] J'admire sur tout l'energie, la

5. The French editions appeared at Amsterdam (1764, 1766, and 1769) and at Yverdon (1767).
6. For the year 1769 we are aware only of two editions (Genève 1769; and Amsterdam 1769).
7. *Philosophische Palingenesie* (Zürich 1769-1770).
8. No complete Italian translation of the *Palingénésie* is known to us. Part of it was translated as *Ricerche filosofiche sopra le prove del cristianesimo* (Venezia 1771).

1. Enceladus was one of the giants of Greek mythology who fought against the gods lead by Zeus and were defeated. According to one account of the legend, Enceladus was killed by Pallas; according to another account he was buried under Aetna by Zeus.

clarté, et la precision de votre style, quoiqu'en puissent dire certains sçavans François, que j'ai vû ici, et dont la célébrité est en quelque façon reconnüe, mais Je ne suis pas fait après tant d'années d'étude à me determiner dans mes jugemens, par ce que les autres sentent, ou croient sentir, mais par ce que je sens en moi-meme. Tout ce qui est bien raisonné, precis, clair, et fortement exprimé est bien écrit pour moi, et la mesure exacte des periodes, l'harmonie, le choix trop scrupuleux des mots, les pretendus *hiatus*, et mille autres niaiseries grammaticales n'éntrent pour rien chez moi: c'est du sçavoir à la chinoise, dont les idées ne vont gueres plus loin, que les signes; et pourvu que la lumiere perce sans obstruction, quand je ne cherche autre chose, qu'à m'éclairer, que m'importe la forme plus, ou moins élegante des fenetres, qui la transmettent? L'eloge, que je viens de faire de votre ouvrage est le resultat d'un examen raisonné, mais general; si je voulois prendre les choses en detail, sur tout dans les deux parties Theologique, et metaphysique nous ne serons pas toujours d'accord; vous croyez sans doute en les retrecissant de les avoir bien lié avec votre physique palpable; Je crois en les étendant bien plus loin, que vous, et en montant du palpable, à l'intelligible de pouvoir passer les bornes étroits de la chair, et du sang, pour les lier avec ma physique plus exaltée que la votre, bien plus heureusement. Vous me paroissés deprimer la religion, et la metaphysique pour les rendre palpables, pendant qu'il est plus convenable, et plus philosophi-que à mon avis d'exalter la physique avec Leibnitz, et Mallebranche[2] pour la faire atteindre à la foi, dont les objets selon St Paul *excedent tout entendement*. Les miracles selon vous ne sont pas des operations immediates de la divinité, mais les suites d'un plan naturel préétabli, qui se developpe en lieu, et tems; les peines de la vie future, quoique énoncées comme éternelles dans l'evangile, ne peuvent pas l'etre; et tous ceux, qui admettent des mysteres en fait de religion audela de certaines bornes tracés dans votre livre, et qui ne sont pas reduisibles au systeme palpable, que vous avez établi, sont des gens, qui n'ont autre motif de croyance, que le merite pretendu de tout croire sans distinction. Jean le clerc[3] avoit aussi autrefois crû, comme vous, qu'en adoptant le systeme de la durée bornée des peines d'enfer, il leveroit bien de difficultés, que la raison trouve dans la conduite de dieu, *parce qu'il est naturel*, dit il, *de se determiner du côté, ou il y a moins de difficultés.*[4]

2. For a biography of Nicolas Malebranche (1638-1715), the philosopher of the Congregation of the Oratory, see André (1886); for a bibliography of his writings, see Malebranche (1962-1967, 20:291-331); and for literature on Malebranche, see Malebranche (1962-1967, 20:333-451). For a recent study on Malebranche, which also investigates the reception of his thought during the eighteenth century, see Alquié (1974). For Malebranche's speculations on physics and his influence in this field, see Brunet (1934), Gueroult (1954), and A. Robinet (1964). Needham owned some of Malebranche's most famous works; see *Catalogue* (1782, pt.1:39,59).

3. In 1683 the Genevan scholar and Armenian theologian Jean Le Clerc (1657-1736) was expelled from his town for his heterodox ideas. He settled in Holland, where he was soon made Professor of Hebrew and Philosophy at the Remonstrant College at Amsterdam. The editor of a number of journals and religious and classical texts, Le Clerc was very influential in biblical criticism. For a general introduction to his life and work, see Barnes (1938), which also contains a bibliography of Le Clerc's writings; for a list of studies on Le Clerc, see Geisendorf (1966:407); and for more recent works on Le Clerc, see Sina (1978), Bentley (1978), Pitassi (1982), and Simonutti (1982).

4. In his 'Défense de la bonté & de la sainteté divine, contre les objections de Mr. Bayle', published in the *Bibliotheque choisie, pour servir de suite à la Bibliotheque universelle*, Année MDCCVI, 9:103-71 (here quoted from the edition of Amsterdam 1719). Le Clerc argued that Bayle should have embraced the sect of Origene, because in his *Dictionaire* Bayle had shown that this sect presented

Voici la reponse, que lui fit Bayle,[5] qui, quoique sceptic étoit bien au fait du vrai esprit de christianisme.[6] 'C'est ainsi, qui parlent ceux, qui cherchent à ruiner tous les mysteres de la religion; ils posent pour fondement, que les interpretations de l'écriture les moins exposées aux difficultés sont les meilleures. Mais l'esprit du christianisme a toujours été contraire à cela, et cet esprit s'est conservé heureusement dans les communions Protestantes: elles souscrivent de tout leur cœur à cette belle maxime, qui fût lüe dans la conference de Fontaine-bleau: *aux choses de la foi il ne faut pas toujours choisir ce qui est suivi de moins de difficultés; mais plûtot il faut poser ce qui est conforme aux paroles des saintes écritures, et à la tradition de l'eglise, encore qu'il s'y trouve plus de difficultés.* Que deviendront la permission du Peché, la chute de notre premier Pere, et ses suites, si nos idées naturelles sont la mesure commune de la bonté, et de la sainté de dieu, et de la bonté, et de la sainté humaine que deviendra l'existence meme de la divinité, si on doit rien accorder, que ce que la raison comprend?'[7] Vous voyez, mon cher ami, que si nous étendons notre foi bien au de la dela votre, ce n'est pas pour nous procurer un merite imaginaire par un excés de credulité, mais c'est uniquement parce que nous nous croyons obligés de nous soumettre à tout ce, que dieu nous a révélé clairement sans trop nous appuyer sur notre raison, dont nous reconnoissons la foiblesse meme dans les choses naturelles. Reduire les mysteres de la religion au vil taux de nos foibles conceptions, ou en rejetter tout le merveilleux avec Rousseau pour s'attacher à la seule morale de l'evangile, ne me paroit guere differer, puisque l'un ou l'autre systeme aneantit totalement le merite de la foi, si fortement recommandée dans les saintes écritures. En un mot si vous admettez un être simple intellectuel, tel que l'esprit humain, comme une chose possible, pourquoi pas admettre avec Leibnitz des êtres simples materiels, c'est à dire denués de toute intelligence, mais doués de certaines forces inferieu-res, qui produisent par leurs combinaisons, et leurs actions reciproques tous les phenomenes materiels de l'univers? Si vous croiez avec St Paul, que *in ipso*

fewer philosophical difficulties than others. Le Clerc's argument was the following: 'On auroit crû qu'il auroit dû donc l'embrasser, plûtôt que de dire qu'il est faux, & de prendre pour vrais ceux qu'il avoit détruits, par ses objections. Il étoit naturel de se déterminer du côté, ou il y avoit moins de difficultés, si l'on avoit pour but d'établir quelque chose, & non pas de détruire tout' (pp.138-39). Needham probably quoted parts of these sentences by Le Clerc from Bayle (1725-1727, 3:994), who had reproduced them.

5. The most authoritative biography of Pierre Bayle (1647-1706) is contained in the first volume of Labrousse (1963-1964), which also contains an extensive bibliography on Bayle; for a review of recent studies on him, see Jossua (1967). Bayle and Le Clerc corresponded with one another (Labrousse 1961:375), but soon their relationship fell into deep and bitter conflicts over biblical criticism, the divinity of scriptures, and mutual accusations of holding heterodox ideas. On such contrasts, see Barnes (1938:228-37) and Labrousse (1963-1964, 1:259-60, 262-65, and 2:328-31).

6. This sentence by Needham and Bonnet's answer in letter 41 are revealing of the complexity of eighteenth-century reactions to Bayle's work. Indeed his image oscillated from that of a skilful and irreligious sceptic, a champion of incredulity, and a precursor of the Enlightenment to that of a tolerant philosopher and devoted Christian. For the reputation, diffusion, and puzzling interpreta-tions of his work in eighteenth-century France, see Rétat (1971); and for his influence in the Netherlands and in Germany, see Thijssen-Schoute (1959).

7. Needham quoted this passage (with some alterations) from the 'Reponse pour Mr. Bayle à Mr. Le Clerc, au sujet du 3. & du 13. articles du 9. tome de la Bibliotheque choisie' (Bayle 1725-1727, 3:994).

vivimus movemur, et sumus,[8] pourquoi pas croire toute suite, qu'il est libre comme cause premiere toujours agissant de donner tel branle aux parties de la nature, qu'il voudra, et de produire par une operation immediate un miracle, ou en autres termes un mouvement ou contraire aux mouvemens ordinaires, ou plus accéléré, ou enfin different de ce que nous voyons? Vous croiez peutêtre qu'il est convenable à sa sagesse de se fixer un plan physique immuable, et de laisser agir la nature toute seule, mais il y des exceptions et des deviations meme dans la nature, tels que les monstres &c. qui sortent de plan commun, mais que sont compris dans un plan à nous invisible, et beaucoup plus etendu. De meme je me persuade, que dans les choses de la religion, il ne deroge nullement de sa sagesse prise selon toute son étendue en produisant de tems en tems des exceptions locales par des volontés, qui paroissoient speciales pour nous, mais qui marquent en meme tems son domain souverain. Cela se fera, si vous voulez, par un plan bien plus étendu que le votre, et dont l'unité ne sera pas derangée par un certain petit nombre de miracles, parce que le tout sera fondé sur une harmonie préétablie entre la physique, dont il est le maitre, et la morale, qui est fixée par des relations vraiment immuables eternellement. C'est ainsi qu'au lieu de restraindre les vües de la divinité, je cherche plûtot à les étendre, et loin de la croire assujettie à une pure necessité materielle indigne de sa toute puissance, je me persuade qu'elle se perd pour moi bien au de la du palpable dans le moral, et l'intellectuel, dont les bornes dependent de la creation prise en general. Tout ce que je viens de dire est si conforme à nos connoissances, qu'à moins de pouvoir demontrer, que la metaphysique de Leibnitz est absurde, et que dieu n'opere jamais rien immediatement, vous ne pourez jamais établir votre plan physique, et palpable, ni nous convaincre, que l'ame separée de tout corps organisé quelconque, et devenüe pur esprit, ne pourra pas sentir, et raisonner placée dans quelque autre point de vüe, ou par l'intervention d'une combinaison systematique des êtres simples materiels, differente du systeme corporel, qu'elle anime maintenant, ou par l'operation immediate de la divinité. Avant de finir cette lettre, qui est deja peutêtre trop longue, il ne me reste qu'une seul remarque à faire sur ce que vous vous trouvez dans la nécessité d'établir avec M[r.] de Buffon, et moi la distinction réelle assés clairement marquée par les phenomenes entre la classe inferieure des corps organisés vitaux, et la classe superieure des animaux sensitifs. Cependant vous devez vous souvenir, qu'il y a bientot vingt ans, que vous nous avez fait la guerre en quelque façon, de ce que nous avancions dans ce tems, lui dans son histoire naturelle,[9] et moi dans mes observations microscopiques,[10] que les êtres microscopiques n'étoient pas de vrais animalcules, mais seulement des êtres vitaux organisés sans aucune puissance sensitive. Cela est si certain, que Spalanzani travaillant sous votre

---

8. Actus apostolorum xvii.28.

9. In the *Histoire naturelle* (1749-1789, 2:259-63), Buffon had argued that microscopic animalcules resulted from chance combinations of organic particles and were therefore not true animals.

10. In his early works, Needham (1748:637-39, 644-45; 1750:196-200, 215-17) had argued that microscopic animalcules arose from decomposed organic materials through the action of a vegetative force. Later he drew a sharp distinction between these 'vital beings', which are devoid of sensation, and true animals, which possess a sensitive principle (see Needham's notes in Spallanzani 1769, pt.1:150-56, 165-70).

direction ne cherche rien avec plus d'ardeur dans tout son ouvrage, qu'à prouver, que toute cette classe microscopique est evidemment douée, comme tous les autres animaux, d'une vraie puissance sensitive, et spontanée.[11] Ainsi quoique je n'ai pas eu le bonheur de vous plaire par tout, en cela au moins nous sommes d'accord, et vous étes dans la nécessité aussi bien que M[r.] Spalanzani d'avouer, que nous avons raison quelquefois. Il y avoit meme un tems, comme je puis prouver par des lettres anterieures à votre correspondence avec lui,[12] qu'il étoit en tout, et par tout d'accord avec moi, tant pour les phenomenes, que pour les consequences, que j'ai tiré, mais il a depuis changé sa façon de voir, et il s'est refugié de notre camp dans le votre.[13] Adieu, mon cher ami, et soyez persuadé, que quoique nous ne soyons pas d'accord dans nos manieres de voir, et de raisonner en tout, et par tout, il n'y a personne sur la terre, qui vous aime, et qui vous respecte plus que

votre ami très sincere, et confrere
Needham.

Ce que je viens de vous marquer, jai écrit *currente calamo*; ainsi ne vous attachez pas trop à mon style; mais soyez un peu content de moi, si vous m'entendez asses bien pour comprendre mes principes, et les raisons, pourquoi je ne puis absolument être d'accord avec vous sur tout ce que vous avez avancé dans un ouvrage, qui d'ailleurs doit être infiniment precieux aux yeux de tout bon estimateur du vrai merite. À propos il y a quelque tems, que je suis priё par un ami intime de recommander à vos attentions un jeun homme de bonne famille, qui voiage en Italie, et se trouve à present à Rome. Il est de la Flandre françoise, il s'appelle M[r.] d'Eurick,[14] et il doit repasser par Geneve, ou il compte de fixer pour quelques mois. J'ai quelques raisons de le croire affecté de la maladie epidemique de ce siecle, et gaté du coté de la religion par les ouvrages de Voltaire, et ceux des autres impies. Cependant il a la plus grande opinion de vous, non sans raison, et desire ardemment de vous connoitre. Vous reduirez peutêtre son imagination un peu trop ardente à la raison, et sa raison trop entreprenante à la foi. Je le connois un peu, l'ayant vu, et conversé avec lui en passant par douai à Bruxelles l'année passée. Il merite vos soins de toutes les façons, et ce qui doit vous interesser encore en sa faveur par une espece de

---

11. See chapters 2 and 3 of Spallanzani's *Saggio di osservazioni microscopiche* (1765, pt.1:9-30; 1769, pt.1:11-45).

12. Spallanzani first wrote to Needham in 1761 (see letter 15, n.4, and letter 52, n.24). Bonnet's correspondence with Spallanzani did not begin until 1765 (see Castellani 1971 and *Epistolario*).

13. A number of Spallanzani's laboratory notes, which form the basis for his famous *Saggio* (Spallanzani 1765), show that in the early stages of his investigations, 1761-1763, he was indeed inclined to support Needham's theory of generation, but not ultimately; see Pancaldi (1972:49-72 and 1982) and Spallanzani (1978a:77-276). See also section 2.iv of the Introduction. For Spallanzani's later denials of his initial acceptance of Needham's views, see his letters to Bonnet of 24 August 1765 and 8 March 1770 (*Epistolario*, 1:63, 227-28), Spallanzani (1776, 1:289-93 n.a), and Spallanzani (1777, 2:72-76 n.a).

14. Possibly Pierre-Joseph-Jean van Heurck (d.1779), the son of Jean-Charles van Heurck (1708-1766).

sympathie est qu'il a presque perdu la vüe naturellement foible par un excés d'application. Encore un fois adieu, et ne m'oubliez pas aupres de mes amis Les Messieurs Trembley, et M[r.] Tronchin[15] votre ancien procureur general, aussi bien que Milord,[16] et Miladi Stanhope,[17] si vous les voyez quelquefois. Souvenez vous aussi de moi auprès de M[r.] de Saussure et tous mes autres amis.

J'ai encore une question à vous faire. Serez vous mecontent de moi, si je ferai un extrait apart de vos raisonnemens sur la religion, en laissant tout ce, qui peut choquer nos catholiques en matiere de foi, pour le faire reimprimer ici? Je crois, qu'un extrait de cette nature separé de toutes vos Theses, ou hypotheses philosophiques, qui precedent cette partie de votre palingenesie, pourra faire beaucoup du bien parmi la jeunesse, d'autant que je n'ai rien vu encore sur le sujet si clair, si court, si precis, et si comprehensif. Repondez moi, aussitot que votre loisir vous le permettra.

MANUSCRIPT
BPUG, MS Bonnet 66:161r-164r.

41

Bonnet to Needham – Genthod, 17 February 1770

Genthod le 17.e Fevrièr 1770.

Je le sçavois bien, mon cher et digne Ami et Confrère; que vous étiés toujours prêt à rendre justice au Travail et aux intentions de ceux même qui n'adoptent pas toutes vos Opinions. L'obligeante Lettre à laquelle je réponds, m'a reproduit mon bon Ami Néédham tel que je l'avois toujours connu. Le plaisir qu'il a gouté à la lecture de mes *Recherches sur le* CHRISTIANISME,[1] ajoute beaucoup à celui que

15. The Genevan patrician Jean-Robert Tronchin (1710-1793), a mathematician who was elected in 1760 as Geneva's Attorney General, was a good friend of Bonnet since the early years when they both attended the informal *société de gens de lettres* set up by the Genevan philosophers (Savioz 1948b:117). Tronchin was instrumental in Bonnet's visiting Voltaire in May 1754 (Savioz 1948b:178). Bonnet admired very much Tronchin's famous attack against Rousseau contained in the *Lettres écrites de la campagne*, which was published anonymously in 1763 (Sonntag 1983:361, 408), but could not appreciate Tronchin's political activities around 1768 (Sonntag 1983:762, 810). However he considered Tronchin as 'l'un des plus beaux génies et des hommes les plus éloquents que Genève ait produits' (Savioz 1948b:117).

16. For a biography of Philip, second Earl Stanhope (1714-1786), see Newman (1969:102-28). Stanhope had an undistinguished political career in the House of Lords but was a respected mathematician. Elected a Fellow of the Royal Society in 1735, Stanhope declined its presidency when it was offered to him in 1772. The Stanhopes resided in Geneva from 1763 to 1773, having moved there so that their dying son Philip could receive medical treatment from the famous physician and friend of Bonnet's, Théodore Tronchin (1709-1781).

17. For a biography of Grizel Hamilton, later Lady Stanhope (1719-1811), see Newman (1969:102-28). Daughter of Charles Lord Binning and grand-daughter of the sixth Earl of Haddington, she married the second Earl Stanhope in 1744. In Geneva Lady Stanhope's home became a centre for visiting travellers from England.

1. See letter 37, n.1.

m'ont donné les Lettres que j'ai reçües sur ce sujet d'un assés grand nombre de Sçavans ou de vrais connoisseurs.

Je vous assure, mon cher Ami, que je me suis fort félicité de n'être point *Ecclésiastique*; quoi que Personne au Monde ne respecte plus que moi cet état. Je me disois souvent en composant mes *Recherches*, que j'étois dans le cas de l'illustre Addisson, qui n'avoit pas voulu se consacrer à l'Eglize pour servir mieux l'Eglize et la RELIGION.[2]

J'ai regardé comme un devoir sacré d'employer le peu de Connoissances et de Talens que DIEU m'a départi, a établir les grandes Preuves de cette REVELA-TION, qui est le Fondement le plus solide de nos plus chères esperances. J'y étois encore déterminé par un motif particulier. Certains Incrédules avoient cru trouver dans mon *Essai Analytique* et ailleurs des raisons de présumer que je rejettois intérieurement la RÉVELATION.[3] Ils se plaisoient à me produire comme un de leurs Confrères; et je vous laisse à juger si leurs prétentions étoient bien raisonnables. Ne m'étois-je pas expliqué très clairement et très fortement dans le Chapitre XXIV de l'*Essai Analytique*?[4] N'avois-je pas donné dans la Préface[5] du même Ouvrage les meilleures Preuves de l'*Immatérialité* de l'Ame? ᵃMais; Descartes et Montesquieu avoient été accusés d'Athéisme,[6] et ils avoient donné pourtant de très bonnes Preuves de l'éxistence de DIEU.ᵃ Ce ne sont pas seulement

---

2. Bonnet is probably alluding to the last lines of the poem 'An account of the greatest English poets', written by Addison (1721, 1:41) in his youth:

> I've done at length; and now, dear Friend, receive
> The last poor present that my Muse can give.
> I leave the arts of poetry and verse
> To them that practise 'em with more success.
> Of greater truths I'll now prepare to tell,
> And so at once, dear Friend and Muse, farewell.

In the biography prefixed to the edition of Addison's *Works*, Thomas Tickell (1686-1740), Addison's friend and literary executor, commented as follows: 'In the close [of "An account of the greatest English poets"] he insinuates a design he then had of going into holy orders, to which he was strongly importuned by his father. His remarkable seriousness and modesty, which might have been urged as powerful reasons for his choosing that life, proved the chief obstacles to it. These qualities, by which the priesthood is so much adorned, represented the duties of it as too weighty for him; and rendered him still the more worthy of that honour, which they made him decline. It is happy that this very circumstance has since turned so much to the advantage of virtue and religion, in the cause of which he has bestowed his labours the more successfully, as they were his voluntary, not his necessary employment. The world became insensibly reconciled to wisdom and goodness, when they saw them recommended by him with at least as much spirit and elegance, as they had been ridiculed for half a century' (Addison 1721, 1:xi-xii).

3. In the *Palingénésie* Bonnet devoted a short section to the clarification of his 'Raisons pourquoi l'Auteur n'est pas Matérialiste'. There he stated, 'Non; je ne suis point *Matérialiste*; je ne crois point à la *matérialité* de l'Ame; mais je veux bien qu'on sçache, que si j'étois Matérialiste, je ne me ferois aucune peine de l'avouer' (Bonnet 1769a, 1:50; and B.O., 7:34/15:50-51).

4. Bonnet (1760:451-93) and B.O., 6:335-68/14:205-56.

5. Bonnet (1760:i-xxiv) and B.O., 6:vii-xxiv/13:vii-xxxvi.

6. In 1749, for instance, the Jansenist La Roche summarised his attack on Montesquieu thus: 'Ajoutons à cette analyse: 1° que ceux que nous appelons les messieurs de la *religion naturelle* n'en ont proprement aucune, puisque c'est n'avoir aucune religion, que de n'avoir que celle qu'on se fait en suivant une raison aveugle et corrompue; 2° que l'ouvrage dont il s'agit n'est pas moins contraire aux saines maximes du gouvernement temporel qu'à la religion de Jésus-Christ et aux saintes règles de l'Evangile' (Montesquieu 1875-1879, 6:137). On Montesquieu's personal religious ideas, see Shackleton (1956); and for his position on religious questions during his youth, see Kra (1970). See also letter 30, n.8.

des *Incrédules*, qui avoient suspecté ma Croyance: des Théologiens n'en avoient pas présumé plus favorablement ou plus charitablement; et je suis persuadé que vous n'en êtes point surpris. Ces Théologiens n'étoient point des *Néédhams*.

J'espère donc qu'aujourdhui il n'y aura plus de doutes sur ma Croyance, et qu'on me fera la grace de me croire Chrétien. J'ai toujours pensé, que les Philosophes Laics étoient plus tenus encore que les Clercs de consacrer leurs veilles à la défense de la RÉLIGION: c'est qu'ils sont bien mieux placés pour la déffendre, et qu'ils peuvent inspirer bien plus de confiance. Vous avés pu voir que c'est cette confiance que j'ai tâché d'inspirer par tout à mes Lecteurs. Dans cette vuë, je ne me suis jamais produit que sous l'aspect d'un *simple Chercheur*. Mais, je souhaitois en même tems de mettre dans ma marche un interet ou un agrément dont mes plus Illustres dévanciers s'étoient trop dispensés.

Je vous scais le plus grand gré d'avoir si bien saisi ma manière et mon Style. Ces Sçavans François dont vous me parlés, et qui me reprochoient *la mésure exacte des Périodes et le choix trop scrupuleux des Mots*, ne me paroissent pas avoir beaucoup médité sur l'emploi et sur l'analogie des Mots.[7] Ils ignorent trop, qu'il en est des Mots en Philosophie rationelle, comme des Signes en Géometrie ou en Algèbre. J'oserois défier ces Messieurs de substituer d'autres expressions aux miennes sans alterer plus ou moins les Idées. *ᵇLa plupartᵇ* des François pensent trop peu profondément pour juger du degré d'éxactitude et de précision que le Style philosophique éxige. Ils préfèrent trop souvent de parler à l'Oreille plutot qu'à l'Entendement. Comme ils n'ont guères analysé leurs Idées, et qu'ils n'ont sur les Sujets philosophique que des Idées assés vagues et malᶜ digerées, il est tout naturel qu'ils se méprennent sur l'emploi d'une Langue qu'ils croyent posseder bien. Si je voulois écrire là-dessus, je pourrois leur dire des choses auxquelles ils n'ont jamaisᵈ songé. Je l'ai assés insinué page IX de la Préface de la *Palingénésie*,[8] et Art. XXI de l'*Analyse Abregée*.[9] *ᵃVeuillés relire ces endroits, et vous conviendrés que les Sçavans dont nous parlons n'apprendroient pas à l'Auteur, ce qui caractérise un Livre bien fait et bien pensé.ᵃ* J'aurois souhaité que vous eussiés fait causer un peu ces *Virtuoso*: s'ils vous retombent sous la main, n'y manqués point. Vous jugerés bientot s'ils sont faits pour m'entendre. L'immortel Montesquieu n'auroit pas jugé comme eux: j'en ai de bonnes preuves. Il est à mon avis le premier Ecrivain de la Nation: c'est qu'il est celui

7. The identity of the scholars who criticised Bonnet's style has not been established, nor is it known whether the criticism appeared in a review of the *Palingénésie*. It is interesting to note, however, the following comment in a review of Bonnet (1762): 'Comme écrivain, il ne lui manque que d'avoir vécu quelque temps à Paris pour y prendre ce que nous appelons ton, ce qu'on appelait urbanité à Rome, et à Athènes l'atticisme' (*C.L.*, 5:414). A similar comment was also made in the review of Bonnet (1764) in *C.L.* (6:198-99).

8. 'Au reste; on juge aisément que depuis environ vingt-sept ans que je ne cesse point de composer pour le Public, j'ai eu des occasions fréquentes de m'occuper de la méchanique du style en général & de celle du style philosophique et particulier. J'ai donc médité souvent sur les signes de nos idées, sur l'emploi de ces signes & sur les effets natureles de cet emploi. J'ai reconnu bientôt que ce sujet n'avoit point été creusé ou anatomisé autant qu'il méritoit de l'être, & qu'il avoit avec les principes de la Science psychologique des liaisons secretes que les meilleurs Ecrivains de Rhétorique ne me paroissent pas avoir apperçues. Je ne me livrerai pas ici à cette intéressante discussion: elle exigeroit des détails qui me jeteroient fort au-delà des bornes d'une Préface' (Bonnet 1769a, 1:viii-ix; and B.O., 7:ii-iii/15:vii).

9. Bonnet (1769a, 1:54-57) and B.O., 7:36-38/15:55-58.

qui avoit le plus de précision, de justesse et de profondeur dans l'Esprit: il ne sacrifioit ni au nombre ni à l'harmonie: il sçavoit que les Mots ne sont pas de simples Sons.

Je vous remercie fort, mon digne Ami, du petit Projet que vous avés formé d'imprimer séparément à Bruxelles mon Morceau sur la RÉVÉLATION. Rien ne pouvoit mieux me prouver le cas que vous voulés bien faire de cet Ecrit. Des Personnes dont je respecte le jugement et les vuës m'avoient déjà sollicité de consentir à cette réimpression séparée. Mes Libraires y avoient aussi été invités de l'Etranger. Quoi que ce Morceau eusse été calculé pour faire corps avec le reste de l'Ouvrage, *dans les vuës secretes que je m'étois proposé sur les Incrédules;* je n'ai pas laissé de ceder à ces obligeantes sollicitations. J'ai beaucoup plus fait: j'ai donné à ce Morceau une Forme toute nouvelle; j'y ai fait quelques additions plus ou moins importantes, et quantité de petites Notes, propres à faciliter l'intelligence du Texte à la plupart des Lecteurs. À l'heure que je vous écris, notre* Presse roule *à force* sur cette nouvelle Edition:[10] elle sera finie vers le commencement d'Avril, et je me hâterai de vous en faire parvenir un Exemplaire. Vos louables vuës seront donc remplies, et mieux que vous ne l'auriés pu faire à Bruxelles. Ne suivés donc point votre Projet: il seroit superflu.

Je ne vous comprends point, mon bon Ami, dans vos Remarques critiques sur mon Livre: que *veulent dire* ces expressions; *je crois en étendant mes Idées bien plus loin que vous, et en montant du palpable à l'intelligible de pouvoir passer les bornes étroites de la Chair* &c. Je vous avouerai ingénument, que jamais je n'ai aspiré un instant à *passer les bornes de la Chair*: c'est que j'étois très sur de n'y pas réussir dans cette Vie. Mais; s'il vous est donné de *franchir* de telles *bornes*, je vous suivrai de l'Oeil en restant dans ma Chair infirme.

Je ne conçois pas mieux vos reproches; *que je retrécis la Métaphysique, et que je déprime la* RÉLIGION, pour les rendre palpables &c. Il est vrai que j'ai désiré ardemment de rendre la Métaphysique et la RELIGION *palpables* aux Incrédules, et je croirois n'avoir pas travaillé en vain si j'avois eu le bonheur d'y réussir. Mais; je n'imaginois pas, qu'en présentant la Métaphysique et la Réligion sous le point de vuë que j'ai choisi, je les *retressissoit et les déprimoit*. J'étois bien plus éloigné encore d'imaginer, que pour être utile aux Hommes, il fallut absolument leur débiter des Choses qui *excédassent tout Entendement*. Etois-ce la un bon moyen d'obtenir un quart d'heure d'audience de ces Incrédules Philosophes auxquels je m'adressois.

Que voulés-vous dire encore, mon cher Ami, quand vous ajoutés; *qu'il étoit plus convenable et plus philosophique d'éxalter la Physique avec Leibnitz et Mallebranche, pour la faire atteindre à la* FOI? Je vous répondrai qu'il est vrai encore, *que je n'ai pas éxalté la Physique pour la faire atteindre* à ce que vous nommés *la foi*. C'est que j'aurois craint de tomber dans quelque Galimäthias qui auroit détruit la Physique et la FOI.

Mais; si vous pensés sérieusement *que j'ai déprimé la* RELIGION; comment

---

10. Charles Bonnet, *Recherches philosophiques sur les preuves du christianisme. Nouvelle édition, où l'on trouvera quelques additions, & des notes propres à faciliter l'intelligence de l'ouvrage à un plus grand nombre de lecteurs* (Genève 1770).

pouvés-vous me proposer de réimprimer séparément mon Ecrit sur la RELIGION, comme un Ecrit qui vous *paroit propre à faire beaucoup de bien parmi la Jeunesse; d'autant que vous n'avés rien vu encore sur le Sujet de si clair, de si court, de si précis et de si compréhensible?*

Je n'ai point du tout décidé sur l'Eternité des Peines: mais, j'ai laissé parler mon Coeur.[11] Si j'avois décidé pour cette Eternité, les Incrédules se seroient mocqués de moi et m'auroient traité d'Hypocrite. Je suis étonné que vous argumentiés du propos de Baile: ignoriés-vous, qu'il ne vouloit faire taire ici la Raison, que pour anéantir plus surement la FOI?[12] À ce qu'il me paroit, mon bon Ami, vous n'êtes pas si fin que lui [a]:aussi n'avoit-il pas votre droiture et votre bonhommie[a]. Au reste; avant que de prononcer sur le sens de quelques Passages de l'Ecriture, il convient de s'assurer si les Mots ont réellement la valeur que les apparences semblent leur donner. Et si ces apparences choquoient évidemment des Notions certaines, ne seroit-il pas plus raisonnable de soup-conner un autre Sens. Pensés-vous que le subtil et adroit dialecticien que vous m'opposés, fut bien porté à prendre ici le mot d'*éternel*[13] comme vous le prenés? J'ai lieu de présumer qu'il n'auroit pas été mécontent de moi, et qu'il ne m'auroit pas reproché de n'avoir pas dit des choses, *qui excèdent tout Entendement*. Je crois que Leibnitz ne m'auroit pas plus désaprouvé: il est bien clair, qu'il ne paroissoit admettre l'Eternité des Peines, que pour ne choquer point les Théologiens qu'il vouloit gagner; puis que ce Dogme ruinoit son Système de l'Optimisme. Il étoit possedé de l'Esprit de conciliation.

Nos Principes sur la FOI doivent differer autant que nos Principes sur la Génération. Je suis très assuré que notre amitié n'en souffrira jamais. Je tiens qu'il n'y a aucun mérite à croire des choses *inintelligibles*; parce que croire de telles choses, c'est ne rien croire. Le mérite consiste ici à rechercher dans l'ECRITURE ce qui est *intelligible et pratique*, pour le *croire* et le *pratiquer*. Je ne conçois point, que l'ETRE SOUVERAINEMENT SAGE ait voulu éxercer l'obéissance des Hommes par des mots vuides de sens. Si ce fripon de Baile, qui n'étoit point un *Néédham*, vouloit immoler la Raison sur l'Autel de la FOI, c'est qu'il sçavoit très bien, qu'après le sacrifice, les Philosophes et les Gens d'Esprit ne voudroient plus de la FOI. O mon Ami; que vous m'étonnés en me citant avec tant de confiance et de simplicité[g] ce rusé dialecticien!

Vous m'attaqués encore sur ce que j'ai dit des Miracles:[14] j'en suis surpris; car *j'exaltois ici la Physique pour atteindre à la* FOI. [h]Voyés, je vous prie, comment

---

11. Bonnet (1769a, 1:308-19) and B.O., 7:228-38/15:334-47.

12. Bonnet's rhetorical question, typical of many eighteenth-century discussions on Bayle, foresha-dowed what has become, among some contemporary historians, a dilemma between Bayle as a sceptic and therefore a non-believer and Bayle as a sceptic and therefore a believer; see, e.g., Popkin (1959), Labrousse (1963-1964, 2:293-316), and Jossua (1967:405). The latter explicitly states that Bayle's total pyrrhonism leads to total faith. In more recent years, Paganini (1980) has avoided this historiographical polarity in his own interpretation by viewing Bayle's thought as being based on a dialectical relationship between rational criticism and religious fideism.

13. Bayle's reflections on the *eternité des peines* may be found in Bayle (1725-1727, 3:873, 878, 1075, and 4:27) and in the articles 'Origene' (remarks C and E) and 'Socin' (remark L); see Bayle (1720, 3:2124b, 2125-28, 2612a). It is interesting to note that Bonnet's friend, the theologian Jacob Vernet (1766a, 1:120-22), believed that the Scriptures did not provide enough information to determine whether or not punishment was eternal.

14. Bonnet (1769a, 2:176-201) and B.O., 7:461-79/16:194-224.

vous raisonnés:[h] *à moins*, dites-vous, *de pouvoir démontrer que la Métaphysique de Leibnitz est absurde, et que* DIEU *n'opère jamais rien[a] immédiatement, vous ne pourrés jamais établir votre Plan physique et palpable.* Où avés-vous vû dans mon Livre, que je décidasse *que* DIEU *n'opère jamais immédiatement?* Il me paroit que vous [i]avés bien peu donné d'attention à ma marche[i]: aucun Ecrivain peut être n'a pris un ton moins décisif que moi. Mais; vous qui voulés qu'on *éxalte la Philosophie*, pourquoi trouvés vous mauvais, que j'aye dit, que s'il est possible que DIEU ait tout operé par un *Acte unique*, il est raisonnable de penser qu'Il l'aura fait? Je montre en même tems les fondemens de cette possibilité, et je n'excluds point les Actes particuliers comme absurdes. Prenés la peine de relire avec plus d'attention les Parties XVII et XVIII.[15] Voici donc la difference qui est entre votre Opinion et la mienne: je suppose que DIEU a été assés Intelligent et assés Puissant pour avoir tout préordonné par une seule Volonté ou par un seul Acte; tandis que vous préferés de Lui faire mettre de tems en tems le Doigt à la Machine. En vérité, mon cher Chanoine, vous n'avés pas bonne grace de me reprocher *de retrécir la Métaphysique*.

Où avés-vous pris encore dans mon Livre, que je *décidois que l'Ame séparée de tout Corps organisé ne pourroit penser?* Mais; vous[j] qui ne permettés point qu'on s'écarte de l'ECRITURE, me dirés-vous pourquoi elle auroit enseigné aux Hommes le Dogme si fondamental de la *Résurrection*, si l'Homme étoit appellé à être un *Esprit pur?* Arrangés-vous donc avec vous même: arrangés-vous encore avec le grand Leibnitz sur lequel vous-vous appuyés si souvent, et dont la Métaphysique vous paroit si démontrée. Mais, cette Métaphysique qui vous plait tant[k] la possedés-vous assés? Vous en parlés à un Homme qui est actuellement occupé à l'approfondir plus que jamais.[16] Comment avés-vous oublié, qu'un des Points capitaux de cette Métaphysique est, qu'il ne se trouve dans l'Univers entier *aucune Ame* qui soit *séparée* de tout *Corps organique?* Ecoutés Leibnitz lui même et convenés de votre oubli: *je tiens que chaqu' Ame est toujours accompagnée d'un Corps organique, et que toutes les Substances simples seront toujours unies à des Corps organiques diversement transformables.*[17] Vous êtes Epigéniste: Leibnitz regardoit toute *Epigénèse* comme une *absurdité.* Relisés ce que j'en ai dit dans la Partie VII,[18] et pesés encore le passage suivant: *je suis d'avis, que les Loix du Méchanisme toutes seules ne sçauroient former un Animal, et qu'on ne sçauroit jamais produire un Corps organique, sans aucune préformation. Je crois que les Corps organiques sont enveloppés les uns dans les autres à l'infini.*[19] Eh bien! Mon Ami, qu'en dites vous? Etiés-vous bien fondé à

15. Bonnet (1769a, 2:157-260) and B.O., 7:435-524/16:157-290.

16. See the following works by Bonnet: 'Recueil de divers passages de Leibniz sur la survivance de l'animal, pour servir de supplément à la partie VII. de la Palingénésie philosophique, et réflexions sur ces passages' in B.O., 8:245-68/18:3-39, and 'Vue du Leibnitianisme' in B.O., 8:277-314/18:52-107.

17. This quotation is a combination of two different passages from Leibniz's 'Lettre à M. Arnauld' of 1690 and from the 'Lettre à Mr. des Maizeau' of 1711 (Leibniz 1768, 2, pt.1:46, 66).

18. Bonnet (1769a, 1:263-307) and B.O., 7:195-227/15:285-333.

19. This quotation is a combination of different sentences from Leibniz's 'Considérations sur le principes de la vie, & sur les natures plastiques' (Leibniz 1768, 2, pt.1:43). In his 'Recueil de divers passages de Leibniz sur la survivance de l'animal', Bonnet wrote: 'J'invite mon célèbre Ami Mr. NEEDHAM, qui voudroit étayer son Epigénèse de l'autorité de LEIBNITZ, à méditer un peu ce Passage & sur-tout ces expressions si tranchantes; *je suis d'avis, que les Loix du Méchanisme toutes seules ne sauroient former un Animal, là où il n'y a rien encore d'organisé*' (B.O., 8:258/18:22-23).

argumenter contre moi de la Doctrine de Leibnitz? *ᵃNe me faites donc plus l'injure de me traiter autant en Ecolier*, en me citant si mal à propos ce Platon de la Germanie, dont les Principes sont si diamètralement opposés aux vôtres. Et puis, venés-moi dire encore d'*éxalter la Physique avec Leibnitz.ᵃ*

Je ne sçais comment vous lisés*ˡ*; mais, je rencontre*ᵐ* à chaque pas*ⁿ* dans votre Lettre des *preuves démonstrativesᵃ*, que vous ne m'avés *ᵒpoint du tout saisiᵒ* ou que vous *ᵖne m'avés lu que du pouceᵖ*. En voici un autre éxemple singulièrement frappant. *Vous-vous trouvés*, me dites vous, *dans la nécessité d'établir avec M.ʳ de Buffon et moi la distinction réelle entre la Classe inférieure des Corps organisés vitaux, et la Classe supérieure des Animaux Sensitifs.* Quelcun qui ne m'auroit point lu, se douteroit-il que j'ai dit précisément le contraire? Voilà donc comment vous me lisés, et ensuite vous-vous pressés de tirer des Conséquences sur ma manière de penser, et vous ajoutés avec confiance; *ainsi quoi que je n'aye pas eu le bonheur de vous plaire partout; nous sommes au moins d'accord en cela, et vous êtes dans la nécessité d'avouer, que nous avons raison quelque fois.* Veuillés donc me relire encore, puis que vous m'avés si mal lu. Prenés-moi à la page 88 du Tome II et lisés ce qui suit. 'J'aurois pu donner facilement des explications purement méchaniques de tous ces Phénomènes aussi nouveaux qu'embarassans: je me serois même debarrassé ainsi de plus grandes difficultés. Mais j'aurois cru choquer d'autres Phénomènes qui semblent attester que le *Polype* n'est pas une simple *Machine organique.*'[20] J'aurois donc cru choquer les Phénomènes du Polype, si j'avois regardé cet Etre comme une simple Machine organique; c'est à dire, si je lui avois refusé le Sentiment, et que je l'eusse regardé simplement comme un *Etre vital.* Voyés encore ce que j'ajoute pag: 106, 107, 108, et la grande Note tirée de notre Ami M.ʳ Spallanzani;[21] et avoués que vous ne m'aviés pas bien lu. Que pretendois-je donc, en appliquant, comme je l'ai fait, l'Irritabilité au Polype, &c? Je le dis moi même très expressément, pag: 88: *pour montrer cependant à mon Lecteur, que j'ai envisagé mon Sujet sous le plus de faces qu'il m'a été possible, je hazarderai ici une Solution méchanique*; &c.[22] Y étes-vous à présent, mon bon Ami: je vous conjure d'être à l'avenir plus attentif à mon Texte, quand il vous arrivera de me relever. Vous pourriés autrement me faire dire ce que je n'ai jamais pensé; et vous en seriés plus fache que que*ᵃ* moi. Je remarque, que vous suivés plutot le fil de vos Idées, que celui des Idées des Auteurs que vous consultés. Vous ne portés guères votre vuë que sur un seul côté de l'Objet, et quand quelque chose vous frappe, c'est toujours si fortement, qu'il ne vous reste plus assés d'attention pour voir ce qui l'avoisine.

Tenés-moi compte, mon estimable Ami, des détails dans lesquels je viens d'entrer, et qui vous prouvent que votre jugement ne m'est pas indifferent. Je vous ai relevé avec cette franchise que vous aimés et que j'aime. Je vous l'avois déja fait observer dans une de mes Lettres: vous n'avés point sous les Yeux les Auteurs que vous cités ou que vous relevés: vous-vous fiés trop à votre Mémoire: vous m'en faisiés vous même l'aveu. Cette méthode est très vicieuse et vous exposeroit à des reproches fréquens de la part des Auteurs. La Lettre que je vous écris vous en fournit de nouvelles preuves.

20. Bonnet (1769a, 2:88) and B.O., 7:388/16:86.
21. Bonnet (1769a, 2:107-109n) and B.O., 7:400-401 n.1/16:105-107 n.1.
22. Bonnet (1769a, 2:88) and B.O., 7:388/16:86.

*a*Votre Ami Sabatier est un négligent, et de plus un *impoli*: c'est M.ʳ Spallanzani qui me prie de vous le dire.²³ Vous n'avés pas oublié ce Ballot de votre dernier Ouvrage, que j'expédiai sur votre ordre à ce M.ʳ Sabatier. M.ʳ Spallanzani ne recevant point son Exemplaire, écrivit en droiture à ce dernier à Turin. Il n'a jamais eu de lui ni Exemplaire ni Réponse.*a* *q*Il a donc été reduit à l'emprunter votre Ouvrage.*q* Sa lecture a produit un grand effet sur son Esprit, et que vous n'aviés peut être pas prévu: ça été de l'affermir plus que jamais dans ses Principes et dans les miens. Vous pouvés compter qu'il vous refutera publiquement,²⁴ solidement et fortement. Il pense de cet Ouvrage précisément ce que j'en pense, et ce que je vous en ai écrit.

Mes Libraires ont donné une 2.ᵈᵉ Edition de la *Palingénésie*.²⁵ J'en ai profité pour publier une Lettre très intéressante que M.ʳ de Saussure m'a adressé sur les *Animalcules des Infusions*,²⁶ et*a* qui n'est point du tout favorable à vos Opinions. Vous ne pouvés douter que les Observations que renferme cette Lettre n'ayent été bien faites; vous connoissés l'Observateur. Mais; je n'espère pas que vous abandonniés jamais vos Idées. Vous n'avés pas même voulu prendre la peine de me suivre pied à pied dans mes *Considerations sur les Corps Organisés*. Le *Poulet*²⁷ tout seul auroit du suffire pour vous ouvrir les Yeux. Et combien d'autres Faits, que j'ai rassemblés et décrits avec soin, et qui concourent à combatre votre étrange Système. M.ʳ de Haller n'est pas plus content que moi de tout ce que vous avés exposé en dernier lieu sur la *Vitalité*: il lui paroit que vous choqués ouvertement la Nature.²⁸ Peut être vous l'aura-t-il écrit lui même.

Notre Ami M. Spallanzani vient de mettre au jour sa Traduction Italienne de la *Contemplation de la Nature*.²⁹ Il l'a enrichie de Notes curieuses et d'une sçavante Préface sur les progrès et sur l'utilité de l'Histoire Naturelle. Les *Corps Organisés* ont été aussi traduits en Italien à Florence,³⁰ et prennent fort en Italie.

23. In his letter of 23 December 1769 to Bonnet, Spallanzani wrote: 'Ce n'est pas de M.r Sabatier de Turin que je tiens le Livre de l'Epigeniste (au contraire il ne s'est deigné non plus de repondre à ma lettre) mais c'est un des mes Amis de Milan, qui me l'a preté. Si vous avez occasion d'ecrire au nouveau chenoine Needham, apprenez lui la politesse de M.r Sabatier' (*Epistolario*, 1:215).

24. In the letter cited above (n.23) Spallanzani had expressed his intention thus: 'Je vois bien que dans mon Ouvrage il foudra que je parle de nouveau de son Roman' (*Epistolario*, 1:215).

25. Charles Bonnet, *La Palingénésie philosophique, ou idées sur l'état passé et sur l'état futur des êtres vivans* [...] *et qui contient principalement le précis de ses Recherches sur le christianisme* (Genève, Lyon 1770).

26. The letter by Saussure, dated 28 September 1769, is published in Bonnet (1770a, 1:428-30) and contains a long section on Needham; see also B.O., 7:324-28/15:475-80, and section 2.iv of the Introduction. This letter was also published by Spallanzani (see Spallanzani 1776, 1:148-52; and Spallanzani 1777, 1:172-76). For Needham's comments on Saussure's letter, see his own letter to Joseph Berington of 1 May 1772 (WCRO, Throckmorton MSS, CR 1998/Gate box, folder 8).

27. Bonnet is alluding to Haller's observations on incubated chicken eggs; see Haller (1758) and letter 22, n.8.

28. In his letters to Bonnet, Haller does not actually seem to have used such an expression in relation to Needham. He was indeed reluctant to read the book by the 'tenebreux Needham' and when he did, he simply stated in [October 1769], 'J'ai lu l'ouvrage de notre ami Needham, qui a fort menagé son ami Buffon. Je vois qu'il soutient encore sa vie mitoyenne, separée du sentiment, mais qui ne paroit pas convenir aux phenomenes des polypes' (Sonntag 1983:838).

29. See letter 39, n.2.

30. We do not know of a Florentine edition of this book by Bonnet, but only of a later Venetian one: *Considerazioni sopra i corpi organizzati* [...] *recata dal francese dal P.F.F.N.N., sacerdote professo carmelitano scalzo della Provincia di Toscana* (Venezia 1781).

Je voudrois pouvoir vous dire ce que le grand Morgagni[31] m'en a écrit.

Voltaire' a entrepris tout seul une *Encyclopédie* qu'on dit n'être que *litteraire*.[32] Vous croyés-bien qu'il ne s'en tiendra pas à la *pure littérature*, et qu'il fera de fréquentes excursions sur des sujets plus graves.

Vous avés les sincères complimens et les voeux de notre Maison et de M.ʳˢ Trembley et de Saussure.

Sçavés-vous que c'est à l'illustre Van-Swieten[33] que vous devés votre Place de Bruxelles? Il me l'a appris lui même,[34] et vous jugés bien que je n'ai pas manqué de lui dire[35] toute la reconnoissance que vous lui en auriés témoigné si vous l'eussiés sçu, et tous mes sentimens pour vous. Vous les connoissés, mon vertueux Ami, et vous êtes très sûr qu'ils ne varieront jamais.

[ADDRESS] Bruxelles, M.ʳ Néédham, de la Societé Royale d'Angleterre.

MANUSCRIPTS
BPUG, MS Bonnet 73:122r-124r; MS Bonnet 85:187v-193r.

31. For a biography of the Italian anatomist Giambattista Morgagni (1682-1771), from 1715 Professor of Anatomy at Padua University and considered the founder of pathological anatomy, see Giordano (1941) and the old, but well-informed, Fabroni (1778-1805, 12:7-58). For a list of Morgagni's published works, see Zanelli (1931); for a bibliography of works on him, see Premuda (1967); and for indications about his manuscripts, see Mazzolini and Ongaro (1983). See also the short, but accurate biography by Luigi Belloni, *D.S.B.*, 11 (1974) 510-12. For works published after this date, see Ongaro (1981) and the literature cited therein. Significant portions of Morgagni's correspondence, which constitute also an important source on the Italian scientific movement in the eighteenth century, have been published by Rocchi (1875), Corradi (1876), Bilancioni (1914), and Hintzsche (1964). Morgagni seems to have written only one letter to Bonnet (see Usuelli 1972:55). It is dated 'Patavii IV. Idus Julii 1766' and contains answers to some questions on embryology that Bonnet had addressed to him. Morgagni also declared that he had been teaching the theory of preformation for fifty-four years.

32. *Questions sur l'encyclopédie par des amateurs* ([Genève] 1770-1772). This work forms part of what is now known as the *Dictionnaire philosophique* (see V.O., vols.xvii-xx). For a review of recent studies on this work by Voltaire, see Virolle (1971) and especially Schwarzbach (1982).

33. The Dutch Catholic physician Gerard van Swieten (1700-1772) was a pupil of Boerhaave and from 1745 Court physician of Maria Theresa and one of her closest advisers. He was also the great reformer of Vienna's Medical Faculty, of censorship, and of the Court Library; for details see Brechka (1970), the collective volume edited by Lesky and Wandruszka (1973), and Peter W. van der Pas, *D.S.B.*, 13 (1976) 181-83, which lists all of his major works. For secondary literature on van Swieten, see Lesky and Rohl's paper in Lesky and Wandruszka (1973:181-94).

34. Bonnet's reference to van Swieten's having given him this information could not be found in the letters of van Swieten still preserved in the BPUG. It could well be that van Swieten's letter to Bonnet is now missing. For Needham's appointment at Brussels, see Mailly (1883, 1:9-19) and section 9 of the Introduction.

35. On 4 November 1769, Bonnet wrote to van Swieten: 'L'estimable M. Needham vous doit d'autant plus, que vous avés eu la délicatesse de lui laisser ignorer la main genereuse dont partoit le Bienfait. Il en seroit bien reconnoissant' (BPUG, MS Bonnet 73:93v). Bonnet's comment to Needham suggests that van Swieten played a significant role in Needham's appointment at Brussels, but this is not confirmed by official documents. When Maria Theresa received Prince Kaunitz's report of 24 October 1768 on the establishment of a 'Société des sciences et des belles-lettres à Bruxelles', for which Needham had been proposed as Director (see letter 35, n.1), she wrote in the margin, 'J'aprouve en tout le plan comme le prince Kaunitz le propose, l'ayant communiquée à Vanzuite [van Swieten], et l'ayant voulue lire moi-même, c'est la raison pourquoi cela a tant tardée, j'ai lue avec plaisir tout cet arrangement' (Gachard 1838:169). From the information that is at present available, the only possible inference is that van Swieten had warmly supported Needham's candidacy when discussing Kaunitz's report with Maria Theresa.

EDITIONS
'Votre Ami Sabatier [...] en ai écrit' published in Castellani (1973:100).

TEXT NOTES
a. B: *omitted b.* B: Bien *c.* B: peu *d.* B: peut-être pas *e.* B: la *f.* B: signifient en particulier *g.* B: bonne foi *h.* B: Pardonnez si j'insiste sur votre manière de raissonner: *i.* B: m'avez lu avec trop peu d'attention *j.* B: vous, mon estimable Ami, *k.* B: tant, soufrez que je vous le demande, *l.* B: m'avez lu *m.* B: rencontre presque *n.* B: page *o.* B: pas bien saisi *p.* B: m'avez lu trop rapidement *q.* B: M.ʳ Spallanzani ne recevant point votre Ouvrage à été réduit à l'emprunter. *r.* B: V.***

42

Bonnet to Needham – Genthod, 1 June 1770

Genthod le 1.ᵉʳ de Juin 1770.

M.ʳ de Constable[1] m'a envoyé ici ce matin, mon bon Ami, votre Lettre du 22.ᵉ d'Avril,[2] et je me suis hâté de lui exprimer en réponse à La Lettre très polie dont il avoit accompagné la votre, mes regrets, mes excuses et mon respecte.[3] Comment aviés vous ignoré ou comment vous avois-je laissé ignorer, que depuis plus de trois ans je n'habite plus la Ville, pas même en Hiver? Le dernier Hiver est le 4.ᵐᵉ que j'ai passé consécutivement à la Campagne.[4] La triste situation de notre infortunée République et les maux de ma pauvre Femme qui ont fort accru, nous ont rendu nécessaire le séjour de la Campagne. Vous devés donc comprendre à present que je ne sçaurois satisfaire aux *Recommandations* de mes Amis de l'Etranger. Depuis plus d'un an, je n'ai été qu'une seule fois en Ville, et encore pour les funerailles d'une proche Parente. Je suis ainsi forcé, mon cher Ami, de vous prier, de ne m'adresser plus à l'avenir de ces Voyageurs que la curiosité attire dans notre Ville. Malgré toute la disposition que j'ai à vous obliger, je ne pourrois leur être d'aucune utilité. Je fais la même prière à tous mes Amis du dedans et du dehors, et je me refuse de tout mon pouvoir aux Curieux, que la lecture de mes Ecrits porte à désirer de me voir. Je vis dans une retraite où je jouis de moi même, et de tems en tems de quelques Amis. Veuillés donc n'oublier point ce que je viens de vous écrire.

Parce que vous m'aviés fait une fort longue Lettre, je vous fis le 15.ᵉ de Fevrier

1. William Constable, Esq. (1721-1791), an English Catholic aristocrat, inherited a large fortune at his father's death. He travelled extensively on the Continent for ten years with his sister Winifred and purchased many paintings and antiques. When he returned to England, he refurbished his residence at Burton Constable in Yorkshire. In 1770 he set off on a new continental tour. At Lyon he met Rousseau and later corresponded with him. On his final return to England, he devoted himself to study, became acquainted with Hume and Joseph Priestley (1733-1804), and was elected a Fellow of the Royal Society. According to Kirk (1909:129), he 'was a complete Deist, if not Atheist'. For further biographical information see Kirk (1909:57), Chichester-Constable and Courtois (1932:157-58), de Beer and Rousseau (1967:136-38), and the long note in Leigh, 6712.

2. This letter by Needham cannot be traced.

3. Constable's letter is not preserved among Bonnet's papers in the BPUG.

4. Three days after the rejection of the *Projet de Règlement* (15 December 1766), Bonnet, like many other patricians, left Geneva. He settled in his father-in-law's country-house at Genthod, where he had previously spent his summers (Savioz 1948b:225).

une fort longue Réponse. Ce n'est pas ma coutume de répondre si au long: mais je vous le devois. Je vous dispense d'une *fort longue* Réplique: je ne pourrois y dupliquer. Si néanmoins votre Réplique étoit courte, ma duplique le seroit aussi.

Je viens de vous faire expédier par une Voiture mes nouvelles *Recherches sur les Preuves du* CHRISTIANISME.[5] Elles sont le fruit de ma Solitude et du désir que j'ai de me rendre aussi utile au Public que je le puis dans mes circonstances. J'espère que cet Ouvrage qui n'est en vente que depuis peu de jours, vous parviendra vers le commencement du mois prochain. Recevés-le, mon digne Ami, comme une nouvelle marque des Sentimens de la véritable estime et du sincère attachement de l'Auteur.

[ADDRESS] Bruxelles, M.ʳ l'Abbé Néédham de la Soc: Royale d'Angleterre, celle de Flandres &c.

MANUSCRIPT
   BPUG, MS Bonnet 73:141*v* (not included in copy B).

43

Needham to Bonnet – Brussels, 26 June 1770

à Bruxelles le 26. Juin 1770.

Je suis très faché, mon cher Monsieur, ami, et confrere, que Mʳ· de Constable seigneur d'un très grand merite a été malheureusement privé de l'avantage, qu'il s'étoit proposé en vous voyant frequemment pendant son sejour à Geneve.[1] Je ne pouvois pas prevoir votre triste situation, dont vous me parlez, d'autant plus, que vous m'en n'avez fait aucune mention, et que vous éties dans la coutume autre fois de vous rendre de tems en tems à la ville, meme en été. Quant aux malheureuses dissensions civiles, qui troublent votre patrie, j'ai les appris, il est vrai, par les gazettes, mais j'ai crû qu'elles auront été une raison de plus pour vous fixer à Geneve, afin de travailler de concert avec les autres sages de votre republique pour tâcher de les assoupir. Vous étes bien à plaindre, mais malgré toutes nos precautions, nous ne pouvons jamais nous garentir contre les maladies morales aussi naturelles à l'homme pendant son sejour ici bas, que les maladies physiques. Vous en avez actuellement un exemple frappant en angleterre, qui est d'autant plus à craindre dans ses effets, qu'il se montre sur un champ bien plus étendu. Mʳ· de Constable me ne parle pas de vos troubles actuelles; apparemment qu'ils ont cessé, et le calme s'est remis encore une fois

---

5. See letter 41, n.10.

1. In a letter of 1770 to Rousseau, Constable wrote: 'At Geneva I saw many people who did themselves the honor to call themselves your friends, all did justice to your merit, few spoke of you without tears [...] & I was surprised what has become of your enemies. The greatest only gently suggested a difference in opinion. I did not see Bonnet' (Chichester-Constable and Courtois 1932:173).

chez vous. Il a trouvé à la fin le moyen avec grande difficulté de percer jusqu'à la personne de Voltaire, dont il n'est pas du tout content.[2] Il l'envisage comme un fanatique plein de mechancété; c'est tout dire. Il s'occupe, dit il, à faire une nouvelle encyclopedie, dont il a deja composé, ou compilé six volumes in folio, qui paroitront vers la fin de l'année.[3] *Scribendi cacoethes et in ægro corde senescit.*[4] Il est bien plus content de votre Rousseau, qu'il a vu très souvent à Lyons.[5] Je vous enverrai bientot une peinture assés vive de ces deux hommes extraordinaires, qui part d'une main de maitre, qui ne veut pas paroitre, et dont je ne suis que l'editeur. Elle s'imprime actuellement ici sous ma direction.[6] Avant de la recevoir vous en aurez un extrait, que je vous enverrai par la poste; je vous prierai meme de la faire inserer dans vos journaux helvetiques. J'attends avec grande impatience vos nouvelles recherches sur les preuves du christianisme. Je vous ai promis une replique à votre avant derniere lettre; je ne sçai quand je pourrai la faire; depuis quelque tems je m'occupe de notre nouvelle acadamie, dont j'ai l'honneur d'etre le directeur; je viens de donner un memoire sur le meilleur preservatif à employer pour garentir les bêtes à cornes contre la maladie contagieuse, qui regne depuis 25. ans dans les pais septentrionaux de l'europe:[7] il a été generalement gouté ici, et on commence à mettre en pratique ce que je propose. Il consiste à fournir sans cesse tant dans les prairies, aussi bien qu'aux étables des grosses masses de sel de Roche, afin que les bêtes les trouvent à lêcher à discretion &c. Mes preuves et ma façon de raisonner en consequence

2. In the same letter to Rousseau quoted above (n.1), Constable described his meeting with Voltaire thus: 'I saw Voltaire, & did not applaud, we disagreed at the Door of my Coach. [...] Il voulut m'engager, mais j'etais content: nous nous quittames. ... il a dans sa Contenance L'Esprit ... mais il y a aussi La Dureté' (Chichester-Constable and Courtois 1932:174; see also the commentary to Best.D16389).

3. See letter 41, n.32

4. Juvenal, VII, 51.

5. See Constable's letters to Rousseau (Chichester-Constable and Courtois 1932:158-76).

6. Needham sent to Bonnet the *Extrait d'un discours prononcé a Pekin cent ans après la mort d'un poete historiographe et celle d'un orateur-philosophe ou le parallele*, which was published with a separate title page in the anonymous book *Les Vrai quakers, ou les exhortations, harangues, & prédictions des vrais serviteurs du Seigneur Dieu* (Londres 1770). A second edition of this book appeared in 1771. Both editions are listed by Conlon (1981:78, 81), but no identification of the authors is given. Needham had copies of the two editions in his library (see *Catalogue* 1782, pt.1:56; pt.2:23). In his éloge of Needham, Mann (1783:xli) listed as one of the books edited by Needham *Les Vrais quakers, par le Chevalier Colmon: à Bruxelles, chez d'Ours, 1771, in-8vo. 195 pages.* The author of *Les Vrais quakers* was indeed Henri-Camille Colmont de Vaulgrenand (1735-1794); see M. Jacquet, *D.B.F.*, 9 (1961) 312-13. But the author of the *Extrait* was Needham himself, as also appears from the contents of letters 44 and 46. Bonnet recognised at once the true authorship of the *Extrait*. On 18 December 1770, he wrote to Haller: 'Le bon Néédham m'envoye en Juillet dernier l'*Imprimé* que je joins à mon Paquet avec la Lettre qui l'accompagnoit [this letter cannot be traced]. Vous y verrés que cet Imprimé est une sorte d'Extrait d'un gros Ouvrage, que le Docte Abbé m'annonçoit dans une Lettre précédente comme un Ouvrage de *main de Maître*. Remarqués ces expressions. Au Style lâche, embarassé et incorrect de l'*Imprimé*, il ne me fut pas difficile de reconnoître l'Abbé lui même. Je fus faché par l'interet vrai que je prends à lui qu'il se fut exposé à rompre si lourdement une lance avec des Adversaires aussi redoutables que le sont Voltaire & Rousseau. Je lui en écrivis [here letter 44] donc avec toute la franchise possible, et je ne parus point m'appercevoir qu'il étoit lui même l'Auteur de cet Ouvrage qu'il me donnoit pour être de main de Maître' (Sonntag 1983:911-12).

7. *Mémoire sur la maladie contagieuse des betes a cornes, où on cherche un remede préservatif le plus simple, le plus éfficace, le plus général, & le moins couteux* (Bruxelles 1770). On this work by Needham, see the extract published in the *Mémoires de l'Académie impériale et royale des sciences et belles-lettres de Bruxelles*, 2 (1780) xxiv-xxviii, and Mailly (1883, 2:3-5).

d'un nombre de faits, que j'ai produit, ont été approuvées. Je vous enverrai un exemplaire avec la critique de Voltaire, et Rousseau, dont je vous ai parlé cy dessus. Vous m'avez engagé à écrire une lettre assés longue à M^r. Vanswieten[8] sur ce qu'il vous avoit marqué, que je dois en partie les graces, que la cour de vienne m'a faites, à ses soins. C'étoit une lettre, comme je crois, assés honnête pour lui temoigner mes reconnoissances, et lui offrir mes services. Il y a pour le moins deux mois, que ma lettre est partie, cependant je n'ai reçu encore aucune reponse, et je m'étonne très fort de son silence sans pouvoir deviner à quoi l'attribuer. Depuis je lui envoye deux exemplaires de mon dernier memoire, dont je n'entends plus parler. Adieu, mon très cher, et respectable ami, prions tous les jours, que dieu nous reunisse dans un autre monde plus heureux que celui, et qu'il nous éclaire ici autant qu'il est necessaire pour nous conformer à sa sainte volonté. Nos differences en fait de philosophie sont des choses très indifferentes par leur nature, celles de la religion sont plus graves; cependant si les catholiques ont raison, dieu, que vous aimez de tout votre coeur, vous pardonnera vos erreurs involontaires, si vous le priez sincerement de vous éclaircir sur ce point autant qu'il est necessaire pour vous conformer à sa sainte volonté. Encore une fois je vous remercie de toutes vos bontés pour moi, et j'ai l'honneur d'être avec l'attachement le plus vrai

votre très sincere ami, et serviteur obligé Needham.

Souvenez vous de moi auprès de Madame, de Messieurs Trembley, Tronchin,[9] Saussure et tous nos amis de Geneve. En parlant de l'ouvrage, que je vous destine, et de son extrait, que vous receverez incessamment il faut avoir la bonté de ne jamais me nommer comme l'editeur.

[ADDRESS] A Monsieur / Monsieur C. Bonnet de la / Société Royale de Londres &c. / correspondant de l'academie des sciences / à Paris &c. / à Geneve.

MANUSCRIPT
  BPUG, MS Bonnet 30:271r-272v.

44

Bonnet to Needham – [Genthod], 29 September 1770

De ma Retraite le 29.e Septembre 1770.

Il arrive souvent, mon cher Ami et Confrère, d'avoir tant de Réponses à faire, que je parois paresseux ou négligent, quoi que je tâche de n'être ni l'un ni l'autre. Je réponds donc assés tard à votre Envoi du 17.e de Juillet,[1] et vous voulés bien ne compter point avec moi. Vous connoissés mon amitié, et je connois la votre. Quand notre petit Commerce épistolaire seroit interrompu

---

8. Needham's letter to van Swieten could not be traced.
9. See letter 40, n.15.

1. This letter by Needham of 17 July 1770 cannot be traced (see also letter 43, n.6).

pendant plusieurs années, nos sentimens réciproques n'en soufriroient surement aucune altération.

De deux choses l'une, mon bon Ami; ou vous-vous êtes bien prévenu en faveur de cet Imprimé que vous aviés joint à votre Paquet; ou je ne suis point du tout Juge de cet Imprimé.[2] Vous me l'annoncés comme un Ouvrage *de main de Maître*, et je n'y reconnois point la main *d'un Maître*. Je soupçonne que votre attachement pour l'Auteur, et la justice que mérite ses louables intentions, ont beaucoup influé sur le jugement trop avantageux que vous portés de cette Pièce.

Je ne le vous dissimule donc point: elle m'a paru écrite trop foiblement pour faire impression sur les Lecteurs que vous avés principalement en vuë. Les Phrases en sont d'une longueur qui ne pourra manquer de déplaire. Il s'y trouve de fréquentes incorrections, et des tours qui ne sont point dans l'Analogie de la Langue Françoise, et qui même la choque de front. J'y apperçois encore nombre d'Expressions qui ne sont pas plus dans la *propieté* du langage, et qui décèlent par tout un Anglois travesti en François. En un mot; tout cela est bien froid et bien languissant.

Voilà pour le Style. Je ne contredirai pas le fond des Choses. Elles ne sont malheureusement que trop vrayes; mais, elles me semblent trop dépourvues d'interet. Toutes ont été dites et repètées mille fois, et d'une manière plus fine et plus agréable. Ce n'est pas ainsi, à mon avis, que les Hommes auxquels en veut l'Anonyme, doivent être peints. L'Historien des *Cacouacs*[3] avoit fourni un meilleur modèle, et à moins que de faire aussi bien que cet Ingénieux Ecrivain, il ne convient guères de s'en mêler. Les Adversaires ont Bec et Dents, et manient supérieurement la Plume. On leur donne trop davantages, quand on ne les

---

2. See letter 43, n.6.

3. In the *Mercure de France* of October 1757 (pp.9-15), there appeared an anonymous 'Avis utile' written by Odet Joseph de Vaux de Giry, abbé de Saint-Cyr, announcing the discovery of 'une nation de sauvages, plus féroce et plus redoutable que les Caraïbes ne l'ont jamais été. On les appelle Cacouacs [in a note the author clarified: 'Il est à remarquer que le mot grec κακός qui ressemble à celui de Cacouacs, signifie-*méchant*']. [...] leur armes consistent dans un venin caché sous leur langue; à chaque parole qu'ils prononcent, même du ton le plus riant, ce venin coule, s'échappe et se répand au loin.' The 'Avis utile' went on to say that 'quelques-uns de ces monstres sont venus en Europe; ils se sont appliqués à contrefaire le ton de la bonne compagnie, pour s'y introduire et s'y mieux cacher'. This anti-philosophes satire was taken up by Jacob-Nicolas Moreau (1717-1803), who published an anonymous pamphlet – the one alluded to by Bonnet – entitled *Nouveau mémoire pour servir à l'histoire des Cacouacs* (Amsterdam 1757). Moreau did not regard the Cacouacs/philosophes as savages but as cultivated men, and wittily portrayed their manners, life-styles, and ideas, showing that they represented a true menace to moral order. Moreau drew mainly on the works of Rousseau, Diderot, d'Alembert, and Voltaire. As a result of this publication Moreau was, in his own words, 'traité d'impie par les jansénistes et de plat dévot par les philosophes' (J.-N. Moreau 1898-1901, 1:54). He republished the work in J.-N. Moreau (1785, 1:46-136). Moreau was born in Saint-Florentin of an ancient professional family. In 1741 he entered the legal profession, but during the 1750s he turned to political journalism in which he strongly supported current French foreign policy and thus began a brilliant career. In 1759 he was called to Versailles and appointed *avocat des finances*. In 1770 he became Librarian to Marie-Antoinette, and in 1774 he received the title of *historiographe de France*. Through prince Starhemberg he was elected a foreign member of the Brussels Academy of Sciences (Mailly 1883, 1:140). During the French Revolution he was jailed for five months and his possessions were confiscated. The main source for Moreau's life is his autobiography, which lists all of his published works (J.-N. Moreau 1898-1901, 1:xxx-lx). For a shorter biography, see Paul Benhamou in Sgard (1976:283-84); and for Moreau's ideas on the role of an *historiographe de France*, see Gembicki (1972). For the Cacouac episode, see Best. D.app.160 and Diaz (1958:282-83 n.2).

combat pas avec autant d'Esprit et de Sel qu'ils en répandent dans leurs nombreuses Diatribes.

Je vous l'avouerai même: je préférerois de beaucoup que les Ecrivains Chrétiens se bornassent à établir solidement les grandes Preuves de la Révélation, sans s'embarasser le moins du monde des Ironies et des Sarcasmes des Incrédules. Je souhaiterois donc qu'on ne repoussat pas l'Ironie par l'Ironie, et qu'on s'attachat uniquement à deffendre bien le Tronc de l'Arbre contre ceux qui s'efforcent d'en faire tomber au moins quelques Feuilles.

Ce que je dis-ici, je l'ai moi même pratiqué dans la *Palingénésie* et dans ces nouvelles *Recherches sur les Preuves du* CHRISTIANISME, que vous devés avoir enfin reçuës. Je n'y ai pas même supposé l'éxistence des Incrédules: les Mots d'*Incrédules* et d'*Incrédulité* ne se trouvent même nulle part dans ces deux Ouvrages. La Charité Chrétienne nous ordonne la douceur et la moderation, et nous interdit ces petites vengeances que la Philosophie moderne compte pour rien, parce qu'elle s'en permet trés souvent de plus fortes. Nous devons chercher à faire du bien, même aux Incrédules qui nous font le plus de mal. Nous devons tacher de les éclairer et de les toucher, et ce ne sera assurément pas par des railleries et par des sarcasmes que nous pourrons esperer d'y parvenir. Ils nous rendront guerre pour guerre, et de quel profit cette guerre cruelle sera t-elle au Genre humain? Tout ce polémique insensé ne servira jamais qu'à alimenter cet amour propre malheureux qui l'inspire et l'éxalte. Un Ami sincère de la Vérité et de la Vertu a un meilleur emploi à faire de son tems et de ses talens.

Vous n'avés pas oublié, mon cher Ami; que je vous présentai les mêmes refléxions, quand vous publiates votre première Brochure contre l'Auteur[4] du *Dictionnaire Philosophique.* Si j'avois été à vos côtés quand vous écriviés cette Pièce, j'aurois fait les plus grands efforts pour vous arracher la Plume de la main. Vous donnates lieu à cet Auteur de lacher une douzaine d'autres Brochures, toutes plus dangereuses les unes que les autres: le Peuple lut avec avidité ces Brochures et ne lut pas les votres.[5]

Je reviens à votre Anonyme. Il trace les Portraits de Voltaire et de Rousseau. Vous scavés à quel point les Portraits doivent être finis, et combien ceux-ci le sont il peu! Veuillés en juger par les remarques suivantes.[6]

4. Voltaire.

5. This is an allusion to the Voltaire-Needham controversy on miracles. See letter 21, n.1 and n.2, and section 5 of the Introduction.

6. The following examples discussed by Bonnet are taken from pp.85-86 of the *Extrait* (see letter 43, n.6). The second edition does not differ from the first. '[Voltaire] Doué d'une part d'un naturel gai, violent, leger & capricieux; doué de l'autre, d'une conception aisée, d'une vaste mémoire, d'un esprit saillant, d'une intelligence moins capable d'inventer que d'imaginer, moins ingénieuse à trouver qu'habile à exprimer & à imiter; & d'une plus grande délicatesse & justesse d'oreille que de jugement, il fut Poëte en naissant, & vécut tel. Il s'appliqua à l'étude des belles Lettres & aux genres agreables seulement: il devint élegant Auteur, & conteur plaisant. Poëte dramatique, il voulut être Poëte de bon ton & de bonne compagnie, un esprit-fort, un génie universel: si bien qu'à trente ans il joua l'homme de Cour, à cinquante ans le Philosophe, à soixante & dix le bouffon & l'impie.

'Suasoure [Rousseau] sortit d'une famille plus obscure: ses Parents, pauvres mais instruits, lui donnerent eux-même la premiere éducation: né opiniâtre, triste, altier, sauvage, chaud, & sensible depuis l'épiderme jusqu'au fond de l'ame, il se montra d'abord *Penseur ingénieux*, Sophiste éloquent & fécond; puis ayant donné à l'observation de la nature & à l'étude de la sagesse humaine, tous les moments, que lui laissoient les occupations, qui lui produisoient de quoi subsister avec décence, il

Doué d'un Esprit saillant: on n'a jamais dit un *Esprit saillant*; mais on dit une *Pensée saillante*.

Une Intelligence moins capable d'inventer que d'imaginer: celà est-il bien clair? Découvre-ton ce que l'Ecrivain voudroit exprimer? Le Lecteur apperçoit-il la difference qu'on met ici entre *inventer* et *imaginer*?

Il fut Poëte en naissant et vécut tel: qu'est-ce je vous prie que vivre en Poëte? Homère, Milton, Pope, Racine, ne *vivoient*-ils donc pas *en Poëtes*?

Il voulut être Poëte de bon Ton et de bonne Compagnie: qu'est-ce encore qu'un Poëte *de bon Ton et de bonne Compagnie*? On entrevoit à peu près ce que l'Auteur veut dire; mais, étois-ce ainsi qu'il falloit le dire?

Si bien qu'à trente ans: ce *Si bien* est-il bien propre à figurer dans un Portrait?

Il joua l'Homme de Cour: on joue le Dévot, et on *ne joue pas l'Homme de Cour*.

Sensible depuis l'épiderme jusqu'au fond de l'Ame: il falloit donc mettre *jusqu'au fond des moelles*; car il n'y point d'opposition entre l'*épiderme* et l'Ame.

Puis ayant donné: rien de plus inélégant que ce tour.

Peintre le plus chaud: je ne sçache pas qu'on ait jamais dit d'un Peintre *qu'il étoit chaud*: mais, on a dit, *qu'il y avoit de la chaleur* dans certaines Peintures. Un Anglois ne peut guères saisir ces nuances de la Langue Françoise: pourquoi aussi un Anglois veut il faire des Portraits en François?

Une des plus vives lumières en matière de Raisonnement: de bonne foi Rousseau est-il cela? Connoissés vous un Auteur plus *anti-logique* ou qui se contredise plus ouvertement?

Depuis le dernier jusqu'au premier des Etres:[7] quelle indécence n'y a-t-il point à mettre ici le PREMIER DES ETRES dans la même phrase avec *le dernier*.

Consacra son Siècle: le Siecle de *Montesquieu* peut-il être consacré par l'éloquence d'un Ecrivain qui a fait à la Societé la plus profonde playe? J'ajoute; que *consacrer son Siècle* est d'une grande incorrection.

J'aurois bien d'autres Remarques à faire sur ce très court Imprimé: le tems me manque, et celles ci vous suffiront pour vous faire juger de ce que je supprime. Vous ne serés donc pas surpris que je n'aye pas fait courir ce petit Ecrit, et vous me pardonnérés ma franchise en consideration du motif et des sentimens que vous a voués pour sa vie le Palingénésiste.

[ADDRESS] Bruxelles; M.ʳ l'Abbé Néédham, de la Societé Royale d'Angleterre.

---

devint Orateur-Philosophe, le Peintre le plus chaud du sentiment le plus vrai, & une des plus vives lumieres en matiere de raisonnement. Il vécut longtems ignoré & comme s'ignorant lui-même.'

7. The following examples are taken from pp.102-103 of the *Extrait* (see letter 43, n.6): 'Les excès de Tévilaor [Voltaire], une fois connus, persuaderent enfin au reste de ses Partisans qu'il avoit effectivement écrit pour lui seul, & contre tout le monde; qu'il n'avoit prêché la tolérance que par intolérance: en un mot que c'etoit un persécuteur cruel & hypocrite, qui vouloit être seul à persécuter, qui persécutoit en riant; en recommandant d'une part le pardon des injures, la douceur & l'humanité, & de l'autre en écrivant sans relâche d'horribles satyres & de noires calomnies contre tout l'univers, depuis le dernier jusqu'au premier des êtres, pourvu qu'il se crut en sureté.

'Sausoure [Rousseau] ne perdit aucun de ses admirateurs; sa mort, ne fit que lui rendre ceux que l'envie & l'espece de son amour-propre lui avoient fait perdre pendant sa vie: sa personne trop peu puissante pour être recherchée, trop misantrope, trop altiere pour se former un parti, trop honnête pour être crainte, trop infortunée pour être haïe plus d'un moment, dut être & fut bientôt oubliée, même de son vivant: mais son éloquence immortelle consacra son nom, sa langue & son siecle.'

MANUSCRIPT
  BPUG, MS Bonnet 73:169*v*-170*r* (not included in copy B).

45

Needham to Bonnet – Brussels, 23 October 1770

à Bruxelles, Le 23. d'oct: 1770.

Vous dites très bien, mon cher ami & confrere, dans une de vos dernieres lettres, dont je me rappelle la substance, que nos principes sur la foi doivent differer, autant que nos principes sur la generation; et je dois ajouter que notre façon de voir en fait de critique differe pour le moins autant que nos sentimens physiques, ou Religieux. Je ne suis pas du tout prevenu en faveur de l'imprimé, que je vous ai fait parvenir, et vous n'etes pas moins bon juge sur les points, que vous attaquez, pour l'avoir critiqué de la façon, que vous le faites. Votre malheur est à mon avis, qu'ayant acquis un gout exquis en fait de style, et donnant trop dans le luxe litteraire des François de ce malheureux siecle, vous vous attachez tant au colori, que les choses vous echappent sans daigner meme les regarder assés pres pour les apprecier selon leur juste valeur. En nous prenant comme nous sommes tous deux formés, et constitués par education vous François, pour ainsi dire, et moi anglois il n'est pas étonnant, que de mon coté je m'attache entierement à la vérité, et la justesse des traits, et de contours, et vous principalement au colori. Sans cela comment peut il arriver, que vous preferez les vingt satyres indecentes, et ridicules de Voltaire remplies d'absurdites, d'inepties, d'ordure, et de blasphemes aux trois lettres, ou hors d'œuvres, pour ainsi dire, qui m'ont échappés à Geneve,[1] sur tout à la parodie de sa troisieme lettre sur les miracles, dont la justesse et la vérité a été par tout estimée, et meme à Geneve. Jamais de ma vie je me suis attaché en lisant aux delicatesses d'un style recherché, mais toujours à la façon de tous mes compatriotes aux choses contenües, dont je ne demande en fait d'expression, que l'energie, et la clarté. Or les portraits faits d'après nature de Voltaire, et Rousseau, et mis en contraste ne sont pas communs, comme vous pensés, et si vous croyez de les avoir vu peints avec plus de justesse, ou d'une maniere plus fine, et plus agreable vous etes jusqu'à ce moment de tant des personnes à qui j'ai montré l'ouvrage en manuscrit, le seul de votre sentiment. Il a été meme lu, et relu par l'auteur de la vie de Louis treize[2] ouvrage très estimé des François, en ma presence sans

---

1. See letter 21, n.1. For the Voltaire-Needham controversy on miracles, see section 5 of the Introduction.

2. The Jesuit historian Henri Griffet (1698-1771) published in 1758 the *Histoire du regne de Louis XIII, Roi de France et de Navarre* (Paris). This and his treatise on historiographical method (Griffet 1769) are the works for which he is chiefly remembered. For a biography of Griffet, see *B.U.* (17:534-35) and especially Bouchard (1861-1863); for a bibliography of his works, see Sommervogel (1960, 3:1814-25). Bonnet's opinion of Griffet's *Histoire* was not as high as Needham's. As he wrote to Haller: 'Il [Needham] s'appuye pour le *Style* sur l'Authorité de l'Historien de Louis XIII a qui il avoit donné la Pièce *à revoir*, et qui n'y avoit trouvé que *quelques legères fautes*. Admirés, mon illustre Ami, le jugement de ce Censeur; mais vous n'ignorés pas combien l'Historien en question a été

qu'il ait vu les defauts impardonables, dont vous me parlez, le peu de defauts qu'il m'a marqué en fait du style ont été corrigés suivant son avis. Il peut après tout, qu'il ne soit pas aussi parfait, comme vous l'exigéz, mais tous les defauts possibles, tels que ceux, dont vous vous plaignés, ne me feront jamais mepriser un ouvrage, dont le fond est excellent, ni toute l'harmonie des phrases mesurées de Voltaire, ni ses antitheses, ni les pretendues charmes de son style me forceront jamais d'approuver les faussetes, et les absurdités renfermées dans ce qu'il a donné autrefois, et donne encore journellement au public. En un mot, si vous éties peintre, je vous dirai, que malgré tout ce qu'un monde enchanté peut dire, je prefererai toujours les tableaux de Poussin avec ses couleurs mattes à ceux de Michel ange de Caravaggio, dont toute la valeur, et la force consistent dans le seul colori composé de tout ce qu'il y a de plus brillant, et des ombres qui me choquent par leur faux tranchant avec la lumiere. Du reste vous ferez de ce, que j'ai cru pouvoir vous faire plaisir, et que je vous ai envoyé tout ce que vous voulés, vous le cacherés aux yeux de vos amis, ou vous les produirés avec vos remarques, cela doit m'etre indifferent, car il est autant impossible que je voye les choses par vos yeux, comme il est impossible que vous les voyés avec les miens. L'ouvrage en attendant ne fera pas moins son chemin, et si tout le monde ne pense pas comme moi en fait des connoissances de toute espece, tout le monde ne pense pas comme vous non plus, et chacun aura son parti. La seule chose qui me fait de la peine pour ce moment est que je n'ai pas reçu vos nouvelles recherches sur les preuves du christianisme, et dieu sçait quand je les recevrai. C'est en cela pour la plûpart que nous sommes bien d'accord ensemble, mais ce n'est pas tant votre style, que j'admire, que les choses qu'il renferme et la force de vos raisonnements. Ou faites moi l'avoir au plûtot en écrivant à votre correspondent à Paris de me l'envoyer par le carosse sans delai, ou dites moi à qui je dois m'adresser pour l'avoir en le payant. Adieu, mon cher ami, et confrere, ayés la bonté de ne pas m'oublier aupres de Madame, et nos amis communs, et soyés toujours persuadé de l'amitie fondée sur l'estime de celui, qui a l'honneur d'etre

votre ami sincere, et très humble serviteur
Needham.

Notre nouvelle academie va prendre des nouvelles forces; elle a changé sa peau, comme les vers à soye, pour la premiere fois; le nouveau ministre[3] la favorise d'une maniere distinguée, je viens de donner un memoire[4] par ses ordres

---

relevé lui même sur son *Style*. Nous laisserons donc le trop complaisant Abbé s'applaudir de sa nouvelle progéniture, et nous souhaiterons qu'il ne soit pas écorché tout vivant par les principaux Aristarques de la Secte *philosophesque*' (Sonntag 1983:913).

3. A short biography of count, later prince Georg Adam Starhemberg (1724-1807), Minister Plenipotentiary in the Austrian Netherlands from 1770 to 1783, is given in Wurzbach (37:200-202). Eichwalder (1971) has studied Starhemberg's diplomatic and political activity both before and after his years at Brussels, while de Boom (1932:320-47) has analysed his political activity as Minister Plenipotentiary in the Austrian Netherlands.

4. A few days after the arrival of prince Starhemberg in Brussels on 9 June 1770, Needham requested an audience with the new Minister Plenipotentiary (Mailly 1883, 1:35). It must have been on that occasion that he was asked to write a mémoire. It seems likely that this is the undated mémoire in Needham's own handwriting, still preserved in AARB (Needham), and bearing the title 'Mémoire sur la Société littéraire de Bruxelles, fait et présenté à S.A. le Ministre plénipotentiaire de S.M.I.R.A., par M. Needham, directeur de ladite société', which was later published by Gachard

sur les moyens les plus prompts et les plus efficaces pour son avancement; elle sera fondée par des lettres patentes, par des pensions, et par un fond approprié à son necessaire. La conduite de M^r· Vanswieten, dont je vous ai parlé dans ma derniere lettre m'étonne; je ne demande pas de personne, qu'il me previent, mais j'ai droit, il me semble, d'exiger une reponse honnete à une lettre très polie, dont vous etes la cause par ce que vous m'avez dites sur le compte de ce célèbre medecin.

MANUSCRIPT
BPUG, MS Bonnet 30:273r-274r.

46

Needham to Bonnet – Brussels, 16 July 1773

à Bruxelles, le 16 Juillet 1773.

Je profite, mon cher Monsieur, ami, et confrere, d'une occasion heureuse, qui se presente, pour vous temoigner mes égards constants en vous faisant parvenir une brochure[1] assés curieuse, dont je suis depuis peu l'editeur. Écrivés moi quelques mots par la poste, non pas de reconnoissance, car je m'assure que notre amitie reciproque n'a jamais été interrompüe un seul instant, mais uniquement pour me marquer l'etat de votre santé, et de celle de mes amis de Geneve, pour qui je m'interesse. Dites moi aussi en quatre mots à quoi vous vous occupés maintenant, et quel est le dernier resultat de toutes vos recherches sur la generation des abeilles? Car il n'y a pas long tems, que j'ai trouvé une brochure[2] sur cette matiere, ou il y a des memoires adressés de votre part à l'academie des sciences à Paris, entremelés parmi plusieurs autres écrits portant des observations en apparence contradictoires, qui m'empechent de sçavoir à quoi je dois me tenir sur ce sujet. Il va paroitre dans le courant du mois prochain un nouvel

(1840:58-65).

1. *Lettre de Pekin, sur le génie de la langue chinoise, et la nature de leur écriture symbolique, comparée avec celle des anciens Egyptiens* (Bruxelles 1773). This work is divided into two parts. The first (paginated in Roman numerals) contains an unsigned *Avis préliminaire* by Needham (pp.ii-iv), a group of certificates authenticating Needham's depiction of the characters on the so-called 'bust of Isis' (pp.v-ix), and two reviews that had appeared in the *Journal des sçavans* concerning two works by Guignes (pp.ix-xxxviii). The second part (paginated in Arabic numerals) consists of the *Lettre sur les caractères chinois par le Reverend Pere***, de la Compagnie de Jesus*, the anonymous author of which was Father Cibot (b.1727); see Davin (1961:393-95). This *Lettre* was the answer to the enquiries that are mentioned by Needham and Bonnet in 1764 (see letter 17, n.2; letter 18; and section 6 of the Introduction).

2. Adam Gottlieb Schirach, *Histoire naturelle de la reine des abeilles, avec l'art de former des essaims* [...] *On y a ajouté la correspondance de l'auteur avec quelques sçavans, & trois Mémoires de l'illustre M. Bonnet de Genève sur ses découvertes. Le tout traduit de l'Allemand ou recueilli, par J.J. Blassière* (La Haye 1771). This work was translated into Italian as *Storia naturale della regina delle api* (Brescia 1774). For a discussion of this work, see section 10 of the Introduction; for Bonnet's mémoires on bees, see letter 49, n.6.

ouvrage[3] de M[r.] Le Comte de Buffon sur les elemens de la matiere, dont M[r.] Daubenton[4] vient de me parler dans une lettre,[5] qui le caracterise comme l'ouvrage le plus sublime, qui ait jamais sorti de sa plume, et appuyé des experiences, qui, dit il, me feront le plus grand plaisir. On l'imprime actuellement à l'imprimerie Royale, et je l'attend avec impatience. Notre nouvelle academie des sciences, et belles lettres, dont j'ai l'honneur d'etre le directeur, vient d'etre fondée radicalement par des lettres patentes[6] de sa Majesté Imperiale sous le titre d'Imperiale et Royale, qui conferent en meme tems aux membres jusqu'a des titres, et des prerogatifs de Noblesse. Elle est actuellement composée de 16. membres du Pais, et cinq étrangers, et jusqu'à present tout paroit promettre assés bien pour l'avenir. Ayés la bonté de saluer de ma part votre aimable famille, Messieurs Trembley, de Saussure &c. et soyés persuadé de l'estime, et de l'attachement, avec le quel j'ai l'honneur

d'etre, cher ami, et confrere,
votre très humble, et très obeissant s[e]rvit[eu]r
Needham.

MANUSCRIPT
BPUG, MS Bonnet 32:141r.

47

Bonnet to Needham – [Genthod], 18 September 1773

À la Campagne le 18.[e] de Septembre 1773
Je vous tiens le plus grand compte, Monsieur mon cher et célèbre Ami, de vous être souvenu si obligeamment de moi, à l'occasion de ces Lettres sur[a] la Langue Chinoise,[1] dont je suis redevable à votre amitié. [b]J'ai été d'autant plus sensible à ce procedé amical, que je vous devois depuis très longtemps une Réponse. Mais, il faut bien que je vous l'avoue; je ne sçavois comment vous faire cette Réponse. Vous m'aviés écrit des choses qui m'avoient étonné et presque affligé, et que je n'avois assurément pas mérité. Je vous avois communiqué quelques petites

3. Buffon's work, of which Daubenton (see n.4 below) had given advance notice, was 'Des élémens', which contained two parts, 'De la lumière, de la chaleur et du feu' and 'De l'air, de l'eau et de la terre', and was published in 1774 in the *Supplément* (1:1-125) to the *Histoire naturelle* (1749-1789).

4. For a short biography of Louis-Jean-Marie Daubenton (1716-1800), *garde et démonstrateur* of the natural history collection at the Jardin du Roi and Buffon's main collaborator in the *Histoire naturelle*, see Camille Limoges, *D.S.B.*, 15 (1978) 111-14, which lists Daubenton's major scientific works and the main secondary literature. See also Farber (1975).

5. This letter could not be traced.

6. The Lettres Patentes of Maria Theresa, which changed the Société littéraire de Bruxelles into the Académie impériale et royale des sciences et belles-lettres, were dated 16 December 1772. The first meeting of the new Academy was held in the Royal Library on 13 April 1773. The main official documents regarding the foundation are listed in *L'Académie* (1973:16-18); some are published in Gachard (1840); and a history of them is given by Mailly (1883, 1:52-80).

1. See letter 46, n.1.

Remarques Critiques sur une Brochure[2] que vous m'aviés adressée contre Voltaire et Rousseau. Cette Brochure n'étoit que l'annonce d'un plus grand Ouvrage Polémique dont vous ne me disiés point que vous étiés l'Auteur, et dont vous me demandiés mon jugement. Je crus que l'amitié qui nous lie, m'imposoit la Loi de vous satisfaire, et de vous dire ma pensée avec cette franchise qui plait tant à l'amitié et qu'elle inspire toujours. Mes Remarques portoient sur les Choses et sur le Style, et toutes tendoient, en general à engager l'estimable Auteur à prendre un autre tour pour combattre ces deux fameux Polémistes. Je ne voulois pas que l'honnête Apologiste fut exposé à des Critiques qui auroient nui à l'importante Cause qu'il entreprenoit de deffendre. Quelle fut donc ma surprise, lors que je vis par votre Lettre que loin d'entrer dans l'Esprit et le but de de mes Remarques, vous me témoigniés de la manière la plus forte combien elles vous avoient déplu, et combien vous les désapprouviés. Vous alliés même jusqu'à me dire; *que je faisois tant de cas du Coloris, que je préferois les vingt Satyres indécentes et ridicules de Voltaire, remplies d'absurdités, d'inepties, d'ordures et de blasphêmes, aux trois Lettres du hors d'Oeuvre qui vous étoient échappés.*[3] Je parle de cette Lettre que vous m'écrivites de Bruxelles le 23.ᵉ d'Octobre 1770. Cette tirade et bien d'autres que renfermoient la même Lettre, contrastoient si prodigieusement avec ma manière de sentir et de penser et avec mon attachement pour vous, que je n'eus plus la force de vous écrire. Je ne vous en étois pas demeuré moins attaché; car mon Coeur n'est pas fait pour nourrir aucun genre de ressentiment; bien moins encore contre un Ancien Ami, qu'il aimera toujours à obliger. Je m'étois donc prescrit un Silence absolu, en attendant quelqu' heureuse occasion qui m'invitat à le rompre. Vous me la fournissés, cette occasion; je vous en remercie, mon bon Ami, et j'en profite. Je viens donc à l'obligeante Lettre qui accompagnoit votre Envoi, qui m'a été remis le mois dernier. Je ne vous aurois même rien dit du tout de votre précédente Lettre, si je n'avois pas eu à vous rendre raison de mon long silence.[b]

Vous m'avés fait plaisir en me ramenant à l'importante Question de l'*Origine des Chinois*, qui avoit fait autrefois la matière de quelques uns de nos Entretiens. Vous-vous rappellés, que j'avois été fort frappé du Travail du profond de Guignes.[4] J'avois même fait un Extrait suivi de son intéressant Mémoire. J'y avois joint les Conjectures de l'illustre Mairan;[5] et en repassant dans mon Esprit toutes ces analogies, il m'avoit paru très probable, que ces Chinois, dont l'Antiquité étoit si vantée par nos Philosophes à Brevet, n'étoient qu'une Colonie de l'Ancienne Egypte. Votre Isis étoit venu à l'appui de tout cela, et j'étois

2. See letter 43, n.6.
3. This is not an exact quotation from Needham's letter (see letter 45).
4. See letter 14, n.2.
5. For a short biography and list of the major publications of the French physicist Jean-Jacques Dortous (also Dortus) de Mairan (1678-1771), see *B.U.* (26:161-63); Sigalia C. Dostrovsky, *D.S.B.*, 9 (1974) 33-34; J. Moreau (1947); and Guerlac (1977). A disciple of Malebranche, a member of the Académie des sciences from 1718, and Secretary of the same body between 1741 and 1743, Mairan attended the Paris salons, kept up a vast correspondence, and also had historical interests. Ten of Mairan's letters to Bonnet are preserved in the BPUG (see also Marx 1976:343-44 and Savioz 1948b: 199-200). Bonnet is alluding to Mairan's conjecture that the Chinese were a colony of the Egyptians. Mairan expressed this view in his *Lettres de M. de Mairan, au R.P. Parrenin, missionnaire de la Compagnie de Jesus, à Pekin. Contenant diverses questions sur la Chine* (Paris 1759).

chaque jour dans l'attente de quelque nouvelle Découverte, qui accroîtroit la somme des probabilités que présentoit ce riche sujet. J'ai été un peu déçu de mes espérances par la Lecture de la sçavante Epitre de votre Missionnaire de Peking.[6] Ce morceau précieux m'a semblé plus instructif, plus précis, et pourtant plus clair que tout ce que j'avois lu jusqu'ici sur la Langue Chinoise. Je serois tenté de le proposer comme un excellent Manuel à l'usage de ceux qui s'occupent de ces épineuses Recherches. L'Auteur me paroit aussi impartial qu'éclairé. Je vois à la page 19 un Fait qui n'est point favorable à votre conjecture sur les *Caractères* de l'*Isis* de Turin.[7] *Dès que des Lettrés du premier ordre ont décidé que l'Inscription de cette Isis n'est pas Chinoise, et qu'ils ne pouvoient pas l'expliquer*; il me semble qu'il seroit contre les Règles de la bonne Critique de soutenir la conformité des Caractères de cette Inscription *[b]avec ceux[b]* de l'*Ancien Chinois.*

L'ingénieux Missionnaire ouvre une autre route pour parvenir à la véritable Cause des Analogies qu'on croit appercevoir entre certains Hiéroglyphes Egyptiens et certains Caractères Chinois. Il présume; que les deux Peuples ayant par Noë une même origine, ont pu facilement se rencontrer dans l'expression *Hiéroglyphique* de certains objets; sans qu'on puisse légitimement en inferer que l'un de ces Peuples est une Colonie de l'autre.[8] Je ne pense pas qu'on puisse refuter solidement l'opinion du Missionnaire; car comment débrouiller des Choses si profondément enfoncées dans l'abîme des temps! Peut être néanmoins qu'en fouillant plus avant dans la Science Hiéroglyphique des deux Peuples, on parviendra un jour à éclaircir un peu plus le Mystère.

Je lis à la page 28 l'étrange Conjecture du Sçavant Missionnaire sur le Caractère Chinois qui exprime l'*union.*[9] Comment a-t-il été possible qu'il ait

6. *Lettre sur les caracteres chinois par le Reverend Pere* **** [Cibot], dated 'Pe-king ce 20 Octobre 1764' (see letter 46, n.1. and section 6 of the Introduction).

7. 'Voici qui est plus décisif: l'ensemble de tous ces Caracteres [of the so-called 'bust of Isis'] n'a rien de Chinois. Un coup d'oeil sur quelque livre que ce soit, suffit pour s'en convaincre. Qu'on les compare avec les cinq différentes écritures dont nous avons parlé plus haut, on n'y trouvera pas mieux son compte. [...] Enfin pour n'avoir rien à me reprocher à cet égard, j'ai fait copier une suite d'inscriptions anciennes qui passent chez les Antiquaires pour être du tems des *Chang*, c'est-à-dire de plus de 1500 ans avant Jesus-Christ. [...] Ou je suis bien trompé, ou qui les comparera avec les symboles de l'*Isis*, y trouvera autant de différence qu'entre une page d'Arabe & une de Tartare' ([Cibot] 1773:19).

8. Cibot suggested five possible lines of investigation that could establish a relationship between Chinese and Egyptians. The one alluded to by Bonnet was the following: 'La croyance d'un Dieu créateur, rédempteur, rémunérateur; la tradition de l'état d'innocence, du péché originel, du déluge; le culte religieux par la priere, les offrandes & les sacrifices étant communs à tous les anciens peuples, par leur descendance commune de Noë. Je m'attacherois à ces grands objets, non-seulement pour consoler ma foi, mais encore pour avoir un point fixe de confrontation, & me donner une regle assurée de vérification' ([Cibot] 1773:21).

9. 'Parmi les anciens Caracteres Chinois qui ont été conservés, on trouve celui-ci Δ qu'on a écrit depuis /Δ. Selon le Dictionnaire de *Kang-hi* ce Caractere signifie *union*. Ecoutons les Chinois sur son analyse *(aa)*. Selon *choue-ouen*, ce Livre si vanté, Δ est *trois unis en un*. Il dérive de ce caractere des caracteres ∧ *jou* entrer, pénétrer & —Ч un, d'où il conclut que Δ c'est trois unis, pénétrés, fondus en un. *Lieou chou tsing hoen* qui est une explication raisonnée & savante des plus anciens caracteres s'exprime ainsi: "Δ signifie union intime, harmonie, le premier bien de l'homme, du Ciel & de la terre, c'est l'union des trois. *Tsni (Tsai* signifie principe, puissance, habilité) Dans le *Tao*; car uni, ils dirigent ensemble, crient & nourrissent. L'image ㍉.(trois) unis en une seule figure n'est pas si obscure en elle-même, cependant il est difficile d'en raisonner sans se tromper, il n'est pas aisé d'en parler." Je connois la délicatesse de notre siecle, & la rigueur des plus sages critiques, dès qu'il s'agit de religion. Malgré cela j'ose conjecturer que le caractere Δ pourroit avoir été chez les anciens

prétendu y découvrir le Mystère de la *Trinité*, révélé, selon lui, par Noë à ses Descendans. Ne sautoit il pas aux yeux, que si le Patriarche avoit si bien connu ce Mystère, Moyse l'auroit connu aussi; et si Moyse l'eut si bien connu, comment ne l'auroit-il pas énoncé directement dans le Pentateuque! Cette Conjecture, presque bizarre, dépare un peu l'intéressant Ecrit du Missionnaire, et je ne sçaurois croire que vous l'adoptiés. Combien est-il évident, que le Mystère dont il s'agit est propre au Christianisme! Ce seroit, à mon avis, abuser beaucoup de l'Interprétation, que de prétendre que ce Mystère est contenu dans ces paroles de la Genèse; *faisons l'Homme à notre image … il est dévenu semblable à l'un de nous*; ou dans les *trois Hommes* qui visitèrent Abraham.

Je goute fort la Conjecture du Missionnaire exposée page 30.[10] Cette distinction entre les *grands* et les *petits* Hiéroglyphes peut mener loin, et elle est puisée dans la marche la plus naturelle de l'Esprit. On ne peut se refuser à admettre que la première Ecriture n'ait été une *Peinture* ou du moins une *Esquisse* des Objets les plus familiers. Il aura bein fallu dans la suite réduire ou simplifier cette Peinture, &c. &c.

Je fais sur la Conjecture de la page 33 touchant l'*Agneau*[11] la même Remarque que sur celle qui a pour objet la *Trinité*. Je suis faché de trouver de pareilles choses dans ce bon Ecrit. Je vous écris à mésure que je le lis; car je n'avois pu le lire encore. Le bon Père, qui se donne à la fin de sa Lettre pour *fort neuf et fort ignorant en toutes sortes de Sciences et de littérature*,[12] cite pourtant dans ses Notes les Amien Marcellin, les Josephe, les Eusèbe, les Bochart &c &c. et combien d'autres traits dans son Ecrit qui décèlent une grande Erudition![13] Je n'aime pas que la modestie employe des expressions qui pourroient la rendre suspecte. Il ne faut pas que la bonne Monnoye aye l'air d'une fausse Monnoye; cela mettroit trop de défiance dans le Commerce.

Les Notes[14] de l'Auteur ont intéressé mon Attention. Je regrette qu'elles ne soyent pas plus étendues et plus nombreuses. On voit que sa Tête ne demande qu'à se vuider, et qu'elle ne laisse distiller la Science Chinoise goutte à goutte que parce que le Propriétaire en bouche les principales ouvertures. Je désirerois fort qu'on le déterminât à ouvrir le maître robinet.

Ce qu'il dit dans la *Note S* sur la destruction des Monumens Chinois[15] à

Chinois le symbole de la très-adorable Trinité' ([Cibot] 1773:28).

10. 'Il est incertain si les figures & symboles élémentaires des Caracteres Chinois n'ont pas été réduits en petit dès les premiers temps pour la commodité de l'écriture. Peut-être qu'il en aura été de même en Egypte, & que les Hiéroglyphes composés d'images & de figures, n'auront été employés que dans les grands monumens, les obélisques, &c. & que sur les petites pieces, comme momies, bas-reliefs, inscriptions, on se sera servi d'Hiéroglyphes abrégés & réduits à quelques traits en la façon des Caracteres Chinois' ([Cibot] 1773:30).

11. 'Selon *Tchangtsien*, critique fameux, les anciens Chinois se saluoient en s'abordant par ces deux mots *vou yang, sans agneau*; on donnera tel sens qu'on voudra à ce salut singulier, mais il me paroît que le Caractere *yang*, *agneau* est employé dans plusieurs Caracteres, de façon à faire conjecturer que la signification qui y étoit attachée indiquoit l'Agneau sans tache immolé pour le salut du monde' ([Cibot] 1773:33).

12. [Cibot] (1773:35-36).

13. For instance [Cibot] (1773:38).

14. [Cibot] (1773:37-46).

15. 'Dans les grandes révolutions qui ont donné à la Chine de nouveaux maitres, presque tous les monumens en cuivre ont été fondus, les bibliotheques des Empereurs détrônés ont été brûlées avec leur Palais, de sorte qu'il ne reste presque plus de monumens anciens. [...] A un changement

chaque nouvelle Dynastie, est bien désavantageux à l'authorité de l'Histoire de la Chine, et bien désolant pour les Amateurs de la plus haute Antiquité. Si l'on y ajoute l'Incendie des Livres par *Chi-hoang-ti*, l'an 213 avant N.S. on aura de la peine à ne tomber point dans le scepticisme sur l'Histoire de la Chine. La difficulté de fixer d'une manière certaine le sens des plus anciens caractères, est une autre source feconde de Pyrronisme dans ce Genre de Critique &c.

Des Planches[16] étoient un accompagnement fort nécessaire de cet Ecrit. J'ai parcouru avec plaisir celles qu'il renferme. Les Planches 5, 6, 7, &c démontrent à l'Oeil que *l'Ancienne Ecriture* étoit une *Peinture réduite*. J'en avois déja vu quelques éxemples frappans dans le Mémoire de Mr. de Guignes:[17] mais ils sont rassemblés ici en bien plus grand nombre.

En considerant attentivement les Figures des Planches 9, 10, 11, &c qui mettent en parallèle les *anciens Caractères* Chinois avec les *Hiéroglyphes* Egyptiens, on ne peut s'empêcher de reconnoître, qu'il est entre les uns et les autres des Rapports ou des Analogies plus ou moins remarquables. On sent, que si l'on poussoit plus loin cet intéressant Parallèle, les Analogies se multiplieroient. Tout ceci sera, sans doute, beaucoup plus approfondi par M.ʳ Court de Gebelin[18] dans son Grand Ouvrage du *Monde primitif analysé et comparé avec le Monde moderne*.[19] Vous en avés-vu apparemment le *Plan raisonné*,[20] et vous aurés jugé

de Dynastie on détruit tout ce qui rappelleroit le souvenir de la famille détrônée. On ne fait pas même grace aux tombeaux' ([Cibot] 1773:44).

16. [Cibot] (1773) contains a total of twenty-seven plates by Cibot and two by Needham.

17. Bonnet must be alluding to the three plates accompanying Guignes's *Mémoire* of 1764, and not to those that were printed with the summary of 1759 (see Guignes 1759a and 1764; see also letter 14, n.2).

18. For a biography of the French Protestant savant and historian Antoine Court de Gébelin (1725-1784), see *B.U.* (9:373-76) and Dardier (1890), which also contains a full list of his publications. For his activities as mediator between the French central political power and French Protestants in the years 1763-1784, see P. Schmidt [1908] and Lods (1899); for his support of Mesmer, see Viatte (1928, 1:225-26); and for his ideas on the origin of language, see Harnois ([1928]:57-59) and Borst (1957-1963, 3, pt.2:1447). Court de Gébelin wrote only one letter to Bonnet (BPUG, MS Bonnet 26:282; also mentioned by P. Schmidt [1908]:xii). When Court de Gébelin died, Charles-Etienne François Moulinié (1757-1836) enquired whether Bonnet would contribute to the edition of his manuscripts; see Marx (1976:631 n.20). Needham owned the first six volumes of Court de Gébelin's work *Monde primitif* (see n.19 below and *Catalogue* 1782, pt.1:19). Bonnet seems to have admired at least parts of this work (see Sonntag 1983:1145-46).

19. Antoine Court de Gébelin, *Monde primitif, analysé et comparé avec le monde moderne* (Paris 1773-1782). Although Court de Gébelin obtained financial support for this work from the Académie française both in 1780 and 1781, its publication resulted in a financial loss. For the work's editorial history and financial difficulties, see P. Schmidt ([1908]:111-18); and for a historical evaluation, see Viatte (1928, 1:186-88) and Baldensperger (1940).

20. *Plan général et raisonné des divers objets et des découvertes qui composent l'ouvrage intitulé Monde primitif, analysé et comparé avec le monde moderne, ou recherches sur les antiquités du monde* [1773]. This work (which we were unable to locate) set out the programme that Court de Gébelin only partially realised in the nine-volume work cited above (n.19). It was republished in the first volume of the *Monde primitif*. In a critical review of the *Plan général* that appeared in the *Journal des sçavans* (November 1773, pp.726-34), the anonymous author (probably Guignes) accused Court de Gébelin of arrogance and cast doubts on his claims that with his method of investigation man's original language could be understood. He added: 'Toutes ces promesses sont admirables; mais nous serions tentés de croire que l'Auteur ne parle pas sérieusement, si dans une matière aussi importante & aussi délicate il étoit permis de plaisanter. Nous osons le dire: l'intelligence de sa langue primitive & son génie allégorique ne sont que de pures imaginations. L'homme le plus habile dans les langues orientales qui sera en état de lire & d'entendre les livres, pourra, dans l'examen qu'il fera des racines de ces

facilement de ce que nous pouvons nous promettre des laborieuses Recherches de l'infatigable et sçavant Auteur. Il ne me paroit pas partisan de la méthode ingénieuse de M.ʳ de Guignes. Voici ce qu'il écrivoit en dernier lieu à un Ami qui me l'a communiqué.[21]

'Les principes de M.ʳ de Guignes sur les rapports des Egyptiens avec les Chinois me servent singulièrement, quelle que soit la cause de ces rapports; parce que le Chinois se trouvant semblable à l'Egyptien qui étoit lui même Phénicien, Hébreu, Arabe, Scithe &c tout se retrouve semblable. Quant à la conséquence qu'en tire M.ʳ de Guignes que les Chinois sont Colonie Egyptienne, elle me paroit conforme à celle de Rudbeck[22] qui voyant les rapports du Suedois avec les Egyptiens en conclud que ceux-ci étoient Colonie Suedoise: il faut plus que des mots pour établir le rapport d'origine de deux Peuples: or il y a entre les Chinois et les Egyptiens une si prodigieuse différence surtout pour la Religion et la Mythologie, qu'on peut bien douter s'ils sont venus l'un de l'autre. Sans Osiris et Isis, et sans le Sacerdoce et la fameuse Croix, point d'Egyptiens: quoi de pareil chés les Chinois? Il est impossible de se tirer de là. On trouveroit mieux son compte à dire avec Schmidt le jeune, que l'Inde fut peuplée par une Colonie Egyptienne.'[23] Mais M.ʳ de Guignes ne s'étoit pas borné au Parallele des Caractères ou des Hiéroglyphes des deux Peuples: il les avoit encore comparés, comme M.ʳ de Mairan, dans le rapport à la Religion, aux Coutumes, au Gouvernement, aux Sciences, aux Arts, &c.[24]

Puis que vous avés lu mes *Mémoires sur les Abeilles* insérés dans l'*Histoire Naturelle*

langues, parvenir à une racine primitive qui sera l'origine des autres; mais ces recherches ne pourront jamais s'étendre que sur quelques mots & non le conduire à la connoissance entière de la langue primitive. On ne peut appercevoir que des lueurs & quelques traits, qui, après un sérieux examen, ne pourront être présentés que pour des conjectures; que penser donc de celui qui, entraîné par une imagination vive, ose annoncer toutes ces recherches pour des découvertes réelles, ose les étendre sur des Livres tels que ceux de Moyse?' (p.733). In his own review of this work, Grimm (*C.L.*, 10:211-13) remarked, 'Sa vanité, qui perce à travers son ouvrage, fait de temps en temps sourir le lecteur' (p.212).

21. It has not been possible to determine who communicated the following passage to Bonnet from Court de Gébelin's letter.

22. The Swede Olaf Rudbeck the younger (1660-1740) was the son of the famous anatomist Olaf Rudbeck (1630-1702). Born in Uppsala, he studied there and obtained his M.D. In 1687 he visited Holland and attended the lectures of Boerhaave, whose ideas on botany and medicine he introduced at Uppsala University. In 1695 he was commissioned by king Charles XI (1655-1697) to undertake a scientific journey in Lapland. On his return to Uppsala he devoted himself to his academic career, and studied mainly botany and languages. He was also a great collector. Many of his manuscripts and his entire plant collection were destroyed in the great fire of 1702. He was Linnaeus's patron and teacher. For more details, see the anonymous 'Vita' in the *Acta Societatis Regiae Scientiarum Upsaliensis. Ad annum MDCCXL* (1744:124-32) and *B.U.* (37:31-32). Like his father he had a great interest in language, which he studied analogically. According to Borst (1957-1963, 3, pt.1:1339-40) his contemporaries ridiculed his linguistic theories. In his *Specimen usus linguae Gothicae* (Upsalis 1717), for instance, after listing Chinese and Gothic words and noting their similarity, Rudbeck wrote, 'Frequens me ipsum quoque admiratio subiit, quaenam tanti linguarum in gentibus maxime dissitis consensus causa, quaeve esset origo: sed mirari hoc desinent omnes, quum argumentis haud levibus probatum viderint, Chinae veteris incolas Scythas fuisse seu Gothos' (Rudbeck 1717:71).

23. Schmidt held the thesis mentioned in the text in his essay, 'De commerciis et navigationibus Ptolemaeorum', which received the 1762 prize of the Académie des inscriptions and was also published in his *Opuscula quibus res antiquae praecipue Aegyptiacae explanantur*, pp.123-379 (Carolsruhae 1765). See especially pp.164-84.

24. Bonnet is alluding to Mairan (1759) and Guignes (1759a and 1764).

de la Reine Abeille que M.ʳ Blassière[25] a publiée; vous êtes donc très au fait, mon cher Alethophile, des étranges Questions qui se sont élevées dans ces derniers temps sur l'*Origine* de ces Mouches industrieuses. Vous aurés remarqué que mes Raisonnemens sont par-tout *conditionels* ou qu'ils reposent tous sur la supposition que les Faits ont été bien observés et vérifiés. Je ne suis point du tout garant de la vérité de la supposition. Les Observateurs de Lusace[26] sont en opposition sur divers Points essentiels avec celui du Palatinat.[27] Ils m'ont adressé de longues Epitres et m'ont pris pour Juge. Je les ai renvoyés au Suprême Arbitre de ces Controverses, la Nature, et je leur ai indiqué quelques Expériences par lesquelles ils devroient l'interroger. Ce ne sont point des Naturalistes consommés dans l'*Art de voir*; cet Art si peu connu encore, et qui suppose tant de Qualités conspirantes de l'Esprit et du Corps. J'avois éxhorté l'Observateur du Palatinat à chercher des *Ovaires* dans les Abeilles ouvrières: il m'assure en avoir trouvé; mais je me défie à bon droit de son habileté dans des dissections qui exigeroient la Main de l'étonnant Lyonet.[28] J'avois prié l'Académie des Sciences de Paris de faire repèter ces Expériences de Lusace:[29] croiriés vous qu'il ne s'est rencontré Personne dans cetteᶜ Compagnie qui ait voulu entreprendre ce Travail. L'état actuel de mes Yeux me l'interdit. L'Académie de Bruxelles ne pourroit-elle s'occuper de cet objet? Il ne seroit assurément pas indigne de son attention. Il enveloppe des Vérités importantes dansᵈ l'Histoire de la Génération.

J'ignorois ce nouvel Ouvrage de M.ʳ de Buffon *sur les Elémens de la Matière*.[30] La Question de l'origine de l'*Etendue matérielle* est, sans contredit, une des plus difficiles de la Métaphysique transcendante[*b*]. Je crois même, après y avoir longtemps réfléchi, que cette Question ne sçauroit être décidée par des Hommes. Newton admettoit des *Atomes insécables*:[31] Leibnitz les rejettoit comme n'expli-

25. See letter 46, n.2.

26. On Adam Gottlob Schirach and on Johann Gottlob Wilhelmi, see letter 51, n.2. and n.6.

27. On Johann Riem, see letter 51, n.12.

28. The authoritative biography of Pierre Lyonet (1706-1789), the famous entomologist and outstanding illustrator of The Hague, is provided by van Seters :1962:185-200), which contains a full list of Lyonet's writings, drawings, and manuscript correspondence. See also the bibliographical information provided by Nissen (1969-1978, 1:265) and the papers by Freeman (1962:178-82) and van Seters (1963). While Bonnet was carrying out his investigations on aphids in the early 1740s, Trembley and Lyonet were duplicating his experiments on the Bentinck estate. Trembley kept Bonnet constantly informed of all of the observations made by Lyonet, and Bonnet's admiration for Lyonet's capacities as an observer dates from these early years. He also greatly admired the quality and accuracy of Lyonet's plates in his *Traité anatomique de la chenille, qui ronge le bois de saule*, published in The Hague in 1762. Suspicious of any form of speculation and of an excessive use of hypotheses, Lyonet did not share Bonnet's ideas on generation. On Bonnet and Lyonet, see van Seters (1962:99-104) and Marx (1976:410-11).

29. Bonnet is alluding particularly to Schirach's experiments, described in Schirach (1767 and 1771). By placing worker honeybees and a piece of comb containing larvae and honey in an empty hive and by keeping it closed for several days, Schirach observed, after a few days, that the bees has started building a queen's cell. After about twenty days, he noticed that a new queen appeared in the hive and concluded that honeybee larvae could develop into queen's larvae and finally into queens if they were suitably housed and fed. On 16 October 1769, Schirach wrote to Bonnet in German giving him details of most of his original observations. Bonnet had Schirach's letter translated and subsequently informed the French public of Schirach's findings in his 'Lettre sur les Abeilles, adressée à Messieurs les auteurs du Journal des sçavans' published in *Journal des sçavans* (November 1770, pp.746-53). On Schirach's experiments, see section 10 of the Introduction.

30. See letter 46, n.3.

31. In the *Principia*, Bk. III, rule III, Newton (1713:358) called them 'particulas indivisas'.

quant rien, et recourroit aux fameuses *Monades*,[32] qui ont ouvert un Abîme de nouvelles Difficultés. M.ʳ Euler, frappé de ces Difficultés, combat les *Monades*, et soutient que la Matière *est actuellement divisée à l'infini*.[33] Autre Abîme de Difficultés, et plus profond encore. Pour traiter philosophiquement de pareilles Questions, il ne faut point d'Eloquence; mais il faut une Logique très éxacte, beaucoup de précision dans les Idées et dans le Style, un grand fond de la meilleure Métaphysique, et point du tout de *Molécules organiques*.

Notre estimable Ami l'Abbé Spallanzani va publier un Ouvrage sur les *Animalcules des Infusions*,[34] qui vous étonnera beaucoup et n'étonnera pas moins l'illustre Inventeur des *Molécules organiques*.[35] M.ʳ Mulller,[36] habile Observateur Danois, m'a envoyé un Ecrit Latin sur ces Animalcules, qui en expose la *Nomenclature*.[37] Il est le premier Naturaliste qui ait entrepris de classer ces Etres microscopiques.

La Fondation de l'Académie de Bruxelles ajoutera aux traits déja si nombreux qui illustreront le Régne de Marie Thérése. En vous nommant Directeur de sa nouvelle Académie, cette grande Reine montre qu'elle sçait honnorer la vertu

32. See, for instance, 'Principia philosophiae, seu theses in gratiam Principis Eugenii' (Leibniz 1768, 2, pt.1:20-21) and 'Système nouveau de la nature & de la communication des substances, aussi bien que de l'union qu'il y a entre l'ame & le corps' (Leibniz 1768, 2, pt.1:50, 53).

33. For a biography of Leonhard Euler, see Wolf (1858-1862, 4:87-134); for a bibliography of his works, see Eneström (1910-1913); and for secondary sources on his mathematical works, see May (1973:141-47). An excellent introduction to Euler's scientific works is provided by A.P. Youschkevitch, *D.S.B.*, 4 (1971) 467-84, which contains a useful list of secondary sources and gives information both on Euler's incomplete and monumental *Opera omnia* and on his correspondence, which is only partially published. For works on Euler published after 1971, see Truesdell (1972), which contains an annotated bibliography of secondary sources; Sheynin (1972b); De Martino (1978); and Harman (1983). In his autobiography, Bonnet transcribed most of the correspondence he exchanged with Euler in 1761-1762 and 1770 (Savioz 1948b:195-204, 290-303), which concerned mainly their disagreement on the mechanism of sensation and on the nature of response of the nervous fibres. On this topic see also Savioz (1948a:202-204), Rocci (1975:96-97), and Anderson (1982:19-20). Bonnet is alluding to Euler's treatment of the question of infinite divisibility and his criticism of the Leibnizian position, which was discussed by Euler in letters 123-127 of the *Lettres à une princesse d'Allemagne*, 2:202-203 (Saint Petersbourg 1768-1772). In one passage Euler argued as follows: 'Si la divisibilité à l'infini est une propriété de l'étendue en géneral, il faut nécessairement qu'elle convienne aussi à tous les êtres individuels étendus; ou bien si les êtres actuels étendus ne sont pas divisibles à l'infini, il est faux que la divisibilité à l'infini soit une propriété de l'étendue en géneral. On ne sauroit nier l'une ou l'autre de ces consequences sans renverser les principes les plus solides de toutes nos connoissances; & les Philosophes, qui n'admettent pas la divisibilité à l'infini dans les êtres réels étendus ne devroient pas l'admettre non plus dans l'étendue en géneral, mais comme ils accordent le dernier, ils tombent dans une contradiction ouverte' (Euler 1768-1772, 2:209-10).

34. Bonnet is alluding to Spallanzani's researches on infusions, which were not published until 1776 in the first volume of the *Opuscoli di fisica animale, e vegetabile*.

35. Buffon.

36. For a biography of the famous Danish zoologist Otto Frederik Müller (1730-1784), one of the first field naturalists and the first author to provide a classification of Infusoria, see E. Snorrason, *D.S.B.*, 9 (1974) 574-76, and especially Anker (1943), who has fully studied Müller's travels abroad and his contacts with contemporary scientists. In their correspondence, Bonnet and Müller discussed Needham's theory of generation; and while Müller declared 'je suis infiniment éloigné des sentimens de Mr. Needham' (13 April 1771, BPUG, MS Bonnet 30:288r), he also confessed that he could not explain the phenomena of generation of fungi and infusoria. Needham's microscopical observations are mentioned by O. Müller (1773-1774, 1, pt.1:21 and 1786:vi).

37. The first part of the first volume of Müller's *Vermium terrestrium et fluviatilium, seu animalium infusoriorum, helminthicorum, et testaceorum, non marinorum, succinta historia* (Havniae, Lipsiae 1773-1774).

et la sçavoir. Aujourd'hui le Commerce mène en France à la Noblesse; et il est bien*ᵇ* plus encore dans la nature de la Chose, que les Lumières et les Talens litteraires y conduisent.

Je me repose actuellement, si l'on peut se reposer quand on a toujours quelques Epîtres à composer. Je retranche le plus qu'il m'est possible de ma Correspondance, qui s'étoit beaucoup trop étendue rélativement à mes forces et à mes circonstances. Je bois les Eaux de Spa depuis la mi-Juillet. Feu l'illustre van-Swieten me les avoit conseillées pour mes yeux, affoiblis depuis si longtemps. J'en éprouve du soulagement.

Vous me disiés dans votre précédente, que vous n'aviés pas reçu mes *Recherches sur le Christianisme* de la 1.ʳᵉ Edition. Il a fallu bientôt en faire une 2.ᵈᵉ, où j'ai inséré un morceau important *sur les Preuves de l'existences de* DIEU,³⁸ qui manquoit à la première et à la *Palingénésie*. Je vais faire ensorte que vous receviés bientôt cette Edition. Cet Ouvrage a été traduit en Allemand, en Italien, en Hollandois et on le traduit a present en Anglois.³⁹

*ᵇ*Ma Femme vous présente ses honneurs et ses voeux empressés; Nos Amis vous remercient de votre bon souvenir, et vous font leurs sincères complimens.*ᵇ* Recevés, Monsieur mon cher et célèbre Ami, le renouvellement des assurances des sentimens pleins d'éstime et d'attachement que vous a voués

[ADDRESS] Bruxelles; M.ʳ Néédham, des Societés Royales d'Angleterre et de Bruxelles

MANUSCRIPTS
   BPUG, MS Bonnet 74:97*v*-98*v*; MS Bonnet 85:193*r*-196*v*.

TEXT NOTES
   a. B: *sur le genie de b*. B: *omitted c*. B: cette illustre *d*. B: pour

48

Needham to Bonnet – Brussels, 28 October (September) 1779

Monsieur, et très cher ami

Je ne crains pas de vous qualifier de ce titre, quoique j'ai negligé depuis trop long tems de repondre à votre derniere lettre, que je conserve neanmoins precieusement. Les obstacles, et les difficultés, que j'ai rencontrées dans le soutien, et la direction de notre nouvelle Academie en absorbant le tems, que j'ai été accoutumé de consacrer à mes amis, en ont été en partie la cause. Tant de mouvemens en dedans, et tant de travaux immediatement attachés à mon

38. Chapter 3 of the *Recherches philosophiques sur les preuves du christianisme. Seconde édition, où l'on trouvera quelques additions, en particulier sur l'existence de Dieu & des notes propres à faciliter l'intelligence de l'ouvrage à un plus grand nombre de lecteurs*, pp.50-92 (Genève 1771); B.O., 7:437-49/16:160-78.

39. *Philosophische Untersuchung der Beweise für das Christenthum* (Zürich 1769); *Ricerche filosofiche sopra le prove del cristanesimo* (Venezia 1771); *Philosophische navorschingen van de bewyzen voor het Christendom* ('sGravenhage 1771). The English translation appeared much later: *Philosophical and critical inquiries concerning Christianity* (London 1787).

office m'ont reduit presqu'à l'etat d'Horace Philosophe par accès en depit de la
légéreté de son genie Poetique; *oblitusque meorum, obliviscendus et illis.*[1] Mais si
malgré tout ce que je viens d'alleguer, vous persistés à croire, que dans le grand
nombre de connaissances, que j'ai faites en parcourant plus d'une fois notre
continent, je devrai en faire une exception en votre faveur, en vertu de notre
ancienne amitie; j'avouerai volontiers mon tort à votre égard personellement
sans résumer pour repondre pertinemment à votre derniere lettre, la question,
qui partageoit autrefois nos opinions Philosophiques, à laquelle, selon ce que
l'abbe Lambinet[2] me mande, vous croiés devoir attribuer mon silence. Car je
vous avouerai volontiers loin d'avoir été affecté par une pareille cause, je
suis las jusqu'à l'excés de toutes ces recherches inutiles, et tous ces debats
interminables. Bref, il y a bien du tems, que jetté par terre mon bouclier, et mes
armes offensives en tournant mon dos à mes adversaires, et Spalanzani, comme
vous le sçavés, est resté maitre du champ de bataille. Voulés vous que je vous
dise un secret, qui me régarde, et que je n'ai dit encore à personne? J'ai appris
de ma plus tendre jeunesse à considerer la science morale, comme la premiere,
et la seule vraiment utile parmi toutes les autres. En arrivant à Paris pour la
premiere fois l'année 1746. j'ai rémarqué, que la nouvelle Philosophie de ce Pais
un peu trop analogue au caractere leger de la nation, tendoit, comme l'Aliboron
aux ailes renversées de Palissot vers la terre au lieu de monter au ciel, ou le
système sublime de Newton l'appelloit. Hypothese pour Hypothese, celle des
germes preexistans écartant toute idée de generation équivoque valoir bien, ou
meme plus qu'une autre pour assurer la morale de la puissance creatice de dieu,
et de la dependance entiere du monde de son conservateur. De meme en
metaphysique l'hypothese des idées innées imaginée par descartes, quoique
fausse en elle-meme servoit assés bien pour tranquilliser l'esprit inquiet de
l'homme sur la presence intime de dieu, *in quo vivimus movemur et sumus,*[3] et sur
l'immutabilité de nos principes moraux en general. Le seul malheur étoit, qu'en
prenant ces deux hypotheses, qui n'etoient en effet que des pars *succedanea*, pour
la vraie, et l'unique base de la morale, les faux Philosophes, qui en voyoient la
foiblesse, ou pour le moins l'incertitude, ont conçu la folle esperance en les
renversant de pouvoir sapper les fondemens de toute religion tant naturelle, que
révélée, et de la detruire radicalement. En effet le système des idées innées
étoit exactement analogue à celui des germes préexistans, et une résource en
metaphysique de la meme espece precisement, que l'autre avoit été en Physique
pour fixer, et pour arrêter, s'il étoit possible, les récherches trop épineuses, et
meme dangereuses de l'esprit humain sur la premiere origine des choses, et sur

1. Horace, *Epistulae*, XI, 8.
2. The bibliographer and historian Pierre Lambinet (1742-1813) was born at Tournes, near
Mézières. He studied at the Jesuit College at Charleville, first entering the Society and later
becoming a member of the order of Prémontré. In the late 1770s he moved to Liège and then to
Brussels, where he was tutor to the sons of the Count de Cruyckenburg. There he made contact
with Needham, who presented at the Academy Lambinet's 'Notice de quelques manuscrits qui
concernent l'histoire des Pay-Bas, faite à la Bibliothèque publique de Berne, en juin 1779' (Mailly
1883, 2:110), which probably contained the results of research carried out during Lambinet's tour
of Switzerland in 1779. For short biographies of Lambinet and lists of his writings, see *B.U.* (23:59-
60) and Michel Gilot in Sgard (1976:217).
3. Actus apostolorum xvii. 28.

la source, d'ou dérivent nos operations intellectuelles. Du reste il est très sur que descartes inventeur de ce systeme des idées innées, et victime de sa bonne volonté avoit des intentions très saines en l'imaginant au depens meme de la vérité, aussi bien qu'en privant la matiere de toute espece d'activité pour ne lui accorder, que des qualités insubstantielles et purement negatives, si on excepte ce qu'il appelle son étendüe solide en quoi il fait consister très mal à propos son essence. J'ai dit *très mal à propos*, quoiqu'il ne cherchoit par là qu'à poser une forte barriere destructive cependant de toute union naturelle, entre le corps, et l'esprit, parce qu'en confondant le Phenomene de l'etendüe, qui n'est qu'une pure relation, avec la solidité, qui n'est autre chose que la puissance réactive de la matiere, provenant de ce degré d'activité reelle, absolüe, et substantielle, qui lui est propre, et qui derive de l'essence meme de ses premiers principes combinés ensemble, il en a fait une composition chimerique et contradictoire, dont les adversaires de la morale ont profité pour obscurcir nos principes les plus certains.—Voyant par consequent du commencement meme de ma carriere Philosophique, et prevoyant que ces differentes resources cartesiennes, et autres en faveur de la religion pouvoient fort aisement nous manquer, en meme tems que la morale, sans laquelle la société ne peut subsister, periclitoit, si on ne prenoit pas les precautions de la pourvoir d'un second retranchement plus fort que le premier, j'ai voulu en prevenir les suites funestes.—Pour le faire plus efficacement j'ai crû devoir poser le systême, que j'ai établi d'après la nature, comme je me flatte, fondé sur les forces actives de premiers principes de la matiere agissants par essence, & reagissans réciproquement selon des loix posées par la divinité, et aussi certains dans leurs effets généralement parlant, que les forces, qui gouvernent le système planetaire. Simples, et par consequent substantiels dans le sens le plus energique du mot, parce que l'essence d'une composition quelconque comme composition, éternellement divisible selon les idées vulgaires, est toujours rélative, toujours fugitive, toujours indéterminée, pendant que la parfaite unité est seule substantielle; il en suivoit, que je devrai leur assigner des forces actives pour s'assimiler conformement aux Phenomenes selon les occasions, d'ou les composés s'élevent par une coactivité entre eux, et pour se separer pareillement toujours selon des circonstances en dehors déterminées, et par des loix immuables, ce qui constitue la decomposition, vulgairement dite *corruption*. Cette ouverture m'a conduit au premier degré de l'echelle des êtres simples essentiellement distingués les uns des autres par leurs attributs, et par l'espece d'activité propre à chacun, dont le premier échelon sont des agens simples constitutifs de la matiere, insensitifs cependant, et privés de toute espece de connoissance; le second échelon en montant à un dégré superieur d'activité sont les ames des bêtes, et ainsi du reste comprenant l'intelligence, dont les dégrés varient les uns au dessus des autres par des nuances inconnües à nous autres mortels, aussi bien que les bornes du total.—Cela posé, et le tout se réglant par des loix immuables, ce que prouve dans une vüe generale la face constante de la nature pendant tant de generations passées, je me suis apperçu d'abord, que quoiqu'il m'etoit impossible d'expliquer en detail le comment de chaque operation, c'étoit le seul moyen de substituer quelque chose de solide au système des germes preexistants méchamment ébranlé par les faux Philosophes, en leur accordant tout ce qu'ils prétendoient avancer contre cette hypothese, qui paroissoit un peu surannée. On étoit alors en état de leur répondre, que meme en la réjettant ils ne gagnoient rein du coté de l'impiété, qu'ils proposoient secretement d'établir sur ses ruines, et que soit que le tout a été fait du commencement, ou que chaque corps organisé se faisoit comme les autres corps, à mesure, les effets toujours constants demontroient l'uniformité des causes, la stabilité des loix établies par la divinité, et l'absurdité de la generation équivoque. De meme le grand Newton en developpant les loix du Monde Planetaire, et en les substituant aux idées pueriles de nos pieux ancêtres, qui le faisoient mouvoir par le ministere des Anges, loin d'affoiblir le pouvoir legislatif du Createur n'a fait autre chose, que de la confirmer d'une maniere inebranlable en le rendant meme plus sensible, et plus analogue à nos idées de sa puissance supreme. De meme encore le celebre Lock en exterminant le systême des idées innées, quoiqu'il a paru sommeiller à la fin, quand il s'est précipité tête baissée dans le materialisme, n'a fait en réalité aucun tort à la morale, parce que soit que certaines idées fussent innées, ou qu'elles soient formées à mesure, les premiers principes de la Morale sont immuables, et leur universalité, qu'on observe chez toutes les nations policées, identique dans toutes les têtes bien organisées demontre, qu'ils derivent d'une relation necessaire entre la constitution de l'univers tant morale que Physique, et les êtres pensants, qui constituent la société. Du reste je ne crois pas, qu'il soit necessaire à un esprit comme le votre de vous faire remarquer, que mon systême de generation differe *toto cælo* de celui de M[r.] de Buffon, aussi bien que ma Theorie de la terre, qui ne ressemble en rien à la sienne;[4] cette Theorie, que j'ai établie d'après la nature combinée avec l'histoire sacrée de la Creation pour obvier aux mauvaises consequences, que les Impies tirent tous les jours de la sienne contre la chronologie de Moyse me paroit avoir plû à nos meilleurs Physiciens de ce jour, et lui-meme se trouve actuellement reduit à revenir sur ses pas depuis les nouvelles decouvertes faites récemment en Auvergne, en Allemagne, en Ecosse, en Italie, et presque par tout ailleurs.[5] Non seulement il adopte dans ses ouvrages

4. Needham is referring to Buffon's latest work on the theory of the Earth. On 10 April 1779, four different issues of *Les Epoques de la nature* were published at the same time. One of them, entitled 'Histoire naturelle des époques de la nature', was contained in the *Supplément* (5:1-254) to Buffon's *Histoire naturelle* (1749-1789). For an editorial history and an illuminating historical analysis of this work, see Roger's critical edition, Buffon (1962:ix-clii).

5. Needham is referring to the discovery of numerous extinct volcanoes and volcanic formations that had been made in Europe since the publication of Buffon's initial theory in 1749. The existence of such formations lent support to Needham's notion of mountain-building via an internal expansive force rather than by water currents, as on Buffon's view. Needham probably had in mind the recent paper by Nicolas Desmarest (1725-1815) entitled 'Mémoire sur l'origine & la nature du basalte à grandes colonnes polygones, déterminées par l'histoire naturelle de cette pierre, observée en Auvergne', published in 1774 in the *Histoire de l'Académie royale des sciences. Année M.DCCLXXI. Avec les Mémoires*, pp.705-75. In this mémoire, Desmarest reported his own observations on the extinct volcanoes of Auvergne, which had first been discovered by Jean-Etienne Guettard (1715-1786) in 1751 (see Guettard 1756). Desmarest also reviewed reports by other naturalists of volcanic formations in Germany, Ireland, Scotland, and Italy (which he had also visited). For further contemporary discussions of volcanoes in Scotland, see Da Costa (1761) and Pennant (1771), where Joseph Banks's observations on Scottish volcanoes are reported; for those in Germany, see Raspe (1776); and for those in Italy, see Hamilton (1776). For secondary literature on the origins of volcanic geology, see Geike (1905:127-75), de Beer (1962), K. Taylor (1969), Porter (1977:123-24, 162-63), and Ellenberger (1978).

posterieurs mes idées sur la force expansive developpant la terre par degrés, et sur l'activité du feu comme agent universel depuis le commencement du monde,[6] mais il s'accorde avec moi sur l'explication, que j'ai donnée de six jours de la generation du ciel, et de la terrre pris pour six periodes d'un tems inconnu, ou *six états de notre globe*, comme St Gregoire de Nysse[7] s'exprime, conformement aux plusieurs autres textes de la Bible, ou le mot *dies* au singulier porte ce meme sens; d'ou il suit que la chronologie de Moyse n'est pas la chronologie de notre planette, mais celle du genre humain, et qu'on a beau vouloir l'ebranler en donnant une antiquité quelconque à la terre.

Maintenant, mon cher ami, vous voyez complettement mon but, et la parfaite unité de mon plan dans toutes mes entreprises. Il se peut qu'en faveur de mes bonnes intentions le bonheur d'avoir atteint la vérité, comme J'incline à le croire, a été la recompense de mes penibles travaux toujours dirigés à reconcilier les verités revelées avec les vérités naturelles; mais sans m'attacher avec fanatisme à mes idées ce qui me console est que mes systêmes, dans la supposition que les votres ne puissent pas se tenir contre les ennemis de la morale, sont le *ne plus ultra* de tous leurs raisonnemens, et un second retranchement d'autant plus inexpugnable, qu'ils on beau vouloir en portant leurs recherches aussi loin que l'esprit humain peut monter, se passer de la divinité, on la rencontre par tout, et la nature sans elle se reduira toujours au zero: *si ascendero in cælum, tu illic es, si descendero in infernum ades.*[8] Bien loin par consequent, comme M^r L'abbe Lambinet de me mander d'après vos craintes à mon égard, d'avoir rénoncé à votre amitie, parce que nos sentimens étoient differens dans quelques points de Physique je ne vous ai jamais perdu de vüe, et vous m'avez toujours été cher, parce que je ne pouvois pas ignorer, que nous tendions de meme, quoique par des routes differentes dans le cours de nos récherches Philosophiques, au seul bien solide, l'affermissement de la morale Evangelique. Nous differons de meme dans notre croyance en matiere de Foi divine, qui fait une partie selon moi essentielle de la morale prise dans toute son étendüe, en tant que la soumission de la part de notre entendement à l'autorité divine par la Foi est autant un sacrifice necessaire, et un devoir indispensable envers dieu, que la soumission du cœur par la pratique de la vertu aux preceptes de la charité. Cette difference neanmoins ne diminüe en rien cette bienveillance que je vous dois à tous égards. On peut errer dans cette partie de nos devoirs innocemment, si on se trompe après avoir fait tant par nos prieres, que par nos récherches toutes les demarches

6. Buffon never cited Needham in *Les Epoques de la nature*. However there is no doubt that in the late 1760s they discussed problems relating to the theory of the Earth (see letter 29, n.5). This does not necessarily imply that Buffon's ideas were derived from Needham, as Needham suggests in his letter (see section 7 of the Introduction).

7. In his *Apologia in Hexaemeron*, Gregory of Nyssa (1863, 1:61-124) expressed the view that the creation of the world was simultaneous and that it took place according to an order (τάξις) that had been completely foreseen by God in his prescience, because in God coexisted thought (το νοηθὲν) and act (ἐνέργεια) (see Gregory of Nyssa 1863, 1:69A). A critical edition of the *Apologia in Hexaemeron* has not yet been published in the series of Gregory's *Opera* begun by Werner Jaeger. For a study of Gregory of Nyssa's interpretation of the book of Genesis, see Alexandre (1976); and for a review of contemporary interpretations of Gregory's theory of biblical exegesis, see Gargano (1981:13-44).

8. Psalmi 138, 8.

necessaires pour decouvrir la vérité, et si on est devant dieu toujours dans la disposition de l'embrasser, aussitot qu'elle se découvrira, en depit de toute consideration humaine quelconque. Dans le cas d'une ignorance invincible, qui est toujours rélative aux moyens, et aux facultés personeles, *chacun sera jugé,* comme St Paul dit, *selon la loi, qu'il connoit, et non pas selon la loi, qu'il ne connoit pas.*[9] C'est la doctrine de tous nos Theologiens Catholiques les plus célebres, qui n'est nullement contraire à cet autre principe general, *hors de la vraie église point de salut,* parce qu'une régle generale souffre mille exceptions, et c'est ainsi que la justice, et la paix de la charité s'embrassent selon l'expression du psalmiste; *justitia et pax osculatae sunt.*[10]—Les plus grands talens meme n'excluent pas necessairement cette espece d'ignorance invincible, parce que, malgré que l'affaire de la religion soit malheureusement pour la plupart des hommes faineans par nature plûtot une affaire du gout, que du raisonnement, en quoi ils sont condannables, on peut se tromper innocemment meme en se servant de toute la force de sa raison; et dieu connoit seul nos defauts, il est seul en état d'apprecier nos pechés; quant aux hommes; *delicta quis intelligit?*[11]—M[r.] L'abbé Lambinet me mande en meme tems, que vous desirés d'avoir mes deux memoires, dont j'ai detaché heureusement quelques exemplaires du second volume de nos ouvrages Academiques, qui va paroitre incessamment avec le troisieme, sur *la Fourmi,*[12] et sur *les mouches à miel.*[13] Vous y verrez quelques observations nouvelles, mais je ne vous en dirai rien en détail pour vous prevenir en leur faveur; ils parleront pour eux mêmes, et s'ils ne sont pas en état de se soutenir par leurs propres forces, dont une partie est dirigée contre les Impies, ou plûtot contre ceux, qui en sont la dupe, ils ne meriteront aucune Apologie de ma part. Peutetre ai j'y parlé quelquefois avec trop d'emphase, trop de vivacité conformement à la nature de mon esprit, qui s'irrite naturellement par l'amour que je porte au genre humaine contre la mauvaise Philosophie, sur tout quand elle attaque la Providence; c'est mon grand defaut, et si le monde ne veut pas me le pardonner, au moins mes amis me le pardonneront en faveur de mes bonnes intentions. Mandés moi, si vous avez quelque correspondant à Paris, à qui je pourrai les adresser d'ici, et qui est en état de vous les faire parvenir sans delai à Geneve. J'en ferai toute suite à la récette de votre reponse un paquet avec une autre petite piece de ma façon, dont il ne me reste que peu d'exemplaires; et j'y ajouterai deux autres de dits memoires pour Messieurs de Saussure, et Trembley, à qui je vous prie de les presenter de ma part avec mes très sinceres complimens. Excusés les taches, les fautes, et les ratures, que j'étois dans la necessité de faire dans cette lettre, dont la longueur peutetre vous ennuyera, je n'ai pas ni votre

---

9. Epistola ad Romanos ii.12-14.

10. Psalmi 84, 11.

11. Psalmi 18, 13.

12. John Turberville Needham, 'Observations sur l'histoire-naturelle de la fourmi, à l'occasion desquelles on releve quelques méprises de certains auteurs célebres', *Mémoires de l'Académie impériale et royale des sciences et belles-lettres de Bruxelles,* 2 (1780) 295-312. This mémoire was read on 18 December 1776.

13. John Turberville Needham, 'Nouvelles recherches sur la nature et l'économie des mouches à miel, suivies de quelques instructions pratiques, propres à perfectionner cette partie de culture rurale', *Mémoires de l'Académie impériale et royale des sciences et belles-lettres de Bruxelles,* 2 (1780) 323-87. This mémoire was read on 9 December 1777. It is discussed in section 10 of the Introduction.

parfaite connoissance de la langue Françoise, ni votre talent à dicter sans faute, pas meme une lettre, encore moins un ouvrage entier. Il n'y a que vous, mon cher Monsieur, dans le monde entier peutetre, qui possede cette heureuse faculté. Il est tems donc, et plus que tems de la finir, ce que je ne pourrai pas faire d'une maniere plus conforme à mon cœur, qu'en vous rénouvellant les sentimens de respect, et d'attachement, avec lesquels

j'ai l'honneur d'etre, mon cher Monsieur,

votre ami tres sincere, et très obeissant serviteur
Needham.

*a*de Septembre*a*
Bruxelles, Le 28. Oct: 1779
place de grands Sablons

P.S. Si vous avez quelque chose de nouveau, outre la nouvelle edition complette de vos ouvrages,[14] et celle de ceux de M*r.* de Saussure, qui s'impriment actuellement,[15] et aux quelles je désire de souscrire tant pour mon instruction, que par forme de temoignage de mon estime, je vous prie de me l'adresser par la premiere bonne occasion.

MANUSCRIPT
BPUG, MS Bonnet 35:100*r*-103*r*.

EDITIONS
'[J]e vous avouerai volontiers' and 'je suis las […] bataille' published in Castellani (1973:101).

TEXT NOTES
a. 'de Septembre' is written in another hand above the date. That Needham did not write this letter on 28 October is confirmed by the fact that Bonnet discussed its contents in a letter to Spallanzani written on 23 October 1773 (see Castellani 1971:387-88).

49

Bonnet to Needham – Genthod, 8 November 1779

À Genthod prés de Genève le 8.*c* Novembre 1779.

Jamais, Monsieur mon cher et bon Ami, je n'ai douté le moins du monde de la droiture de vos intentions ni de la sincérité de votre attachement aux principes religieux que je vous connois. Vous sçavés que je vous ai toujours rendu justice à cet égard et en public et en particulier. J'avois très bien remarqué que votre *Epinégésisme* ne ressembloit point du tout à celui de nos Matérialistes modernes, et que vous subordonniés votre *force végétatrice* à la CAUSE PREMIERE. J'avois très bien vu encore, que vous supposiés partout des Loix constances, émanées du grand ETRE, qui régissoient le Système organique et déterminoient les réproductions de tout genre.

14. Charles Bonnet, *Œuvres d'histoire naturelle et de philosophie* (Neuchâtel 1779-1783). Two editions of Bonnet's collected works were published simultaneously, one in 8 vols. in 4° and the other in 18 vols. in 8°.
15. The first volume of Saussure's masterpiece, *Voyages dans les Alpes* (Neuchâtel, Genève 1779-1796) appeared in 1779. Needham owned a copy of this volume (*Catalogue* 1782, pt.1:16).

Vous me confirmés tout cela dans votre bonne Lettre, et vous me dites ce que vous nommés *votre secret*, et qui ne pouvoit en être un pour moi. Mais j'apprends avec plaisir, que vous jugés mon hypothèse des *germes* conforme a la bonne Philosophie. Il vous paroit seulement que la votre prête moins aux difficultés des Incrédules. Cela doit bien être, puis qu'ils ne sçauroient l'attaquer sans renoncer aux formations méchaniques qui leur plaisent tant. Mais, si vous n'êtes pas exposé aux assauts de ces nouveaux Philosophes, vous n'êtes guères à l'abri des objections de Philosophes que vous estimés et qui le méritent.

Au fond; il ne s'agit pas de sçavoir quelle est l'hypothèse qui nous met le plus à l'aise ou la chaussure qui convient le mieux à notre pied. Il s'agit uniquement de sçavoir quelle est l'hypothese que la Nature paroit avouer.

Si vous avés reçu les *Opuscules de Physique animale et végétale*[1] que notre célèbre Ami l'Abbé Spallanzani vous envoya en 1776, vous y aurés vu une multitude d'expériences bien faites qui contredisent de la maniére la plus directe vos propres expériences et l'hypothèse que vous en avés déduite. Le sage Auteur vous a suivi pas à pas, et partout il a interrogé la Nature comme vous le desiriés et comme elle demandoit à l'être.

J'ai remanié pour la cinquième fois cette grande et belle matière dans les amples Notes que j'ai ajoutées dans cette nouvelle Edition de mes *Considérations sur les Corps organisés* qui composent le IIIme Vol: de mes Oeuvres[2] de l'Edit: in 4.to et le Vme et VIme de l'Edit: in 8.vo. J'écrirai incessamment à Hardouin, Libraire de Paris, de vous envoyer *franco* le plutot possible ces premiers Vol: de la Collection générale^a de mes Ecrits. ^bElle s'imprime par souscription à Neuchatel en Suisse chés Fauche Libraire du Roi de Prusse, et elle m'engage^b dans un travail bien plus pénible que vous ne l'imaginés; car combien de choses à corriger ou à perfectionnner dans mes petits^a Ecrits! Que de découvertes qu'on a faites depuis leur publication, et dont il falloit bien que je donnasse le précis? Vous verrés dans les *Corps organisés* l'emploi que j'ai tâché d'en faire et la singulière convergence des nouveaux faits vers les principes que je ^cm'étois faits^c dans un temps où nous les ignorions encore. Vous y verrés aussi l'éloge de votre procedé à l'occasion des fameuses Anguilles du *Bled rachitique*.[3]

Vous jugerés de ce que je fais pour le perfectionnement de mes Oeuvres quand je vous dirai; que ces premiers Vol: dont je viens de vous parler, et qui ont paru cette année, contiennent plus de six cent pages in 4to d'additions. J'en suis au IVme de l'in 4to qui contiendra la *Contemplation de la Nature*. Il y en aura huit, et

---

1. Spallanzani's *Opuscoli di fisica animale, e vegetabile* (see letter 36, n.4) was translated into French by Jean Senebier (1742-1809) with the title *Opuscules de physique animale et végétale* (Genève 1777).

2. The most important notes regarding Spallanzani are the following: B.O., 3:90-99 n.1, 120-21 n.1, 152 n.1, 225-27 n.1, 411-27 n.1, 440-44 n.1, 546-49 n.2/5:232-45 n.1, 279-81 n.1, 333 n.1 and 6:16-18 n.1, 317-39 n.1, 360-65 n.2, 545-50.

3. B.O., 3:346 n.2/6:217 n.2. Bonnet praised Needham's public admission of the erroneous nature of his former views on the origins of eels in blighted wheat, which Needham had argued were formed by vegetation but which Roffredi had shown were larvae that came from eggs (see letter 6, n.4, and letter 14, n.8). Needham's retraction read in part: 'Je n'ai d'autre apologie à faire pour mes erreurs, que de dire qu'alors, (il y a plus de trente ans de ma découverte) il étoit très-aisé & très-naturel de se tromper sur la nature & l'origine d'un être si singulier, dont la vie renouvellée à plaisir après un très-long & très-parfait desséchement, étoit un phénomene qui n'entroit pas du tout dans l'idée que les philosophes de ce temps s'étoient faite de la vitalité animale' (Needham 1775a:226).

seize de l'in 8to. Ce travail si considérable ne peut aller bien vite: vous n'avés pas oublié que le triste état de mes yeux me force à éxécuter tout par Lecteur et par Secretaire.

D'autres occupations encore viennent souvent à la traverse. Avés vous vu dans les Journaux de Rozier de 1777 et 1779 mes expériences sur les admirables Réproductions du Limaçon[4] et de la Salamandre,[5] et les réfléxions philosophiques dont elles sont accompagnées? J'ai publié aussi en 1775 dans le même Journal trois Mémoires sur les Abeilles,[6] où je rends compte des nouvelles découvertes faites en Luzace et dans le Palatinat, que les Swammerdam, les Maraldi et les Réaumur[7] étoient bien éloignés de soupçonner. Je montre com-

4. 'Expériences sur la régénération de la tête du limaçon terrestre', *Observations sur la physique, sur l'histoire naturelle et sur les arts*, September 1777, 11:165-79; republished in B.O., 5, pt.1:246-66/11:1-34. A second mémoire on the same subject was first published in B.O., 5, pt.1:267-83/11:35-61.

5. 'Mémoire sur la reproduction des membres de la salamandre aquatique', *Observations sur la physique, sur l'histoire naturelle et sur les arts*, November 1777, 10:385-405, republished in B.O., 5, pt.1:284-313/11:62-109; 'Expériences sur la reproduction des membres de la salamandre aquatique. Second mémoire', *Observations sur la physique*, January 1779, 13:1-18, republished in B.O., 5, pt.1:314-39/11:110-50. Later Bonnet published a 'Troisième mémoire sur la reproduction des membres de la Salamandre aquatique' in B.O., 5, pt.1:340-58/11:151-79.

6. 'Premier mémoire sur les abeilles, où l'on rend compte d'une nouvelle découverte fort singulière, qui a été faite en Luzace sur ces mouches', *Observations sur la physique, sur l'histoire naturelle et sur les arts*, April 1775, 5:327-44, republished in B.O., 5,pt.1:68-93/10:107-48; 'Second mémoire, contenant la suite des decouvertes faites en Luzace sur les abeilles', *Observations sur la physique*, May 1775, 5:418-28, republished in B.O., 5, pt.1:94-108/10:149-73; 'Troisième mémoire sur les abeilles, où l'on expose les principaux résultats des nouvelles expériences qui ont été faites sur ces mouches dans le Palatinat', *Observations sur la physique*, July 1775, 6:23-32, republished in B.O., 5, pt.1:109-22/10:174-95. All three mémoires were first published in Schirach (1771:181-254) and translated into Italian in Schirach (1774:186-263).

7. The most authoritative biography of the Dutch physician and naturalist Jan Swammerdam (1637-1680) is Schierbeek (1967), which lists all of Swammerdam's works. Hermann Boerhaave's biography, however, which is prefixed to the first volume of Swammerdam (1737-1738), remains our main source for his life. For more bibliographical information, see Nissen (1969, 1:401-402) and Mary P. Winsor, *D.S.B.*, 13 (1976) 168-75. Among the literature published after this date, see Smit (1981) and Lindeboom (1981 and 1982). Bonnet is alluding to the 'Tractatus de apibus: sive descriptio accurata ortus, generationis, sexus, oeconomia, operum, atque utilitatis apum' edited by Hermann Boerhaave and translated into Latin by Gaub in Swammerdam's masterpiece, the *Biblia naturae* (Leydae 1737-1738, 1:367-550), which was published over fifty years after his death. The splendid tables (XVII-XXVI) regarding the anatomy of the bee are all in volume ii (see figs.18, 19). For a historical evaluation of Swammerdam's contribution to this particular subject, see Bodenheimer (1928-1929, 1:353-64), Cole (1944: 288-95), Théodoridès (1968:26), Müller-Graupa (1938:358-59), Schierbeek (1967:154-61), and Baldini (1980:166-67). See also section 10 of the Introduction.

For a biography of the Italian astronomer Giacomo Filippo Maraldi (1665-1729), who was a member of the Académie des sciences, see the éloge by [Fontenelle] (1731:116-20), *B.U.* (26:410-11), and Fabroni (1778-1805, 8:295-320), who lists all of his published works. Although he was a professional astronomer, Maraldi had a keen interest in bees, which he could observe in glass-hives in the gardens surrounding the Paris astronomical observatory directed by his uncle Gian Domenico Cassini (1625-1712). While he was making his observations, he was unable to consult either the *Apiarium* (1625) of Federico Cesi (1585-1630) and Francesco Stelluti (1577-1646) owing to its rarity, or the great work by Swammerdam, which was not published until 1737-1738, but which he knew of from Swammerdam's (1682:96-98) own description. On 16 November 1712, Maraldi read a paper at the Academy entitled 'Observations sur les abeilles', which was subsequently published in *Histoire de l'Academie royale des sciences. Année MDCCXII. Avec les Mémoires*, 1714:299-335. An abridged English translation of Maraldi's work was published in 1742; see Fraser (1951a:51). Maraldi made valuable observations on the organisation of the colony, the building of combs, the structure of cells, and the anatomy of bees. As far as the problem of fertilisation is concerned, he stated that he could not discover 'jusqu'à present de quelle maniere se fait cette fécondation, si c'est

ment ces faits si nouveaux et si opposés à tout ce que ces grands Observateurs avoient pensé, rentrent dans les principes que j'avois exposés sur la Génération. J'ai donné encore plusieurs autres Mémoires au même Journal, entr'autres sur le *Taenia*,[8] sur les Germes et leur accroissement avant la fécondation,[9] sur la fécondation des Plantes[10] où je célèbre votre découverte,[11] &c. Tous ces Mémoires seront rassemblés dans le Vme Vol: de mes Oeuvres.

Je remercie l'Abbé Lambinet de vous avoir parlé de ma part de vos Mémoires sur les Abeilles et sur les Fourmis, que je suis très impatient de lire. Vous m'obligerés beaucoup, mon cher Ami, de me les faire parvenir. Adressés-les *au Sr Hardouin, Libraire, rue des Prêtres, St Germain Lauxerrois*, à Paris qui les adressera à mes Editeurs à Neuchatel.

L'Ouvrage de Mr de Saussure sur ^dla Théorie de la Terre^d [12] commencera à paroître le mois prochain. Il sera de trois Volumes in 4to, qui s'impriment, comme mes Oeuvres, ^apar souscription^a chés Fauche à Neuchatel. Vous lirés avec avidité cet excellent Livre, que l'Auteur, qui me touche de fort près me lit en manuscript. Vous y trouverés une foule d'observations intéressantes sur les Montagnes, qui vous prouveront la sagacité et la bonne Logique de l'Observateur, si elles ne vous étoient pas déjà très connues.

Mon illustre Ami l'Auteur des Polypes[13] vient de publier trois nouveaux

---

dans le corps de la femelle, ou bien si c'est à la maniere des Poissons, après que la femelle les a posés' (p.332), but he did demonstrate that drones were males.

In the fifth volume of his *Mémoires pour servir à l'histoire des insectes*, published in 1740, Réaumur devoted nine mémoires (v to xiii) to the study of all aspects of a bee colony. For a historical evalution of Réaumur's researches in this field, see Bodenheimer (1928-1929, 1:439-44), Grassé (1956), Torlais (1958b), Théodoridès (1959:70-76 and 1968:27-31), and Baldini (1980:167-71). See also section 10 of the Introduction.

8. 'Nouvelles recherches sur la structure du taenia', *Observations sur la physique, sur l'histoire naturelle et sur les arts*, April 1777, 9:243-67; republished in B.O., 5, pt.1:178-212/10:282-337.

9. 'Maniere dont on peut concevoir la nutrition & l'accroissement des germes avant la fécondation dans l'hypothese de l'emboîtement', *Observations sur la physique, sur l'histoire naturelle et sur les arts*, March 1774, 3:174-80; republished as 'Mémoire sur les germes' in B.O., 5, pt.1:1-11/10:1-17.

10. 'Idées sur la fécondation des plantes', *Observations sur la physique, sur l'histoire naturelle et sur les arts*, October 1774, 4:261-83; republished in B.O., 5, pt.1:24-59/10:33-93.

11. '[L]e savant Needham [...] découvrit, que la poussiere des étamines étoit beaucoup plus composée qu'on ne l'avoit d'abord imaginé. Il prouva par des observations bien faites, que chaque grain de cette poussiere étoit lui-même une tres-petite boîte, qui renfermoit dans une espece de vapeur ou de liqueur prodigieusement subtile, un nombre innombrable de grains d'une petitesse extrême, qu'il regarde, à bon droit, comme les vrais agens de la fécondation. Mais il se trompa beaucoup sur la maniere de cette fécondation, comme je l'ai montré dans les *Considérations sur les corps organisés*' (Bonnet 1774b:261-62, and B.O., 5, pt.1:25/10:39). Bonnet is referring to Needham's theory of pollination, which was based on a series of microscopical observations Needham carried out on *farina faecundans* or pollen grains (Needham 1743:639-40 and 1745:60-84). By placing a drop of water on pollen grains of the common white lily, Needham was able to observe that 'a Train of Globules, involved in a filmy Substance' was ejaculated by these minute bodies (Needham 1745:74). Having observed this burst of minute globules in pollen grains of other species of flowers, Needham inferred that it was a universal mechanism and concluded that these globules fertilised the flower's ovaries. He also put forward a hypothesis about the mechanism of impregnation, suggesting that the globules must pass into the channels of the pistil leading to the ovary (Needham 1745:79-80). Needham's theory, though criticised by some authors, remained current up to the 1820s. For Needham's theory of pollination, see Sachs (1890:431-32) and A. G. Morton (1981:243-44).

12. See letter 48, n.15.

13. Abraham Trembley.

Volumes de son *Instruction d'un Père à ses Efans*,[14] qui contiennent des réfléxions sur la Religion Judaïque et sur la Religion Chrétienne propres à perfectionner également l'Esprit et le Coeur. L'admirable caractère moral de l'Auteur y est empreint à chaque page. L'Ouvrage a été imprimé à Genève ches Barthélemy Chirol. Je tacherai de vous le faire parvenir; mais dites-moi auparavant si vous avés les deux premiers Volumes qui parurent en 1775 et qui roulent sur la Nature?[15]

Votre Académie travaille-t-elle au gré de vos désirs? Et le Souverain accorde-t-il *ªaux talensª* les encouragemens dont ils ne peuvent guères se passer?

Ne me faites point d'excuses ni sur la longueur de vos Lettres ni sur votre François: vous êtes toujours assés clair pour qu'il ne me soit jamais difficile de saisir votre pensée.

M.ʳˢ Trembley et de Saussure, qui sont très sensibles à votre bon souvenir, me chargent de beaucoup de compliments pour vous. Ils recevront avec bien de la reconnoissance les Mémoires que vous leur promettés.

Je ne dois pas vous laisser ignorer que l'Abbé Spallanzani m'a fait cet Eté une bonne visite.[16] Vous imaginés bien tout le plaisir que j'ai eu à le recevoir dans ma retraite champêtre. Il a fait des découvertes qui vous étonneront beaucoup. Les principales roulent sur la *fécondation artificielle* et sur la *prééxistence du foetus à la fécondation.* J'en ai dit quelque chose dans mes nouvelles Notes sur les *Corps organisés.*[17] J'ai été charmé de connoître personnellement cet excellent Naturaliste qui fait tant d'honneur à l'Italie.

Ne doutés jamais, mon cher et célèbre Ami, des sentimens si vrais que vous a voués.

[ADDRESS] Bruxelles; M.ʳ l'Abbé Néédham, Directeur de l'Academie Impériale.

MANUSCRIPTS
BPUG, MS Bonnet 75:224*v*-225*r*; MS Bonnet 85:196*v*-198*v*.

EDITIONS
'Si vous avés [...] à l'être' published in Castellani (1973:102).

TEXT NOTES
a. B: *omitted b.* B: Cette entreprise typograhique m'a engagé *c.* B: avois adoptés *d.* B:les Alpes

14. Abraham Trembley, *Instructions d'un père à ses enfans, sur la religion naturelle et révelée* (Genève 1779).
15. Abraham Trembley, *Instructions d'un père à ses enfans, sur la nature et sur la religion* (Genève 1775). Needham owned this work (*Catalogue* 1782, pt.2:51). For comments on it, see Wernle (1923-1925, 2:147-50).
16. Spallanzani left Pavia for a journey to Switzerland on 12 July 1779 and returned to Scandiano at the end of September. He was a guest of Bonnet at Genthod for about ten days; see Di Pietro (1979:48-51). Bonnet described Spallanzani's visit as 'une époque dans ma vie littéraire, que je me rappellerai toujours avec interêt' (Castellani 1971:384).
17. The note on *fecondation artificielle* is in B.O., 3:440-44 n.2/6:360-65 n.2, where Bonnet refers to Spallanzani as 'le confident le plus secret de la Naturë'; and that on the *preexistence du foetus* is in B.O., 3:120 n.1/5:279 n.1. Spallanzani's first paper on artificial insemination appeared with the title 'Fecondazione artificiale' in the *Prodromo della nuova enciclipedia italiana*, pp.129-34 (Siena 1779), edited by Alessandro Zorzi. The second dissertation in volume ii of Spallanzani's *Dissertazioni di fisica animale, e vegetabile* (Modena 1780) was also devoted to the same subject. For Spallanzani's experiments on artificial insemination and the interest they aroused, see Poynter (1968), Sandler (1973), Castellani (1977, 1978, and 1979), Castellani's commentary in his editions of Spallanzani (1978a:649-55 and 1978b:44-120), and Di Pietro (1976:206-10).

50

Needham to Bonnet – Brussels, 25 November 1779

Bruxelles, Le 25. Novembre 1779.

Le systême de l'Epigenese, Monsieur et très cher ami, est si necessairement lié avec mes principes tant Physiques, que metaphysiques, qu'il n'est pas possible de le rejetter sans renoncer à toute la chaine de mes idées; ainsi loin d'avoir saisi le veritable sens de ma lettre, il vous a paru à tort, que je l'avois embrassé sans aucun égard à la vérité uniquement pour me mettre plus à mon aise vis à vis les ennemis de la Religion. Tout ce que j'ai voulu dire en consequence de ce que l'Abbé Lambinet m'avoit mandé de votre part étoit, que loin d'avoir rompu toute correspondence avec vous à cause de la difference de nos sentimens à cet égard j'etois assez disposé à traiter mon système, comme une chose totalement indifferente en elle meme, abstraction faite de ma vüe principale en faveur de la morale. Sans entrer par consequent dans la question, qui nous partage pour décider dogmatiquement quel de deux systêmes est plus conforme à la bonne Philosophie, il me suffisoit en vous régardant toujours, comme un de plus respectables de mes amis, que nous tendions tous deux, quoique par des routes differentes au meme but, et qu'en fait de morale, quel que puisse être leur merite Physique, l'un valoit autant que l'autre. Ainsi comme il falloit necessairement opter entre ces deux opinions, qui n'admettent aucun milieu; mon dessein étoit non pas de m'attirer de vains applaudissemens par des noveautés mal-fondées conformes au gout dépravé de nos sophistes modernes; non pas meme d'étayer la religion par des opinions fausses, ou peu probables; mais en énonçant librement mes sentimens réels sur le sujet en question de démontrer en meme tems en depit de mal-intentionnés, qu'ils étoient également conformes à la bonne morale, comme à la bonne Physique.—J'ai lû et relû tout ce que vous avez donné dans le journal de Rozier;[1] vous en serez convaincu, quand vous aurez parcouru mon memoire sur les abeilles;[2] j'ai consideré suffisamment toutes les experiences de notre ami Spalanzani dans ses opuscules de la Physique animale,[3] que j'ai trouvé ici parmi nos libraires; cependant loin de changer de sentiment à cet égard, j'ai cru pouvoir meme sans blesser le respect, et l'amitie, que je vous dois à tant de titres, vous accuser d'un peu trop de predilection en faveur de votre systeme, comme vous le verrez dans le dit memoire sur les abeilles.—J'ai dit que j'ai trouvé ici parmi nos libraires l'ouvrage de l'Abbé Spalanzani; car quant à l'exemplaire, dont vous parlez, comme adressé à moi de sa part, il n'est me jamais parvenu. Je vous prie de lui marquer cela à la premiere occasion, car ne l'ayant jamais remercié de ce present, qu'il m'avoit destiné, et que je n'ai pas réçu, je pourrai passer dans ses idées pour un ingrat. Ce n'est pas du tout mon caractere, et vous m'obligerés meme en lui temoignant toute ma réconnoissance pour son bon souvenir d'un ancien ami, qui l'estime, et qui

1. See letter 49, nn. 4, 5, 6, 8, 9, and 10.
2. See letter 48, n.13.
3. See letter 36, n.4, and letter 49, n.1.

connoit son merite.[4]—Il est inutile de dire davantage par raport à nos differentes façons de voir en Physique certains objets; cette lettre n'est gueres autre chose qu'une simple lettre d'avis pour vous annoncer le depart aujourdhui par la diligence, qui va à Paris, d'un paquet contenant quelques uns des mes derniers ouvrages addressés pour vous les faire tenir ensuite, à votre libraire le sieur Hardouin. Vous y verrez mes sentimens actuels, et si l'occasion se presente dans vos publications futures d'y inserer certaines parties de ce que je vous envoye, vous me ferez le plus grand plaisir en me justifiant contre la fausse idée, que le malheureux auteur du systême de la nature a donné de mes observations microscopiques.[5] Je vous ne ferai pas un denombrement en detail de ces pieces; chaque parcelle y contenüe porte son adresse; il y en a pour vous, et pour nos amis Messieurs Saussure, et Trembley, que je vous prie de saluer très cordialement de ma part. Je connois deja les deux premiers volumes de M[r.] Trembley sur la nature, qui font déjà partie de ma bibliotheque choisie, et je les ai lû avec un plaisir, qui me fait desirer de posseder au plûtot les trois volumes suivants.[6] Je me trouverai ainsi complettement satisfait, quand je possederai ensemble tout ce qui est sorti de la plume, compris vos ouvrages, et ceux de M[r.] de Saussure, d'un si celebre, et si digne triumvirat. Vous ne serez pas faché de sçavoir peutetre, que M[r.] du Luc[7] travaille aussi de son coté à Londres pour illustrer

4. This entire sections 'J'ai dit que [...] merite' is transcribed in Bonnet's letter to Spallanzani of 11 January 1780 (see Castellani 1971:392). Spallanzani certainly did send a copy of his *Opuscoli* to Needham in 1776 and wrote him a letter (*Epistolario*, 2:92), which Needham apparently did not receive.

5. In this packet of publications he was sending to Bonnet, Needham included his *Idée sommaire, ou vüe générale du systeme physique, & metaphysique de Monsieur Needham sur la génération des corps organisés* (Bruxelles 1776; 2nd ed., Bruxelles 1781). This work, which was devoted to demonstrating that Needham's system did not support materialism, consisted of a long note that Needham had included in [Blaise Monestier], *La Vraie philosophie* (Bruxelles 1774; Bruxelles 1775; pp.460-70) of which Needham was the editor. This note had also been published separately in the *Journal ecclésiastique* (March 1744, pp.234-50). In the *Idée sommaire*, Needham added to this note a revised version of a letter he had published in the *Journal encyclopédique* (15 January 1771, I, pt.2:292-97) in opposition to d'Holbach's *Système de la nature* (1770) and a 'Remarque sur la reponse de M. de Voltaire au système de la nature'. Needham was provoked into defending his views against materialism by d'Holbach's favourable reference to Needham's observations. In the second chapter of the *Système de la nature*, where d'Holbach argued that matter possesses inherent active forces, he included the following example: 'En humectant de la farine avec de l'eau & renfermant ce mélange, on trouve au bout de quelque tems à l'aide du microscope qu'il a produit des êtres organisés qui jouissent d'une vie dont on croyoit la farine & l'eau incapables. C'est ainsi que la matiere inanimée peut passer à la vie qui n'est elle-même qu'un assemblage de mouvemens' ([Holbach] 1770, 1:23). D'Holbach continued in a footnote: 'Voyez les *Observations microscopiques* de M. Néedham, qui confirment pleinement ce sentiment. Pour un homme qui réfléchit, la production d'un homme, indépendamment des voies ordinaires, seroit-elle donc plus merveilleuse que celle d'un insecte avec de la farine & de l'eau? La fermentation & la putréfaction produisent visiblement des animaux vivans. La génération que l'on a nommée *Equivoque*, ne l'est que pour ceux qui ne se sont pas permis d'observer attentivement la nature' (p.23, n.5). Needham's opinion of d'Holbach's materialist manifesto is summed up in the following comment: 'Le triste & sombre *systême de la nature* vient de sortir de l'abîme de l'impiété: le monde recule d'horreur aux blasphêmes y lancées contre son Créateur' (Needham 1781:21). For the editorial history of the first edition of d'Holbach's *Système de la nature*, see Vercruysee (1971:A6). For d'Holbach's materialism, see Naville (1967); and for Needham's relationship to d'Holbach and to materialism more generally, see Marx (1973a), Roe (1983 and 1985), and section 4 of the Introduction.

6. See letter 49, n.14 and n.15.

7. The Genevan meteorologist, geologist, and natural philosopher Jean-André de Luc (1727-

votre Patrie. M[r.] Le Prince de Gallitzin[8] vient de me mander cette nouvelle, en meme tems, qu'il m'envoye le resultat d'une experience faite avec éclat à Petersbourg tout recemment sur les maisons de bois incombustibles inventées en Angletterre par Milord Mahon, et M[r.] Hartley,[9] et dont j'ai ajouté aux autres

1817) was one of the most influential personalities among the burghers in the political crisis in Geneva of 1763-1768 (see Gür 1967). He left his home town in 1773, after the collapse of his family business. He settled in England and was made a fellow of the Royal Society on 10 June 1773. In 1774 he was appointed reader to queen Charlotte (1744-1818), consort of George III. On de Luc (in England often spelled Deluc), see Wolf (1858-1862, 4:193-210); William Jerome Harrison, *D.N.B.*, 14 (1888) 328-29; Robert P. Beckinsale, *D.S.B.*, 4 (1971) 27-29; and Tunbridge (1971). For his contacts with Rousseau, see François (1924); and for his studies on the hygrometer, see Archinard (1977:372-80). Bonnet was one of de Luc's sponsors for membership in the Royal Society (Tunbridge 1971:18), notwithstanding their political differences.

8. The Russian prince Dmitry Alekseevich Golitsuin (often spelled Galitzin or Gallitzin) was sent to Paris by Catherine II (1729-1796) in 1765, where he became friendly with Grimm and Diderot. In 1768 he was appointed ambassador to The Hague, where he remained until his resignation in 1782. Diderot was his guest there for three months in 1773, the same year that Helvétius's posthumous treatise *De l'homme* was published under Golitsuin's auspices by Marc-Michel Rey (see Tourneux 1899:62-68 and Best.D18431). He corresponded with Voltaire and Tronchin. During the French Revolution he settled in Germany. He was not merely a man of the salons, but also a keen mineralogist and an active member of the Academies of St Petersburg and Brussels. He died at Brunswick in 1803. For further information see *B.U.* (15:425-26), and Kuhfuss (1976:116-17). For Golitsuin's election in 1778 to the Brussels Academy, see Mailly (1883, 1:216-17).

9. For a biography of the radical politician and inventor Lord Charles Mahon, later third Earl Stanhope (1753-1816), see William Prideaux Courtney, *D.N.B.*, 54 (1898) 1-5; G. Stanhope and Gooch (1914); and Newman (1969:129-203). For his political career see Turberville (1958:92-95); and for his scientific work, see Beatty (1955). Stanhope was a prolific inventor: he developed a method of roofing houses; perfected a process of stereotyping; invented the iron press that bears his name (both were acquired by the Delegates of the Clarendon Press; see Kubler 1938 and Hart 1966); constructed two calculating machines; experimented on boats without sails, propelled by steam engines; and made electrical experiments, discovering the 'return stroke' (Heilbron 1979:462-64). Needham met the young Lord Mahon while the latter was studying at Geneva in the years 1764-1774 under Georges-Louis Le Sage (1724-1803). Later Needham translated Mahon's *Principles of electricity* (1779) into French (see C. Stanhope 1781). Needham is alluding to Lord Mahon's experiments for safeguarding buildings from fire, which were reported in 1778 in a paper communicted to the Royal Society, 'Description of a most effectual method of securing buildings against fire', *Philosophical transactions*, 68 (1778) 884-94. In Mahon's own words, 'The new and very simple method which I have discovered of securing every kind of building [...] against all danger of fire, may very properly be divided into three parts; namely, *underflooring*, *extra-lathing*, and *inter-securing*, which particular methods may be applied, in part or in whole, to different buildings, according to the various circumstances attending their construction, and according to the degree of accumulated fire, to which each of these buildings may be exposed, from the different uses to which they are meant to be appropriated' (C. Stanhope 1778:884).

The statesman and scientific inventor David Hartley the younger (1732-1813), son of the philosopher, matriculated at Oxford in 1747, obtained his B.A. in 1750, and was a Fellow of Merton College until his death. He represented Hull in Parliament in 1774-1780 and in 1782-1784. A friend and correspondent of Benjamin Franklin (1706-1790), he strongly opposed the war with America. In 1783 he was chosen to act as Plenipotentiary in Paris where, with Franklin, he drafted and signed the definitive treaty of peace between Great Britain and the United States. For a short biography, see R.R. Anderson, *D.N.B.*, 25 (1891) 68-69. In 1774 Hartley presented to the King a pamphlet entitled *An account of the method of securing buildings (and ships) against fire* (London 1774). The proposed method consisted in 'the Application of thin Iron plates under the Floors, and to the Ceilings. The Effect of these Fire Plates, depends partly, upon their preventing the immediate Access of the Fire itself, to the Timbers of the House, and partly, upon their stopping the free Supply and Current of Air, without which, no Fire can get to any great Height, or make any destructive Progress' (Hartley 1774:3). A successful experiment was carried out on 2 September 1776 on Wimbledon Common. The Lord Mayor of London, who attended the experiment, laid a foundation stone for the erection of a pillar commemorating Hartley's invention (see Hartley 1834:25-26).

pieces à votre adresse un extrait imprimé.[10] Voici comme S. E. s'exprime[11] sur le compte de M[r.] du Luc. 'Vous avez donné, il y a quelque tems, une nouvelle Theorie de la terre; mais gare l'animadversion de M[r.] du Luc, si elle n'est pas conforme à la sienne, qu'il va donner dans cinq ou six mois peutêtre après nous l'avoir annoncé depuis deux ans dejà, je crois.[12] Ce M[r.] du Luc a pris le ton actuellement à la mode parmi les gens de lettres, et que Voltaire leur a transmis. Il se peut cépendant, qu'il sera plus poli, plus moderé dans ses écrits; mais en parlant, il n'appelle pas autrement M[r.] de Buffon, que radoteur, et de la plus crasse ignorance dans la Physique. Je vous avoüe, que j'en été très scandalisé, d'autant plus qu'il est à present à l'egard de M[r.] de Buffon, ce qu'est Monsieur Pinto[13] à l'égard des Ameriquains;[14] dès qu'il en entend le nom, il devient comme un Energumene.' J'ai cru, que cette nouvelle pouvoit interesser mes amis, ses compatriotes à Geneve.—Du reste quant à ce que vous me demandés touchant notre Academie, il me semble qu'elle est assés bien montée pour le peu de tems, qu'elle existe, et qu'elle meritera de plus en plus la haute Protection, que le Souverain lui accorde. Comptés sur les sentimens d'Amitie, d'estime, et de respect, avec lesquels je serai toujours à vous.

T. Needham.

P.S. Avec des pieces de ma façon J'ai crû devoir joindre quatre autres memoires de mon ami et confrere M[r.] L'abbé Mann,[15] qui font également partie

10. In November 1777 the Austrian Minister Plenipotentiary Georg Adam Starhemberg sent to England the abbé Mann (see n.15 below) to examine the inventions of Hartley and Lord Mahon. Mann described them in the *Mémoire sur les diverses méthodes inventées jusqu'à present pour garantir les édifices d'incendie* (Bruxelles 1778), which was subsequently translated into German, Spanish (Reiffenberg 1850:88), and Italian. It is probable that Needham sent this mémoire to Bonnet.

11. The original of Golitsuin's letter to Needham could not be traced.

12. Jean-André de Luc, *Lettres physiques et morales sur l'histoire de la terre et de l'homme, adressées à la reine de la Grande Bretagne* (Paris, La Haye 1779-1780). De Luc (1779-1780, 5, pt.2:517-611) challenged Buffon's *Les Epoques de la nature*, claiming that there was no evidence suggesting that the Earth was becoming colder, as it should have been according to Buffon's theory of the Earth. De Luc did not discuss Needham's cosmogony or theory of the Earth. On de Luc's geological ideas, see François (1924:212-16), Gillispie (1969:56-66), Rudwick (1972:110-12), and Porter (1977:198-202).

13. Isaac de Pinto (1715-1787), a Jew of Portuguese origin, was born in Amsterdam and had some influence both on economic and diplomatic affairs and on the literary life of his day. During the War of the Austrian Succession, when Dutch territory was invaded by the French, Pinto donated much of his personal fortune to the Public Treasury and gained a strong influence among the advisers of William IV (1711-1751), the first general Stadholder of the Dutch Republic. After the death of William IV, Pinto spent much time in Paris and London. In 1763 he provided John Russell, fourth Duke of Bedford (1710-1771), who was then conducting negotiations that would lead to the treaty of Paris, with confidential information on the affairs of the French East India Company. This must have been valuable because it changed the Duke's final tactics and earned Pinto a pension from the East India House of £500 per annum (see Bedford 1842-1846, 3:184, 257-58; and Sutherland 1947:189-90). In 1771 Pinto published his most important economic treatise, which also included some of his previously published works (Pinto 1771). Some evidence suggests that when in 1780 the Anglo-Dutch connection broke down and the United Provinces joined France, Pinto passed military information regarding Dutch and French vessels to the British Crown (see Fortescue 1927-1928, 6:140). Some information about the life of this neglected personality, with a list of his major publications, is provided by *B.U.* (33:383-85), and J. Zwarts, *N.N.B.W.*, 6 (1924) 1124-28. On Pinto and Diderot, see Freer (1964 and 1966).

14. During the American Revolution, Pinto sided with England and wrote three pamphlets against the rebels; see Pinto (1776a, 1776b, and 1776c).

15. The English scientist, historian, and antiquary Theodore Augustus Mann (1735-1809), Needham's biographer, collaborator, and housemate during his last years, was the keystone of the

de nos memoires Academiques composant les 2. et 3. vol actuellement sous presse.[16] Je me flatte, qu'ils vous paroitront assés interessants pour occuper une partie de votre loisir.

[ADDRESS] A Monsieur / Monsieur Charles Bonnet / membre de plusieurs Academies / à Genthod / près de Geneve.

MANUSCRIPT
BPUG, MS Bonnet 35:104*r*-105*v*.

EDITIONS
'[J]'ai consideré […] nos libraires' and 'J'ai dit […] son merite' published in Castellani (1973:101).

Brussels Academy. For a biography of the abbé Mann, which includes the most complete list of his published works, see Reiffenberg (1850); see also Thomas Seccombe, *D.N.B.*, 36 (1893) 44-46, and Alphonse-François Renard, *B.N.*, 13 (1895-1898) 343-55. For Mann's ideas on economics and his involvement in economic reforms, see Harsin (1935); and for his position and activities at the Brussels Academy, see Mailly (1883) and Marx (1977:56, 61). To Joseph Banks, Mann wrote after Needham's death: 'My old and dear friend's health had declined for a year and half before his death, which happened December the 30th, 1781. The decline of his memory and presence of mind was still more visible than that of his health. He died of dropsy in his breast, in the 69th year of his age, being born in London, Sept 10, 1713. His uprightness and goodness of heart were the sources of the greatest blemishes he had, I mean those of being too credulous, and too easily the dupe of the designing part of mankind. I feel the separation most sensibly' (letter of 26 March 1782, BL, Add.8095; published in Ellis 1843:418). Mann's éloge of Needham, which was published in the *Mémoires de l'Académie impériale et royale des sciences et belles-lettres de Bruxelles*, 4 (1783) xxxiii-xli, contained the following characterisation of Needham as a scientist: 'M. Needham a joui pendant plus de 30 ans d'une réputation distinguée dans le monde savant: il a été compté avec raison entre les premiers Physiciens de ce siecle. Sa sagacité étoit grand; ses vues étoient vastes; il les portoit sur l'universalité des êtres: ses idées en général étoient très-justes, quoique peut-être un peu systématiques. Habile observateur, habile à confirmer ses observations par des expériences, il ne s'arrêtoit jamais aux faits; il généralisoit, & il les réduisoit à son système général. Il voyoit les choses en Grand, & en Physicien éclairé & profond, & il les rapportoit toujours à une Intelligence suprême.

'Sa plume n'étoit ni féconde ni méthodique: ses écrits sont plutôt de grands traits jettés à la hâte, que des traités achevés sur les différens sujets qu'il a maniés. Il pensa avec force, & en écrivant, il consulta plus la chose que l'expression: ses vues philosophiques se trouvent exposées comme elles se présentoient à son esprit, sans méthode & sans ordre. En parlant & en écrivant, il se montroit presque toujours inférieur à sa science' (p.xxxvii).

16. 'Mémoire sur le feu élémentaire, considéré en général dans toute la nature, avec des conjectures sur ses différentes modifications, ses lois d'action, sa fin et ses usages universels', *Mémoires de l'Académie impériale et royale des sciences et belles-lettres de Bruxelles*, 2 (1780) 3-46; 'Mémoire sur l'histoire naturelle de la mer du Nord et sur la pêche qui s'y fait' *Ibid.*, 2 (1780) 159-220; 'Mémoire dans lequel on examine les effets et les phénomènes produits en versant différentes sortes d'huiles sur les eaux, tant tranquilles qu'en mouvement', *Ibid.*, 2 (1780) 258-94; 'Dissertation dans laquelle on tâche de déterminer précisément le port où Jules-César s'est embarqué pour passer en Grande-Bretagne et celui où il y aborda', *Ibid.*, 3 (1780) 231-55.

51

Bonnet to Needham – Genthod, [8]ᵃ March 1780

À Genthod près de Genève le Mars 1780.

J'ai reçu, Monsieur mon cher et célèbre Ami, les divers Mémoires[1] que vous m'avés fait le plaisir de m'envoyer, et dont je vous fais mes plus justes remercimens.

Vous pensés bien que je me suis d'abord adressé aux vôtres, comme à ceux qui piquoient le plus ma curiosité. Je me suis surtout attaché à celui sur les Abeilles; et je vais vous en dire mon jugement en peu de mots; car je suis trop enrhumé pour dicter une longue Lettre.

Vous rejettés l'explication que j'avois donnée de l'expérience de Schirach;[2] je suis bien éloigné de vous en sçavoir mauvais gré: mais j'avois dit et repèté que je ne raisonnois que sur la supposition de la vérité du fait; et j'aurois souhaité que vous l'eussiés rappellé à votre Lecteur.

Vous préférés d'admettre que la Reine pond des oeufs de femelles dans des cellules communes; et vous dites que c'est ce qui avoit trompé l'Observateur de Lusace.[3] Mais pourquoi ne nous donnés-vous aucune preuve directe de votre assertion? Pourquoi vous contentés-vous d'affirmer; *que dans toute portion de couvain il doit se trouver un ou plusieurs oeufs royaux?*[4]

Pourquoi encore n'avés-vous fait aucune attention à ce que m'écrivoit si expressém.ᵗ l'Observateur de Lusace; que toutes les fois qu'il avoit tenté l'expérience avec les seuls oeufs, elle n'avoit jamais réussi; mais qu'elle avoit constamment réussi et en toute saison lors qu'il l'avoit faite avec des Vers de trois à quatre jours.[5] Il étoit même si sûr de son fait, qu'il avoit proposé à son Beaufrère Wilhelmi,[6] qui refusoit opiniatrément de croire, de prendre au hazard un Ver de trois jours, et qu'il s'assureroit par ses propres yeux de sa conversion en Ver royal.[7]

Voilà, mon bon Ami, ce que vous n'aviés pas present à l'esprit lors que vous critiquiés l'Observateur Allemand et que vous me critiquiés à mon tour. Vousᵇ

---

1. See letter 48, n.12 and n.13; and letter 50, n.5, n.10, and n.16.
2. For short biographies of Adam Gottlob Schirach (1724-1773), pastor in Kleinbautzen near Bautzen in Upper Lusatia, author of the well-known *Melitto-theologia* (Dresden 1767), and perpetual Secretary of the newly founded Society of Apiculture, which became a model for similar societies, see *B.U.* (38:329-30) and *A.D.B.* (31:307). For a list of his publications, see Meusel (1802-1816, 12:174-78); for those on bees, see De Keller (1881:159-62); and for an account of his major achievements, see Baldini (1980:196), section 10 of the Introduction, and letter 47, n.29.
3. Schirach.
4. Needham (1780c:356-57).
5. Schirach (1771:189-98). Schirach's letter was published by Bonnet in his first 'Mémoire sur les abeilles'; see Bonnet (1775a:331-36) and B.O., 5, pt.1:74-82/10:118-29.
6. Johann Gottlob Wilhelmi (1721-1796) was born in Bautzen and studied in Leipzig and in Halle. From 1760 he was Pastor in Diehsa. At the death of Schirach in 1773, he was elected Secretary of the Society of Apiculture. For a list of his publications, see Meusel (1802-1816, 15:136-37); and for those on bees, see De Keller (1881:197).
7. Schirach (1771:114-15).

critiqués aussi l'Apoticaire de Cambridge[8] qui affirme avoir vérifié le fait; et vous n'opposés à son expérience et aux nombreuses expériences de l'Observateur de Lusace qu'une simple négative.

Si donc vous avés fait vous même de nombreuses expériences sur ce sujet intéressant, comment est il arrivé que vous ne les ayés point détaillées dans votre Mémoire? Comment n'avés-vous point indiqué votre marche, vos procedés, les précautions que vous avés prisés pour n'être point trompé, les divers faits qui se sont présentés sur votre route &c &c? Voilà ce que j'attendois de votre habileté dans l'art d'observer et ce que je n'ai point trouvé dans votre Mémoire. Ce n'est pas ainsi que vous avés traité d'autres sujets d'Histoire naturelle qui ont rendu votre nom célèbre. Je vous condamne donc pour réparation de ce, à composer un autre Mémoire sur les Abeilles où vous nous racontiés en détail tout ce que vous avés fait et tout ce que vous avés-vu.

Vous assurés, pag: 358 qu'il est parfois *des Reines de la taille des Abeilles communes*.[9] Comment, je vous prie, vous en êtes vous assuré? Quelles observations bien faites vous ont donné la preuve de ce fait si nouveau? Votre Ecrit est aussi muet sur ce point que sur le précédent.

Vous parlés *de la distribution des oeufs faite par les ouvrières*:[10] avés-vous vu cela, et comment êtes-vous parvenu à le voir?

Vous dites encore *que la Reine dépose très souvent depuis deux jusqu'à soixante oeufs dans une alvéole ordinaire*.[11] Toujours de simples assertions et point de ces détails qui constatent les faits.

J'ai suspecté, comme vous, l'expérience de l'Observateur de Lauter[12] sur la

8. Bonnet is referring to John Debraw, Apothecary to Addenbrook's Hospital in Cambridge, who published a paper entitled 'Discoveries on the sex of bees, explaining the manner in which their species is propagated; with an account of the utility that may be derived from those discoveries by the actual application of them to practice', in the *Philosophical transactions*, 67 (1777) 15-32. The paper attracted considerable attention, and the following year its results were confirmed by Polhill (1778:107-10). It was reprinted as an appendix to the second volume of Spallanzani (1784, 2:357-72) and translated into Italian in 1779; see De Keller (1881:46) and Harding (1979:93). The general point made by Debraw was that after the queen had laid the eggs in the hive, these were fertilised by the drones (see n.17 below). Debraw (1777:20) also confirmed Schirach's discovery: 'The trials made by Mr. SCHIRACH seem to evince the truth of his conlusions in the most satisfactory manner, singular as they appear to be at first sight; and indeed in my own judgement, from the constant happy result of my numerous experiments, which I began near two years before Mr. SCHIRACH's publication, and repeated every season since. I am enabled to pronounce on their reality.' Although Needham (1780c:347-52) accepted as correct Debraw's explanation of fertilisation, he did not accept his confirmation of Schirach's experiments: 'Il [Debraw] adopte néanmoins, on ne sait pas trop pourquoi, les erreurs de M. Schirach, et il prétend même avoir des preuves certaines du changement d'une abeille neutre en reine-mere, d'après des expériences qu'il a faites; mais qu'il n'articule pas, de crainte, dit-il, d'ennuyer ses lecteurs, par la longeur de son Mémoire' (Needham 1780c:352).

9. 'Or, il est très-certain, qu'on voit par fois des Reines de la taille des abeilles communes, comme on y trouve des faux-bourdons de la même taille en grande quantité, & par la même raison, pour avoir été laissées par la mere abeille, sous la forme d'œufs, sans discernement dans les alvéoles communs où elle les a déposés' (Needham 1780c:358).

10. 'De même, il est indubitable, par ce que j'ai vu moi-même & par ce qui m'a été communiqué d'ailleurs, qu'outre les œufs courans, dont chacun occupe sa cellule respective, après la distribution faite par les abeilles ouvrieres, la Reine dépose très-souvent, sur-tout vers la fin de l'automne, depuis deux jusqu'à soixante œufs quelquefois, dans un alvéole ordinaire' (Needham 1780c:358-59).

11. See n.10 above.

12. For a short biography of the German agronomist Johann Riem (1739-1807), who won the 1768 prize at the Academy of Sciences at Mannheim for his dissertation on beekeeping and was the

ponte des Abeilles communes. Mais cet Observateur m'avoit écrit qu'il avoit disséqué des Abeilles communes dans lesquelles il avoit trouvé des ovaires.[13] Ces Abeilles étoient elles donc de ces Reines à petit corsage dont vous parlés?

Les petits Faux-bourdons n'étoient pas inconnus à feu mon illustre Maître et Ami Reaumur; mais il les jugeoit accidentels.[14] La découverte de Cambridge prouveroit qu'ils sont bien de l'institution de la Nature;[15] et cette découverte rend très bien raison du grand nombre des Mâles. Ici notre Academicien François[16] avoit trop donné à l'analogie; et il semble qu'on ne puisse plus se refuser à croire avec l'Apoticaire Anglois, que les oeufs des Abeilles sont fécondés à la manière de ceux des Poissons à écailles.[17] Mais n'est-il pas très singulier,

founder of the Society of Apiculture at Kaiserlautern, see *B.U.* (36:12). For a list of his publications on bees, see De Keller (1881:149-50). Riem corresponded extensively with Bonnet and sent him two long manuscript mémoires concerning his observations on bees carried out in 1769 and 1770 (BPUG, MS Bonnet 30:89r-116r and 135r-160v), which were summarised by Bonnet (1775c; see also B.O., 5, pt.1:109-22/10:174-96). Riem's correspondence of 1771-1772 was partly edited or summarised by Bonnet in B.O., 5, pt.1:123-42/10:196-226. Bonnet complained to Haller about the length of some of Riem's letters: 'Mr Riem m'assomoit par ses Lettres *Gallico-germaniques* de 100 ou 150 pages: ma Santé n'y pouvoit suffire. Je lui ai demandé quartier en lui témoignant ma juste reconnoissance de la peine qu'il prenoit de m'instruire' (Sonntag 1983:1011).

13. In his 'Quatrième mémoire sur les abeilles', Bonnet reported Riem's observation as follows: 'J'avois fort exhorté notre Cultivateur [Riem] à disséquer des Ouvrieres pour tâcher de découvrir leurs ovaires, et je luis avois fait sentir l'importance de cette dissection. Il m'a répondu, qu'il l'avoit fait, et qu'il avoit choisi ses Sujets parmi les Ouvrieres de l'expérience précédente: qu'il s'étoit aidé du microscope, et qu'en présence de deux témoins qu'il me nomme, il avoit ouvert six Ouvrieres, dont deux seulement lui avoient offert un ovaire analogue à celui de la Reine. Il avoue qu'il auroit dû disséquer un plus grand nombre d'Ouvrieres, pour mieux constater un fait si nouveau et si essentiel; mais il s'excuse sur des occupations qui ne lui ont pas laissé le tems de se livrer à ce travail anatomique' (B.O., 5, pt.1:126-27/10:202).

14. Acutually Réaumur (1734-1742, 5:590) only once saw smaller drones: 'Il m'est arrivé une seule fois de voir de ces petits mâles, et j'en ai même conservé un dans mon recueil d'insectes secs.' Maraldi (1714:333) had made a similar observation: 'Nous avons trouvé depuis peu une grande quantité de Bourdons, beaucoup plus petits que ceux que nous avions remarqué auparavant, et qui ne surpassent point la grandeur des petites Abeilles, de sorte qu'il n'auroit pas été aisé de les distinguer dans cette Ruche des Abeilles ordinaires sans le grand nombre que nous y en avons trouvé.'

15. Debraw (1777) was indeed correct in believing that the drones had a special function in the process of fertilisation, but he was wrong in believing that this occurred in the hive after the eggs had been laid; see n.17 below.

16. Réaumur.

17. Debraw (1777:23) observed 'a whitish liquor left in the angle of the basis of each cell, containing an egg' and conjectured that this could be the prolific fluid of drones. As noted by Debraw, a similar observation had already been made by Maraldi (1714:332), who described it as 'matiere blanchâtre dont l'œuf est environné au fond de l'Aveole peu de temps aprés sa naissance'. Furthermore Debraw (1777:23) observed in his glass-hives several bees 'inserting the posterior part of their bodies each into a cell, and sinking into it, where they continued but a little while'. In order to establish whether those bees were drones or workers, Debraw devised several experiments, one of which consisted in placing the queen and worker bees only or the queen and drones only in glass-hives. The results he obtained led him to conclude that the drones impregnated the eggs in the hive and that these 'like the spawn of fishes, most probably owe their fecundation to an impregnation from the males' (Debraw 1777:17). On this point see Bonnet's long note in B.O., 4, pt.2:274-76 n.8/9:134-36 n.8. Some years later Debraw's conclusions were challenged by the Genevan naturalist François Huber (1750-1831) who, in a series of letters addressed to Bonnet, published in 1792, correctly pointed out, first, that in the months from September to April, 'hives are generally destitute of males, yet, notwithstanding their absence, the queen then lays fertile eggs' and, second, that the whitish liquor observed by Debraw was 'an illusion arising from the reflection of the light, for nothing like a fluid was visible, except when the solar rays reached the bottom of the cells' (Fran.

que M.ʳ de Reaumur et moi qui avions observé les Abeilles pendant plusieurs années et dans des ruches de verre de la construction la plus favorable, nous n'ayons jamais surpris un seul Faux-bourdon, parmi des centaines, dans l'importante opération dont il s'agit, tandis que nous avions observé cent et cent fois la femelle unique occupée à pondre? C'étoit en particulier sur ce point si essentiel que j'esperois de trouver de nouvelles observations dans votre Mémoire.

Vous prouvés bien dans celui sur les Fourmis ce que vous voulés prouver: mais Salomon se passe à merveille de nos justifications:[18] car ne reste-t-il pas toujours vrai qu'il a pu renvoyer le paresseux à la Fourmi? Est-il un Animal plus actif et plus laborieux? Ici encore, je m'attendois à lire de nouveaux faits rélatifs à l'Histore de cet Insecte si intéressant.

Votre *Idée sommaire*[19] m'a fait plaisir en ce qu'elle m'a présenté en raccourci ce que j'avois vu ailleurs dans un détail un peu trop grand. Vous sçavés tout ce que notre celèbre Ami Spallanzani vous oppose et qu'il tient des mains de la Nature elle même.

Je n'ai pu lire jusqu'ici de l'Abbé Mann que son Ecrit sur le feu.[20] Il m'a paru plein de bonne Physique; mais je n'y ai pas apperçu des choses absolument neuves. Vous sçavés combien d'excellents écrits nous possedons en ce genre, et où la même doctrine se retrouve à quelques modifications près.

Au reste; il s'est glissé dans son Mémoire et dans les votres bien des anglicismes et des incorrections qui choqueront les oreilles Françoises. Ils ne choquent pas les miennes, parce que je sçais tout ce qu'on doit pardonner à un Etranger qui n'écrit pas dans sa propre langue.

J'avois chargé Hardouin de vous envoyer mes *Oeuvres*: l'a-t-il fait?

Le Rhume me presse: je ne puis plus dicter: je finis mon cher et célèbre Ami, en vous renouvellant les assurances de mon parfait attachement.

[ADDRESS] Bruxelles; M.ʳ Néédham, Directeur de l'Académie Impériale.

MANUSCRIPTS
    BPUG, MS Bonnet 75:236v-237r; MS Bonnet 85:199r-200v.

TEXT NOTES
    a. For the day of this letter, see letter 52. *b.* B: Vous avez

Huber, 1808:14-15).
    18. Bonnet is alluding to the following passage by Needham (1780b:298-99): 'Salomon ne parle de la fourmi, que dans un seul endroit de ses ouvrages, où il la propose comme un exemple de reproche aux paresseux; par conséquent, pour se mettre au fait de ses sentimens à cet égard, & pour détromper ceux, qui croient faussement pouvoir conclure de-là, que la fourmi travaille en été, pour se nourrir en hiver, le plus court sera de citer le texte entier de ce Roi philosophe; il se trouve dans le livre des Proverbes, Chapitre sixieme, Vers. 6, 7 & 8. *Vade ad formicam, ô piger, & considera vias ejus, & disce sapientiam: quae cum non habeat ducem, nec praeceptorem, nec principem, parat in aestate cibum sibi, & congregat in messe quod comedat.* On voit d'abord, qu'il ne s'agit nullement dans ces paroles d'une nourriture préparée d'avance très-inutilement pour une saison éloignée, pendant laquelle elles doivent rester engourdies par le froid, sans pouvoir faire usage de leurs facultés naturelles, comme les physiciens le savent très-bien aujourd'hui, mais qu'il s'agit uniquement d'une nourriture accumulée en été pour la jeune race, qui ne peut sortir de la fourmiliere, que lorsque ses forces le lui permettent.'
    19. See letter 50, n.5.
    20. See letter 50, n.16.

52

Needham to Bonnet – Brussels, 17 March 1780

Bruxelles Le 17. Mars 1780.

Je dois commencer ma reponse à votre lettre du 8. courant, mon très cher, et respectable ami, par vous remercier de l'ordre, que vous avez bien voulu donner au sieur Hardouin de m'envoyer vos ouvrages. J'en reçu les premiers volumes en 8vo.[1] ou il ne manque rien que votre portrait, qui selon les annonces devroit accompagner cette edition. Si c'est un present de votre part, car il ne s'explique pas sur ce point, Je vous dois un surcroit de reconnaissance pour un don, dont Je ne suis pas en état d'en rendre l'equivalent; si c'est au contraire un effet de ce, que je vous ai proposé de souscrire pour vos œuvres en les payant comme de raison, J'aurais préfére la belle edition[2] en 4to. que j'ai vüe l'autre jour chez un ami. Daignés me satisfaire sur ce doute, afin que je puisse m'arranger en consequence avec ce Libraire.—Ma tâche maintenant est de repondre à vos observations sur mes deux Memoires article par article.

Vous me faites le plus grand plaisir possible en m'assurant, que vous etes bien éloigné de me sçavoir mauvais gré de ce que je réjette l'explication, que vous avez donnée de l'experience de Schirac.[3] C'est une preuve de plus de votre disposition amicale envers moi, et de votre tolerance Philosophique en general; je vous remercie de tout mon cœur de m'avoir ôté un certain embarras à ce sujet, que j'ai souffert jusqu'à l'arrivée de votre lettre. Vous me réprochés neanmoins en meme tems de n'avoir pas rémarqué, que vos explications n'etoient fondées, que sur la supposition de la vérité du fait: or c'est un réproche, que je n'ai pas mérité certainement; vous en trouverez la preuve à la page 332. de mon memoire,[4] ou j'ai dit clairement & positivement, que vous paroissés douter de ces prétendus faits de Schirach en les traitant hypothetiquement avant d'en donner des explications conformes à vos idées sur la generation des corps organisés. Une fois dit, et cela en commençant d'en parler, il étoit très inutile de le répéter dans la suite.—Je préfere, dites vous d'admettre, que la Reine pond des œufs des femelles dans les cellules communes, et vous me demandés ensuite pourquoi je n'ai pas donné aucune preuve directe de mon assertion: il me semble au contraire à moi, que je l'ai prouvée suffisamment par le resultat des observations de M^r. Riem faites en 1769, et 1770.[5] qui vaut bien un Schirach; par la nature de la chose, ou le discernement attribué sans preuves à la Reine pour distinguer avant meme la ponte de chaque œuf, ceux des femelles, ceux

---

1. In 1779 the first six volumes of the 8° edition of Bonnet's *Œuvres d'histoire naturelle et de philosophie* appeared.

2. See letter 48, n.14.

3. See letter 47, n.29.

4. 'En effet, M. Bonnet lui-même, malgré sa bienveillance naturelle envers ses correspondans, paroît douter de ces prétendus faits de M. Schirach, en les traitant hypothétiquement avant d'établir la nouvelle Théorie qui, selon lui, doit s'ensuivre' (Needham 1780c:332).

5. Riem's observations were summarised by Bonnet in his 'Troisième mémoire sur les abeilles'; see Schirach (1771:240-44), Bonnet (1775c:24-26), and B.O., 5, pt.1:110-13/10:176-81.

des faux bourdons, et ceux des ouvrieres, les uns des autres, n'a pas l'apparence meme de probabilité; et enfin, ce qui est encore plus positif, par ce que j'eu entre mes mains un magasin de toute sorte d'œufs entassés sans ordre dans une seule cellule commune. Cette vérité est connüe avec certitude dans ce Pais par plusieurs de nos cultivateurs des mouches à miel, dont je pourrai en nommer un en particulier très distingué à Louvain, et elle prouve en meme tems de la maniere la plus directe, que la Reine pond ses œufs sans les distribuer avec ce discernement suppossé par M^r· de Reaumur,[6] chacun apart dans sa propre cellule, et enfin que ce sont les ouvrieres, qui les discernent après la ponte pour en effectuer la distribution requise; car La Reine, et les faux bourdons, comme vous sçavés, ne travaillent jamais. (voyés pages 340. 358. 359.[7]

C'est pour ces raisons, que j'ose affirmer, sans que vous ayés droit de me taxer de temerité, que dans toute portion de couvain, *quand l'experience de Schirach a le bonheur de reussir*, il doit se trouver un ou plusieurs œufs Royaux. J'ai dit, *quand elle réussit*, car elle manque très souvent, et elle a manquée jusqu'à sept fois chez un Physicien de mes amis, dont l'habilité au sujet des recherches sur les abeilles est très célébre dans ce pais. M^r· Riem lui-meme confirme ces observations tant pour ce qui régarde l'accumulation des œufs de differente sorte dans une cellule commune, que pour ce qu'on doit penser sur l'experience de Schirach, qui manque assés souvent, à sçavoir quand l'hazard veut, qu'il ne se trouve pas un œuf royal dans la portion du couvain, mise apart pour la production d'une nouvelle race.[8] Quant à la pretendüe reproduction d'une nouvelle Reine par la metamorphose d'un ver neutre de trois jours en femelle il le nie formellement après des essais à diverses fois répetés inutilement. Il me semble après tout cela, que j'en ai suffisamment donné des preuves, et que mon memoire ne se reduit pas à des simples assertions. Voyés en pages 356. 357. 358. 359.[9] En effet qu'elle autre espece de preuve pourrés vous me demander, quand il est impossible d'ouvrir d'avance chaque cellule de la dite portion du couvain pour en y voir le contenu sans le gater? Ou peut on mieux faire, quand on ne peut pas voir tout par soi-meme, que d'employer les observations des autres en pesant les temoignages quelquefois contraires pour en adopter ceux, qui paroissent les plus conformes au cours connu de la nature? Bien d'autres en Hollande, comme ailleurs, et sur tout le Prince de Gallitzin à la Haye ont vu mon memoire dans tout un autre jour, que mon bon ami à Geneve, et il leur semble, que j'ai rempli complettement la tâche, que je me suis proposée en plaçant pour devise à la tête, *non fumum ex fulgore, sed ex fumo dare lucem.* Hor[10]

Vous me demandés ensuite pourquoi je n'ai fait aucune attention à ce que l'observateur de Lusace vous ait écrit,[11] que toutes les fois, qu'il avoit tenté l'experience avec les seuls œufs, il n'avoit jamais reussi, mais qu'il l'avoit constamment, et en toute saison, lorsqu'il l'avoit faite avec des vers de trois ou quatre jours. Ayés la bonté de révenir sur vos pas, vous trouverés à la page

6. Réaumur (1734-1742, 5:471-74).
7. Needham (1780c:340, 358, 359).
8. Schirach (1771:240), Bonnet (1775c:24), and B.O., 5, pt.1:110/10:176.
9. Needham (1780c:356, 357-59).
10. Horace, *Ars poetica*, 143.
11. See letter 51, n.5.

357.[12] que j'en ai donné une notice exacte; que j'ai réjetté ce pretendu fait fondé sur les observations directement contradictoires de M[r.] Riem un observateur bien plus vrai, et plus judicieux, que Schirach; que son beaufrere Wilhelmi, qui travailloit avec lui, refusoit constamment de le croire,[13] dans quel refus il persiste, autant que puisse le sçavoir depuis dix ans jusqu'à ce jour; et qu'enfin il n'est pas possible d'ajouter foi à celui, qui vous a presenté comme un fait, dont il pretendoit avoir été temoin oculaire, une faussété notoire; à sçavoir, comme un ver de trois jours ne vous ait pas paru, comme de raison, transportable d'une cellule commune à une cellule royale, que les ouvrieres detruisoient trois cellules communes pour les arrondir ensuite en forme de cellule Royale à l'entour de son ver de trois jours. Or mes propres experiences aussi bien que celles des autres dans ce pais voyés page 336.[14] demontrent, que les ouvrieres à cette occasion batissent une ou plusieurs cellules Royales en entier, et apart, aux quelles un ver de trois, ou quatre jours n'est nullement transportable par leurs forces unies, ce qui les mette dans la nécessité d'employer, et d'y placer avec discernement un œuf Royal. *Semel decipi incommodum est iterum stultum*,[15] et certainement je ne veux pas m'exposer à un pareil réproche.

Vous observés de plus que je critique aussi l'observateur de Cambridge, et cela par une simple negative. Or en cela je vous demande mille pardons, Le contraire paroit pages 347. &c. et Page 354.[16] J'en ai donné mes preuves, qui vous doivent paraitre demonstratives, contre la possibilité physique de l'existence des œufs dans les ouvrieres, *des œufs visibles à la simple* vüe contenus dans les ovaires invisibles aux lentilles les plus fortes, à moins que le contenu puisse être immensement plus grand que le contenant. Ce que vous y ajoutés après de l'observateur de Lauter, qui a vu, selon qu'il le pretend des ovaires dans ces ouvrieres, n'est d'aucun poids, parce qu'on ne doit pas croire sur sa parole un imposteur une fois demasqué, et parce qu'il est le seul parmi tous les plus grands observateurs, qui les a pu decouvrir. Comment en effet croire un homme sujet déjà à caution contre des temoignages si unanimes?

Vous m'accusés ensuite de n'avoir pas traité le sujet des abeilles, comme j'ai traite d'autres sujets d'histoire naturelle. Il n'etoit pas possible de les traiter exactement de meme. Le sujet, que je propose dans mon memoire n'est pas neuf, il est plûtot un objet des conclusions fondées sur des observations déjà

---

12. 'C'est encore une illusion de croire que la nouvelle Reine, qu'on trouve dans les caisses de Mr. Schirach, soit nécessairement le produit d'un ver neutre de deux ou trois jours, et que la cellule royale, qui doit lui servir de berceau, soit formée des débris de trois autres cellules communes. Mr. Riem assure positivement que, non-seulement la cellule royale est entiérement bâtie de nouveau, mais que la jeune Reine provient toujours d'un œuf royal, que les ouvrieres savent démêler parmi les autres déposés sans regle par la mere-abeille, dans les alvéoles. C'est un fait dont j'ai vérifié moi-même la vérité, pour ce qui regarde la construction de la nouvelle cellule royale' (Needham 1780c:357).

13. Wilhelmi's doubts were expressed in a letter addressed to Bonnet dated 9 March 1770 and published by Bonnet in his 'Second mémoire [...] sur les abeilles'; see Schirach (1771:219-20), Bonnet (1775b:418-23), and B.O., 5, pt.2:94-101/10:150-60. See also Schirach (1771:197), Bonnet (1775a:335), and B.O., 5, pt.2:80/10:127.

14. Needham (1780c:336).

15. Reminiscent of Cicero, *De inventione rhetorica*, I, 37, 71: 'Primo quidem decipi incommodum est, iterum stultum.'

16. Needham (1780c:347, 351-53).

faites obscurcies par des pretendues observations plus modernes contradictoires les unes aux autres, aussi bien qu'au sens commun. Il falloit donc debrouiller ce chaos dans mon memoire pour en tirer le vrai, et pour en écarter le faux. C'est en le faisant, que je pretends en avoir mis l'objet en plein jour, et fixer par des raisonnements justes les bornes de notre croyance sur tant de choses absolument disparates. Cela ne veut pas dire, que j'ai manqué d'y ajouter mes propres observations pour completter mes recherches d'une maniere meme decisive en faveur de mes assertions, ou certainement vous ne me rendez pas justice en les traitant comme de simples negatives denuées des preuves très suffisantes. Vous les avez devant vous ces observations, qui me sont propres, à la fin de mon memoire, après avoir mis en ballance celles des autres. Voyés pages 356. et seq.[17]

Quant aux Reines de la petite taille, on ne les connoit plus particulierement, que depuis qu'on se familiarise avec les abeilles d'une maniere tout à fait nouvelle d'après la methode de deux Wildmans.[18] Mais, quoiqu'on dise la dessus, et quoique peutêtre j'ai trop avancé sur la foi des autres en affirmant page 358.[19] que cette difference de taille descend jusqu'à donner des Reines quelquefois, qui n'excedent pas celle des ouvrieres, c'est toujours un accident, qui n'est pas sans probabilité. Cependant qu'il soit vrai, ou faux pris à la lettre, il n'affecte nullement mes conclusions, ou les observations sur lesquelles mes assertions principales sur cette partie de l'economie rurale sont baties. On le croira d'après les raports courans, ou on ne le croira pas, les grandes verités établies dans mon memoire ne seront pas moins evide[ntes et] elles en sont totalement independantes.

Vous observés encore que je parle de la distribution des œufs dans leurs cellules respectives faite par les ouvrieres, et vous demandés, si j'ai vu cela, et comment je suis parvenu à le voir? Je parle en effet de cette distribution, mais c'est d'apres les observations de Mr Riem, qui l'affirme positivement, et c'est encore pour avoir vu moi-meme plusieurs œufs entassés ensemble dans une cellule commune, dont les ouvrieres de toute necessité, comme j'ai observé cy-devant, sont les distributrices, puisque la Reine et les faux bourdons ne se mêlent jamais des travaux d'aucune espece, comme tous les naturalistes le connoissent.

---

17. Needham (1780c:356-61).

18. Thomas Wildman moved to London from Plymouth in 1766, where he 'achieved fame by trick performances with bees which had been previously subdued by diving' (Harding 1979:88-89). In 1768 he published *A treatise on the management of bees* (London), which shows a good knowledge of continental beekeeping. It was translated into French, German, and Italian (see De Keller 1881:196-97). His nephew Daniel Wildman published a less ambitious work, *A complete guide for the management of bees* (London 1773), which ran to twenty editions and was also translated into French, German, and Italian (see Harding 1979:91-92). On both the Wildmans, see Fraser (1951a:57-58). The method envisaged by the Wildmans for rendering bees easier to handle is described by Needham (1780c:365-66) himself thus: 'La maniere [...] de les [the bees] étourdir [...] est de poser la ruche pleine sur une ruche vuide, ouverture contre ouverture, qu'on entoure ensuite d'un linge pour boucher l'interstice entre deux, et de frapper continuellement avec un bâton sur la ruche supérieure, où les abeilles se trouvent avec leur gâteau, jusqu'à ce qu'elles soient étourdies, et tombent toutes dans la ruche vuide.

'On connoît, quand il est temps de l'ouvrir, pour les faire glisser ensuite sur un drap propre, par la cessation entiere du bourdonnement, que le bruit, et le choc continuel du bâton cause jusqu'au moment de la stupéfaction complette.'

19. See letter 51, n.9.

Cette consequence est donc aussi certaine, comme si je l'avais vu moi-meme, et quant à la question, que vous me faites comment je suis parvenu à le voir, elle se resout, d'elle-meme, puisqu'il est très facile en rompant un certain nombre de cellules d'y decouvrir les magasins. M^r. Riem en parle tout, comme moi, après les avoir vu pareillement; voyés page 359,[20] ou je le cite comme temoin oculaire de ce fait, dont je me rends en meme tems garand.—Il est sans doute singulier que des observateurs de votre trempe, et de celle de M^r. de Reaumur n'aient jamais vu la fecondation des œufs, telle qu'on vient de la constater aujourdhui, mais cela meme sert à nous convaincre, que les plus habiles ne sont pas toujours les plus fortunés dans les recherches, qu'on se propose de faire en histoire naturelle. On en voit des exemples tous les jours; ce qui se presente à l'un par quelque heureux hazard ne se presentera pas à un autre. Mais, comme vous le remarqués très bien, la chose n'est pas moins certaine, et le celebre M^r. Maraldi l'avait plus que suspecté, comme j'ai observé, page 345.[21]

Dans vos reflexions, qui régardent mon memoire sur la fourmi, vous croyés que Salomon peut se passer à merveille de nos justifications;[22] je le crois de meme, mais c'etoit pour deraciner une erreur vulgaire commune au Peuple, et aux Philosophes, sur le compte de ce Roi Physicien. C'est la moindre partie de mon memoire, et une chose qui n'y entre qu'incidemment pour faire valoir mon respect pour les livres sacrés. L'important est d'avoir rédressé une erreur en histoire naturelle sur l'economie de cet insecte, qui sembloit attaquer la sagesse de dieu, et les causes finales. Tout le monde, et plus particulierement les Philosophes, qui en tiroient de tres mauvaises consequences l'avoient embrassée. J'ai resolu clairement, et nettement ce probleme en établissant le vrai inconnu avant moi, et en écartant le faux. Comment pourrés vous dire après cela, que je n'y donne aucuns nouveaux faits relatifs à l'histoire naturelle de cet insecte. En vérité je ne comprends rien à votre critique à ce sujet.—Vous voulés enfin pour conclure que je travaille de nouveau mon memoire sur les abeilles; je crois au contraire d'avoir tout dit, qu'on puisse dire pour le present sur cette matiere en établissant des verités chancellantes, en écartant le faux merveilleux de certains naturalistes, et en reduisant le tout à la simple nature. Que pourrés vous demander de plus de moi au milieu de tant de nuages, qui sont venus de la Saxe pour obscurcir un sujet si interessant et pour les Physiciens, et pour les Economistes?—Du reste je suis très aise, que mon idée sommaire[23] vous ait fait plaisir; nous ne serons jamais peutetre d'accord avant la vie future sur la metaphysique des choses; cela importe très peu pour le present, et il ne diminue en rien le respect, que je vous ai toujours voué. Quant à Spallanzani, soit dit entre nous, son caractere, et sa manière de raisonner ne me plairont jamais. En

---

20. Needham (1780c:359).

21. Needham (1780c:345-46). Maraldi (1714:332) had stated: 'Nous n'avons pû découvrir jusqu'à present de quelle maniere se fait cette fécondation, si c'est dans le corps de la femelle, ou bien si c'est *à la maniere des Poissons*, aprés que la femelle les a posés. La matiere blanchâtre [see letter 51, n.17] dont l'œuf est environné au fond de l'Alveole peu de temps aprés sa naissance, semble conforme à la derniere opinion, aussi-bien que la remarque faite plusieurs fois d'un grand nombre d'œufs qui sont restés inféconds au fond de l'Alveole et autour desquels nous n'avons point vû cette matiere' (italics added).

22. See letter 51, n.18.

23. See letter 50, n.5.

faisant son entrée dans la carriere des recherches Physiques l'année 1751. avant que vous avez fait sa connaissance, il m'avoit adressé une lettre à Rome[24] pour me faire beaucoup de complimens sur mes nouvelles decouvertes microscopiques, qui venoient de paraitre en 1750. et pour me prier en meme tems de lui permettre de communiquer au public la confirmation, qu'il étoit prêt à faire d'après ses propres experiences de la vérité exacte de mes observations sous la forme des lettres adressées à moi nommement.[25] Apparemment croyant, que j'avois acquis par cet ouvrage quelque célébrité dans la republique des lettres, il vouloit s'accrocher à moi pour s'y placer parmi les autres. La permission, chose de peu de consequence, lui avoit été accordée, mais les lettres en question n'ont jamais parües. Il l'a cru convenable de rebrousser chemin en s'adressant à vous pour y parvenir plûtot en raison de votre plus grande célébrité. En cela, puisqu'il étoit determiné à faire fortune à tout prix, il n'avoit pas tort, quoiqu'il se trouve par là en contradiction avec lui meme. C'est donc un homme, qui souffle froid et chaud, et sa conduite à cet égard est l'inverse precisement de ce que tout Philosophe, qui aime le vrai, doit tenir pour maxime, *amicus Plato, sed magis amica veritas*.[26] Il dependoit de moi, au lieu de lui répondre d'une maniere honnête, comme j'ai fait une fois, mais que je ne ferai jamais plus, de publier sa lettre,[27] qui lui n'auroit pas faite certainement honneur, mais je le laissai pour ce qu'il est, et, j'abandonne pour toujours un homme, en qui il m'est impossible d'avoir pour l'avenir la moindre confiance. Vous m'aves forcé en le pronant de trahir mon secret. Adieu je vous estime, et je vous respecte de tout mon cœur.

Needham.

[a]Replique sur les Abeilles.
[word illegible] contre Mr Spallanzani[a]

[ADDRESS] A Monsieur / Monsieur Charles Bonnet / de plusieurs Academies / à Genthod / près Geneve

MANUSCRIPT
    BPUG, MS Bonnet 35:106r-109v.

EDITIONS
    'Quant à Spallanzani [...] mon secret' published in Castellani (1973:102).

TEXT NOTES
    a. Written in another hand at the head of the letter.

24. This is a mistake on Needham's part, because his correspondence with Spallanzani did not begin until 1761; see Needham's mention of Spallanzani's letter in letter 15 (see also Castellani 1973:102 n.63). Spallanzani's first letter to Needham cannot be traced, but Needham's reply, dated 29 August 1761, is preserved in the BCRE (see Castellani 1973:79-80).

25. In his reply to Spallanzani's first letter, Needham had written, 'Quant à cé, que vous me demandés, de pouvoir adresser vos lettres contenantes vos observations à moi, c'est me faire beaucoup d'honneur, et meme plus que je merite' (29 August 1761; Castellani 1973:79). These letters were never written, because Spallanzani soon abandoned Needham's theory and became a preformationist (see letter 40, n.13, and section 2.iv of the Introduction).

26. Attributed to Aristotle.

27. See n.24 above.

53

Bonnet to Needham – Genthod, 18 April 1780

À Genthod le 18ᵉ d'Avril 1780.

Cet Exemplaire de mes Oeuvres, mon cher et célèbre Ami, que vous avés reçu d'Hardouin étoit bien *donum Amici*: vous n'en devés donc point la valeur au Libraire qui vous l'a expedié de ma part.

Les fraix si considérables que cette entreprise typographique occasionne aux Editeurs m'a porté à me contenter d'un fort petit nombre d'exemplaires de la grande Edition et c'est ce qui m'a privé du plaisir de faire tous mes présens en Exemplaires de cette Edition. Ce n'est pas néanmoins que je ne leur livre tous mes Manuscripts *gratis*, comme je l'ai toujours fait à tous mes Libraires. Mais j'ai été éfrayé de la grandeur des fraix. C'étoit même cette considération qui me porta en 1775 à résister si fortement aux sollicitations de l'Entrepreneur. Vous avés-vu cela dans ma Préface générale.[1]

Le Portrait que vous demandés sera distribué avec les Volumes VII et VIII de l'Edition in 8.° et vous en serés content. Celui qui avoit été fait pour être placé au devant du 1.ᵉʳ Vol: avoit des défauts essentiels qui nous avoient forcé de le supprimer.

Je ne puis répondre actuellement aux divers articles de votre bonne Lettre qui concernent les Abeilles. Je le ferai, j'espére, un autre jour. Je me borne à vous répéter*ᵃ*, que votre réponse à Schirach m'auroit paru plus satisfaisante si elle n'avoit consisté que dans une suite d'expériences bien faites et instituées par vous même.

Que diriés-vous, si Schirach avoit toujours pris la précaution de s'assurer qu'il n'avoit point d'oeufs dans le petit gâteau où se trouvoit le Ver commun de trois jours?

*ᵇ*Vous faites une singulière équivoque sur l'*Observateur de Lauter*, au sujet des ovaires qu'il prétendoit avoir découvert dans les Ouvrières: vous me dites; que son témoignage *n'est d'aucun poids, parce qu'on ne doit pas croire sur sa parole un Imposteur une fois démasqué.*[2] Mais, mon bon Ami, cet Homme que vous nommés un *Imposteur* et dont le témoignage ne vous paroît d'aucun poids, est ce même Riem sur les observations duquel vous-vous appuyés si fréquemment. Vous le preniés apparemment pour Schirach; mais Lauter est dans le Palatinat et non dans la Lusace. D'ailleurs le terme plus que dûr d'*Imposteur* ne conviendroit pas plus à Schirach qu'à Riem. Nous devons présumer que l'un et l'autre ont dit de bonne foi ce qu'ils ont cru avoir bien observé.*ᵇ*

*ᶜ*Le reproche que vous faites à M.ʳ Spallanzani est plus grave encore. Je vous

---

1. 'Je ne songeois point du tout à publier une Collection complette de mes Écrits, lorsqu'un Libraire étranger vint en 1775, me solliciter dans ma retraite de consentir à cette entreprise & d'y concourir. Je me refusai d'abord à ses sollicitations; & j'insistai fortement auprès de lui sur les considérations qui me paroissoient les plus propres à le détourner de son dessein. Comme il me promettoit une belle édition en grand format, je craignois avec fondement, que le débit ne répondit pas aux frais considérables dans lesquels une pareille entreprise l'engageroit' (B.O., 1:iii/1:iv).

2. See letter 52.

renvoie la dessus[c] à la grande Note que j'ai placée à la fin du Chapitre VI du Tom: II des *Corps organisés*[d].[3] Vous y verrés que le Professeur de Reggio, puis de Modène, m'écrivoit expressément; que lors qu'il vous écrivit, (apparemment dans l'epoque dont vous me parlés) il vous dit; que vous entendiés ses Lettres dans un sens trop favorable pour vous &c. [b]Du reste; ce n'est point à moi à prononcer sur ce qui s'est passé entre vous deux; puis que je n'ai pas vû votre commerce épistolaire. Mais, je vous avouerai, que je ne sçaurois me persuader que M.[r] Spallanzani aît pu être inspiré par le motif si peu philosophique que vous lui supposés. Il m'a paru trop honnête et trop vrai dans tous le cours de ma propre correspondance qui dure sans interruption depuis quinze ans.[b] Quoi[e] qu'il en soit de ce qu'il peut vous avoir écrit et de la manière dont vous l'avés interprété; il s'agit toujours de sçavoir si les nouvelles expériences de l'Observateur de Reggio ne détruisent pas les conséquences que vous aviés tirées des votres et que je n'avois pu adopter. Or; il me semble que pour décider cette question il ne faut qu'ouvrir les *Opuscules de Physique*[4] de votre Antagoniste. Il a interrogé plusieurs fois la Nature d'après vos propres procedés; et toujours ses réponses ont été directement contraires à vos résultats. Convenés-vous des faits vus et revus tant de fois par M.[r] Spallanzani ou avés-vous découvert de nouveaux faits qui leur soyent opposés?

Soufrés que j'ajoute; que je n'ai pas prôné[f] le Naturaliste de Reggio; je n'ai fait que rendre justice aux grandes Vérités dont il a enrichi l'Histoire naturelle, et que vous êtes bien capable d'apprécier.

Adieu, mon cher et célèbre Ami; je vous embrasse bien cordialement.

[ADDRESS] Bruxelles; M.[r] Néédham, Directeur de l'Académie Impériale.

MANUSCRIPTS
BPUG, MS Bonnet 75:240v-241r; MS Bonnet 85:201r-201v.

EDITIONS
'Le reproche [...] d'apprécier' published in Castellani (1973:104-105).

TEXT NOTES
a. B: réitérer *b.* B: *omitted* *c.* B: À l'egard de ce que vous me dites sur l'Abbé SPALLANZANI, je vous renvoie *d.* B: *Corps Organisés,* de la nouvelle Edition *e.* B: Mais, quoi *f.* B: trop célébré

3. B.O., 3:411-27 n.1/6:317-39 n.1. This long note, which was added in the *Œuvres* edition of Bonnet's *Considérations sur les corps organisés*, contains a reconstruction of the Needham-Spallanzani controversy from Bonnet's point of view.
4. See letter 36, n.4, and letter 49, n.1.

Appendices

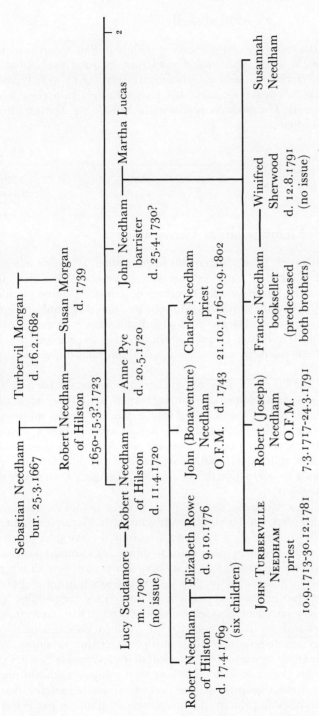

APPENDIX A. NEEDHAM'S GENEALOGY[1]

Sebastian Needham
bur. 25.3.1667
— Turbervil Morgan
d. 16.2.1682

Robert Needham
of Hilston
1650-15.3?.1723
— Susan Morgan
d. 1739

Robert Needham
of Hilston
d. 11.4.1720
— Anne Pye
d. 20.5.1720

John Needham
barrister
d. 25.4.1730?
— Martha Lucas

Lucy Scudamore — Robert Needham
of Hilston
d. 17.4.1769
m. 1700
(no issue)

Robert Needham
of Hilston
d. 17.4.1769
— Elizabeth Rowe
d. 9.10.1776
(six children)

John (Bonaventure)
Needham
O.F.M. d. 1743

Charles Needham
priest
21.10.1716-10.9.1802

Robert (Joseph)
Needham
O.F.M.
7.3.1717-24.3.1791

Francis Needham
bookseller
(predeceased
both brothers)
— Winifred
Sherwood
d. 12.8.1791
(no issue)

Susannah
Needham

JOHN TURBERVILLE
NEEDHAM
priest
10.9.1713-30.12.1781

1. Modified from the 'Pedigree of the Family of Needham of Hilston' in Bradney (1904-1932, 1:58). Further information was obtained from WDA, SEC. 12/14/17; the wills of Martha and Robert (Joseph) Needham in PAL, D.1 and D.6.WF.LXLVI; C. R. S., 9:163-65; 12:21, 35, 36, 38, 82, 240; 28:101n, 130-31n, 150n, Foley (1877-82, 5:320, 335-36; 7:538); Gillow (1885-1903, 5:157-60); Thaddeus (1898:278); Kirk (1909:171-72); and Anstruther (1968-77, 4:195-96). See also the biographical sources listed in Needham's biographical note (at the beginning of this volume). We would like to thank the following individuals for their help in determining the details of Needham's life and family: Elisabeth Poyser, Westminster Diocesan Archives, London; Fr. Justin McLoughlin O.F.M., Provincial Archives O.F.M., London; and Rev. Michael Sharratt, Ushaw College, Durham.

2. There were seven other children of this marriage: Sebastian Needham S.J. (b. 1671, d. 4 Jan. 1743); Jane Needham (d. 16 Sept. 1695, no issue); Susan Needham (m. George Pinkard); Mary Needham (d. 15 Nov. 1718, m. Richard Langhorne); Ursula Needham (bur. 1 June 1749, m. Thomas Belchier); Elizabeth Needham (d. 2 Aug. 1718, m. Thomas Jenkins); Turberville Needham (d. 7 Aug. 1700, no issue)

APPENDIX B

NEEDHAM deposited the following sealed mémoire with Jean-Paul Grandjean de Fouchy, Secretary of the Paris Académie des sciences, in June 1748. It was written shortly after Needham's joint microscopical observations with Buffon had ended and while he was continuing his own infusion researches (see Introduction, section 2.ii). The mémoire is now in the SPKB (Slg. Darmstädter FIC 1740 (1) J. T. Needham).

Juin 9. 1748.
Needham

Memoire sur la Generation.

Apres avoir vû la systeme de M^r· de Buffons sur la generation, ayant fait infuser dans l'eau un grand nombre de matieres vegetales, et animales de differente espece, et principalement les semences, et germes de semences d'une grande quantité de plantes, j'ai vu dans toutes ces infusions un amas de globules, corps longs &c. en mouvement semblables a ceux qu'on voit dans la semence des mâles, et qu'on qualifie d'animaux, et qui sont du meme genre, quoique d'une differente espece, comme ces memes corps mouvants d'infusions different entre eux memes.

Je me suis assuré, que l'air, et l'eau n'ont aucune part a tous ces effets pour leur production, si non comme element de leur vegetation, et qu'ils viennent de la matiere meme animale ou vegetale. Car j'ai trouve dans ces memes infusions plusieurs filets, qui s'etendoient du fond des Phioles, ou etoit l'infusion, et qui produisoient ces globules, &c. J'ai vu meme naitre ces filets, et j'ai poursuivie avec la microscope leur differentes gradations pendant tout le tems de leur accroississement jusqu'a la production de ces globules, &c. que j'ai vu naitre et sortir de la maniere suivante.

De sein d'une matiere gelatineuse, dans la quelle se resolvent les vegetaux, et les animaux il sort des filets, ou des tiges, et qui font la moisissure ordinaire, qui portent des branches, comme les plantes; ces filets sont des veritables plantes microscopiques, qui tendent continuellement à se dilater, et s'etendre avec un accroissisement fort prompt quand la tige, et les branches cessent de s'allonger, ses extremités se gonflent jusqu'à ce qu'elles s'ouvrent, alors tous les globules &c. sortent avec impetuosité, et se repandent de tous cotés avec toutes les apparences d'un mouvement spontané. Ces globules en perdant leur mouvement apres plusieurs heures se decomposent encore, et se resolvent dans une matiere gelatineuse, d'ou il en nait de nouveaux, mais plus petits, et ainsi de suite.

Par ces experiences et par une infinite d'autres dont je supprime le detail, j'es peut demontrer, que les vegetaux, et les animaux sont composes pour la plus grande partie de cette matiere gelatineuse, que j'appelerai *matiere generative*, dont les particules ont dans elles un principe de mouvement, et d'union, par le quel elles forment ces filets, et ces globules &c. dans les infusions vegetales, ou animales, et dans la semence des animaux, et si elles se trouvent avec un certain melange de principes, et dans une matrice convenable elles sont propres par des certaines lois, a lesquelles elles sont assujettie a produire tantot les corps des plantes, tantot des animaux, tantot la partie mechanique des hommes. Par consequence la hypothese des germes contenu en germes est fausse et insoutenable &c.

Il y a deja trois mois, que je commencé ces experiences, et que j'ai fait une grande partie de ces decouvertes; j'ai communiqué à mesure mes observations a Mr de Buffons, Mr de Reaumur, M^r D'aubenton, Mr Monnier le medecin, et plusieurs autres, mais comme on a commencé a parler de cette systeme nouvelle, et que mes experiences sont plus connu que j'ai voulu d'abord pour m'assurer mes propres decouvertes, J'ai pris la precaution de sceller, et signer cette petite memoire, que j'ai mis entre les mains de Mr de Fouchy secretaire perpetuell de l'academ[ie] Royalle de sciences.

Turbervill Needham
de la societé Royalle de
Londres.

Paris Juin. 9. 1748.

[ADDRESS] N° 19 / Memoire sur la / generation par Mr Needham / de la societé Royalle / de Londres / addressé a Mr de Fouchy secretaire / perpetuell de l'Academie Royale / des sciences.

[In Fouchy's hand] Le 9 Juin 1748. ce paquet cacheté / m'a été remis pour estre déposé au secrétariat / et y avoir recours en cas de besoin / Grandjean De Fouchy   N° 19 / sec^e perp^l de l'ac R. des Sciences

Appendix C

Although the papers and letters that were in Needham's possession at his death (Mann 1783:xli) have never been located, several Needham manuscripts and a number of letters he wrote to others have been preserved in various library archives. Because Needham's life and work, in comparison to Bonnet's, have previously not been studied in great detail, we offer the following as a list of the extant Needham manuscript materials that are currently known to us.

Manuscripts

'Compendium logicae, traditum a nobili domino domino Turberwillo Needham, scriptum vero ab auditore ejus obsequentissimo Oswaldo Lancaster, inchoatum die 10° julii anno 1736'. [Student notes from Needham's course on logic at Douai.] BD.

Seven letters to the Royal Society, reporting on scientific observations, dated 1743 (five) and 1760 (two). Two were published as Needham (1743) and Needham (1760b). RS (L&P. I. 167, 193, 204, 244; L&P. IV. 6, 17; Fo. 2.8).

'Memoire sur la Generation', dated 9 June 1748; deposited with Jean-Paul Grandjean de Fouchy, Secretary of the Paris Académie des sciences. Published here as Appendix B. SPKB (Slg. Darmstädter Fic 1740 [1] J. T. Needham).

'Ideae quaedam generales de mundi systemate cum earum ordine quodam metaphysico', sent to Albrecht von Haller in 1759. BNM (B. II. 3151/19). Published by Monti (1985).

Attestation (in Needham's hand), certifying that twenty-nine of the characters on the 'bust of Isis' and several on other monuments could be found in the Vatican Library's Chinese dictionary, dated 25 March 1762 and signed by ten of Needham's colleagues. SAL (Thomas Jenkins F.S.A. Nine Letters to Norris 1758-1772) and BL (Add. 21416).

'Remarks upon the Athanasian Creed' (in James Boswell's hand), written by Needham in 1765. The original was sent to Boswell by Needham to be passed on to John Wilkes. YUL (Boswell Papers).

'Recherches sur les Mines [...]', [1769] (one copy in Needham's hand and a second copy in another hand). A brief report on this study was published in *Mémoires de l'Académie impériale et royale des sciences et belles-lettres*, 1777, 1:li-liii. AARB (Needham).

'Mémoire sur la Société littéraire de Bruxelles, fait et présenté à S. A. le Ministre plénipotentiaire de S.M.I.R.A., par M. Needham, directeur de ladite société', [1770]. Published by Gachard (1840:58-65). AARB (Needham).

'Sommaire du Mem. sur la maladie contagieuse des bêtes à cornes', [1770] (not in Needham's hand). Published as Needham (1780a). AARB (Needham).

'Memoire sur la Province de Luxembourg', [1773] (not in Needham's hand).

Published as Needham (1777). AARB (Needham).

'Examen par l'abbé Needham et le prévôt de Saint-Pierre de Louvain, de Marci du projet de François Du Rondeau […] sur l'établissement d'une salle électrique à Bruxelles, à l'instar de celle de Paris […]', [1778]. AGR (Secrétairerie d'État et de Guerre, n° 2134).

'Etat present de l'Academie', [1779]. AARB (Needham).

'Rapport fait à l'Academie Imperiale et Royale de Bruxelles sur le Fanal de Bidiston', [date unknown] (not in Needham's hand). AARB (Needham).

'Mémoire sur un phenomene d'optique', [date unknown] (not in Needham's hand). AARB (Needham).

Correspondence

One letter to James Parsons, 1746. WIHM (Autograph Letters).

Twelve letters to Emanuel Mendez Da Costa, 1747-1780 (with drafts of Da Costa's replies). BL (Add. 28540).

Eight letters to Paolo Frisi, 1751-1780. BAM (Y 153. Sup., lett. 11, 44-50).

Two letters to Ferdinando Bassi, 1752. BUB (Cod. 233, vol. II).

One letter to John Ellis, 1755. Partially published in Savage (1948:12-13). LSL (MS 276).

One letter to Gerard Bernard, 1756. UCLC (Corr. 4 vi 1756).

One letter to the Royal Society, accompanying a memoir by Claude-Siméon Passemant, 1760. RS (L&P. IV. 57).

Five letters to Joseph de Guignes, 1761. BL (Add 21416).

One letter to William Norris, 1762. SAL (Correspondence 1761-1770).

Extract from one letter to Joseph Wilcocks, 1762 (not in Needham's hand). SAL (Correspondence 1761-1770).

Two letters to and a travel itinerary for James Boswell, 1765. YUL (Boswell Papers).

Two letter to Emanuel Mendez Da Costa, 1765 and 1767. SPKB (Slg. Darmstädter Fıc 1740 [1] J. T. Needham).

Fifty-seven letters to Honoré-Auguste Sabatier de Cabre, 1765-1781. BLUL (Brotherton Collection).

One letter to Pierre-Michel Hennin, [1766]. BIF (Needham).

Two letters to Joseph Berington, 1771-1772 (not in Needham's hand). BDA (C.685).

Three letters to Joseph Berington, 1772-1774. WCRO (Throckmorton MSS, CR 1998/Gate box, folder 8).

One letter to Charles Dillon, 1773. HL (JE 620).

Two letters to Jan Ingen-Housz, 1773-1774. KB (133 B 24, Needham ad Ingen-Housz).

Five letters to Nathaniel Pigott, 1773-1777. VF.

One letter to [Joseph-Ambroise Crumpipen], 1774. AARB (Needham).

One letter to Joseph-Ambroise Crumpipen, 1778. AGR (Secrétairerie d'Etat et de Guerre, no. 2134B).

One letter to Jan Hendrik van Swinden, 1779. UL (BPL 755, Needham ad Swinden).

One letter to Horace Benedict de Saussure, 1780. BPUG (MS Saussure 10).

(For published editions of Needham's letters to Vallisneri, see Paravia 1842:152-60; to Spallanzani, see Castellani 1973; and to Haller, see Mazzolini 1976.)

Bibliography

Abrégé
1798 *Abrégé de l'histoire de Geneve*. Neuchâtel: Chez les Frères Girardet

L'Académie
1973 *L'Académie impériale et royale des sciences et belles-lettres de Bruxelles 1772-1794. Sa fondation. Ses travaux*. Bruxelles: Palais des Académies

Adams, Percy G.
1962 *Travelers and travel liars*. Berkeley, Los Angeles: University of California Press

Adanson, Michel
1770 'Mémoire sur un mouvement particulier découvert dans une plante appelée tremella'. *Histoire de l'Academie royale des sciences. Année MDCCLXVII. Avec les Mémoires* [...], pp.564-72

Addison, Joseph
1721 *The Works of the right honourable Joseph Addison*. 4 vols. London: Printed for Jacob Tonson

Agassiz, Louis
1859 *An essay on classification*. London: Longman, Brown, Green, Longmans, & Roberts, and Trübner & Co.

Alexandre, Monique
1976 'L'exégèse de *Gen*. 1, 1-2a dans l'*In Hexaemeron* de Grégoire de Nysse: deux approches du problème de la matière'. In *Gregor von Nyssa und die Philosophie. Zweites internationales Kolloquium über Gregor von Nyssa*, pp.159-86. Edited by Heinrich Dörrie and others. Leiden: E. J. Brill

[Allamand, Jean-Nicolas-Sébastien]
1771 'Eloge historique de Mr. Albinus'. *Bibliothèque des sciences et des beaux arts*, 36, pt.2:416-65

Allen, Don Cameron
1949 *The Legend of Noah: Renaissance rationalism in art, science, and letters*. Urbana: University of Illinois Press

Alquié, Ferdinand
1974 *Le Cartésianisme de Malebranche*. Paris: Librairie philosophique J. Vrin

Amano, Keitaro
1961 *Bibliography of the classical economics. Part I*. The Science Council of Japan, Economic Series, no. 27. Tokyo

Ambri Berselli, P.
1955 'Lettre di illustri francesi a F. M. Zanotti'. *Strenna storica bolognese*, 5:17-33

Anderson, Lorin
1976 'Charles Bonnet's taxonomy and chain of being'. *Journal of the history of ideas*, 37:45-58
1982 *Charles Bonnet and the order of the known*. Studies in the History of Modern Science, 11. Dordrecht: D. Reidel Publishing Company

André, Yves
1886 *La Vie du R. P. Malebranche, prêtre de l'Oratoire, avec l'histoire de ses ouvrages* [...] publiée par le P. Ingold. Paris: Poussielgue

344   *Bibliography*

Anker, Jean
    1943 *Otto Friderich Müller*. Bibliotheca Universitatis Hauniensis, 2. København:Ejnar Munksgaard

Anspach, Isaac Salomon
    [1793] *Discours* [...] *prononcé le Jeudi 8 d'Août 1793, l'an 2e. de l'Egalité. Après le placement de l'inscription en l'honneur de Charles Bonnet*. n.p.

Anstruther, Godfrey
    1968-1977 *The Seminary priests: a dictionary of the secular clergy of England and Wales 1558-1850*. 4 vols. Ware: St Edmund's College, Durham: Ushaw College (vol. i); Great Wakering: Mayhew-McCrimmon (vols. ii-iv)

Appleton, William W.
    1951 *A cycle of Cathay: the Chinese vogue in England during the seventeenth and eighteenth centuries*. New York: Columbia University Press

Archinard, Margarida
    1977 'L'apport genevois à l'hygrométrie'. *Gesnerus*, 34:362-82

Badaloni, Nicola
    1967 'Storia della natura e storia dell'uomo in uno sconosciuto vichiano del 700: Antonio Vallisneri junior'. *Critica storica*, 6:783-820

Baker, Henry
    1742 *The Microscope made easy*. London: Printed for R. Dodsley
    1753 *Employment for the microscope*. London: Printed for R. Dodsley

Baker, John R.
    1952 *Abraham Trembley of Geneva: scientist and philosopher 1710-1784*. London: Edward Arnold

Baldensperger, Fernand
    1931 'Voltaire et la diplomatie française dans les affaires de Genève'. *Revue de littérature comparée*, 11:581-606
    1940 'Court de Gébelin et l'importance de son *Monde Primitif*'. In *Mélanges de philologie et d'histoire littéraire offerts à Edmond Huguet*, pp.315-30. Paris: Pierre André

Baldi, Marialuisa
    1979 *Filosofia e cultura a Mantova nella seconda metà del Settecento*. Firenze: La Nuova Italia

Baldini, Massimo
    1980 'C'era una volta un re [...]'. *Rivista di biologia*, 73:165-77

Balmer, Heinz
    1977 *Albrecht von Haller*. Berner Heimatbücher, 119. Bern: Verlag Paul Haupt

Barnard, John
    1973 *Pope: the critical heritage*. London, Boston: Routledge & Kegan Paul

Barnes, Annie
    1938 *Jean Le Clerc (1657-1736) et la république des lettres*. Paris: Droz

Barr, Mary-Margaret H.
    1929 *A bibliography of writings on Voltaire 1825-1925*. New York: Publications of the Institute of French Studies

Barr, Mary-Margaret H., and Spear, Frederick A.
    1968 *Quarante années d'études voltairiennes. Bibliographie analytique des livres et articles sur Voltaire, 1926-1965*. Paris: Librairie Armand Colin

Barthélemy, Jean-Jacques
    1797 *Œuvres diverses*. 2 vols. Paris: Chez H. J. Jansen

Bartoli, Giuseppe
1762a *Lettera prima sopra il marmo effigiato ed iscritto ch'è collocato nel Regio Museo, e diede occasione ad un libretto del Signor Needham.* Torino: Presso il Mairesse
1762b *Lettera seconda, nella quale si pubblicano i veri caratteri del noto busto, e si spiega una antica pittura d'Ercolano, incisa nella tavola XVII del tomo II.* Torino: Presso il Mairesse

Bayle, Pierre
1720 *Dictionaire historique et critique.* Troisième édition, revue, corrigée, et augmentée par l'auteur. 4 vols. Rotterdam: Chez Michel Bohm
1725-1727 *Œuvres diverses.* 4 vols. La Haye: P. Husson

Bazin, Gilles-Augustin
1744a *Histoire naturelle des abeilles.* 2 vols. Paris: Chez les frères Guérin
1744b *The Natural history of bees.* London: Printed for J. and P. Knapton

Beatty, F. M.
1955 'The scientific work of the third Earl Stanhope'. *Notes and records of the Royal Society of London*, 11:202-21

Bedford, John, Duke of
1842-1846 *Correspondence of John, fourth Duke of Bedford: selected from the originals at Woburn Abbey.* With an Introduction by Lord John Russell. 3 vols. London: Printed for Longman, Brown [etc.]

Belloni, Luigi
1961 'Dalle "Riproduzioni animali" di Spallanzani agli "Innesti animali" di G. Baronio'. *Physis*, 3:37-48
1969 'Il primo ventennio della microscopia (Galilei 1610-Harvey 1628). Dalla microscopia alla anatomia microscopica dell'insetto'. *Clio medica*, 4:179-90
1976 'Asterischi spallanzaniani'. *Physis*, 18:104-11
1977 'Charles Bonnet e Vincenzo Malacarne sul cervelletto quale sede dell'anima e sulla impressione basilare del cranio nel cretinismo'. *Physis*, 19:111-60

Bengesco, Georges
1882-1890 *Voltaire: bibliographie de ses œuvres.* 4 vols. Paris: Librairie Académique Didier

Bentley, Jerry H.
1978 'Erasmus, Le Clerc, and the principle of the harder reading'. *Renaissance quarterly*, 31:309-21

Bernoulli, Daniel II
1787 'Vita Danielis Bernoulli'. *Nova acta helvetica*, 1:1-32

Bertrandi, Ambrogio
1786-1799 *Opere.* Pubblicate, e accresciute di note, e di supplementi dai chirurghi Gio. Antonio Penchienati e Gioanni Brugnone. 11 vols. Torino: Presso i Fratelli Reycends

Besterman, Theodore
1965 'Voltaire, absolute monarchy, and the enlightened monarch'. *Studies on Voltaire*, 32:7-21
1967 'Voltaire's god'. *Studies on Voltaire*, 55:23-41
1976 *Voltaire.* Third edition revised and enlarged. Oxford: Basil Blackwell

Biblioteka
1961 *Biblioteka Vol'tera: katalog knig; Bibliothèque de Voltaire: catalogue des livres.* Moskva, Leningrad: Izdatel'stvo Akademii Nauk SSSR

Bilancioni, Guglielmo (ed.)
1914 *Carteggio inedito di G. B. Morgagni con Giovanni Bianchi.* Bari: Società tipografica editrice barese

Bodemer, Charles W.

1964 'Regeneration and the decline of preformationism in eighteenth century embryology'. *Bulletin of the history of medicine*, 38:20-31

Bodenheimer, Friedrich Simon

1928-1929 *Materialien zur Geschichte der Entomologie bis Linné.* 2 vols. Berlin: W. Junk

Boiteux, Lucas Alexandre

1950-1952 'Le rolle de d'Alembert dans la querelle Rousseau-Hume'. *Annales de la Société Jean-Jacques Rousseau*, 32:143-54

Bonar, James

1932 *A catalogue of the library of Adam Smith.* Second edition. London: Macmillan and Co.

Bonino, Giovanni Giacomo

1824-1825 *Biografia medica piemontese.* 2 vols. Torino: Dalla tipografia Bianco

Bonnard, George A. (ed.)

1961 *Gibbon's journey from Geneva to Rome: his Journal from 20 April to 2 October 1764* London, Edinburgh [etc.]: Thomas Nelson and Sons

Bonnet, Charles

1745 *Traité d'insectologie.* 2 vols. Paris: Chez Durand

1754 *Recherches sur l'usage des feuilles dans les plantes, et sur quelques autres sujets relatifs à l'histoire de la vegetation.* Gottingue, Leide: Chez Elie Luzac, Fils

1755 *Essai de psychologie; ou considerations sur les operations de l'ame, sur l'habitude et sur l'education.* [...] Londres [Leyde]

1760 *Essai analytique sur les facultés de l'ame.* Copenhague: Chez les Freres Cl. & Ant. Philibert

1762 *Considérations sur les corps organisés.* 2 vols. Amsterdam: Chez Marc-Michel Rey

1764 *Contemplation de la nature.* 2 vols. Amsterdam: Chez Marc-Michel Rey

1766a *Betrachtung über die Natur.* Leipzig: J. H. Junius

1766b *The Contemplation of Nature.* 2 vols. London: Printed for T. Longman [etc.]

1769a *La Palingénésie philosophique, ou idées sur l'état passé et sur l'état futur des êtres vivans* [...] *et qui contient principalement le précis de ses Recherches sur le christianisme.* 2 vols. Genève: Chez Claude Philibert et Barthelemi Chirol

1769b *Philosophische Untersuchung der Beweise für das Christenthum.* Zürich: Fuesslin

1769-1770a *Philosophische Palingenesie.* 2 vols. Zürich: Bey Orell [etc.]

1769-1770b *Contemplazione della natura.* 2 vols. Modena: Appresso Giovanni Montanari

1770a *La Palingénésie philosophique, ou idées sur l'état passé et sur l'état futur des êtres vivans* [...] *et qui contient principalement le précis de ses Recherches sur le christianisme.* [2nd ed.] 2 vols. Genève, Lyon: Chez Jean-Marie Bruyset

1770b *Recherches philosophiques sur les preuves du christianisme. Nouvelle édition, où l'on trouvera quelques additions, & des notes propres à faciliter l'intelligence de l'ouvrage à un plus grand nombre de lecteurs.* Genève: Chez Claude Philibert & Bart. Chirol

1770c 'Lettre sur les abeilles, adressée à Messieurs les auteurs du Journal des sçavans'. *Journal des sçavans*, November 1770, pp.746-53

1771a *Recherches philosophiques sur les preuves du christianisme. Seconde édition, où l'on trouvera quelques additions, en particulier sur l'existence de Dieu & des notes propres à faciliter l'intelligence de l'ouvrage à un plus grand nombre de lecteurs.* Genève: Chez Claude Philibert & Barth. Chirol

1771b *Ricerche filosofiche sopra le prove del cristianesimo.* Venezia: Presso Antonio Graziosi

1771c *Philosophische navorschingen van de bewyzen voor het Christendom.* 'sGravenhage: J. Thierry

1774a 'Maniere dont on peut concevoir la nutrition & l'accroissement des germes avant la fécondation dans l'hypothese de l'emboîtement'. *Observations sur la physique, sur l'histoire naturelle et sur les arts*, 3:174-80

1774b 'Idées sur la fécondation des plantes'. *Observations sur la physique, sur l'histoire naturelle et sur les arts*, 4:261-83

1775a 'Premier mémoire sur les abeilles, où l'on rend compte d'une nouvelle découverte fort singulière, qui a été faite en Luzace sur ces mouches'. *Observations sur la physique, sur l'histoire naturelle et sur les arts*, 5:327-44

1775b 'Second mémoire, contenant la suite des decouvertes faites en Luzace sur les abeilles'. *Observations sur la physique, sur l'histoire naturelle et sur les arts*, 5:418-28

1775c 'Troisième mémoire sur les abeilles, où l'on expose les principaux résultats des nouvelles expériences qui ont été faites sur ces mouches dans le Palatinat'. *Observations sur la physique, sur l'histoire naturelle et sur les arts*, 6:23-32

1777a 'Nouvelles recherches sur la structure du taenia'. *Observations sur la physique, sur l'histoire naturelle et sur les arts*, 9:243-67

1777b 'Mémoire sur la reproduction des membres de la salamandre aquatique'. *Observations sur la physique, sur l'histoire naturelle et sur les arts*, 10:385-405

1777c 'Expériences sur la régénération de la tête du limaçon terrestre'. *Observations sur la physique, sur l'histoire naturelle et sur les arts*, 11:165-79

1779 'Expériences sur la reproduction des membres de la salamandre aquatique. Second mémoire'. *Observations sur la physique, sur l'histoire naturelle et sur les arts*, 13:1-18

1779-1783 *Œuvres d'histoire naturelle et de philosophie*. 8 vols. in 10 parts (4°), Neuchâtel: De l'Imprimerie de Samuel Fauche. 18 vols. (8°), Neuchâtel: Chez Samuel Fauche, Libraire du Roi. [Abbreviated as B.O.]

1781 *Considerazioni sopra i corpi organizzati […] recata dal francese dal P.F.F.N.N., sacerdote professo carmelitano scalzo della Provincia di Toscana*. 2 vols. Venezia: Appresso Francesco di Nicolò Pezzana

1787 *Philosophical and critical inquiries concerning Christianity*. London: Printed for J. Stockdale [etc.]

Bonnet, Georges
1930 *Charles Bonnet (1720-1793)*. Paris: Librairie M. Lac

Bork, Kennard B.
1974 'The geological insights of Louis Bourguet (1678-1742)'. *Journal of the scientific laboratories, Denison University*, 55:49-77

Borst, Arno
1957-1963 *Der Turmbau von Babel. Geschichte der Meinungen über Ursprung und Vielfalt der Sprache und Völker*. 4 vols in 6 parts. Stuttgart: Anton Hiersemann

Boscovich, Ruggiero Giuseppe
1980 *Lettere a Giovan Stefano Conti*. A cura di Gino Arrighi. Firenze: L. S. Olschki

Bosdari, Filippo
1928 'Francesco Maria Zanotti nella vita bolognese del Settecento'. *Atti e Memorie della Deputazione di storia patria per le provincie di Romagna*, serie 4, 18:157-222

Bouchard, Ernest
1861-1863 'Notice biographique sur Henri Griffet'. *Bulletin de la Société d'émulation du Département de l'Allier*, 8:363-418

Boufflers, Stanislas Jean de
1806 *Eloge historique de M. l'abbé Barthélemy*. Paris: Chez L. M. Guillaume

Bouillier, Francisque
1868 *Histoire de la philosophie cartésienne*. 2 vols. Paris: Ch. Delagrave et Cie

Bourde, André J.
1967 *Agronomie et agronomes en France au XVIIIe siècle*. 3 vols. Paris: S. E. V. P. E. N.

348   *Bibliography*

Bourguet, Louis
    1728 'Lettre de Mr. L. B. P. à Monsieur Antoine Vallisnieri [...] sur la gradation &
        l'échelle des fossiles'. *Bibliothèque italique*, 2:99-131
    1729 *Lettres philosophiques sur la formation des sels et des crystaux, et sur la génération & le
        mechanisme organique des plantes et des animaux.* Amsterdam: Chez François l'Honoré
    1742 *Traité des petrifications. Avec figures.* Paris: Chez Briasson
    1762 *Lettres philosophiques sur la formation des sels et des crystaux, et sur la génération & le
        mechanisme organique des plantes et des animaux.* Amsterdam: Chez Marc-Michel Rey
Bowler, Peter J.
    1973 'Bonnet and Buffon: theories of generation and the problem of species'. *Journal
        of the history of biology*, 6:259-81
Bradney, Joseph Alfred
    1904-1932 *A history of Monmouthshire, from the coming of the Normans into Wales down to the
        present time.* 4 vols. London: Mitchell Hughes and Clarke
Brady, Frank, and Pottle, Frederick A. (eds.)
    1955 *Boswell on the Grand Tour: Italy, Corsica, and France 1765-1766.* Melbourne, London,
        Toronto: William Heinemann Ltd
Brechka, Frank T.
    1970 *Gerard Van Swieten and his world 1700-1772.* The Hague: Martinus Nijhoff
Browne, Janet
    1983 *The Secular ark: studies in the history of biogeography.* New Haven: Yale University
        Press
Brumfitt, John Henry
    1958 *Voltaire historian.* London: Oxford University Press
Brunet, Pierre
    1934 'Un grand débat sur la physique de Malebranche au XVIIIe siècle'. *Isis*, 20:367-
        95
Bucher, Heini W.
    1958 *Tissot und sein Traité des nerfs.* Zürcher medizingeschichtliche Abhandlungen, N.
        R. 1. Zürich
Budé, Eugène-Guillaume-Théodore de
    1893 *Vie de Jacob Vernet, théologien genevois 1698-1789.* Lausanne: G. Bridel
Buess, Heinrich
    1942 'Zur Entwicklung der Irritabilitätslehre'. In *Festschrift für Jacques Brodbeck-Sandreu-
        ter* [...] *zu seinem 60. Geburtstag*, pp.299-333. Basel
    1958 'Zur Entstehung der *Elementa physiologiae* Albrecht Hallers (1708-1777)'. *Gesnerus*,
        15:17-35
Buffon, Georges Louis Leclerc, comte de
    1749-1789 *Histoire naturelle, générale et particulière, avec la description du cabinet du roy.* 31
        vols. Paris: De l'Imprimerie Royale
    1750-1772 *Allgemeine Historie der Natur nach allen ihren besondern Theilen abgehandelt.* 8 vols.
        Hamburg, Leipzig: G. C. Grund und A. H. Holle
    1954 *Œuvres philosophiques.* Texte établi et présenté par Jean Piveteau. Corpus général
        des philosophes français, t.xli, 1. Paris: Presses Universitaires de France
    1962 *Les Epoques de la nature.* Edition critique par J. Roger. Mémoires du Muséum
        national d'histoire naturelle, Série c, Sciences de la Terre, t.x. Paris: Editions du
        Muséum
Burnet, Thomas
    1681 *Telluris theoria sacra: orbis nostri originem & mutationes generales, quas aut jam subiit,
        aut olim subiturus est, complectens. Libri duo priores de diluvio & paradiso.* Londini: Typis
        R. N. Impensis Gualt. Kettilby

1684 *The Theory of the Earth: containing an account of the original of the Earth, and of all the general changes which it hath already undergone, or is to undergo, till the consummation of all things. The two first books concerning the Deluge, and concerning Paradise.* London: Printed by R. Norton, for Walter Kettilby

1692 *Archaeologiae philosophicae: sive doctrina antiqua de rerum originibus.* Londini: Typis R. N. Impensis Gualt. Kettilby

[Butler, Samuel]

1757 *Hudibras. A poem written in the time of the civil wars; Hudibras. Poëme ecrit dans le tems des troubles d'Angleterre.* [Translated by John Towneley; edited by John Turberville Needham.] 3 vols. London

Byron, John

1768 *The Narrative of the honourable John Byron* [...] *containing an account of the great distresses suffered by himself and his companions on the coast of Patagonia, from the year 1740, till their arrival in England, 1746.* [...] London: Printed for S. Baker and G. Leigh [etc.]

Cabeen, David Clark

1947 *Montesquieu: a bibliography.* New York: The New York Public Library

1955 'A supplementary Montesquieu bibliography'. *Revue internationale de philosophie*, 9:409-34

Candaux, Jean-Daniel

1979 'Voltaire: biographie, bibliographie et éditions critiques'. *Revue d'histoire littéraire de la France*, 79:296-319

1980 'La révolution genevoise de 1782: un état de la question'. *Etudes sur le XVIIIe siècle*, 7:77-93

Caraman, [Victor-Antoine Charles de Riquet], duc de

1859 *Charles Bonnet philosophe et naturaliste. Sa vie et ses œuvres.* Paris: A. Vaton

Casini, Paolo

1958 'Studi su Diderot'. *Rassegna di filosofia*, 7:5-26, 150-73, 234-54

1978 'Les débuts du newtonianisme en Italie, 1700-1740'. *Dix-huitième siècle*, 10:85-100

1980 'Ottica, astronomia, relatività: Boscovich a Roma, 1738-1748'. *Rivista di filosofia*, n.18:354-81

Castellani, Carlo

1969 'Il "mistero della generazione" nell'opera di Charles Bonnet e nelle sue lettere a Lazzaro Spallanzani'. *Revista de la Sociedad mexicana de historia natural*, 30:345-71

1969-1970 'L'origine degli infusori nella polemica Needham, Spallanzani, Bonnet'. *Episteme*, 3:214-41; 4:19-36

1971 (ed.) *Lettres à M. l'abbé Spallanzani de Charles Bonnet.* Edizione critica condotta sugli originali, introduzione e note di Carlo Castellani. Milano: Episteme editrice

1972 'The problem of generation in Bonnet and Buffon: a critical comparison'. In *Science, medicine, and society in the Renaissance: essays to honor Walter Pagel*, 2:265-88. Edited by Allen G. Debus. 2 vols. New York: Science History Publications

1973 'I rapporti tra Lazzaro Spallanzani e John T. Needham'. *Physis*, 15:73-106

1977 'Il problema della generazione in alcuni inediti spallanzaniani'. *Contributi*, 1:91-101

1978 'Appunti per uno studio della biologia post-spallanzaniana: 1780-1820'. *Physis*, 20:5-29

1979 'Una rilettura ottocentesca di Spallanzani: la *Nouvelle théorie de la génération* di Prévost e Dumas (1824)'. *History and philosophy of the life sciences*, 1:215-59

Catalogue

1777 *A catalogue of several valuable libraries, lately purchased, including the books of natural history, philosophy and physick, of M. Matty.* [...] London: By Benjamin White

1782 *Catalogue des livres de feu M. l'abbé Needham*. Bruxelles: Chez Lemaire

1789 *Catalogue des livres de la bibliothèque de feu M. le Baron d'Holbach*. Paris: Chez De Bure

1800 *Catalogue des livres de la bibliothèque de feu l'abbé Barthélemy*. Paris: Chez Bernard et Thuret

Ceitac, Jane

1956a *L'Affaire des natifs et Voltaire*. Thèse de l'Université de Lausanne. Genève: Librairie E. Droz

1956b 'Négociations sur le projet secret de Tronchin avant le projet de conciliation de 1768'. *Schweizerische Zeitschrift für Geschichte*, 6:456-91

Cesi, Federico, and Stelluti, Francesco

1625 *Apiarium* [or *Melissographia*]. Romae

Cetto, Benedetto

1776 *De argumentis e Sinensium annalibus pro Hungarorum origine demonstranda desumtis dissertatio*. Viennae: Typis Schulzianis

Chichester-Constable, Cecil Hugh, and Courtois, Louis-J.

1932 'Jean-Jacques Rousseau et William Constable (Correspondance inédite)'. *Annales de la Société Jean-Jacques Rousseau*, 21:157-76

Chouillet, Anne-Marie *see* Chouillet, Jacques

Chouillet, Jacques

1979 'Etat présent des études sur Diderot'. *L'Information littéraire*, 31:103-14

Chouillet, Jacques, and Chouillet, Anne-Marie

1980 'Etat actuel des recherches sur Diderot'. *Dix-huitième siècle*, 12:443-70

Christophersen, Halfdan Olavs

1930 *A bibliographical introduction to the study of John Locke*. Oslo: Norske Videnskaps-Akademi

[Cibot]

1773 *Lettre de Pekin, sur le génie de la langue chinoise, et la nature de leur écriture symbolique, comparée avec celle des anciens Egyptiens*. [Edited and with a preface by John Turberville Needham.] Bruxelles: Chez J. L. Bourbes

Cioranescu, Alexandre

1969 *Bibliographie de la littérature française du dix-huitième siècle*. 3 vols. Paris: Editions du Centre National de la Recherche Scientifique

Claparède, David

1765 *Considerations sur les miracles de l'evangile, pour servir de reponse aux difficultés de Mr. J. J. Rousseau, dans sa 3ᵉ. lettre ecrite de la montagne*. Genève: Chez Claude Philibert

Claparède, Edouard

1909 *La Psychologie animale de Charles Bonnet*. Genève: Librairie Georg & Cie

Cocchi, Antonio

1737 *Elogio di Pietro Antonio Micheli*. Firenze: Per Gio. Gaetano Tartini e Santi Franchi

Cole, Francis Joseph

1944 *A history of comparative anatomy from Aristotle to the eighteenth century*. London: Macmillan

Collier, Katherine Brownell

1934 *Cosmogonies of our Fathers: some theories of the seventeenth and the eighteenth centuries*. New York: Columbia University Press

[Colmont de Vaulgrenand, Henri-Camille]

1770 *Les Vrais quakers, ou les exhortations, harangues, & prédictions des vrais serviteurs du Seigneur Dieu: à un mechant frere, specialement au sujet de ses maximes sur le luxe, & de ses persécutions contre un frere dans le malheur. Ouvrage à la suite du quel on a inseré un mémoire* [by Needham] *vraiment curieux par son étonnante analogie avec ce qui précede.* Londres

1771 *Les Vrais quakers, ou les exhortations, harangues, & prédictions des vrais serviteurs du Seigneur Dieu à un mechant frere, specialement au sujet de ses maximes sur le luxe, & de ses persécutions contre un frere dans le malheur. Ouvrage posthume à la suite duquel on a joint le Parallele* [by Needham] *le plus-curieux des deux celébres littératuers; & plusieurs pieces critiques, morales & philosophiques, sous le titre de Correspondance entre un oncle & son neveu.* Londres, Paris: L. Parault; Bruxelles: A. d'Ours

A concise
1766 *A concise and genuine account of the dispute between Mr. Hume and Mr. Rousseau: with the letters that passed between them during their controversy.* London: Printed for T. Becket and P. A. De Hondt

Condillac, Etienne Bonnot de
1754 *Traité des sensations.* 2 vols. Londres, Paris: de Bure aîné

Conlon, Pierre M.
1967 'La Condamine the inquisitive'. *Studies on Voltaire*, 55:361-93
1981 *Ouvrages français relatifs à Jean-Jacques Rousseau 1751-1799. Bibliographie chronologique.* Genève: Librairie Droz

Corpus
1979- *Corpus des notes marginales de Voltaire.* Berlin: Akademie-Verlag

Corradi, Alfonso (ed.)
1876 *Lettere di Lancisi a Morgagni e parecchie altre dello stesso Morgagni ora per la prima volta pubblicate.* Pavia: Stabilimento tipografico successori Bizzoni

Costa, Gustavo
1967 'Boscovich e Spallanzani. (Documenti di una polemica)'. *Rivista critica di storia della filosofia,* 22:294-302

Court de Gébelin, Antoine
1773-1782 *Monde primitif, analysé et comparé avec le monde moderne.* [...] 9 vols. Paris: Chez l'Auteur, Boudet [etc.]

Courtheoux, Jean-Paul
1957 'Observations et idées économiques de Réaumur'. *Revue d'histoire économique et sociale,* 35:347-69

Courtois, Louis-J.
1923 'Chronologie critique de la vie et des œuvres de Jean-Jacques Rousseau'. *Annales de la Société Jean-Jacques Rousseau,* 15:1-366

Courtois, Louis-J. *see also* Chichester-Constable, Cecil Hugh

Coyer, Gabriel-François
1782-1783 *Œuvres complettes de M. l'Abbé Coyer.* 7 vols. Paris: Chez la Veuve Duchesne, Libraire

Cramer, Marc
1962 'Jean Jallabert (1712-1768) inventeur de l'électrothérapie'. *Musées de Genève,* nr. 25, 3:12-14

Cranston, Maurice
1957 *John Locke: a biography.* London: Longmans Green and Co.
1962 'Rousseau's visit to England, 1766-7'. *Essays by divers hands being the Transactions of the Royal Society of Literature,* N. S., 31:16-34

Croft, William
1902 *Historical account of Lisbon College.* With a Register compiled by Joseph Gillow. London: S. Anselm's Society

Crucitti Ullrich, Francesca Bianca
    1974   La 'Bibliothèque italique': cultura 'italianisante' e giornalismo letterario. Milano, Napoli:
            Riccardo Ricciardi editore
Curto, Silvio
    1962-1963   'Storia di un falso celebre'. Bollettino della Società piemontese di archeologia e di
            belle arti, N.S., 16-17:5-15
Cuvier, Georges
    1819-1827   'Eloges historiques de Charles Bonnet et H. B. de Saussure'. In Recueil des
            éloges historiques lus dans les séances publiques de l'Institut royal de France, 1:383-430. 3 vols.
            Strasbourg, Paris: F. G. Levrault
Da Costa, Emanuel Mendez
    1761   'An Account of some productions of nature in Scotland resembling the Giants-
            Causeway in Ireland: in a letter to the Right Reverend Richard Lord Bishop of
            Offory, F.R.S.'. Philosophical transactions, 52:103-4
Dardier, Charles
    1890   Court de Gébelin. Notice sur sa vie et ses écrits. Nîmes: Imprimerie Clavel et Chastanier
Darnton, Robert
    1979   The Business of Enlightenment: a publishing history of the Encyclopédie 1775-1800.
            Cambridge, Mass.: The Belknap Press of Harvard University Press
David, Madeleine-V.
    1961   'En marge du mémoire de l'abbé Barthélemy sur les inscriptions phéniciennes
            (1758)'. Comptes rendus des séances de l'Académie des inscriptions et belles-lettres, pp.30-42
    1965   Le Débat sur les écritures et l'hiéroglyphe aux XVIIe et XVIIIe siècles, et l'application de
            la notion de déchiffrement aux écritures mortes. Paris: S. E. V. P. E. N.
Davin, Emmanuel
    1961   'Un éminent sinologue toulonnais du XVIIIe siècle le R. P. Amiot, S. J. (1718-
            1793)'. Bulletin de l'Association Guillaume Budé, quatrième série, numéro 3: 380-95
Davis, Walter W.
    1974   Joseph II: an imperial reformer for the Austrian Netherlands. The Hague: Martinus
            Nijhoff
Dawson, Warren R.
    1932   'An eighteenth-century discourse on hieroglyphs'. In Studies presented to F. LL.
            Griffith, pp.465-73. London: Egypt Exploration Society
    1935-1938   'Louis Poinsinet de Sivry on hieroglyphs'. Mélanges Maspero. Mémoires publiés
            par les membres de l'Institut français d'archéologie orientale du Caire, 66, pt.1:367-71
De Beer, Gavin
    1962   'The volcanoes of Auvergne'. Annals of science, 18:49-61
De Beer, Gavin, and Rousseau, André-Michel
    1967   'Voltaire's British visitors'. Studies on Voltaire, 49:5-201
De Boom, Ghislaine
    1932   Les Ministres plénipotentiaires dans les Pays-Bas autrichiens, principalement Cobenzl.
            Académie royale de Belgique. Classe des lettres. [...] Collection in-8°, série 2, t.xxxi.
            Bruxelles: Maurice Lamertin
Debraw, John
    1777   'Discoveries on the sex of bees, explaining the manner in which their species is
            propagated; with an account of the utility that may be derived from those discoveries
            by the actual application of them to practice'. Philosophical transactions, 67, pt.1:15-
            32

De Dominicis, E.

1978 'Ambiguità di Locke? Rassegna di recenti studi lockiani'. *Bollettino dell'Istituto di Filosofia dell'Università di Macerata (1976-1977)*, pp.163-217. Roma: Edizioni Abete

De Keller, Augusto

1881 *Bibliografia universale di apicoltura*. Milano: Ulrico Hoepli

Delany, Mary

1861-1862 *The Autobiography and correspondence of Mary Granville, Mrs Delany*. [...] Edited by [...] Lady Llanover. 3 vols of the first series + 3 vols of the second series. London

Delaporte, François

1977 'Des organismes problématiques'. *Dix-huitième siècle*, 9:49-59

Della Torre, Giovanni Maria

[1760] *Praeclarissimo viro Abbati Noleto publico physicae professori*. [Neapoli]

1763 *Nuove osservazioni intorno la storia naturale*. Napoli

1776 *Nuove osservazioni microscopiche*. Napoli

Delsedime, Piero

1971 'La disputa delle corde vibranti ed una lettera inedita di Lagrange a Daniel Bernoulli'. *Physis*, 13:117-46

De Luc, Jean-André

1779-1780 *Lettres physiques et morales sur l'histoire de la terre et de l'homme, adressées à la Reine de la Grande Bretagne*. 5 vols in 6 parts. Paris: Chez la Veuve Duchesne; La Haye: Chez De Turne

De Martino, Domenico

1978 'Spazio e tempo in Leonhard Euler'. In *Filosofia, scienza, politica nel Settecento francese*, pp.259-92. A cura di Paolo Rossi. Firenze: Cooperativa Editrice Universitaria

Descartes, René

1644 *Principia philosophiae*. Amstelodami: Apud Ludovicum Elzevirium

1664 *Le Monde de Mr Descartes, ou le traité de la lumiere, et des autres principaux objets des sens*. Paris: Chez Theodore Girad

1897-1910 *Œuvres*. Publiées par Charles Adam & Paul Tannery. 12 vols. Paris: Leopold Cerf

Deshautesrayes, Leroux

1759 *Doutes sur la dissertation de M. de Guignes, qui a pour titre: Memoire, dans lequel on prouve que les Chinois sont une colonie égyptienne*. Paris: Chez Laurent Prault et Duchesne

Desmarest, Nicolas

1774 'Mémoire sur l'origine & la nature du basalte à grandes colonnes polygones, déterminées par l'histoire naturelle de cette pierre, observée en Auvergne'. *Histoire de l'Académie royale des sciences. Année M.DCCLXXI. Avec les Mémoires* [...], pp.705-75

Desnoiresterres, Gustave

1875 *Voltaire et Genève*. Paris: Didier

Diaz, Furio

1958 *Voltaire storico*. Torino: Giulio Einaudi editore

Diderot, Denis

1749 *Lettre sur les aveugles, à l'usage de ceux qui voyent*. Londres

1964 *Eléments de physiologie*. Edition critique, avec une introduction et des notes, par Jean Mayer. Paris: Librairie Marcel Didier

1971 *Le Rêve de d'Alembert*. Texte intégral [...] présenté et annoté par Jean Varloot. Paris: Editions sociales

Diderot, Denis, and d'Alembert, Jean Le Rond (eds.)

1751-1765 *Encyclopédie, ou dictionnaire raisonné des sciences, des arts et des métiers, par une société de gens de lettres. Mis en ordre et publié par M. Diderot [...] et quant à la partie mathématique, par M. d'Alembert.* 17 vols. Paris: Briasson, David, Le Breton, Durand (vols i-vii); Neufchastel: S. Faulche (vols viii-xvii)

Dieckmann, Liselotte

1970 *Hieroglyphics: the history of a literary symbol.* St. Louis, Missouri: Washington University Press

Diermanse, P. J. J. *see* Meulen, Jacob ter

Di Pietro, Pericle

1976 'La "fecondazione artificiale" nel Settecento attraverso il carteggio tra Lazzaro Spallanzani e Giuseppe Bufalini'. *Physis,* 18:383-406

1977 'Inventario delle lettere a Lazzaro Spallanzani conservate a Modena ed a Reggio Emilia'. *Atti e memorie della deputazione di storia patria delle antiche provincie modenesi,* S. X, 12:155-72

1979 *Lazzaro Spallanzani.* Modena: Aedes Muratoriana

Doney, Willis

1978 'Some recent work on Descartes: a bibliography'. In *Descartes: critical and interpretive essays,* pp.299-312. Edited by Michael Hooker. Baltimore, London: The Johns Hopkins University Press

Donvez, Jacques

1955 'Une idée voltairienne: Versoix, ville de tolérance'. *La Revue française de l'élite européenne,* no 67:16-23

Dougherty, Frank William Peter

1980 'Buffon's gnoseological principle'. *Zeitschrift für allgemeine Wissenschaftstheorie,* 11:238-53

Dübi, Heinrich

1893 'Zwei vergessene Berner Gelehrte aus dem 18. Jahrhundert'. *Neujahrs-Blatt der Litterarischen Gesellschaft Bern aus das Jahr 1894,* pp.3-40

Duchesneau, François

1979 'Haller et les théories de Buffon et C. F. Wolff sur l'épigenèse'. *History and philosophy of the life sciences,* 1:65-100

Dufour, Théophile

1925 *Recherches bibliographiques sur les œuvres imprimées de J.-J. Rousseau.* 2 vols. Paris: L. Giraud-Badin

Duhamel Du Monceau, Henri-Louis

1758 *La Physique des arbres; où il est traité de l'anatomie des plantes et de l'économie végétale.* 2 vols. Paris: Chez H. L. Guerin & L. F. Delatour

Edit

1768 *Edit du 11. Mars 1768.* [Genève]

Eichwalder, Reinhard

1971 'Georg Adam Fürst Starhemberg (1724-1807) Diplomat, Staatsmann und Grundherr'. *Österreich in Geschichte und Literatur,* 15:193-203

Ellenberger, François

1978 'Précisions nouvelles sur la découverte des volcans de France: Guettard, ses prédécesseurs, ses émules clermontois'. *Histoire et nature,* 12/13:3-42

Ellis, Henry (ed.)

1843 *Original letters of eminent literary men of the sixteenth, seventeenth, and eighteenth centuries.* London: The Camden Society

Eneström, Gustaf
1910-1913 *Verzeichnis der Schriften Leonhard Eulers*. Jahresbericht der Deutschen Mathematiker-Vereinigung. Ergänzungsband 4. Leipzig: Druck und Verlag von B. G. Teubner

Euler, Leonhard
1768-1772 *Lettres à une princesse d'Allemagne sur divers sujets de physique & de philosophie*. 3 vols. Saint Petersbourg: de l'Imprimerie de l'Académie Impériale des Sciences

Exposé
1766 *Exposé succinct de la contestation qui s'est élevée entre M. Hume et M. Rousseau, avec les pieces justificatives*. Londres [Paris]

Eynard, Charles
1839 *Essai sur la vie de Tissot*. Lausanne: M. Ducloux

Fabroni, Angelo
1778-1805 *Vitae Italorum doctrina excellentium qui saeculis XVII. et XVIII floruerunt*. 20 vols. Pisis: Excudebat Carolus Ginesius; [Lucae: Typis Dominici Marescandoli]

Falletti, N.-Charles
1885 *Jacob Vernet théologien genevois 1698-1789*. Genève: Imprimerie Charles Schuchardt

Fantuzzi, Giovanni
1771-1794 *Notizie degli scrittori bolognesi*. 9 vols. Bologna: S. Tommaso d'Aquino
1778 *Notizie della vita e degli scritti di Francesco Maria Zanotti*. Bologna

Farber, Paul Lawrence
1975 'Buffon and Daubenton: divergent traditions within the *Histoire naturelle*'. *Isis*, 66:63-74

Farley, John
1977 *The Spontaneous generation controversy from Descartes to Oparin*. Baltimore, London: The Johns Hopkins University Press

Feil, Joseph
1861 'Versuche zur Gründung einer Akademie der Wissenschaften unter Maria Theresia'. *Jahrbuch für vaterländische Geschichte*, 1:319-407

Feiling, Keith Grahame
1959 *The Second Tory Party 1714-1832*. London: Macmillan [1st ed. 1938]

Fellows, Otis E., and Milliken, Stephen F.
1972 *Buffon*. New York: Twayne Publishers

Ferrier, Jean-Pierre
1922 *Le Duc de Choiseul, Voltaire et la création de Versoix la Ville*. Genève
1926 'L'interdiction de commerce et l'expulsion de France des Genevois en 1766'. *Etrennes genevoises*, pp.76-99
1927 'Un pamphlet genevois du XVIIIe siècle. Le Dictionnaire des Négatifs – 1766'. *Etrennes genevoises*, pp.75-85
1951 'Le XVIIIe siècle. Politique intérieure et extérieure'. In *Histoire de Genève des origines à 1798*, publiée par la Société d'Histoire et d'Archéologie de Genève, pp.401-82. Genève: Alexander Jullien

Foley, Henry
1877-1882 *Records of the English Province of the Society of Jesus*. 7 vols in 8. London: Burns and Oates

Fontana, Felice
1980 *Epistolario, 1. Carteggio con Leopoldo Marc'Antonio Caldani 1758-1794*. A cura di Renato G. Mazzolini e Giuseppe Ongaro. Trento: Società di Studi Trentini di Scienze Storiche

[Fontenelle, Bernard le Bovier de]
  1731 'Eloge de M. Maraldi'. *Histoire de l'Académie royale des sciences. Année MDCCXXIX. Avec les Mémoires* [...], pp.116-20
Formey, Jean-Henri-Samuel
  1769 *Entretiens psychologiques, tirés de l'Essai analytique sur les facultés de l'ame de Mr. Bonnet.* Berlin: Chez Joachim Pauli
  1789 *Souvenirs d'un citoyen.* 2 vols. Berlin: Chez François de La Garde
Fortescue, John (ed.)
  1927-1928 *The Correspondence of king George the Third from 1760 to December 1783.* 6 vols. London: Macmillan and Co.
François, Alexis
  1924 'Jean-Jacques Rousseau et la science genevoise au XVIIIe siècle: ses rapports avec les naturalistes De Luc'. *Revue d'histoire littéraire de la France,* 31:206-24
Frängsmyr, Tore
  1983 'Linnaeus as a geologist'. In *Linnaeus: the man and his work,* pp.110-55. Edited by Tore Frängsmyr. Berkeley: University of California Press
Fraser, Henry Malcolm
  1951a *Beekeeping in antiquity.* 2nd ed. London: University of London
  [1951b] *Anton Janscha on the swarming of bees.* Teddington: The Apis Club, 3/6
  1958 *History of beekeeping in Britain.* London: Bee Research Association
Freeman, R. B.
  1962 'Illustrations of insect anatomy from the beginning to the time of Cuvier'. *Medical and biological illustration,* 12:174-83
Freer, Alan J.
  1964 'Isaac de Pinto e la sua *Lettre à Mr. D[iderot] sur le jeu des cartes*'. *Annali della Scuola Normale Superiore di Pisa,* S. 2, 33:93-117
  1966 'Ancora su Isaac de Pinto'. *Annali della Scuola Normale Superiore di Pisa,* S. 2, 35:120-27
Freshfield, Douglas W., with the collaboration of Montagnier, Henry F.
  1920 *The Life of Horace Benedict de Saussure.* London: Edward Arnold
Frisi, Paolo
  1771 *Colombiade.* Milano: Marelli
Fritzsche, Oskar William
  1905 *Die Pädagogisch-didaktischen Theorien Charles Bonnets.* Innaugural-Dissertation [...] der Universität Leipzig. Langensalza: Druck von Hermann Beyer & Söhne
Gachard, Louis
  1838 'Rapport du prince de Kaunitz à Marie-Thérèse, sur l'érection d'une société des sciences et des belles-lettres à Bruxelles'. *Annuaire de l'Académie royale des sciences et belles-lettres de Bruxelles,* 4:151-78
  1840 'Documens relatifs à l'histoire de l'ancienne Académie impériale et royale de Bruxelles'. *Annuaire de l'Académie royale des sciences et belles-lettres de Bruxelles,* 6:36-109
Gagnebin, Bernard
  1955 'Le médiateur d'une petite querelle genevoise'. *Travaux sur Voltaire et le dix-huitieme siècle,* 1:115-23
Gaissinovitch, A. E.
  1961 *K. F. Vol'f i uchenie o razvitii organizmov (v svjazi s obshchej èvoljuciej nauchnogo mirovozzrenija).* Moskva: Izdatel'stvo Akademii Nauk SSSR
Galiffe, Jean-Barthélemy-Gaïfre
  1877 *D'un siècle à l'autre. Correspondances inédites entre gens connus et inconnus du XVIIIe et du XIXe siècle.* Genève: Jules Sandoz, éditeur

Garbari, Maria

1981 *Libertà scientifica e potere politico in due secoli di attività dell'Accademia Roveretana degli Agiati*. Rovereto: Accademia Roveretana degli Agiati

Gargano, Guido-Innocenzo

1981 *La Teoria di Gregorio di Nissa sul Cantico dei Cantici. Indagine su alcune indicazioni di metodo esegetico*. Roma: Pont. Institutum Studiorum Orientalium

Gargett, Graham

1980 *Voltaire and Protestantism*. Studies on Voltaire, 188. Oxford: The Voltaire Foundation

Gasking, Elizabeth

1967 *Investigations into generation, 1651-1828*. Baltimore: Johns Hopkins Press; London: Hutchinson Publishing Group

Gaspari, Gianmarco (ed.)

1980 *Viaggio a Parigi e Londra (1766-1767). Carteggio di Pietro a Alessandro Verri*. A cura di Gianmarco Gaspari. Milano: Adelphi edizioni

Gaullieur, Eusèbe-Henri

1855 'Charles Bonnet considéré comme homme politique'. *Etrennes nationales*, 3:16-41

[Gaultier, Jean Baptiste]

1751 *Les Lettres persannes convaincues d'impiété*. n.p.

Gauthier, Henri

1906 'Un précurseur de Champollion au XVIe siècle'. *Bulletin de l'Institut français d'archéologie orientale*, 5:65-86

Gay, Peter

1958 'Voltaire's *Idées républicaines*: a study in bibliography and interpretation'. *Studies on Voltaire*, 6:67-105

1965 *Voltaire's politics: the poet as realist*. New York: Random House [1st ed. Princeton: Princeton University Press, 1959]

Geike, Archibald

1905 *The Founders of geology*. 2nd ed. London: Macmillan and Co.

Geisendorf, Paul-F.

1966 *Bibliographie raisonnée de l'histoire de Genève des origines à 1798*. Genève: Alex. Jullien

Gembicki, Dieter

1972 'Jacob-Nicolas Moreau et son "Mémoire sur les fonctions d'un historiographe de France"'. *Dix-huitième siècle*, 4:191-215

Gens, A.

1978 'Die Kontroverse von R.A.F. de Réaumur und J.Th. Klein über Bau und Wachstum der Schneckenschalen'. *Janus*, 65:167-81

Gerbi, Antonello

1955 *La Disputa del nuovo mondo. Storia di una polemica 1750-1900*. Milano, Napoli: Riccardo Ricciardi Editore

Gianformaggio, Letizia

1979 *Diritto e felicità: la teoria del diritto in Helvétius*. Milano: Edizioni Comunità

Gibbon, Edward

1966 *Memoirs of my Life*. Edited from the manuscripts by Georges A. Bonnard. London: Nelson

Gillispie, Charles Coulston

1969 *Genesis and geology*. Cambridge, Mass.: Harvard University Press [1st ed. 1951]

Gillow, Joseph
    1885-1903 *A literary and biographical history, or bibliographical dictionary of the English Catholics: from the breach with Rome, in 1534, to the present time.* 5 vols. London, New York: Burns & Oates

Giordani, Francesco
    1973 'La teoria dell'inoculazione di S. A. Tissot vista alla luce delle recenti scoperte nel campo dell'immunologia'. *Rivista di storia della medicina,* 17:59-67

Giordano, Davide
    1941 *Giambattista Morgagni.* Torino: U. T. E. T.

Glock, Johann Philipp
    1891 *Die Symbolik der Bienen und ihrer Produkte in Sage, Dichtung, Kultus, Kunst und Bräuchen der Völker.* [...] Heidelberg: Verlag Theodor Groos

Gode-von Aesch, Alexander
    1941 *Natural science in German romanticism.* New York: Columbia University Press

Gooch, G. P. *see* Stanhope, Ghita

Gottdenker, Paula
    1980 'Three clerics in pursuit of "little animals"'. *Cio medica,* 14:213-24

Gould, Stephen Jay
    1977 *Ontogeny and phylogeny.* Cambridge, Mass.: The Belknap Press of Harvard University Press

Goulding, Richard W.
    1913 'John Achard, a duke's tutor and friend'. *The National review,* 62, no.367:85-101

Grass, Nikolaus
    1948 'Die Innsbrucker Gelehrtenakademie des 18. Jh. und das Stift Wilten'. *Tiroler Heimatblätter,* 23:13-19

Grassé, Pierre-P.
    1956 *Réaumur et l'analyse des phénomènes instinctifs.* Les Conférences du Palais de la Découverte, Série D, no 48. Paris: Librairie du Palais de la Découverte

[Greene, Edward Burnaby]
    1766 *A defence of Mr. Rousseau, against the aspersions of Mr. Hume, Mons. Voltaire, and their associates.* London: Printed for S. Bladon

Gregory of Nyssa
    1863 *Opera* (Migne). 3 vols. Paris: Apud J.-P. Migne

Griffet, Henri
    1758 *Histoire du regne de Louis XIII, Roi de France et de Navarre.* 3 vols. Paris: Chez les Libraires Associés
    1769 *Traité des différentes sortes de preuves qui servent à établir la vérité de l'histoire.* Liège: Chez J. F. Bassompierre

Griffith, Reginald Harvey
    1922-1927 *Alexander Pope: a bibliography.* 1 vol. in 2 parts. Austin: The University of Texas

Grimsley, Ronald
    1963 *Jean d'Alembert (1717-1783).* Oxford: Clarendon Press

Guasco, Ottaviano
    1768 *De l'usage des statues chez les anciens. Essai historique.* Bruxelles: Chez J. L. de Boubers

Guerinot, Joseph Vincent
    1969 *Pamphlet attacks on Alexander Pope 1711-1744: a descriptive bibliography.* London: Methuen

Guerlac, Henry

1977 'The Newtonianism of Dortus de Mairan'. In *Essays and papers in the history of modern science*, pp.479-90. Baltimore, London: The Johns Hopkins University Press

Gueroult, Martial

1954 'Métaphysique et physique de la force chez Descartes et Malebranche'. *Revue de métaphysique et de morale*, 59:113-34

Guettard, Jean-Etienne

1756 'Mémoire sur quelques montagnes de la France qui ont été des volcans'. *Histoire de l'Académie royale des sciences. Année M.DCCLII. Avec les Mémoires* [...], pp.27-59

Guibert, Albert Jean

1976 *Bibliographie des œuvres de René Descartes publiées au XVIIIe siècle*. Paris: Editions du C.N.R.S.

Guignes, Joseph de

1759a *Mémoire dans lequel on prouve, que les Chinois sont une colonie égyptienne*. Paris: Chez Desaint & Saillant

1759b *Réponse aux doutes proposés par Monsieur Deshautesrayes, sur la dissertation qui a pour titre: Mémoire dans lequel on prouve que les Chinois sont une colonie égyptienne*. Paris: Chez Michel Lambert

1760 *Mémoire dans lequel on prouve, que les Chinois sont une colonie égyptienne*. Nouvelle édition. Paris: Chez Desaint & Saillant

1764 'Mémoire dans lequel [...] on essaye d'établir que le caractère épistolique [...] des Egyptiens se retrouve dans les caractères des Chinois, & que la nation chinoise est une colonie égyptienne'. *Histoire de l'Académie royale des inscriptions et belles-lettres, avec les Mémoires* [...], 29:1-26

1774 'Lettre à Messieurs les auteurs du Journal des Sçavans, concernant un ouvrage de M. de P*** intitulé: Recherches philosophiques sur les Egyptiens & sur les Chinois [...]'. *Journal des sçavans*, April, pp.218-28

1780 'Observations sur quelques points concernant la religion & la philosophie des Egyptiens & des Chinois'. *Histoire de l'Académie royale des inscriptions et belles-lettres, avec les Mémoires* [...], 40:163-86

Guillemin, Henri

1942 *Les Philosophes contre Jean-Jacques 'Cette affaire infernale'. L'affaire J.-J. Rousseau-Hume-1766*. Paris: Librairie Plon

Gür, André

1967 'La négociation de l'édit du 11 mars 1768, d'après le journal de Jean-André Deluc et la correspondance de Gédeon Turrettini'. *Schweizerische Zeitschrift für Geschichte*, 17:166-217

Guy, Basil

1963 *The French image of China before and after Voltaire*. Studies on Voltaire, 21. Oxford: The Voltaire Foundation

Guyot, Charles

1955 *Le Rayonnement de l'Encyclopédie en Suisse française*. Neuchâtel: Secrétariat de l'Université

Haber, Francis C.

1959 *The Age of the World: Moses to Darwin*. Baltimore: The Johns Hopkins Press

Hall, A. Rupert

1982 'Newton's revolution'. *British journal for the philosophy of science*, 33:305-15

Hall, Roland

1978 *Fifty years of Hume scholarship: a bibliographical guide*. Edinburgh: University Press

Hall, Roland, and Woolhouse, R.
  1970 'Forty years of work on John Locke (1929-1969): a bibliography'. *Philosophical quarterly*, 20:258-68

Haller, Albrecht von
  1751 *Réflexions sur le systême de la génération, de M. de Buffon.* Genève: Chez Barrillot & Fils
  1753 'De partibus corporis humani sensilibus et irritabilibus'. *Commentarii Societatis regiae scientiarum gottingensis. Ad annum MDCCLII,* 2:114-58
  1756a *Deux mémoires sur le mouvement du sang et sur les effets de la saignée, fondés sur des expériences faites sur des animaux.* Lausanne: M.-M. Bousquet [etc.]
  1756b *Sammlung kleiner Hallerischer Schrifften.* Bern: E. Haller
  1757-1766 *Elementa physiologiae corporis humani.* 8 vols. Lausannae: Sumptibus Marci-Michael Bousquet (vol. i), S. d'Arnay (vol. ii), F. Grasset (vols iii-v); Bernae: Societatis Typographicae (vols vi-viii)
  1758 *Sur la formation du cœur dans le poulet; sur l'œil; sur la structure du jaune.* [...] 2 vols. Lausanne: Chez Marc-Mich. Bousquet et Comp.
  1762-1768 *Opera minora emendata, aucta, et renovata.* 3 vols. Lausannae: Grasset
  1764 'Mémoire sur les yeux de quelques poissons'. *Histoire de l'Académie royale des sciences. Année MDCCLXII. Avec les Mémoires* [...], pp.76-95
  1772 *Sammlung kleiner Hallerischer Schriften.* 2nd ed. 3 vols. Bern: E. Haller
  1773-1775 (ed.) *Epistolarum ab eruditis viris ad Alb. Hallerum scriptarum.* 6 vols. Bernae: Sumptibus Societatis Typographica
  1775-1777 *Briefe über einige Einwürfe nochlebender Freigeister wieder die Offenbarung.* 3 vols. Bern: Typographische Gesellschaft

Halley, Edmund
  1692 'An account of the cause of the change of the variation of the magnetical needle; with an Hypothesis of the structure of the internal parts of the Earth: as it was proposed to the Royal Society in one of their late meetings'. *Philosophical transactions,* 16:563-78

Hamers-van Duynen, S. W.
  1978 *Hieronymus David Gaubius (1705-1780). Zijn correspondentie met Antonio Nunes Ribeiro Sanches en andere tijdgenoten.* Amsterdam: Van Gorcum

Hamilton, William
  1776 *Campi Phlegraei. Observations on the volcanos of the two Sicilies as they have been communicated to the Royal Society of London.* 2 vols. Naples

Hankins, Thomas L.
  1970 *Jean d'Alembert: science and the Enlightenment.* Oxford: Clarendon Press

Hanks, Lesley
  1966 *Buffon avant l'"Histoire Naturelle".* Paris: Presses Universitaires de France

Harding, Joan P. [M.], and others (eds.)
  1979 *British bee books: a bibliography 1500-1976.* By International Bee Research Association. London

Hardouin, Jean
  1733 *Opera varia.* Amstelodami: Apud Henricum Du Sauzet; Hagae Comitum: Apud Petrum De Hondt

Harman, P. H.
  1983 'Force and inertia: Euler and Kant's *Metaphysical foundations of natural science*'. In *Nature mathematized,* vol.1, pp.229-49. Edited by William R. Shea. Dordrecht: D. Reidel Publishing Company

Harms, Ernest
  1956 'Simon-Andred [*sic*] Tissot (1728-1797). The Freudian before Freud'. *The American journal of psychiatry*, 112:744

Harnois, Guy
  1928 *Les Théories du langage en France de 1660 à 1821*. Paris: Société d'Edition 'Les Belles Lettres'

Harsin, Paul
  1935 'Un économiste aux Pays-Bas au XVIIIe siècle, l'abbé Mann'. *Annales de la Société scientifique de Bruxelles*, 53:149-227

Hart, Horace
  1966 *Charles Earl Stanhope and the Oxford University Press*. London: Printing Historical Society

Hartleben, Hermine
  1906 *Champollion: sein Leben und sein Werk*. 2 vols. Berlin: Weidmannsche Buchhandlung
  1909 (ed.) *Lettres de Champollion le jeune*. Bibliothèque égyptologique, vols 30 and 31. 2 vols. Paris: Ernest Leroux éditeur

Hartley, David
  1774 *An account of the methods of securing buildings (and ships) against fire*. London
  1834 *An account of the invention and use of fire-plates, for the security of buildings and ships against fire*. London: James Cochrane, and Co.

Havens, George R., and Torrey, Norman L.
  1959 *Voltaire's catalogue of his library at Ferney*. Studies on Voltaire, 9. Genève: Institut et Musée Voltaire

Hawkesworth, John
  1773 *An account of the voyages undertaken by the order of his present majesty for making discoveries in the southern hemisphere, and successively performed by Commodore Byron, Captain Carteret, Captain Wallis, and Captain Cook*. [...] 3 vols. London: Printed for W. Strahan and T. Cadell

Hazen, Allen Tracy
  1973 *A bibliography of Horace Walpole*. Folkestone, London: Dawsons of Pall Mall

[Heathcote, Ralph]
  1767 *A letter to the Honorable Mr. Horace Walpole, concerning the dispute between Mr. Hume and Mr. Rousseau*. London: Printed for B. White

Heilbron, John L.
  1979 *Electricity in the 17th and 18th centuries: a study of early modern physics*. Berkeley: University of California Press

Hemmerle, Josef
  1957 'Die Olmützer Gelehrtenakademie und der Benediktinerorden'. *Studien und Mitteilungen zur Geschichte des Benediktinerordens*, 67: 298-305

Herrlinger, Robert
  1959 'C. F. Wolffs *Theoria generationis* (1759). Die Geschichte einer epochemachenden Dissertation'. *Zeitschrift für Anatomie und Entwicklungsgeschichte*, 121:245-70

Hintzsche, Erich
  1964 (ed.) *Albrecht von Haller, Giambattista Morgagni. Briefwechsel 1745-1768*. Bern: H. Huber Verlag
  1965 (ed.) *Albrecht von Haller, Ignazio Somis. Briefwechsel 1745-1776*. Bern: H. Huber Verlag
  1966 'Albrecht von Hallers Tätigkeit als Enzyklopädist'. *Clio medica*, 1:235-54
  1977 (ed.) *Albrecht von Hallers Briefe an Auguste Tissot 1754-1777*. Bern: H. Huber Verlag

Hoffheimer, Michael H.
  1982 'Maupertuis and the eighteenth-century critique of preexistence'. *Journal of the history of biology*, 15:119-44
[Holbach, Paul Henri Thiry, baron d']
  1770 *Système de la nature, ou des loix du monde physique, & du monde moral.* 2 vols. Londres
Huber, François
  1792 *Nouvelles observations sur les abeilles, adressées à Charles Bonnet.* Genève: Barde et Manget
  1808 *New observations on the natural history of bees.* Second edition. Edinburgh: Printed for John Anderson [etc.]
Huber, Friedrich
  1959 *Daniel Bernoulli (1700-1782) als Physiologe und Statistiker.* Basler Veröffentlichungen zur Gescichte der Medizin und der Biologie, Fasc. 8. Basel: Benno Schwabe & Co.
Humbert, Edouard
  1858 'Charles Bonnet disciple de Montesquieu'. *Bibliothèque universelle. Revue suisse et étrangère*, 63e année, nouv. pér., 1:525-51
Hume, David
  1932 *The Letters of David Hume.* Edited by J. Y. T. Greig. 2 vols. Oxford: At the Clarendon Press
  1954 *New letters of David Hume.* Edited by Raymond Klibansky and Ernest C. Mossner. Oxford: At the Clarendon Press
Im Hof, Ulrich
  1980 'Ancien régime'. In *Handbuch der Schweizer Geschichte*, 2:673-784. 2 vols. Zürich: Buchverlag Berichthaus
  1982 *Das Gesellige Jahrhundert. Gesellschaft und Gesellschaften im Zeitalter der Aufklärung.* München: Verlag C. H. Beck
Irsay, Stephen d'
  1928 'Der philosophische Hintergrund der Nervenphysiologie im 17. und 18. Jahrhundert'. *Archiv für Geschichte der Medizin*, 20:181-97
Isenberg, Karl
  1906 *Der Einfluss der Philosophie Charles Bonnets auf Friedrich Heinrich Jacobi.* Inaugural-Dissertation [...] der Universität zu Tübingen. Borna, Leipzig: Buchdruckerei Robert Noske
[Ivernois, François d']
  1782 *Tableau historique et politique des révolutions de Genève dans le dix-huitiéme siécle.* Genève
Iversen, Erik
  1961 *The Myth of Egypt and its hieroglyphs in European tradition.* Copenhagen: GEC GAD Publishers
Jacob, Margaret C.
  1981 *The Radical Enlightenment: pantheists, freemasons and republicans.* London: George Allen & Unwin
Jallabert, Jean
  1748 *Experiences sur l'electricité, avec quelques conjectures sur la cause de ses effets.* Genève: Chez Barrillot & Fils
Janssens-Knorsch, Uta Eva Maria
  1975 *Matthieu Maty and the Journal Britannique 1750-1755.* Amsterdam: Holland University Press
Jessop, Thomas Edmund
  1938 *A bibliography of David Hume and of Scottish philosophy from Francis Hutcheson to Lord Balfour.* London: A. Brown & Sons

Jossua, Jean-Pierre
  1967 'Actualité de Bayle. Réflexions sur quelques études récentes'. *Revue des sciences philosophiques et théologiques*, 51:403-39

A journal
  1767 *A journal of a voyage round the World in His Majesty's Ship The Dolphin, commanded by the honourable Commodore Byron.* [...] London: Printed for M. Cooper

Kaegi, Werner
  1942 'Voltaire und der Zerfall des Christlichen Geschichtsbildes'. In *Historische Meditationen*, pp.221-48. Zürich: Fretz & Wasmuth Verlag

Karmin, Otto
  1920 *Sir Francis d'Ivernois 1757-1842: sa vie, son œuvre et son temps.* Genève: Revue Historique de la Révolution Française et de l'Empire

Keilin, David
  1959 'The problem of anabiosis or latent life: history and current concept'. *Proceedings of the Royal Society of London*, Series B, 150:149-91

Keim, Albert
  1907 *Helvétius: sa vie et son œuvre.* Paris: Félix Alcan

Kennicott, Benjamin
  1770 *The Ten annual accounts of the collation of Hebrew MSS of the Old Testament, begun in 1760 and compleated in 1769.* Oxford: Fletcher and Prince
  1776-1780 *Vetus Testamentum Hebraicum, cum variis lectionibus.* Edidit Benjaminus Kennicott. [...] 2 vols. Oxonii: E Typographeo Clarendoniano

Kerby-Miller, Charles (ed.)
  1950 *Memoirs of the extraordinary life, works, and discoveries of Martinus Scriblerus.* [...] New Haven: Published for Wellesley College by Yale University Press

Kirk, John
  1909 *Biographies of English Catholics in the eighteenth century.* Edited by John Hungerford Pollen, S. J., and Edwin Burton, D. D. London: Burns & Oates

Klingenstein, Grete
  1974 'Vienna nel Settecento. Alcuni aspetti'. *Quaderni storici*, 27:803-13
  1976 'Despotismus und Wissenschaft'. In *Formen der europäischen Aufklärung. Untersuchungen zur Situation von Christentum, Bildung und Wissenschaft im 18. Jahrhundert*, pp.126-57. Herausgegeben von Friedrich Engel-Janosi, Grete Klingenstein, Heinrich Lutz. Wien: Verlag für Geschichte und Politik
  1978 'Akademikerüberschuß als soziales Problem im Aufgeklärten Absolutismus'. In *Bildung, Politik und Gesellschaft. Studien zur Geschichte des europäischen Bildungswesen vom 16. bis zum 20. Jahrhundert*, pp.165-204. Herausgegeben von Grete Klingenstein, Heinrich Lutz, Gerald Stourzh. Wien: Verlag für Geschichte und Politik

Knight, William Stanley
  1925 *The Life and works of Hugo Grotius.* The Grotius Society Publications, no. 4. London: Sweet & Maxwell

Knox, Thomas Francis
  1878 *The First and second diaries of the English College, Douai.* London: David Nutt

Kra, Pauline
  1970 'Religion in Montesquieu's *Lettres persanes*'. *Studies on Voltaire*, 72:5-224

Krauss, Werner
  1963 'La correspondance de Formey'. *Revue d'histoire littéraire de la France*, 63:207-16

Krönert, Gisela *see* Müller, Kurt

Kubler, George A.

1938   *The Era of Charles Mahon third Earl of Stanhope, stereotyper 1750-1825.* New York: J. J. Little and Ives Company

Kuhfuss, Walter

1976   'Le manuscrit de La Haye'. In *La correspondance littéraire de Grimm et de Meister (1754-1813),* pp.113-18. Colloque de Sarrebruck (22-24 février 1974) [...] publiés par Bernard Bray, Jochen Schlobach, Jean Varloot. Actes et Colloques, 19. Paris: Editions Klincksieck

Labrousse, Elisabeth

1961   *Inventaire critique de la correspondance de Pierre Bayle.* Paris: Librairie philosophique J. Vrin

1963-1964   *Pierre Bayle.* Vol.i: *Du Pays de Foix à la Cité d'Erasme.* Vol.ii: *Hétérodoxie et rigorisme.* Archives internationales d'histoire des idées, 1, 2. La Haye: Martinus Nijhoff

Lang. S. *see* Pevsner, Nikolaus

Launay, Jean-Louis-Wenceslas de

1775   'Précis d'un mémoire qui porte pour titre: Recherches sur l'origine des fossiles accidentels du Brabant [...] lû à l'Académie impériale & royale des sciences & belles-lettres de Bruxelles, par M. Néedham [...]'. *Observations sur la physique, sur l'histoire naturelle et sur les arts,* 6:113-24

Lavalleye, Jacques

1973   *L'Académie royale des sciences, des lettres et des beaux-arts de Belgique 1772-1972: esquisse historique.* Bruxelles: Palais des Académies

Le Clerc, Jean

1719   'Défense de la bonté & de la sainteté divine, contre les objections de Mr. Bayle'. *Bibliotheque choisie, pour servir de suite à la Bibliotheque universelle.* Année MDCCVI, 9:103-71. Amsterdam: Chez les Wetsteins

Le Goff, F.

1863   *De la philosophie de l'abbé De Lignac.* Paris: Librairie Hachette

Lehmann-Haupt, Helmut

1973   'The microscope and the book'. In *Festschrift für Claus Nissen zum siebzigsten Geburtstag 2. September 1971,* pp.471-502 Wiesbaden: Guido Pressler

Leibniz, Gottfried Wilhelm

1693   'Protogaea', *Acta eruditorum,* pp.40-42

1710   *Essais de theodicée sur la bonté de Dieu, la liberté de l'homme et l'origine du mal.* Amsterdam: Chez Isaac Troyel, Libraire

1749   *Protogaea sive de prima facie telluris et antiquissimae historiae vestigiis in ipsis naturae monumentis dissertatio ex schedis manuscriptis [...] edita a Christiano Ludovico Scheidio.* Goettingae: Sumptibus Ioh. Guil. Schmidii, Bibliopolae Universit.

1768   *Opera omnia.* 6 vols. Genevae: Apud Fratres de Tournes

Lelarge de Lignac, Joseph-Adrien

1751   *Lettres à un Amériquain sur l'histoire naturelle, générale et particuliere de monsieur de Buffon.* 5 vols. Hambourg [Paris]

1756   *Suite des lettres à un Amériquain, sur les IVe & Ve volumes de l'Histoire naturelle de M. de Buffon; et sur le Traité des animaux de M. l'Abbé de Condillac.* 4 vols. Hambourg [Paris]

1760   *Le Témoignage du sens intime et de l'expérience, opposé à la foi profane et ridicule des fatalistes modernes.* 3 vols. Auxerre: Chez François Fournier

Lesky, Erna

1959   'Albrecht von Haller und Anton de Haen im Streit um die Lehre von der Sensibilität'. *Gesnerus,* 16:16-46

Lesky, Erna, and Wandruskzka, Adam (eds.)
 1973 *Gerard van Swieten und seine Zeit*. Studien zur Geschichte der Universität Wien,
  Bd. 8. Wien [etc.]: Verlag Hermann Böhlaus
[Lévesque de Pouilly, Jean-Simon]
 1794 *Eloge de Charles Bonnet*. Lausanne: Chez J. P. Heubach
Lewis, Wilmarth Sheldon
 1961 *Horace Walpole*. London: Rupert Hart-Davis
Lignac *see* Lelarge de Lignac, Joseph-Adrien
Lindeboom, Gerrit A.
 1981 'Jan Swammerdam als microscopist'. *Tijdschrift voor de Geschiedenis der Geneeskunde,
  Natuurwetenschappen, Wiskunde en Techniek*, 4:87-110
 1982 'Jan Swammerdam (1637-1680) and his *Biblia Naturae*'. *Clio medica*, 17:113-31
Linnaeus, Carl
 1744 *Oratio de telluris habitabilis incremento. Et Andraeae Celsii, Oratio de mutationibus
  generalioribus quae in superficie corporum coelestium contingunt*. Lugduni Batavorum: apud
  Cornelium Haak
 1749-1769 'Oratio de telluris habitabilis incremento'. In *Amoenitates academicae seu
  dissertationes variae physicae, medicae, botanicae* [...], 2: 430-78. 7 vols. Holmiae, Lipsiae:
  Apud Godefredum Kiesewetter (vol.i); Holmiae: Apud Laurentium Salvium (vols.ii-
  vii)
 1781 'On the increase of the habitable Earth'. In *Select dissertations from the Amoenitates
  Academicae, a supplement to Mr. Stillingfleet's tracts relating to natural history*, 1:71-127.
  Translated by F. J. Brand. 2 vols. London: G. Robinson and J. Robson
Locke, John
 1959 *An essay concerning human understanding*. Collated and annotated, with prolegomena,
  biographical, critical, and historical by Alexander Campbell Fraser. 2 vols. New
  York: Dover Publications
Lods, Armand
 1899 'Court de Gébelin et la représentation des églises réformées auprès du gouverne-
  ment de Louis xv (1763-1766)'. *Société de l'Histoire du Protestantisme Français. Bulletin
  historique et litteraire*, 48:244-75
Löwith, Karl
 1949 *Meaning in history: the theological implications of the philosophy of history*. Chicago: The
  University of Chicago Press
Lopez, Cecilia L.
 1970 *Alexander Pope: an annotated bibliography, 1945-1967*. Gainesville: University of
  Florida Press
Lough, John
 1968 *Essays on the Encyclopédie of Diderot and d'Alembert*. London, New York: Oxford
  University Press
Lucretius
 1768 *De la nature des choses*. Traduction nouvelle, avec des notes par M. L.* G**
  [Lagrange]. 2 vols. Paris: Bleuet
Lukina, Tat'jana A.
 1975 'Caspar Friedrich Wolff und die Petersburger Akademie der Wissenschaften'.
  *Beiträge zur Geschichte der Naturwissenschaften und der Medizin: Festschrift für Georg
  Uschmann*. Acta Historica Leopoldina, no.9: 411-25
Lullin, Amadeus
 1766 *Dissertatio physica de electricitate, quam, favente Deo, Praeside D. D. Hor. De Saussure
  Philosophiae Professore*. [...] Genevae: Typis Steph. Blanc & J. P. Bonnant Typog.

Lundsgaard-Hansen-von Fischer, Susanna

1959 *Verzeichnis der gedruckten Schriften Albrecht von Hallers*. Berner Beiträge zur Geschichte der Medizin und der Naturwissenschaften, nr. 18. Bern: Paul Haupt

Lyonet, Pierre

1762 *Traité anatomique de la chenille, qui ronge le bois de saule*. [...] La Haye: Au depends de l'Auteur. Se vend chez Pierre de Hondt [etc.]

Maccabez, Eugène

1903 *F. B. de Félice 1723-1789 et son Encyclopédie. Yverdon 1770-1780*. Bâle: Imprimerie Emile Birkhauser

Maggs, Barbara Widenor

1974 'Answers from eighteenth-century China to certain questions on Voltaire's sinology'. *Studies on Voltaire*, 120:179-98

Mahon, Charles *see* Stanhope, Charles

Maillet, Benoît de

1748 *Telliamed ou Entretiens d'un philosophe indien avec un missionnaire françois sur la diminution de la mer, la formation de la terre, l'origine de l'homme, &c. Mis en ordre sur les mémoires de feu M. de Maillet, par J. A. G****. Amsterdam: Chez l'Honoré et fils, Libraires

Mailly, Edouard

1883 *Histoire de l'Académie impériale et royale des sciences et belles-lettres de Bruxelles*. Mémoires couronnés et autres Mémoires publiés par l'Académie royale des sciences des lettres et des beaux-arts de Belgique. Collection in-8° tomes 34 et 35. Bruxelles: F. Hayez

Mairan, Jean-Jacques Dortous (Dortus) de

1749 *Dissertation sur la glace, ou explication physique de la formation de la glace, & de ses divers phénomènes*. Paris: De l'Imprimerie Royale

1759 *Lettres de M. de Mairan, au R. P. Parrenin, missionnaire de la Compagnie de Jesus, à Pekin. Continant diverses questions sur la Chine*. Paris: Chez Desaint et Saillant

1767 *Nouvelles recherches sur la cause générale du chaud en eté & du froid en hiver, en tant qu'elle se lie à la chaleur interne & permanente de la terre*. [Paris]

1768 'Nouvelles recherches sur la cause générale du chaud en eté & du froid en hiver, en tant qu'elle se lie à la chaleur interne & permanente de la terre; en supplément & correction au mémoire qui fut donné sur ce sujet dans le volume de 1719, page 104'. *Histoire de l'Académie royale des sciences. Année M.DCCLXV. Avec les Mémoires* [...], pp.143-266

Malebranche, Nicolas

1962-1967 *Œuvres complètes*. Direction, André Robinet. 20 vols. Paris: Librairie philosophique J. Vrin

Mann, Theodore Augustus

1778 *Memoire sur les diverses méthodes inventées jusqu'à présent, pour garantir les édifices d'incendie*. [...] Bruxelles: Impr. académique

1780a 'Mémoire sur le feu élémentaire, considéré en général dans toute la nature, avec des conjectures sur ses différentes modifications, ses lois d'action, sa fin et ses usages universels'. *Mémoires de l'Académie impériale et royale des sciences et belles-lettres de Bruxelles*, 2:3-46

1780b 'Mémoire sur l'histoire naturelle de la mer du Nord et sur la pêche qui s'y fait [...]'. *Mémoires de l'Académie impériale et royale des sciences et belles-lettres de Bruxelles*, 2:159-220

1780c 'Mémoire dans lequel on examine les effets et les phénomènes produits en versant différentes sortes d'huiles sur les eaux, tant tranquilles qu'en mouvement [...]'. *Mémoires de l'Académie impériale et royale des sciences et belles-lettres de Bruxelles*, 2:258-94

1780d 'Dissertation dans laquelle on tâche de déterminer précisément le port où Jules-César s'est embarqué pour passer en Grande-Bretagne et celui où il y aborda [...]'. *Mémoires de l'Académie impériale et royale des sciences et belles-lettres de Bruxelles*, 3:231-55

1783 'Notice historique de la vie et des ouvrages de M. l'abbé Needham'. *Mémoires de l'Académie impériale et royale des sciences et belles-lettres de Bruxelles*, 4:xxxiii-xli

1788 'Extrait d'un rapport de M. l'abbé Needham touchant les moyens de fondre & d'affiner le fer avec les braises des charbons de terre; fait le 29 Avril 1779'. *Mémoires de l'Académie impériale et royale des sciences et belles-lettres de Bruxelles*, 5:xx-xxi

Manzini, Paola
1981 *Catalogo dei manoscritti di Lazzaro Spallanzani*. Reggio Emilia: Cassa di Risparmio

Maraldi, Giacomo Filippo
1714 'Observations sur les abeilles'. *Histoire de l'Académie royale des sciences. Année MDCCXII. Avec les Mémoires* [...], pp.299-335

Marchand, Jean
1960 'Bibliographie générale raisonnée des œuvres de Montesquieu'. *Bulletin du bibliophile*, N.S., pp.49-62

Marchenay, Philippe
1979 *L'Homme et l'abeille*. Nancy: Berger-Levrault

Marcu, Eva
1953 'Un encyclopédiste oublié: Formey'. *Revue d'histoire littéraire de la France*, 53:296-305

Markgraf, F., and Steiger, R.
1969 'F. Allamand und seine botanischen Beobachtungen'. *Taxon*, 18:421-24

Marx, Jacques
1973a 'Des anguilles à la philosophie mécanique. Deux réfutations peu connues du *Système de la Nature*'. *Tijdschrift voor de studie van de Verlichting*, 1:69-87

1973b 'La préformation du germe dans la philosophie biologique du XVIIIe siècle'. *Tijdschrift voor de studie van de Verlichting*, 3-4:397-428

1974 'L'art d'observer au XVIIIe siècle: J. Senebier et Ch. Bonnet'. *Janus*, 61:201-20

1975 'Voltaire et les sciences'. *Episteme*, 9:270-84

1976 *Charles Bonnet contre les Lumières: 1738-1850*. Studies on Voltaire, 156-57. Banbury: The Voltaire Foundation

1977 L'activité scientifique de l'Académie impériale et royale des sciences et belles-lettres de Bruxelles 1722-1794'. *Etudes sur le XVIIIe siècle*, 4:49-61

Mason, Haydn Trevor
1963 *Pierre Bayle and Voltaire*. London: Oxford University Press

Massa Piacentini, Maria
1941 'Priorità e contributo di Giovanni Maria Della Torre agli studi vesuviani'. *Atti della reale accademia ligure di scienze e lettere*, 1:124-36

Masson, Pierre Maurice
1916 *La Religion de J. J. Rousseau*. 3 vols. Paris: Librairie Hachette

Matteucci, Nicola
1953 '*Genève* nelle polemiche dell'*Encyclopédie*'. *Il Mulino*, nn.25-26:726-44

Maupertuis, Pierre Louis Moreau de
1744 *Dissertation physique à l'occasion du négre blanc*. Leiden

1745 *Vénus physique*. n.p.

1756 *Œuvres de Mr. de Maupertuis*. Nouvelle edition corrigée & augmentée. 4 vols. Lyon: Chez Jean-Marie Bruyset

May, Kenneth O.
1973 *Bibliography and research manual of the history of mathematics*. Toronto: University of Toronto Press

Mayer, J.
1954 'Robinet, philosophe de la nature'. *Revue des sciences humaines*, N. S., Fasc. 72, pp.295-309

Mazzolini, Renato Giuseppe
1972 'Il carteggio tra Charles Bonnet e Felice Fontana'. *Physis*, 14:69-103
1973 'Il carteggio tra Carlo Allioni e Lazzaro Spallanzani. (Contributo all'epistolario spallanzaniano)'. *Physis*, 15:280-324
1974 'Lettere di Lazzaro Spallanzani ad Antonio Vallisneri iunior. (Contributo all'epistolario spallanzaniano)'. *Physis*, 16:377-95
1976 'Two letters on epigenesis from John Turberville Needham to Albrecht von Haller.' *Journal of the history of medicine and allied sciences*, 31:68-77
1977 'Sugli studi embriologici di Albrecht von Haller negli anni 1755-1758'. *Annali dell'Istituto storico italo-germanico in Trento*, 3:183-242
1980 *The Iris in eighteenth-century physiology*. Berner Beiträge zur Geschichte der Medizin und der Naturwissenschaften, N. F. 9. Bern: Verlag Hans Huber

Mazzolini, Renato Giuseppe, and Ongaro, Giuseppe
1983 '*Quasi tradens se totum*: i manoscritti morgagnani della Biblioteca Palatina di Parma'. *Annali dell'Istituto e Museo di storia della scienza di Firenze*, 8:101-105

Meister, Richard
1947 *Geschichte der Akademie der Wissenschaften in Wien 1847-1947*. Wien: Druck und Verlag Adolf Holzhausens Nfg.

Metzger, Hélène
1969 *La Genèse de la science des cristaux*. Nouveau tirage. Paris: Albert Blanchard

Meulen, Jacob ter, and Diermanse, P. J. J.
1950 *Bibliographie des écrits imprimés de Hugo Grotius*. La Haye: Martinus Nijhoff
1961 *Bibliographie des écrits sur Hugo Grotius imprimés au XVIIe siècle*. La Haye: Martinus Nijhoff

Meusel, Johann Georg
1802-1816 *Lexikon der vom Jahr 1750 bis 1800 verstorbenen Teutschen Schriftsteller*. 15 vols. Leipzig: Bey Gerhard Fleischer

Meyer, Paul H.
1952 'The manuscript of Hume's account of his dispute with Rousseau'. *Comparative literature*, 4:341-50

Meyer-Steineg, Theodor
1923 'Hieronymus Dav. Gaub über die natürlichen Heilkräfte'. *Archiv für Geschichte der Medizin*, 15:114-20

Micheli, Pietro Antonio
1729 *Nova plantarum genera iuxta Tournefortii methodum disposita*. Florentiae: Typis Bernardi Paperinii

Milliken, Stephen F. *see* Fellows, Otis E.

Misch, Manfred
[1974] *Apis est animal – apis est ecclesia. Ein Beitrag zum Verhältnis von Naturkunde und Theologie in spätantiker und mittelalterlicher Literatur*. Europäischen Hochschulschriften, Reihe 1, Bd.107. Frankfurt am Main: Verlag Peter Lang

Moeschlin-Krieg, Beate
1953 *Zur Geschichte der Regenerationsforschung im 18. Jahrhundert*. Basler Veröffentlichungen zur Geschichte der Medizin und der Biologie, 1. Basel: Benno Schwabe

[Monestier, Blaise]

1774 *La Vraie philosophie.* [Edited and with a note by John Turberville Needham.] Bruxelles: J. L. de Boubers

1775 *La Vraie philosophie.* [Edited and with a note by John Turberville Needham.] Bruxelles: Chez Valade

Montagu, Edward Wortley

1763 *Observations upon a supposed antique bust at Turin. In two letters, addressed to the right honourable the Earl of Macclesfield, President of the Royal Society.* London: Printed for T. Becket and P. A. de Hondt

Montesquieu, Charles-Louis de Secondat, baron de la Brède et de

[1748] *De l'esprit des loix.* 2 vols. Genève: Chez Barrillot, & Fils

1875-1879 *Œuvres complètes de Montesquieu.* Avec les variantes des premières éditions, un choix des meilleurs commentaires et des notes nouvelles par Edouard Laboulaye. 7 vols. Paris: Garnier Frères, Libraires-éditeurs

1914 *Correspondance de Montesquieu.* Publiée par François Gebelin avec la collaboration de André Morize. 2 vols. Paris: Librairie Ancienne Honoré Champion

Monti, Maria Teresa

1985 'Un inedito di John Turberville Needham: Ideae quaedam generales de mundi systemate'. *Rivista di storia della filosofia*, n.3:503-29

Moreau, Jacob-Nicolas

1757 *Nouveau mémoire pour servir à l'histoire des Cacouacs.* Amsterdam

1785 *Variétés morales et philosophiques.* 2 vols. Paris: de l'Imprimerie de Monsieur, aux dépens de l'Auteur, et pour ses seuls amis

1898-1901 *Mes souvenirs.* [...] Collationnés, annotés et publiés par Camille Hermelin. 2 vols. Paris: Librairie Plon

Moreau, Joseph (ed.)

1947 *Malebranche. Correspondance avec J.-J. Dortous de Mairan.* Edition nouvelle. [...] Paris: Librairie philosophique J. Vrin

Morellet, André

1822 *Mémoires inédits de l'abbé Morellet,* [...] *sur le dix-huitième siècle et sur la révolution; précédés de l'Eloge de l'abbé Morellet, par M. Lémontey.* [...] Deuxième édition, considérablement augmentée. 2 vols. Paris: A la Librairie Française De Ladvocat

Mortier, Roland

1954 *Diderot en Allemagne (1750-1850).* Paris: Presses Universitaires de France

Morton, A. G.

1981 *History of botanical science.* London [etc.]: Academic Press

Morton, Charles

1769 'Extract from the Journals of the Royal Society, June 23, 1768, respecting a Letter addressed to the Society by a Member of the House of Jesuits at Pekin in China'. *Philosophical transactions*, 59:489-504

Mossner, Ernest Campbell

1980 *The Life of David Hume.* Second edition. Oxford: At the Clarendon Press

Moureaux, Philippe

1974 'Charles de Cobenzl, homme d'état moderne'. *Etudes sur le XVIIIe siècle*, 1:171-78

Müller, Hans-Heinrich

1975 *Akademie und Wirtschaft im 18. Jahrhundert.* Berlin: Akademie-Verlag

Müller, Kurt (ed.)

1967 *Leibniz-Bibliographie. Die Literatur über Leibniz.* Bearbeitet von Kurt Müller. Veröffentlichungen des Leibniz-Archivs, 1. Frankfurt am Main: Vittorio Klostermann

Müller, Kurt, and Krönert, Gisela

1969 *Leben und Werk von Gottfried Wilhelm Leibniz. Eine Chronik.* Veröffentlichungen des Leibniz-Archiv, 2. Frankfurt am Main: Klostermann

Müller, Otto Friderich

1773-1774 *Vermium terrestrium et fluviatilium, seu animalium infusoriorum, helminthicorum et testaceorum, non marinorum, succinta historia.* 2 vols in 3 pts. Havniae, Lipsiae: Apud Heineck et Faber

1786 *Animalcula infusoria fluviatilia et marina* [...] *opus hoc posthumum quod cum tabulis aeneis L in lucem tradit vidua ejus nobilissima cura Othonis Fabricii.* Havniae: Typis Nicolai Möllerei

Müller-Graupa, Edwin

1938 'Der Hochzeitsflug der Bienenkönigin. Die Geschichte eines biologischen Problems von Aristoteles bis Meeterlinck'. *Sudhoffs Archiv*, 31:350-64

Murphy, Terence

1976a 'Jean Baptiste René Robinet: the career of a man of letters'. *Studies on Voltaire*, 150:183-250

1976b 'A propos de la correspondance de Jean-Baptiste Robinet'. *Revue de synthèse*, 97:123-24

Nathorst, Alfred Gabriel

1909 'Carl von Linné as a geologist'. *Annual report of the Board of Regents of the Smithsonian Institution* [...] *for the year ending June 30 1908.* Washington: Government Printing Office

Naville, Pierre

1967 *D'Holbach et la philosophie scientifique au XVIIIe siècle.* Nouvelle édition revue et augmentée. Paris: Gallimard

Needham, John Turberville

1743 'A letter from Mr. Turbevil Needham, to the President; concerning certain chalky tubulous concretions, called malm: with some microscopical observations on the farina of the red lily, and of worms discovered in smutty corn'. *Philosophical transactions*, 42 (1742-1743):634-41

1745 *An account of some new microscopical discoveries.* London: Printed for F. Needham

1746a 'Extract of a letter from Mr. Turbervill Needham to Martin Folkes, Esq.; Pr. R. S. concerning some new electrical experiments lately made at Paris'. *Philosophical transactions*, 44 (1746-1747): 247-63

1746b *A letter from Paris, concerning some new electrical experiments made there.* London: Printed for C. Davis and M. Cooper

1747a *Nouvelles découvertes faites avec le microscope* par T. Needham, *traduites de l'Anglois. Avec un memoire sur les polypes à bouquet, et sur ceux en entonnoir* par A. Trembley. Leide: De l'Imp. d'Elie Luzac

1747b 'Part of a letter from Mr. Turberville Needham to James Parson M.D. F.R.S. of a new mirror, which burns at 66 feet distance, invented by M. de Buffon F.R.S. and Member of the Royal Academy of Sciences at Paris'. *Philosophical transactions*, 44 (1746-1747): 493-95

1748 'A summary of some late observations upon the generation, composition, and decomposition of animal and vegetable substances; communicated in a letter to Martin Folkes Esq; President of the Royal Society'. *Philosophical transactions*, 45:615-66

1749 *Observations upon the generation, composition, and decomposition of animal and vegetable substances.* London

1750 *Nouvelles observations microscopiques, avec des découvertes intéressantes sur la composition & décomposition des corps organisés.* Paris: Chez Louis-Etienne Ganeau

1752 'Observations des hauteurs faites avec le baromètre, au mois d'août 1751, sur une partie des Alpes, en présence & sous les auspices de Mylord Comte de Rochford Envoyé extraordinaire de S. M. Britannique à la cour de Turin'. *Journal britannique*, 8:356-71

1754 'Lettre aux journalistes. Eclairissement à ce sujet. Extrait d'un écrit singulier de M. Lauder contre Milton: Réflexions sur le plagiat reproché à ce Poëte, & sur le zéle des Anglois pour l'honneur de sa memoire'. *Journal étranger*, November 1754, pp.212-35

1760a *Observations des hauteurs, faites avec le baromètre, au mois d'Aoust 1751, sur une partie des Alpes, en presence, et sous les auspices de Milord Comte de Rochford.* [...] Berne: Chez Abr. Wagner fils

1760b 'An account of a late discovery of asbestos in France'. *Philosophical transactions*, 51 (1759-1760):837-38

1761 *De inscriptione quadam Aegyptiaca Taurini inventa et characteribus Aegyptiis olim et Sinis communibus exarata idolo cuidam antiquo in Regia Universitate servato.* Romae: Ex Typographia Palladis

1762 *Réponse* [...] *aux deux lettres de Monsieur Bartoli antiquaire de S. M. le Roi de Sardaigne.* Turin: Imprimerie royale

1763 *Lettres et autres écrits concernant l'incendie arrivée à l'Académie royale de Caen, le 16 d'Août 1763.* Caen: P.-J. Yvon

[1765a] *Reponse d'un theologien au docte proposant des autres questions.* [Genève]

[1765b] *Parodie de la troisieme lettre du proposant, adressée à un philosophe.* [Genève]

[1765c] *Projet de notes instructives,* véridiques, *théologiques, historiques & critiques sur certaines brochures polémiques du tems, adressées aux dignes editeurs des doctes ouvrages du proposant.* [Genève]

[1766] *Parodie de la troisieme lettre du proposant, adressée à un philosophe. Par Mr. N****.* Seconde edition corrigée & augmenté. [Genève]

1769a *see* Spallanzani (1769)

1769b *Questions sur les miracles, à M. Claparede, Professeur de Théologie à Genève, par un proposant: ou extrait de diverses lettres de M. de Voltaire, avec des réponses par M. Néedham.* [...] Londres, Paris: Chez Crapart

1770a *Mémoire sur la maladie contagieuse des betes a cornes, où on cherche un remede préservatif le plus simple, le plus éfficace, le plus général, & le moins couteux.* Bruxelles: De l'Imprimerie royale

1770b *see* [Colmont de Vaulgrenand] (1770)

1771a 'Lettre de M. N***, [...] adressée aux auteurs de ce Journal'. *Journal encyclopédique*, 1:292-97

1771b *see* [Colmont de Vaulgrenand] (1771)

1773 *see* [Cibot] (1773)

1774a *see* [Monestier] (1774)

1774b 'Lettre de M. Needham, à M. l'abbé Rozier, auteur des Observations sur la physique, sur l'histoire naturelle & sur les arts.' Followed by 'Des principes de M. Needham, sur la génération des corps organisés, & sur les premiers eléments de la matiere, contenue dans une note, qui se trouve à la fin de l'ouvrage intitulé: *La vraie philosophie,* par M. l'abbé M.... dont il est l'éditeur'. *Journal ecclésiastique, ou bibliothèque raisonnée des sciences ecclésiastiques*, March 1774, pp.234-50

1775a 'Lettre ecrite à l'auteur de ce Recueil'. *Observations sur la physique, sur l'histoire naturelle et sur les arts,* 5:226-28

1775b *see* Launey (1775)

1775c *see* [Monestier] (1775)

1776 *Idée sommaire, ou vüe générale du systeme physique, & metaphysique de Monsieur Needham sur la génération des corps organisés.* Bruxelles: Chez Pauwels

1777 'Recueil de quelques observations physiques, faites principalement dans la Province de Luxembourg, en 1772, pendant un voyage astronomique avec M. Pigot'. *Mémoires de l'Académie impériale et royale des sciences et belles-lettres de Bruxelles*, 1:155-77. [Read 25 May 1773]

1780a Extract of Needham's *Mémoire sur la maladie contagieuse des bêtes à cornes* [1770a]. *Mémoires de l'Académie impériale et royale des sciences et belles-lettres de Bruxelles*, 2:xxiv-xxviii

1780b 'Observations sur l'histoire-naturelle de la fourmi, a l'occasion desquelles on releve quelques méprises de certains auteurs célebres'. *Mémoires de l'Académie impériale et royale des sciences et belles-lettres de Bruxelles*, 2:295-312. [Read 18 December 1776]

1780c 'Nouvelles recherches sur la nature et l'économie des mouches à miel, suivies de quelques instructions pratiques, propres à perfectionner cette partie de culture rurale'. *Mémoires de l'Académie impériale et royale des sciences et belles-lettres de Bruxelles*, 2:323-87. [Read 9 December 1777]

1781 *Idée sommaire, ou vue générale du système physique & métaphysique de Monsieur Needham, sur la génération des corps organisés.* Bruxelles: Chez Lemaire

1783a 'Recherches sur la question: si le son des cloches, pendant les orages, fait éclater la foudre en la faisant descendre sur le clocher, dès que la nuée chargée de matiere électrique, est audessus de l'endroit où l'on sonne'. *Mémoires de l'Académie impériale et royale des sciences et belles-lettres de Bruxelles*, 4:57-72. [Read 20 November 1781]

1783b 'Recherches sur les moyens les plus efficaces d'empécher le dérangement produit souvent dans la direction naturelle des aiguilles aimantées, par l'electricité de l'atmosphere'. *Mémoires de l'Académie impériale et royale des sciences et belles-lettres de Bruxelles*, 4:73-87. [Read 20 December 1781]

1788 *see* Mann (1788)

Needham, John Turberville (ed.)
see [Butler] (1757); [Colmont de Vaulgrenand] (1770, 1771); [Cibot] (1773); [Monestier] (1774, 1775); Pownall (1781)

Needham, John Turberville (trans.)
see Stanhope, C. (1781)

New, Melvyn
1970 'Laurence Sterne and Henry Baker's *The Microscope made easy*'. *Studies in English literature*, 10:591-604

Newman, Aubrey
1969 *The Stanhopes of Chevening: a family biography.* London: Macmillan

Newton, Isaac
1713 *Philosophiae naturalis principia mathematica.* Editio secunda auctior et emendatior. Cambridge: [C. Crownfield]
1739-1742 *Philosophiae naturalis principia mathematica. Perpetuis commentariis illustrata, communi studio PP. Thomae Le Seur & Francisci Jacquier.* 3 vols. Genevae: Typis Barrillot

Nissen, Claus
1969-1978 *Die zoologische Buchillustration. Ihre Bibliographie und Geschichte.* 2 vols. Stuttgart: Anton Hiersemann

Nous soussignés
1766 *Nous soussignés Ministres Plenipotentiaires.* [...] [Genève]

Olmi, Giuseppe
1981 '"In essercitio universale di contemplatione e prattica": Federico Cesi e i Lincei'. In *Università, Accademie e Società scientifiche in Italia e in Germania dal Cinquecento al Settecento*, pp.169-235. A cura di Laetitia Boehm e Ezio Raimondi. Annali dell'Istituto storico italo-germanico, Quaderno 9. Bologna: il Mulino

Ongaro, Giuseppe
   1973 'Lazzaro Spallanzani e Antonio Vallisneri iunior. (Contributo all'epistolario spallanzaniano)'. *Physis* 15: 197-229
   1981 'I rapporti tra Giambattista Morgagni e Lazzaro Spallanzani'. *Contributi*, 5:125-34
Ongaro, Giuseppe *see also* Mazzolini, Renato Giuseppe
Oudin, Charles
   1911 *Le Spinozisme de Montesquieu: étude critique*. Paris: Librairie générale de Droit & de Jurisprudence
Paganini, Gianni
   1980 *Analisi della fede e critica della ragione nella filosofia di Pierre Bayle*. Firenze: La Nuova Italia
Palmer, Robert Roswell
   1959-1964 *The Age of the democratic revolution: a political history of Europe and America, 1760-1800*. 2 vols. Princeton: Princeton University Press
   1961 *Catholics and unbelievers in eighteenth century France*. New York: Cooper Square Publishers [1st ed. Princeton: Princeton University Press, 1939]
Pancaldi, Giuliano
   1972 *La Generazione spontanea nelle prime ricerche dello Spallanzani*. Quaderni di storia e critica della scienza, N.S. 1. Pisa: Domus Galilaeana
   1982 'La generazione spontanea fra sistema ed esperimento: Spallanzani e la generazione degli infusori (1761-1765)'. In *Lazzaro Spallanzani e la biologia del Settecento: teorie, esperimenti, istituzioni scientifiche*, pp.283-94. A cura di Giuseppe Montalenti e Paolo Rossi. Firenze: Leo S. Olschki Editore
Paquot, Jean-Noël
   1763-1770 *Mémoires pour servir à l'histoire litteraire des dix-sept provinces des Pays-Bas, de la Principauté de Liège, et de quelques contrées voisines*. 18 vols. Louvain: De l'Imprimerie Académique
Paravia, Pier-Alessandro
   1842 *Della vita e degli studi di Giuseppe Bartoli*. Torino: Stabilimento tipografico Fontana
Pauw, Corneille de
   1773 *Recherches philosophiques sur les Egyptiens et les Chinois*. 2 vols. Berlin: Chez G. J. Decker
Pennant, Thomas
   1771 *A tour in Scotland, MDCCLXIX*. Chester: Printed by John Monk
Perkins, Jean A.
   1965 'Voltaire and the natural sciences'. *Studies on Voltaire*, 37:61-76
   1981 'Censorship and the Académie des sciences: a case study of Bonnet's *Considérations sur les corps organisés*'. *Studies on Voltaire*, 199:251-62
Pevsner, Nikolaus, and Lang, S.
   1956 'The Egyptian revival'. *The Architectural review*, 119:242-54
Pierce, S. Rowland
   1965 'Thomas Jenkins in Rome'. *The Antiquaries journal*, 45:200-229
Pighetti, Clelia
   1960 'Cinquant'anni di studi newtoniani (1908-1959)'. *Rivista critica di storia della filosofia*, 15:181-203
Pigott, Nathaniel
   1776 'Astronomical observations made in the Austrian Netherlands in 1772 and 1773'. *Philosophical transactions*, 66, pt.1:182-95

1777 'Observations astronomiques, faites aux Pays-Bas Autrichiens en 1772 et 1773'. *Mémoires de l'Académie impériale et royale des sciences et belles-lettres de Bruxelles*, 1:1-25

Pinto, Isaac de
1771 *Traité de la circulation et du crédit*. Amsterdam: Chez Michel Rey
1776a *Lettre de Mr. de ***** a Mr. S. B.* [...] *au sujet des troubles qui agitent actuellement toute l'Amérique Septentrionale*. La Haye: Chez Pierre-Frederic Gosse
1776b *Seconde lettre* [...] *à l'occasion des troubles des Colonies, contenant des réflexions politiques sur les suites de ces troubles, et sur l'état actuel de l'Angleterre*. La Haye: Chez Pierre-Frederic Gosse
1776c *Reponse* [...] *aux observations d'un homme impartial, sur la lettre a Mr. S. B.* [...] La Haye: Chez Pierre-Frederic Gosse

Pirenne, Henri
1972-1975 *Histoire de Belgique des origines à nos jours*. 5 vols. Bruxelles: La Renaissance du Livre

Pitassi, Maria Cristina
1982 'L'écho des discussions métaphysiques dans la correspondance entre Isaac Papin et Jean Le Clerc (1684-1685)'. *Revue de théologie et de philosophie*, 114:259-75

Pitou, Spire
1972 'Voltaire, Linguet, and China'. *Studies on Voltaire*, 98:61-68

Piuz, Anne-Marie
1974 'La Genève des Lumières'. In *Histoire de Genève*, pp.225-54. Publiée sous la direction de Paul Guichonnet. Toulouse: Privat; Lausanne: Payot

Plantefol, Lucien
1969 'Duhamel du Monceau'. *Dix-huitième siècle*, 1:123-37

Poinsinet de Sivry, Louis
1778 *Nouvelles recherches sur la science des médailles, inscriptions et hiéroglyphes antiques*. Maestricht: Chez Jean-Edme Dufour et Philippe Roux

Polhill, Nathaniel
1778 'A letter [...] to Mr. John Belchier, F.R.S. on Mr. Debraw's improvements in the culture of bees'. *Philosophical transactions*, 68, pt.1:107-10

Pomeau, René
1969 *La Religion de Voltaire*. Nouv. ed. Paris: Librairie Nizet

Poncelet, Polycarpe
1766a *La Nature dans la formation du tonnerre, et la reproduction des êtres vivans*. [...] Paris: Chez P. G. Le Mercier & Ch. Saillant
1766b *La Nature dans la reproduction des êtres vivans, des animaux, des végétaux, mais plus particulierement du froment*. [...] Paris: Chez P. G. Le Mercier & Ch. Saillant
1779 *Histoire naturelle du froment*. [...] Paris: Chez G. Desprez

Pope, Alexander
1733 *An essay on Man*. In *Epistles to a friend*. *Epistle III*. Dublin: Printed by S. Powell, for George Risk [etc.]
1734 *An essay on Man*. In *Epistles to a friend*. *Epistle IV*. London, Dublin: Printed and Re-printed in Dublin by George Faulkner [etc.]

Popkin, Richard H.
1959 'Pierre Bayle's place in 17th-century scepticism'. In *Pierre Bayle le philosophe de Rotterdam*, pp.1-19. Etudes et documents publiés sous la direction de Paul Dibon. Amsterdam: Elsevier Publishing Company

Porter, Roy
1977 *The Making of geology: Earth science in Britain 1660-1815*. Cambridge: Cambridge University Press

Postigliola, Alberto
1978 'Montesquieu e Bonnet: la controversia sul concetto di legge'. In *La Politica della ragione. Studi sull'Illuminismo francese*, pp.43-69. A cura di Paolo Casini. Bologna: Società editrice il Mulino

Pottle, Frederick A. *see* Brady, Frank

Pownall, Thomas
1781 *Memoire adressé aux souverains de l'Europe, sur l'état présent des affaires de l'ancien & du nouveau monde*. Traduit le l'Anglois par M***. [Edited and with a Preface by John Turberville Needham.] Londres, Bruxelles: Chez E. Flon

Poynter, Frederick Noël Lawrence
1968 'Hunter, Spallanzani, and the history of artificial insemination'. In *Medicine, science and culture: historical essays in honor of Owsei Temkin*, pp.97-113. Edited by Lloyd G. Stevenson and Robert P. Multhauf. Baltimore: The Johns Hopkins Press

Prandi, Dino
1952 *Bibliografia di Lazzaro Spallanzani*. Firenze: Sansoni Antiquariato

Premuda, Loris
1967 'Versuch einer Bibliographie mit Anmerkungen über das Leben und die Werke von G. B. Morgagni'. In G. B. Morgagni, *Sitz und Ursachen der Krankheiten*, pp.163-95. Edited and translated by Markwart Michler. Bern, Stuttgart: Verlag Hans Huber

Projet
1766 *Projet de Règlement de l'Illustre Médiation, pour la pacification des dissentions de la République de Genève*. [Genève]

Prononcé
1767 *Prononcé des Puissances garantes du Reglement de 1738*. [Genève]

Punt, Hendrik
1977 'Bernard Siegfried Albinus (1697-1770) und die anatomische Perfektion'. *Medizinhistorisches Journal*, 12:325-45
1983 *Bernard Siegfried Albinus (1697-1770) on 'human nature': anatomical and physiological ideas in eighteenth-century Leiden*. Amsterdam: B.M. Israël B.V.

Purchas, Samuel
1657 *A theatre of politicall flying-insects*. London: Printed by R. I. for Thomas Parkhurst

Questions
1767 *Questions sur les miracles, en forme de lettres. A Monsieur le professeur Cl.... Par un proposant*. Genève

Rae, John
1895 *Life of Adam Smith*. London: Macmillan and Co.

Raitières, Anna
1981 'Lettres à Buffon dans les "Registres de l'Ancien Régime" (1739-1788)'. *Histoire et nature*, 17-18:85-148

Rappaport, Rhoda
1964 'Problems and sources in the history of geology, 1749-1810'. *History of science*, 3:60-78
1974 'Guettard, Lavoisier, and Monnet: geologists in the service of the French monarchy.' Ph.D. dissertation, Cornell University, 1964. Ann Arbor: University Microfilms
1978 'Geology and orthodoxy: the case of Noah's flood in eighteenth-century thought'. *British journal for the history of science*, 11:1-18
1982 'Borrowed words: problems of vocabulary in eighteenth-century geology'. *British journal for the history of science*, 15:27-44

Raspe, Rudolf Erich

1776 *An account of some German volcanos, and their productions.* [...] London: Printed for Lockyer Davis, Holborn, printer to the Royal Society

Rather, Lelland Joseph

1965 *Mind and body in eighteenth-century medicine: a study based on J. Gaub's De regimine mentis.* London: Wellcome Institute of the History of Medicine

[Ratte, Etienne-Hyacinthe de]

1774 'Eloge de M. Jallabert'. *Assemblée publique de la Société royale des sciences tenue* [...] *le 8 Décembre 1773*, pp.7-17. Montpellier: De l'Imprimerie de Jean Martel Ainé

Ravier, Emile

1937 *Bibliographie des œuvres de Leibniz.* Paris: Librairie Félix Alcan

Ray, John

1693 *Three physico-theological discourses, concerning I. The primitive chaos, and creation of the World. II. The general deluge, its causes and effects. III. The dissolution of the world, and future conflagration.* Second edition. London: Printed for Sam. Smith

Réaumur, René-Antoine Ferchault de

1734-1742 *Mémoires pour servir à l'histoire des insectes.* 6 vols. Paris: De l'Imprimerie Royale

Reeves, James

1976 *The Reputation and writings of Alexander Pope.* London: Heinemann

Régley

1755 *Histoire de Louis Mandrin.* Chambéry: Gorrin

1779 *Eloge historique du brave Crillon, discours qui a remporté le prix d'éloquence de l'Académie d'Amiens.* Paris: Vve Duchesne

Reiffenberg, Frédéric-Auguste-Ferdinand-Thomas de

1850 'Eloge de l'abbé Mann'. *Annuaire de la Bibliothèque royale de Belgique*, 11:76-125

Representation

1765 *Representation des Citoyens & Bourgeois remise à Messieurs les Sindics le 7 Février 1765.* [Genève]

Representations

1763 *Representations des Citoyens et Bourgeois de Geneve au Premier Sindic de cette république; avec les réponses du Conseil à ces representations.* [Genève]

Rétat, Pierre

1971 *Le Dictionnaire de Bayle et la lutte philosophique au XVIIIe siècle.* Bibliothèque de la Faculté des Lettres de Lyon, xxviii. Lyon: Imprimerie Audin

Rihs, Charles

1962 *Voltaire: recherches sur les origines du matérialisme historique.* Genève: Librairie E. Droz; Paris: Librairie Minard

Ritter, Eugène

1904 'Voltaire et le pasteur Robert Brown'. *Bulletin de la Société de l'histoire du protestantisme français*, 53:156-63

1916-1917a 'Rousseau et le professeur Vernet'. *Annales de la Société Jean-Jacques Rousseau*, 11:114-51

1916-1917b 'Rousseau et Charles Bonnet'. *Annales de la Société Jean-Jacques Rousseau*, 11:159-88

Ritterbush, Philip C.

1964 *Overtures to biology: the speculations of eighteenth-century naturalists.* New Haven: Yale University Press

Rivoire, Emile
1897 *Bibliographie historique de Genève au XVIIIe siècle*. Vols vi and vii of *Mémoires et documents publiés par la Société d'histoire et d'archéologie de Genève*. Genève: J. Jullien, Georg & Cie; Paris: Alphonse Picard

Robinet, André
1964 'Du rôle accordé à l'expérience dans la physique de Malebranche'. In *Mélanges Alexandre Koyré*, 2:400-410. Paris: Hermann

Robinet, Jean-Baptiste-René
1761-1766 *De la nature*. 4 vols. Amsterdam: Chez E. van Harrevelt

Rocchi, Gino (ed.)
1875 *Carteggio tra Giambattista Morgagni e Francesco M. Zanotti*. Bologna: Presso Nicola Zanichelli

Rocci, Giovanni
1975 *Charles Bonnet. Filosofia e scienza*. Firenze: G. C. Sansoni editore

Roddier, Henri
1950 *J.-J. Rousseau en Angleterre au XVIIIe siècle*. Paris: Editions contemporaines Boivin

Roe, Shirley A.
1975 'The development of Albrecht von Haller's views on embryology'. *Journal of the history of biology*, 8:167-90
1979 'Rationalism and embryology: Caspar Friedrich Wolff's theory of epigenesis'. *Journal of the history of biology*, 12:1-43
1981 *Matter, life, and generation: eighteenth-century embryology and the Haller-Wolff debate*. Cambridge, New York: Cambridge University Press
1982 'Needham's controversy with Spallanzani: can animals be produced from plants?' In *Lazzaro Spallanzani e la biologia del Settecento: teorie, esperimenti, istituzioni scientifiche*, pp.295-303. A cura di Giuseppe Montalenti e Paolo Rossi. Firenze: Leo S. Olschki Editore
1983 'John Turberville Needham and the generation of living organisms'. *Isis*, 74:159-84
1984 '*Anatomia animata*: the Newtonian physiology of Albrecht von Haller'. In *Transformation and tradition in the sciences: essays in honor of I. Bernard Cohen*, pp.273-300. Edited by Everett Mendelsohn. Cambridge, New York: Cambridge University Press
1985 'Voltaire versus Needham: atheism, materialism, and the generation of life'. *Journal of the history of ideas*, 46:65-87

Roffredi, Maurizio
1769 'Lettres [...] sur les nouvelles observations microscopiques de Mr. Néedham, & ses notes sur les recherches de Mr. Spallanzani'. *Mélanges de philosophie et de mathématique de la Société Royale de Turin pour les années 1760-1769 (Miscellanea Taurinensia)*, 4:109-60
1775a 'Mémoire sur l'origine des petits vers ou anguilles du bled rachitique'. *Observations sur la physique, sur l'histoire naturelle et sur les arts*, 5:1-19
1775b 'Seconde lettre, ou suite d'observations sur le rachitisme du bled, sur les anguilles de la colle de farine, & sur le grain charbonné'. *Observations sur la physique, sur l'histoire naturelle et sur les arts*, 5:197-225

Roger, Jacques
1963 *Les Sciences de la vie dans la pensée française du XVIIIe siècle: la génération des animaux de Descartes à l'Encyclopédie*. Paris: Armand Colin
1968 'Leibniz et les sciences de la vie'. *Studia leibnitiana supplementa*, 2:209-19

Rogers, Charles
1876 *Boswelliana: the commonplace book of James Boswell*. London: Printed for the Grampian Club

Rosso, Carrado
    1954 'Il "paradosso" di Robinet'. *Filosofia*, 5:37-62
    1976 'Montesquieu présent: études et travaux depuis 1960'. *Dix-huitième siècle*, 8:373-404

Rostand, Jean
    1951 *Les Origines de la biologie éxpérimentale et l'abbé Spallanzani*. Paris: Fasquelle Editeurs

Rothschuh, Karl Eduard
    1953 *Geschichte der Physiologie*. Berlin, Gottingen, Heidelberg: Springer

Rousseau, André-Michel *see* De Beer, Gavin

Rousseau, Jean-Jacques
    1764 *Lettres écrites de la montagne*. Amsterdam: Chez Marc Michel Rey
    1959- *Œuvres complètes*. Edited by Bernard Gagnebin, Marcel Raymond. 4 vols. Paris: Bibliothèque de la Pléiade. [Abbreviated as R.O.]
    1965- *Correspondance complète de Jean Jacques Rousseau*. Edited by R. A. Leigh. Genève: Institut et Musée Voltaire (vols i-xiv); Banbury, Oxford: The Voltaire Foundation (vols xiv-). [Abbreviated as Leigh]

Rovillain, Eugène E.
    1927 'L'Angleterre et les troubles de Genève en 1766-1767'. *Zeitschrift für Schweizerische Geschichte*, 7:164-203

Rudbeck, Olof
    1717 *Specimen usus linguae Gothicae, in eruendis atque illustrandis obscurissimis quibusvis Sacrae Scripturae locis: addita analogia linguae Gothicae cum Sinica, nec non Finnonica cum Ungarica*. Upsalis: Impressum â Joh. Henr. Werner

Rudolph, Gerhard
    1964 'Hallers Lehre von der Irritabilität und Sensibilität'. In *Von Boerhaave bis Berger. Die Entwicklung der kontinentalen Physiologie im 18. und 19. Jahrhundert*, pp.14-34. Herausgegeben von K. E. Rothschuh. Stuttgart: Fischer

Rudwick, Martin
    1972 *The Meaning of fossils: episodes in the history of palaeontology*. London: Macdonald; New York: American Elsevier Inc.

Sachs, Julius von
    1890 *History of botany (1530-1860)*. Authorised translation by Henry F. F. Garnsey, revised by Isaac Bayley Balfour. Oxford: At the Clarendon Press

Saladin, Michel-Jean-Louis
    1790 *Mémoire historique sur la vie et les ouvrages de Mr J. Vernet*. [...] Paris: Chez Bossange [etc.]

Sandler, Iris
    1973 'The re-examination of Spallanzani's interpretation of the role of spermatic animalcules in fertilization'. *Journal of the history of biology*, 6:193-223

Saussure, Horace-Bénédict de
    1779-1796 *Voyages dans les Alpes, précédés d'un essai sur l'histoire naturelle des environs de Geneve*. 4 vols. Neuchâtel: Chez S. Fauche (vols i, iii, iv); Genève: Chez Barde (vol. ii)
    [1793] *Eloge historique de Charles Bonnet*. n.p.

Savage, Spencer
    1948 *Catalogue of the manuscripts in the Library of the Linnean Society of London*. Part IV. *Calendar of the Ellis Manuscripts*. London: Printed for the Linnean Society by Taylor and Francis Ltd.

Savioz, Raymond
    1948a *La Philosophie de Charles Bonnet de Genève.* Paris: Librairie philosophique J. Vrin
    1948b *Mémoires autobiographiques de Charles Bonnet de Genève.* Paris: Librairie philosophique J. Vrin
    1950 'Montesquieu et le philosophe genevois Charles Bonnet'. *Revue des sciences humaines,* N.S., Fasc. 60:270-76
Schaeffer, Jacob Christian
    1761 *Piscium Bavarico-Ratisbonensium pentas. Cum tabulis IV. aeri incisis icones coloribus suis distinctas exhibentibus.* Ratisbonae: Impensis Mantagii et Typis Weissianis
    1762-1763 *Fungorum qui in Bavaria et Palatinatu circa Ratisbonam nascuntur icones nativis coloribus expressae.* 2 vols. Ratisbonae: Typis Zunkelianis
Schazmann, Paul-Emile
    1976 *The Bentincks: the history of a European family.* Translated by Steve Cox. London: Weidenfeld and Nicolson
Schierbeek, Abraham
    1967 *Jan Swammerdam (1637-1680): his life and works.* Amsterdam: Swets & Zeitlinger
Schiller, Joseph
    1978 *La Notion d'organisation dans l'histoire de la biologie.* Paris: Maloine
Schirach, Adam Gottlob
    1767 *Melitto-theologia. Die Verherrlichung des glorwürdigen Schöpfers aus der wundervollen Biene.* Dresden: Gedruckt in der Waltherischen Hof-Buchdruckerey
    1771 *Histoire naturelle de la reine des abeilles, avec l'art de former des essaims.* [...] *On y a ajouté la correspondance de l'Auteur avec quelques sçavans, & trois Mémoires de l'illustre M. Bonnet de Genève sur ses découvertes. Le tout traduit de l'Allemand ou recueilli, par J. J. Blassière.* La Haye: Chez Frederic Staatman
    1774 *Storia naturale della regina delle api.* [...] Brescia: Per Giammaria Rizzardi
Schmidt, Friedrich Samuel
    1765 *Opuscula quibus res antiquae praecipue Aegyptiacae explanantur.* Carolsruhae: In Officina Macklottiana
    1768 *Dissertatio de sacerdotibus et sacrificiis Aegyptiorum.* Tubingae: Apud Joh. Georg Cottam
Schmidt, Paul
    [1908] *Court de Gébelin à Paris (1763-1784): étude sur le protestantisme français pendant la seconde motié du XVIIIe siècle.* St. Blaise, Roubaix: Foyer Solidariste de Librairie et d'Edition
Schoock, Martin
    1643 *Admiranda methodus novae philosophiae Renati des Cartes.* Ultraiecti: Ex Officina Joannis van Waesberge
Schubert, Anna
    1909 *Die Psychologie von Bonnet und Tetens mit besonderer Berücksichtigung des methodologischen Verfahrens derselben.* Inaugural-Dissertation [...] der Universität Zürich. Zürich: Druck von J. J. Meier
Schuster, Julius
    1941 'Der Streit um die Erkenntnis des organischen Werdens im Lichte der Briefe C. F. Wolffs an A. von Haller'. *Sudhoffs Archiv für Geschichte der Medizin,* 34:196-218
Schwarzbach, Bertram Eugene
    1982 'The problem of the Kehl additions to the *Dictionnaire philosophique*: sources, dating and authenticity'. *Studies on Voltaire,* 201:7-66
Sebba, Gregor
    1964 *Bibliographia cartesiana: a critical guide to the Descartes literature 1800-1960.* The Hague: Martinus Nijhoff

Sénac, Jean-Baptiste
   1749 *Traité de la structure du cœur, de son action, et de ses maladies.* 2 vols. Paris: Briasson

Senebier, Jean
   [1801] *Mémoire historique sur la vie et les écrits de Horace Bénédict Desaussure.* Genève: Chez J. J. Paschoud

Sénelier, Jean
   1950 *Bibliographie générale des œuvres de J.-J. Rousseau.* Paris: Presses Universitaires de France

Sgard, Jean (ed.)
   1976 *Dictionnaire des journalistes (1600-1789).* Sous la direction de Jean Sgard avec la collaboration de Michel Gilot et Françoise Weil. Grenoble: Presses Universitaires

Shackleton, Robert
   1956 'La religion de Montesquieu'. *Actes du Congrès Montesquieu,* pp.287-94. Bordeaux: Imprimerie Delmas
   1961 *Montesquieu: a critical biography.* London: Oxford University Press

Shankland, Peter
   1975 *Byron of the wager.* London: Collins

Sharratt, Michael
   1973 'John Manley's letter book'. *Ushaw magazine,* 84:12-17

Sherwood, James
   1746 'A letter from Mr. James Sherwood, surgeon, to Martin Folkes, Esq; President of the Royal Society, concerning the minute eels in paste being viviparous'. *Philosophical transactions,* 44:67-69

Sheynin, O. B.
   1972a 'D. Bernoulli's work on probability'. *Rete,* 1:273-300
   1972b 'On the mathematical treatment of observations by L. Euler'. *Archive for history of exact sciences,* 9:45-56

Sigorgne, Pierre
   1767 *Institutions léibnitiennes, ou, précis de la monadologie.* Lyon: Les Frères Perisse

Simonutti, Luisa
   1982 'Questioni di filosofia nel carteggio di due teologi protestanti: Jean Leclerc e Isaac Papin'. *Annali della Scuola Normale Superiore di Pisa,* classe di lettere, Serie 3, vol.12, pt.1:269-358

Sina, Mario
   1978 *Vico e Le Clerc: tra filosofia e filologia.* Napoli: Guida editori
   1980 'Il rinnovamento degli studi lockiani'. *Cultura e scuola,* 19:111-18
   1982 *Introduzione a Locke.* Bari: Editori Laterza

Singer, Charles
   1953 'The earliest figures of microscopic objects'. *Endeavour,* 12:197-201

Sirven, Paul
   1934-1942 *Vittorio Alfieri.* 4 vols. Paris: Les Presses Universitaires de France

Sloan, Phillip R.
   1979 'Buffon, German biology, and the historical interpretation of biological species'. *The British journal for the history of science,* 12:107-53

Smeaton, William Arthur
   1978 'The chemical work of Horace Bénédict de Saussure (1740-1799). With the text of a letter written to him by Madame Lavoisier'. *Annals of science,* 35:1-16

Smit, Pieter
1981 'Jan Swammerdam (1637-1680) und seine Beobachtungen zur Metamorphose der Insekten'. In *Hallesche Physiologie im Werden*, pp.35-43. Herausgegeben vom Wolfram Kaiser und Hans Hübner. Halle (Saale): Wissenschaftliche Beiträge der Martin-Luther-Universität Halle-Wittenberg

Smith, Adam
1759 *The Theory of moral sentiments*. London: Printed for A. Millar; Edinburgh: A. Kincaid and J. Bell
1764 *Métaphysique de l'ame, ou théorie des sentimens moraux*, traduite de l'anglois de M. Adam Smith, [...] par M***. 2 vols. Paris: Chez Briasson
1774-1775 *Théorie des sentimens moraux. Traduction nouvelle de l'anglois de M. Smith [...] par M. l'abbé Blavet.* [...] 2 vol. Paris: Chez Valade
1976 *The Theory of moral sentiments*. Edited by D. D. Raphael and A. L. Macfie. Oxford: Clarendon Press
1977 *The Correspondence of Adam Smith*. Edited by Ernest Campbell Mossner and Ian Simpson Ross. Oxford: At the Clarendon Press

Smith, Davis Warner
1965 *Helvétius: a study in persecution*. Oxford: Clarendon Press
1971 'Helvétius's library'. *Studies on Voltaire*, 79:153-61
1973 'La correspondance d'Helvétius'. *Dix-huitième siècle*, 5:335-61

Smith, Robert
1738 *A complete system of opticks*. 2 vols. Cambridge: Printed for the Author, and sold there by Cornelius Crownfield

Smith, Warren Hunting (ed.)
1967 *Horace Walpole writer, politician, and connoisseur: essays on the 250th anniversary of Walpole's birth*. New Haven, London: Yale University Press

Soleto, Rocco
1966 'La dottrina della generazione secondo Charles Bonnet (1720-1793)'. *Medicina nei secoli*, 3, nr.4:9-18
1968 'La maladie des yeux de Charles Bonnet dans sa correspondance épistolaire avec van Swieten'. In *Verhandlungen des XX. Internationalen Kongresses für Geschichte der Medizin, Berlin, 22.-27. August 1966*, pp.848-49. Hildesheim: Georg Olms

Solinas, Giovanni
1967 *Il microscopio e le metafisiche: epigenesi e preesistenza da Cartesio a Kant*. Milano: Feltrinelli

Sommervogel, Carlos
1960 *Bibliothèque de la Compagnie de Jésus*. 12 vols. Bruxelles: Réimpression anastatique. Imprimerie Polleunis et Ceuterick

Sonntag, Otto (ed.)
1983 *The Correspondence between Albrecht von Haller and Charles Bonnet*. Studia Halleriana, 1. Bern [etc.]: Hans Huber Publishers

Spallanzani, Lazzaro
1765 *Dissertazioni due*. Modena: Per gli Eredi di Bartolomeo Soliani Stamp. Ducali
1768a *Prodromo di un opera da imprimersi sopra le riproduzioni animali*. Modena: Nella Stamperia di Giovanni Montanari
1768b *Programme ou précis d'un ouvrage sur les réproductions animales*. Genève: Chez Claude Philibert
1769 *Nouvelles recherches sur les découvertes microscopiques, et la génération des corps organisés. Ouvrage traduit de l'Italien de M. l'abbé Spallanzani par M. l'abbé Regley. [...] Avec des notes, des recherches physiques et métaphysiques sur la nature et la religion, et une nouvelle théorie*

de la terre. Par M. de Needham. [...] Londres, Paris: Chez Lacombe

1770 *Prolusio.* Mutinae: Ex Typographia Johannis Montanari

1776 *Opuscoli di fisica animale, e vegetabile.* 2 vols. Modena: Presso la Società Tipografica

1777 *Opuscules de physique animale et végétale. Traduits de l'italien.* [...] 2 vols. Genève: Chez Barthelemi Chirol

1779 'Fecondazione artificiale'. In *Prodromo della nuova enciclopedia italiana,* pp.129-34. Siena: Per Vincenzo Pazzini-Carli e figli e Luigi e Benedetto Bindi

1780 *Dissertazioni di fisica animale, e vegetabile.* 2 vols. Modena: Presso la Società Tipografica

1784 *Dissertations relative to the natural history of animals and vegetables. Translated from the Italian.* [...] 2 vols. London: Printed for J. Murray

1958-1964 *Epistolario.* A cura di Benedetto Biagi. 5 vols. Firenze: Sansoni antiquariato. [Abbreviated as *Epistolario*]

1978a *Opera scelte.* A cura di Carlo Castellani. Torino: U.T.E.T.

1978b *I giornali delle sperienze e osservazioni relativi alla fisiologia della generazione e alla embriologia sperimentale.* A cura di Carlo Castellani e Vincenzo G. Leone. Milano: Episteme editrice

Spear, Frederick A.

1980 *Bibliographie de Diderot. Repertoire analitique international.* Genève: Librairie Droz

Spear, Frederick A. *see also* Barr, Mary-Margaret H.

Speck, Johannes

1897 *Bonnets Einwirkung auf die deutsche Psychologie des vorigen Jahrhunderts.* Innaugural-Dissertation [...] der Universität zu Berlin. Berlin

Spink, John Stephenson

1934 *Jean-Jacques Rousseau et Genève: essai sur les idées politiques et religieuses de Rousseau dans leur relation avec la pensée genevoise au XVIIIe siècle.* Paris: Boivin & Cie, Editeurs

Stanhope, Charles (Lord Mahon)

1778 'Description of a most effectual method of securing buildings against fire'. *Philosophical transactions,* 68, pt.2:884-94

1779 *Principles of electricity.* [...] London: Printed for P. Elmsly

1781 *Principes d'électricité.* [...] Ouvrage traduit de l'Anglois, par Mr. l'abbé N[eedham]. Londres, Bruxelles: Chez Emmanuel Flon

Stanhope, Ghita, and Gooch, G. P.

1914 *The Life of Charles, third Earl Stanhope.* London: Longmans, Green and Co.

Starobinski, Jean

1975 'L'Essai de psychologie de Charles Bonnet: une version corrigée inédite'. *Gesnerus,* 32:1-15

Steiger, R. *see* Markgraf, F.

Stelluti, Francesco *see* Cesi, Federico

Stokes, Evelyn

1969 'The six days and the Deluge: some ideas on Earth history in the Royal Society of London 1660-1775'. *Earth science journal,* 3:13-39

Strózewski, Stanislaus

1905 *Bonnets Psychologie in Ihrem Verhältnis zu Condillacs Traité des sensations.* Inaugural-Dissertation [...] der Universität Tübingen. Berlin: Druck von Emil Rieger

Suringar, Gerard Conrad Bernard

1867 'Het bijeenbrengen eener verzameling van natuurlijke voorwerpen [...]'. *Nederlandsch tijdschrift voor geneeskunde,* tweede reeks, 3/2:265-84

Sutherland, Lucy S.
  1947 'The East India Company and the Peace of Paris'. *The English historical review*, 62:179-90

Swammerdam, Jan
  1682 *Histoire generale des insectes*. Utrecht: Chez Guillaume de Walcheren
  1737-1738 *Biblia naturae; sive historia insectorum, in classes certas redacta, nec non exemplis, et anatomico variorum animalculorum examine, aeneisque tabulis illustrata*. [...] 2 vols. Leydae: Apud Isaacum Severinum [etc.]
  1758 *The Book of nature; or, the history of insects*. [...] Translated from the Dutch and Latin original edition, by Thomas Flloyd. Revised and improved by notes from Réaumur and others, by John Hill. London: Printed for C. G. Seyffert

Targioni-Tozzetti, Giovanni
  1858 *Notizie della vita e delle opere di Pier' Antonio Micheli*. Pubblicate per cura di Adolfo Targioni-Tozzetti. Firenze: Felice Le Monnier

Taylor, Kenneth L.
  1969 'Nicholas Desmarest and geology in the eighteenth century'. In *Toward a history of geology*, pp.339-56. Edited by Cecil J. Schneer. Cambridge, Mass.: M.I.T. Press

Taylor, Samuel S. B.
  1981 'The Enlightenment in Switzerland'. In *The Enlightenment in national context*, pp.72-89. Edited by Roy Porter and Mikuláš Teich. Cambridge: Cambridge University Press

Tega, Walter
  1971 'Meccanicismo e scienze della vita nel tardo Settecento'. *Rivista di filosofia*, 62:155-76

Temkin, Owsei
  1964 'The classical roots of Glisson's doctrine of irritation'. *Bulletin of the history of medicine*, 38:297-328

Thaddeus, Rev. Father
  1898 *The Franciscans in England 1600-1850*. London, Leamington: Art & Book Co.

Théodoridès, Jean
  1959 'Réaumur (1683-1757) et les insectes sociaux'. *Janus*, 48:62-76
  1968 'Historique des connaissances scientifiques sur l'abeille'. In *Traité de biologie de l'abeille*, 5:1-34. Edited by Remy Chauvin. 5 vols. Paris: Masson et Cie

Thijssen-Schoute, C. Louise
  1959 'La diffusion européenne des idées de Bayle'. In *Pierre Bayle le philosophe de Rotterdam*, pp.150-95. Etudes et documents publiés sous la direction de Paul Dibon. Amsterdam: Elsevier Publishing Company

Tiraboschi, Girolamo
  1781-1786 *Biblioteca modenese*. [...] 6 vols. Modena: Società tipografica

Tissot, Samuel Auguste André David
  1809-1813 *Œuvres complètes de Tissot*. [...] Nouvelle édition, publiée par M. P. [Alexandre-Pascal] Tissot, précédée d'un Précis historique sur la vie de l'auteur et accompagnée de notes, par M. J.-N. Hallé. [...] 11 vols. Paris: Allut

Tobin, James Edward
  1945 *Alexander Pope: a list of critical studies published from 1895 to 1944*. New York: Cosmopolitan Science & Art Service

Toellner, Richard
  1967 'Anima et irritabilitas. Hallers Abwehr von Animismus und Materialismus'. *Sudhoffs Archiv*, 51:130-44

1971 *Albrecht von Haller: über die Einheit im Denken des letzten Universalgelehrten.* Sudhoffs Archiv, Beiheft 10. Wiesbaden: Franz Steiner

Torlais, Jean

1932 'Un maître et un élève. Réaumur et Charles Bonnet'. *Gazette hebdomadaire des sciences médicales de Bordeaux,* nr.41: 641-55; nr.42:657-59

1958a 'Chronologie de la vie et des œuvres de René-Antoine Ferchault de Réaumur'. *Revue d'histoire des sciences,* 11:1-12

1958b 'Réaumur et l'histoire des abeilles'. *Revue d'histoire des sciences,* 11:51-67

1961 *Réaumur, un esprit encyclopédique en dehors de l'Encyclopédie.* Edition revue et augmentée. Paris: Albert Blanchard

Torrey, Norman L. *see* Havens, George R.

Tourneux, Maurice

1899 *Diderot et Catherine II.* Paris: Colman Lévy

Trembley, Abraham

1744 *Mémoires pour servir à l'histoire d'un genre de polypes d'eau douce, à bras en forme de cornes.* Leide: Chez Jean & Herman Verbeek

1775 *Instructions d'un père à ses enfans, sur la nature et sur la religion.* 2 vols. Genève: J. S. Cailler

1779 *Instructions d'un père à ses enfans, sur la religion naturelle et révélée.* Genève: B. Chirol

[Trembley, Jean]

1794 *Mémoire pour servir à l'histoire de la vie et des ouvrages de M. Charles Bonnet.* Berne: Chez la Société typographique

Trembley, Maurice (ed.)

1943 *Correspondance inédite entre Réaumur et Abraham Trembley.* Genève: Georg & Cie

[Tronchin, Jean-Robert]

1763 *Lettres écrites de la campagne.* [Genève]

Trousson, Raymond

1977 'Quinze années d'études rousseauistes'. *Dix-huitième siècle,* 9:343-86

Truesdell, C.

1972 'Leonard Euler, supreme geometer (1707-1783).' *Studies in eighteenth-century culture,* 2:51-95

Tunbridge, Paul A.

1971 'Jean André de Luc, F.R.S. (1727-1817)'. *Notes and records of the Royal Society of London,* 26:15-33

Turberville, Arthur Stanley

1938-1939 *A history of Welbeck Abbey and its owners.* 2 vols. London: Faber and Faber

1958 *The House of Lords in the age of reform 1784-1837.* London: Faber and Faber

Turner, G. L'E.

1974 'Henry Baker, F.R.S.: founder of the Bakerian Lecture'. *Notes and records of the Royal Society of London,* 29:53-79

Usuelli, Luca

1972 'Sui rapporti Morgagni-Bonnet'. *Episteme,* 6:49-55

Valceschini, Silvio

1977 *Un poète et naturaliste au pouvoir: Albert de Haller Vice-gouverneur d'Aigle en 1762-1763.* Aigle: Association Musée Suisse du Sel

Vallisneri, Antonio

1733 *Opere fisico-mediche stampate e manoscritte del kavalier Antonio Vallisneri raccolte da Antonio suo figliuolo.* [...] 3 vols. Venezia: Appresso Sebastiano Coleti

Vanderblue, Homer B.
1939 *The Vanderblue Memorial collection of Smithiana*. The Kress Library of Business and Economics, N.2. Boston: Harvard University Press

Van Seters, W. H.
1962 *Pierre Lyonet 1706-1789: sa vie, ses collections de coquillages et de tableaux, ses recherches entomologiques*. La Haye: Martinus Nijhoff
1963 'Lyonet's Kunstboek'. *Medical and biological illustration*, 13:255-64

Vartanian, Aram
1950 'Trembley's polyp, La Mettrie, and eighteenth-century French materialism'. *Journal of the history of ideas*, 11:259-86
1953 Review of *Abraham Trembley of Geneva: scientist and philosopher*, by John R. Baker. *Isis*, 44:387-89

Venturi, Franco
1969-1979 *Settecento riformatore*. 3 vols. Torino: Giulio Einaudi editore
1982 '*Ubi libertas, ibi patria*: la rivoluzione ginevrina del 1782'. *Rivista storica italiana*, 94:395-434

Vercruysse, Jeroom
1971 *Bibliographie descriptive des écrits du baron d'Holbach*. Paris: Lettres modernes Minard

Vernes, Jacob
1765 *Examen de ce qui concerne le christianisme, la réformation evangélique, et les ministres de Genève, dans les deux premieres lettres de Mr. J. J. Rousseau, écrites de la montagne*. Genève: Chez Claude Philibert

Vernet, Jacob
[1761] *Lettres critiques d'un voyageur anglois sur l'Article Genève du Dictionaire encyclopédique; et sur la Lettre de Mr. D'Alembert à Mr. Rousseau. Publiées avec une Preface par R. Brown Ministre Anglois à Utrecht*. Utrecht: Chez J. C. Ten Bosch
1766a *Lettres critiques d'un voyageur anglois*. [...] Troisième édition corrigée, et augmentée [...]. 2 vols. Copenhague
1766b *Mémoire presenté à M.ʳ le Premier Sindic*. [...] n.p.

Vernière, Paul
1954 *Spinoza et la pensée française avant la révolution*. 2 vols. Paris: Presses Universitaires de France

Vian, Louis
1872 *Montesquieu: bibliographie de ses œuvres*. Paris: Durand et Pédone-Lauriel

Viatte, Auguste
1928 *Les Sources occultes du romantisme: illuminisme-théosophie 1770-1820*. 2 vols. Paris: Librairie Ancienne Honoré Champion

Vigouroux, Fulcran-Grégoire
1889 *La Cosmogonie mosaïque d'après les pères de l'église suivie d'études diverses relatives à l'ancien et au nouveau testament*. 2nd ed. Paris: Berche et Tralin, éditeurs

Virolle, Roland
1974 'Où en sont les études sur le *Dictionnaire philosophique* de Voltaire?' *L'Information littéraire*, 26:60-67

'Vita'
1744 'Vita Olavi Rudbeck'. *Acta Societatis Regiae Scientiarum Upsaliensis. Ad annum MDCCXL*, pp.124-32

Voltaire, François-Marie Arouet de
1759-1763 *Histoire de l'empire de Russie sous Pierre le Grand*. 2 vols. n.p.
1765 *Collection des lettres sur les miracles. Ecrites à Geneve, et à Neufchatel. Par Mr. le Proposant*

Théro, Monsieur Covelle, Monsieur Néedham, Mr. Beaudinet, & Mr. de Montmolin, &c.
Neuchâtel [Genève]; republished Neuchâtel [Amsterdam], 1767

1765-1775 *Nouveaux mélanges philosophiques, historiques, critiques, &c. &c.* 19 vols.
[Genève]

1766 *Lettre curieuse de M. Robert Covelle, célèbre citoyen de Genève, à la louange de M. V....,
professeur en théologie dans ladite ville.* Dijon: Chez P. Brocard

1768 *Les Singularités de la nature.* Basle [Genève]

1769 *Dieu et les hommes, œuvre theologique; mais raisonnable, par le Docteur Obern. Traduit par
Jacques Aimon.* Berlin: Chez Christian de Vos

1770 *Dieu. Réponse de Mr. de Voltaire au Systême de la nature.* Au Château de Ferney

1770-1772 *Questions sur l'encyclopédie par des amateurs.* 9 vols. [Genève]

1775 *Piéces détachées, attribuées à divers hommes célèbres.* 3 vols. [Genève]

1776 *Commentaire historique sur les œuvres de l'auteur de la Henriade, &c. Avec les pièces
originales & les preuves.* Basle: Chez les Héritiers de Paul Duker

1883-1885 *Œuvres complètes de Voltaire.* [Edited by Louis Moland.] Nouvelle édition. 52
vols. Paris: Garnier Frères, Libraires-Editeurs. [Abbreviated as V.O.]

1968-1977 *Correspondence and related documents.* Definitive edition by Theodore Bester-
man. Vols.85-135 of *The Complete works of Voltaire.* Genève: Institut et Musée
Voltaire (vols 85-99); Banbury, Oxford: The Voltaire Foundation (vols 100-135).
[Abbreviated as Best.D]

Voss, Jürgen
1976 'La contribution de Jean-Daniel Schoepflin à la fondation de l'Académie de
Bruxelles'. *Académie royale de Belgique. Bulletin de la Classe des lettres et des sciences morales
et politiques,* 5e Série, 62:320-40

Wallis, Peter, and Wallis, Ruth
1977 *Newton and Newtoniana 1672-1975: a bibliography.* Folkestone: Dawson

Walpole, Horace
1935- *The Yale edition of Horace Walpole's correspondence.* Edited by W. S. Lewis. London:
Oxford University Press. [Abbreviated as *W.C.*]

1936 *The Duchess of Portland's museum.* With an introduction by W. S. Lewis. New York:
The Grollier Club

Wandruszka, Adam *see* Lesky, Erna

Warder, Joseph
1713 *The True Amazons: or the monarchy of bees: being a new discovery and improvement of
those wonderful creatures.* The Second Edition with Additions. London: Printed for
John Pemberton

Waszink, Jan Hendrik
1974 *Biene und Honig als Symbol des Dichters und der Dichtung in der griechisch-römischen
Antike.* Rheinisch-Westfälische Akademie der Wissenschaften, Vorträge G 196.
Opladen: Westdeutscher Verlag

Wernle, Paul
1923-1925 *Der schweizerische Protestantismus im XVIII. Jahrhundert.* 3 vols. Tübingen:
Verlag von J. E. B. Mohr

Westfall, Richard S.
1976 'The changing world of the Newtonian industry'. *Journal of the history of ideas,*
37:175-84

1980 *Never at rest: a biography of Isaac Newton.* Cambridge: Cambridge University Press

Whiston, William
1696 *A new theory of the Earth, from its original, to the consummation of all things. Wherein the
Creation of the World in six days, the universal Deluge, and the general conflagration, as laid*

down in the Holy Scriptures, are shewn to be perfectly agreeable to reason and philosophy. London: Printed by R. Roberts for Benj. Tooke

Whiteside, Derek Thomas

1962 'The expanding world of Newtonian research'. *History of science*, 1:16-29

Whitman, C. O.

1895a 'Bonnet's theory of evolution: a system of negations'. *Biological lectures delivered at the Marine Biological Laboratory of Wood's Hole, 1894*, pp.225-40. Boston: Ginn & Co.

1895b 'The palingenesia and the germ doctrine of Bonnet'. *Biological lectures delivered at the Marine Biological Laboratory of Wood's Hole, 1894*, pp.241-72. Boston: Ginn & Co.

Whyte, Lancelot Law (ed.)

1961 *Roger Joseph Boscovich S. J., F.R.S., 1711-1787: studies of his life and work on the 250th anniversary of his birth*. London: George Allen & Unwin

Wilcocks, Joseph

1792 *Roman conversations; or, a short description of the antiquities of Rome, and the characters of many eminent Romans*. 2 vols. London: Printed for W. Brown

1797 *Roman conversations*. [...] Second edition, corrected [...] containing some account of the Life of the Author. [Edited by Weeden Butler, the elder.] 2 vols. London: R. Bickerstaff

Wildman, Daniel

1773 *A complete guide for the management of bees*. London

Wildman, Thomas

1768 *A treatise on the management of bees*. London: T. Cadell

Wilson, Arthur M.

1972 *Diderot*. New York: Oxford University Press

Wirz, Charles-Ferdinand

1979 'Rousseau: les éditions, les recherches biographiques'. *Revue d'histoire littéraire de de la France*, 79:351-73

Wittkower, Rudolf

1977 *Allegory and the migration of symbols*. Boulder, Colorado: Westview Press

Wolf, Abraham (ed.)

1927 *The Oldest biography of Spinoza*. London: George Allen & Unwin

Wolf, Rudolf

1858-1862 *Biographien zur Kulturgeschichte der Schweiz*. 4 vols. Zürich: Orell, Füssli & Comp.

Wolff, Caspar Friedrich

1759 *Theoria generationis*. Halle: Hendel

Woodward, John

1695 *An essay toward a natural history of the Earth: and terrestrial bodies, especially minerals: as also of the sea, rivers, and springs. With an account of the universal Deluge: and of the effects that it had upon the Earth*. London: Printed for Ric. Wilkin

Worsley, Richard

1781 *The History of the Isle of Wight*. London: Printed by A. Hamilton

Zanelli, Renato

1931 'Catalogo ragionato delle edizioni morgagnane in ordine cronologico'. In *Le Onoranze a G. B. Morgagni, Forli, 24 maggio 1931*, pp.137-47. Siena: Stab. tip. S. Bernardino

Zanobio, Bruno

1959 'Le osservazioni microscopiche di Felice Fontana sulla struttura dei nervi'. *Physis*, 1:307-20

1961 'Ricerche di micrografia dell'eritrocità nel Settecento'. In *Actes du Symposium international sur les sciences naturelles, la chimie et la pharmacie du 1630 au 1850* (Florence-Vinci 8-10 Octobre 1960), pp.159-79. Firenze

Zanotti, Francesco Maria

1779-1802 *Opere*. 9 vols. Bologna: Nella Stamperia di San Tommaso d'Aquino

Index

An asterisk indicates bio-bibliographical information.